THE FALL
RUSSIAN M

THE FALL OF THE RUSSIAN MONARCHY

Sir Bernard Pares was the foremost English expert on Russia of his generation. He was born in 1867, and educated at Harrow and Trinity College, Cambridge. Before the First World War, and again after the Revolution, he paid regular and sustained visits to Russia and acquired an unrivalled knowledge of the country, its history and its people. From 1914 until 1917 he was attached to the Russian Army, and in 1917 to the British Ambassador in Petrograd. Between 1908 and 1917, he was Professor of Russian History, Language and Literature at Liverpool University, and he held the same position at London University from 1919 to 1938. His most famous books were *History of Russia* (1926), *My Russian Memoirs* (1931) and *Russia* (1940). He was knighted in 1919 and died in 1949.

THE FALL OF THE RUSSIAN MONARCHY

Bernard Pares

PHOENIX
PRESS

5 UPPER SAINT MARTIN'S LANE
LONDON
WC2H 9EA

A PHOENIX PRESS PAPERBACK

First published in Great Britain
by Jonathan Cape in 1939
Cassell edition published in 1988
This paperback edition published in 2001
by Phoenix Press,
a division of The Orion Publishing Group Ltd,
Orion House, 5 Upper St Martin's Lane,
London WC2H 9EA

A CIP catalogue record for this book
is available from the British Library.

Printed and bound in Great Britain by
Clays Ltd, St Ives plc

ISBN 1 84212 114 6

Plans nos. I, II, III and IV from Youri Danilov's *La Russie dans la Guerre mondiale*, by kind permission of Messrs. Payot, Paris
Plan V from a plan by General Golovin in *The Slavonic and East European Review*
Plan VI by kind permission of Herr Baedeker

CONTENTS

PLAN I. TANNENBERG

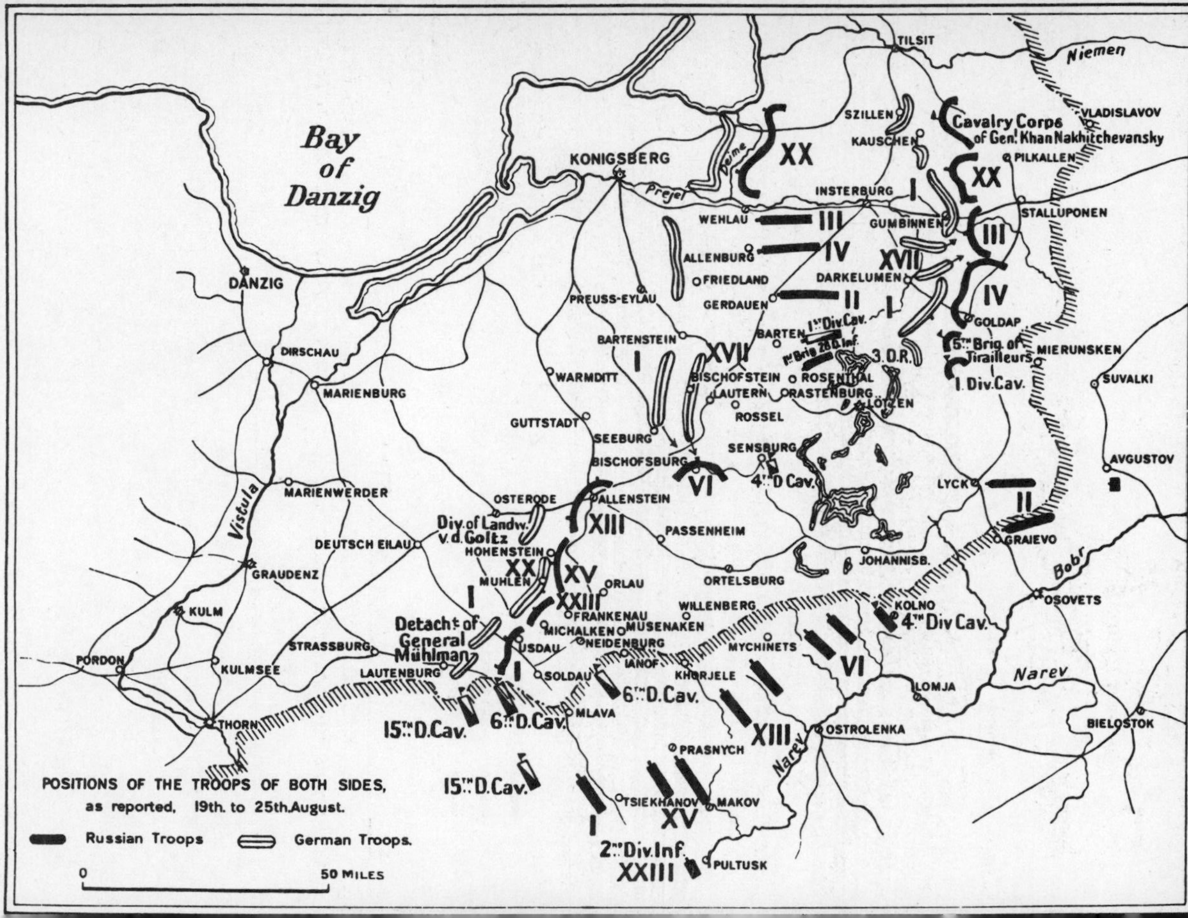

PLAN II. THE GALICIAN BATTLE OF 1914

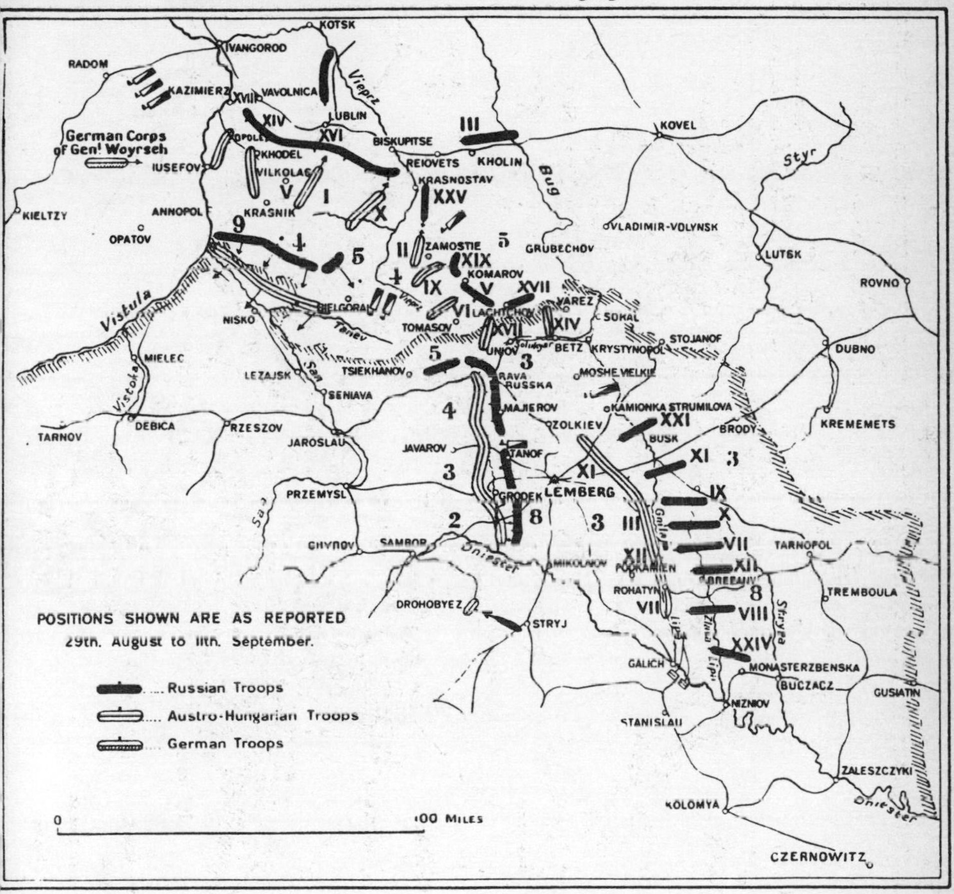

PLAN III. BATTLE OF LODZ, 1914

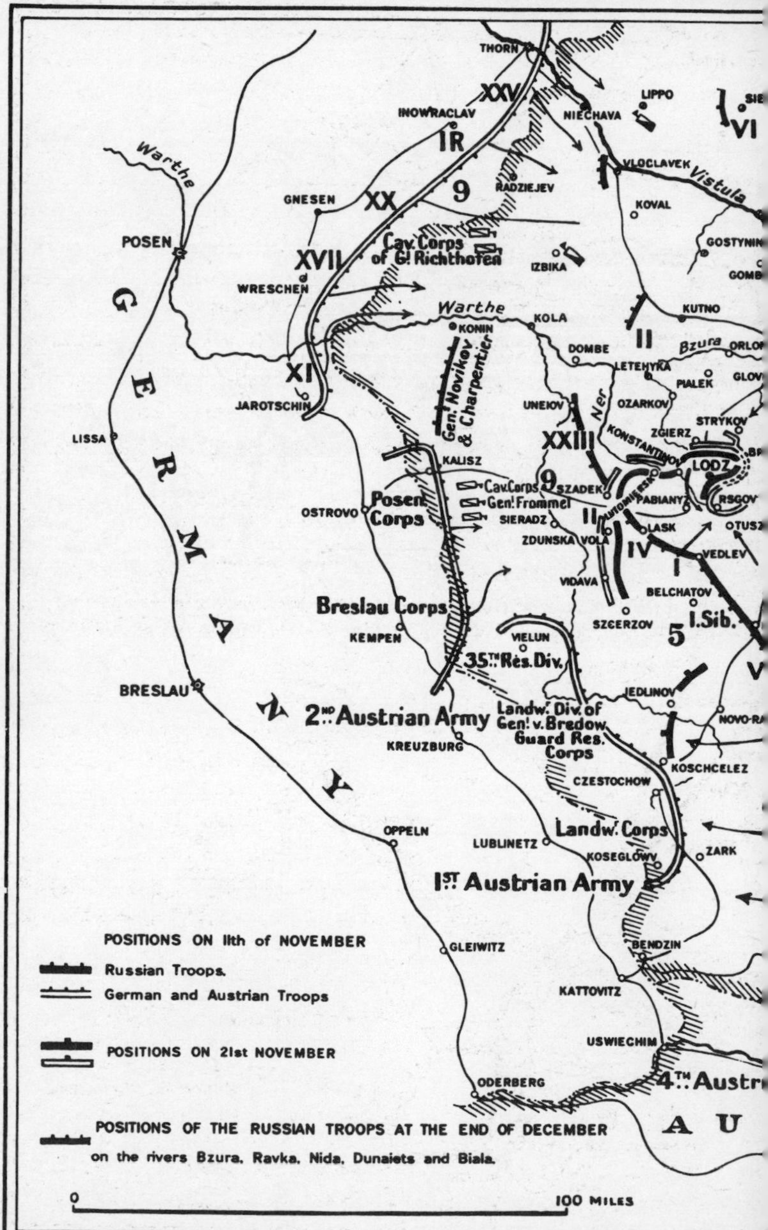

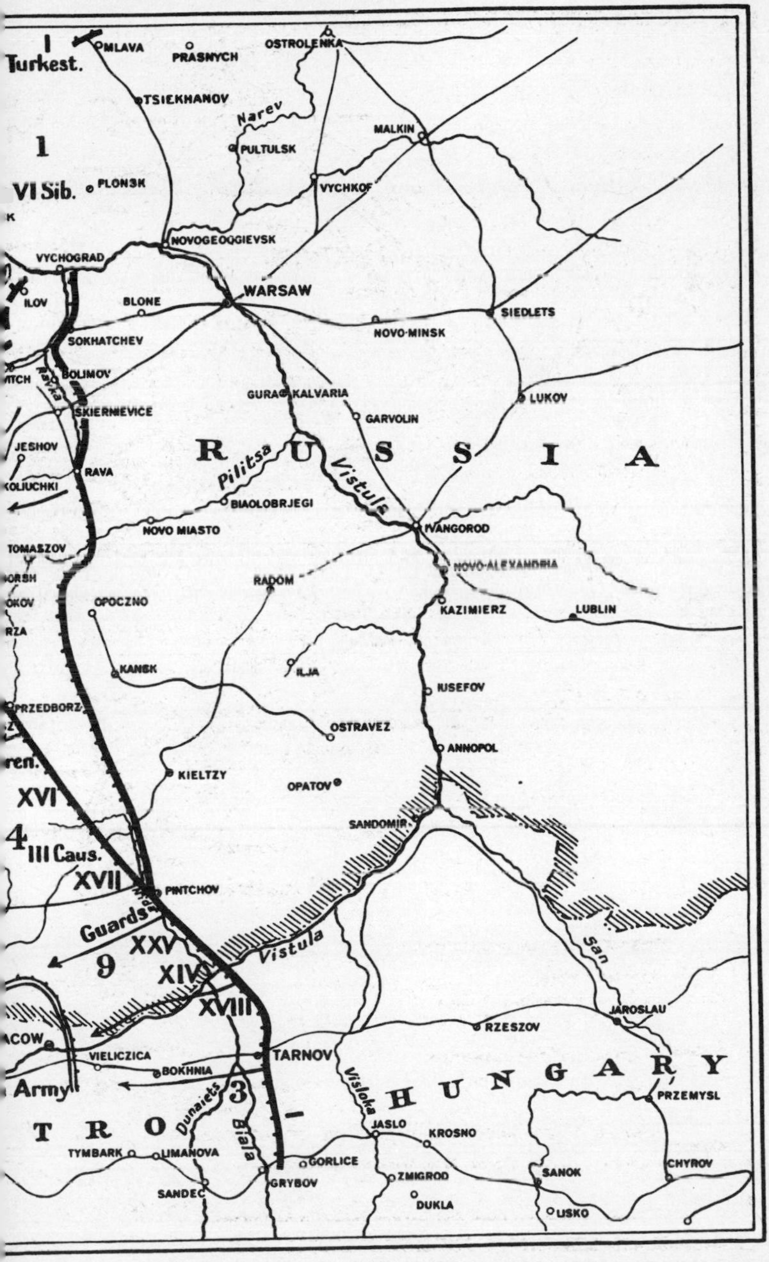

I Turkest.
MLAVA
PRASNYCH
OSTROLENKA
TSIEKHANOV
Narev
1
PULTULSK
MALKIN
VI Sib.
PLONSK
VYCHKOF
NOVOGEOGIEVSK
VYCHOGRAD
WARSAW
ILOV
BLONE
SIEDLETS
SOKHATCHEV
NOVO-MINSK
BOLIMOV
GURA KALVARIA
LUKOV
SKIERNIEVICE
GARVOLIN
JESHOV
R U S S I A
RAVA
Pilitsa
Vistula
KOLIUCHKI
BIAOLOBRJEGI
IVANGOROD
NOVO MIASTO
TOMASZOV
NOVO-ALEXANDRIA
RADOM
OPOCZNO
KAZIMIERZ
LUBLIN
KANSK
ILJA
IUSEFOV
PRZEDBORZ
OSTRAVEZ
ANNOPOL
XVI
KIELTZY
OPATOV
SANDOMIR
4
III Caus.
XVII
PINTCHOV
Guards
XXV
9
Vistula
San
XIV
XVIII
JAROSLAU
RZESZOV
TARNOV
VIELICZICA
BOKHNIA
Army
3
Dunaiets
Visloka
H U N G A R Y
PRZEMYSL
T R O
JASLO
KROSNO
Biala
TYMBARK
LIMANOVA
GORLICE
ZMIGROD
SANOK
CHYROV
SANDEC
GRYBOV
DUKLA
LISKO

INTRODUCTION

From 1904 till 1919, I was following out a plan of study of contemporary history in Russia. Up to the War, I spent three or four months of each year there, and sought out anyone who had played or was playing a part of any importance in public events, not for a newspaper interview, but for materials for history. Russians of all shades of opinion were very ready to be approached in this way, and once they realized the object I had in view they continued to keep in touch with me, and, with that pleasant friendliness and honesty which most of them have when telling of themselves, they were entirely frank and full in their information. For three years (1906 to 1908) of this work, I had an invaluable colleague in my friend, Samuel N. Harper, now Professor of Russian in the University of Chicago. We usually paid our visits to public men together, which ensured greater accuracy in the notes which we afterwards made of them, always set down before we went to bed. As soon as we knew a number of different persons concerned in the same event, this method enabled us to suggest corrections in the accounts which were given us, and it was almost as if we were able to hear and cross-examine what would later be recorded in their memoirs. I was also very fortunate throughout in being myself present at many of the principal events, (which is sometimes noted by the sign † in the text) together with these personal contacts, I was following the public life of the country closely in the published materials.

After the Revolution, when I had completed the general history of Russia on which I had been engaged, I felt that I ought to set down all that I myself knew at first hand of the contemporary period which was my special subject of study, and this was done in *My Russian Memoirs* — necessarily a more or less unconnected record. I wanted these materials anyhow to be available for future historians; but I also hoped that when I had completed my own evidence, I might set it aside and make a thorough study of all other published materials which had by now become accessible to me on this, the most critical period in Russian history. This has been a work of more than eight years, and the present book is the result of it.

I know of no period of history which is so rich in first-hand materials. This is, of course, due to the Revolution. It is true that a good many materials which I was following up have been lost for ever; for instance, being allowed to live with any regiment that I liked at the Russian front during the War, I found it easy to obtain a lien on the regimental records; but these for the most part seem to have disappeared. On the other hand, the Revolution opened access to a vast number of materials of infinitely greater value, many of which, without it, could hardly have ever become known to the public — private letters of the most personal kind passing between the chief actors in the period, diaries and other personal records. Here, as a student of history, I must pay the warmest tribute to Professor Michael Pokrovsky, the communist historian, to whom fell the priceless opportunity of making the greater part of this rich material accessible. Pokrovsky carried his extreme views into his historical studies, and they have now been discarded in the Soviet Union; but he had those instincts of scholarship which have always been so precious to the academic world of Russia, and in organizing the work of research and publication conducted under his leadership, he did not forget that he was a historian. I am in close touch with many of the scholars and public men of the emigration, and I have never heard a complaint that the materials taken from their private archives have been distorted, while several have gone out of their way to testify to their accuracy. In many of the most personal of these materials, the authenticity stands out of itself and can be verified from other sources.

I will analyse these materials now; and will remind the reader of some of them, as they become important to the narrative. First among them I should rank the *verbatim* report of the Investigating Commission of the Provisional Government which carried on its work in the eight months of 1917 between the March and November Revolutions. The new Minister of Justice, Kerensky, who was himself true to the high traditions of the Russian Bar, set up this commission directly after the abdication of Nicholas II; and its published records cover the period from March 31st (New Style) to October 24th; its work only came to an end with the Communist Revolution of November 7th. The Provisional Government was entirely liberal and democratic, and the work of the commission was entrusted to trained jurists of high standing. Those who gave evidence before it were ordinarily not examined as under any kind of prosecution, though they included imprisoned ex-Ministers of the Tsar and others who were in prison. They were questioned with great courtesy and consideration, but plainly and exhaustively; and the questions put to them were, for the most part, exactly those which would be of the greatest interest to the future historian. Those under examination, on their side, fully responded to this treatment; and some of them, including some who were most guilty of administrative abuses, with a Russian readiness, accepted the invitation to write down in full in prison all that they knew. The examination included not only nearly all the chief members and ex-members of the Cabinet, most of whom were still at liberty, but generals, high police officials, and also those parasites of the old vicious regime, who had most shamelessly exploited its corruption. There is also the evidence of members of the Duma and other distinguished public men. The whole forms a series of seven volumes, of some five hundred pages each, which enable us to check and compare the statements of nearly all of those who were most concerned in the fall of the monarchy. Particularly interesting are, on the one side, the records of the warnings given by one honest Minister after another, each of which was often followed by dismissal, and on the other hand, the fullest details, often given with remarkable objectivity and verified from other sources, by the chief villains of the piece. Especially interesting are the frank accounts of Protopopov, Beletsky (these two occupy a whole volume), Komissarov and Manuilov, the dignified records of Dzhunkovsky, Naumov, Ignatyev and Pokrovsky, and the soldierly accounts of the actual revolution by Generals Ivanov and Dubensky.

Of a like importance are the intimate and extensive personal letters written in English day by day, and sometimes twice daily, by the Empress Alexandra to her husband during their long periods of separation, and — to a lesser extent — his much shorter replies. Before the War, the imperial couple were seldom parted, and during the first year of it, Alexandra's letters are mostly concerned with personal and family interests; but from then onwards they are the chief source of all for this history, for they contain, by no means all, but an exhaustive number of the political demands of Rasputin which the Empress forwarded to her husband for authoritative execution in the sphere of administration, and a simple comparison of the dates with those of the most important subsequent political events enables us to see how many of them were carried out.

When the sovereigns were together, Rasputin had even more opportunities of approach to them; and notes in the Empress's letters make it clear that Anna Vyrubova, who was her principal intermediary with Rasputin, in spite of certain signs of the Empress's jealousy, was also authorized to communicate other demands of Rasputin direct to the Emperor; but there is much more than enough in the Empress's own letters to establish Rasputin's predominating influence in political affairs. As we gather from Nicholas's correspondence with his mother, these letters were still in his possession at Tobolsk, and were being re-read by him there.[1] After the assassination of the imperial family at Ekaterinburg, they were discovered in a black leather suitcase, and among those who were intimate with and devoted to the family there has never arisen any question as to their authenticity. In fact, there is such a wealth of personal detail, for instance, of nicknames for members of the leading reigning families in Europe, and sometimes what might almost be called code expressions, that these letters could not have been counterfeited. It is these letters that convinced me, when editing the English edition of them, that for this study we had such a mine of information as could hardly be hoped for in any other similar subject.

No inquirer into the details of this story, even the most indifferent, could have escaped the feeling that the greatest responsibility was demanded in the utilization of this most private and personal source of history. These letters are love letters of a middle-aged woman, who is as much in love with her husband as when they were engaged, and they are inspired throughout with the deepest tenderness and passion. Nothing could have been more painful to the Empress than that they should ever have seen any other eyes than those for which they were intended, and no one could read them without the sense that he is intruding into the most

[1] M.F. to N. Nov. 21st/Dec. 4th, 1917, p. 303

private sanctuary. For all that, these letters are also her triumphant vindication against unfounded accusations of her personal character, which were almost universally accepted at the time. Once they were published, they were in the hands of historians and had to be recognized as giving the chief cue to the fall of the monarchy; and as they have revealed in its completeness the part which the Empress played in this event, they are indispensable evidence of that side of her activity, for which she must answer before the bar of history. And the repercussions of that activity have proved to be a source of ruin for millions of human beings.

There have recently been published a number of letters which passed between the Emperor and his mother, the Dowager Empress Maria Fedorovna, sister of our own Queen Alexandra, from his childhood to his end. They present a more favourable picture of him than any other first-hand materials, with the exception of the admirable record of Count Kokovtsev, and show a good deal more judgment and resolution than he was ordinarily credited with, but they relate mostly to his earlier years, and during the most important part of my period, his mother, though never alienated, had already been more or less cut off from him by the jealousy of the younger Empress.

Nicholas's diaries have been partially published by the Soviet Government. They have a good deal more value than has been allowed to them, especially for the Revolution and the period of captivity. Nicholas talked with himself with complete honesty but, as was natural, with few words. The man who had made almost an art of self-restraint in speech was not likely to do more, and the inference of want of feeling, which has sometimes been drawn from them, is not justified.

Nearly everyone who was at all intimate with the extremely narrow circle of the imperial home has written a book. Among others, which are of little value, one must pay attention to the rather absurd memoirs of Anna Vyrubova because she was the recognized intermediary with Rasputin, though she says as little of that as possible in her book. She is the flimsiest of witnesses; her testimony to the Investigating Commission could hardly have been more evasive and misleading but there are a number of passages relating to the home life and even to politics where there is no reason to doubt her.

The outstanding book on that part of the subject is that of Pierre Gilliard, the perfect picture of a perfect family life, of which the real centre of interest was the nursery; and after all the nursery was the centre of all Russia's troubles. While Gilliard does full justice to that little isle of blessedness in a sea of troubles, with all his devotion to his employer friends he keeps a level head and understands all the enormous issues involved. For the captivity of the family in Tsarskoe Selo we have Gilliard's diary and that of the loyal Count Benckendorff, besides the record of Kerensky as Minister of Justice and later Prime Minister. For the imprisonment at Tobolsk and at Ekaterinburg we have on the royalist side again Gilliard's diary and the outstanding record of Nicholas Sokolov, the trained legal investigator who tracked out all the details of the story amongst abnormal difficulties, and on the Soviet side a much shorter account by P. M. Bykov, Chairman of the Soviet of Ekaterinburg, which in all the chief essentials agrees with that of Sokolov. Letters of the Empress out of captivity have been preserved by Anna Vyrubova and others. After Sokolov's death, Captain Paul Bulygin, who had accompanied him in his difficult investigation, summarized his record, with a few additions, in *The Murder of the Romanovs*, which also contained Kerensky's account of the earlier days of the captivity of the imperial family. Bulygin himself made an abortive attempt to rescue the family in Ekaterinburg, for which this devoted Jacobite nearly paid with his life.

Among the more intimate records must be ranked very high *At the Court of the Last Tsar*, by A. A. Mosolov, head of the Emperor's Civil Chancery under the Minister of the Court. His chief, Count Fredericksz, has been described even by the scandal-mongering Count Witte as 'nothing less than a knight', and Mosolov's book, one of the most understanding in our library on the subject, is fully worthy of his chief. Still, even a courtier in constant intercourse was precluded from any real intimacy by that atmosphere which he describes as one of 'Austrian etiquette' and his colleague Voeykov, Commandant of the Palace, as a world of 'lay figures'.

The well-known letters of the Kaiser to the Tsar are of great importance for the history of Russian policy up to and during the Japanese War; and a number of letters from the various Grand Dukes to the Tsar published in French translation are of value —

in particular the two long plain-spoken warnings from two of the Michael branch of the family, the Grand Dukes Nicholas and Alexander. Alexander Mikhailovich has also separately written his own reminiscences (*Once a Grand Duke*) and we have a record by the younger Grand Duchess Maria Pavlovna (there were two Grand Duchesses of this name) entitled *Things I Remember*; though these are not first-hand sources of information, they are of quite considerable interest. One can hardly say the same of *Souvenirs de Russie* by Princess Paley or *The Real Tsaritsa* by Lili Daehn, both of whom belonged intimately to the narrow circle of Anna Vyrubova. The first of these owed such currency as it attained chiefly to a quite ridiculous attack which it made on the personal honour of Sir George Buchanan.

For the history of Rasputin we have Rodzyanko's book *The Reign of Rasputin*, very important, though the statements are sometimes loose and confused or even inaccurate. Two of the assassins of Rasputin have disputed the dubious honour of having killed him, Prince Felix Yusupov and Vladimir Purishkevich — it was Purishkevich who actually fired the fatal shot — and Basil Maklakov, eminent politician and barrister, who was in close touch with the conspirators, has published his comments, so that we are able to trace every detail of that episode. More important are the books of two men who were in different periods close intimates of Rasputin, the monk Illiodor (*The Holy Devil*), who first befriended him and then fought him tooth and nail, and Aaron Simanovich, who was Rasputin's secretary and business man. Though he repeats a number of entirely unfounded scandals, Simanovich gives details of Rasputin's methods and his political views and conduct, which can often be verified from other sides. There is also a not very valuable but interesting book by Rasputin's daughter *The Real Rasputin*. A very full investigation of all the materials relating to Rasputin was made by Fülöp-Miller; but his big book on the subject, *Der Heilige Teufel*, though embodying a whole lot of good spade work, is unfortunately written up in a journalistic style, entirely misplacing some of the chief episodes of the story and even transforming parts of the record into imaginary conversations for which the author alone is responsible.

I have spoken so far of those materials which deal with the hidden part of the story; and the reader who reads this book to the end will probably share the view that we find the real explanation of the fall of the monarchy in them. I have left unmentioned a number of the ordinary materials for the history of the period, which have long been accessible and have already been utilized by myself and others. But when we pass to the records of the public men of the time we find several that are of the highest value. For the earlier part there is little that bears on the inner history of Russian policy except the memoirs of the ablest statesman of the period, Count Witte; and Witte's book is marred by his undisguised personal hostility both to the Emperor and to Witte's own successor, Stolypin, and also by a kind of cynical indifference; for example, beyond boasting of his achievements, which were very great indeed, he seems hardly to care to explain to his readers a number of first-class problems with which he was dealing and his way of dealing with them; his chapters on the gold reserve, the gold standard and the liquor monopoly are almost trifling. Witte ceases to be a source after 1905; but for the period which followed, almost up to the World War, we have one of the best of all the books on the subject, that of Count Kokovtsev. This is an admirable piece of work and does as much credit to the character as to the industry and the fidelity of the writer. Kokovtsev had a habit of recording all his conversations with the Emperor (from 1904 to 1914) immediately afterwards, and his book is not only a most kindly, but the best portrait of Nicholas II. For the history of the Russian Empire for those ten years it will remain the best of all the sources. Izvolsky, Minister of Foreign Affairs from 1905 to 1910, never brought his memoirs up to the point where they would have the most historical value and hardly touches the important questions of foreign policy in his period of office. Much better, though by no means entirely satisfactory, is the record of his successor, Sergius Sazonov (Foreign Minister from 1910 to 1916). Sazonov's book is entirely honest and faithfully reflects his own limitations; its chief defect is due to his loyalty to his deposed sovereign, and he has written down only a very small part of what he knew of the causes of the fall of the monarchy. An almost hectic interest attaches to the notes taken by the assistant secretary of the Cabinet, Yakhontov, during the most heated period of the constitutional crisis of 1915, which was the culmination of the whole story. The same may be said of the very remarkable memorandum which Protopopov drew up after his fall and shortly before his execution by the Bolsheviks; it contains a vivid picture of his last days of office, and he also gives the frankest account of his views and intentions in the sphere of policy.

General Polivanov, who was Assistant War Minister from 1906 to 1912, throws the most light on the day to day life of the Cabinet and Duma in the time of Stolypin; and in the record of his work as War Minister in the critical months from June to September 1915, his short, plain and soldierly notes supplement and greatly extend what we learn from Yakhontov about the constitutional crisis of 1915. On the other hand the book of Vasilyev, the last Director of the Police Department before the Revolution, (*Police Russe et Révolution*), can hardly be treated as sincere on the subject of Rasputin, to whom he indirectly owed his appointment, and sometimes shows a surprising inaccuracy or even ignorance. But it contains some of the most official information on the murder of Rasputin, and a priceless record of the March Revolution from the angle of the police.

Among the 'public men' — members of the Duma and others outside the Government — the first place should have belonged to Rodzyanko, President of the Duma, who published in English translation his book with the title *The Reign of Rasputin*, for which perhaps the author was not responsible; but Rodzyanko wrote in exile and apparently without records, except for his very important notes on his audiences with the Emperor, which he is able to relate in full — and they are the chief things that we want from him. In other respects his book is sometimes loose and confused. Equally, his judgments, especially of men, are often hasty and inadequate. Milyukov is of course a great source of information which I have utilized in other ways, but his *History of the Second Russian Revolution*, except for its interesting summary of the causes, is inadequate for our purpose and was written too early. Kerensky also has written widely; and several of his publications are available in English. His translated memoirs have been issued in English translation (his son is an excellent translator) under an entirely inappropriate title *The Crucifixion of Liberty* — by the way, how would one set about crucifying liberty? In spite of this title, the book is most interesting, though it is a personal autobiography and almost bears the character rather of a speech than of a literary work; and it is the frankest account of all the writer's most intimate instincts and political beliefs. Among the 'public men' far the best contribution to our knowledge and understanding of the events which lead up to the Revolution is that of Basil Shulgin. He recalls the picture with all its lights and shades; and one, who like myself saw it as it was unfolding, will recognize it as the true perspective throughout; Shulgin has a remarkable gift of narrative and a quite unusual understanding of others entirely remote from him in their political outlook. Among other materials I have found of use the diary kept throughout by my friend Valery Carrick — in my opinion the greatest Russian political caricaturist of his time (he did some joint work with Sir F. Carruthers Gould) and always instinctively the friend of the man in the street.

Both the British and French Ambassadors played prominent parts in this story and both have left records of it. The British Ambassador, Sir George Buchanan, wrote *My Mission to Russia* so near to the time that he was certainly hampered by restrictions on the publication of official documents; and in his strong personal loyalty to the fallen sovereigns, like his friend Sazonov, he abstained from saying much that he might have said. Besides this he had a kind of baffling simplicity, which both in speech and in writing made his remarks seem commonplace, where knowledge of the circumstances would show the reader the justice and wisdom of his judgments. His daughter's book, *The Dissolution of the Empire*, is a sketch of the Russian Society of the time and a defence of the slandered memory of her noble father. Paleologue, the French Ambassador on the other hand is a brilliant writer and his book *La Russie des Tsars pendant la Grande Guerre* is the more valuable because it is in the form of a diary; but one cannot help feeling that the diary has been greatly touched up afterwards; and though his book is far richer both in detail and in knowledge of Russia, his judgments have not the value of those of his British colleague. Here may be mentioned the book of R. H. Bruce Lockhart (*Memoirs of a British Agent*) who as Deputy British Consul General in Moscow rendered brilliant service to the Allied cause in the War, but it is heavily coloured by the requirements of a best seller.

Turning to the military writers, the British reader owes a special debt to the Senior British Military Attaché, Sir Alfred Knox (*With the Russian Army*). This is one of the most valuable of all our original authorities. Knox knew the Russian Army through and through; and it was General Sukhomlinov, who, as Minister of War seems to have done what he could to block him in his work, that described him as the ablest military attaché whom he had known. Knox's book also is largely in diary form; and its historical value is the greater because he left these day-to-day jottings uncorrected by knowledge acquired after the event. Young historians have recognized his objectivity, his sound sense and the far-reaching wisdom of many of his judgments. But Knox's book is not a history of the War; and that more difficult task has been ably executed by General Danilov (*La Russie dans la Guerre Mondiale*), who as Quarter-Master-General of the Grand Duke Nicholas was responsible for drawing up the orders for operations from the beginning of the War till September 1915, a period which, with the exception of Brusilov's offensive, saw the major part of the fighting. Danilov had his prejudices; he was always in favour of a knock-out blow to Germany. There was another school of military thought among those opposed to Austria, from whose distinguished group so many won promotion to the highest posts, and this group included a much younger soldier, at the outset of the War almost the youngest general in the Russian Army, Golovin, who in spite of his youth was more than once thought of for the highest military posts. Golovin is a first-rate military historian, and has published special studies of the most important phases of the War on the Eastern Front — Tannenberg, the Russian conquest of Galicia, and Brusilov's offensive — and also a careful survey of the conditions in which the Russian army fought in his *Russia and the Great War*. The Russian commander who showed the greatest intellect was Brusilov: and we have his *My Reminiscences* published in English under the title *A Soldier's Notebook* which, written without all the necessary records, give us a full and fascinating picture of his experiences and of his military ideas. Brusilov's judgment on the psychology of the Russian soldiers in the War goes deeper than that of his military colleagues. General Gurko's book *Russia in* 1914-17 is slighter and more exclusively personal. But our picture would have been quite incomplete without the records of the chief German commanders. Hindenburg's book *Out of My Life*, though it does not give much of the military detail, is of absorbing personal interest and is full of a broad humanity.

It is Ludendorff who gives the detail essential to our understanding of the course of the military struggle; and nothing is more striking in his book *My War Memories* than the tribute he pays again and again to the courage and chivalry of the Russian troops. General Hoffmann's war papers and summary are an excellent supplement to these two, confirming them on all points and equally impressive in his tribute to the Russian fighting man.

As a summary of the whole subject, there should be mentioned the work of a young Russian scholar, Florinsky (*The End of the Russian Empire*). The arrangement of the subject is unsatisfactory; for each phase of the national life of Russia through the World War is taken separately throughout, and of all things the army is put last, so that it is very difficult to trace the ups and downs of the story, and this encourages conclusions based too readily on the turn which things finally took; but Florinsky has made a scholarly research into the economic conditions produced by the War, for which later students will be greatly indebted.

To this I have to add my own evidence. Much of it is incorporated in *My Russian Memoirs*; but it has also been of great value to me to have had so many personal contacts, in some cases quite frequently, with leading characters of this period; and the personal knowledge obtained in this way has been of great use in checking other statements. I have thought that this should be indicated in some way; and I have therefore marked with the sign † in the index the names of those with whom I was personally acquainted. The names in the index are also accentuated to indicate the correct pronunciation. Where my evidence bears directly on any question of major importance, I have similarly shown this in the text of the book. Apart from this, it has been possible since the Revolution — especially in two visits for the purpose to Paris in 1935 and 1938 and two to Leningrad in 1936 and 1937 — to obtain much supplementary material and to verify at first hand some points on which I was in doubt. In particular, Alexander Guchkov before his death dictated to me a very full account covering the whole of his political career. And I have specially profited by detailed conversations with Count Kokovtsev, General Golovin, Paul Milyukov, Alexander Kerensky and Vladimir Burtsev. Where necessary these sources are indicated in footnotes.

In general, as so much of what I have written is based directly on the statements of those concerned or of others who had close knowledge of the events in question, it is essential to indicate the references; but I have been anxious not to irritate the reader with voluminous footnotes, and usually give only the name of the author and the reference. The titles of the various sources are given in full above in a special table, with such abbreviations as I have used in the footnotes. References are indispensable as a guarantee of good faith or for verification by serious students; but I hope the general reader will simply disregard them throughout. There are much fewer in the earlier chapters, as there the main events have long been ascertained and made public. In the later I am digging out details at first hand, of which I have not seen a consecutive narrative, even in Russian.

The question of dates offers great difficulty. As is known, throughout this period all dates of internal Russian history were given in the Old Style, which in the twentieth century was thirteen days *behind* the New (in the nineteenth century, twelve). On the other hand, military events are ordinarily given in the New, especially by writers now in the emigration who have published their books in other languages than Russian. But this is not always consistent. What is one to say of a Foreign Minister (Sazonov) who gives the dates of the crisis and the declaration of war in the New Style, but gives the principal events of Russian internal politics in the Old? Where dates had to be recovered through all sorts of private materials, for instance, letters, and in some cases were given incorrectly, this difficulty was increased. One cannot have one calendar for the War and another for the internal politics; and to give the date in the Old Style for such an event as the Battle of Tannenberg could only be confusing. I found that the only way, even for my own sanity, was to make a day to day diary of the whole of the period, and thought it obviously best to draw it up in the New Style, which has now, I am glad to say, been adopted in Russia. This may be taken into account when I am giving, for instance, references to letters from the Empress which can only be verified in the Old Style, and in such cases I have given both dates.

As some of the different sources have been published in more than one language, I have indicated in the table of references which edition has been utilized. In some cases — for instance with Witte and Kokovtsev — two-volumed works in Russian have been abridged into one volume. Where obtainable, I have of course preferred the Russian. For all translations from the Russian, I am myself responsible, and in two cases I have altered the English version to be in closer accordance with the Russian. The translations of Russian political verse are my own. Where they contained puns, I have had to find equivalents in English, but never with any departure from the meaning of the original.

I should be at a loss how to acknowledge all the help that I have had in this study, extending over so many years; to the many Russians who have so freely put themselves at my disposal and have spared no pains in giving me of their best, to colleagues who have helped me in the verification of details, especially in the bibliography, to those who have read through a part or even the whole of the book, to those who have lent me photographs for its illustration and to my friends the publishers with whom I have collaborated in all the details of its production.

The story which emerges from this material is as tragic as anything I have ever known. Following the events throughout while they were evolving and later filling in one gap after another in my knowledge of them, I have become quite convinced that the cause of the ruin came not at all from below, but from above. This is what was actually said by some of the chief actors in the course of the story; as even the loyal Gilliard sums it up, 'Everything was done to provoke a revolution, and nothing to anticipate its sequels.[1] This had to be made clear to the reader. The Tsar had many opportunities of putting things right, and several times he was on the point of taking them; the reader will find out why he did not. So far from a dictation of events from below, this passive people went on enduring long after it ought to have ceased to do so; and even when the crash came, it had done so little to shape it in any way, that it was left to the last-minute decision of a single regiment to determine the issue — and then, when the defenders with their own hands have removed the last of their ramparts,

> The ocean, overpeering of his list,
> Eats not the flats with more impiteous haste.

So far from diminishing the force of the Revolution, this adds to it a finality which could never have been obtained from a

[1] GILLIARD, 142.

successful conspiracy. It was only later that brooding over that surging waste of waters, a master mind was to write on it a new word.

But, once more, the initiative comes from above; and there — 'above' — we are faced with the strangest of human tangles, the complicated and abnormal relations of three persons — Rasputin, the Empress and the Emperor: set in an ascending order of authority and a descending order of influence. Yet, it is impossible to treat this story as an intimately personal episode, because we are dealing with the most critical events in the history of a people covering an enormous part of the surface of the earth. This is what we have to remember, as we watch the doings in the remote little palace at Tsarskoe Selo.

SCOTO VIATORI
COMES VIAE

And let me speak to th' yet unknowing world,
How these things came about. So shall you hear
Of carnal, bloody, and unnatural acts,
Of accidental judgements, casual slaughters,
Of deaths put on by cunning, and forc'd cause,
And in this upshot, purposes mistook,
Fall'n on the inventors' heads.

Hamlet, v, 2

CHAPTER I

NICHOLAS II AND HIS TASK

The King is come, deal mildly with his youth.
Richard II., II. I

AUTOCRACY really ended in Russia on November 1st, 1894, when the last autocrat died. The question was, what was to succeed it?

No one had expected the death of Alexander III. If one takes in the direct line the five immediate ancestors of Nicholas II, one will notice that three of the five were assassinated, and only two died in their beds; but these were precisely the two who were capable of producing what might be called an aura of autocracy: a powerful psychological force, which with the vast majority of the nation for the time being removed ideas of assassination and revolution into a misty background, though the memory was always there.

There was an amazingly ingenious and impressive equestrian statue of Alexander III, the work of a brilliantly clever sculptor, Prince Paul Trubetskoy, which throughout the reign of his son stood in the square before the Nicholas station of St. Petersburg. A huge, powerful, bearded man, clothed in that Russian military uniform that recalls the loose costume and top boots of the Russian peasant, forcibly gripped with his legs the loins of a small, spirited and vicious Cossack horse — the whole a very picture of masterful rule. The picture simply showed autocracy in the life; autocracy might call for your approval or your indignation, but this was the true presentation of it, and it was later to be left standing after the Revolution of 1917.

The tradition that a system of autocracy should produce a succession of autocrats is entirely fallacious. Often enough in monarchical countries the heir apparent has been in constant friction with his reigning father; but the predominance in the domestic circle of such a strong and narrow-minded man as

Alexander III was enough to crush out any sproutings of will-power in his successor. Mosolov, who was close to the family, tells us that they were all 'in veritable terror'[1] of him. They might see him 'tying an iron poker into knots'[2] or merely bending a fork, as he did to amuse and impress two Austrian officers.[3] The close domestic atmosphere of this family, united in obedience, was the school which taught how everything should be done rightly. In the family chamber music, we are told, the big bear appropriately played the big bassoon.

In this atmosphere Nicholas grew up as a slight young man with a singular gentleness of disposition and manner. 'Nicky', writes one of his most intimate cousins, Alexander Mikhailovich, 'smiled his usual tender, shy, slightly sad smile',[4] all the more appealing because of the beauty of his frank blue eyes. Unlike his father, who was a second son, he well knows the nature of the overwhelming task that awaits him, which he never regards as other than 'a heavy cross'; and he must know that he has none of the force of his father's character to face it. His own nature, as Izvolsky has put it, is one of 'nuances and half tones'.[5] He does not forget that he was born on the day that commemorates Job. He is simple in all his ways, but truly religious, and this sense grows more and more on him through life. He is deeply conscientious, but he is instinctively distrustful of himself. His mother in her wise letters to him often emphasizes the responsibility of any act of his in public, and he responds: 'One has to be cautious with everyone at the outset.'[6] It is his tutor, General Danilevsky, known at the Court as 'the Jesuit', who is credited with having implanted in him 'an impenetrable reserve'.[7] He has an excellent quickness of mind: 'a great capacity for grasping his interlocutor's thought', writes Mosolov.[8] Though his education like that of other prospective sovereigns had consisted in the main of a mass of superficial and patchy impressions, he could see at once not only the point but the implications of any step which was suggested to him. Alexander Guchkov, who was later to become his special bugbear as the leader for patriotic reform, said of him: 'He can understand with half a word what particular idea you are trying

[1] Mosolov, 72. [2] G. D. Alexander, 73. [3] ibid., 80.
[4] G. D. A. M., 91. [5] Izvolsky, 278. [6] N. to M. F., 36.
[7] Mosolov, 6. [8] ibid., 10.

to plant on him'[1] — surely one of the most indispensable qualities for a constitutional sovereign.

But far the most striking of his characteristics was a conquering personal charm which had for its basis an innate delicacy of mind. There is practically not a single one among the innumerable records of contact with him that does not emphasize this quality. It is useless to give names, for no reference to him is without this note. One may quote a few of them just to give the colour of expression: 'With his usual simplicity and friendliness', writes Kokovtsev.[2] 'A rare kindness of heart', says Sazonov.[3] 'A charm that attracted all who came near him', writes Buchanan, who adds that he always felt that he was talking 'with a friend and not the Emperor'.[4] 'Charming in the kindly simplicity of his ways', says young Yusupov.[5] Take for instance a man who hated him and at the bottom of his heart despised him, his ablest statesman, the masterful Witte, whose glaring vulgarity might have excluded him from any appreciation of this quality.

> If one may say so [he writes in his spiteful memoirs] a spirit of good will came out of him in bright rays. He heartily and sincerely wished happiness to Russia as a whole, to all the nationalities composing Russia, to all his subjects, for undoubtedly he had an extremely good, kind heart . . . I can say that I have never in my life met a man of finer breeding.[6]

And again:

> The Emperor Nicholas II has a peculiar gift of charm. I do not know anyone who was not charmed by him the first time that they were presented to him. He charms both by simple kindness, by his manner of address and particularly by his wonderful good-feeling; for I have never in my life met anyone who had nicer manners than our Emperor.[7]

Nice manners are hardly the feature which one would expect to find as the outstanding characteristic of an autocrat. Like many others who had met him, the writer himself when speaking to him depended on memory to realize that he was conversing with an Emperor. 'In his cast of mind', writes Sokolov, 'he was a living

[1] Guchkov to B. P. [2] KOKOVTSEV, I, 118. [3] SAZONOV, 36.
[4] BUCHANAN, I, 170. [5] YUSUPOV, 25. [6] WITTE, I, 12.
[7] ibid., I, 70.

negation of the idea of autocracy.'[1] But much the fullest picture of this most pleasant personality is to be found in the memoirs of Count Kokovtsev, a masterly work full of sincerity, fairness and understanding. Kokovtsev was a simple and straightforward bureaucratic official, who for ten years, first as Minister of Finance and later as also Prime Minister, possessed in full the confidence and affection of his sovereign. His accurate notes vividly recall the very different personalities of the two men. The charm in these conversations is all supplied by Nicholas, and it is omnipresent. Everywhere there is humour, good sense, a compelling kindliness, a quick intelligence and an excellent memory. Nowhere is there strength. The quality was one of appeal; it was as if he were almost asking you to be pleased in his company.

The training of the future sovereign was closely domestic and very strict. He got up ordinarily at six o'clock; camp beds were the custom of the imperial family. In the rigid etiquette of his education it was apparently prescribed that the teacher should not put the pupil any questions; at least that is what the most famous of his tutors, Pobedonostev, told Witte. Among one of the practices enjoined on him was that of keeping a diary, a habit which he religiously continued till the very end of his life. Many passages of this diary have now been made public. The entries are ordinarily very short. They nearly always contain references to the weather, which in this case are anything but perfunctory. Nicholas was entirely an out-of-door man. He found his greatest pleasure with his gun in the woods or swimming or rowing. Physical exercise was an absolute necessity to him, and he walked very fast. He had a close eye for the sky, the sun and the clouds, and at many points he writes of the weather with genuine feeling and delight. In his diary he delights in 'the yellowing trees', 'the tracings of the hoar frost', and he continues his enthusiastic comments such as 'a wonderful sunny frosty day', 'a radiant day', 'weather wonderful', after abdication and even in prison. Anything to do with the army, of which he was an enthusiastic and undiscriminating admirer, and especially the big military parades, is described with something like rapture. The short early notes do not tell so much about his life, except that it was very much

[1] SOKOLOV, 57.

restricted, with occasional simple and unaffected references to a night out with some regimental mess and once an honest record of how he was carried home.

But soon appears what is later to be the mainspring of his personal life.

On Aug. 20th/Sept. 1st 1891, he writes:

> O Lord, how I want to go to Ilyinsky . . . otherwise if I do not see her now I shall have to wait a whole year, and that will be hard.

He is speaking of the one love of his life (for his passing affection for the dancer Kseshinskaya — also honestly recorded in his diary — was nothing more than a fancy). At Ilyinsky, the Moscow country house of his uncle Sergius and his aunt Elisabeth, was then staying his aunt's sister Princess Alix of Hesse-Darmstadt, one of the younger daughters of Princess Alice of England, and grand-daughter of Queen Victoria.

> My dream [he writes on Dec. 21st/Jan. 2nd, 1892] is some day to marry Alix H. I have loved her for a long while, and still deeper and stronger since 1889 when she spent six weeks in St. Petersburg. For a long time I resisted my feeling, trying to deceive myself by the impossibility that my dearest dream will come true.

And in the same passage he describes it as

> 'that dream and that hope by which I live from day to day'.

From what he writes it is evident that at one time he thought her destined to marry the eldest son of King Edward of England, but now the only barrier that remains is the question of religion. 'It is all in the hands of God,' he ends this entry. 'Relying on His mercy, I look forward to the future calmly and obediently.'

Religion was in this case a very real obstacle. The early picture of Princess Alix is of a young girl, unusually reserved and shy, almost careless of appearances, absorbed in her own thoughts, in which religion had far the deepest place of all. No nature was ever more whole-hearted. She was capable, as few people are, of sustained and concentrated contemplation, especially on religion. Very beautiful and stately, of the fair-haired German or English type, she was almost indifferent to anything but the great realities of life. On her side she loved Nicholas as deeply as he could ever have loved her. In one of her later letters she dates this absorbing affection even from childhood. It is perhaps not realized that throughout her life she looked up to him, and no wonder — for she had none of the charm which was so strong in him — and she was boundlessly grateful for his love. But religion meant everything to her, and princess or not, any change of confession could only be to her the most vital matter of conscience that is possible.

She had failed to leave any good impression in the very alien higher society of St. Petersburg in 1889, and this with her lover's family had added to the obstacles to their marriage. Other suggestions were made to Nicholas in vain, and in 1894 his decision prevailed with his parents, and he was allowed to go and make his proposal. Yet it would not be the first time that the orthodox confession could prove to have a conquering attraction for German Protestant princesses. The brilliant and cynical Catherine the Great, originally Princess of Anhalt-Zerbst, familiar as she was with Catholicism, Lutheranism, and Calvinism, so far as there was any religion in her nature, gave herself wholeheartedly to the Orthodox Church, which she described enthusiastically as a great oak with roots deep in the ground. Alix's own elder sister Elisabeth is a far more outstanding example. Married to the morose Grand Duke Sergius, and treated with an appearance of churlishness which excited general pity, Elisabeth found much more than consolation for this willingly accepted bondage in Russian Orthodoxy, to which after her husband's assassination she gave herself up entirely, becoming the head of an order of deaconesses founded by herself under the title of Martha and Mary, and devoting herself to every kind of good work. This was to come later; but Alix, too, when she once got a grasp of the spiritual power of Russian religion, was to embrace it with a fervour which was to carry her to its furthest extravagances, but at the same time to give her an absolute sureness of herself for the rest of her life.

In April 1894 Nicholas and Alix met in Coburg, whither Queen Victoria had herself come, to help in removing the last difficulties. The last remains of the obstacle were still there.

> Heavens, what a day! [writes Nicholas in his diary] After coffee about ten, we went to Aunt Ella to the rooms of Ernie

> and Alix. She looked particularly pretty, but extremely sad. [How many references are there later to those great, sad, blue eyes!] They left us alone, and then began between us that talk which I had long ago strongly wanted and at the same time very much feared. We talked till twelve, but with no result; she still objects to changing her religion. Poor girl, she cried a lot. We parted more calmly. [April 5th/17th]

Three days later with the comforting presence of 'Granny' (as Nicholas also affectionately calls Queen Victoria) the clouds are all removed.

> Wonderful, unforgettable day in my life [he writes on April 8th/20th] the day of my engagement to my darling, adorable[1] Alix. After ten she came to Aunt Miechen and after a talk with her we came to an understanding. O God, what a mountain has rolled from my shoulders . . . The whole day I have been walking in a mist, without fully realizing what has actually happened to me. Wilhelm [the Emperor of Germany] sat in the next room and waited with the uncles and aunts till our talk was over. I went straight with Alix to the Queen [Victoria] and then to Aunt Mary, where the whole family was simply enraptured. After lunch we went to Aunt Mary's church and had a thanksgiving service . . . I cannot even believe that I am engaged. [April 10th/22nd] At ten came my wonderful Alix, and we went together to the Queen to drink coffee. It was a cold, raw day, but in my heart it was bright and joyful.

To his mother he writes:

> I gave her your letter and after that she couldn't argue any more . . . The whole world is changed for me: nature, mankind, everything; and all seem to be good and lovable and happy.[2]

In her reply she writes: 'It has been a real battle! But God has helped you to this great victory'; and it is now that she asks Alix to give her the name of 'Mother dear' (in English), which so often recurs in later letters.[3]

'Granny', at home or in her pony cart, is a constant feature in this courtship, and she insists that the young couple shall come

[1] The Russian word is *nenaglyadnaya*, which means 'I cannot look enough at her'.
[2] N. to M. F. 75. Ap. 10th/22nd.
[3] M. F. to N. 77. Ap. 14th/26th.

and continue it in England. Alix had never considered herself anything else but an Englishwoman. Her mother had died in her prime in 1878, when the child was only six years old, and from that time it was Queen Victoria who was the central figure in all her education and had given her the instincts which were to grow with her throughout life. The future Empress of Russia was in the deepest sense a Victorian Englishwoman. The lovers were together at Walton-on-Thames, and to 'dear Walton' Alix constantly looks back in her later correspondence with her husband. They picnicked on the banks of the Thames, they were together again at Windsor. This, if they had known it, was the only honeymoon they were ever to have.

At the very outset of their engagement Alix captured her lover's diary; throughout her life she did everything to make him feel her presence when he was far from her, and she now entered in advance at various points, where they later interrupt the narrative, favourite quotations, English or German, which were to make him feel that she was with him when she was far away. To one of the earliest of these entries she constantly returns in later life when writing to her husband:

> Hush, my dear, lie still and slumber,
> Holy Angels guard thy bed!
> Heavenly blessings without number
> Gently falling on thy head!
> Better, better every day.
> With unending true devotion,
> Better far than I can say.[1]

On his way back while at sea he comes on the following entry under July 14th/26th:

> My thoughts are ever with you, and my love grows deeper day by day . . . sleep sweetly, and let the gentle waves rock you to sleep — your Guardian Angel is keeping watch over you. A tender kiss.[2]

And on July 16th/28th from Marie Corelli:

> For the past is past and will never return — the future we know not — and only the present can be called our own.[3]

[1] N. diary, *Dnevnik Imperatora Nikolaya Vtorago*, Berlin, 1923, 62.
[2] ibid., 72.
[3] ibid., 73.

This habit continues; it is that she takes command of his soul, and her love for him from the start is like that of a mother. She pities him — no wonder — to think of the crushing burden which is to fall upon that tender, lovable nature.

In the autumn Alexander III fell ill. He was still in middle life and no one realized at first that his life was in danger. As he quickly got worse, it was a question whether his future daughter-in-law could arrive in time in Russia to see him alive. Summoned hastily, Alix reached Livadia in Crimea on October 11th/23rd. This was later to be her dearest home, and from the first she was struck by the marvellous climate, the vineyards and flowers; but also from the very first, while all thoughts are concentrated on the dying Emperor, she stirs up her lover to take a more prominent part in all that is being done to tend the patient.

> Sweet child, pray to God [she writes in an inset in his diary for October 16th/28th]. He will comfort you, don't feel too low, He will help you in your trouble. Your Sunny is praying for you and the beloved patient . . . Be firm and make the doctors, Leyden or the other G., come alone to you every day and tell you how they find him and exactly what they wish him to do, so that you are the first always to know . . . Don't let others be put first and you left out . . . Show your own mind and don't let others forget who you are.'[1]

The illness went swiftly to its appointed end. John of Kronstadt, the favourite priest of the Emperor, was with him when he died. The betrothal had taken place in the Emperor's bedroom. The future Empress made her first appearance as fiancée of the new sovereign in the countless funeral services and unending railway journeys between Livadia and St. Petersburg. Any face would be sad at that time, but hers, with her deep devotion to her betrothed and her deep religious feeling at this moment of sorrow, was the saddest of all, and her natural shyness was emphasized more than ever. This was how she was shown to Russia, and even simple peasant women drew their ominous conclusions. The spiteful Witte, who learned to hate her, draws a sharp contrast between that sad and burdened face and the beauty of her aunt Alexandra, the future queen of England.

[1] N. diary, *Dnevnik Imperatora Nikolaya Vtorago*, Berlin, 1923, 83.

Still in the atmosphere of mourning took place the wedding on November 26th.

> Never [writes the young wife in her husband's diary on Nov. 27th/Dec. 8th] did I believe there could be such utter happiness in this world, such a feeling of unity between two mortal beings. I love you — those three words have my life in them.

And again on Dec. 9th (Nov. 27th O.S.):

> No more separations. At last united, bound for life, and when this life is ended we meet again in the other world to remain together for all eternity. Yours, yours.

And what was the nature of the 'official' honeymoon, when her husband, long before he had expected it, had to take over what must have been the most onerous task in the world, for which he was only very partially prepared — that of Tsar of Russia? He has hardly any time to be with her. He is gathering what he can from his father's advisers, and of course before all things from his mother. At every turn comes the interruption of new duties. Her husband she adores, but what is all round her is not the Russia which she is to get to love so deeply; it is official St. Petersburg with its cold etiquette and heartless routine and a society with which she cannot be in any sympathy. That he is utterly overburdened goes without saying; yet it is the most critical steps that are awaited at the beginning of a new reign. He is all day in the limelight, with his devoted wife left in the background. Is it surprising that her first impressions — for she knew all his kindliness and his weakness — were full of fear.

> I feel [she once said to a confidante] that all who surround my husband are insincere, and no one is doing his duty for Russia. They are all serving him for their career and personal advantage, and I worry myself and cry for days on end, as I feel that my husband is very young and inexperienced, of which they are all taking advantage.[1]

It was in these first days that originated the alienation between wife and mother. It was inevitable that Maria Fedorovna with

[1] *Dnevnik Imperatora Nikolaya Vtorago*, Berlin, 106.

her wise head and tact and with her own and her son's loyalty to the late Emperor, however she might wish to avoid it, should be forced into a closeness of communion which left the young wife alone.

These are the conditions in which Nicholas II mounted the throne of Russia, and we must turn from this narrow domestic atmosphere, as he had to do, to study the task which lay before him. The record of this ordinary, though so genuine love affair, so typical of the middle class of Victorian England, is the only rightful preface to the story which follows; but the contrast is tremendous.

It would take us too far to try to give anything like a full summary of what was wrong with Russia; besides, I have myself written my own account of it elsewhere.[1] There is a very good attempt, short and telling, in the first pages of Milyukov's *History of the Second Russian Revolution.*[2] The Russian Revolution, according to Milyukov, really contained much more of Pugachev, Razin and Bolotnikov (these were the great leaders of servile revolts) than of any realization of modern watchwords. The State idea, he explains, was borrowed from abroad and was far in advance of the intelligence of the population. It developed a service class of local land tenants of the State who were less squires than officials of the central government, and who were rewarded for their state services, principally military, not originally by the ownership, but by the tenure of land. This system developed a series of burning questions which were much more social than political. Meanwhile, the superstructure of the State was recent and artificial; the very capital itself grew up as a creation of autocracy and bureaucracy at a corner of the Empire.

The Russian autocracy in its origin was a perfectly genuine creation of national needs, above all of the need of national defence — first to shake off the Tartar yoke, which for two hundred and forty years (1240-1480) lay so heavy upon the country, not only politically but socially and economically, and for centuries after that to repel almost yearly invasions in which numbers of peasants — men, women and children — were dragged

[1] PARES, *A History of Russia.*
[2] MILYUKOV, *Istoria Vtoroy Russkoy Revolutsii,* 1 ff.

away into slavery. It was this purely military need that essentially shaped the social development of Russia. As time went on, and particularly in the seventeenth and eighteenth centuries, every function of state service was defined: priests were to pray; the service gentry were to fight; the merchants were to pay; and the peasants were to till. It was a wholly artificial system of class compartments, divisions which could not possibly be regularly maintained, and it was in this system that lay the origins of class war.

The vast majority of the population was the peasantry, still in 1894, over seventy-five per cent of the whole. The gentry were a mere sprinkling; so later was the growing, constantly repressed educated class; the merchants, who were given nothing more than an artificial organization, were only a kind of supplement. The Church was indeed a reality, and still more so religion, but the official Church in the eighteenth century and yet more under Peter the Great became a function of the State, and thereby was sharply separated from the ideals which it professed.

The running sore of this system, of which it was an essential part, was serfdom; for even at the final emancipation in 1861 about a third of the population were serfs. The peasants, as has been explained, had been brought into serfdom for the needs of the state service, and this was done in the most elementary way by planting among them officials whose first duty was military service and whose obligation it was to lead their serfs into battle and to levy from them the taxes of the State, which ultimately came to lie almost exclusively on the peasantry. For this purpose the 'service squire' received an absolute authority which made of him in the end not only the master, but the tax gatherer, the recruiting officer, the chief of police and the magistrate. This vicious system, so far from being reformed by Peter the Great (1682 — 1725) was by him in every way stereotyped. The essence of serfdom was that the peasantry could not leave the soil: one of the ridiculous effects of this was that the development of the reconquered fertile lands of the south, which had originally been the centre of the Russian State, was left until the population was free to gravitate thither after 1861. It was under Peter's father that was taken the most fatal step of all, by which all descendants of the peasantry were declared to be riveted to the soil.

When Milyukov speaks of Pugachev, Razin and Bolotnikov he, like the peasants themselves, is recalling the memories of the men who at different times in vain challenged the official regime. The peasants, largely owing to the old communal system by which they held and administered their village property in common, had a culture and tradition of their own. Closely defined as an underdog class into which no one could pass except by social degradation, they had in the most marked degree the psychology of their class and loyalty to it. That the peasants were really in the long run all-important, came in the end to be recognized by anyone and everyone; and indeed the very name *narod* (the people) was ordinarily understood as specially applying to the peasantry. There was in all the best peasants' minds — and many peasants had a peculiarly shrewd and far-seeing intelligence — a clear sense of the wrong that had been done to them. Historically they were correct when they regarded the state officials who ruled over them as intruders, and they looked forward to the time when the land should be restored to them in its entirety. As life cannot be prevented from growing, the peasantry in every way broke through the barbed wires of official prohibition. By extensive side-industries, especially on the poor soil of the north, they accumulated what they could of property, though even this was at the mercy of their masters. By the nature of their conditions they became not only masters of evasion, but also of escape, and flowed of themselves into the vast hinterland where government control was almost nominal. It was the underdog people of Russia that made Siberia Russian, and it was they who created the phenomenon of the Cossacks — frontier warriors, traders and thieves, who at least in frontier conditions could command their own lot. To a low hill on the banks of the Volga is still attached the legend of Stephen Razin: one of the most beautiful of Russian peasant songs describes how the famous peasant leader passed the night there and dreamed his dream, and all who should do the same would learn his secret. It was the simplest of all secrets — the class war.

It was on this question of serfdom that Russian public opinion was built up, both political and social, but especially the second. The great social convulsions at the beginning of the seventeenth century produced only a few isolated political critics. The revolutionary changes of Peter the Great, all to the profit of the

State, produced others. It was under Catherine, who at first encouraged and even insisted on criticism, that the first groups of Russian intelligentsia began to form, only to go under with her successor Paul. The French Revolution, on the other hand, was an enormous object lesson for Russia; and Russians charted the very various stages of it, right as far on as Babeuf, with an intelligence and accuracy which we in England never attempted. The common interests and common life of Europe produced by the wars of Napoleon and also the common romantic movement in literature carried things much farther; and Alexander I, the triumphant opponent of Napoleon, was at the end of his reign to see the beginnings of the first truly political conspiracy, that of the Decembrists in 1825, which took the place of the more or less meaningless palace revolutions that had preceded it. However, even the Decembrists had no real programme, or rather they had a whole number of them, often quite incompatible; and the vengeance of the State under Nicholas I marked the end of the gentry as the leaders of political revolt. With Nicholas I (1825–1855) the ball passed to the incipient middle class, just as it had done in England under the Tudors; but one could not yet speak of a revolutionary movement, only of a movement of thought which produced potential leaders for the future. One thing was obvious to all who had any intelligence, whether sovereigns, administrators, generals or thinkers: the peasant question would have to be dealt with, or the State would ultimately collapse, as Catherine herself had foretold. It must not be thought that the sovereigns were behind others in this conviction. Nicholas I set up no less than five commissions on it, and when a bureaucracy of serf-owners obviously blocked the way, he characteristically made it a military question, with himself as commander-in-chief, and he did, in detail, introduce salutary improvements, though unfortunately to mend the system and not to change it. Meanwhile the thinkers were practically convinced of the need for a radical change. The existence of serfdom had produced two types of them. There was the 'conscience-stricken gentleman' who realized the iniquity of the source of his own privileges, and there was the 'man of mixed class' who was forcing his way from the bottom towards the top. Their psychologies were entirely different; the one was an altruist who wished others to be as happy as himself, the other was a pusher who attempted to make himself and others happy. The one was psychologically a liberal, the other a revolutionary.

The Crimean war, with its record of official incompetence and of the heroism of the serf army, as told so vividly by Tolstoy in his first-hand *Tales of Sevastopol*, put the seal on the matter. The question was at last really dealt with, and the initiative was taken throughout by Alexander II, who was the grandfather of Nicholas II. This Tsar was not a strong man, but he was honest, and he was strong on this subject; and he utilized his own position as autocrat to drive this reform through past the army of vested interests which surrounded him, confirming at point after point the views of a small liberal minority among them, on which he put the stamp of his own authority. But the Acts of Emancipation of 1861 — seven years before Nicholas II was born — were in themselves a revolution. The service squire's authority over the peasants was cancelled entirely, and from that time he was a stranger in their midst, though still living among them with all the memories of his past authority. More than that, the question of landed property, on which peasant opinion was the very opposite to that of the gentry, was settled on a rough principle of half and half, going far further than anything that has been attempted even up to the present day in England. About half of each estate became peasant property, to be paid for by instalments spread over nearly fifty years. By a later decree of 1893 it could never pass into other hands, and was held conjointly on the old communal system. The other half remained to the gentry, who from the day of the Emancipation were a dying class as far as their importance to the country was concerned. It was as if a barbed wire were run through the middle of each estate, with the two rival interests on each side of it: on the one the squire with his family, on the other the mass of the peasants. And it was to become obvious that whenever police authority was withdrawn, the peasants would pass over the barrier and take the rest. The squire was put in the position of a stingy landowner, making money off the peasants by renting to them portions of his own remaining holding; they, on the other hand, were forced to accept his terms if only to recover the cultivation of what they had been tilling before the Emancipation. In this struggle the peasant got the best of it. The squire in many cases left it to his steward and lived on his rents elsewhere, and by the time of the Revolution of 1917 the peasants, whether with or without rent, were in occupation of between four-fifths and five-sixths of the cultivated land in the country.

The Emancipation was a revolution; it abolished the old foundations and left everything in the air. Half and half was a compromise; if half, why not all? Such was the view of the innumerable young students, who thronged to the universities under Alexander II while the long drawn settlement of the peasant question was forming public opinion in Russia. Again, the peasants were to repay the State by a long series of instalments for the land which they had obtained. Was the price too high? Should there have been any payment at all? Room was left for any theory or conjecture on the subject; and the peasant question had made economic theory the favourite study of nearly all young students at the University.

One other point — the benevolent autocrat who made the Emancipation retained the old communal system, which even in the view of Russian reactionaries was a desirable feature of the life of old patriarchal Russia. But at the same time — largely, it is true, to secure the independence of the peasants from their former squires — the communal system itself was taken under the special protection and control of the Ministry of the Interior, and the peasant class, with much of its old distinctiveness, was retained as a bottom rung of the official system.

The Emancipation, however, was an act of enormous beneficence and set free economic forces which were entirely to transform Russia, even shifting the whole centre of gravitation of the population to the rich lands of the south, where the unworked reserves of coal and iron invited free labour. There, as elsewhere in the Empire, the Emancipation was the beginning of modern development and modern capitalism. Russia went through her fever of railway speculation just as England had done earlier, but in spite of all mistakes and blunders, the arrears of development were so great that the process once started could not be stopped, and economic progress, rapid enough at first, went at a greater and greater rate.

Meanwhile, to replace the service squire in every one of his numberless capacities, it was necessary to create a whole new social order. This was a task which the tired Emperor and the tired bureaucracy could not avoid, and willingly or unwillingly they had to carry through all sorts of first-class reforms on all sides. The whole judicial system was transformed on the basis of trial by jury, with public debates by trained barristers. Local government on the principle of election and responsibility to the public, with a power to levy rates, was gradually set up in all the older provinces of the Empire. The State budget was made public; universities received the right of electing their own officials; the army was put on a modern basis of conscription with no privileges whatever for birth or rank, and exemptions which only took account of sole breadwinners or of education; instruction in literacy went forward nowhere faster than in the army. Truly, a great record of liberal reform without the real existence of a liberal party, more or less synchronizing in date with the great transformation of England in the first Reform Ministry of Gladstone [1867–1874].

But as to principle, everything, as has been pointed out, was left in the air, and it was on the basis of these reforms that the revolutionary movement developed in Russia. If the old was condemned as bad, why not an entirely new world? The movement naturally concentrated at first exclusively on the peasantry. Now that they were in the limelight, every deficiency in their life showed up larger. Were they really better off? Anyhow, they were at present cultivating much less land than before. How was it possible under archaic conditions to get a living out of a reduced holding with one horse or possibly none? The great Russian literature of the reign of Nicholas I had mainly been concentrated on peasant life. The students themselves, of whom a large number held bursaries of the State, came in larger proportion from the peasantry than perhaps in any other European country, and they realized that it still paid the greater part of the taxes, thereby securing to them a free education. They recognized their debt; and their university comrades from the gentry class recognized their shame. The growing fatigue of the government led to reaction. Student protests led to wholesale exclusions, and hundreds of young men and women with vague and often contradictory ideas, but thinking all the harder for that, went down to the country in the hope of producing a peasant rising, a social revolution. The peasants met them with stolid incomprehension and indifference, and often themselves delivered them to the authorities; and the most fiery of the agitators returned disgruntled to the towns to conduct a war on the official system as a whole, not with, but for the people, by sporadic assassinations which ultimately culminated in the murder of the liberator Emperor. Alexander II was killed on the very day when he had at last signed an act calling members of the newly established elective County Councils (Zemstva) to a part in the work of legislation.

This was how Alexander III came to the throne, when his son Nicholas was thirteen years old. There is a vivid picture of how the new Emperor at the moment when life was declared extinct in his father gave his first imperious orders, and, calling his wife to him, drove rapidly off to his own palace, surrounded by a troop of cavalry. As Rambaud has put it, Alexander III mounted the throne as a soldier mounts a breach.[1] As far as public thought was concerned, the thirteen years of his reign were one long period of repression. This gigantic man, brother-in-law of our own King Edward VII, with his clear and limited mind and his strong will, never left any doubt as to what he would allow. He was capable of sharp outbursts or vigorous abuse; as there was no question that his will would be executed, he dealt with each incident once for all, and ordinarily retained no ill feeling afterwards. He had no disturbing changes of mind and purpose; he was his own prime minister, as an autocrat should necessarily be. He chose his colleagues for their special qualifications and kept them strictly within the limits of their tasks; so long as they retained his confidence, he retained their services. The government was to recover, the country was to progress; therefore there was to be no war. He was his own foreign minister, Giers remaining only an executant as he had been under Gorchakov. However great his antipathy to all that was republican, Alexander was even ready for a kind of insurance alliance with republican France to guarantee peace. The public thought of the country he made no effort to understand; he was restoring the autocracy.

Peace was indeed secured, and the country did indeed proceed on its further development. Alexander gave his special confidence

[1] RAMBAUD, *Histoire de Russie*, 756.

to his ablest and most practical statesman, Sergius Witte, who, rising from comparatively modest beginnings, became first Minister of Railways and later of Finance, and was in the course of eleven years at that Ministry to direct with singular courage and insight the whole economic advance of Russia, which had long been waiting for such a leader; and Witte on his side had a real faith in autocracy as it functioned under his master, and sincerely believed it to be the best form of government for Russia. But as far as the public was concerned, there was silence — what was officially termed at that time, 'the public calm'. Public thought was commanded to stand still, and in the stunning effect produced by the murder of the last Tsar this, for a time at least, harmonized with the public mood. The few revolutionaries — hardly more than a hundred[1] — who had taken part in the assassination of Alexander II were rounded up, and revolution in the words of the revolutionaries themselves, became 'a cottage industry'. The aura of authority was restored. On no one was this lesson more strikingly ingrained than on the heir to the throne, the future Nicholas II, brought up in the awesome presence of his father in a close atmosphere of domestic regulations, and immensely impressed by his father's powerful personality. The Russian autocracy became for Nicholas a sacred trust, inviolable as his coronation oath.

No period can live without some idea, however lacking in content; and the official creed of this one was, characteristically enough, a brilliant contradiction, constructed on a negation of accepted commonplaces. Its author was Constantine Pobedonostsev, a jurist of first-rate ability and of absolute integrity, who after taking a useful part in the great law reform of 1864, had become more and more reactionary as the revolutionary movement developed. Pobedonostsev was a firm believer in the old patriarchal Russia of Tsar, Church and people, undisturbed by any perplexing modern ideas or developments. He pointed to perversions of the modern European press with the simple implication that absolute silence was better. He pointed to the manipulations of modern parliamentary life with the implication that the principle of national representation was essentially evil. Pobedonostsev was an inverted Nihilist, pleading the cause of the

[1] So one of them told me.

existing autocracy. He had an immense personal prestige with the sovereign, who under this system was the only person that counted. He had been the preceptor of his elder brother, the original heir to the throne, and, after his death, of Alexander III himself: he remained in something like the same close personal relation with Alexander's son Nicholas. He was the dominator of the Church, and through it of the nation's expression of thought for a quarter of a century, from 1881 to 1904, which meant that all free public expression was stifled at birth. The periodicals had to worm their way as best they could between Scylla and Charybdis: either they risked being stopped by the government for saying too much, or they risked losing their readers by saying too little. One of the noblest representatives of Russian public thought, Prince Eugene Trubetskoy, member of a family of outstanding intellectual distinction, compared the Russia of this day to the valley of bones in the prophecies of Ezekiel, and asked if these bones could live. Independent thought necessarily became cynical in a country where patriotism and religion alike meant subservience. Such legislation as there was in this period was in the main simply prohibitive, or preventive — for instance in 1889 new local officials, called Land Captains, were introduced to drill the peasants, and the exceptions continually made to the working of the great reforms of the last reign became so numerous that what was called exceptional law had itself to be codified.

If there was Pobedonostsev, there was also Witte, carrying out in this and the next reign a full programme to regulate the enormous economic advances due to the liberation of free labour by the Acts of Emancipation. Witte put the finances of the State on a sound basis, especially in its relations with foreign credit, by introducing the gold standard. He was practically alone in his championship of this idea, except for the steady support both of Alexander III and, in this respect, of his successor[1]. To guarantee this stability Witte amassed a colossal gold reserve — a very essential condition in a still mainly agricultural country which possessed hardly any floating capital. Armed with these reforms, Witte welcomed foreign enterprise into Russia on the broadest scale. The French, in their anxiety for a Russian alliance, lent enormous sums to the Russian Government. The Germans

[1] Witte to B. P.

preferred to work from outside, covering Russia with a network of able and thoroughly trained economic experts. What Witte wanted was that foreign industrialists should themselves come into Russia and set up their factories there, thus benefiting the native population and spending their money in the country, and this was the way in which during this period the British and the Belgians made a real contribution to the construction of a new Russia.[1] Witte gave those who would follow this way large concessions, temporary exemptions from taxation, large government orders and even subsidies; on the other hand insisting on the institution of crèches, schools and hospitals in the interests of labour. It should be mentioned in this connection that his predecessor Nicholas Bunge (1881-87), an admirably broadminded and intelligent statesman of finance, had already set up a comprehensive provision for the regulation and safeguarding of labour; the government controlled the conditions of labour by laws limiting hours of work, especially for women and minors, by demanding conditions of health, and by instituting factory inspectors to safeguard the rights of workers. Witte not only acquired for the government a number of important railway lines, but extended the railway mileage more during his Ministry than was done in the same period in any other country. The most important of his enterprises was the Trans-Siberian railway, begun in 1891, which set going a new stream of settlement in Siberia. Finally, he fought German exploitation by an alternative hostile Tariff and in 1894 brought his opponents to reasonable terms.

Towards the very end of Alexander III's short reign of thirteen years came domestic events which indicated that a new period was at hand. In 1891 opened one of those series of three years of famine which were so common in Russia. Famine in Russia was largely a matter of disorganization. The northern, so-called consuming, provinces could not feed themselves; even half way between St. Petersburg and Moscow seldom a week passed in the summer without one night of frost. It was, then, a question of making the producing provinces feed the consuming, and that was a matter of transport, and Witte was before all things a great builder of railways. But Witte was not Minister of the Interior,

[1] The view of the Socialist, Tugan-Baranovsky, author of the best history of the Russian factory.

and three years of famine in the consuming provinces themselves were not only a terrible national disaster, but gave fuel for every kind of criticism. A new law of 1890, by which the government restricted still further the Zemstva or County Councils of Alexander II, marked the lowest point in their development; but the urgent appeal of a national famine stirred them again into action; and one man after another who was to play a part in the years that followed, for instance the restless and enterprising Alexander Guchkov, learned his first lessons of public service in the work of relief. Ever since the institution of these Zemstva on an elective basis, critics had asked when the 'building would be crowned' — that is, when the principle of election and responsibility to the public would also be applied to national affairs. It was at this time that the strong Tsar died and Nicholas II came to the throne.

CHAPTER II

FIRST STEPS: THE JAPANESE WAR

Do not for ever with thy veiled lids,
Seek for thy noble father in the dust.
Hamlet, I, 2

NICHOLAS came to the throne on November 1st, 1894, and was crowned in Moscow on May 14th, 1896. We shall not dwell long on the earlier years of his reign. The story of them has been told elsewhere, and up to 1902 there is not very much to tell. For these years the materials are fairly simple; and there is comparatively little to give us an intimate knowledge of the internal workings of the government. There is no such wealth of sources as we have on what follows; and indeed the profoundly disturbing forces which were to intervene later were not yet in operation. This early period is chiefly important to us for the lessons which it taught and which it is was quite possible to turn to full account; for though the foundations of the State were to be most seriously shaken in 1905, the storm was weathered, the monarchy was saved, and definite progress, if slow yet substantial, was resumed on all the main lines. We will therefore content ourselves with noting the significance of the chief developments and events.

The new sovereign set himself to continue the recuperation of Russia which had marked the reign of his father, to whose example he was full of filial fidelity; and the influence which counted for most with him in that period, was that of his mother. But his uncles also at first asserted themselves and later his cousins,[1] and it was only with time and strong backing from his wife that he gradually brought them to some measures of discipline. It was generally moral irregularities which vexed his Victorian partner that served as occasions for such emphasis of authority, and this was not likely to make her more popular.

As it was the decisions of the sovereign, however given, that decided the course of events in Russia, the evolution of his

[1] G. D. ALEXANDER, 195.

character must be the first subject of our study; and the study of a character chiefly made up of 'half tones' is extremely difficult. With the knowledge of detail which we now possess, it seems clear that accession to the throne produced a profound effect on this gentle and sensitive man. At the bottom, we have the tremendous contrast, which has been illustrated in the last chapter, between what he was and what was expected of him — a contrast which probably was never absent from his mind. He must have been afraid of his own indecision and weakness. And the various phases in his development as a sovereign seem to have been founded on fear, a constant fear from which he could never escape except by separation from the throne and a return to his natural self. This was not any sense of physical fear; he was often to show later that he had none of that; in fact probably few have shown or felt such a complete indifference to their personal fate. 'I have never seen such a fatalist,' wrote one of his suite, who saw him pass through one of his greatest trials, but the same witness testified that his sleep, his appetite, his manner, were in no way affected by it.[1] Mosolov writes: 'He unfailingly remained outwardly imperturbable'.[2] To one of his Ministers in a moment of confidence he said that he had wrestled with and suppressed any instinct of personal irritation.[3] There are signs that in some of the deepest things of life he could show strength; but it was the colossal responsibility that overawed him, compelling him to be that which he would not otherwise have been. Many, especially among his suite, even imagined him to be almost heartless; but that was not the truth, for in moments of self-revelation, we can see how deeply he felt, and that the true cause of the general misapprehension was his self-distrust and self-suppression. To his naturally so friendly and genial nature it was intensely distasteful to show displeasure. He had a natural aversion to an argument, to anything that was in any way unpleasant.[4] The result was silence, and the silence was misunderstood. But those who were nearest to him were alike amazed by his extraordinary power of self-control. The idea that he was stupid, was a sheer illusion confined to revolutionaries who knew nothing about him. The idea that he was weak, must

[1] General Dubensky, *Padenie*, vi, 405.
[2] Mosolov, 14.
[3] Izvolsky, 204-6.
[4] Mosolov, 9.

itself be qualified. We find him refusing to oblige even his mother by ill-considered generosity to a well-born suitor at the expense of the treasury, on the ground that in such a case 'charity becomes most unjust'.[1] Also, with no loss of affection or of balance he defends himself firmly against some of her criticisms of his policy. He is clearly in a high degree conscientious; and throughout his reign he worked dutifully day by day through the innumerable reports which were presented to him, including for instance a fortnightly summary of the police conditions in the Empire.[2] The comments which he wrote on the margin of these reports showed no lack of intelligence, and seldom any of resolution. 'Your first decisions', wrote one of his cousins to him, 'are generally right.' Two of his Ministers, Kokovtsev and Polivanov — the two who have given the fullest records of official intercourse with him — were both impressed by the straight answer which they would get to a straight question. No one who was near him had any doubt of his earnest solicitude for all his subjects, most of all for the humblest of them. Before a new kit for the infantry soldier was introduced in the army, Nicholas donned the complete equipment and in the comparative solitude of his residence in Crimea made a forced march of eight or nine hours[3] — Count Fredericksz tells us that he ordinarily walked as fast as a horse, and apparently Drenteln was the only one of his attachés who could keep up with him.

In his preferences among foreign peoples and their rulers, much his strongest attachment was to the family of his aunt Alexandra of England and particularly to King George V and Queen Mary. He writes of them with an intimate affection:

> It was a great joy to see them again [Nov. 6th/18th, 1888], how nice it is to feel as if one were among one's own family [June 24th/July 6th, 1893].

There is much that he admires in England; the sense of responsibility, the open-air life — he asks why there cannot be something like Rotten Row in Russia.[4] This does not at all extend to British politics, and least of all to British foreign policy in the

[1] N. to M. F., 97.
[2] Vasilyev, 56.
[3] Mosolov, 22.
[4] N. to M. F., 72.

earlier part of his reign. On the Boer War he writes (Nov. 9th/21st, 1899):

> the Anglo-Boer War interests me terribly: I wish all possible success to these poor people in this unequal and unjust war.

He has a steady and sincere liking for the French and their ways, which was natural enough to this delicate-minded man, and this throws an amusing light on the vulgar tirades against them which he is constantly receiving from his cousin Wilhelm.

> The good French people were very touching [on his visit to Paris and Compiegne, Sept. 13th/26th, 1901, p. 153] . . . Everything was done sensibly and calmly and without any fuss whatever; the soldiers looked very happy; many smiled when I approached them and during the review they all nodded their heads in answer to Alix's bows while she drove round: just as our own men do . . . We had lunch on the spot . . . and after saying good-bye to the courteous Frenchmen, left by train . . .

This special friendliness includes their rulers — in particular Presidents Faure and Poincaré.

The Germans, on the other hand, thoroughly bore him. On his passage from France into Germany in 1896 (Oct. 2nd-14th) he writes:

> After, began German helmets, and it was unpleasant to look out of the window. At every station in France one heard 'Hurrah', and saw kind and jolly faces, but here everything was black, dark, and boring. Happily it was time to go to bed; by daylight it would have been even more depressing.[1]

Their entertainments, the ladies' tastes in clothes come in for his satire. Least tolerable of all to him is the exuberance of Wilhelm, though as ruler to ruler he endeavours to be courteous.

> I think, no matter how disagreeable it may be, we are obliged to let him wear our naval uniform: particularly since he made me last year a captain in his own navy and what's worse I'll have to greet him as such at Kronstadt. *C'est à vomir* [July 23rd/Aug. 5th, 1897].

And later:

[1] N. to M. F., 124-5.

> Thank God, the German visit is over, and one may definitely say without boasting that it went off successfully . . . He so much liked the *Standard* [Nicholas's yacht] that he said he would have been happy to get it as a present [Aug. 1st/13th, 1897; N. to M. F., 128-30].

At the funeral of Queen Victoria:

> Don't you think that the German Emperor is trying to appear as the 'chief mourner' in England? I am trying to keep the golden mean [Jan. 16th/29th, 1901, N. to M. F. 150]

It is Mosolov who best sums up the main motif in the life of Nicholas: 'He was literally the lover of his life's partner'.[1] If Nicholas was easy to misjudge, far more so was Alexandra. At her earliest visits to St. Petersburg as a child her shyness and aloofness had set the tongues of society wagging against her, and of this she was well aware. We know how long Nicholas's parents had been opposed to the marriage, and how she was presented to the people as their future sovereign. With her wholeheartedness — as Kokovtsev puts it, 'her sharply defined soul'[2] — she was even more unreservedly devoted to him than he to her. In her own words, she loved him 'as man was rarely loved'. She devoted herself absolutely to his country with a truly Russian patriotism 'far above all her contemporaries'[3] and what she loved was the common folk of Russia. His religion she embraced with the enthusiasm of a convert. She revered and made also her own that autocratic authority of his which seemed so foreign to him. But a sovereign of Russia was bound to live in constant fear: on a train, in their yacht, the slightest mischance — such as is common enough in Russia — might have a sinister meaning. All social ceremony was intensely distasteful to her, and she would sit evidently ill at ease till it was over. 'She felt', writes Mosolov, 'that the fewer people she saw, the better.'[4] Even on their travels, when loyal crowds were gathered to greet them as they stopped at a station, the blinds of the carriages would be drawn. Gradually the Court came to be completely in eclipse; and her place was partially taken by her cousin, the elder Grand Duchess, Maria Pavlovna, of whom she was intensely

[1] Mosolov, 30.
[2] Kokovtsev, II, 342.
[3] G. D. Alexander, 301.
[4] Mosolov, 49.

jealous. This great lady was eminently qualified to lead society, and once on being congratulated on her tact by Mosolov replied: 'One ought to know one's job; you can pass that on to the Grand Court.[1] All this emphasized the seclusion of the imperial couple and tended to prevent the people, and more particularly the educated public, from realizing the strongest weapon of authority which their sovereign possessed, his conquering personal charm. Though the Empress gave birth in succession to four charming girls, her health early began to suffer. The long desired heir did not come.

Nicholas was singularly open to reasonable argument — much more so than his father. The trouble was that he was so much so, that each new impression might efface the last. Many a time in this reign the issue depended almost upon a chance, and it was so with the first example that occurred. Something has been said already of the movement of public opinion, which had been springing up under the influence of the great famines of 1891-93 led by the elected zemstva or county councils, which had been legally instituted by Nicholas's grandfather, Alexander II. On the occasion of the coronation, addresses of congratulation poured in from these county councils, and one of them in particular expressed the hopes of intelligent public opinion. It came from the fortress of Russian liberalism, the zemstvo of Tver, and was drafted by Fedor Rodichev, a typical English liberal of the period of Gladstone and one of the foremost barristers in Russia. Twice before, each time with the co-operation of Rodichev, the Tver zemstvo had said the word that counted: when it asked the Tsar Liberator Alexander II to give his loyal people such self-government as he had given to the Bulgarians,[2] namely, a constitution, and when it greeted the initiative of the Liberal Minister, Loris Melikov, as opening 'a happy future for our beloved country'.[3] In his address to Nicholas II he expressed the hope 'that the voice of the people's need will always be heard from the height of the throne' and 'that the rights of individuals and public institutions will be firmly safeguarded'. The young Tsar appears at first to have seen no harm in this pronouncement; but he was warned by Pobedonostsev, and under his schooling, when replying to the

[1] Mosolov, 78.

[2] Svatikov, *Obshchestvennoe Dvizhenie v Rossii* (1700-1895), 93. The Harkov zemstvo made the same request.

[3] ibid., 122.

addresses, he spoke of 'senseless dreams of the participation of zemstvo representatives in the affairs of internal administration',[1] and declared: 'I shall maintain the principle of autocracy just as firmly and unflinchingly as it was preserved by my unforgettable dead father'[2] (Jan. 17th, 1896). What was lacking was the personality and will power of the father. The scene is thus described by a friend of Count Lamsdorff, who was later to become Nicholas's Minister for Foreign Affairs:

> A little officer came out; in his cap he had a bit of paper; he began mumbling something, now and then looking at that bit of paper, and then suddenly he shouted out: 'senseless dreams'; here we understood we were being scolded for something. Well, why should one bark?

Such was the impression left by the spirit of Pobedonostsev in the mouth of Nicholas.[3]

From the side of the revolutionaries, the reply to Nicholas's challenge came in the organization of a new party, that of the S.R.s or Social Revolutionaries. The S.R.s were soon probably the largest of Russian political parties and certainly the most typically Russian. They were not Marxists, but drew their traditions from the *narodniks*, or men of the seventies, whose work among the peasantry they were to continue on a much more effective basis, often as employees of the zemstva in such fields as public health and education. They were patriotic, and many of them were religious. They were revolutionaries, but a parliamentary regime would convert them into ordinary radicals. They were not doctrinaire and indeed were often very vague in their political ideas. The one practical part of their programme was that the land should belong exclusively to those who worked on it. Some of them, but only a minority, were terrorists. The Party admitted of the use of this weapon, and it was exercised by a special section which later forced the attention of the public by many political assassinations — Witte himself has even suggested that the Terrorists, on the whole, chose suitable victims[4] — but these methods the Party discountenanced at times when there were more peaceful means of obtaining its objects.

[1] Svatikov, 191. [2] ibid., 197.
[3] *Slavonic Review*, xii, 35, 350 footnote; P. Struve, *My Contacts with Rodichev*; Krasny Arkhiv, iii (46), 26.
[4] Witte, ii, 433.

Nicholas was from the outset a fatalist, and became more and more so. But it seemed as if fate made every effort to strengthen this instinct in him. At his coronation one of the highest decorations of the Empire, the St. Andrew, which he was wearing, came loose and fell on the floor before him.[1] But this was nothing to what was to follow immediately afterwards. The usual distribution of small presents to the vast crowds, principally peasants, who had come to witness the coronation was most unaccountably held on a vast field full of ditches, which had earlier been cut up for military exercises. The crush was such that thousands of peasants were pressed into these ditches, and the actual number of dead was estimated at two thousand.[2] Official stupidity concealed this terrible disaster as far as possible from the young sovereign when he made his way towards the spot, so that he had at first no idea whatever of its dimensions and he and the young Empress attended the ball given that evening by the French Ambassador. When he learned of the extent of the disaster, he wished to retire to a monastery to pray for his people; but from this he was unwisely dissuaded.

Once the measure of the catastrophe became known, it was the occasion for a war of cavilling and recrimination between the two authorities which shared the responsibility. On one side was the Ministry of the Court, headed by the old and amiable Count Vorontsev-Dashkov, who would naturally have the sympathy of the Dowager Empress; on the other, clearly more directly responsible, were the police authorities of Moscow, at the head of whom stood the Governor General, the Grand Duke Sergius, married to the sister of the young Empress. The question was never really cleared up, but it led to the resignation of the Court Minister, for which Alexandra was held responsible, and the intrigues which it started were to set the tone for incessant rivalries and manœuvres of Ministers during this reign.

In his selection and treatment of Ministers Nicholas was throughout the very opposite of his father; his choices were often haphazard and sometimes incomprehensible. When receiving them, he almost invariably gave them the impression that he was particularly pleased with them, which the peculiar charm of his person turned into a conviction. While they were with him, he

[1] Izvolsky, 261. [2] Witte, I, 58.

seemed constitutionally incapable of saying anything to them which might cause them unpleasantness, and more usually than not their dismissal arrived as a complete surprise by post afterwards. Such a sovereign could not give them the security, which they would have felt with his predecessor, that they were trusted so long as they were retained, a condition which Witte rightly regarded as a first essential to the functioning of the principle of autocracy. They never knew when they were being undermined by some purely casual interloper entering the palace by backstairs influence.

There is one point which requires special emphasis, for without it the rest of the story cannot be understood. Autocracy, to an intelligent person such as Witte, had its own set of rules, which had been given it by the greatest of its bureaucratic statesmen Speransky, the Minister of Alexander I. The autocrat decides everything, but on the basis of official information and advice served up to him by those qualified to give it, who have themselves been appointed by him for this purpose. Speransky, who would have done very much more if his master had not failed him, left as his principal creation the Council of State (1811), a sort of House of Lords or rather of life lords, chosen solely on the basis of service to the State, principally bureaucratic. It had its own traditions and the appointments to it were usually well founded. It had a closely regulated procedure; any question referred to it by the sovereign passed first through the whole body, then through one or more relevant departments of it, according as to whether the question was administrative, economic, financial or judicial;[1] then it returned to the whole body, and finally was laid before the sovereign — with every solution of it that had been proposed, detailed in writing. It was even possible for a single member to insist on sending up his opinion. Then the sovereign was absolutely free to choose which opinion he thought best, without any relation whatever to numbers or majorities.

But he also had a right to settle any question straight off himself, without referring to this body at all. This, in periods of government by favourites, was the course naturally followed. For instance, all the worst regulations on two sore subjects, the Jews

[1] The four departments were respectively named: Laws, Civil and Religious Affairs, State Economy, and Trade and Industry.

and the Press, were issued in temporary ordinances which never passed through the Council of State and indeed, with its traditions, could hardly have done so even in times of reaction. Even this course did not prejudice the position of a Minister so long as the sovereign did nothing in his province behind his back. But that was exactly what was happening all the time throughout the reign of Nicholas II. The responsible Minister never knew when something might not be ordained direct by the Emperor in total contradiction to the advice which he had given.

This, unfortunately, was perfectly legal; and anyone who wanted to flatter the Tsar — his wife or anyone else — might advise a weak sovereign to show his strength in this way. The point of the whole matter lay precisely in the fact that this way of settling questions was still legal. The sovereign might be as weak as water, he might change his mind every five minutes, but the thing which he said last, was the thing that was done, and the government of the Empire at once reflected in full every variation of his will.

This aspect of Nicholas's reign is well illustrated by his relations with old Prince V. P. Meshchersky; they exchanged some most interesting letters, which are now likely to become accessible to the public, edited by Dr. Victor Frank. Meshchersky was a contemporary and intimate friend of the Tsarevich Nicholas, elder brother of Alexander III. This prince before his early death was betrothed to the future Empress Marie Feodorovna, and he entrusted her to Alexander on his death bed. Some intimate letters passed between him and Meshchersky, and the downright and loyal Alexander took over also this friendship in a remarkable letter to Meshchersky of Jan. 14th/26th, 1867. He writes:

> For all your vexation and unpleasantness that you have had on my account, I give you my friendship because you have fully deserved it,

and signs himself 'Your friend, Alexander'. Some time after he became Tsar, in 1887, he was approached by Meshchersky with a proposal to issue a daily paper, *The Citizen* (*Grazhdanin*), which would contain at least parts of the personal diaries which Meshchersky was apparently already sending to the Emperor. Alexander fully approves of this proposal and even sanctions Meshchersky's suggestion of engaging attachés of the chief Russian embassies abroad as correspondents of his paper. This, however, is the only time when he appears to have written to Meshchersky while Tsar, and there are reasons to think that Alexander was later more reserved with Meshchersky. The Empress Maria, with her excellent sense of who was disinterested and who was not, detested him.[1]

In 1902, evidently after a new approach of Meshchersky, Nicholas II, who has now been on the throne for nearly eight years, in his turn adopts this friendship. He declares it to be

> the direct consequence of the education of [given me by] my dear father. His testament has passed wholesale into me and filled all my being. You have appeared, and have at once revived and further strengthened that testament. I have somehow grown in my own eyes.

It is quite clear that Meshchersky, who appears as an old rugged councillor, is advising Nicholas to be more sure of his own autocracy. In fact the Tsar writes at the top of one of these early letters, 'I have become more confident in myself'. On this footing there were many further communications and several private meetings, and Nicholas speaks more than once of 'the secret defensive alliance' which has been formed between the two. Meshchersky considers it his task to keep the autocrat in Nicholas up to the mark; and Nicholas several times reassures him, in words which evidently leave some doubt in his correspondent, that his autocracy is in full vigour. Going past his responsible Ministers, he repeatedly asks Meshchersky for draft decrees, for announcements on the appointment of Ministers or on the most critical problems of his reign; but the correspondence shows that these are generally delayed by Nicholas and seldom issued in the form which Meshchersky has given to them. Sometimes the answers of Nicholas are very sensible and discriminating. At one point (May 1st/13th, 1903) he asks his friend to remember that 'I have my own opinion and my own will'. Shortly afterwards (May 23rd/June 4th) he writes that he is deeply hurt by Meshchersky's suggestion that he is listening to flatterers and adds, 'I beg you always to remember this', and a little later (June 21st/July 3rd), 'the contents of your letter surprised me but did not convince me'. More

[1] Kokovtsev to B. P.

than once he warns the Prince on tactless personal articles in *The Citizen*: 'How often have I told you not to do this (that is, mention names)! Even peasants don't do that'. And when Meshchersky proposes that a decoration should be bestowed in acknowledgment of a flattering article by the French politician, M. Paul de Cassagnac, he comments 'Such services, all the same, are not rewarded by Orders'. The correspondence is interrupted from 1905 to 1913, which is just the date when the Tsar is again returning to his full belief in his autocracy; but there is only one more letter shortly before the War, in which he advises Meshchersky to see Gregory (Rasputin), adding 'he is angry with you'. Meshchersky died just before the War. Meanwhile *The Citizen* was regularly supplied to Nicholas and we know from him that it was the only paper which he always read regularly.

Meshchersky can by no means be regarded as disinterested. We find in his correspondence an insistent demand for a money grant for a friend, and he had a whole troop of clients whose claims he was always pushing by this backstairs avenue. This rugged 'friend of your father' had a very sinister reputation on the fringe of Russian politics, and it was not only his politics but his morals that were generally challenged.

Alexander III was his own prime minister by right of his autocracy. In the new reign only the principle of autocracy was retained, and there was no prime minister, which meant chaos in governmental decisions. This set the Ministers free to wage war on each other, and, incidentally, to make any use possible of the backstairs influence which was now in fashion. If Witte is accurate, no better instance can be found of the way things were done or were not done, than an incident which he relates in his memoirs from the end of 1896.[1] The Russian ambassador in Constantinople, Nelidov, goes to St. Petersburg and urges on the Emperor a plan for seizing the Bosphorus in full time of peace. Nelidov is to 'create incidents' in Constantinople and dispatch a telegram, not to St. Petersburg, or to the government, but only to its financial representative in London, with a cryptic message about the purchase of corn. On the receipt of this message, which is at once to be transmitted to St. Petersburg, flotillas are to start from Odessa and Sevastopol and seize the Bosphorus. Nicholas, according to

[1] WITTE, I, 88-92.

Witte, liked the idea and approved of it, and Nelidov went back to Constantinople to 'create his incidents'. Witte, when the matter had been under consideration, had made a most energetic protest and insisted on submitting an 'individual opinion'. He informed Pobedonostsev, who said: 'Jacta est alea. God help Russia!' Of course the result would have been a European war; but fortunately the sovereign was dissuaded and the whole project was called off. If Nicholas could be put under the restraint of a constitution, which was obviously best suited to his character and qualities, such a danger could hardly arise.

The policy of the early years of the reign was a simple continuation of what had gone before — with one big difference, that the driving force, the will of the autocrat, had dropped out. The two Ministers who counted most were those who have just been mentioned, Pobedonostsev and Witte — in fact the principal achievements of Witte mostly fell into this reign.

Pobedonostsev stood for sheer reaction and hostility to every kind of intellectual initiative. There is a Russian word *nachalstvo* which means 'initiative' and it had come to be used exclusively for anyone in authority, especially of the Government: every other initiative was regarded as dangerous. The chief objects of Pobedonostsev's suspicious animosity were the Press and the students. The Press was bound hand and foot with all sorts of ordinances, nominally 'temporary', administered not by a Cabinet, but by a few Ministers — for instance, restricting retail sales and even forbidding certain persons to act as editors. The power of unlimited fines was in the hands of the local Governors, who taxed the provincial Press to the limit of existence for almost anything which might arouse public interest. In this period there was a constant succession, peculiarly emphasized in 1898-99, of student sallies and student repressions, with exclusions from degrees, which practically starved the victims of any chance of remunerative employment. The Government, this time in the person of the Minister of the Interior, was almost equally hostile to the zemstva and town councils.

Justice was another sphere for the encroachments of the Government. Judges and law officers of the crown, according to the reform of 1864, could not be removed; so the Government adopted a practice of appointing deputies, whose tenure was not guaranteed.

Among the peasants had been set up in 1889, instead of the former elected Justices of the Peace, the new type of official called the Land Captain, who without any legal training exercised both judicial and administrative functions, often with confusion of the two, and was justly regarded by the peasants as an attempt to return to the old control of serfdom.

Pobedonostsev's speciality was the province of religion; and he attempted to drive all the inhabitants of Russia wholesale into a groove of the narrowest official Orthodoxy. All religions suffered under him, including the Orthodox Church itself. In Catholic Poland, where religion almost came to blend completely with nationality, his oppression met with a resistance that could not be overcome. In Ukraine and White Russia, there were large numbers of Uniats, who accepted the headship of the Pope but were authorized to worship in the Orthodox way; these had remained Russian under Polish rule, but it only needed a change of persecutor to alienate them. German Lutherans of the Baltic continued to suffer from the persecution which came over, somewhat relaxed, from the last reign. There were some twenty millions of Mussulmans, who also suffered from Pobedonostsev, and even the heathen nomad tribes as well. The official word 'missionary' came into odium as representing an agent of the Government, who might be rewarded with a state decoration for the number of his forced conversions.

As with religions, so with nationalities, of which there were something like 120 in Russia. The non-Russian population was officially styled by the offensive name *inorodtsy* or aliens, and were harassed in every way. Even in the University of Warsaw, Poles were taught their native literature in Russian; the porters at the railway stations were punished for speaking in any other language; Russian was even the official language of the village offices of local government. Poles were prevented from occupying estates near the frontier of the Empire, and in mixed Russo-Polish districts, such as Lithuania and White Russia, the discrimination was even more oppressive. It is true that Nicholas was not unfriendly to the Poles; but the old regulations still stood.

The Poles gained somewhat from Nicholas's personal sympathies, but the Finns, on the other hand, had their worst time in his reign. The Finns, who had been annexed to Russia in the time of

Napoleon with the guarantee of all their national institutions, had acted throughout with remarkable correctness; but this was sorely tried by the innovations of the reign of Nicholas. He resented their exemption from Russian military service and, not without reason, regarded their proximity to the capital as a danger to the national defence. The increasing encroachments of Nicholas, which were disturbing to foreign opinion, brought him an almost sharp reminder from his mother, at the time resident in England, to which he replied with some spirit. It was only after prolonged pressure that revolutionary acts, even of terrorism, began to appear in Finland.

The Baltic Germans, who had rendered immense services in the administration of the empire and at the same time retained their high local culture, continued to suffer, in a milder way, from the stupid Russifying policy of Alexander III.

But at all times and in both reigns the favourite object of persecution was the Jewry of Russia, which was in 1914 nearly one half of the whole Jewish population of the world. And here Nicholas was as bad as Alexander. It was not so much a question of what rights the Jews did not possess, but whether they had the right to exist at all. But for special exemptions, the Jewish population was confined to the so-called Jewish Pale of Settlement, where they had lived under Polish rule before the partitions of Poland; but these exemptions were a fruitful source of demoralization for the Russian police, for by systematic bribery the Jews were able to evade all restrictions. As a Russian police officer would say, 'water cannot be prevented from flowing'. They were forbidden to employ Christian servants; the Jew who would accept Orthodoxy had a right to a free divorce; the schools of their area, supported chiefly by their taxes, admitted only a very low proportion of their children.

For all Russia, one of the greatest grievances was what is called administrative *proizvol*, a word which means high-handedness or arbitrariness. With no effective restraint in the practice of law, the police could do what they liked; and it was even illegal to put a member of this body on trial without the permission of his superior officer.

Yet meanwhile public life was growing and expanding in all directions. Since the emancipation, the peasants had gone in large numbers to the main towns in a methodical and regulated way; they were under obligation to send back part of their wages to discharge the dues of the village commune and could, if they wished, return later to resume their place among its members, probably sending a son or a nephew to take up the place which the man had made for himself in the town. From the same date, population had been streaming southwards to the vast undeveloped resources of South Russia, to work in the mines and industries which were growing up there. All this development had only been waiting for such a statesman as Witte to regulate it; and he continued to cover Russia with new railways, invite new foreign capital and extend Russian trade. The Trans-Siberian greatly facilitated migration to Siberia. This had been in the past illegal. But when Nicholas's new Minister of the Interior, Goremykin, called his attention to it and suggested further methods of restriction, Nicholas, very sensibly, asked to see the figures and commented that this seemed to be a natural development which called for assistance rather than restriction.

The industrial development of Russia had brought with it the first elements of modern socialism. After the assassination of Alexander II, George Plekhanov, who had headed the more moderate section of the revolutionaries and did not see any sense in terrorism, organized a 'League for the Liberation of Labour', which became the germ of Russian Marxism. In 1889 the small groups of Russian Marxists, men of a high education and often of a high scholarship, combined with other elements, such as the Jewish Revolutionary Party, known as the 'Bund', to form a Social Democratic Party for Russia. Plekhanov and his chief collaborators had to live in exile; but they exercised an extensive influence over Russian public thought by imported socialist literature; and to the growing forces of industry, Marxism, if intelligibly interpreted, came like a special gospel of their own.

Throughout Russia, however, the national interest took for the most part another channel, that of English liberalism, which received such a strong impetus from the more ardent members of the zemstva and town councils. In this field such different elements as country gentry and peasants, town merchants, university professors and students, found a simple avenue of public service, consisting of devoted work for the unprivileged, and leading in the opposite direction to that of class war. The town councils were a little slower than the zemstva to work for reform, but as soon as they began to do so, they found an even wider scope for their activity and in this work, the old capital, Moscow, in particular, played a leading part. Around the work of these councils of local government gathered an ever extending fringe of public interest. The professional class began to organize groups with the same tendencies as the zemstva; and between them they developed a liberal public opinion, which would serve as a basis for further organized advance. These various elements produced a group of liberal thinkers and workers, known as the 'League of Liberation'; and later they published outside Russia an organ named 'Liberation', which was brought into the country with the same difficulties as the revolutionary literature and was read there with the same avidity.

The episode of the Bosphorus related by Witte was for many years the last stir of Nicholas II's activity on the side of the west; and in 1900 he suggested to the other Powers a kind of moratorium in Europe by the summoning of a conference at The Hague to preserve and stabilize peace. Witte, almost our sole authority for the inner history of this period, has suggested that this was proposed because Russia, engaged in reorganizing her infantry, could not then afford to counter certain increases of artillery which were being planned in Austro-Hungary;[1] but we need not accept this explanation, and the move was probably at the time entirely sincere. However, it marked a new turning away of Russia from Europe. This was in keeping with the general lines of policy in the last reign; but there was a difference between father and son: Alexander had secured himself against war by the friendship of France, but kept the manifestations of that friendship within strict limits, whereas Nicholas publicly announced it as an alliance. Alexander had been in favour of developing the Asiatic part of the Empire and Nicholas, while heir to the throne, had been sent on a journey of education to the Far East which had left a very great impression on him, the more so as he was only saved by Prince George of Greece from assassination by a fanatic in Japan, but he allowed his policy to drift into sheer adventure. In this, he had the full encouragement of his cousin the Kaiser.

[1] WITTE, I, 143.

Nicholas's accession had synchronized with the war between Japan and China. Since 1868 Japan had rapidly reconstructed her public services and public life on Western models. She aimed at expansion into Korea, which was under Chinese suzerainty. The consequent struggle between China and Japan became especially acute in three crises, those of 1882, 1884, and 1894. The third crisis led to a war in which the Japanese were easily victorious, and imposed their own terms. Witte's conception of Russian foreign policy — which was not at all in his province — was an economic co-operation between the three chief continental Powers, Germany, France and Russia, as a check to British economic predominance. In accordance with this idea, these three Powers intervened in the dispute between Japan and China and upset the treaty of peace, depriving the Japanese of any gain of territory on the main land. Witte with much ingenuity brought about a visit of the Chinese statesman, Li-Hung-Chang, to Moscow in 1896 during the coronation of Nicholas, and there, in return for a guarantee of the integrity of Chinese territory and an offer to meet the Chinese war indemnity to Japan by a loan which he secured from France, he arranged a concession to run the Trans-Siberian railway to Vladivostok through Manchurian territory, including a strip on both sides of the line to be administered by Russia in the interests of the railway. The shrewd old Chinese statesman warned him at the time that if the Russian hand ever stretched farther southwards towards the sea there would be trouble, and Witte was himself opposed to any policy of expansion on that side.

Not so Nicholas. On a visit to Russia, the Kaiser Wilhelm asked him, while out on a drive, whether he would agree to a German seizure of Kiao-Chow; according to Witte, Nicholas, in relating the incident, defended his agreement by the plea that it was awkward to refuse a guest. On the ground of the murder of two German missionaries, Germany secured a ninety-nine years lease of Kiao-Chow, and Nicholas, in spite of Witte's opposition and his own guarantee of the intregity of China, decided to occupy Port Arthur, for which he secured a similar lease of twenty-five years. Witte, according to his own account, showed his moral weakness by helping to carry through the policy he had opposed, which he did by actually bribing Li-Hung-Chang.[1]

[1] WITTE, I, 128.

England, France and Italy now made similar demands on Chinese territory. This orgy of international spoliation of China produced a vehement resistance in the Boxer movement, which for some time endangered the safety of the embassies and legations in Peking. An international force of Germans, French, British, Russians and Japanese was sent to restore order; the Russian lease of Port Arthur was extended to ninety-nine years, and a branch line was run to connect it with the Trans-Siberian.

The most outstanding of the Ministerial feuds of this reign was between Witte and Plehve. Witte stood high above all his colleagues and rivals by virtue of sheer ability. He was too able and too clever to condone either inefficiency or stupidity, and it was his fate to watch a progressive demolition of that great edifice, the Russian Empire. But his moral significance was far inferior to his intellectual. He stood for self, and he had a genius for intrigue. 'A man of double thoughts', writes Sazonov[1] The most acute description of his methods comes later from Nicholas himself, who instinctively distrusted him and completely saw through him:

> As soon as he was back [in Russia] a peculiar atmosphere full of all sorts of rumours and gossip and insinuations began to form around him.[2]

Witte has quite justly been accused of turning his Ministry of Finance into a 'State within a State',[3] and encroaching on the functions of his various colleagues. He was constantly intervening in foreign affairs, once going so far as even to mobilize the Emperor of Germany in favour of his views. But his main enemy was the Ministry of the Interior, which had control both of the police and the zemstva, and was the most powerful of the organs of government. Any Minister might now have his own list of candidates for the offices of all his colleagues, and this was all the simpler because Nicholas, before making an appointment, frequently asked for suggestions. Witte was able to drive from the Ministry of the Interior a bureaucratic official, Goremykin, who, he suggested, was pandering to liberalism in an extremely mild project for the extension of the zemstvo system of elective local government to some other parts of the Empire. Witte was able to replace

[1] SAZONOV, 289. [2] N. to M. F., 221. [3] e.g. IZVOLSKY, 118.

him by his own candidate, Sipyagin, who was very correct from the reactionary point of view; but in 1902 Sipyagin was assassinated by a terrorist S.R., and Witte, though consulted on the vacancy, was this time unable to keep out his bitterest rival. Vyacheslav Plehve, another product of bureaucracy, was a law officer who, after dabbling in official liberalism in the time of the great reforms, first put himself upon the ladder by sweeping up in the most efficient way the remains of the organization which had assassinated Alexander II.

In his struggles with Plehve, Witte inconsistently enough decided to play as his card the growing activity of the zemstva. The work of famine relief had given the greatest stimulus to their activity; their most important functions were public health and primary education, matters which had practically escaped the attention of the central government. The zemstvo work was a school which gave to many Russians a very valuable preparation for future participation in national affairs, on the same basis of election and responsibility to the public. The zemstvo policy was founded on a well conceived statistical campaign which, like all other functions of this work, was regarded almost as a mission. Once they knew their field, the zemstva achieved most remarkable results. There were rural districts of the great province of Moscow in which the school was brought to within two miles of every village and the cottage hospital within three. The zemstvo of Tver achieved an admirable development of cottage industries; it planned a staff of agricultural experts to advise the peasants as to the quality and possibilities of their soil; it set up the first provincial hospital built on the principle of isolation of various diseases. The zemstvo of Saratov, with its bacteriological station, succeeded in almost entirely expelling the epidemics which made their way into this province from neighbouring Asia. Probably the most universally commended zemstvo was that of Vyatka, managed practically by peasant farmers, who were almost the only population.

Questions of public health took little account of boundaries of provinces; and since the joint effort against the famines of 1891-93, the zemstva did more and more to organize a common programme, which was at first purely economic. The lead clearly belonged to the provincial zemstvo of Moscow, which was still the natural centre of the life of the nation. For nine years (1895-1902) the chairman of this central zemstvo was Dmitry Shipov, a man capable of uniting persons of the most various views in comradely work. From time to time, important economic questions roused the Government to set up special conferences, of which the most prominent local men were naturally members, and Shipov seized such occasions to organize private meetings of zemstvo chairmen for concerted action. Plehve, as Minister of the Interior, was entirely against the zemstva doing anything in common. Witte, however, set up in 1903 local committees under the cover of his own Ministry 'on the agricultural industry', in which the leading role fell to the zemstvo men. It was impossible that economic questions should fail to lead on to politics. A common programme, circulated by the Moscow zemstvo, resulted in a general demand for an overhauling of the economic life of the country, and for those civil liberties and that freedom of publicity which could alone give reality to reform. Witte was, however, outplayed by his rival. The committees were cut short, and the organizers, men of the highest rank and standing, received the imperial reprimand. Tver, the fortress of Russian Liberalism, came in for special punishment. A local zemstvo of Tver (that of Novo-Torzhok) had been particularly forward with the construction of hospitals (including the first open door asylum) and the intelligent development of cottage industries. It had proposed also to introduce agricultural specialists to advise the peasants. New items of a zemstvo budget could be struck out by the local Governor within a given time limit. He let this expire and then forbade the proposal. The zemstvo protested, and a reactionary official named Stürmer who had an estate in the district, was sent down to reduce it to submission. This bully dismissed the elected zemstvo Board and replaced it by nominees of the crown.

The conjunction of a different cause of dissatisfaction led to Witte's dismissal from office. He had opposed throughout the reckless policy by which Russia was drifting into war with Japan. On this subject Nicholas was in the hands, not of his natural adviser, his own Minister for Foreign Affairs, Count Lamsdorff, who shared the views of Witte, but of a group of irresponsible persons, among whom the only Minister was the Home Minister, Plehve; and Witte received his congé more for his wise warnings on this subject than for any other reason. Plehve remained supreme and conducted a policy of all-round repression, including an instigated pogrom in Kishinev and the wholesale flogging of peasants in Ekaterinoslav. The most extraordinary of all his devices was a fictitious movement of police socialism conducted by his confidant Zubatov, by which the workers were encouraged to think that the Government itself would help them against their own employers. Zubatov worked this programme in Moscow, and its principal agent in St. Petersburg was a priest named Gapon. Witte records how he warned Plehve that his general policy must lead to his assassination; Plehve tells Kuropatkin that the country is on the brink of revolution, and that the one thing that can stop it is 'a small victorious war'.[1]

Russia had now taken the place of China in the struggle for Korea. Russian policy was directed by a group of adventurers surrounding the Emperor, of whom the most prominent was a harebrained officer named Bezobrazov. No real account was taken of military considerations; Russian military policy for years past had been based on the possibility of an attack on the western frontier by Germany. Nicholas's War Minister, Kuropatkin, was lacking in decision though he dissented from this policy.

The issue between Russia and Japan was clear enough. There had been various treaties relating to Korea, arranging now for joint influence in Korea, now for division of spheres, now for the abstention of both. Russia had meanwhile obtained control of Manchuria; and the Japanese would have been content to leave her that control if they themselves had a free hand in Korea. The directors of Russian policy, and particularly the Emperor, regarded this as an impertinence, and claimed to dominate in both questions. The greatest of Japanese statesmen, Ito, who had played the chief part in the transformation of his country, came himself to St. Petersburg to get an agreement, and was treated with the most marked discourtesy, whereupon his London colleague obtained a treaty with England by which, if France and Germany again intervened to help Russia against Japan, England would take the side of Japan. This agreement was really an insurance against a world war, and it did actually succeed in localizing the conflict.

[1] Witte, I, 262.

When war between Russia and Japan became inevitable, the Japanese diplomacy and army moved hand in hand. The Japanese Minister left St. Petersburg just at the moment when the ice first allowed Japanese troops to embark in the north of Korea, thereby settling the Korean question straight off. At the same time, without any declaration of war, Admiral Togo effectually blockaded Port Arthur, which was then invested, thereby securing from the outset a command of the sea. This left only the question of Manchuria; and on three converging lines the Japanese advanced from the coast northward. So far the conduct of Russian policy was in chaos. An incompetent favourite, Admiral Alexeyev, had been appointed Russian Viceroy in the Far East, and at first was also Commander-in-Chief. This was so resented by Russian public opinion that the War Minister, Kuropatkin, was sent to take command in his stead. Admiral Alexeyev still remained Viceroy. Before Kuropatkin started, Witte solemnly advised him on reaching Manchuria to arrest the Admiral and send him under escort to St. Petersburg. Kuropatkin had proved a competent War Minister, but as general in command he was sadly lacking in resolution; his former chief Skobelev had warned him against ever seeking an independent command. Alexeyev was for driving the Japanese into the sea; but Kuropatkin, who had an army quite inferior both in numbers and in quality, was for retiring until he should be strong enough to advance in turn. Any differences between Alexeyev and Kuropatkin could only be settled by reference to Nicholas himself, who had no serious knowledge of military affairs. The three converging Japanese columns, marching through mountainous country, were allowed to meet at Liao-Yang, where Kuropatkin after a competent, but mechanical defence made a competent, but mechanical retreat.

Nicholas was most anxious to go to the war himself, which he could not of course have done except as Commander-in-Chief. He was dissuaded with difficulty. The question was to arise again in another connection with all-important consequences; and his motives were then fatally misunderstood. His wish, though anything but a wise one, was prompted now, as in the later instance, by sheer chivalry. On Sept. 23rd/Oct. 6th, 1904, he wrote to his mother:

> My conscience is often very troubled by my staying here instead of sharing the dangers and privations of the army. I asked Uncle Alexey yesterday what he thought about it: he thinks my presence with the Army *in this War* is not necessary — still, to stay behind in times like these is very upsetting to me.[1]

Meanwhile the long siege of Port Arthur came to an end by what was little short of treachery on January 1st, 1905. The defence had been vigorous, able and even heroic. The Russian private soldier did his part as so often before, and numbers of the best officers in the Russian army won their spurs in that defence. It was vigorously conducted as long as the brilliant chief of Engineers, Kondratenko, was alive, but after his death the commander, Stössel, without consulting his colleagues, sent out the white flag.

The surrender, of course, released large Japanese forces to join their comrades in the north before Mukden. The interval might have been utilized by Kuropatkin who by now, for the time, had superior forces, but he neither moved himself nor gave any real support to those of his lieutenants whom he authorized to do so. There was again the same almost automatic concentration of the Japanese in front of him at Mukden, the same competent and routine-like defence, and the same competent and routine-like retreat (Feb. 23rd-Mar. 14th, 1905).

As a last desperate move, the Russian Baltic fleet had been sent half round the world to reopen the naval issue. Its commanders were under no misapprehension as to their chances of success. After a whole Odyssey of misadventure, which included firing on the British fishing fleet on the Dogger Bank, this fleet went with docile courage to its doom in the Sea of Japan. Admiral Togo never had to join issue at all. His ships steamed rapidly across the Russian fleet at a distance of 7000 yards, and in three-quarters of an hour had put most of them out of action (May 27th, 1905).

By the time that the Russian fleet was practically annihilated at Tsushima, a great movement of national protest was in full progress in Russia. The main forces of the army had never been sent eastwards, and there was still less hope of sending them now. The Japanese, on their side, had advanced as far as they could make

[1] N. to M. F., 177.

good their hold. The President of the United States, Theodore Roosevelt, intervened with an offer of mediation. He was in a position to refuse further American credit to Japan. With a sore heart Nicholas dispatched Witte, who had always opposed the war, to make the best job he could of patching up a peace; he was given one limitation — he was on no account to agree to a financial indemnity, which would in Asia be taken for tribute. He was extremely adroit in his handling of the negotiations and managed to secure the sympathy of American public opinion. He had, of course, to abandon all claims on Korea. He had to cede Port Arthur, with the southern half of Manchuria, and half of the island of Sakhalin. As Izvolsky puts it, 'No diplomat by profession could have done it',[1] and his outstanding services brought him the title of Count.

What are the lessons of this war? They are two. The first is fully brought out in the best account of the war in English, that of General Sir F. Maurice.[2] It is that on the Japanese side, army and nation worked in the closest co-operation throughout, and that with the Russians it was just the opposite. The other is the bankruptcy of the vain hope of the Russian Government that Russia could evade all questions of reform at home by plunging her head into Asia to realize a dream of imperial expansion. As soon as the head peeped out on to the Pacific, it received a crushing blow from exactly that Asiatic nation which had been most eager to learn and assimilate the most useful lessons that Europe could teach it. The failure of the Far Eastern enterprise of Russia and the victory of progressive Japan sent back a wave that stirred all European Russia and even beat against the walls of the last great fortress of absolutism in Europe, the Prussian Empire of Germany.

[1] IZVOLSKY, 24.
[2] In the *Cambridge Modern History*, vol. XIII

CHAPTER III

THE FOUNDATIONS SHAKEN

THE LIBERATION MOVEMENT

And like a man to double business bound,
I stand in pause where I shall first begin,
And both neglect.

Hamlet, III, 3

PLEHVE and his friends had their war, but it was neither small nor victorious, and in the course of it Plehve himself was blown sky high on July 28th, 1904, by a bomb launched by a terrorist S.R. named Sazonov, while on his way to report to the Emperor, apparently armed with a number of documents to accuse Witte himself of being a revolutionary. This, together with the war, set going a new national movement — or rather two parallel movements, never clearly enough distinguished from each other, one for reform and the other for revolution.

The very hesitations of Nicholas were proof that he did not feel any real confidence in a policy of sheer reaction. His first instinct was to replace Plehve by a reactionary, and in his correspondence with Meshchersky (soon to be broken off) we come across the sinister name of Stürmer. His final choice fell upon Prince Svyatopolk-Mirsky, a man of the highest integrity, liberal by instinct, who had the respect of all who knew him. At once it was seen how the public responded to any move in its direction, and there followed a short period of general optimism, known as 'the Russian Spring'.

The reform movement was a natural outcome of Shipov's attempt to co-ordinate the work of the zemstva, and of the conclusions of nearly all the committees of 1903 on the agricultural industry. Shipov was pressed to call another conference of zemstvo representatives. Mirsky did everything to make this easy for him. The conference was unanimous on all points except for one important detail. Its programme was a national plea for civil liberties: of person (from arbitrary arrest), of conscience, of speech, of press, of meeting and of the formation of associations. The conference also asked unanimously for a representative national assembly, and it was divided only on the question as to whether this assembly should be legislative or consultative (November 1904). Such unanimity in the legally elected representatives of local government was in itself impressive. The Emperor debated the questions thus raised with his advisers, including Witte, who still occupied a comparatively honorary post as Chairman of the Committee of Ministers, — that is, Chairman in the absence of the sovereign. He was advised against granting a national assembly. He issued two pronouncements: in one he ordered the zemstva to mind their own business, and not interfere in politics; in the other he announced his intention of initiating a programme of reforms himself; it was obvious that he could only do this through the machinery of the bureaucracy, which was exactly what the country wanted to see reformed.

The requests of the zemstva — not as yet demands — were taken up with a convincing unanimity by almost the whole of the educated public. The lawyers, celebrating the fortieth anniversary of the introduction of trial by jury, held a banquet at which they endorsed the zemstvo programme and formed themselves into a 'union' to assist its fulfilment. At that time professional bodies had the right of meeting in conference, though only for the discussion of professional questions. This made the present unanimous expression of opinion all the more striking. It was a general agreement of all professional opinion, expressing itself freely and without regard for established authority. One after another, the authors, the professors, the journalists, the doctors, and the engineers took the same action as the lawyers. The unions thus formed, a creation of the professional class, were the first trade unions in Russia; for this reason even under Communism trade unions in Russia are still called professional unions.

It was now for the masses to move, and obviously the town workers had a much better chance of doing so than the scattered and backward peasantry. This class was still in the process of formation and can hardly have amounted at this time to as much as five millions. Much of it was still half-peasant, being founded on the go-away industries of the peasantry which brought them to the towns. But it represented a higher standard of information and public intelligence, and above all it was concentrated. Plekhanov and his emigrant colleagues, who led the Social Democrats or S.D.s from abroad and had devoted their energies principally to the town workers, also desired the introduction of democratic principles into the government of Russia, which would obviously simplify their task, and were prepared to co-operate with the middle class for that purpose. Plekhanov was in favour of a latitude for local groups and of basing the whole movement as far as possible on the rank and file of the working population; but a younger man of great intellect and vigour, Vladimir Ulyanov, known under his press name of Lenin, challenged this view. Lenin's elder brother had joined in a plot to assassinate Alexander III and had been executed. The early report on his character by his headmaster, who curiously enough was the father of Alexander Kerensky, describes him as a boy of seriousness, purpose and aloofness; and even in his early conspirative revolutionary work there was always the claim and the dominance of a leader. He was a thorough scholar, a keen and acute thinker and, whatever the problems he had to face and the variety of tactics required to meet them, he always knew where he was going. He wished to have a closely knit leading group and a close party discipline, which would monopolize all the initiative. At a party conference begun in Brussels and completed in London in 1903, there was a sharp split between the two theories, followed by struggle for control. When the cause of liberty was moving forward, the public atmosphere favoured the moderates, who were prepared to work with other parties. Lenin, however, did not believe that illiterate Russia could be won for Marxism that way. He foresaw, in the long run, a great war resulting from the capitalist struggle for markets, in which all the old authorities might be swept away. At present neither the Mensheviks of Plekhanov nor the Bolsheviks of Lenin had any but an almost negligible following, but their motto of the socialization of the means of production, however vaguely understood or interpreted, made an intimate appeal to the comparatively small, but fast growing class of town workers.

It was not, however, through the official exponents of Marxism that the masses now expressed themselves, but in another way, namely through the bastard organization of Father Gapon in St. Petersburg, which owed its origin to the absurd 'police socialism' of the dead Plehve. The workers had been glad to utilize any facilities which enabled them to meet. Gapon's organization was based on a representation of one person for every thousand workers. Though originally working in contact with the police, he decided to mobilize it in support of the general national programme with special emphasis on the needs of the workers, which indeed had also been specially emphasized in the zemstvo conference of November 19th. He planned a peaceful demonstration in the form of a march to the Winter Palace, carrying church banners and singing religious and national songs. Owing to the idiocy of the military authorities, the crowd was met with rifle fire both at the outskirts of the city and on the palace square. The actual victims, as certified by a public commission of lawyers of the Opposition, was approximately 150 killed and 200 wounded; and as all who had taken a leading part in the procession were then expelled from the capital, the news was circulated all over the Empire. It resulted in a very epidemic of strikes of all kinds, which when it reached the non-Russian populations took on an aspect of separatism; and by this passive movement alone, apart from the many disorders that broke out, the government authority almost ceased to function in such parts. One feature of this period, which became more and more prominent, was the enormous number of isolated murders of ordinary police officials in the twilight, the murderer almost always escaping.

The Government found no real way of dealing with these disorders. Immediately after the bloody work of January 22nd, General Dmitry Trepov, City Prefect of Moscow, was sent for and was appointed as, first, Governor General of St. Petersburg, and later also Assistant Minister of the Interior, with an absolute control over all the police of the Empire. Apart from sending from the capital all the leaders of the march to the Winter Palace, apparently his only idea was to organize a deputation of workmen to the Tsar to beg pardon for the march. Nicholas entertained them to tea, and gave them a warning to transmit to their class as a whole. Trepov was a brave man; a student shot at him point blank as he was starting from Moscow, and he stood fire without flinching; but he was nothing else, and all his antecedents were those of a police officer. Things got worse and worse till they culminated in the assassination of the Grand Duke Sergius, who till lately had been Governor General in Moscow, and was still in charge of the troops there. He had hardly a friend or an admirer, and he had managed to alienate nearly every class in Moscow, from the merchants to the students. His cousin, Alexander Mikhailovich, writes of him: 'Try as I will, I cannot find a single redeeming feature in his character'.[1] This blow came near home, for the Grand Duke was the uncle of the Emperor and married to the sister of the Empress. The act, for which the terrorist section of the S.R.s was responsible, was committed in broad daylight in the Kremlin. The assassin, Kaliayev, made no attempt to escape, and showed the greatest courage under examination and trial. The widow of the victim, the Grand Duchess Elizabeth, a beautiful and saintly woman, came to see him in prison and asked to plead for his life on the sole condition that he should express his sorrow for his act.[2] This he refused, saying that his execution would be of more use to his cause, and he went to his death with the same courage. Further details, which came out later, only tended to throw further odium on the police; for the man, Azef, who as organizer of the terrorist section of the S.R.s, sent Kaliayev to his death, turned out to be playing the double role of terrorist and police agent. He was exposed by the persistent investigations of that extraordinary revolutionary scholar, Burtsev, and the result was a resounding scandal.

The answer of the sovereign to this challenge was of vital consequence to what followed, but it is perhaps the very best instance of his hesitations. The details have only recently been made clear by the invaluable record of Count Kokovtsev, then Minister of Finance.[3] It was essential to Kokovtsev to organize a French loan to Russia, and he was at this time receiving M. Netzlin, the head of a French group of bankers. Netzlin, disturbed by the disorders in Russia, was asking for some security of union between the Government and the people; and Kokovtsev, with the help of Witte, utilized this plea to secure an audience for Netzlin with the Emperor. Netzlin spoke plainly to the Emperor

[1] G. D. ALEXANDER, *Once a Grand Duke*, 158.
[2] ibid., 159-60.
[3] KOKOVTSEV, I, 64.

and came back radiant at his reception; but instead of the expected act of conciliation appeared an imperial manifesto reasserting the autocracy and calling on all loyal citizens to rally round the throne. Nicholas had asked Meshchersky to supply such a manifesto, though he had not used a word of it. It was natural enough that he should give expression to his indignation at the murder of his uncle and brother-in-law; but the two statesmen were confounded. They approached him again, and the manifesto was almost immediately followed by the greatest concession of the reign, the institution of a national assembly to be called the Imperial Duma and to consist of the 'best men invested with the confidence of the population'. With this was issued a third document, which directed the new Minister of the Interior, Bulygin, to welcome any opinions from the population as to the form which this assembly should take. The impulse which prompted this was certainly well-meaning. It had been the custom in old days, sometimes to welcome such expressions of opinion from public men of high standing. But while the Tsar was thinking in terms of patriarchal Russia, the educated public was thinking of British and French constitutions, and this document was taken as a direct invitation to form political parties and draw up programmes.

Though there is no sign that he had intended it, Nicholas had caused a split among his critics and opponents. In the clamour of various party conferences, the divisions in their ranks became evident. It was at this point that came the news of the final act of the war, the annihilation of the Baltic fleet at Tsushima. This at once closed the ranks of the public. Shipov invited all the leaders to a coalition congress, and it asked the Emperor without delay to receive a deputation from the public as a whole. The request was granted, and the reception took place on June 19th. The spokesman chosen was a man of the highest credit and integrity not associated with any party, Prince Sergius Trubetskoy, a member of a great and noble-minded family, and he found a way of impressing the sovereign with the absolute necessity of union with the people. In historic and prophetic words he pointed out that if this was not achieved without delay, there would be a movement against 'all that were called masters', and he ended: 'Do not linger, Sir. Great is your responsibility before God and Russia.'

The Emperor at last found himself in intimate contact with men who were really representative of the public, and this was by no means the only time that he proved responsive to it. His face changed while Trubetskoy was speaking, and very simply he gave an answer which must have been as little expected by himself as it was by his hearers:

> Throw away your doubts. My will, the Tsar's will, to call together representatives of the people is unchangeable. I every day follow and stand for this work. You may tell this to all who are near to you, living whether in the country or in the towns. I hope you will co-operate with me in this task.[1]

The Tsar's reply was taken as a mandate for further public discussions. Hitherto the zemstva had led the movement for reform; now the town councils of Russia joined hands with them, and on July 19th was opened in Moscow a joint congress of representatives of both of them. It is interesting to note what were the leading principles of this comparatively united public opinion. They were typically English; there remained the open question, how far they could find their realization in the Russian Empire. A Grand Remonstrance was passed, calling attention to the violations by the Government of its own laws; and a wisely drafted plan for a constitution, based largely on English models and including all the civil liberties which had been called for in November 1904, was accepted in principle — 'at the first reading', as it was put by the proposer, Professor Muromtsev. An appeal to the public drafted by the veteran of Russian Liberalism, Ivan Petrunkevich, was passed for the use of political meetings; it contained words that were also to become pathetically prophetic:[2]

> The path which we have pointed out is a path of peace, it is to lead the country to a new order of things without convulsions, without bloodshed, without thousands of unnecessary victims.†

These words, representing at this moment the universal desire of the population, issued by the only persons who could claim to be its elected representatives, may now be regarded as the noble epitaph of the liberal movement in Russia.

A month later (August 19th) was issued the Government's own

[1] PARES, *Russia and Reform*, 510. [2] ibid., 515.

draft scheme for the Duma. The Emperor had called together his chosen advisers, selected of course from that narrow bureaucratic circle which alone was known to him, and he himself presided at their discussions. There was no voting; for by the principle of autocracy the Emperor settled everything. He comes out as a very intelligent and sensible chairman, usually swayed by all that was happening towards the more liberal and intelligent view. But the draft as a whole could not possibly meet the wishes of the public. The Duma was to be only consultative; in general it was to work in departments, co-operating with the various Ministries; its franchise was absurd: practically the whole professional class and other very large sections of the population were left out. The disorders, therefore, continued and increased as the summer passed. The Government did restore self-government to the universities and allowed meetings there; but as such meetings were forbidden elsewhere and the students were at present the most revolutionary element in the country the meetings took place in their class-rooms, where all were admitted and work became impossible. In the Black Sea the battleship *Potemkin* mutinied, killed its officers, fired on Odessa and ultimately took refuge in the Rumanian port of Constandza.

The movement for the formation of professional unions, begun at the end of the previous year, had now spread on to the great mass of the population, and there were unions of factory workers, railway men, etc. Early in the year, chiefly through the organizing genius of Professor Milyukov, all the unions had gathered together into a Union of Unions, of which he was the first president. This was a very remarkable man, who had helped to bring the professional class to the support of the zemstva. He aimed at creating a Liberal party in Russia, relying on the more progressive of the zemstvo men and the more moderately minded in the professional class. Milyukov was a first-rate historical scholar, and in his political views he was a product of the English liberalism of his time, to which throughout a hard life he always remained faithful. As with another scholar, Thomas Masaryk, it was the conditions of his country that drove him into politics, but he brought into them the doctrinaire assuredness of the professor and pursuing a well-thought-out programme with a remarkable talent for organization, he tended to reduce Russian Liberalism to a formula bounded by his not too broad conception of it and to ask allegiance for tactics which were sometimes peculiarly shortsighted. But whatever may or may not have been in Milyukov, he stood throughout as a tower of Russian liberalism to which he gave shape and direction in a country which, more than most others, had need of this. He was the foremost and worthy representative of those principles of the liberal era in Europe — freedom, the sanctity of the individual, reason and persuasion — which responded to a deep desire of the Russian people; and from them not the hardest buffetings of public life could ever estrange him, shift his moral balance or disturb his extraordinary equanimity, or even, in a long political life, of the measure rather of a British than of a Russian statesman, diminish his unfailing energy and activity. His first entry into politics was an order of house arrest for a public lecture which he had given under auspices such as those of our University Extension. The almighty Plehve paid a visit to his prisoner, and, struck by his ability, asked him if he might be inclined to occupy the post of Minister of Public Instruction. Milyukov replied that he would prefer that of Minister of the Interior, which was Plehve's own post.[1]

Liberalism was a matter of faith in those days — not, as in democratic countries, something to be assumed; and there was one outstanding man who had worked his way to it through other theories. This was Peter Struve, who was not only a scholar of exceptional learning and insight, but one of the most profound thinkers of his time. For Struve, thinking was a matter of conscience, a continual and responsible wrestle, to be essayed only with a complete intellectual honesty. He had been one of the earliest Marxists, though never a hard and fast doctrinaire. At one time he had worked with Lenin, and it was he who had supplied him with books when he was in prison. This was for him a stage in his development, and he was now on his way to become the principal leader of intellectual Liberalism. The old Zemstvo Liberals still mistrusted him a little; but he had been chosen to edit their organ *Liberation*, which was published at first at Stuttgart and later in Paris.

Meanwhile, under the title of a Peasants' Union, the S.R.s, discarding for the time questions of forms of government, were

[1] Milyukov to B. P.

managing to secure an almost complete adherence of the peasants to a simple programme for restoring all the land to them.

Trepov had no way of dealing with such problems other than the motto expressed in a famous order of his, 'Not to spare the cartridges', which was warmly commended by Nicholas.[1] The Government arrested the Congress of Railway men, and as a result all the railways ceased to function. This inevitably brought the whole life of the country to a standstill; it must be remembered that the food supply of the capital depended on the railways. Everyone more or less automatically joined in the general strike, and the paralysis of the whole country was most impressive, nowhere more so than in St. Petersburg. Originally there was no organization of the strike, but in the course of it was created a body based on the same principle as that of Gapon, namely election of one from each thousand of factory workers, but led by the Marxist S.D.s and the S.R.s. The president was an able and magnetic lawyer named Nosar under his pseudonym Hrustalev, and the vice-president was Leon Trotsky, then a Menshevik Social Democrat.

It was in the late summer that the Japanese War was brought to an end by the Treaty of Portsmouth in America (August 29th). This, as we know, was the work of Witte, and he was now recognized as the coming man in Russia. He arrived there during the General Strike. It was even impossible for the Ministers to reach the Tsar's summer palace at Peterhof otherwise than by water. Witte presented a memorandum in which he laid before the Emperor two alternatives: either to set up a military dictatorship or practically to grant a constitution by making the Duma legislative instead of consultative and by declaring that no law would have force without its assent. The Emperor consulted his advisers, among others the Grand Duke Nicholas Nikolayevich, who was the obvious choice for military dictator, and the Grand Duke, a very excitable and outspoken man, threatened to shoot himself, then and there, if this task were committed to him. Here is the incident as recorded by Mosolov.[2]

> If the Emperor does not accept the Witte programme [he said to Count Fredericksz], if he wants to force me to become

[1] N. to M. F., 187.
[2] Mosolov, 90.

> Dictator, I shall kill myself in his presence with this revolver. I am going on to the Tsar; I only called here to let you know my intentions. You must support Witte at all costs. It is necessary for the good of Russia and of all of us.

The Empress ever afterwards regarded the Grand Duke as responsible for the Russian constitution. The Tsar had no way out, and accepted Witte's second alternative. Thus came to be issued the famous manifesto of October 17th/30th, 1905, drafted in the main by Witte, with a government communication which was entirely his work, containing the whole programme of civil liberties — a frank adoption of the maximum programme of Shipov's Zemstvo Conference, with a legislative Duma.[1] The Emperor gave way with the greatest reluctance. He was deeply and simply religious: and what stuck in his mind most of all was that he was proving untrue to his coronation oath, to his father's memory, and to his obligations to his infant son born in this year. He and the Empress prayed long and silently together over the great issue. But he did at the time frankly accept the implications of what he was doing, for in a letter of November 1st/14th to his mother, he wrote: 'That, of course, would be a constitution'; and she, whom he might well regard as the truest representative of the traditions of his father, replied on November 14th: 'I am sure you could not act otherwise than you have done.'

Anyhow this was the end of the direct influence of Pobedonostsev, who finally retired from office. As to Witte, the question is more complex. In his memoirs he claims that at that time not only the conservative *Novoe Vremya*, but such reactionaries as Durnovo and even Meshchersky were in favour of the concession,[2] and he still supports it with such arguments as that a river cannot flow backwards and that this was the legitimate antidote to revolution;[3] he even expresses the view that Russia will inevitably become a constitutional state, like those of western Europe;[4] but to me when I later asked him his opinion on the subject he replied: 'I have a constitution in my head; but as to my heart' — and he spat on the floor.

The change included the introduction into Russia of the Cabinet System, namely of a Prime Minister with control over and responsi-

[1] See the full text, which is printed as an Appendix.
[2] Witte, I, 448-9. [3] ibid., I, 438. [4] ibid., II, 282.

bility for his colleagues; Witte had refused to take office on any other terms. As he already held the more or less honorary post of President of the *Committee* of Ministers, it was easy to adopt a slight alteration in title and to make him Prime Minister under the name of President of the *Council* of Ministers. It must be said at once that this was in principle one of the greatest of all the changes which took place, and the one which the Emperor most resented.

As the new Prime Minister, Witte was in a most unenviable position. It is true that the Manifesto at once had an enormous effect, rallying to the throne all such moderate elements as Shipov and his friends, who later, led by Alexander Guchkov, formed a 'League of October 17th', the germ of the future party of Octobrists or conservative reformers. Milyukov had at this very moment completed his arrangements for the creation of a great Russian Liberal party under the name of Constitutional Democrats, which the public shortened to 'Cadets'. But neither the Octobrists nor the Cadets had much trust in Witte. He had stolen their programme without really believing in it, except as the only way of stopping a revolution. He now interviewed them in turn to secure their support. The Octobrists refused to join him; he had appointed as Minister of the Interior and Head of Police an extremely able and well-known reactionary named Durnovo, because, as he explained, none but a man with police antecedents could secure the life of the sovereign. The Cadets he threatened to outbid with a Bill for the compulsory expropriation of land which was never issued. The reactionaries were of course bitterly opposed to him and lampooned him in a very clever periodical entitled *Saint Witte's Dance*, and with the active assistance of the police, they organized a whole series of pogroms or armed attacks on the Jews, whose cause, to his credit, had always been championed by Witte; Nicholas took these as a genuine expression of public opinion.[1] Witte had no easier time with the new Soviet, which, representing the factory population of St. Petersburg, was perhaps his most immediate and dangerous enemy.

Meanwhile the conflagration had now reached the mass of the peasants. The S.R.s had remarkable success with their foundation of a Peasant Union; and in the course of the late autumn and early winter, when the crops had been harvested, peasants gathered in

[1] N. to M. F., 190

masses on one estate after another, always led by an S.R. agitator, and quietly escorted the squire out of the district, often burning his house down, to make it not worth his while to come back. In one district after another sprang up what were called peasant republics; these 'republics' were not so much a challenge to Tsardom as simply institutions of local self-government by the peasants themselves, directed by a very clear, if rude, instinct of public order, and sometimes very well managed.

In the capital people were discussing whether Witte would arrest Hrustalev, or Hrustalev would arrest Witte; but the Soviet had no practical ideas other than the declaration of new general strikes on various issues, such as an amnesty for a mutiny which had been put down in Kronstadt and the repeal of martial la v in Poland, and it never obtained any real direction of the masses, so that these various attempts at repeating the original General Strike ended in failure. At one point the Soviet ordered the withdrawal of all individual accounts from savings banks; Witte in reply threatened to arrest any editor who printed this order. Ultimately the Government took courage, and on the declaration of a post and telegraph strike, it arrested the bulk of the Soviet, as many as a hundred and ninety members (Dec. 16th). Those who were left called another general strike, but almost immediately called it off. The original summons reached Moscow and resulted in the outbreak of an armed movement, during which students and workmen set up loose barricades in the streets and for a time dominated the greater part of the city (Dec. 22nd to Jan. 1st). Here too, however, there was no real organization; the revolutionaries never secured the main railway stations, and the Semenovsky regiment of the Guard and other troops were brought into the city and without any great difficulty suppressed the rising. This, as far as the two capitals were concerned, was the real end of the movement on its revolutionary side. Most fortunately for the Government, the unhappy Japanese War had been liquidated before the principal outburst of revolution in Russia, and the public at this time was definitely alienated by the futility and disorder of revolution. There followed, like a series of echoes, local mutinies or outbreaks, which were most serious among the defeated and demobilized troops returning from the Far East; the most ruthless of these movements — on both sides —

was an uprising of the Lettish and Estonian peasants in the Baltic provinces against their German landowners, and when order was at last restored, landowners accompanied the punitive columns and the reprisals were not less cruel. Military columns were also sent down to the principal centres of disorder among the Russian peasantry; villages were bombarded with machine guns, and the country was brought to submission.

We have a light on Nicholas's mind throughout this period in his letters to his mother, or at least on so much of it as he showed to her, not forgetting that she was the wife of his strong father. They also throw an interesting light on his relations with Witte.

He writes on Sep. 29th/Oct. 12th, 1905:

> At Björkö Witte came to see me — he was very charming and interesting. After a long talk [no doubt, on his brilliant peace negotiations] I told him of his new honour — I am creating him a Count. He went quite stiff with emotion and then tried three times to kiss my hand!

She writes on October 16th:

> I am sure that the only man who can help you now and be useful is Witte, because he should be well disposed again *now*.

On Oct. 19th/Nov. 1st, Nicholas writes in full on the issue of the famous October Manifesto:

> You remember, no doubt, those January days when we were together at Tsarskoe — they were miserable, weren't they? But they are *nothing* in comparison with what has happened now . . . All sorts of conferences took place in Moscow, which Durnovo permitted, I do not know why . . . God knows what happened in the universities. Every *kind* of riffraff walked in from the streets, riot was loudly proclaimed — nobody seemed to mind . . . It makes me sick to read the news! . . . But the Ministers, instead of acting with quick decision, only assemble in council like a lot of frightened hens and cackle about providing united ministerial action . . . Trepov made it quite plain to the populace by his proclamations that any disorder would be ruthlessly put down . . . One had the same feeling as before a thunderstorm in summer! . . . Through all those horrible days, I constantly met Witte. We very often met in the early morning to part only in the evening when night fell . . . There were only two ways open; to find an energetic

soldier and crush the rebellion by sheer force . . . That would mean rivers of blood, and in the end we should be where we had started . . . The other way out would be to give to the people their civil rights, freedom of speech and press, also to have all laws confirmed by a State Duma — that of course, would be a constitution. Witte defends this very energetically . . . Almost everybody I had an opportunity of consulting, is of the same opinion. Witte put it quite clearly to me that he would accept the Presidency of the Council of Ministers only on the condition that his programme was agreed to, and his actions not interfered with . . . We discussed it for two days and in the end, invoking God's help I signed . . . In my telegram I could not explain all the circumstances which brought me to this terrible decision which nevertheless I took quite consciously . . . I had nobody to rely on except honest Trepov. There was no other way out than to cross oneself and give what everyone was asking for . . . All the Ministers are resigning and we have to find new ones, but Witte must see to that . . . We are in the midst of a revolution with an administrative apparatus entirely disorganized, and in this lies the main danger.

On Oct. 27th/Nov. 9th:

It is strange that such a clever man should be wrong in his forecast of an easy pacification. I do not quite like his way of getting into touch with various extremists, especially as all these talks appear in the press next day.

On Nov. 10th/23rd, he writes:

Everybody is afraid of taking courageous action; I keep on trying to force them — even Witte himself — to behave more energetically. With us nobody is accustomed to shouldering responsibility: all expect to be given orders which, however, they disobey as often as not.

On Dec. 1st/14th:

He (Witte) is now prepared to order the arrest of all the principal leaders of the outbreak. I have been trying for some time past to get him to do it, but he always hoped to be able to manage without drastic measures.

On Dec. 8th/21st:

Please don't worry so much about us. Of course I am not going through an easy time, but God is my strength and

> gives me peace of mind . . . So many Russians now-a-days have lost that spirit . . . Civic courage, as you know, is at the best of times noticeable here only among the few. Now it hardly seems to exist at all.

On Dec. 15th/28th he describes the Moscow rising:

> The abscess was growing gradually, causing much pain and suffering, and now it has burst . . . He declares that the chief difficulty is to find enough troops.

On Dec. 19th/Jan. 1st, writing of the savage rising in the Baltic Provinces, he uses the phrase, 'Terror must be met by terror'. He had made a similar comment on the margin of a report, and it has always been used by the revolutionaries to prove that he was a bloodthirsty tyrant, which is entirely out of keeping with his character.

On Jan. 12th/25th, 1906, he writes:

> As for Witte, since the happenings in Moscow he has radically changed his views; now he wants to hang and shoot everybody. I have never seen such a chameleon of a man. That, naturally, is the reason why no one believes in him any more . . . Durnovo the Minister of the Interior is doing splendid work.

These were the conditions in which Russia proceeded to the election of its first national assembly. In the middle of the Moscow rising, when Witte could not yet know how the cat was going to jump, he made his last big concession. The October Manifesto had promised that the election should really be nation-wide, and Witte on December 24th practically gave universal suffrage. It is true that it was indirect, as suffrage naturally was in such a backward country as Russia (Nicholas had rightly rejected as 'fantastical' a proposal of direct suffrage by Prince A. D. Obolensky). The illiterate peasants would choose their literate betters and send them to take part in the next stage of the election. This, of course, involved prolonged discussions among the electors themselves. The bearings of the Government's law were best understood by the Cadets, as many of them were experts in the constitutions of Western Europe. In each province a majority of the electors could capture the whole representation of the province. Extremists of both sides were now discredited, the Government by its renewed repressions, the revolutionaries by their futility. It was not, then, surprising that the Cadets were the dominant party in the first Russian Duma. The S.R.s elected a large number of peasant representatives, but did not appear under their own name in the Duma; their leaders, who were well known to the police, could hardly come out in public. Of the S.D.s, who suffered from the same difficulty, the Mensheviks had a good deal of success among the factory workers; the Bolsheviks at first unwisely boycotted the elections, and by the time they decided to take an active part in them, it was too late.

There was nothing in the conduct of Witte that more irritated the Emperor than his last concession of December 24th. Witte he regarded as playing the role of a modern prime minister and reducing his sovereign to a nullity. Durnovo, meanwhile, was always undermining Witte at the powerful Ministry of the Interior, and after the General Strike Trepov, with no loss of the confidence of his sovereign, had become commandant of the Imperial palace. He was more than that. The dismissed head of the police of the Empire, who had found it impossible to work with Witte, was now the special confidant of the sovereign to whom all Witte's proposals were submitted before confirmation. On Jan. 26th/Feb. 8th Nicholas writes to his mother:

> Trepov is absolutely indispensable to me; he is acting in a kind of secretarial capacity. He is experienced and clever and cautious in his advice. I give him Witte's bulky memoranda to read, then he reports on them quickly and concisely. This is of course a secret to everybody but ourselves.[1]

What a start for a constitutional Prime Minister! It is the refuge of a weak man who feels that his power is being filched from him by an unscrupulous Minister, cleverer than himself.

Witte tried to rectify his position by a number of efforts to recover the good will of the Tsar. The October Manifesto had laid down certain principles, but they were still to be put into shape. This was obviously a task for the Duma, without whose consent, so the Manifesto declared, no law was to be made in Russia. Witte, however, set about drafting a number of arbitrary additions to

[1] N. to M. F., 212.

the fundamental laws, which were to be placed outside the competence of the Duma; for instance, it was not to touch the army and navy, which remained prerogatives of the sovereign, and even more important was its exclusion from any part in the obtaining of foreign loans. Witte, as he has himself explained in his memoirs, put his enormous personal credit with foreign bankers into the scale in order to secure so large a loan that the Government would not be dependent on grants from the Duma.[1] Germany refused to help him, but France did, much to the indignation of the Russian Liberals and revolutionaries.

Another of the most important of the new additions was an adaptation of Article 14 of the Austrian constitution (numbered Article 87 by Witte), by which the Government was free, in any matter of emergency during a vacation of the Duma, itself to issue any law to deal with that emergency, on condition of presenting it to the Duma for confirmation within two months of its next meeting. Article 87 was to be the occasion for innumerable protests and many conflicts in the future. For one other task Witte was indispensable, namely, bringing back the defeated army from the Far East, and this he achieved in a masterly way, but his credit was gone and not to be recovered. More than once he offered his resignation, and ultimately he was dismissed on the eve of the opening of the Duma. Nicholas writes of him later (Nov. 1906):

> As long as I live, I will never trust that man again with the smallest thing. I had quite enough of last year's experiment. It is still like a nightmare to me.[2]

The new Prime Minister was Goremykin. The present-day materials and especially the invaluable record of Kokovtsev enable us to understand the significance of this otherwise enigmatic public figure. As a politician, in the broad sense, Goremykin was a nullity. 'An insignificant person,' writes Witte of him.[3] He was already too old for his job; but he was very wily, knew the bureaucratic machine thoroughly, and was opposed to all change, which he usually evaded by an attitude of cynical indifference. But the reason why he should be selected rather than any one else — and this is extremely important to the rest of the story — was that he constantly and effusively insisted on the principle that

[1] WITTE, II, 193. [2] N. to M. F., 221. [3] WITTE, I, 195.

Ministers were no more than servants of the Tsar, and that if they were called upon to carry out a measure which seemed to conflict with their own better judgment, all they were to do after advising against it was simply to carry it out. 'Any attempt to alter the imperial view', he explained to Kokovtsev, 'will be quite useless and only dangerous to you.'[1] We can well understand what an appeal such an attitude made to the Empress, who constantly speaks of Goremykin affectionately as 'the old man', a nickname which he shared with the most trusted and loyal of all the personal servants of the Emperor, Count Fredericksz, the Minister of the Court.

The Minister of Finance was again Kokovtsev, honest, intelligent and devoted to the service of the State. Izvolsky speaks of 'his universally recognized probity'.[2] Buchanan describes him as 'the best type of the old bureaucracy'.[3] But the most striking figure in the new Ministry was Peter Stolypin, who came not from the bureaucracy, but from another reserve that the Government possessed for the highest offices, namely the local governors. In the troubled months at the end of 1905 the part played by Stolypin was outstanding; he was responsible for the most turbulent province of Russia, that of Saratov. Accompanied by a small and competent staff, he travelled from place to place restoring order by his sheer presence and personality. He stopped a riot of reactionaries with the words: 'Is that how you show your loyalty to your sovereign?' And he saved a revolutionary and insurgent village from destruction by advancing alone among a shower of bullets and begging them not to compel him to use his power. At one moment one of the agitators seized him by the arm; Stolypin turned round with the words: 'Hold my coat', which were obeyed.[4]

There is no need here to dwell long on the short life of the First Duma. It was indeed the cream of the Russian intelligentsia and the peasants in particular had obeyed the imperial summons to choose men who had the confidence of the population and were generally too shrewd to be led away by party cries. But the revolutionary basis on which the success of the reformers had so much depended, had fallen away from beneath them; the country

[1] Kokovtsev to B. P.
[2] Izvolsky, 93.
[3] Buchanan, I, 162.
[4] Izvolsky, 97.

was sick of revolution. So few were the competent public men in Russia that the elections to the Duma depleted the zemstva of most of their best men. The Cadets never had a basis of organization in the country; there was no real possibility of frequent public meetings, and they had only insignificant party funds. Hardly any of them had any experience of administration; they were mostly professional men who hoped to carry the fortress of autocracy by expressions of principle.

The first and best act of the Duma was to put the needs of the country clearly before the sovereign. Adopting English precedents — as it did, not only now, but throughout its existence — the Duma replied to 'the King's Speech' made to it by the Emperor when receiving it at the Winter Palace and containing little more than general expressions of good will, by an 'Address to the Throne' — such was the title actually chosen. It was drafted so ably as to carry the support of all the different groups in the House, it was steered through the debate with exceptional ability by the young Liberal, Vladimir Nabokov and was adopted almost unanimously. While embracing all the main demands of the public, it was capable of circulation throughout Russia in microscopic form on a post card. Much fuss was made by the Government as to whether the Duma had a right to address the sovereign, but it was ultimately received by the Minister of the Court. Goremykin then led his heterogeneous colleagues down to the Duma and read a lecture, after the manner of an old schoolmaster, in which he dismissed the most important demand of all, relating to land for the peasants, as 'inadmissible'. Nabokov at once proposed a vote of censure, and this led to a debate in which one abuse of the Government after another was laid bare. The Ministers present, with the exception of Stolypin, proved quite incapable of defending themselves, being as new to this environment as anyone else.†

So far everything had proceeded on the English model, and after the vote of censure presumably the Government ought to resign. It did not do so, and Government and Duma sat looking at each other, each wondering what step it dared to take, and what support it would receive from the country. Ultimately, in order to win such support, the Duma raised the land question in two Bills, respectively from the Cadet and Labour Parties, both of which were based on the principle of compulsory expropriation of land: the first with compensation and the second without. The Government next invited the peasants to look to it for support rather than to the Duma. The Duma now decided to make its own appeal to the country, but this was precisely one of those things which the fundamental laws forbade it to do.

With the Government there was a crisis of indecision. Trepov, who had the ear of the Emperor, actually advised him to treat with the Liberals and call them to office, and it is almost clear from a half finished utterance of his that he hoped they would find the task of governing too difficult for them, and would pave the way for a military dictatorship.[1] Stolypin, on the other hand, who defined his position as 'a constitutionalist (under the Manifesto of October), but not a parliamentarist', urged that a Cadet Ministry would in a few months have destroyed all the prestige of the Government, and that the loss would be irreparable.[2] Stolypin was for dissolving this Duma under the existing law and calling another under the same conditions. It is significant that the strongest plea against dissolution was made by the Foreign Minister, Izvolsky, recently appointed to direct Russian foreign policy towards friendship with France and England. The Emperor had long been yearning to dissolve the Duma, in which of course he had the full support of Goremykin. He was not prepared for a 'leap into the unknown'[3] and he felt that in face of the challenge to his authority, resistance at all costs was better than surrender. He still hesitated and consulted various advisers. Kokovtsev strongly counselled against any adoption of English parliamentarism. Stolypin had negotiated with some of the leading 'public men' for what was to be called later a 'Ministry of Confidence', a blend of the more reasonable holders of office with men who represented the more moderate shades of public opinion. Trepov and Izvolsky were frankly for a cabinet composed exclusively of the latter with Muromtsev, the President of the Duma, at its head. Muromtsev was indeed approached — as he understood, on behalf of the sovereign. He referred the matter to Milyukov as leader of the dominant party in the Duma.[4] Shipov, who was also approached, had but few supporters in the Duma and gave the same answer.[5] Milyukov was out to carry the whole position by

[1] Izvolsky, 211. [2] Stolypin to B. P. [3] Kokovtsev, I, 200. [4] Muromtsev to B. P. [5] Shipov to B.P.

moral pressure and demanded a Cadet Ministry, with himself at its head. Here he made one of the crucial mistakes of his career. Conversation had passed between Trepov and Milyukov, and Milyukov has himself owned to having 'set very hard conditions'.[1] It was in the middle of this that the Duma decided to appeal to the public against the Government, which Milyukov had done his best to prevent; and it was this appeal which finally decided the Emperor. On July 20th the Cabinet was summoned for 8 p.m. Goremykin and Stolypin had been sent for, separately, to Tsarskoe Selo. Goremykin was received first and advised the appointment of Stolypin as Prime Minister and the dissolution of the Duma; and he returned to the Cabinet in the mood — as he put it, of 'a schoolboy on holiday' — to announce this decision, which was published directly afterwards.[2]

The Duma continued to rely on its moral strength and on the country. The Cadets and the Labour Party made a hurried dash for Viborg over the Finnish border — an act of half bravery very prejudicial to the liberties of Finland — and there adopted an appeal to the country to demand that the dissolution be withdrawn—clearly an unconstitutional act, as the sovereign unquestionably had the right to dissolve. In the meantime, until the Duma was restored, they called on the country to refuse recruits to the army and taxes to the Treasury, and to recognize no foreign loans contracted in its absence.† There was no organization to carry out this programme and the initiative was left to any given village. It was a piece of political bluff. The country was in a state of inertia and took no action.

Stolypin ruled in the vacuum which his own advice had created, and the dangers of his position at once became evident. As he put it at the time to the writer, he had two fronts; he was against revolution and he was for reform; his task, he added, was probably a superhuman one. He declared that he wanted 'to show the country that it had parted company for ever with the old police order of things', and that was impossible without the support of the Duma.[3] He had called another on the same franchise; but, as we now know from Kokovtsev, it was already determined to abolish universal franchise, and in the interval before the next Duma, which was to be elected under the same conditions as the

[1] Milyukov to B. P. [2] KOKOVTSEV, I, 209 & ff. [3] Stolypin to B. P.

first, an able bureaucrat, Kryzhanovsky, was instructed to draw up a new electoral law within much narrower limits. Stolypin, so Kokovtsev tells us, hesitated long before agreeing to this step.[1] He, Kokovtsev and even the reactionary Minister of Justice, Shcheglovitov, fully realized that this was a direct breach of the new constitution, which in particular guaranteed that no law relating to the Duma should be passed without its consent. Meanwhile all who had signed the Viborg appeal, that is, the great majority of the Duma, were put on trial, and this under Russian law excluded them from re-election. All sorts of other exclusions, sometimes of whole categories, such as those peasants who alternated between town work and country in the course of the year, were put in practice by right of so called interpretations of the existing law by the highest legal Court, the Senate. Local governors, whom it was practically impossible for Stolypin to control, went to all lengths in their methods for securing a subservient Duma.

Stolypin dealt drastically, and for the time successfully, with the revolutionaries. He utilized Article 87, to set up field courts martial, which dealt with all acts of terrorism in two or three days, nearly always inflicting the death sentence. It may be noted that the number of death sentences was very much less than that of the murders of police and officials; but it must also be remembered that the death penalty obtained in Russia only under martial law, and in time of peace it was only inflicted for political crimes; civil murder was punished by transportation to Siberia. An attempt to assassinate Stolypin in his villa outside St. Petersburg narrowly failed to kill him, and crippled his daughter for life; with his face spattered with ink he showed the greatest courage and presence of mind in attending at once to the victims of the bomb.[2]

On the other hand Stolypin with equal vigour attacked the question of reform. The Government, in his view, had made the greatest mistake in evading it.[3] Again utilizing Article 87, which was never meant to apply to matters of such permanent importance, he carried through by edict one of the greatest reforms for which Russia had been waiting ever since the Emancipation, equalizing the peasants with other classes in civil rights, in particular those of election, and authorizing them to separate at will from the peasant commune, whose control many of them described as 'a

[1] Kokovtsev, I, 232-3. [2] ibid., I, 223. [3] Stolypin to B. P.

second serfdom'. He went on to attack the root question of land, and on November 22nd he issued an edict by which any peasant could claim his share of the village holding as personal property and could pass it on to his heirs. It was a colossal change in the whole economy of Russia, aiming, as Stolypin made clear, at the creation of a class of peasant yeomen; but its initial regulations were so shadowy and inadequate, that it was only to have its full effect later.

Stolypin worked in an atmosphere of continuous unrest. Reactionaries such as Trepov had not demanded the dissolution of the Duma, and the constitutionalist Stolypin had had to do it for them; but now that the dissolution had passed without consequences, they asked why the Duma should go on existing at all, and were continually pressing their view on the sovereign, with the flattering prayer that he would restore his full autocracy. Fantastic schemes were drawn up, by which if there were to be any national assembly, education and intelligence were to be excluded as far as possible, and the peasant members were to be chosen by lot, so as to represent the rank and file. Surely, the peasant disorders of 1905 ought to have cured the reactionaries of their touching faith in a patriarchal peasantry. The Emperor, to his credit, disregarded such advice.

It is true that the centre of gravity still lay with the peasantry; and few things in their history are as interesting as the way in which they approached the political position and dealt with the problem presented to them by the new General Election. They had chosen their 'best men' for the First Duma, and it had been sent flying in a few months. They were entirely opposed to the dissolution. On the the other hand, they had not any intention of committing themselves to any party view or of indulging in further disorders. In the circumstances the peasants, more or less generally, decided to send to the Second Duma men who on the one hand would continue the demand for reform, and on the other, would do it in such a way as to give no excuse for a second dissolution. For this purpose they very ingeniously selected, in the main, revolutionaries who would be prepared to do the talking and suffer for it, instructing them meanwhile to keep the Second Duma in being as long as possible. There were all sorts of interesting features of this election. In one district the peasants, like the constituents of Middlesex in the time of Wilkes, persisted in re-electing an ex-member of the First Duma, the Labour leader Aladin excluded for his part in the Viborg appeal. As members of the Duma could not be imprisoned except by sentence of a law court, they elected in many cases prominent labour leaders who had been imprisoned without such a sentence, and the Government was compelled to set them free and let them sit in the Duma. In several other details this election was a very satisfactory test of their political maturity.[1]

When, however, the Second Duma met on March 5th, 1907, the effects of the Viborg exclusions were painfully manifest. Russia was anyhow weak enough in trained politicians, and its parliamentary experience was confined to the First Duma, which was now excluded almost wholesale. The Cadets, who had led in the First Duma, were now represented in the main by secondary men, with the notable exceptions of Rodichev, who had been in England when the Viborg appeal was signed, and two new men, Andrew Shingarev and Basil Maklakov, who were to play distinguished parts later. Shingarev was a model provincial medical officer trained in the work of the county councils, upright, intelligent and clear-headed, who was to grow beyond recognition in the atmosphere of the Duma. Maklakov, one of the most brilliant members of the Russian bar, had a natural gift of oratory which, under the discipline which he gave to it, developed into a real political power. This time the revolutionary parties entered the Duma under their own flags, as Social Democrats or Social Revolutionaries. There was also a small group of reactionaries, largely pushed through by police pressure, including a most remarkable die-hard, Vladimir Purishkevich, and a brilliant young Conservative, Basil Shulgin.

The reactionaries, now triumphant and even exultant, were out to destroy the Duma altogether. Their tactics were crude and simple; they determined to compromise it before Russian and foreign opinion by raising as often as possible in debate the question of terrorism. The Duma was there to perform such duties as examining the credits for building railways or making bridges, and all theoretical subjects lay outside its competence, except by inference. However, the challenge was one which many revolu-

[1] Smirnov, *Kak proshli Vybory v Vtoruyu Gosudarstvennuyu Dumu* (How the Elections to the Second Imperial Duma went).

tionaries in the Duma could not refrain from taking up, and on May 30th the subject was debated in full. The Duma contained no less than nine different parties, and each put forward its own theoretical view. None was accepted, and the House remained without an answer to this burning question.

Meanwhile the police had been busy in the same cause and announced, one after the other, the discovery of two plots implicating the two main revolutionary parties, the S.R.s and the S.D.s. The charges were widely debated at the time, but it was only after the revolution of 1917 that the full publication of police details on the subject has proved conclusively the provocative character of both plots; in fact the manœuvre was later brought in its nakedness before the Cabinet and severely condemned. In the case of the S.R.s, a police agent, Ratimov, approached them with the offer of information which would enable them to assassinate the Emperor; and in accordance with a decision of both revolutionary parties that there should be no terrorist acts during the sitting of the Duma, no action was taken.[1] In the case of the S.D.s a female police agent, Shornikova, who managed to become secretary of the organization, drew up on police instructions two copies of an appeal for mutiny in the army; one she deposited with the police, and the other she handed to an S.D. member of the Duma at a moment when she had arranged that the police should come and arrest the whole group. Gerasimov, Head of the Petrograd Okhrana, told Stolypin that the police copy had been taken from the other.[2] Stolypin had done what he could to find a working basis with the Second Duma; as he said ironically at this time, it was taking him more trouble to prevent the dissolution of the Second Duma than to obtain the dissolution of the First. He met Basil Maklakov and others, who replied to him with truth, that the Duma was beginning to understand its responsibilities. The Emperor was waiting with the greatest impatience for a chance of dissolving it; he was infuriated by a speech full of insults to the Russian army. Stolypin had to demand a special sitting to debate the Shornikova plot, and to obtain the surrender of the S.D. members. The Duma refused to deprive them of their immunity

[1] Gerasimov, *Padenie*, III, 24.
[2] Kokovtsev, I, 272; Gerasimov, *Padenie*, III, 4-7; Dzhunkovsky, *Padenie*, V, 87-99.

from arrest as Members without further investigation of the charge, and while a commission for the purpose was hastily examining the evidence, the Second Duma was dissolved. The President, F. A. Golovin, himself only learned the news from a journalist.[1]

Troops had been brought into St. Petersburg; and the second dissolution was taken lying down both by the Duma and by the country, except for sporadic disorders. An imperial manifesto accused the Duma of having plotted against the sovereign, and this was followed up almost immediately by the publication of a new electoral law, which abolished all semblance of universal suffrage and threw the elections for the most part into the hands of a dying class, the country gentry. The one saving clause, not noticed by either side at the time, was that no change was made in the competence of the Duma, which still remained a legislative body, though the Emperor from this time onwards more than once contemplated reducing its functions to consultation only.

This last act of the revolutionary period, 1904-7, opened a new epoch which was to be as different as possible from anything anticipated at the time; but it was followed by a whole series of repressions, individually or of whole classes, which lingered on into the new period, and left throughout it a feeling of suppuration, an instinct that something all-important was suppressed.

Maurice Baring, probably the acutest observer of the Russian public at this time, leaving Russia typically enough shortly before the inevitable blow fell, made a singularly prophetic guess: 'In ten years we shall know'. Ten years later in 1917, if Russia had possessed a Duma elected by universal suffrage, it seems almost impossible that events would have followed the course which they actually took after the March Revolution of that year.

[1] Golovin to B. P.

CHAPTER IV

RECOVERY

STOLYPIN AND THE THIRD DUMA

He was a man, take him for all in all:
I shall not look upon his like again.
Hamlet, I, 2

THE change in the electoral law was essentially a *coup d'état*. The new law[1] was preposterous. Of the towns, where voting had been direct, nearly all lost their members, and were merged in the country constituencies; where the town representation was retained, all the electors were divided into two categories, monstrously unequal, each of which elected to the same number of seats; on the one side were the owners of large property, on the other all the rest, including of course the professional class. A member for the first of these categories in St. Petersburg, when I asked him how he could explain a certain step of his to his constituents, replied: 'My constituents could all be gathered together in one room.' In the country the centre of gravity was completely shifted to the country gentry; this was done by giving them, though they were only a sprinkling, a majority of the 'electors'. Thus even the peasant members of the Third and Fourth Dumas were really elected by the gentry. When one looked up the statistics in a province such as Vyatka, where there were hardly any gentry at all, one saw to what lengths the law had gone in misrepresentation. This was still more patent in the non-Russian regions of the Empire. The Poles, who had provided the ablest group in the Second Duma, had their representation arbitrarily cut down from thirty-six to fourteen, and in Warsaw, where there were hardly any Russians except the military and officials, one member was chosen from them and one from the Polish inhabitants. In border districts everything was done to give the predominance to the small

[1] A careful and sound analysis of it was made by my companion in Russia, Professor S. N. Harper of Chicago University.

Russian population. All those who had been kept out of the second elections by the arbitrary interpretations of the Senate, such as the migratory peasants, were formally excluded by the new law. One direct violation of the constitution was that all questions as to the validity of the elections were to be settled in future not by the Duma, but by the Minister of the Interior; the local governors obtained a corresponding control.

This wholesale falsification of the principle of election did not look as if it could lead to anything good; yet those who knew Russia at the time could be sure that practically any national assembly would be in opposition to the Government, even if it had consisted exclusively of ex-Ministers. Stolypin, on his side, had made every effort to broaden the basis of his Cabinet by negotiating with such public men as Guchkov, Nicholas Lvov and Paul Vinogradov; but though in some cases he induced them to visit the sovereign, such men were bound in conscience to refuse, because it was quite impossible for them to get even a minimum of guarantee that the principles which they represented would be respected, so that they could only have been regarded as individual captives of the reaction.[1]

The country was stunned by the second dissolution and received it inertly. Members of the dissolved Second Duma were carefully watched by the police. The popular song of the moment was Gorky's 'Na dne' (At the bottom). The disappointment of so many aspirations led to a comparative breakdown not only of public but of private morality. I travelled through one third of European Russia immediately after the second dissolution. Open challenges of a crude and chaotic kind were offered to the government authority in outlying parts. Mail steamers were robbed of Government funds, bands of brigands were active, such as the 'Forest Brethren' of Vyatka, who robbed the Government and gave to the poor.

Yet this phase did not last long. The disillusionment acted as a cold douche. There were some very remarkable Liberal political thinkers at this time, and they set themselves to examine with absolute honesty the causes of their failure.[2] 'The power', wrote Peter Struve, 'dropped from our unprepared hands.' The remedy

[1] Guchkov to B. P.
[2] In *Vekhi* (Landmarks), Moscow, 1909.

they found in a deepening of personal discipline, a deeper understanding of the issues involved and the forces opposed to them. Meanwhile the more intelligent members of the public set about such practical work as could at least extend their activity in the management of their own affairs. The politicians explored the situation to see what was left that could still be saved out of the wreck. There was a very great deal. There was still some kind of a national assembly, which could not fail in some respect to reflect the opinions and interests of the country. If the franchise of the Duma had been radically altered, its competence remained untouched, and it was still a legislative assembly. The first two Dumas in their heat and haste had let themselves be dissolved without living long enough to use their most powerful weapon, the yearly examination of the budget, which involved prolonged and public discussion of all important questions. The parliamentary reports were ordinarily still exempt from the censorship; indeed, there were numbers of peasants who learned to read from the Duma debates. No party made more use of the Duma as a forum than the Social Democrats.

All these conditions were acutely appreciated by the new man of the moment, Alexander Guchkov. The Cadets had had their period and they had failed hopelessly. Their leader, Paul Milyukov, was too doctrinaire to lead an attack in detail. Guchkov, grandson of a serf, son of a merchant and magistrate of Moscow, was a restless spirit always coming into prominence on this or that issue of the moment, now going through Macedonia or Armenia in times of disorders, now riding along the Great Wall of China at the time of the Boxers' rising, now fighting for the Boers against England in South Africa, now remaining in Mukden to transfer the care of the wounded to the advancing Japanese, now returning to say a bold word for enlightened and patriotic Conservatism in the whirl of 1905, now summoned and entertained by the Emperor and Empress and fearlessly advising the Tsar to establish a link between himself and his people by summoning some kind of national assembly, though his ideas then hardly went beyond the old Zemsky Sobor of the 16th and 17th centuries.[1]

Guchkov's chief quality was a daring gallantry; he was at ease with himself and enjoyed stepping forward under fire with a

[1] Guchkov to B. P.

perfect calm whenever there was anything which he wished to challenge; his defect was his restlessness; without actually asking for it, he was instinctively always in the limelight, always trying to do too much. He had the easy organizing ability of a first-rate English politician; he was quietly proud of his democratic origin, and all his actions were inspired by an ardent love for Russia and the Russian people, in whose native conservatism, common sense and loyalty he fully shared. He was an enemy of class privileges, and at this time he claimed for his country some such measure of consultation as was secured for Germany by the Reichstag. Guchkov led the Octobrists or party of patriotic reform, and for them no less than for the Cadets the political model was England; but while the Cadets preached English political principles, the Octobrists were much more akin to the ordinary instincts of English public life.

The composition of the Third Duma, which met in the autumn of 1907, gave plenty of scope to Guchkov's methods. Elected in the main from the educated classes, it contained a whole number of men who had stood high in the service of the Government itself. Several had been trained in the Ministry of Agriculture by the Liberal Minister, Ermolov; for instance, the future president of the Third Duma, Nicholas Homyakov, a liberal-minded Conservative, son of the famous Slavophil and one of the wisest public men in Russia. Alexeyenko, the new president of the Duma budget commission, was recognized as one of the first financial authorities in Russia. Von Anrep, high in the public system of education, might have been Minister at any time if the sovereign had ever been ready to entrust the Education Office to a Liberal. Milyukov had been arbitrarily excluded from membership of the first two Dumas, though he had more or less led them from outside, and thus he had been saved from signing the Viborg Appeal, though he was really responsible for that tactical mistake. Now he entered the Duma and set himself with singular courage and self-restraint to the ordinary tasks of a leader of the Opposition. With him were the brilliant Basil Maklakov, who maintained the highest level of eloquence of all the many orators produced by the Duma, and Alexander Shingarev, who became one of the ablest critics of the budget, always pleading the cause of the peasantry. The Third Duma naturally had a much larger proportion of Rights or Conservatives; but these fell into two very different groups, one purely reactionary led by the hysterical and witty Purishkevich, and the other consisting of independent country Tories, among whom Basil Shulgin, a young man gifted with insight, tolerance and humour, was full of political promise.

Guchkov spent the first months in organizing his Octobrists, who were always more of an association than a party. He had behind him about a third of the House, 153 members, occupying the centre. With able management he was in a position to rule most of its decisions. To the right of him were the nationalists (89) and reactionaries (50), to the left the 54 Cadets, still representing the flower of the professional class, a small section of Poles (18), a somewhat inchoate Labour group (13), and a small section of Social Democrats (20). These last had also their outstanding spokesman in the Georgian, Chkheidze, a little man with the bitterness of the national wrath within him, fearless, outspoken and witty; with him, as time went on, hardly anyone in the Duma would have wished to dispense.

Guchkov followed definite tactics from the start. The Tsar's original idea of the Duma had been a series of commissions dealing with various subjects and seldom sitting together. Muromtsev, the Cadet President of the First Duma, who was the real creator of its internal regulations, had adopted this basis of commissions while maintaining the importance of the subsequent discussions of every subject by the whole body. Muromtsev had been professor of Roman Law in the University of Moscow and was one of the most distinguished of Russian scholars. He had imprinted his instinct of equity on the choice of these commissions; on each of them every party or group was entitled to that measure of representation which corresponded to its number of members in the House, a practice already followed in zemstva and town councils. There was also a Semioren Konvent, or regular meeting of all the group leaders to discuss in advance the conduct of public business. Each commission appointed a president and a reporter. The Duma had the right to information from the Ministers on all questions of administration, which was an enormously important factor in its own political education; and these explanations were given by the Minister or his representative to the relevant commission, with its own chairman in the chair. The conclusions of the commission had to be laid before the whole assembly by the reporter of the commission; and once agreement had been obtained in commission, it was very unlikely that the House would alter its decisions, composed, as it was, of the best experts of all parties. As the Octobrists were the guiding Party most, not all, of the chairmen and reporters were Octobrists. The importance of these commissions will be evident. It was particularly clear in discussions of the budget, which Guchkov utilized to the full. If a Minister were to carry his estimates through the Duma, he had at least to satisfy the chairman of the commission, and to have the goodwill of the official reporter. This could not be won by any personal manœuvre. On several occasions Stolypin offered high office to these men; in each case the offer was referred to the leader, and ultimately was not accepted.[1] It was, therefore, very important that the Minister should himseif come to the Duma and not merely send a representative; and Stolypin always encouraged his colleagues to do so.[2] In its attitude to the various Ministers the Duma first took account of the respect which each of them paid to its opinions. It was not a recommendation to a Minister that he should have to tell his sovereign that he had failed to get his estimates through the Duma.

The most important of all the commissions was that of the budget under Alexeyenko, who had no ambition to become Minister of Finance and much preferred his position of official critic. Ministers who came with perfunctory explanations found that they had to change their tone in this atmosphere. But the place where Guchkov's tactics became most clear was the Duma commission for Imperial Defence. The First and Second Dumas, in their hurry, had overlooked their first-class opportunity of overhauling all the responsibilities in the disastrous Japanese war. Guchkov had lived, so to speak, on the outskirts of the army, and was in close touch with many of the best officers, military or naval, such as the future War Minister, Polivanov, and the future Admiral, Kolchak, men with the best instincts of their profession. These men burned to wipe out the national disgrace by restoring the armed forces of Russia, a desire which Guchkov shared to the full. The Admiralty was a kind of Augean stable, and Kolchak, with a group of other able young officers, aimed at setting up a

[1] Guchkov to B. P. [2] KOKOVTSEV, I, 346.

regular naval staff. For this purpose he sought the co-operation of the Duma, and with its help was successful; the project was confirmed by the Emperor. It is true that the affairs of the fighting services were specially reserved in the fundamental laws as a prerogative of the sovereign, which made Guchkov's task a delicate one; but the budget gave the opportunity for raising almost any question, and once the Duma had taken the line of being clearly as patriotic as the Government in this matter, it was hardly possible for the Government to protest. Where the Duma could be assured that the estimates would be well applied, it would not only accept them but increase them. Nicholas was devoted to his army, and this new attitude, so different from the vituperation of it in the Second Duma, could not fail to appeal to him. To Stolypin he said: 'This Duma cannot be reproached with an attempt to seize the power, and there is no need at all to quarrel with it.'[1]

The crisis of Guchkov's first year of work, the best of his career, came at the end of the first session in June 1908. Speaking on the naval and military estimates, reading in a quiet voice from a carefully prepared manuscript, Guchkov actually called on the various Grand Dukes to resign their posts as inspectors of the various branches of defence on the patriotic ground that as members of the Imperial family they were not subject to criticism, and that thus they stood in the way of all proposals of reform:

> If we consider ourselves entitled and even bound to turn to the people and to the country and demand from them heavy sacrifices for this work of defence, then we are entitled to address ourselves also to those few irresponsible persons from whom we have to demand no more than the renunciation of certain terrestrial advantages, and of certain satisfactions of vainglory which are connected with those posts which they at present hold.[2]†

The Government made no defence of those attacked, for which the War Minister was later dismissed;[3] and the spirited Grand Duke Nicholas, far the best soldier among the Grand Dukes, and Chairman of the Tsar's own committee of Imperial Defence, wrote to him, saying that as no answer had been given in the Duma, he

[1] Kokovtsev, I, 343. [2] *The Russian Review* (Nelson's), II, I, 121.
[3] N. to M. F., 240.

resigned his post.[1] It was a dangerous thing for Guchkov's future influence with his sovereign to strike at the Imperial family itself; but though the Grand Dukes were allowed to remain Inspectors-General of the various arms, they were limited in their initiative, especially in the matter of contracts.

Guchkov's speech was followed up by another, equally telling, by Von Anrep on behalf of the Duma commission of education. Avoiding all exaggeration and speaking with full knowledge and authority, Anrep gave a just picture of that Ministry, which fully confirmed the general opinion that it was less a Ministry for public instruction than a Ministry for the prevention of it. We may note that while these debates were in progress King Edward VII was the guest of his nephew at Reval, and possibly the Duma's choice of this moment was not made without appreciation of the coincidence.

This was the best year of the Third Duma, for these speeches fixed its consequence with the public, which contrasted their great moral success with the failures of the First and Second Dumas. The Duma apparently had come to stay. However unrepresentative, it had succeeded in expressing what everyone was thinking. In the years which followed, till the Third Duma came to the end of its legal term in 1912, this initial success was followed up in the most important fields of legislation.

There was no doubt that in any change of Ministry Stolypin would be replaced by reactionaries. He had one deadly enemy who was always working for this. Witte, who had made such an extremely bad guess in December 1905, was now earnestly trying to make his peace with the sovereign and with the extreme Rights. He was full of spite at being successfully replaced; this runs through all the latter part of his memoirs and quite spoils them. Neither the Duma nor the public placed any faith in him, nor as it seems did the reactionaries, and certainly not his sovereign. Guchkov never made any agreement with Stolypin;[2] but he much preferred him not only to any alternative Premier, but to most of his colleagues in the Ministry. This resulted in a practical understanding between the two which meant in the main a general co-operation between the Government and the Duma, a basis on which detailed work of reform could be done on many sides.

[1] *Lettres des Grands-Ducs*, 9-14, N. N. to N.

[2] Guchkov to B. P.

Stolypin was not what is called a great man; he had evident limitations, of intellect rather than understanding; though not really unscrupulous, he found his way to the political objects which he had set himself by simple energy and directness. But he was essentially a big man, with a broad and simple nobility, devoted to his sovereign, generous to his colleagues, frank and fearless in his dealings with his adversaries. He was an eloquent and straightforward speaker with a strong and pleasant voice. This large-built bearded man had something of the charm of a big naive friendly bear; and his common sense and his courage made a strong appeal to those who worked with him. Izvolsky describes him as 'gifted with a very clear and healthy turn of mind that enabled him to comprehend the general significance of matters submitted to him for his decision; his capacity for work and his moral power of endurance were prodigious'.[1] Buchanan calls him 'an ideal minister to transact business with' and adds 'his promises were always kept'.[2]

Stolypin had none of the ambiguities of promoted bureaucrats. It was the first time that the Cabinet had, not a mere chairman like Goremykin, or a dictator like Witte, but a real leader. Kokovtsev bears striking testimony to 'the unquestionable personal nobility of Stolypin', his straightness, his clear head and his courage,[3] even when carefully marking any disagreements in detail between the two, or his own occasional mild resentment at minor misunderstandings. We get the same picture of a leader from the brief soldierly notes of General Polivanov, who, as far as the Cabinet and the Duma were concerned, was almost Acting War Minister from 1906 to 1912 – in other words, the whole period of Stolypin's Premiership, and kept a short diary of each day's happenings. Stolypin stands out from all the other Ministers by the warmth and vigour which he felt and inspired, like the captain of a team working devotedly for his country. Nicholas writes of him to his mother on Oct. 11th/24th 1906, 'I cannot tell you how much I have come to like and respect this man![4] Goremykin's advice was truly sound when he said this was the only man for the place'. The secretary of the Cabinet, Lodyzhensky, giving a striking picture of successive ex-premiers after the revolution of

[1] IZVOLSKY, 98-9.
[2] BUCHANAN, I, 160.
[3] KOKOVTSEV, I, 203.
[4] N. to M. F., 220.

1917, describes the atmosphere of solidarity which Stolypin inspired, and the vigour and earnestness of his speeches in the Cabinet debates. 'Stolypin's time', he says, 'was a time of great creative work.'[1] No less notable were Stolypin's speeches in the Duma. No one had been able to shout him down in the First Duma. To the Second he had said: 'We are not frightened', and again, 'You want great convulsions, but we want a great Russia'. In the Third Duma he was completely at home, and even toward the end had his own party in it. He had a fine presence — a big powerful man with a direct approach to every question and an evident sincerity which appealed even to his antagonists, not excluding the revolutionaries.

Under these conditions great problems could be attacked. The most important of those now pending was the land reform of Stolypin, based on the principle of individual peasant property. Up to 1906 no public man had been found to come out boldly for this principle. Witte, who began as an adherent of the old communal system, was too sensible not to see its grave defects. He became a convert to individual farming and favoured it in the practice of his Ministry, but he never really challenged existing prejudices. The reactionaries had even now not lost the illusion of a patriarchal peasantry, and stood for the commune. The revolutionaries, of course, wanted to keep the commune as a road into modern socialism. The Liberals, who really believed in individual holdings, had pandered to the revolutionaries in this matter to keep their support. Meanwhile the peasants themselves, who were the people most concerned, had in several cases followed Western Europe by breaking up the communal holding into individual farms, even when this had to be done in spite of the law. Stolypin had roots in two districts, Kovno in the west and Saratov in the south-east, where this movement was favourably received. Directly after his appointment as Premier, he had decided to take up this, the thorniest of all questions. It was all wrong, he said to me at that time, that every proposal of reform should come from the opposition. In defiance of all party views and utilizing the questionable Article 87, he had in November 1906 authorized any peasant to claim his portion of the holding, and to have it all together in one place. This meant a complete

[1] LODYZHENSKY, *Padenie*, VI, 156.

disturbance of the existing strip system, one of the worst features of the commune. A peasant might quite commonly be in occupation of a hundred and fifty strips scattered over several square miles, which, if he had only one horse, or perhaps not that, became an absurdity.[1]

Stolypin's first edict of 1906 was so crude as to be unworkable. It was the more intelligent of the peasants who saw the value of it; but if they went to the commune and claimed their portion as individual property, it would resent the loss of a good taxpayer and fob him off with some remote or useless part of the village holding, and appeal could only be made to the hated Land Captain, which was worse than useless; or his neighbours might even burn down his new farm. This man was probably one of the most important villagers, in several cases the actual leader of the riots of 1905,[2] and he would go off and do some hard thinking. In the end he would come to the conclusion that the best thing he could do, would be to convince his neighbours of the value of the opportunity and get them to utilize it too. In the language of the time, instead of asking to 'divide out' for himself, he would set himself to persuade them all to 'divide up'.

Stolypin's law was of course challenged in the shortlived Second Duma, and he brought it up before the Third. Its land commission was under the chairmanship of Shidlovsky, born in the year of the Emancipation, and associated throughout his life with the cause of peasant reform. The commission introduced material improvements in the working of the law. The principal expert employed, Andreas Kofod, was a brilliant ex-student of the Danish Academy of Agriculture, who had worked long in the land service of the Russian government and was indifferent to all political theories. He had discovered peasant communities which without any help and even against the law had made the change for themselves, and he had been sent by Witte to make a historical study of the question in the archives of most of the countries of Western Europe. From now onwards the reform went forward by leaps and bounds. It could not be imposed on any village, for by the old communal law, which was in this respect retained, a two-thirds majority of a village was required before any new distribution, but this one was final. The cleverest

[1] PARES, *My Russian Memoirs*, 218. [2] ibid., 217.

of all Stolypin's colleagues was the Minister of Agriculture, Krivoshein, who, with his very able assistant, Rittich, a model permanent official, put Government assistance in surveying, well-sinking, etc., behind any village which adopted the reform. His Ministry welcomed the temporary help of all sorts of volunteer land surveyors, quite irrespective of their political views — some of the best of them were revolutionaries; and these carried the movement forward with such enthusiasm as had never before been associated with any Government measure since the Emancipation.[1]

The results were astonishing. By 1914 there was already a yeoman population of 8,700,000 households,[2] with a strong sense of property, and consequently with a strong instinct of public order. On the new farms the men were full of a new and businesslike energy. The cattle took on an altogether healthier appearance. Districts outside the village, which might, therefore, at any time have changed ownership under the old dispensation, were now for the first time carefully cultivated and planted with fruit trees. Such peasants as had no taste for agriculture and sought other work were now quite free to do so; they made their way to the towns with the capital obtained from the sale of their holdings and added materially to their prosperity. Some revolutionaries had attempted in vain to base a modern agricultural co-operation on the old communal system; even their model villages took up with ardour the new reform; and now the principle of co-operation flourished everywhere, for once the peasant had some property with which to co-operate, he sought association with his fellows for buying machinery or for marketing goods. No instinct is more in the genius of the Russian peasant than that of co-operation. In this the common life of the old system had played its part. But it was conceived on principles which were attributed to English models; that is, the co-operation was free; and in this form it grew up of itself and flourished everywhere.

Equally important was the work of the Minister of Finance, Kokovtsev. This Ministry showed the same desire for co-operation with the Duma, which with its high standard of education and the financial experience of so many of its members, was much more

[1] See the *Russian Review*, (Nelson's) 1, 18-26 and 56-74.
[2] FLORINSKY, 16.

qualified to make effective criticism of the budget than either of its predecessors. Kokovtsev, who had always resented the 'wolfish appetites' of adventurers[1], was an entire believer in the benefits of financial publicity. He frankly recognized the Duma's power over the public purse and set himself to co-operate with it in the heartiest way. He genuinely enjoyed his visits to the Duma, and to its budget commission, which he has described as a happy memory.[2] With a complete grasp of his work, thoroughly honest, sensible, able and practical, he welcomed reasonable criticism; though not actually an orator, he was a particularly clear and engaging speaker, and his memoirs often reveal the simple pleasure which he took in his successes in the tribune. There was one moment of friction when annoyed at an inexpert criticism he burst out with the words: 'Thank heaven we have not got a Parliament',[3] for his position, like Stolypin's was 'constitutionalist but not parliamentarist'. But in fact it was probably the parliamentary aspect of his skirmishes with his opponents that he enjoyed the most. Alexeyenko and he treated each other with respect. His most regular opponent was the Cadet, Shingarev, and on one occasion when he was absent, Kokovtsev, in making his statement on the budget, said that he felt quite lost at not having Shingarev to follow him and tell him that he had not done enough for the peasantry: a little incident which is typical of the whole atmosphere of this Duma and of the education which both Ministers and Duma were giving each other.

Everything in the Russian budget depended on the crop, and the period of the Third Duma was marked by a succession of fine harvests. This was largely due to greatly improved culture, and to the rapid development and far higher yield of Siberia. In these years, for once in a way, there was a growing surplus. Agriculture profited enormously by the reform of Stolypin and Krivoshein; and industry was advancing fast with increasing steadiness. There can be no doubt that economically the seven years from 1907 to 1914 were, so far, the most prosperous period in Russian history. The incidence of taxation was slowly and surely shifting to the growing industry, which in itself helped to relieve agriculture.

There was also at this time a strong movement in the commercial

[1] KOKOVTSEV, I, 67. [2] ibid., I, 287. [3] ibid., 306.

public for emancipation from government control and the development of private initiative. Much more solid than the previous organization of professional unions, and founded with quite a different purpose, was the institution of regular congresses not only of individual industries and trades, but of all of them conjointly; and the common congress of all set up a permanent office with a staff and a statistical organization, which were a vast improvement on anything previous. The congress usually met during the sessions of the Duma, of which many of its participants were members, and sometimes its debates were the more interesting and important of the two. This was definitely a movement away from the old system of protection with its Chinese walls, a direction which had been prepared in the eleven years of Witte's administration of finance. Economically, as in other ways, Russia was fast becoming more European, and now reflected much more visibly the position of the world market, with the difference that there remained still so much to do in the development of the vast natural resources of the country that slumps in Russia were of less consequence that elsewhere. Having the unwonted luxury of a surplus and no necessity for an appeal to foreign loans, Kokovtsev was able to proceed freely to productive expenditure. The railway system, now put under public control, was greatly improved, and for the first time yielded a profit. With the help of the Duma, the forest wealth of Russia was also regulated.

In two other fields the co-operation of Government and Duma gave valuable results. The best era in Russian educational policy was as far back as Alexander I (1801-1825), when the modern ladder system, with easy transfer from one grade of school to another, was at the bottom of all that was done. Nicholas I (1825-1855) had replaced this by a jealous system of closed compartments. The reign of Alexander II (1855-1881) marked a partial and somewhat half-hearted restoration of the ladder system. Alexander III was in this respect quite reactionary, and so were nearly all the Ministers of Education of Nicholas II. The general atmosphere of health created by the Duma meant a return toward the system of free access[1]. The Duma was largely based on the zemstvo, which had done so very much to promote primary education. Zemstvo and Duma were alike ardent adherents of

[1] See N. Hans, *History of Russian Educational Policy.*

the principle of free access. The Duma greatly raised the salaries of primary teachers, and carried a Government Bill establishing the principle of free primary education, which with the necessary provision of schools was ultimately to become compulsory by 1922.[1]

In the sphere of religious tolerance the Duma was also wholeheartedly liberal. Here, in spite of two mildly liberal successors in the seat of Pobedonostsev, there were still very great obstacles to be overcome. No die-hard can be more stubborn than the Orthodox die-hard, and but little ground was actually gained. But the breath of reform was strong within the Church itself; and the liberal movement was so general that the Tsar came near consenting to its two principal claims, the summons of a Church Council to purify the Church, especially from its subservience to the secular authorities, and the restoration of the Patriarchate as the symbol and instrument of its independence. These things were not done; and we now know that Rasputin assured his sovereign that it was enough that there was 'an anointed Tsar'. At least there was a definite move of the Left wing of the Russian Church towards closer friendship with the Right wing of the Anglican. But there was much more than that; and without the atmosphere of 1905-14 there would have been no preparation for the more or less unanimous adoption of an entirely liberal policy for the reconstruction of the Russian Church, which followed immediately after the March revolution of 1917.

May an Englishman, bred in the tradition of Gladstone, to whom the Duma was almost a home with many friends of all parties, recall that vanished past? At the bottom was a feeling of reassurance, and founded on it one saw a growing courage and initiative and a growing mutual understanding and goodwill. The Duma had the freshness of a school, with something of surprise at the simplicity with which differences that had seemed formidable could be removed. One could feel the pleasure with which the Members were finding their way into common work for the good of the whole country. In the First Duma peasants had picked out as their chief impression the realization that Russia was a great family, that there were so many others with thoughts and hopes like their own. 'It went past like a dream' one of them said

[1] KERENSKY, C. L., 132.

to me. The Second Duma was fast growing more and more into a family when it was prematurely dissolved. The Third Duma, though its horizon was much more limited, did come to stay, and its membership was better qualified to take practical advantage of the education which it offered. Some seventy persons at least, forming the nucleus of the more important commissions, were learning in detail to understand the problems and difficulties of administration and therefore to understand both each other and the Government. One could see political competence growing day by day. And to a constant observer it was becoming more and more an open secret that the distinctions of party meant little, and that in the social warmth of their public work for Russia all these men were becoming friends.

The most perceptible success of the Duma so far lay in the creation of an atmosphere of confidence. The Duma was establishing itself as an indispensable part of the organization of public life, and the Emperor himself took a certain pride in it as his own creation. Those surrounding him continued their attempts to prejudice it in his eyes, but having once rejected the occasion to abolish it in his *coup d'état* of 1907, he was increasingly less likely to do so now. In 1912 he said to me: 'The Duma started too fast; now it is slower, but better', and in answer to a rather audacious question he added benevolently: 'And more lasting.' That was the general judgment of others, and the result was a growing vigour of initiative not only in practical affairs, but also in thought and expression. The censorship was subject to criticism in the Duma, and at no time did it work with more respect for public opinion. In the provinces, it is true, there continued to be monstrous cases of arbitrary fines imposed by the local governors. Though there was no preliminary censorship, the iniquitous provision of the so-called press reform of Alexander II still obtained, by which newspapers could be crushed with such fines by the administrative officials. In the capital, however, it was very different; and serious monthlies, such as even *Byloe* (*The Past*) of the revolutionary Burtsev, could be published freely. Criticism took heart; and the Russian mind, with its quick intelligence and biting humour, is peculiarly effective in criticism. Also, great works of scholarship began to be published, such as the inimitable history of Russia by Klyuchevsky, which though full of intelligent patriotism and religion, had so far only circulated in notes of students. Typically enough, the first volume came out in the year of the First Duma. The practical removal of a ban on many great works of scientific and statistical study meant an enormous increase of the intellectual wealth of the country.

It is in this new atmosphere that the most trustworthy chronicler of the period, Kokovtsev, gives us the best picture of Nicholas at his best. Kokovtsev possessed the fullest confidence and even the affection of his sovereign, and up till now the firm trust of the Empress. At his first appointment she had said to him: 'I want to see you only to tell you that the Emperor and I beg you always to be perfectly frank with us, and to tell us the truth without troubling as to whether it will sometimes be unpleasant to us. Believe me, even if it is sometimes unpleasant for the moment, we will afterwards be grateful to you.' She added that if she heard any complaint against him, she would always send for him and and tell him herself.[1] Nicholas's relations with his Minister were throughout those of a very real and simple affection; at moments of difficulty he more than once embraced him. 'Remember, Vladimir Nikolayevich', he had said in November 1905, when temporarily parting company with him during Witte's Premiership, 'the doors of this study are always open to you at your first wish',[2] and on his reappointment in May 1906, Nicholas welcomed him back with the words, 'As you see, I was right when I told you we should soon meet again'.[3] When Kokovtsev sends him his proposed budget speech for the Third Duma, it is returned to him after two weeks with a whole number of careful markings and the words 'God grant that the Duma may give a calm examination to this excellent statement, and appreciate what an improvement we have reached in so short a time after all the trials which have been sent us.' Sukhomlinov, the new War Minister, is constantly complaining that Kokovtsev is too sparing of military credits; Kokovtsev replies that a great proportion of the existing credits has remained unspent. Nicholas calms down the two Ministers who happen to have the same Christian name, 'Here I am between two Vladimirs who don't always agree', he says,[4] and on one occasion he even insists that the War Minister should himself thank

[1] KOKOVTSEV, I, 22.
[2] ibid., I, 106.
[3] ibid., I, 118.
[4] ibid., II, 122.

Kokovtsev. On another occasion he shows Kokovtsev an extraordinary demand from Witte for a large gratuitous grant from the Treasury, with the words: 'Don't fall in a faint.' He agrees to be generous, and well knowing Witte's malicious enmity to his successor at the Ministry of Finance, he adds, 'I shall tell him you have persuaded me'. Is it surprising that Kokovtsev thought, with another wife who was indifferent to politics, Nicholas would have made an excellent constitutional sovereign.[1]

There is a curious episode, illustrating the characters of Nicholas, Stolypin, and Guchkov. Guchkov was told by a fellow member of the Duma that Stolypin had spoken of him disparagingly. He asked Stolypin, who authorized him to give his informant the lie direct. Guchkov thought that, if he did this, his informant would challenge Stolypin to a duel and, as duels were legally forbidden, this would prejudice Stolypin's position as Prime Minister. He himself had a liking for duels and decided to draw the fire on himself; so at their next meeting at the Duma, he roundly abused his informant, ending in his usual quiet voice, 'Count, how long are you going to let me insult you?' The duel for which he asked, duly followed, he slightly wounded his antagonist; and though he was at the time President of the Duma, he insisted on undergoing his punishment. At his next report to the Emperor, he felt that Nicholas understood the position and was about to amnesty the offence. He begged him not to do so, in the interest of law, and himself went to the fortress to undergo his term of imprisonment. Nicholas understood his desire and let him go there, and after a fortnight sent Kokovtsev in person to tell him that by imperial order he was released.[2]

Guchkov fought another duel which had a serious sequel later. A certain Col. Myasoyedov, known for his shamelessly loose life and more than questionable speculations, was intimate with the Sukhomlinovs.[3] Guchkov, in his investigations as chairman of the Duma commission of imperial defence, had convinced himself that Myasoyedov was a spy in the service of Germany. He denounced him as such in the *Novoe Vremya* and welcomed Myasoyedov's challenge. The duel was fought in the island suburbs. Guchkov coolly awaited his opponent's shot, and then discharged his revolver in the air and walked off without shaking hands, to show

[1] Kokovtsev to B. P. [2] Guchkov to B. P. [3] POLIVANOV, 111.

he did not regard his opponent as worthy to take part in a combat of honour. We shall see that Guchkov was right in his suspicions.

The atmosphere of co-operation was soon to be disturbed. At the outset of the Third Duma Guchkov had lost the goodwill of the Empress. In an address from the Duma he had insisted on the omission of the word 'autocrat'. Stolypin said to him at the time: 'If you were to write to me leaving out "His Excellency", I should not mind; but if you were to strike it out, I should naturally not like it.'[1]

To no cause did the Duma contribute more than to the reform and rehabilitation of the army and navy. Guckhov was himself chairman of its commission of national defence. It acted on the principle that it was ready not only to accept, but to increase estimates for national defence, if it obtained proper guarantees that the sums would be effectively applied. It was, for instance, due in the main to the Duma that the Russian army possessed any, however inadequate, equipment of machine guns in 1914. Near the beginning of 1910 both Witte and the reactionaries frightened the Emperor with the idea that his prerogative of sole control over the military forces was slipping out of his hands. Stolypin was cautioned against too great an intimacy with the Octobrists, and his co-operation with Guchkov decreased. Guchkov had a large dose of adventure in his composition; and it was his political defect that he was often overdoing his cleverness and attempting too much. It was in this spirit that he left the virtual leadership of the Duma to become its President. No doubt, he hoped to utilize the access which the President had to the sovereign — to become a kind of tribune of the people at the palace; but Nicholas was not likely to be influenced in that way. Stolypin, meanwhile, who as Minister took an active part in the Duma debates, relied more particularly on the newly formed group of Nationalists, independent Tories like Shulgin who, under the influence of parliamentary life, were more and more breaking away from the largely subsidized section of sheer reactionaries, such as Purishkevich and Markov.

Stolypin was increasingly feeling the effects of the bureaucratic intrigues of the capital. He had brought thither his own bouquet of country health, simplicity and directness. As provincial

[1] Guchkov to B. P.

Governor he had used his common sense to deal with emergencies as they arose; he had no love for red tape, and too little respect even for the restrictions imposed by law, as he had shown when he had used the convenient Article 87 to make such vital changes in the structure of the country as were involved by his peasant legislation and by his Land Settlement. He was satisfied with his broad instinct of common sense and justice. He called on all officials to pay their taxes, and discharge all other obligations like ordinary citizens. At any injustice, he set up a vigorous government inquiry. He well knew that he had thus made innumerable enemies in the official world.[1]

In 1910, developing his narrowly understood policy of 'A Great Russia', he introduced a nationalist Bill threatening the parliamentary institutions of Finland, which had existed long before its annexation in 1809 and had at the time been guaranteed by a special promise of Alexander I. The Bill extended the competence of the Duma to 'common affairs' relating to the Empire as a whole, and the House was to be supplemented by a small though proportionate number of Finnish members, who would of course be drowned in the majority. This was a severe blow aimed at Finnish self-government; Finland was far better off with a parliament of her own. Stolypin upheld his proposal on the ground of national defence. The Finnish frontier was only some twenty miles from the Russian capital, and it was thither that the majority of the First Duma had repaired to make their demonstration against the Government in 1906. Stolypin asked[2] how England would regard an autonomous State as near as Gravesend.

There was no occasion at all for this measure; for the Finns had been remarkably loyal in spite of the strong pressure on their acknowledged rights. Nicholas's mother, well knowing how much such measures damaged Russia with friendly foreign opinion, had always advised strongly against them. Liberal opinion in Russia was, of course, warmly engaged in defence of the Finns. It stood for free play for all forces within the Empire and the Finnish liberties were almost a barometer of the fortunes of liberalism in Russia. Curiously enough, consideration for the minor nationality was also the constant advice of Rasputin, whose word already counted at the palace. But the chauvinism of the Russian

[1] Stolypin to B. P. [2] Stolypin to B. P.

nationalists was now enlisted against Finnish liberties. Milyukov, in perhaps the best speech of his life, made a fine defence of them in the Duma; but he committed the great tactical mistake of withdrawing his party from the voting. The Octobrists alone were not able to modify the Bill to any effect.

In the spring of 1911 Stolypin submitted another very controversial Bill to the legislature. The zemstva had originally only been introduced in the home provinces of Russia, and he now proposed to extend them to the so-called western provinces, which had a mixed population of Russian and Polish landowners, a Jewish middle class and Russian peasantry. This was, in the main, the proposal which had cost Goremykin his place near the beginning of the reign. But in his zeal for the predominant partner, Stolypin so manipulated the machinery of election as to prejudice both Poles and Jews, in this case magnifying the peasantry at the expense of the gentry, which was exactly the opposite to what had been done with the elections to the Duma itself. The whole business was a muddle which only showed how much Stolypin had lost touch. After a great deal of tension, the Bill was just carried through the Duma; its passage through the Council of State was expected to follow of itself; but here Stolypin's enemies, alleging that they were acting at the express wish of the Emperor, contrived a surprise, and the Bill was defeated. This time Stolypin committed the mistake of losing his temper, and resigned. There was a sharp crisis; he was begged to return, but would only do so on his own conditions, after a heated discussion with the Emperor. On his demand, the leaders of the revolt were given a holiday from their parliamentary duties; but it was never made clear whether they had exaggerated in saying that they were acting at the wish of the Emperor, who had so often asked the advice of Meshchersky or other unofficial counsellors. Stolypin now suspended the sittings of both Houses for three days and, in this artificial 'vacation' he used his favourite Article 87 to enact his law in the form in which it had been with difficulty accepted by the Duma. Guchkov told him that this was a mockery of both Houses and, as a mark that they were parting company, he resigned the Presidency of the Duma.[1] Kokovtsev had urged that he should introduce the Bill again, and warned him that Nicholas would never forgive the

[1] Guchkov to B. P.

pressure which had been put upon him.[1] Stolypin had made a cardinal mistake; and this was not a thing which Nicholas or those who surrounded him were likely to forget. He had even forced Nicholas to exercise his authority under pressure. He was exhausted with the intrigues of the capital, and dwelt on the thought of resignation.[2]

Stolypin's enemies were especially numerous within the official world, whose material interests he had so boldy challenged. He had told Guchkov that he felt sure he would be assassinated by a police agent.[3] His health was seriously impaired. In September, Nicholas paid a ceremonial visit to Kiev, and both Stolypin and Kokovtsev were in attendance. Elaborate measures for the protection of the Emperor were taken by those responsible; but it was so evident that the safety of the Ministers was not included in them that Stolypin remarked to Kokovtsev: 'We are superfluous.'[4]

One Bogrov, who like Azef worked on the fringes of the revolutionaries and the police, had given false and detailed information of a plot against the life of the Emperor. The police followed up the false scent, and with unpardonable negligence admitted Bogrov with a police ticket to the gala performance in the theatre on September 14th; and here, just as Stolypin had said good-bye to Kokovtsev with the words, 'I wish you could take me with you', Bogrov fired at him point blank. Nicholas himself thus describes the scene in a letter to his mother:

> Olga and Tatyana were with me at the time. During the second interval we had just left the box, as it was so hot, when we heard two sounds as if something had been dropped. I thought an opera glass might have fallen on somebody's head and ran back into the box to look. To the right I saw a group of officers and other people. They seemed to be dragging someone along. Women were shrieking and, directly in front of me in the stalls, Stolypin was standing; he slowly turned his face towards us and with his left hand made the sign of the cross in the air. Only then did I notice that he was very pale and that his right hand and uniform were blood-stained. He slowly sank into his chair and began to unbutton his tunic . . . People were trying to lynch the assassin. I am sorry to say the police rescued him from the crowd and took him to an isolated room for his first examination . . . Then the theatre

[1] Kokovtsev, I, 458. [2] Stolypin to B. P. [3] Guchkov to B. P. [4] Kokovtsev, I, 479.

> filled up again, the national anthem was sung, and I left with the girls at eleven. You can imagine with what emotions.[1]

The Emperor called on him as he lay dying in hospital but was not allowed to see him. Kokovtsev was constantly at the bed-side of his friend. He died in great pain on September 18th, and Nicholas paid respect to his body. But none of the Court had attended the prayers for his recovery.

The brief diary of Polivanov, usually confined to business, contains a touching homage to his leader.[2]

> *Tuesday, 6/19th September.* The *Novoe Vremya* has come out with a black border. What a distressing feeling! Not to speak of the loss for Russia, I feel a personal bereavement. I was under the charm of this man. I delighted in him, I was proud to think that he was satisfied with my work. When I said good-bye to him on August 24th (Sept. 6th) after the Cabinet meeting, as usual I tried to catch his eye. He stood by his chair, tall and upright, and his fine face looked healthy and tanned . . . It was on the 27th (Sept. 9th) that for the last time I heard his manly voice on the telephone.

It was Kokovtsev who succeeded him as Prime Minister. He was kindly received by the Empress; but when he spoke to her of Stolypin, she begged him 'not to mention that man'.[3] Kokovtsev urged that Stolypin had died for the Emperor, but in reply she complained that he had 'overshadowed his sovereign', and begged the harmless and loyal Kokovtsev to avoid that mistake. The big man had done a great deal more than serve his sovereign; he had saved his sovereign's throne.

The circumstances of Stolypin's death called forth indignant protests, especially from Guchkov. An official inquiry resulted in a claim for the trial of those responsible — including the Assistant Minister of the Interior, Kurlov, who was charged with the control of the police. When Kokovtsev brought the report of the commission to the Emperor, Nicholas had just been relieved from the threat of a terrible family misfortune in the death of his dearly loved boy, and, in spite of Kokovtsev's gentle reproaches, he declared that he could not punish anyone at such a moment;[4] so that the ugly suspicions of foul play remained in the public mind and were never cleared up.

[1] N. to M. F., 265-7.
[2] Polivanov, 105
[3] Kokovtsev, ii, 8. and to B. P.
[4] Kokovtsev to B. P.

CHAPTER V

RASPUTIN

But in the gross and scope of my opinion,
This bodes some strange eruption to our State.

Hamlet, I, I

THE RISE OF RASPUTIN

THE monarchy had been saved; the country was prosperous; and Russia had — shall we say — half a constitution. From now onward, we must trace what happened in closer detail.

By 1907 the home life of Nicholas and his family had long since fixed itself on definite lines; and it is like something apart and beautiful in the midst of that tragic story which we are henceforth following. Even later when the clouds are thickening, the Empress writes to her husband: 'Heavy trials everywhere, but at home in our nest bright sunshine'.[1] And in another letter she thanks him humbly for all the 'happiness and love you have given me all these (21) years',[2] and again, 'Thank you on my knees for all your love, affection, friendship and patience'. 'The life of Their Majesties', writes Vyrubova, 'was a cloudless happiness of mutual unlimited love'.[3]

We have a perfect picture of this family happiness in the charming book of the tutor of the young Tsarevich, Pierre Gilliard. This was a man of a natural nobility of heart and mind, who was quickly recognized by his employers for all that he was, and was soon put on the footing of a devoted servant and friend. 'That man is a pearl', writes Alexandra later;[4] and he was to prove his worth to the full, when later he followed the family after the abdication into prison and exile and would have followed them to death had he been allowed. It is to his simple and noble record that we owe it that the most difficult and obscure part of all this subject is as well covered as any other. Perhaps the most striking feature

[1] Ap. 8th/21st, 1915.
[2] Ap. 7th/20th.
[3] VYRUBOVA, 30.
[4] A. F. to N., July 1st/14th, 1916.

of it is that Gilliard, living on end in this restricted atmosphere and full of loyalty and love for the family, yet retains a perfect balance of intellect, and that of the events outside which he could not see, he forms as just an estimate as any writer on this period.

Gilliard, who was a Swiss, had been teaching French to the children of the Leuchtenberg family when in September 1905 he was summoned to teach the same language to the Emperor's daughters. Later in 1912 his teaching was transferred to the boy Tsarevich then eight years old, and he gave his first lesson on the very eve of the child's terrible and critical illness at Spala in Poland. So delighted were the imperial couple with Gilliard that not long afterwards they conferred on him the greatest honour which it was in the power of these devoted parents to give, by appointing him tutor of the boy, a post which was ordinarily held by a Russian General or some other high Russian dignitary. Their choice bears witness to the unerring insight which they had into his character and into the tasks with which they set him to deal.

We have another parallel record of very different value, that of Anna Vyrubova, one of the two daughters of the Emperor's Chief of his Personal Chancery, Taneyev, a post which had been in the Taneyev family under five Russian sovereigns. The estate of Anna's father near Moscow was close to that of the Empress's elder sister and aunt by marriage, the Grand Duchess Elizabeth — she was referred to in the family correspondence as Ella — and it was here that Anna first met the Empress Alexandra. In 1901, when she was seventeen, she nearly died of typhus. In the crisis of her illness she imagined that she saw a vision of the favourite Orthodox priest of the time, John of Kronstadt, who had been present at the bedside of Alexander III in his last moments. Directly afterwards she received a visit from him, and shortly after that from the young Empress. Two years later she received the *chiffre*, which gave her court rank, and in February 1905 she was appointed a *Fräulein* on the personal suite of the Empress. Two years later, on May 13th, 1907, Anna married a naval officer named Vyrubov, whose nerves had been shattered in the Battle of Tsushima. It was with great hesitation that she took this step, and her doubts, which she probably communicated to the Grand Duchess Militsa, led to her first sight of Rasputin, whom she met in the house of the Grand Duchess. Rasputin gave an uncannily good forecast of the marriage; but both the Emperor and the Empress reminded her that her word had been given, and the marriage took place in their presence and with their encouragement. It turned out hopelessly, and in fact was never consummated, and a year later Anna Vyrubova, as she now was, obtained a divorce. From then onwards Anna lived in a small and uncomfortable house in Tsarskoe Selo, only about a few hundred yards from the small Alexander Palace in which the imperial couple spent most of their life. The Empress, as is evident from her letters, felt a debt to her as one that had been maimed and bruised, and she became a kind of lame duck of the family, coming across to the palace daily. As time went on, with the gradual process by which all other outside contacts disappeared from the family life, Anna remained as the one constant witness of it. She spent much of the day there, singing duets with the Empress, listening with the family to the pleasant readings of the Emperor, or joining in when they were sorting post cards, glueing them into albums or collecting stamps. Much of the family reading was in English, for instance the *Daily Graphic* or mediocre novels such as those of Florence Barclay, and Anna appears to have picked up some words of the language — as was even the case to a lesser extent with Rasputin. It was in the August of 1907 that Anna first joined in the yearly yachting trip, this time to the Skerries, after which the charming Nicholas said to her: 'Now you have subscribed to come with us regularly.' In 1909 for the first time she accompanied them to their real home in Livadia, of which the girls used to say: 'In Livadia it is pleasure, in St. Petersburg it is service.'

Anna Vyrubova has written a description of the family life in which one will find a mass of stupidities. Gilliard has described her as 'a child, excitable, with no mind or sense'.[1] She was the typical woman worshipper of a woman, dividing the whole world into 'theirs' and 'ours', hopelessly prejudiced, entirely devoid of judgment and in the highest degree loose and inaccurate in her statements. Her examination by the Investigating Commission is one continuous evasion: She is 'not particularly interested in Rasputin'. The imperial couple only regarded him as one who would pray for them. He had nothing to do with politics, and she never talked politics to him. Protopopov she 'hardly knew'. The

[1] GILLIARD, 54.

gentle President feels driven to ask her whether she thinks that telling stories is a bad fault.[1] But, as time went on, as the only confidante in that close circle, she came to be of national and even of international importance. She seems to have been quite disinterested in the political connections in which she came to be plunged, but without any understanding of the issues in question. 'Besides', writes Simanovich of a document which he sent her for the Emperor, 'she understood nothing and sent it on'. He describes her as 'an ideal gramophone disc';[2] Protopopov also calls her 'a gramophone'.[3] Paléologue, to whom she was sent by the Empress to ascertain his views in the crisis of 1915, says that he felt as if he were 'speaking to a phonograph', and gives a lively picture of how she seemed to be repeating his words after him without comprehension, in order not to forget them.[4] The idea that she influenced the Empress would be absurd. She was a medium, a vehicle, a means of communication, and as such one of the most disastrous that could be imagined. For all that, she has her great value for our knowledge of that inner life.

There are side lights on the subject, such as the comparatively insignificant book of Lily Daehn, who was an occasional guest, and — what is far more valuable — the notes of Ministers and others who, with the growing seclusion, came to be almost the only penetrators into that quiet family life. These notes are the more important because here was to be found the only key to all that was to happen.

Kokovtsev gives his testimony as to Nicholas's remarkable clearness of head and his swift understanding of any issues that were presented to him. Nicholas lived apart from his people, but he was working for them all the time. He was a hard worker and enjoyed his work. He had a great sense of order in the arrangement of his papers. Work done, he is essentially an open air man, giving himself hard walking exercise in his park, plunging with keen enjoyment into his beautiful swimming bath, or driving at reckless pace at Livadia. In his park, at Tsarskoe, as everywhere, his favourite company was his children, to whom he was at once Emperor, father and comrade. He was a kind and wise disciplinarian, always with a ready humour. Gilliard recounts how when

[1] VYRUBOVA, *Padenie*, III, 247.
[2] SIMANOVICH, 162.
[3] PROTOPOPOV, *Padenie*, II, 215.
[4] PALÉOLOGUE, II, 46-8.

instructing the sprightly Olga, who was the eldest child and much the most like her father, he failed to exclude from her notice the improper French word *merde*, which has often been rendered in French *Cambronne*, because the general of that name is reputed to have shouted it back to the advancing English when they called on him to surrender at Waterloo. Olga has gone to her father to ask him what the word means, and meeting Gilliard in the park the Emperor says: 'What curious words you are teaching my children!' But he tells Gilliard that he has already put the matter right with Olga. He has explained to her that it is a word which it would not be very good for her to use, but that in certain circumstances it is the glory of the French army.[1]

Besides him in this home circle rises the figure of Alexandra, who is the cloud-wrapt heroine of this tragedy, a subject which might have been coveted by Sophocles, and here it is that we need all the light that either Gilliard or Anna Vyrubova can give us. 'That is how I came to Russia,' said the Empress sadly, to her infatuated Anna, after a full description of her mournful entry, where, as Anna comments, the marriage was the continuation of the funeral. She hated etiquette, especially the unnatural and un-Russian etiquette of the stilted Russian Court at that time; such company made her feel terribly shy. She was entirely at home with the poor and the simple and with those several young officers whom she came literally to mother in an exactly Victorian sense. But she could not abide ceremony, which was only too obvious to all taking part in it, for instance to the French Ambassador, Paléologue, at a public dinner to Poincaré.[2] To foreign diplomats she gave the impression that she was thinking all the time: 'When are you going to get out of my house?' As time went on, her whole mental poise depended on whether a conversation was taking a turn agreeable to her or not; but it would be a very great mistake to describe hers as a mediocre mind or as simply a sick mind. 'The Empress is no fool,' said Rasputin, who sometimes spoke with an exaggerated contempt of her husband's abilities. 'Une tête d'homme,' says Vyrubova, and from her letters and from the testimonies of responsible statesmen one can only get the same impression or that anyhow she had a remarkably penetrating and even discriminating sense for anything that affected her deepest-seated

[1] Gilliard, 46. [2] Paléologue, I, 5.

interests — in particular, the official 'autocracy' of her husband. The essence of her nature and of her intellect was that she was absolutely whole-hearted. Kokovtsev speaks of 'her absolute repudiation of compromise', Gilliard of her 'direct and open nature'.[1] She was an entirely good woman and entirely Victorian, which was one of the chief reasons of her unpopularity in the society of St. Petersburg — lightminded, unhealthy and amoral.

Her great desire was to give an heir to the Russian autocracy. Four daughters followed at short intervals on each other, all of them delightfully healthy, simple and charming girls. In 1900, during the sovereigns' visit to France, the Grand Duchess Militsa, a Montenegrin princess married to Peter Nikolayevich, brought to them at Compiègne an adventurer in mysticism, a professional soul doctor, Philippe Vachot of Nizier, a mild little man with a gentle manner and persuasive eyes, whom they later brought to Russia. He was denounced by the official representative of the Russian police in France, Rachkovsky, who showed him up as a simple charlatan; Philippe had twice been prosecuted in France for practising medicine without a licence. This was put right by obtaining him the recognition of the Military Academy of Medicine in St. Petersburg, a very fine school, and Rachkovsky was dismissed from his post. Nicholas, as we know, was devoted to the memory of his father and there were talks now of *séances* in which Alexander's spirit was resuscitated. Philippe, it appears, claimed to be able to determine sex, and in 1902 a year after the birth of the fourth daughter, Anastasia, the Empress believed herself to be *enceinte*, but nothing happened. During the Japanese War Philippe, who became the tool of politicians, is said to have actually interfered in such questions as the command of the army, and the Empress was unwillingly persuaded to let him go back to France where he later died in obscurity; but before he went, he gave her a bell, as a symbol that she should warn off from the Tsar advisors who did not share her views, and he prophesied to her: 'You will someday have another friend like me who will speak to you of God'.[2] This incident is more than once recalled in her later letters to her husband.

Petersburg was at this time full of the most unhealthy kind of

[1] GILLIARD, 25.
[2] VYRUBOVA, 81; A. F. to N., June 16th/29th, 1915.

mysticism; and where such tendencies existed at Tsarskoe Selo, they were a constant subject of gossip and embroidery. Alexandra herself, when asked, declared that spiritualism was 'a great sin';[1] but both Nicholas and his wife were deeply religious, and Alexandra, who had refused to embrace Orthodoxy without full conviction, plunged into its extreme limits with the fervour of a convert. There were other mystics who played upon this sense, such as the vague figure of one Papus, who appears to have been in some way an associate of Philippe, and a strange incoherent cripple named Mitya Kolyaba, who was brought from Kaluga to the Theological Academy in St. Petersburg.

On August 12th, 1904, in the midst of the disasters of the Japanese War, took place the event which more than anything else determined the whole later course of Russian history. On that day was at last born the heir to the throne, long expected and fervently prayed for. The Empress believed that she owed his birth directly to the intercession of Saint Seraphim, a pious old man of Sarov near Nizhny-Novgorod, who had been very irregularly canonized in the preceding year on the insistence of Nicholas himself. Pobedonostsev, still Minister of Religion, was said to be opposed to it. The birth was a peculiarly easy one, but it was almost at once discovered that the boy suffered from a terrible hereditary disease which the mother herself had for the first time brought into the Russian reigning family. It was hæmophilia, which had already assaulted several of the closest kinsfolk of Alexandra — one of her uncles, one of her brothers and the three boy children of her sister Irina, wife of Prince Henry of Prussia. This disease, though palliatives have been suggested, remains to this day without a known remedy. It consists in a thinness of the blood which does not allow it to coagulate, so that there is no assured means of stopping bleeding when once it has begun. It is accompanied by an extreme brittleness of the veins; and a simple blow, which does not penetrate the skin, sets up an internal swelling causing the acutest agony, so that the victim, however courageous, cannot but cry out with pain. At such times a machine called a 'triangle' was used for days to straighten the leg and the effect was excruciating. Every possible resource at the disposal of a sovereign was exhausted in trying to find a cure for this terrible disease; but

[1] VYRUBOVA, 80.

all the medical authorities — the highest as the most honest — had to admit that it was incurable. Nicholas and Alexandra were the most devoted of parents. Alexandra regarded herself as guilty and was herself practically the nurse of her boy; she bathed him daily, and she would rock his cradle with one hand while signing an official report of some charitable institution with the other. The boy's malady henceforth lay at the bottom of all her thoughts, and it is from this time that Vyrubova dates her constantly recurring heart attacks. With the whole of her absolute nature she set herself to win from God what science had refused to her and what could only be a miracle. 'God is just,' she would say.[1] It was a spiritual wrestle. In her aloofness she had always sought special consolation in religious services; and those of the Orthodox Church touched the very depths of her nature. Hours and hours she spent in solitary prayer in the crypt of the small Fedorovsky Cathedral close to the palace, and these prayers had come to be the continuous concentration of a mother's love.

Towards the end of 1903 there were rumours in St. Petersburg of the advent of a new and great prophet named Gregory Rasputin, a peasant of thirty-one, of the village of Pokrovskoe in the province of Tobolsk, just beyond the Ural mountains. He was declared to have foretold three months of drought, which had duly followed his prophecy.

Siberia was the home of many strange things. It had regularly been used as a place of deportation; since Peter the Great, first fallen court favourites, later unruly peasants and finally the cream of the revolutionary intelligentsia had all been sent thither. Latterly large numbers of peasants had gone there of themselves, against the law which fastened them to their village communes, usually preceded by picked men of adventure, the so called *hodoki* or walkers, who reconnoitred the ground first and found it good. There was something of the pilgrim fathers in these men; and in fact Russian Siberia was a creation not of the Russian Government, still less of the Russian nobility, which had no footing there, but of the Russian people, anxious to get away from the tight control of the centre and advancing into a no man's land which they thus made Russian. All the elements of opposition were represented there. These were almost the only individualists whom

[1] KOKOVTSEV, II, 349.

Russia produced, and always by the road of opposition. The country itself, so far from being a miserable wilderness, was indeed a land of milk and honey which fostered men and women of an extraordinary physical vigour, often accompanied by a strong mental initiative. Russian Siberia, in its metal resources, is probably the most richly endowed part of the world. The climate of itself teaches work and vigour. One finds there a store of unlimited physical appetites and potentialities. The Church too had used Siberia as a place of exile, and here too it was the home of the repugnant under-dog. There were all sorts of religious vagaries to be found in this part, and in particular the most challenging of all the heretics, the *khlysts*, who whipped themselves into a fury of erotics and fanatacism at their secret but regular orgies. This sect had been pronounced illegal, and members of it could be prosecuted before the courts.

In the rich and hungry physical life of this region, in the village of Pokrovskoe, was born Gregory, son of Efim; like many peasants he had no surname, and Rasputin, which means 'the dissolute', appears to have been a nickname attached to him by his fellow villagers, though others explain it by an older name of the village, Palkino Rasputye, the last word meaning a dividing of the ways. His father kept a great number of horses, and both he and Gregory have been accused of being horse thieves; but one of the earliest stories of his boyhood tells of his uncanny discovery of a horse theft by another.[1] What is quite clear, is that he shocked the whole village by his sexual insolence. Then came a sudden change in his life. He was employed to drive a traveller to the neighbouring monastery of Verkhoturye, where a number of *khlysts* were confined in ecclesiastical imprisonment. He was later frequently charged with membership of this sect. This charge was never brought home; but it can at least be said that both his practice and his whole mentality were strongly suggestive of its truth. In any case the rest of Rasputin's life was an extraordinary alternation of erotics and devotion. His conduct in the village became so notorious that Bishop Antony of Tobolsk commissioned the village priest to inquire into it, with the result that the case was handed over to the civil authorities. Meanwhile Rasputin, as he appears to have done earlier, disappeared into the wilds of Russia.

[1] Fülöp-Miller, 15.

Here too he was true to an historical type. Always, throughout Russian history, there had been *stranniki* or wanderers who, without any ecclesiastical commission, lived in asceticism, depriving themselves of the most elementary of human needs, but gladly entertained by the poor wherever they passed. Some of them went barefoot even throughout the winter and wore chains on their legs.[1] This self-denial gave them a freedom to address as peasant equals even the Tsars themselves, and there are many instances of their bold rebukes scattered over Russian history.

Rasputin wandered over all Russia and much farther afield. It was certainly at least twice that he made the traditional journey of Russian peasant pilgrims to Jerusalem. He is known to have roamed both in the Balkans and in Mesopotamia.[2] In Russia itself he got to have a knowledge of all the principal monasteries and even some kind of an indistinct smattering of the canon law. These were the antecedents of the rumours of his power in 1902. There was at that time at the religious academy of St. Petersburg an exceptional young man who was training for the monkhood and came to be known later as the monk Illiodor. He tells us that it was on December 29th, 1903, that Rasputin appeared at the Academy, a stocky peasant of middle height with ragged and dirty hair falling over his shoulders, tangled beard, and steely-grey eyes, deep set under their bushy eyebrows, which sometimes almost sank into pin points, and a strong body odour.[3] He appeared as a man who had been a great sinner and was now a great penitent, drawing an extraordinary power from the experiences through which he had passed. As such he was received by Theophan, a simple man of the most saintly life, who was Inspector of the Academy and for a time confessor to the Empress. Another of his early supporters was the sturdy and vigorous Bishop of Saratov, Hermogen.

Rasputin soon had more powerful backing. On one of his wanderings he was found in Kiev, sawing wood in a courtyard, by one of the principal adepts of fashionable mysticism in St. Petersburg, the Grand Duchess Militsa, who had earlier helped to bring Philippe to Russia. Rasputin was soon established as a

[1] I met one such, who declared his independence and contempt of all Church authority.

[2] Simanovich to B. P.

[3] ILLIODOR, 5; compare SIMANOVICH, 301; YUSUPOV, 51-2, and KOKOVTSEV, II, 35-9.

social favourite. One of his first patrons there was the vigorous, but excitable Grand Duke Nicholas, for whom he is said to have cured a dog! It was at Militsa's house that Anna Vyrubova met Rasputin for the first time to consult him on the prospects of her marriage.

Let us now return to the family life at Tsarskoe Selo. Here everything centred round the health of the little heir to the throne, who was the centre of this close family.[1] Olga was now a sprightly girl with a will of her own and a charming sense of mischief, thoroughly Russian in character and in many ways taking after her father. The second girl Tatyana was taller and more stately; she was her mother's child and especially looked after her and even replaced her as a deputy with her sisters, who sometimes called her 'the little mother' or 'the governess'. Maria, who had promise of great beauty, was a plump and friendly creature of unlimited good nature whom the others sometimes called the big bow-wow (*le gros toutou*). The youngest girl, Anastasia, was spirited, sly and playful; she would get under the dinner table and pinch the legs of some elderly statesman until her father pulled her out by her hair. She has been described as 'a little inextinguishable volcano, with a world of her own'. The four girls were devoted to each other and used to write joint letters to their friends signed by their four initials, OTMA. They never really grew up. Mosolov describes their conversation as like that of children of 10 or 12.[2] They were also devoted to both their parents, who kept them under a firm and kindly English discipline with camp beds and cold baths. Each of them had a dressing-gown of the colours of the regiment of which they were respectively honorary colonels, which gave them great delight. Their whole life, for instance such details as their birthday presents, was regulated with an almost parsimonious simplicity. None of them except Tatyana had any strong consciousness of their rank. Their mother was so fearful of the looseness of Petersburg society that she did not encourage them to any girl friendships,[3] though of course they occasionally met their cousins; but they were perfectly happy, talking among themselves or to any of the poor whom they met, 'with that simplicity which was their charm'.[4] Rasputin's daughter Matrena or Mara, who met them

[1] GILLIARD, 44.
[2] MOSOLOV, 247.
[3] ibid., 61.
[4] GILLIARD, 188.

frequently, speaks of them as 'bent on doing their duty with all their strength'.[1]

But the whole of this united family was haunted by a constant terror. The little Alexis grew up into a charming boy, lively and spirited, with beautiful curly hair and blue eyes, like a little cherub, and a closely knit frame. He had healthy, open air tastes like his father and was always wanting to play like other children: yet the slightest accident — and there were many — might at any time be fatal. His mother's eye was on him practically night and day, and she would constantly call him back to her when he was any distance off. He showed every sign of having both a mind and a will of his own, and his sufferings, so unusual for that age, gave him a peculiarly intimate sense of the troubles of others; for instance, he was urgent in begging off a cook who was in disgrace. He felt abashed and confused when on one of his excursions some peasants threw themselves on their knees before him. But this constant care made him secretive and even inclined to cunning. It was here that Gilliard showed his mettle.[2] He begged the parents to give the boy more latitude for the benefit of his character, even at that great risk; and such was the deepness of their care for the child that to their immense credit they agreed. The boy, with his new measure of freedom, was infinitely grateful; but even within a month a fall from a table on to his knees produced a terrible internal swelling, and a crisis which might have been fatal; yet never did either parent by word or thought reproach the tutor or go back from the decision they had taken.

It was the boy's illness that brought Rasputin into the palace. He was strongly recommended by Militsa and her sister Anastasia,[3] who were at that time intimate with the Empress, and he soon had the almost worship of the simple Vyrubova. The date of his entry at the palace is fixed by a note in the Emperor's diary. On Nov. 1st/14th, 1905, significantly just after the signing of the Constitutional Manifesto, he writes 'We have got to know a man of God — Gregory — from the Tobolsk province'.

What was the nature of Rasputin's influence in the family circle? The foundation of it all was that he could undoubtedly

[1] MARIE RASPUTIN, 103.
[2] GILLIARD, 20-3.
[3] Later the wife of the Grand Duke Nicholas.

bring relief to the boy, and of this there was no question whatsoever. As his last nurse Teglova put it to Sokolov, 'Call it what you will, he could really promise her (the Empress) her boy's life while he lived'. Mosolov speaks of his 'incontestable success in healing'. Did the boy like him? Gilliard says not. At the family table he once asked the domestic chaplain, Father Vasilyev: 'Is Gregory Efimovich a saint?' The Emperor asked the chaplain to answer and the Empress looked fixedly at him. The chaplain discreetly generalized the question by discussing what it took to make a saint, and the Emperor broke off the conversation.[1] Much later, in Siberia after the abdication, when Rasputin's photograph fell on the floor, and the maid, Bitner, explained that she was looking for the 'little icon', the boy laughed and said, 'That's not an icon! Don't look for it.'[2] But for all that, Rasputin, as will be shown by some striking examples, was definitely able to stop the bleeding. Beletsky, Director of the Police Department, who lost his post through Rasputin and regained it through him, tells us that in 1913 he actually took lessons in hypnotism and that Beletsky himself in the period of his hostility put a stopper to this by expelling the teacher from St. Petersburg.[3] Rasputin explains the whole matter to his friend Simanovich: sometimes, he said, he used certain Tibetan drugs which he got from a quack doctor, Badmayev, or even more simple materials; sometimes he pretended to use remedies, but did not; and sometimes he trusted entirely to his will-power.[4] In the later stages, when Rasputin's influence and power were far greater, it was the habit to ring him up from the palace every morning. Once he was rung up because the boy had a headache. Rasputin took the phone and in a soothing voice told the boy a tale about Siberia and bade him go to bed and he would be quite well next day. Beletsky's agent, Komissarov, the watchdog of Rasputin, witnessed the scene.[5] On another occasion, according to Rodzyanko, when some minor operation was in preparation — for no major operation was ever possible owing to the nature of the disease — the Tsar's doctor, Fedorov, had spread out the materials required, carefully disinfected, when he found them covered by a dirty cloak of Rasputin, who in this

[1] Fr. Vasilyev to Beletsky, *Padenie*, IV, 297.
[2] SOKOLOV, 73.
[3] BELETSKY, *Padenie*, IV, 501.
[4] SIMANOVICH 23-4.
[5] BELETSKY, IV, 354.

Houston Public Library
Check Out Summary

Title: Russia under the new Regime : Lenin and t
he birth
Call number: 947.0841 P665
Item ID: R0122742416
Date due: 6/4/2014,23:59

Title: The fall of the Russian monarchy
Call number: 947.083 P228
Item ID: R0125553992
Date due: 6/4/2014,23:59

unsavoury way was blessing the operation.[1] The girls of the family never spoke of Rasputin to Gilliard, and even the malady of the Tsarevich was never mentioned among them; indeed, it was treated as a state secret. Gilliard thought they had no particular respect for Rasputin. Their letters to him would testify otherwise, but no doubt they were written under the direction of their mother, whom they adored. The Emperor himself was by no means always entirely under Rasputin's influence. To Dedyulin, at one time commandant of the palace, who expressed to Nicholas his intense dislike of Rasputin, the Emperor replied: 'He is just a good, religious, simple-minded Russian. When in trouble or assailed by doubts I like to have a talk with him, and invariably feel at peace with myself afterwards'.[2] With the Empress herself Rasputin's influence was greater, and progressively greater until it was an absolute obsession; but nothing could be clearer than its limitations. He was for her a holy man, almost a Christ: she at one time speaks of him as such. It would have seemed treason to her to doubt it, when he appeared at last as an answer to her prayers and accomplished the miracle which the doctors had declared to be impossible; and for that very reason she entirely and absolutely refused to believe that there was any truth at all in what was said against him. In the intimacy of her letters to her husband the nearest approach to any admission of her doubts was where she wrote: 'He was not tipsy' — which he certainly was more than once just before he was summoned to the palace.

It must be realized that the whole family detested the police. The boy in his excursions with Gilliard used to take delight in tricking their watchfulness. The Emperor, when one of them fell at his feet in the Crimea, almost kicked him. It was taken that the police were the enemies of Rasputin, and that the many stories which reached the public were simply their machinations. It is in this finality of the Empress's refusal to believe, that lies the root of the tragedy. I once asked this question of her cousin and brother-in-law, the Grand Duke Alexander Mikhailovich: Did he believe the charges against Rasputin? Why, of course, Rasputin was a disgusting man. What would the Empress have done if she had believed them? She would have been the very first to drive him out. Rasputin himself very well recognized what was required of

[1] RODZYANKO, 102. [2] ibid., 10.

him. At the palace he was the holy man and nothing else; and even if telephoned in the middle of an orgy, he had an extraordinary power of returning at once to sobriety and decency, in order to keep up his character at the palace.

At his first meeting he addressed both the sovereigns as if they were fellow peasants and kissed them, and his manner to them throughout was as if he had the voice of God. But besides that he was also for them the voice of the Russian peasantry; he told them, says Simanovich, 'the tears of the life of the Russian people',[1] among whom he was constantly wandering and of whom he brought back all sorts of curious and interesting tales to the palace; he would use them to put the boy to sleep. And Mosolov hits the mark when he says, in this sense, that the Tsar needed a peasant. Rasputin detested the Russian nobility and made no secret of this. He declared them even to be of another race — not Russian.[2] Nicholas, from the very nature of his strange burden and his own feeling of his incompetence, was always secretive and suspicious. Alexandra never thought of herself as anything but an Englishwoman, the pupil of Queen Victoria, and was disgusted at the immorality of the higher society in the capital. She had no trust in this new world of politics and politicians. In espousing her beloved husband, she had felt that she was espousing the Russian autocracy, which, as she saw with tenderness all his weaknesses, she considered that she herself must defend both for him and for her baby son; but in her patriotism she was utterly and devotedly for Russia; and for her, Russia was the Russian people, and Rasputin was its voice that reached the throne.

For a time his new position made Rasputin more careful about scandal. He had a tremendous success in several of the big salons, and took a peasant's delight in finding this world of luxury and extravagance at his feet. He made a point of humiliating the high and mighty of both sexes. Simanovich speaks of his 'incredible insolence', his 'stable language', his disgusting manners at table, where he would plunge his dirty hands into his favourite fish soup.[3] Nothing is more untrue than the easy explanation that was so often given, that he became the tool of others. He was far too clever to sell himself to anyone. He did not ask for presents and had no need; he had only to accept all that was showered upon

[1] SIMANOVICH, 185. [2] ibid., 34. [3] ibid., 32, 34.

him, and that he did briefly and almost casually, in many cases at once passing on the largess to the poor: his position was that of one who plundered the rich for the poor and was glad to do it.

In his study of Petersburg society he soon found an able coadjutor; in one of his early visits to Kiev, the sacred city of the south, he had made the acquaintance of a little Jewish jeweller, Aaron Simanovich, who has since written his life. The book only claims to have been written from memory and contains all sorts of disgusting scandals for which there is no foundation. But Simanovich, as can be established from other sources, did definitely go into partnership with Rasputin, and ordinarily met him several times daily. Rasputin called him by pet names, 'Simochka' or 'Simoniki', and gave him a ring inscribed 'To the best of Jews'. Simanovich had moved from Kiev to St. Petersburg in 1902, and through Princess Orbeliani, one of the Empress's favourite ladies, got a footing in the palace as a jeweller. He tells us that he utilized the parsimony of the Empress — of which Rasputin also complained to Illiodor — to sell jewels to her at long credit and much under cost price. He found at the Court, as he says, 'an extraordinary ignorance of business',[1] and speaks later of the 'total incapacity of court folk'.[2] Of this he took the fullest advantage, rendering questionable services in the looser life of society, such as organizing cabarets and gambling hells. But Simanovich is not to be dismissed as a villain and nothing else;[3] he had his own fidelities, and, above all — as we shall find from other sources later — he had the courage to prefer the cause of his despised race to his own personal profit. On Rasputin's arrival the two foregathered; and their association was quite recognized and accepted in the inner circle of the Empress, so that it was not a rare thing to find contacts between Simanovich and Vyrubova. He was clever and very well informed; and he tells us himself how he coached Rasputin in the various political and other values in the capital, sometimes even scolding him like a child.[4]

But Rasputin's self-imposed restraint was becoming too much for him. We must remember that he took a real pride in humiliating high society. Playing on the depths of its corrupt sensationalism, he put up the theory that physical contact with himself was

[1] SIMANOVICH, 10.
[2] ibid., 14.
[3] BELETSKY, *Padenie*, IV, 351-2.
[4] SIMANOVICH, 27-8.

in itself a purification. His sexual triumphs were made easy for him. He had 'too many offers' writes Simanovich. Women of high birth sought this humiliation as a new and extravagant sensation. His daughter who admits that he 'had mistresses',[1] only makes the apology that he was 'tempted', and on occasion this was his own only defence. Scandal soon touched the imperial household itself. The girls' governess, Madame Tyutcheva, objected to Rasputin penetrating into their bedroom. The Empress, who in her isolation never in her life saw the evil side of Rasputin, flatly refused to listen to her and, though Nicholas realized that the practice complained of should cease, Tyutcheva was dismissed and spread the scandal in Moscow, particularly in the circle of the Empress's sister, the Grand Duchess Elizabeth. But Rasputin went very much further than this. He actually seduced the nurse of the Tsarevich, who later made a confession, which the Empress dismissed as a kind of hysteria amounting to insanity.[2] Once the restraint was gone, Rasputin's excursions in this field came to be promiscuous.

RASPUTIN AND REACTION

Rasputin had already become a great preoccupation to the principal Ministers. When Stolypin's children were injured by the attempt on his life in 1906, the Emperor had offered him the services of Rasputin as a healer.[3] Later there was an interview between the two at which, according to the account that Stolypin gave to Rodzyanko,[4] Rasputin tried to hypnotize this fine, sturdy and sensible man; Stolypin described how repulsive it was to him. He made a plain report on Rasputin to the Emperor. At the beginning of 1911 he ordered Rasputin out of St. Petersburg, and the order was obeyed. Stolypin's Minister of Religion (Procurator of the Holy Synod), Lukyanov, on the reports of the police, ordered an investigation, and abundant material was forthcoming.[5] From this time, onwards, the Empress hated Stolypin. She sent two of her intimate ladies, Anna Vyrubova

[1] MARIE RASPUTIN, 59. [2] RODZYANKO, 27.
[3] Kokovtsev to B. P. [4] RODZYANKO, 24.
[5] ibid., 23.

and Lily Dachn to Pokrovskoe to vindicate her friend, and they have given their accounts of this visit. Anna Vyrubova brought Rasputin back with her to Kiev on the eve of the assassination of Stolypin. In the remarkable book entitled *Days* by the brilliant young conservative, Shulgin, Rasputin's host relates to the author how he entertained him there. As Stolypin drove through the crowd after the imperial couple, Rasputin calls out, 'Death is after him! Death is driving behind him!' and through the night he is heard muttering the same thought aloud. Stolypin is killed next day.[1] From Kiev Rasputin wandered on to Crimea and the neighbourhood of the imperial palace at Livadia; but he was roughly expelled by the police prefect, Dumbadze, and later returned to St. Petersburg.[2]

The post of Prime Minister was now filled by Kokovtsev. He had not the strength of Stolypin in asserting his authority, and Lukyanov was replaced as Minister of Religion by Sabler, a Rasputin man, who was often reproached with having actually made an obcisance to him; Beletsky treats this charge as generally accepted and Kokovtsev repeats it.[3] Stolypin had also held the predominant post of Minister of the Interior. Here too he had to be replaced. Nicholas had two alternative candidates in mind. One was an ultra-conservative, Nicholas Maklakov, brother of the distinguished Liberal orator of the Duma, whom the Tsar met when staying in the neighbouring province of Chernigov, where Maklakov was governor. The other was Alexis Hvostov, Governor of Nizhny Novgorod, a sheer adventurer who was to play a great part later. Rasputin was actually sent to Hvostov to form a judgment of him shortly before Stolypin's murder; but Hvostov, like many others at the time, did not realize his influence and treated him with contempt. Kokovtsev assured the Emperor that 'no one respected Hvostov', and was able to secure the appointment of his own candidate, Makarov. This was an entirely honest man who later showed a great deal of civic courage; but he was not much more than a good jurist and an eminently respectable official with limited views.

It was now that the sexual exploits of Rasputin were becoming a public scandal of the first order. The saintly Theophan had at first such confidence in Rasputin that he even visited him in his

[1] SHULGIN, 106. [2] RODZYANKO, 26. [3] KOKOVTSEV, II, 32.

village home at Pokrovskoe; what he saw there must probably have enlightened him, and he was himself the recipient of the confession of an injured woman. He spoke up bravely to the Empress; but Rasputin was too strong for him, and he was sent to be Bishop in Crimea and later on to Astrakhan and Poltava: 'I have closed his loop-hole', said the triumphant favourite. According to Rodzyanko,[1] near the beginning of 1911, the Metropolitan Antony, wise and liberal-minded, also made his protest to the Emperor and when told that the imperial family's private affairs did not concern him, replied courageously, 'No sir, this is not merely a family affair, but the affair of all Russia. The Tsarevich is not only your son, but our future sovereign, and belongs to all Russia'. He even said that the Tsar of Russia should live in a palace of crystal, where all his subjects could see him. Antony fell ill after the interview and died shortly afterwards.

The same disillusionment came to Illiodor. This young monk was a man of the most striking personality. A furious fanatic for throne and altar, gifted with a tremendous invective which he had directed against revolutionaries and Jews, he had become a prominent popular preacher of great magnetism, and was followed by bands of devoted adherents; he was also well known and well considered at the Court. He had established a kind of spiritual fortress called Mount Tabor near Tsaritsyn. He was at first very much impressed by the undoubted spiritual powers of Rasputin, and the two for some time worked closely together. They had a third close associate in Illiodor's near neighbour, Hermogen, Bishop of Saratov; this was an older man of great vigour and independence and not without a sound instinct of judgment. In December 1909, Illiodor invited Rasputin down to Tsaritsyn, where together they visited the homes of his followers. He could not help feeling uncomfortable about the multitude of kisses which the bearded Rasputin distributed, especially to the younger and prettier of his parishioners. At Rasputin's request he now accompanied him to Pokrovskoe, and both on the journey and still more in the village he was shocked by the cynicism of Rasputin, whose conduct went to all lengths in sexual licence. Rasputin chaffed Illiodor openly about women, and he was peculiarly frank in his talks about his own past. He had been a drunkard, he said, up to

[1] Rodzyanko, 27-8.

the age of thirty. He described his wanderings and his early meeting with John of Kronstadt, who had taken him very seriously and instead of giving him his blessing had asked himself for Rasputin's. Equally shocking to Illiodor was the way in which Rasputin spoke of the imperial family. They asked him about everything, he said, the War, the Duma, Ministers. They were always ready to listen to 'the rebukes of the muzhik'. Of the Emperor he said: 'he cannot breathe without me'. Nicholas, he asserted, went down on his knees to him and said: 'You are a Christ.' He described how he kissed the Empress in the girls' room. To reinforce his boasts he pointed to his house, the only two-storied one in the village, which he owed to the Grand Duchess Militsa, and also to the portraits of the imperial family, and some letters from the Empress and her children. Alexandra, it appears, had very inadvisedly used some expressions which a cynical reader might interpret into an admission of personal attraction: such as 'My head bows: I feel your hand'.[1] Rasputin showed Illiodor shirts woven for him by the Empress and her daughters, and even gave him three of them; and Illiodor, waiting for a favourable moment, appropriated some of the letters. Rasputin had a wife, two daughters and a half-idiot boy; all of them were known personally in the palace, and the wife visited Petersburg once a year; reference to these visits are to be found in the letters of the Empress to her husband. The wife, says Illiodor, 'knew all her husband's tricks'; to others she said significantly 'he has enough for all'. Through all Rasputin's boasts ran the strain of humiliating the great of the earth. 'The Tsar has washed my hands', he said, 'and you . . .'[2]

On the journey back, when Rasputin's conduct continued to be outrageous, Illiodor was asking himself: 'Is he an angel or a devil?' and *The Holy Devil* is the title which he has given to his book on the subject, to be adopted later by Fülöp-Miller. Correspondence passed between Illiodor and Hermogen on the public attacks on Rasputin, which were now beginning. Illiodor for a time tried to stand up for him. Rasputin on his side tried to propitiate Illiodor; but the confession of a nun, Xenia, of Rasputin's foul treatment of her turned him into an open enemy. Ultimately on December

[1] KOKOVTSEV, II, 42.
[2] ILLIODOR, 23-7.

29th, 1911, Hermogen and Illiodor summoned Rasputin to meet them. It was only on entering the room that he saw he was entrapped. There was his old rival Mitya Kolyaba, who opened the impeachment, seizing on Rasputin. Illiodor followed, and then others. Rasputin, according to Illiodor's account, was completely cowed. Bishop Hermogen demanded imperatively: 'Is this true?' Rasputin hesitated and then murmured: 'It's true, it's true, it's all true.' The burly bishop hit him with his heavy cross, thumped him on the head, and laid on him a prohibition that he was to touch women no more and that he was to keep away from the palace. 'You are smashing our sacred vessels', those were the impressive terms of his indictment. He dragged Rasputin into a small chapel and made him swear on an icon that he would obey these orders. Rasputin next day came to Illiodor crying: 'Save me! Save me!' The two returned to Hermogen, who turned his back, with the words: 'Never and nowhere.'[1]

Rasputin went off with his own version of what had happened to the palace. The result was that Hermogen and Illiodor were both sent to different monasteries. As a bishop, Hermogen had the right of trial by twelve other bishops; but this was over-ridden by the imperial order. Hermogen submitted to the sentence of seclusion, but Illiodor did not. He moved from place to place and continued to denounce Rasputin. The letters of the Empress and her children in his possession passed into other hands, and were copied. Guchkov's Moscow newspaper *Golos Moskvy* (the 'Voice of Moscow') printed a contribution from one Novoselov, a lecturer at the religious academy of the Trinity and St. Sergius and a student of illegal sects, in which he called upon the Synod to deal with Rasputin as a member of the heretical community of Khlysts. His article, which was entitled 'A letter to the Editor', began with these words:

> '*Quo usque tandem!*' . . . Such is the cry of indignation escaping from the lips of all Orthodox men and women against that cunning conspirator against our Holy Church, that fornicator of human souls and bodies — Gregory Rasputin, acting under the holy cover of the Church. '*Quo usque?*' — such are the words which, in anguish and bitterness of spirit, the sons of the Orthodox Church are compelled to address to the Synod,

[1] ILLIODOR, 132 ff.

in view of the unheard-of tolerance exhibited towards the said Gregory Rasputin by the highest dignitaries of the Church . . . How much longer will the Synod remain silent and inactive in the face of this shameful comedy, enacted for years before its very eyes?[1]

The Press took up a general campaign against Rasputin, and the news was full of mothers' complaints and confessions of his victims. By the existing law the old preliminary censorship had been abolished, but the authorities were at liberty to impose arbitrary fines after publication. In this case almost any newspaper was prepared to take the risk; but an order was published forbidding any paper to write about Rasputin. Here the Emperor had broken his own law. The estimates of the Synod were shortly to come before the Duma, which had the right of presenting to the Ministers interpellations signed by a given number of members. Guchkov was still the leader of the predominant party, the Octobrists or conservative reformers; and he put forward an interpellation to the relevant Minister, which would mean an open debate on the whole question of Rasputin.

Guchkov's successor as President of the Duma was a typical country Tory of absolute honesty and integrity, Michael Rodzyanko, who was later to act almost as a minute bell to the sovereign as the danger thickened. He was a man of nearly twenty stone with a great voice which controlled the Chamber, and the chief of all his characteristics was his courage. Faced with the possibility of a full-dress debate on Rasputin, he did what he could to modify the intentions of Guchkov. To a request to Makarov for a copy of Novoselov's pamphlet Rodzyanko received the answer that the Minister had no copies of it at his disposal, neither did he see any reason for circulating it. Rodzyanko therefore went straight to the Minister and found a copy of the pamphlet lying on his desk.[2] 'This proves', he says, 'that even such a perfectly honest man undoubtedly was not entirely free from servility when it came to shielding Rasputin.'

By the intervention of young Prince Yusupov, whose mother was in close contact with both Empresses, Rodzyanko also visited the Dowager Empress,[3] who was terribly distressed. She gave Rodzyanko her blessing, but did not feel she could hope that the

[1] RODZYANKO, 33-4. [2] ibid., 33. [3] ibid., 37-8.

Emperor would listen to a warning. 'He is so pure of heart', she said, 'that he does not believe in evil.' Still, Rodzyanko applied for an audience, and obtained it on March 10th, 1912; he went beforehand with his wife to pray in the Kazan Cathedral, from which Kutuzov had started to face Napoleon just a hundred years before.

Rodzyanko said his word to Nicholas manfully. He spoke of 'the starets, Rasputin, and the inadmissible fact of his presence at Your Majesty's Court'. 'I beseech you, Sire', he said, 'as Your Majesty's most loyal subject, will it be your pleasure to hear me to the end? If not, say but one word and I will remain silent.' With bowed head and with averted gaze the Tsar murmured 'Speak'.[1] He reminded Nicholas of each of those who had suffered for speaking the truth about Rasputin — of Illiodor, of Theophan, and of Bishop Antony of Tobolsk, who had been faced with the choice of seclusion in a monastery or transference to Tver. 'How can the Orthodox Church stand by in silence', said Rodzyanko, 'when Orthodoxy is being destroyed and defiled by the pernicious activities of this rogue?' Nicholas listened to him, interjecting a few questions. Rodzyanko detailed what he knew of the charges against Rasputin.

> 'Have you read Stolypin's report?' asked the Emperor. 'No, I have heard it spoken of, but I never read it.' 'I rejected it,' said the Tsar. 'It is a pity', I replied, 'for all this would not have happened.'[2]

Evidently Rodzyanko had made a great impression: for two days later he was authorized by the Emperor to investigate the matter himself. With great unwillingness Damansky, an official of the Holy Synod and one of the closest adherents of Rasputin, brought him the papers that had been collected by Lukyanov. Rodzyanko at once handed them over to his officials at the Duma, but the very next day Damansky asked for an interview and demanded the papers back.

> He explained [writes Rodzyanko] that the demand came from a very exalted person. 'Who was it, Sabler?' Damansky made a deprecating gesture: 'No, someone much more highly placed . . .' 'Who was it?' I repeated. 'The Empress

[1] RODZYANKO, 41. [2] ibid., 46.

Alexandra Fedorovna.' 'If that is the case, will you kindly inform Her Majesty that she is as much a subject of her august consort as I myself, and that it is the duty of us both to obey his command. I am not therefore in a position to comply with her wishes.'[1]

When Rodzyanko had completed his report, he made a request for another audience. This was refused, and he threatened resignation. By the mediation of Kokovtsev he was instructed to send in the written report. This, as we know, was later studied in Livadia by the Emperor, together with the Grand Duke Ernest of Baden, brother of the Empress. During this visit of the Grand Duke, Sazonov was the Minister in attendance. He has himself described to me how the Grand Duke asked him why the Ministers did not give due warning to the Emperor. Sazonov, thinking that this referred to the dangers to the empire, replied that he had done his best; but the Grand Duke meant something different and said plainly that he was thinking of the Empress. He added the words: 'The Emperor is a saint and an angel, but he does not know how to deal with her.'[2]

Rodzyanko had wished for a joint warning from the highest authorities in the empire, in which he reproaches Kokovtsev for not taking part. Rodzyanko, like others, has justly pointed to the weakness of the 'neutrals'; but Kokovtsev did make his protest and with the same manfulness as Rodzyanko. Nicholas requested him to see Rasputin himself. The interview took place on February 28th.[3] Rasputin made the same curious demonstrations as in his talk with Stolypin, and posed and simpered. He stood there with closed eyes and bowed head, and ultimately in reply to Kokovtsev's demands he answered: 'All right, I'll go.' He added some quite interesting remarks on the subject of the food supply. In reporting to the Emperor, Kokovtsev, who had had charge of prison administration, described Rasputin as the typical Siberian convict. On his next visit to Livadia, as the Empress passed along the circle of guests, she lingered in conversation with each of those standing next to him, who were officials of no particular importance, and passed Kokovtsev with averted face thrusting out a hand for him to salute.[4]

[1] RODZYANKO, 53.
[2] Sazonov to B. P.
[3] KOKOVTSEV, II, 36-7.
[4] ibid., II, 66.

The police were now busy trying to secure the originals of the letters of the Empress and her children to Rasputin, to which the Dowager Empress attached especial importance. By clever manœuvres they secured these letters, and Makarov, as Minister of the Interior, against the warning of Kokovtsev, handed them over, not to the Empress herself, but to the Emperor, which, as the Premier warned him, sealed his fate as a Minister.[1] Nicholas sent a sharp memorandum to Makarov demanding new measures for the control of the Press, and constantly worried Kokovtsev with this request.

Illiodor did not give up the struggle. He at last let himself be taken to imprisonment in the monastery of Florishchevo, and later made a stinging exposure of the life of the monks there. The question of his trial was before the Synod, and he addressed to it a number of vehement letters which sometimes verged on prophecy:

> You have bowed down to the devil [he wrote]. My whole being is for holy vengeance against you. You have sold the glory of God, forgotten the friendship of Christ ... Oh, cheats, serpents, murderers of Christ ... When my vengeance shall take elemental dimensions [this might have been written in 1918], I will tear off your cloaks; for farthings you will pay with milliards ... Traitors and renegades ... Clean the devil's hoofs in hell! ... You are all careerists; you despise the poor; you ride in your carriages, proud and arrogant, you do not stand for the Church, you are not servants of the people, you put present-day prophets to the stake.[2] What they take for God [he writes] is not God. The Synod, as an organ of Holy Christ, no longer exists. Godless, Antichrists, I will not be in spiritual communion with you. ... You are animals fed with the people's blood.[3]

On November 21st he was unfrocked. 'I will not allow myself ever to be pardoned,' he had said, and finally he renounced Orthodoxy, and, disguised as a woman, escaped over the frontier in August 1914 by way of Finland, later to offer his literary wares to American publishers.[4]

[1] Beletsky, *Padenie*, iv, 149; Kokovtsev, ii, 44; Illiodor, 31.
[2] Illiodor, 169-75.
[3] ibid., 168-74.
[4] Illiodor admitted to Burtsev that he had put in 'a bit extra' in this book, especially at the end (Burtsev to B. P.).

Beletsky, Director of the Police Department, who knew most of the inside of this story, reckons that from 1913 Rasputin was firmly established. Simanovich, who knew even more, reckons that Rasputin took five years (1906-11) to gain the power and exercised it for another five (1911-16). Kokovtsev states that Rasputin had no political influence before 1908 but that he was now 'the central question of the nearest future'.[1] Rasputin was constantly saying to the Emperor, 'Why don't you act as a Tsar should?[2] Only the autocracy could serve as cover to him; and he said himself, 'I can only work with sovereigns'.[3] The strong movement for Church reform and the appeal for the summons of a Church Council, which had accompanied the Liberal movement of 1904/07, had been negatived by him with the words 'there is an anointed Tsar', a phrase which is constantly recurring in the Empress's letters. Rasputin, as Kokovtsev has said, was important precisely as confirming in the sovereigns the idea that nothing at all counted except their will and that the people were entirely loyal to it. Loyalty, he says, was measured entirely by agreement with their ideas. With such promptings it was not easy for Nicholas, brought up in strict allegiance to his father's memory and to his coronation oath, to acquire the habit of listening without some irritation even to a loyal and moderate Duma or to Ministers, who reminded him of the changed constitutional position. As early as Sept. 27th/Oct. 10th 1909 he had written to his mother, 'One thing is difficult — to persuade Kokovtsev to get money without the Duma; but we will do it one way or another — no fear'. The humiliation of the spring of 1911 was not forgotten, and there are increasing signs of the approach of a wave of reaction. This irritation is now more openly expressed to Kokovtsev. The Empress had not so far intervened in politics, except for such opinions as a devoted wife might express to her husband, though when it was a question of certifying Philippe as a doctor, she had said that surely the Emperor could do whatever he liked. But she was from the first on her mettle in the defence of Rasputin, and she was now Kokovtsev's personal enemy. Nicholas still retained his affection for him; but he could not fail to feel bitterly offended by the affair of his wife's letters, the almost open publicity given to them, and a

[1] Kokovtsev, II, 21. [2] Simanovich, 54.
[3] ibid., 143.

construction put upon them which he, better than anyone else, knew to be infamous; and Illiodor's book had escaped the attention of the police of Moscow. He speaks to Kokovtsev of 'These gentlemen!' 'This marsh!'[1] 'I am simply stifling', he says, 'in this atmosphere of gossip and malice.' It is at this time (in 1913) that he renews the interrupted friendship with Meshchersky, from whom he looks for moral strength in the reassertion of his autocracy. 'I am beginning to get tired of it', he says significantly to Kokovtsev.[2]

According to the reactionary Minister of Justice, Shcheglovitov, even in October 1911, the Tsar consulted him on reducing the powers of the Duma,[3] and he was constantly demanding of Makarov and of Kokovtsev further restrictions on the Press which, as they well knew, could never have been accepted by it. At least Rasputin remained cut off from the palace. He returned to St. Petersburg in April 1912, but was not received at Tsarskoe. He made flying visits which, according to Rodzyanko, embarrassed the police in their efforts to avert scandal at the public baths and elsewhere. The Emperor now himself began to show a certain coolness to Kokovtsev.

Meanwhile, though the Government drifted after the strong hand of Stolypin had been withdrawn, the country was advancing on its new road of increasing prosperity and increasing contact with Europe. The Duma was becoming more and more the established and indispensable organ of public opinion, of which in spite of its crippling suffrage, it was becoming more and more truly the representative spokesman, and as such it was regarded outside Russia. By a gradual process, the decent habits of parliamentary life were converting the great majority of it – all except the extreme Rights – into a national instrument of progress and reform.

The Third Duma, unlike its predecessors, had lived out its full term of five years, and completed its good work in June 1912. It had an admirable record. It had enabled Kokovtsev, who was still Minister of Finance, to balance the budget regularly and even to spend on productive purposes. Whatever else in parliamentary

[1] KOKOVTSEV, II, 51.
[2] ibid., 143.
[3] SHCHEGLOVITOV, *Padenie*, II, 436.

institutions may be subject to criticism, there can be no doubt of the absolute value of financial publicity and financial criticism; they are in themselves a breath of fresh air and health. Money was saved for the chief needs of national defence; but the greatest progress was in the two vital domains of agriculture and of education. The land settlement programme of Stolypin, administered with rare ability by Krivoshein and Rittich and resting on peasant initiative and peasant support, was creating a whole new population of millions of yeoman farmers; and the work of the Peasant Bank was also giving a strong stimulus to individual farming. Migration to Siberia was increasing rapidly. On this new basis of personal property, agricultural co-operation was springing up of itself everywhere. There was still a wide gap between the Government and the public, which the Duma was rapidly helping to fill up. Kokovtsev, like his predecessor, colleague and friend, Stolypin, was a Duma man, and he firmly maintained to both the sovereigns that the Duma was a necessary factor.[1] Still, it was with great difficulty and only by his personal credit with the Emperor that he succeeded in persuading him to receive the members and thank them for their labours on June 27th, 1912.

Alexandra, however, now hated the Duma because of its discussion of Rasputin. Since the Rasputin crisis, Guchkov had become for ever her special bugbear. 'Hanging is too good for him,' she had said. He stood for the Fourth Duma in two constituencies, but without canvassing; and either by police manipulations or otherwise he failed to secure re-election, and had henceforth to lead his Octobrists from outside.

Rasputin was now far away in his Siberian home. In October the imperial family were at the other end of the Empire at Spala, near the Polish frontier. The boy slipped while getting into a boat and fell upon the gunwale. This set up an acute crisis. There was a turn towards recovery; but by a neglect of which the family loyalty would never reveal the author, the crisis returned in an even sharper form. The doctors could see no hope. The Empress's sister, Princess Irina of Prussia, had come across the neighbouring frontier to visit her and was trying to comfort her. The child was crying out in his agonizing pain.[2] His parents were in despair, and were absorbed in fervent prayer. There was always

[1] KOKOVTSEV, II, 7. [2] GILLIARD, 12-13.

telegraph communication between Rasputin and Anna Vyrubova, and Rasputin telegraphed: 'The illness is not as dangerous as it seems. Don't let the doctors worry him'.[1] From that date, explain it as you will, the boy recovered, though traces of the crisis long remained. It is useless to suggest, as some have done, that Anna Vyrubova promoted the crisis and then administered a remedy, for the reason that even now no real remedy is known.

There is another explanation, equally mysterious. Mosolov relates that at the sharpest moment of the crisis the Emperor's loyal physician, Dr. Fedorov, said to him, 'I do not agree with my colleagues. It is most urgently necessary to apply far more drastic measures; but they involve a risk. What do you think — ought I to say so to the Empress? Or would it be better to prescribe without letting her know?' Mosolov refuses to give an opinion. He reports the account of the telegram from Rasputin. Next day the hæmorrhage has stopped. He delays Fedorov and asks him, 'Did you apply the remedy you spoke of?' In answer, 'He threw up his hands and replied as he went out: "If I had done so, I should not have admitted it: you can see for yourself what is going on here".' Anyhow, if this was Fedorov's secret, it seems to have perished with him.[2]

The Fourth Duma, which was also to last out its full time and continue till the Revolution, was of very similar composition to the Third. There was one remarkable new member in young Alexander Kerensky, a Labour leader with an ardent enthusiasm for liberty which was to govern all his career. Kerensky had the honourable and dangerous calling of counsel for the defence in political cases, and he possessed a natural and spontaneous gift of burning eloquence, direct and fearless, which, while he was speaking, might carry all before him. But as a whole the Duma, deprived of the firm control of Guchkov, was tending to split up into groups. The leading party of the Octobrists itself divided into three sections, and Rodzyanko even thought of resigning the Presidency to lead one of them.

Everything was now making for reaction. A disgraceful incident had taken place in the Lena goldfields. As was later admitted after full investigation, a drunken and half crazy police officer had given orders to fire on quite orderly strikers. The Duma opposition

[1] Vyrubova, 44. [2] Mosolov, 151-2.

sent Kerensky there to examine the matter, and he even had the co-operation of the Governor General, Knyazev, and the Archbishop Innocent. The Government was hard put to it to defend itself, and Makarov's explanation was tactless and irritating.[1]

On December 29th Makarov was replaced by a new Minister of the Interior, Nicholas Maklakov. His views were the opposite of those of his liberal brother, Basil. He gave them himself with frankness and courage after the Revolution to the examining commission. He was whole-heartedly for the Russian autocracy. In the concessions of 1905 'one leg had been lifted', and ever since the life of Russia had been like 'a drunkard's walk, tottering from wall to wall.'[2] He saw the growing discontent, and he claims that he alone was for decisive measures — even for dissolution of the Duma. He had little respect for subservient Right wing politicians and nothing but contempt for the bad scribes of the Government, whose benefits he cut down materially; he thought little better of the police agents, and concurred in their withdrawal from the army; he was no friend of Rasputin's, and claims to have reported against him; but he was an out-and-out champion of absolutism. Nicholas Maklakov had a peculiar relation to the Emperor. He claims to have had no special political ties in the capital when the Tsar visited him as Governor of Chernigov, and their friendship had almost a sentimental origin with the sanctifying connection of an icon. He used to play with the imperial children, jumping at them in the role of 'the amorous panther' — which was sometimes the subject of Press witticisms.

The honest Kokovtsev was not a strong ruler, and had the most doubtful support in the Cabinet, which, since the dismissal of Witte, was in the main appointed by the Emperor. Maklakov with bold proposals and Shcheglovitov with subtle insinuations were always working against him, and Prince Meshchersky with his *Citizen* was always undermining him at the palace. From March 1913 onwards there was frequent friction between the Government and the Duma.

The growing tide of reaction was greatly increased by the tercentenary of the Romanov dynasty, which was celebrated in 1913.[3] In September 1912 special emphasis had been laid on the

[1] N. MAKLAKOV, *Padenie*, III, 128. [2] ibid., III, 87.
[3] KOKOVTSEV, II, 155.

celebration of the defeat of Napoleon's invasion a hundred years before. The Romanov tercentenary had an even greater propaganda value for the monarchy; and it was not likely to be stressed at this time that the Romanovs came to the throne after a great convulsion by a national election with peculiarly solemn preliminaries. The Emperor and Empress travelled back into the past and visited the original home of the Romanovs on the Volga. Rasputin was seen in a most prominent position there; and at the solemn service in the Kazan Cathedral at St. Petersburg he established himself in front of the seats which Rodzyanko, after great difficulty, had secured for the Duma. According to Rodzyanko, Rasputin tried to mesmerize him too. The huge man describes it thus: 'I suddenly became possessed of an almost animal fury, the blood rushed to my heart, and I realized I was working myself into a state of absolute frenzy. I too, stared straight into Rasputin's eyes, and, speaking literally, felt my own starting out of my head . . . "You are a notorious swindler", I said.'[1] He took Rasputin by the scruff of his neck and roughly threw him out of the church. The Emperor showed his personal courage when he rode into Moscow some twenty yards in front of his escort, followed by his family in an open carriage. There was an anxious hush till the outbreak of bells announced that he had reached the Kremlin.[2] In both these celebrations, of 1912 and 1913, the Court authorities, evidently not on their own initiative, went out of their way to minimize the consequence of the Duma.

In the autumn of 1913 an incident in the Duma, probably collusive, when the reactionary member Markov shouted out at the Government, 'You must not steal', led to the protracted abstention of the Ministers. In October Maklakov wrote a letter to the Emperor in which he definitely advocated a *coup d'état*. He proposed to make a menacing speech in the Duma, which was to be followed, if necessary, by dissolution and the abolition of its legislative powers. Nicholas himself was 'pleasurably surprised', but practically all the Cabinet was against Maklakov, and the idea was dropped. Another move in the direction of reaction was the cancelling of the election of a number of local mayors and a proposal, which the Emperor played with, and only dropped at the last moment, to nominate the bully of Tver, the reactionary

[1] Rodzyanko, 76-7.

[2] I witnessed this scene.

Stürmer, as Mayor of Moscow. Kokovtsev manfully met his opponents in the Cabinet with the answer that the mayors 'were not blind executants'.[1] But this was his last success.

Rodzyanko, twice reporting to the Emperor on the Cabinet dissensions, used the expression, 'Your Majesty, you have not a Government'. On the other side, Kokovtsev also appealed to the Emperor for unity in the Government, but could get no satisfaction; and on February 12th, 1914, he was unexpectedly dismissed both from the Premiership and from the Ministry of Finance. Nicholas had been listening to other 'advisers', and at his parting with Kokovtsev, after hearing his criticisms answered, he replied, as so often before: 'You are right, and I am wrong.' He embraced him repeatedly with the words: 'Friends part like this'; but the dismissal stood.[2] Kokovtsev's old antagonist in so many budget debates, the liberal Shingarev, paid him a call of warm sympathy.

Krivoshein, who had much to do with the intrigue and whom the Empress has described as the 'cleverest of them all', did not want the Premiership for himself. He preferred to buttress the aged and incompetent Goremykin, who was acceptable to both the sovereigns for his attitude of a butler, taking instructions to be communicated to the other servants. One cannot but pause to ask what would have been the difference if Kokovtsev had still been Prime Minister in the vital crisis which was to follow later in the same year.

On July 1st, 1914, Nicholas again returned to his idea of a *coup d'état*. The Ministers were all suddenly called to Peterhof, and the Emperor took the chair. He again suggested that the Duma should be reduced to merely a consultative body. Shcheglovitov was a reactionary, but he was a lawyer and Minister of Justice, and, speaking last, he said that he would be a traitor if he gave the Emperor such advice. 'Quite enough,' said Nicholas. 'Clearly we must drop the question.'[3]

Rasputin was since 1912 established in permanent quarters at St. Petersburg at 64 Gorokhovoy. He returned from time to time to Pokrovskoe, and there on June 29th he was stabbed in the stomach by Guseva, a hysterical victim of his lust. Guseva was known to Illiodor and had visited him in his seclusion not long before, but he claims to have had no knowledge of her intentions.

[1] Kokovtsev, II, 237. [2] ibid., II, 293.
[3] Shcheglovitov, *Padenie*, II, 437-8; N. Maklakov, *Padenie*, III, 133.

The wound was a grievous one, even exposing the entrails, but Rasputin recovered. Guseva was officially declared insane.

Meanwhile reaction was again raising the spectre of revolution. A movement of indignation had been rising in the country. In the autumn Guchkov, addressing the Octobrist Party, had come out into open opposition. He foresaw a new violent upheaval which if not firmly directed, would lead to complete anarchy, and he declared that now all means could lawfully be employed against the Government.[1] Throughout the winter all the talk in St. Petersburg had centred round the scandals of Rasputin. Kerensky passing rapidly through the country sounded the general discontent and rallied the forces of Labour. For him the years 1912-14 were taken up with 'strenuous political organizing and revolutionary work'.[2] The days in which all such efforts had to be secretive had ended, he says, with the institution of the Duma, which he describes as 'a powerful weapon for political organization and propaganda'. 'The whole of Russia was now covered with a network of labour and liberal organizations — the co-operatives, trade unions, labour clubs, evening classes, etc.' He was even proceeding fast with the creation of a kind of skeleton staff to take advantage of the expected opportunity for a big move forward.

The measures taken by the Police Department to counter this movement were extraordinary. Its Director, Beletsky, believed in the principle 'Divide et impera', and his application of this principle was to aim at promoting a split in the Marxist (S.D.) Party, whose field lay among the workmen; this was for opposite reasons the direct object of Lenin, who was still living abroad. Beletsky enrolled as a police agent a leading Bolshevik, Malinovsky, and secured his election to the Fourth Duma in 1912. Malinovsky, at the instigation of the Police Department, made violent speeches, even calling for an armed rising. His Menshevik colleagues in the Duma, such as Chkheidze, could not understand either his audacity or his immunity.[3]

The Minister of the Interior, Nicholas Maklakov, was not an administrator but a slap-dash reactionary politician, and took little interest in the detail of the work of his Ministry. The Minister always had two assistants, one of whom, appointed by himself,

[1] Guchkov, *Padenie*, vi, 254. [2] Kerensky, C. L., 162.
[3] Chkheidze, *Padenie*, iii, 492-6

had special responsibility for the Police Department through its Director. This was the post which had been held by Dmitry Trepov and later by Kurlov, who had been accused of negligence in connection with the murder of Stolypin. To this post Maklakov appointed General Dzhunkovsky, an old comrade of the Emperor in the Preobrazhensky Regiment and later an intelligent and humane Governor of Moscow. Dzhunkovsky was before all things a man of honour. With the Tsar's approval he withdrew the police spies from the army and from the schools.[1] He proposed to reorganize the gendarmes into a corps with less odious duties. It was he who persuaded his chief, Maklakov, to clip the wings of the literary hacks of reaction subsidized by the Police Department. It was he who discovered the fraud practised in the provocative plot which had served as an excuse for the dissolution of the Second Duma, and he insisted, again with the approval of the Tsar, on the trial of Shornikova, which however was sidetracked by the guile of the reactionary Minister of Justice, Shcheglovitov. When he also discovered the sinister activities of Malinovsky, he went straight to the President of the Duma, Rodzyanko, and acquainted him with the fact that one of its Members was a police spy. This resulted in the sudden flight of Malinovsky; he returned to Russia after the Revolution, only to be summarily executed by Lenin. Dzhunkovsky dismissed both Beletsky and the Head of the Gendarmes, Gerasimov, who at one time harboured another spy-terrorist, Azef, and later passed into the Opposition.[2]

Since the affair of the Lena goldfields, labour unrest had been growing apace. There were then 700,000 workers out on strike, but in 1914 a million and a half. As is now known, the reports of the German Embassy anticipated a new revolutionary period. Formidable strikes broke out in the capital which, according to General Danilov, were accompanied by actual skirmishes with the troops. Barricades had been set up at the very moment when Germany declared war on Russia.

[1] Dzhunkovsky, *Padenie*, v, 69-70.
[2] ibid., 71-2.

CHAPTER VI

RUSSIA AND THE WORLD WAR

Thereto prick'd on by a most emulate pride.
Hamlet, I, I

WHEN the wanderings of the nations left English and French in immediate neighbourhood, they did nothing more to emphasize the meaning of the word 'foreigner' than they did when they made neighbours of Germany and Russia. The two peoples have hardly anything at all in common. The almost resentful sneer with which the Russian calls attention to 'German accuracy' is matched by a kind of wild fear with which Germans think of Russian hordes and savagery, a nightmare which has never been far from their minds since the surprising Russian raid which for a moment captured Berlin in the reign of Frederick the Great. On his side the Russian, with his anarchical freedom of mind, sees only too clearly the comforting limitations of German industry, self-satisfaction and bourgeois morality.

Individually the Germans have always pecked at Russia as a country out of which profit could be made. They are always 'foreigners' there, in a sense in which we are not. On the other hand, with their colossal personal industry, which would make them work even if there was nothing visible to be got out of it, they have used the advantage of their neighbourhood to know the country through and through in far more detail than the Russians knew it themselves, but always with an objectiveness that is tinged with disparagement and contempt. When there was as yet no German nation in a political sense and only the corporate trade of the Hansa, the Germans organized an exploitation of Russia which was only rarely countered from the other side: for instance when a peculiarly modern-minded Russian Minister of the seventeenth century, Ordyn-Nashchokin, saw what could be made of the organization of Russian trade in Russian interests.

Meanwhile a special friendship between the Romanov and

Hohenzollern dynasties was initiated by Peter the Great, starting from the time when he met the Great Elector in his first visit to Western Europe. Peter in many respects swallowed German influence whole and undigested. He flooded his empire with German words, especially German titles, and everywhere Germans came to be identified with government authority. By his conquest of the long-desired Baltic coast he also swallowed a considerable population of German barons and German traders, which Bismarck is said to have later described as providing the best red-tape officials in the world. He married off daughter or niece to small German potentates; and as he got rid of his only surviving son, these marriages instead of furthering Russian influence in Germany had the opposite effect, and put a succession of German or Germanized sovereigns on the throne of Russia. In the reign of his niece Anne (1730-40), probably the most sinister period in Russian history, Russia was governed by German statesmen, soldiers or favourites.

It was only under Anne that the duel between Russia and Turkey passed from the defensive to the offensive on the side of Russia, and this brought Russia into European combinations on a large scale, generally assuming at least the name of a crusade. At this time the imperial sovereigns of Austria were in anything but cordial relations with Prussia, which they regarded as a pretender. But Austria had the liveliest defensive interest in checking the advance of Russia in the Balkans. Russia had nearly all the cards in her hands — a kinship with the Slav population there and an identity of religious confession not only with the Bulgars and Serbs, but also with the Greeks and the Rumanians. Austria, on the other hand, was nothing but a conglomerate empire based on an identity of sovereign and on a common bureaucracy and army. In the many phases of this long rivalry, it came to be regarded as axiomatic that the preservation of peace in the Balkans depended on finding some temporary accommodation between the rival interests of Russia and Austria.

From Catherine the Great to Nicholas I Russia even exercised an ever recurring influence on German affairs, utilizing the bitter and constant rivalry between the Austrian Emperor and the King of Prussia. Throughout the Napoleonic period, which brought so many quick changes, St. Petersburg was ultimately the dominating factor. The Russian predominance came to an end with the Crimean War, and the whole career of Bismarck, which dates from that period, was a complete reversal of it.

Bismarck, who served as Prussian Minister in St. Petersburg from 1859 to 1862, had formed an estimate of Russia which, under a most plausible cover of friendship, was really a mixture of realism and contempt. He saw all the ingrained weaknesses in the Russian monarchy, that giant with feet of clay: the clay was then a muddy mess of serfdom, on which the whole social structure of the country still rested. He had first to secure the benevolence of Russia to cover his rear when he was carrying out his great programme, which included the three wars of 1864 (against Denmark), 1866 (against Austria) and 1870 (against France). He found a basis for this in the complicity of the three monarchies guilty of the political extinction of Poland, and in 1863 he co-operated with Russia in the suppression of the Polish rising of that year. He was also complacent to Russia when she took advantage of his war against France to quit herself of the prohibition in the Treaty of Paris to refortify on the shores of the Black Sea. As soon as he had won his war and founded his German Empire, his sovereign, the old Emperor William I, paid a visit of thanks to his nephew the Tsar Alexander II. He might well be grateful: for Bismarck's work had entirely altered the whole situation in Europe, to the great disprofit of Russia. Instead of being able to work at will the jealousies of Austria and Prussia, Russia now found on her eastern border granite in place of sand, in the shape of the new military German Empire. From this point onward, Bismarck's task was to veil his new hegemony with a policy of friendliness to both Austria and Russia, to cover the time till he might be compelled to choose between the two; which he was very reluctant to do. After his successful war of 1866 he had most astutely abstained from claiming 'a stone of her fortresses or a foot of her territory'. He had successfully driven Austria out of Germany, and he was really utilizing the existence of a German dynasty and a largely German bureaucracy in a great conglomerate State outside his own borders, to turn it into something like an *annexe* of German policy, with the absorption of as many Slavs and others as possible. This was ultimately to prove the ruin of Austria, which could only be tolerated by Europe in general while it was a mixture of consolation prizes, resulting from wars in the main unsuccessful, and had not yet become the instrument or rather the spearhead of the ambitions of any particular nationality. But Bismarck was much too clever to carry his logic too far. Curiously enough, it was an anti-communist pact, inspired by the explosion of communism in Paris at the end of the Franco-Prussian War, that gave Bismarck a motto for a friendly league of the three autocratic sovereigns of Eastern Europe, a kind of new Holy Aliance till he be compelled to choose between Austria and Russia; but that time came with the Treaty of Berlin in 1878, and the choice then made was sufficiently bold to be obvious to all. For a war waged by Russia and resulting in the liberation of Bulgaria, Austria received a territorial compensation which was more valuable than the gains of Russia herself.

This was the right accorded by Europe to a military occupation of Bosnia and Herzegovina, which was ultimately to lead to the Great War of 1914. It must be made clear that Russian policy in this matter was full of the gravest blunders and greatly assisted the Austrian case. Before the Russo-Turkish War of 1877, at the meeting between the sovereigns of Russia and Austria at Reichstadt on July 8th, 1876, Alexander II had agreed to an eventual annexation of the two Slav provinces by Austria at the expense of Turkey on the presumption of Austrian co-operation in a liberation of the Balkans. There was no Austrian co-operation, and the Treaty of Berlin set up the military occupation of the two provinces by Austria. On at least two other occasions the Russian Government contemplated Austrian annexation of Bosnia. The two provinces had a Slav population; and in this attitude the Russian Government was running dead against the claims of Serbia and the aspirations of traditional Russian policy.

Now that Bismarck had made his position clear, the outcome was a direct alliance with Austria, which, by his ability, was made also to include the new monarchy of Italy. This was the famous *Triplice*. Its object was to guarantee the *status quo* secured for Germany by the Franco-Prussian War; and its result was to establish a kind of embryo Mittel-Europa, holding at arms' length on the two sides its defeated or disappointed rivals, France and Russia. But Bismarck still held on to as much as he could carry of Russian friendship, and he made what has usually been regarded as a treaty of reinsurance with Russia. This lasted to the end of his time and was only dropped by Wilhelm II.

Meanwhile events of enormous internal importance had taken place in Russia, with the emancipation of the serfs and a number of other first class reforms, which it made unavoidable; in particular the introduction of trial by jury, the establishment of local self-government on a basis of election, and the reform of the army on a foundation of universal and equal obligation of military service. The emancipation was in itself an economic revolution; and the Germans, with their far-reaching knowledge of Russia and with the organization of their great industry and energy, outdid all other countries in the part which they obtained in the exploitation of these new conditions. The German consulates-general had staffs which far exceeded those of other countries; and apart from that, there was a corps of travelling experts in the German service who obtained a knowledge of local Russian conditions which the Russian officials had never taken the trouble to get. Individual German efforts received the wholesale backing of the German Government. In this time of economic revolution the values were rapidly changing, and the Germans were quick to seize upon all the new strategic points. The British, who had been so well established here from generation to generation since the sixteenth century, were rapidly being ousted at one point after another. Before the Great War the Germans were established in almost all the dominating positions. They had one great disqualification for which they were to pay dearly; they never took the same interest in the Russian side of the bargains that was habitual with so many of the best English firms, such as Mather and Platt of Manchester. They openly showed their contempt for Russians and Russian ways; and they appeared in one post after another as the jack in office. This went far outside the limits of trade. The large native German population of Russia supplied small officials all over the empire, and the representatives of absentee landlords were often German stewards, religiously squeezing the peasants. It was this more than anything else that explained the genuine national enthusiasm at the beginning of the World War.

Much higher up, the Government possessed a regular supply of administrators in the German barons of the Baltic provinces; but quite apart from Germans in Russia, there was maintained a definite influence and even at times pressure by the German Government on the Russian, directed against any projects of reform. Alexander II was murdered on the day on which he had sanctioned a summons to elect local representatives to take a part in the work of legislation; and the old German Emperor William I, presumably on the advice of Bismarck, strongly and successfully discouraged the first instinct of Alexander III to complete this act as his father's political testament.

Alexander III, though he was a complete reactionary, was in no way German-minded; and his wife, the sister of our own Queen Alexandra, never forgave the Germans for their spoliation of Denmark in 1864. The Tsar himself had a much more recent grievance for the way in which Bismarck had disappointed Russia of the fruits of her triumph over Turkey at the Treaty of Berlin. Though a hot-tempered man, he kept the peace and set himself to consolidate the resources of his empire; but from this time onwards Russian policy assumed that her next international danger would come in the form of an attack launched by Germany with the support of Austria. It was this that brought Alexander III, solely for his own reinsurance, first to encourage French trade in Russia, then to allow military conversations with the French general staff, and, at the very end of his reign, to conclude an alliance with France. It was a measure of defence and common sense; and it overrode the immense political and psychological differences that separated the two governments.

Alexander III's ablest statesman, Sergius Witte, was fully at one with his sovereign in his policy of peace and trade; and he fought the German exploitation of Russia successfully in a tariff war which enabled him to conclude favourable terms in the tariff treaty of 1894. However, he cultivated friendly relations with Germany and conceived the idea of a peaceful and economic bloc of the continental powers, to hold in check the economic predominance of England.[1] When, after a few months' interval, William II ascended the throne of his grandfather, he paid an early visit to Russia and set himself to win the friendship of Witte. He accepted Witte's view, with a great deal of personal flattery, which was very fully appreciated; he even invited Witte to

[1] Witte, ii, 199.

correspond with him direct through the German Embassy whenever he desired. Witte used this opportunity later in a domain for which he was not responsible, that of foreign policy, in order to get the Kaiser to press his views on Witte's own sovereign, a manœuvre which was discovered and treated in the way which it deserved.[1]

No greater contrast could be imagined than between the characters of William II and Nicholas II; and their changing relations have been made manifest in the published letters, in not very good English, of the first to the second. William, thinking along his own lines and taking little account of the thoughts of others, is tactless, full of flattery, at times domineering and often vulgar. Nicholas, very conscious of his own weakness, has, at the same time, a sure instinct which tells him at once when anyone is trying to rush him. It was said of him: 'He hates everyone whom he fears, and there is no one whom he fears more than William.'

William succeeded in restoring the old custom by which each of the two sovereigns put one of his personal attachés at the service of the other. 'The more private and intime affairs', he wrote, 'could as in olden times go directly by them, which makes matters much simpler.'[2] Or, as he puts it later, Nicholas will then be able 'to quickly communicate with me "*le cas échéant*", without the lumbering and indiscreet apparatus of Chancelleries, Embassies, etc.'[3]

In the first place William, like Meshchersky, set himself in this correspondence to flatter in every way Nicholas's confidence in his autocracy and wisdom; for instance, 'I am most astonished at his [Kuropatkin's] short-sightedness in not implicitly obeying your commands.'[4] He is constantly instilling on a willing mind the idea of absolutism: 'The task which has been set us by the Lord of all Lords.'[5] '. . . This way ensures the executive once for all to the "*autocratic Czar*" and not to a leading *Minister* with a board of helpless Colleagues, blindly following his lead.'[6] For the great bulk of your people still place their faith in their *Väterchen* the Czar and worship his hallowed person.'[7] He prances gloriously in the unasked advice which he tenders in the middle of the Tsar's difficulties of 1905, on the plea that he has collected 'the European

[1] WITTE, I, 160.
[2] W. to N., Oct. 25th, 1895, p. 28.
[3] ibid., June 6th, 1904, 120.
[4] ibid., June 6th, 1904, 117.
[5] ibid., Jan. 4th, 1898, 44.
[6] ibid., Feb. 6th, 1905, 162.
[7] ibid., Feb. 21st, 1905, 167.

opinion' which might not be known to Nicholas 'in your solitude at Tsarske'. He gives his prescription of how to deal with the Russian people,[1] and he concludes: 'the people will be deeply touched and cheer you and fall on their knees and pray for you.'[2] He speaks later of 'countries which are happily not yet under the absolute domination of those infernal Parliaments.'[3]

On the question of Russian foreign policy he is equally profuse in his advice. Russia has to go eastward. This was the prescription attributed to Bismarck. 'Russia has nothing to do in the west; she can only catch Nihilism and other diseases, her mission is in Asia; there she represents civilization.' The obvious advantage to Germany and Austria was that this would leave the Balkans to German penetration. William, therefore, from the first combines his doctrine of Russian autocracy with that of eastern empire.

> For that [he writes] is clearly the great task of the future for Russia, to cultivate the Asian Continent and to defend Europe from the inroads of the Great Yellow Race. In this you will always find me on your side, ready to help you as best I can. You have well understood that call of Providence, and have quickly grasped the moment; it is of immense political and historical value and much good will come of it[4] . . . Europe had to be thankful to you that you so quickly had perceived the great future for Russia in the cultivation of Asia and in the Defence of the Cross and the old Christian European culture against the inroads of the Mongols and Buddhism . . . I would let nobody try to interfere with you and attack from behind in Europe during the time you were fulfilling the great mission which Heaven has shaped for you. That was as sure as Amen in Church.[5]

Later, when offering his famous allegorical picture of Russia's mission:

> Will you kindly accept a drawing I have sketched for you showing the Symbolizing figures of Russia and Germany as sentinels at the Yellow Sea for the proclamation of the Gospel of Truth and Light in the East. I drew the sketch in the Xmas week under the blaze of the lights of the Xmas trees![6]

[1] W. to N., Feb. 21st, 1905, 168 ff.
[2] ibid., Feb. 21st, 1905, 180.
[3] ibid., Sept. 26th, 1905, 213.
[4] ibid., March 26th, 1895, 11.
[5] ibid., July 10th, 1895, 13.
[6] ibid., Jan. 4th, 1898, 45.

And on the eve of the Japanese War:

> Therefore it is evident to every unbiased mind that Korea must and will be Russian.[1]

Throughout, William is constantly suggesting that the French are untrue to their alliance with Russia. This he does in the crudest way and sometimes with the most vulgar metaphors. Equally he is always explaining the intrigues of England, on which he sometimes offers, 'only for yourself', secret evidence of his own. There is a delightful passage in which he explains his methods of secret service:

> I have ordered my fleet to shadow the British and when they have anchored to lay themselves near the British Fleet to give them a dinner and make them as drunk as possible to find out what they are about; and then sail off again![2]

However Nicholas had no special reason to be grateful for his friend's incitements to the Japanese adventure, and indeed must have been rather disgusted when the friend himself advised him to make an early peace; and what Nicholas felt, was even more strongly felt by the Russian educated public. William repeatedly boasts of the great services which he had rendered by 'guarding' Russia's rear during the war, presumably from attack by Germany and Austria, against whom had been directed all Russia's military measures of defence since the Treaty of Berlin. The moral was that Nicholas should feel free to denude his western frontier of troops. For such a generous friendship he demanded a high price. In the middle of the war (1904) Witte's successful Tariff Treaty of 1894 was due for revision, and its unhappy author was sent to Berlin to make what was in reality a general surrender. Yet Russia, defeated and with a comparatively empty treasury, could not secure financial aid from Germany and had to turn again to France to meet her need.

The tide was now running fast another way, and William made one more desperate attempt to restore the old friendship. He urgently asked for a treaty of alliance, and after some correspondence arranged for a surprise meeting of their respective yachts at Björkö off the coast of Finland in July 1905. William

[1] W. to N., Jan. 3rd, 1904, 105. [2] ibid., Aug. 25th, 1905, 204.

was accompanied by Tschirschky, an official of his foreign office, bringing with him a draft treaty; the unsuspecting Nicholas had no Minister with him except that of the Navy. William succeeded in forcing Nicholas to accept a treaty of offensive and defensive alliance between Russia and Germany, which was only to be communicated to France after the fact, with an invitation to join if she wanted. The Naval Minister, Birilev, has said that when he was asked to countersign the treaty, the Tsar held his hand over the contents; Nicholas was his Commander-in-Chief, and he held it to be his duty to sign anything that he was told to sign.[1] The Russian Foreign Minister was only informed later.

These were the circumstances in which Witte returned from his success in signing peace with Japan at Portsmouth on far better terms than Russia had a right to expect. Russia was in the thick of the crisis which led to the concession of the constitutional manifesto of October 30th, 1905. It was obvious that of the officials known to him, Nicholas had none but Witte who was capable of dealing with the internal situation. This was understood elsewhere; and on his way back Witte received two invitations to a visit, one from King Edward VII and one from the Kaiser.[2] After obtaining leave from his sovereign, he accepted the second, and stayed for a few days with William at his hunting box at Rominten near the Russian frontier. William flattered him up to the eyes, conferring on him a decoration which he carefully explained was usually reserved for members of ruling families; but he did not speak in more than hints of what had taken place in Björkö, of which the Russian Foreign Minister, Count Lamsdorff, had himself not been informed for a fortnight afterwards. Lamsdorff often consulted with Witte on foreign affairs and generally shared his views; and on Witte's return to Russia the two of them in their different ways, Lamsdorff suavely and Witte crudely, both made it clear to Nicholas that he could not possibly engage in such a treaty without preliminary agreement with the French; and Nicholas, as best he could, shuffled out of the alliance, though William, with the words 'God is our testator' continued to address him as 'your friend and ally'. That was the end of that friendship. Nicholas was no doubt all the more resentful that for the time his hand had been forced.

[1] Izvolsky, 60. [2] Witte, I, 406.

In the Russian public there was more resentment against William's incitements to the disastrous war with Japan than against the Anglo-Japanese Treaty, which, after all, prevented the war from becoming general. In the rising tide of Russian liberalism there was every sympathy with British principles of government. England already had her *Entente* with France, the ally of Russia; and her help was regarded as a possible and very valuable supplement to the economic aid which France supplied and Germany had refused. By the failure of the Japanese War, Russia was driven back into Europe; and Balkan questions, which had always been the chief preoccupation of Russian public opinion, resumed their importance. Izvolsky, as Russian Minister in Copenhagen, and Count Peter Benckendorff, as Russian Ambassador in London, were engaged in doing everything they could to promote friendship between England and Russia; and the new trend became very evident when Izvolsky, though a rather demonstrative Liberal, was appointed Foreign Minister in the Cabinet of Goremykin, which was to face the First Duma in May 1906. Stolypin, who so soon succeeded Goremykin as Premier, definitely and sincerely took as his programme resistance to revolution and the promotion of reform, and he was throughout a firm friend of England. The result of these appointments was seen a year later in the conclusion of the Anglo-Russian Convention on relations with Persia, which removed long-standing difficulties by an agreement based on the integrity of Persian territory. In the same year was established the Anglo-Russian Chamber of Commerce — the first Chamber of Commerce to be set up in Russia, of which, by his sovereign's wish, the Russian Minister of Commerce, Timiryazev, himself became the first President.[1] Two years later the leaders of all the central parties of the Duma, headed by its President, Homyakov, took part in a representative visit to Great Britain, where they received the most cordial welcome from the King, Parliament and public institutions.

The cause of British friendship had a deeper basis with the Russian educated public. At this time the finest political thinker in Russia was Peter Struve, who so often broke new ground for the rest. To Stolypin's appeal in the Duma for a 'Great Russia' he replied with an article both profound and brilliant with the same

[1] Timiryazev to B. P.

title, in which he called for a free development of all the many and various nationalities in Russia, a bold and free utilization of the economic resources of the country, a more intelligent interest in the Slavs of the Balkans, and friendship with France and England.[1] There were initiated Slavonic congresses between the representatives of Slavdom in the various parliaments of Serbia, Bulgaria, Austria, Germany and Russia, and this so called Neo-Slavophil movement followed in the main the lines which Struve had pointed out.

Suddenly into this chorus of friendship fell the bomb of the Austrian annexation of Bosnia. Izvolsky had repeated the mistake of his predecessors by trading away the rights of the Slavs of Bosnia provisionally for Austrian support, presumably in opening the Straits to Russian vessels of war. We now know that Nicholas had never been informed of Russia's previous engagements to Austria. On October 8th/21st, 1908, he writes to his mother:

> But there is something which is really most distressing and which I had no idea of till now; the other day Charykov (Russian Ambassador at Vienna) sent me some secret papers dating back to the Berlin Congress of 1878. It appears from them that, after endless controversy, Russia consented to a possible future annexation of Bosnia and Herzegovina by Austria. I have now received a letter from the old Emperor (Francis Joseph of Austria) calling my attention to this consent, given by Anpapa (Alexander II, Nicholas's grandfather). What an awkward situation! His letter came two weeks ago, and I have not answered it yet. You will understand what an unpleasant surprise this is, and what an embarrassing position we are in. As I said before, I never knew of the existence of such a secret paragraph and never heard about it either from Giers or Lobanov, in whose times all this happened.[2]

Izvolsky was completely outwitted by the Austrian Minister Aehrenthal, for he never got his *quid pro quo* from the other signatories to previous treaties. Austria announced the annexation of Bosnia; and, to make the pill more unappetizing, Bulgaria, who had owed her liberation to the Russian arms, now, clearly acting under cover of the Austrian announcement, declared her final

[1] *The Russian Review*, II, 4 (translation). [2] N. to M. F., 236.

independence of Turkey and gave her sovereign Ferdinand the title of Tsar. The Bosnians, as the close kinsmen of the Serbs, could not properly be willed away in this manner. Stolypin, who was a keen Slav patriot, called Izvolsky sharply to task and seriously thought of resigning.[1] Izvolsky, though a Liberal, defended himself by the plea that foreign affairs were in the exclusive competence of the sovereign and his Foreign Minister. This would appeal to Nicholas, and no doubt helped to secure Izvolsky's retention in office; but the Cabinet were all with Stolypin. Serbia appealed urgently for support to Russia, and the new understanding with England and France was thoroughly tested. It held good, for both France and England gave loyal support; but this was unavailing for Russia; for Germany at this time appeared 'in shining armour' behind Austria, and Russia herself could not take up the challenge so soon after the Japanese War and the internal convulsions of 1905. It was known at the time that no one felt more resentment at this defeat than Nicholas himself. He wrote to his mother on March 18th/31st, 1909, 'Once the matter had been put as definitely and unequivocally as that, there was nothing for it but to swallow one's pride, give in and agree'. He mentions that on this 'the Ministers were unanimous'. He adds next day, 'It is quite true that the form and method of Germany's action — I mean towards us — has simply been brutal, and we shan't forget it. I think they were again trying to separate us from France and England; but once again they have undoubtedly failed. Such methods tend to bring about the opposite result.'[2] Nothing was more striking than the unanimity of all the different Slavonic societies in Russia, associated with the most various and contradictory political views.

From this time onwards, it was generally felt that the Austro-German challenge was sure to be repeated and that next time it would certainly be accepted. The public mind already prepared itself for a defensive war. Meanwhile Austrian agents traversed Poland, getting contact with revolutionary or malcontent feeling and offering to arm the Poles against Russia, taking little trouble to conceal themselves from the Russian authorities.

It was now generally assumed that Germany, with the support of Austria, was determined to break out in one direction or

[1] Kokovtsev, I, 335-6. [2] N. to M. F., 240-2.

another. There were three choices. First there was the way of peaceful penetration in Russia which had already yielded such very solid results. This, of course, excluded the idea of war. Germany had been able to rely on such strong support at Court, in the bureaucracy, and among the upper classes in Russia, that she could almost dare to claim a monopoly of Russian friendship, and she had long been gradually establishing a preponderance in Russian trade relations. A second direction lay south-eastward. Here Germany would make use of Austria; she would absorb Slavonic elements into the Austrian fold, thus joining hands with Turkey, where German influence was already predominant, and, by means of the Baghdad railway, was stretching out an arm in the directions of Egypt and India. This would involve the entirely new claim that Balkan affairs, which it had been an axiom to settle by agreement between Austria and Russia, were now in the sole purview of Austria and Germany, and no Russian sovereign, least of all in a national Russia with a national representation, could afford to admit this claim. Such a course was sure to mean something like open conflict with the Duma, elected on a restricted middle-class franchise. The third way, which has been called in Germany, 'the crusaders' policy', led down the English Channel to the open seas and to colonies, and meant a conflict both with France and England. The economic life of Germany, teeming with energy and full of expert knowledge, imperatively demanded an outlet. It was the misfortune of her central position in Europe that she could not, or anyhow did not, make up her mind as to the choice, and ultimately found herself pursuing both the second and third courses together. The typical merchant of Germany would of course be for continued peaceful penetration of Russia. The sabre-rattling Junker of East Prussia would favour the heroic outlet, past the opposition of England.

There followed a further division of opinions as to the direction of strategy in the event of a world war. Here again there was a choice. The main effort might be launched in an attempt to crush Russia without delay; but the lesson of Napoleon showed that delay was inevitable, and France, who could mobilize far more quickly than Russia, would, by the terms of her alliance, at once be a danger to Western Germany. Thus developed the idea which later took shape, of 'lunching in Paris and dining in St. Petersburg'.

The Tsar did not dismiss Aehrenthal's unfortunate dupe, Izvolsky; both he and his mother felt that that would look like another triumph for Austria and Germany;[1] but Izvolsky, self-centred, nervous and now attacked all round, felt that he had really lost out, and prepared to take cover as Russian Ambassador in Paris. The two possible successors were Charykov and Sazonov, and Izvolsky had already established Sazonov as his assistant. Sazonov was a small, almost timid-looking man of good, though not exceptional, intelligence, but of complete honesty. He was a not too usual example of a diplomat who through good and evil report stood always for one central idea. That idea was the creation of friendship between Russia and England, and it was with this object in view, at a time when such a cause seemed quite hopeless, that he took the decision of entering the diplomatic service while staying at Ventnor in the Isle of Wight.[2] He was profoundly religious, with very much of the Slavophil in him. He was deeply interested in the possibility of a real understanding between Orthodoxy and Anglicanism; one of his friends was Mr. W. J. Birkbeck, then the principal authority in England on the Orthodox Church. He had a broad conception of a common Slavonic policy. These simple convictions gave a real strength to what would not otherwise have been a strong character. Nicholas completely trusted Sazonov, and indeed he was a man of such transparent honesty and devotion that it was impossible to do otherwise. Sazonov's opportunity had come with the now strong trend in Russia towards friendship with England, for the conduct of which he was the most fitting instrument; and the personal friendship which he brought into all these relations made him an ideal co-operator when friendship by the turn of events became alliance.

Sazonov, like his brother-in-law Stolypin, and like Kokovtsev, was one of those Ministers who took the most serious account of the Third Duma, with which he had so much in common. At the institution of the Duma three subjects had been specially 'iron-clad' or marked off as prerogatives of the sovereign; they were the fighting services, foreign loans, and foreign policy. The ingenious Izvolsky, though a professed Liberal, had on this ground tried to cover his rout by claiming to be independent both of the Duma

[1] M. F. to N., 242-3. [2] Sazonov to B. P.

and of the Cabinet. Sazonov, on the other hand, took the Duma fully into his confidence, and did not at this time suffer with his sovereign for doing so. In 1909 he gave the fullest support to an unofficial initiative which resulted in the visit of the leaders of the six central parties in the Duma, headed by their President, to England.† This visit came just after the Bosnian crisis, and just before the celebration of the second centenary of Peter the Great's victory at Poltava. In 1912, after some difficulties, was organized a return visit of British public men to Russia, including representatives of both Houses of Parliament, of Church, army and navy, universities and the business world[1].† In Russia they met with an even greater cordiality from the Emperor, the Duma and the public alike; and from this time forward unofficial committees of a strongly representative kind on both sides continued to work out details of economic and intellectual co-operation between the two countries. There was a much greater interplay than before in trade relations; and England definitely came to count in lightening the political atmosphere in Russia. At each new contact this was unquestionably a factor in the relations between the Tsar and his people and in the gradual progress towards constitutionalism in Russia. These developments were received with open dissatisfaction by official Germany, and the *Hamburger Nachrichten* declared that everything ought to have been done to prevent all this from happening. Sir E. Grey on his side throughout contributed to them as much as Sazonov, but in pursuance of his counsels the movement was scrupulously kept within the limits of a friendship between the two peoples.

Grey, in the clean record of his *Twenty-five Years*, narrates five successive crises which might have led to a world war. The line which he followed was the same throughout. He had the peculiar good fortune — or was it the spell of his own conspicuous honesty? — that throughout these crises the representation of the Great Powers in London remained unchanged, and that he possessed not only the full confidence, but, it may be claimed, even the friendship of these colleagues. At each crisis he asked that the solution should be sought in London, and that is how in the first four instances the danger was successfully averted.

The next crisis again came from the Balkans. As Rambaud,

[1] *The Russian Review*, vol. 1, No. 2.

the historian of Russia, has explained with French lucidity, there was a certain law of gravitation in the Balkans by which those small States nearest to Austria relied on the protection of Russia, and those nearest to Russia sought the support of Austria, which of course also meant Germany; but there was also another movement always growing stronger, by which each sought to be ultimately master of its own destiny.[1] The one thing that had seemed quite impossible was that they should all on this basis unite for a common end; and this, largely by the genius of the Greek Premier, Venizelos, was unexpectedly achieved in 1912, when the Balkan Powers in common went to war with Turkey, to complete their own liberation. Once the enterprise was launched, it was taken for granted in all the European chancelleries that the League would be defeated. The result was the opposite. The Turks were defeated all round and driven to accept terms of peace.

The alliance would have been of little service, if there had not been secured in advance an agreement as to the division of conquests on a basis of national self-determination. The Great Powers had looked on with surprise and apprehension, and had so far confined themselves to an intention, in case of the triumph of Turkey, to safeguard as far as possible the *status quo*. But the occasion for Austria to push her claims further was not likely to be missed; and with German support, she intervened to upset the division of spoils. It will not be forgotten that at the moment when Austria declared her annexation of Bosnia, Bulgaria, obviously by preconcerted arrangement, had declared her absolute independence of Turkey. The Bulgarians had borne a great deal of the brunt of the war. The portion of the settlement challenged by Austria related to Serbia and was directed towards preventing her from obtaining that access to the Adriatic which could have made her independent of Austrian tariffs. It was Austria's object to keep Serbia locked up in a kind of economic ring.

Again followed a European crisis. The Russian policy was badly muddled. Sazonov induced the Tsar to offer his good offices to the former Balkan Allies, Serbia and Bulgaria, for the discussion of their differences in St. Petersburg.[2] This had already been foreseen in their treaty of alliance;[3] but though both parties gave a formal acceptance, it was not likely to lead to any result.

[1] RAMBAUD, *Histoire de Russie*, 782. [2] SAZONOV, 92. [3] ibid., 86.

While Serbia, who engaged the popular sympathy of Russia, was ready to lean on her, Bulgaria had gravitated towards Austria; and Austria might reasonably complain if Russia claimed to settle dissensions in the Balkans without her. The Powers of the Triple Entente, France and England did their best to help; but in their anxiety to avoid a world war, which they could not have justified to their peoples on such grounds, they accepted a compromise by which there was created for the first time an independent Albania. At one point, it even became necessary in the cause of world peace to make a joint naval demonstration of the Powers in the Adriatic to reduce the claims of another of the victorious Powers, Montenegro.

This upsetting of the agreement between the Balkan allies led the Serbs to claim compensation elsewhere in the direction of the Aegean, and this raised again the thorny question of Macedonia, where it was almost impossible to make any discrimination between rival Bulgarian and Serbian interests. The Bulgars took the bull by the horns and strongly attacked their former allies. Their onslaught was beaten off, and Bulgaria now remained isolated as against the other partners. Even Rumania, which had taken no part in the war, joined in against her, and the Turks seized the chance to regain Adrianople. Bulgaria, exhausted by her previous successful efforts in the war, lay helpless; and European diplomacy imposed in London a peace of compromise, of which it has been said that no single transfer of territory was justified on ethnical grounds.

There was an outburst of indignation in St. Petersburg, in which Duma men, headed by their President, Rodzyanko, took an unwise and unseemly part;[1] and Sazonov, who had seen many of his own hopes ruined, had great difficulty in keeping the country out of war. In this he had the firm support of his sovereign; but it is also interesting to note that one of the chief contributing factors was the direct influence of Rasputin. 'Fear, fear War', he said with good reason;[2] and later Alexandra reminds her husband: 'He always said that the Balkans were not worth fighting for.' A reactionary paper, without naming him, even gave him publicly the credit for the preservation of peace.

Bulgaria had made a great mistake, and had paid a very heavy

[1] RODZYANKO, 82. [2] SIMANOVICH, 150.

price for it. Her cause had been separated from that of the other small Slav peoples, and, as in 1909, she placed her hopes of a reversal of her fortunes in Austria and Germany. Russia, meanwhile, cultivated the good will of a junior member of the alliance of the Central European Powers, Rumania; and Sazonov promoted the idea of a marriage between Carol, the future king, and the Tsar's eldest daughter Olga. The imperial family crossed the Black Sea to pay a visit to the Rumanian royal family at Constanza; but Olga, who had a will of her own, obtained a promise from her father that he would leave her free to make her own choice,[1] and her mother, as she explained to Sazonov, was strongly against a foreign marriage.[2] The whole family was entirely devoted to Russia.

During the Balkan complications in the first half of 1913, Austria had increased her forces on the Russian frontier, bringing up to war strength her three corps in Galicia; and to this the Russian Government had replied by suspending the discharge of reservists. Sukhomlinov, the War Minister, nearly succeeded in bringing about a partial mobilization, but this was stopped by Kokovtsev.[3]

Another cause of contention soon arose. Germany admittedly regarded the failure of the Turks in the recent war as showing up the insufficiency of the German military instruction, directed by General von der Goltz – the Kaiser even described it as a 'fiasco'. The German military authorities made a new arrangement by which General Liman von Sanders should take over this work and be appointed commander of the Second Turkish Army Corps, which was stationed in Constantinople. Turkey was also employing British instructors for her fleet; but Admiral Limpus had no such authority as that which was now proposed for Sanders. Bismarck had declared in 1896 that, 'the furtherance of Austria-Hungary's Balkan ambitions is less the affair of Germany than of any other State', and this new and vigorous departure from his view was greatly resented by the Russian Government. German control of the Straits was also little likely to suit either France or England. The German reply to Russian remonstrances was that it was a purely military move undertaken even without the knowledge of the German Chancellor, and that the matter had gone

[1] GILLIARD, 61-2. [2] SAZONOV, 110. [3] ibid., 83; KOKOVTSEV, II, 123-4.

too far for any withdrawal. Sazonov arranged that the Russian Premier, Kokovtsev, who was passing through Berlin on his way back to Russia, should seek an interview with the German authorities. Kokovtsev saw the German Chancellor, Bethmann Hollweg who, while entirely friendly, disclaimed authority for military measures. The French Ambassador in Berlin, it proved, had not been informed of the German intentions. But the Kaiser, who received Kokovtsev next day (Nov. 19th) showed great irritation at Russia's objections and asked if they were an ultimatum. To Davydov, head of the Russian Credit Office, who sat next to him at lunch, he spoke with even greater sharpness. He said to him: 'I must tell you frankly that I fear there will be a clash between Slav and German, and I feel it my duty to apprise you of this fact.'[1] Kokovtsev came to the conclusion that a war in the near future was inevitable. On his return to Russia he reported this in the plainest terms to the Tsar, to which the poor Nicholas, standing by the window and looking out on the Black Sea, replied dreamily: 'In all the will of God.'[2] The crisis was settled by the promotion of Sanders to a higher rank as Inspector General of the Turkish Army, but without command of the Second Army Corps.[3]

In the conviction that a German attack was imminent, Sazonov summoned in February 1914 a conference on imperial defence, at which it became clear that there would be extreme difficulty in parrying the blow. The conference of course became known to the German Government, and has since been represented as a proof of Russia's intention to attack Germany.[4]

Sazonov now energetically sought alliance with England, and Nicholas made the same plea to the British Ambassador, Sir George Buchanan, with the words: 'Then we can sleep safe in our beds' (June 15th, 1914).[5] Sazonov, like his sovereign, pleaded that an alliance would be a strong deterrent to war. Sir Arthur Nicolson, formerly Ambassador in St. Petersburg, who was now at the head of the British Foreign Office, supported this plea. Grey refused; and though the matter is one of opinion, it must be strongly urged that he was right. There were still difficult complications between Russia and England, particularly in the course

[1] KOKOVTSEV, II, 219-29. [2] ibid., 241-2. [3] SAZONOV, 128. [4] ibid., 126. [5] BUCHANAN, I, 187.

of events in Persia and the action of Russian consuls there. Grey's parliamentary situation was curious. He represented a great majority consisting of very diverse elements: on the one hand Liberals like himself, and on the other the growing forces of Labour and also the Irish members. In home politics Grey stood with these forces opposed to the Conservatives; in foreign policy there was a practical identity between the Liberals and the Conservatives, but the other section of the Government majority was often in opposition. It may be represented that it would have been quite impossible for the War to have found England a united nation, if Grey had previously committed her to an alliance with the Government of the Tsar.

The Poles, who could only hope for a restoration of their country to the map of Europe through a world convulsion, were following all these developments with the greatest alertness. In Austrian Poland Pilsudski possessed an agreement with the Austrian Chief of Staff, Conrad von Hoetzendorff, by which Polish legions were to be armed in the Austrian cause. On the other hand Dmowski, the principal leader in Russian Poland, organized a meeting in Austria of Poles from all the three partitions, at which they decided to stand with Russia against Austria — solely for the reason that France was Russia's ally and England might become so.

On June 28th, 1914, the Archduke Francis Ferdinand, heir to the Austrian throne, and his morganatic wife were shot dead during their visit to the Bosnian capital, Sarajevo. The Archduke was disposed in favour of some political recognition of the enormous Slav population (nearly three-fifths of the whole) in what was called the dual monarchy of Austria-Hungary. He had gone to preach an Austrian patriotism in Serbian, that is to say Slavonic, Bosnia. He chose the very anniversary of Serbia's greatest defeat, when she was crushed by the Turks in the battle of Kosovo (1389), a day which she had ever since, in hope of a better fate, observed as her national feast-day.

The tension had somewhat died down when the new President of the French Republic, Poincaré, visited the Tsar at Kronstadt on July 20th. The Tsar, who had a great personal liking for him, gave him the most cordial reception; but there was an unnecessary excitement in the details of the military entertainment.[1] It was

[1] Paléologue, I, 14.

at this moment that the Austrian Ambassador in St. Petersburg unexpectedly returned from his holiday and inquiries were made at the Russian Foreign Office as to the exact time of Poincaré's departure. Too late for the news to reach St. Petersburg before he left, the Austrian Government launched an ultimatum to Serbia couched in the most extravagant terms (July 23rd). The complicity of the Serbian Government in the murder of the Archduke was assumed, and she was called upon to allow Austrian officials to take part in the examination of her own; she was even to submit her schools to an Austrian control of propaganda. Had she agreed to the terms, she could not have remained an independent State. That Austria's intentions were entirely hostile must be concluded from the words of Count Hoyos, Chief of Count Berchthold's Chancellory: 'The Austrian demands are such that no State possessing the smallest amount of national pride or dignity could accept them.'[1] As was inevitable, she made a desperate appeal for the advice and good offices of Russia. The Tsar was all for peace; but replied that 'in no case would Russia remain indifferent to the fate of Serbia'.[2] Sazonov advised the Serbian Premier, Pashich, to accept all of the Austrian terms which were compatible with Serbian independence. Before the advice arrived, Pashich had sent the most conciliatory answer, challenging little more than the Austrian claim that Austro-Hungarian officials should take part in the judicial inquiry into the alleged complicity of the Serbian authorities. On the receipt of the reply, for which a time limit of forty-eight hours had been set by Austria, the Austrian legation left Belgrade.

Sazonov's first effort on hearing of the ultimatum was to obtain an extension of the time-limit. This was refused by Austria. He then tried to get the good offices of Germany, but again without success. Germany followed up the Austrian ultimatum with a declaration that this was a quarrel between Austria and Serbia, which only concerned those two countries. It must be clearly understood that it was on this contention that the Great War was fought. For nearly two hundred years it had come to be taken for granted that, in any radical change in relations in the Balkans, the only way to guarantee European peace was to secure agreement between Austria and Russia. As Sazonov later

[1] Sazonov, 175-6. [2] ibid., 178.

expressly said to the Tsar, no Russian sovereign could have been forgiven by Russia for weakly accepting the arbitrary elimination of this axiom.

Francis Joseph, even before the launching of the ultimatum, had on July 6th written to William II: 'The efforts of my Government must henceforth be directed to the isolation and diminution of Serbia . . . This will only be possible when Serbia, the pivot of Pan-Slavist policy, has ceased to be counted as a political factor in the Balkans.'[1] At a meeting of the Austrian Cabinet on July 7th it was agreed that Serbia should be reduced in size, and the Premier, Count Stürkgh, recommended the dethronement of the Karageorgevich dynasty and some measure of military dependence of Serbia on Austria. The challenge to Russia, though not yet fully known, was in reality direct. More than that, Germany as well as Austria was perfectly aware that this was a moment when Russia was in no way ready for war. The date of the Great War was accurately foretold to me over a year in advance by one of the spokesmen of the Imperial Defence Committee of the Duma, and the ground was given; namely, that in July 1914 Russia would be at the most difficult stage in the radical reorganization of her forces. William II, in a marginal note on the subject used the expression, 'now or never',[2] and in a dispatch of July 24th he wrote: 'Austria-Hungary must have a preponderating influence to the exclusion of Russia in the small Balkan States: otherwise we shall never have peace.'[3] Italy, however, the third partner of the Triple Alliance, made it clear that she did not consider the question one in which her obligations were binding.

On July 28th, Austria declared war on Serbia, and bombarded the Serbian capital Belgrade on the 29th. This of course presumed a preliminary movement of troops, but she did not mobilize against Russia till the 31st. On the 28th Russia decided at a special Council at Krasnoe Selo to prepare for the mobilization of the four Russian military districts on the Austrian frontier, and on the morning of the 29th the order was printed for this partial mobilization. On the 29th came inaccurate news of an Austrian general mobilization. Russia ordered a general mobilization. William

[1] *Austro-Hungarian Diplomatic Documents*, 1919, No. 10, 89.
[2] *Kautsky's Diplomatic Documents*, 1, No. 7, 11.
[3] ibid., No. 155, 168.

had returned from his summer cruise in the fjords of Norway on the 28th. After the humble reply of Serbia to the Austrian ultimatum he had written to his Foreign Minister Jagow: 'Now that Serbia has given in, all grounds for war have disappeared'; though he suggested that Austria should hold a pledge in the shape of some Serbian territory. But he was entirely opposed to a Russian general mobilization, and he telegraphed to Nicholas that military measures by Russia ... would accelerate a calamity 'which both of us desire to avoid'. Nicholas replied offering to refer the whole controversy to the Hague Tribunal (July 29th). He sent the message direct from his Palace at Peterhof to Potsdam, and in the stress of the crisis he omitted to inform Sazonov, so that the telegram was only recovered in January 1915 when it was printed in the Russian *Government Messenger*. This appeal was left without reply on the German side. No reply had been received to the Russian request that Germany would urge Austria to renew negotiations with Russia; the view of the German Government was that it could not interfere. Nicholas countermanded the Russian general mobilization; but according to Buchanan 'the military authorities allowed it ... to proceed without his knowledge'.[1]

On the 27th Sir E. Grey, in reply to a request of Sazonov on the 25th that he would mediate, had proposed to Germany that the question should be referred to a conference of ambassadors in London, a suggestion which was at once accepted by Sazonov. At this time the German Ambassador in London, Lichnowsky, was evidently being kept in the dark by his own Government, and his task was presumably limited to keeping England out of the war. Grey's proposal was not accepted by Germany.

On the 28th the German Ambassador in Petersburg, Count Pourtalès, lunched at the British Embassy with Sir George Buchanan. He was confident that Russia would avoid war, as in the crisis of 1908-09. It has been mentioned earlier that at this time the growing friction between the Russian Government and the Duma and the rising resentment in the country in general had led to strikes in St. Petersburg, and barricades were even being raised in the streets. According to Pourtalès, Russia was on the verge of a revolution and would have to give in again. Sir George

[1] Buchanan, I, 200.

expressed his strong disagreement and ultimately took the German by the shoulders and said to him: 'Count Pourtalès, Russia means it.'[1]

On the 30th came the news that the Austrians had shelled Belgrade. Sazonov proposed to Austria a joint consideration as to whether it was not possible for her to modify the terms of her ultimatum, in which case the Russian military measures should stop; but this, too, was not accepted. News reached St. Petersburg that at 1.0 p.m. there had been published in the *Lokal Anzeiger*, in Berlin, the announcement of a German general mobilization. Directly afterwards this announcement was disavowed by telephone, and this too was at once telegraphed to Russia by the Russian Ambassador, Sverbeyev; but the transit from Germany of this second telegram was considerably delayed.[2]

At two o'clock Sazonov was rung up by the youthful chief of the Russian General Staff, Yanushkevich. He and the War Minister, Sukhomlinov, demanded Sazonov's presence at once. On his arrival they explained to him that a partial mobilization, such as had already been ordered must, in the slow Russian conditions, where railway transport was so inferior to that of Germany or Austria, inevitably dislocate a general mobilization, if that should be declared later. They asked Sazonov at once to represent this to the Tsar.

Sazonov's telephone call to Tsarskoe Selo was answered in person by the Emperor himself, and at 3.10 p.m. the two were in conference. Sazonov reported that in the last two days the position had so much changed for the worse that there was no more hope of preserving peace.[3] He then presented the request of the two Russian generals, explaining the enormous advantage that any delay would give to Germany. The Tsar bowed his head in agreement. He showed Sazonov a masterful telegram which he had received from William in which the suggestion of submitting the conflict to the Hague Tribunal was left without reply. William only declared that unless the Russian mobilization was stopped, he could not accede to the request of Nicholas that he should mediate: nothing was said of the military measures already taken by Austria.

[1] Buchanan to B. P. [2] Sazonov, 198.
[3] ibid., 202.

> He is asking the impossible [said the Tsar]. He has forgotten, or does not wish to remember, that the Austrian mobilization had begun sooner than the Russian, and now asks us to stop ours without saying a word about the Austrian. You know I have already suppressed one mobilization decree, and then consented only to a partial one. If I agreed to Germany's demands now, we should find ourselves unarmed against the Austrian Army, which is mobilized already. It would be madness.

Sazonov expressed his full agreement and repeated his conclusion that war was now unavoidable. After a short silence the Tsar said:

> This would mean sending hundreds of thousands of Russian people to their death. How can one help hesitating to take such a step?

Sazonov assured him that he had on his side done everything that he could to avoid war, even at a great sacrifice of the national pride. The enemy, he said, were 'determined to increase their power by enslaving our natural allies in the Balkans, destroying our influence there and reducing Russia to a pitiful dependence upon the arbitrary will of the Central Powers'. The Tsar, writes Sazonov, 'remained silent and his face showed the traces of a terrible inner struggle. At last, speaking with difficulty, he said: "You are right. There is nothing left us but to get ready for an attack upon us. Give then the Chief of the General Staff my order for mobilization." ' The moment Yanushkevich had received this order by telephone, he mentioned that the telephone was out of order. His meaning, as Sazonov fully understood, was that he expected the Emperor again to countermand his decision. The general mobilization was ordered at 4 p.m.

Grey had in vain asked Germany to moderate the claims of Austria. Sazonov had suggested that both sides should hold their hands, and Nicholas promised William that the Russian troops should not cross the frontier while negotiations were still proceeding. Sazonov even accepted from Grey a modification of his formula for a respite, admitting for the time being the continued presence of Austrian troops in Serbia.[1]

At 11.35 p.m. on July 31st, Count Pourtalès came to the

[1] SAZONOV, 193.

Foreign Office and presented an ultimatum. Russia was to stop her general mobilization in twelve hours and give an explanation of the military measures which she had taken. Nothing was offered on the other side. The next day (Aug. 1st) at ten minutes past seven in the evening Count Pourtalès brought to the Russian Foreign Office a German declaration of war on Russia. This document has a curious history. It was telegraphed in cipher from Berlin in two alternative versions, one for a Russian refusal of the ultimatum, the other for a request for further negotiations. In either case Count Pourtalès was to declare war. The telegram was decoded in the German Embassy, retaining both versions, the second in parentheses; and Pourtalès committed the extraordinary blunder of leaving behind him in the Foreign Office the original message, as decoded, with both alternative versions. To his request for a reply to the ultimatum Sazonov answered with a firm refusal to cancel the general mobilization, but expressed his readiness for further negotiations. Pourtalès seemed hardly to believe his ears, and when Sazonov made it clear that 'no' meant 'no', he delivered the declaration of war. He then lost all control over himself, leaned against the window and burst into tears saying, 'Who would have thought that I should be leaving St. Petersburg in such circumstances', and helped by Sazonov, he tottered from the room.[1]

[1] The whole scene is recounted in Sazonov, 312-3. On my arrival in Russia he himself gave me the account of it in the room in which the scene took place.

CHAPTER VII

SLAV AND TEUTON AT GRIPS

Beware
Of entrance to a quarrel, but, being in,
Bear 't that th' opposèd may beware of thee.
Hamlet, I, 3

THERE can be no doubt that the German challenge — which was recognized as a challenge and as German, not Austrian — raised a great wave of genuine patriotism all over Russia. Those who were there at the time met this on all sides.† It acted as a tonic. The barricades, which had been set up, went down of themselves. Workmen brought in to the authorities leaflets inciting to revolution, which they traced to the German Embassy. It was a dominating building on one of the chief squares surmounted by statues of magnificent horses. It was sacked on August 24th and the horses were thrown down.

On August 2nd, the day after the declaration of war, with the fresh news of the French mobilization, the Tsar met his people at three o'clock at the Winter Palace. The vast circular place in front, one of the largest of public places in Europe, was thronged with an immense crowd of all classes. Inside the palace were the French Ambassador, the heads of the army, the Government and the Chambers of Legislature; and the Tsar, going out on to the balcony, repeated word for word the oath of his predecessor Alexander I on the invasion of Napoleon that he would not make peace until the last foreign soldier had left Russian territory, an oath which he kept to the very end. The vast multitude fell upon their knees and sang 'God save the Tsar' as it had never been sung before and also the beautiful hymn, 'Lord, Save Thy People and Bless Thine Inheritance', calling down the divine protection on Russia in time of war. It was the Square which in 1905 had witnessed 'Bloody Sunday' that now saw this tremendous scene of national enthusiasm. There is a Russian word *sobornost*, typifying the religious unity which may be felt in a great cathedral or at any moment when the community is everything and the individual only has significance as a member of it. Nicholas was as sensible of this great mass-mood as any of his subjects, and what he felt was fully shared by others. It is the Labour leader, Kerensky, who has remarked that at that moment the monarchy had a unique opportunity of identifying itself with the people; for at that moment both alike breathed with the life of Russia. Gilliard, to whom Nicholas spoke freely next day, as he had never done before on politics, describes him as 'transformed';[1] and the Empress, whose sad, prayerful face concealed her burning Russian patriotism, talked freely to Gilliard of the insincerity of William II, adding: 'He will never pardon me this war.'[2]

Rasputin often claimed that he had averted war both in 1909 and in 1912. For reasons of humanity he was opposed to all wars, and with an insight justified by the future, he declared that sovereigns should never make war on each other.[3] He had also always said that 'the Balkans were not worth fighting about'. Specially Vyrubova records that while still lying at Pokrovskoe, recovering from his wound, he now sent a telegram: 'Let Papa not plan war; for with war will come the end of Russia and yourselves, and you will lose to the last man'—not the worst of his prophecies; but she mentions that Nicholas received this message with vexation.[4]

After Rodzyanko's vigorous and patriotic speech at the palace, the Grand Duke embraced him with the words: 'Now, Rodzyanko, I am your friend till death. I will do anything for the Duma. Tell me what you want.'[5] The one-day sitting of the Duma — they wanted no more — which took place on August 8th, corresponded in full in tone with the sitting of the British Parliament where Redmond declared that the defence of Ireland could now be left to the united forces of the north and south, or with that in the French Chamber, summed up by its President in the words 'Sursum corda' (Lift up your hearts). From every side and from every nationality in Russia came the same determination to resist the challenge. The revolutionary Parties, following the general lead of Kerensky, abstained from the actual vote of credits, but offered their whole-hearted energy in national defence. On

[1] GILLIARD, 73. [2] ibid., 74. [3] SIMANOVICH, 143. [4] VYRUBOVA, 49. [5] RODZYANKO, 111.

August 9th the Duma members, postponing all other questions, organized a committee for the wounded and war victims, and many of the more prominent among them set out to take up the posts of heads of the civil or zemstvo Red Cross attached to the various armies. Prince George Lvov, a great Liberal and an excellent Chairman, who had organized this work in the Japanese War, was able in something like a month to prepare a million beds for the wounded.[1]

The same enthusiasm pervaded the army. The mobilization was carried out with surprising rapidity and completeness, and 96 per cent of those called up reported for service.[2] Though the Russian Army rested on the basis of conscription — most fairly distributed by the great reform of 1874 without regard to birth, rank or wealth — there was a special category for volunteers who did not wait for the lot to fall upon them, and many young people of all ages streamed up to the Front. These young folk, with several of whom I wandered in no man's land, would only have joined up for a truly national war. Many of them dreamed of socialism. They turned the war into a combined school of hazard and engineering, asking for all the risky jobs such as scouting or armoured cars; some completed the whole course, passing on to aviation or even to submarine warfare. Several regiments had mascots as young as twelve, some of whom later did most daring feats.

The German ultimatum to Russia had been accompanied by another addressed to France. The declaration of war on Russia was followed in quick succession by the German ultimatum to Belgium (Aug. 2nd), the declaration of war on France (Aug. 3rd), the German entry into Belgium, the British declaration of war on Germany (Aug. 4th), the belated Austrian declaration against Russia (Aug. 6th), the flight of the *Göben* and *Breslau* to Turkish waters on August 10th and the Japanese declaration against Germany on August 22nd. The British Ambassador now took his place by the side of the French as representative of an allied country; and fortunate was it now for Britain that her spokesman was Sir George Buchanan, who embodied in himself the very highest of English character — in a word, the qualities of his chief Sir E. Grey. Between Sazonov, Buchanan and Paléologue reigned

[1] Lvov to B. P. [2] Golovin, 202.

an intimacy of friendship and confidence such as has seldom been associated with diplomacy. They met practically every day to discuss with the utmost frankness every detail of what came to be called everywhere 'the common cause'; and the simple and impressionable Tsar was himself conspicuous in his chivalry to his country's allies. This intimate connection with the democratic countries of the West had at that time an enormous moral significance for Russia; and right down to the ranks of the army ran the instinct that this war, so different from the Japanese, and undertaken for 'the younger brothers' or minor Slavonic nations, together with the new and close contact with the West was bound to bring with it reform in Russia.[1] It was an instinct grounded on realities. The greatest of Russian historians, Klyuchevsky, has written that a community only becomes a nation by going through some tremendous ordeal together. Nowhere was there any doubt of the severity of the test; and it was felt to be a matter of course that the war could only be won by sovereign and people in common.

Of the new spirit there was one significant early sign. The Tsar had himself for purely human reasons wished to share the fate of his army as commander-in-chief at the Front; but he was persuaded by the joint instances of his Premier, War Minister and Foreign Minister to give up this idea in the national interest and to appoint the Grand Duke Nicholas in his stead. On August 14th was issued in the name of the Grand Duke a manifesto to the population of Poland, where most of the fighting would take place. It made a soldierly appeal for the help of all Poles in the scattered divisions of that country, whether under Russian, Austrian or German rule, and gave an unequivocal guarantee that this would be rewarded by autonomy for a reunited Poland. The Emperor, when questioned by Count Wielepolski, declared that the Grand Duke had spoken in his name. Dmowski, leader of the Russian Poles, had already in advance chosen the side of Russia, and, returning from London through Germany, where he was for a time stopped but not recognized, he reached Warsaw just in time to organize an equally frank response from his people. This meant much more than mere words. The Poles who had, so far, often almost pretended that they did not know Russian, now

[1] Danilov, 49.

dashed to the assistance of any stranded car[1] and organized bodies of scouts for the vast no man's land on this side.

On the 17th Nicholas and the Allied Ambassadors visited the sacred city of Moscow, as Russian sovereigns had done before him at the outset of a major war. Gilliard and Buchanan have given us most striking descriptions of the tremendous manifestation of national devotion. Paléologue writes of 'the frantic enthusiasm of the people'. At the same time there was a dead seriousness in Russia in the realization of what was meant by the mere acceptance of the German challenge. It was felt with a kind of awe, not unmixed with a certain audacious joy.[2] German economic penetration had made something like a triumphant progress in the country, and the Russians were almost in the habit of letting the Germans do anything that was necessary for them. Now Germany stood as a great hostile block between Russia and European civilization. The very question of communications presented difficulty. The entry of Turkey into the war, which followed the exploit of the *Göben* and *Breslau* on Nov. 12th, was politically all-important in this sense. Even telegraphic communication with England and France had to find new roads. The question of German exploitation was thus put prominently before the public and was fomented in every way by official propaganda, leading to the most irrational suspicion of every one with a German name and humiliations and even deportation for some of the most loyal of Russian subjects.

But all thoughts were now strained on to the contrast in military power and preparation between Russia and Germany. The disastrous war against Japan was now spoken of generally as a blessing in disguise. It had led to many and great improvements. New military cadres had been established and the training of officers made much more efficient.[3] Knox records that their pay had been raised by twenty-five to thirty-five per cent, with the prospect of pensions.[4] He adds that the relations of officers and men were far better than in Germany.[5] But reserve officers were

[1] My constant experience at the Front.
[2] I was in St. Petersburg at this time.
[3] Danilov, 84.
[4] Knox, xxvi.
[5] ibid., xxxi. This can also be fully confirmed by my own experience with the Russian Army through the major part of the War.

only trained as privates or N.C.O.s; and reserve regiments, with an establishment of twenty-two officers, had only a skeleton formation of four hundred men.[1] According to Golovin, the most eminent of contemporary Russian military historians, Russia exempted from service 48 per cent of the liable male population, as against 3 per cent in Germany and none in France;[2] and only 20 per cent of the people were literate, with no more than 1.1 per cent who had the advantage of a higher education.[3] In this respect the N.C.O.s of Russia could not face any comparison with those of Germany or even of Austria. There were no motor roads, so that all transport had to fall on the railways; and these of course were infinitely less developed than those on the other side of the frontier. The lateral front railways which so often brought up German reinforcements in time to decide the result of an action were entirely lacking on the Russian side; and the most necessary and urgent railway construction, such as that of the Murmansk railway, was postponed almost till its use had disappeared. When the Russians entered enemy territory, they took no trouble to alter the lines to their own broad gauge, so that they could only use captured foreign running material.

The fleet had gained much more than the army from the lessons of the Japanese War, which for it had been much more imperative. The Naval Minister, Grigorovich, appointed as far back as 1908, and the able young group of officers round Captain Kolchak had done much to clean up the Admiralty; and with the help of the Duma and the agreement of the Emperor, for the first time set up a General Naval Staff. Admiral Essen, commanding in the Baltic, with the active help of his chief lieutenant Kolchak, had completed the mining defence of the coast just in time for the war. Five British submarines made the dangerous passage of the Sound into the Baltic, and Max Horton and N. F. Laurence achieved almost legendary exploits, which were the wonder of their Russian comrades.

But at the head of the army there had been a series of hesitations and changes. Between 1905 and 1914 there had been no less than six different Chiefs of Staff.[4] From 1905 to 1909 there had existed an Imperial Committee of Defence headed by the Grand

[1] KNOX, xxi. [2] GOLOVIN, 19. [3] ibid., 23.
[4] DANILOV, 60.

Duke Nicholas, and the functions of the War Minister, who was supposed to be responsible for the supply of the army, were separate from those of the Chief of Staff. After Guchkov's denunciation of the military inefficiency in the Japanese War in 1908, the Grand Duke had resigned this office; and the new War Minister, Sukhomlinov, had obtained control over the Chief of Staff. The officer holding this post at the outbreak of war was General Yanushkevich, one of the youngest generals in the army, who had had no field service and taken no part in strategy; his experience of office had been mainly confined to supply, and apparently he had nothing to recommend him but the personal favour of the Tsar;[1] neither Knox, Danilov or Golovin has anything good to say for him. Danilov himself, who held the next important post of Quartermaster General, which in Russia included the actual instructions for all operations, is described by Knox as the 'hardest worker and strongest brain on the staff'.[2] Polivanov says that he was 'the mainspring of strategical decisions at Headquarters'.[3] Sukhomlinov seems to have himself hoped for the post of Commander-in-Chief, and it was only given to the Grand Duke Nicholas actually a day after the declaration of war. He proposed to take as his Chief of Staff the best strategist in the army, General Alexeyev, but the Tsar said to him, 'I ask and even order you to keep the present Chief of Staff (the wholly unsuitable Yanushkevich) and the Quartermaster General (Danilov)',[4] the nominees of his personal rival the War Minister. He accepted them with his usual chivalry, and he certainly co-operated with them in the heartiest manner, and later took Yanushkevich with him to the Caucasian Front.

Equally absurd was the delay in reforming the Regulation of Military Service which was the base of the whole military system of Russia.[5] The old statute dated from Alexander II. The Duma had made its revision a condition of increasing its estimates. A new regulation of a kind was dished up in 1912. In consequence of this delay, writes Danilov, 'it had hardly any practical influence on the state of the army and on its mobilization'.

The War Minister, Sukhomlinov, who was later to be actually tried for treason, is not regarded as a traitor by any responsible

[1] Danilov, 148. [2] Knox, 42. [3] Polivanov, 238.
[4] Golovin to B. P. [5] Danilov, 61-2.

authority, even the most hostile; but without question he was extraordinarily light-headed, superficial and casual. He had constantly quarrelled with Kokovtsev, the jealous but patriotic guardian of the public purse, complaining that he was stinted in credits, and on each occasion, when he raised this complaint, Kokovtsev pointed to great sums which had remained unexpended. He had nearly hurried the country into a precipitate mobilization in 1912; and on representations of the French Government for the improvement of the Russian railways, he had put forward the most irrational proposals. He strongly disliked the Duma and avoided it as far as possible. He had the ability to please his sovereign with amusing stories and pleasantries; at Court they called him 'General Fly-off' because of his alacrity in anticipating any wishes of the Emperor; but he was not a serious Minister, and he was at loggerheads with the Commander-in-Chief. In consequence of a strengthening of the forces of Austria and Germany, he had been instructed to draw up a programme which would increase the Russian Army by one third in the course of four years. Though this instruction was given in the autumn of 1913, the programme was not ready when a special council met to consider it, nor indeed up to the dismissal of Kokovtsev in February 1914. It was hurriedly passed through the Duma in May.[1]

No changes in the Cabinet were made for the prosecution of the war. The Premier was still Goremykin, the upholder of the 'butler' theory, now seventy-four, expert in all the wiles of the bureaucracy, but extraordinarily cynical and regarding the war as something almost outside his province. The Minister of the Interior was Nicholas Maklakov, who was constantly warning the Emperor of the danger of encouraging any national effort, such as that of the Zemstvo Red Cross, and keeping before him the threat of revolution. The Minister of Justice was the reactionary Shcheglovitov. He and Maklakov had their eyes exclusively fixed on the rear and put before everything else the maintenance of the Russian autocracy. At that time it was assumed that the champions of absolutism were the natural friends of the strongest autocracy in Europe, the German. Very early it was prophesied at the fashionable Yacht Club in St. Petersburg that this war must be fatal to monarchy everywhere; and so of course it has generally

[1] Kokovtsev to B. P.; Kerensky to B. P.

proved. Sazonov, the Foreign Minister, all out for friendship with England and France, had good support from some other Ministers; but the vital Ministry of War remained in the wrong hands.

The purely military disadvantages of Russia were very obvious. Golovin has emphasized the point that large numbers, so far from being a remedy to an insufficient armament, are in themselves a positive disadvantage. The German equipment adjusted armament to numbers in such a way as to produce the greatest efficiency. Russia was hopelessly short of heavy artillery, and even the field equipment of a unit was utterly out of balance: two field batteries per division with one of howitzers against the German fourteen, including two heavy batteries. As to ammunition, there was in peace time practically no reserve beyond the prescribed 1000 shell per gun.[1] There were hardly any aeroplanes at all, and a great shortage of telephones, telegraph and wireless. Transport was so bad that the Zemstvo Red Cross had to supplement it by national effort. In the medical services five surgeons were nominally attached to each regiment of 4000 men, but in fact they often numbered no more than three, and these with the devastating slaughter which was to be expected from the German guns, could not be spared to go up to the front line, so that here again the amateur organization of the Zemstvo Red Cross had often to fill the gap. The successful mobilization was all the more surprising, because of the enormous distances which an average Russian recruit had to travel.

The German and Austrian plan of operations was known to the Russian General Staff before the war. Russian Poland protruded far westward like a great belly, and the plan was to amputate it from the main body of the empire by attacks from north and south — that is to say, if Germany decided to attack Russia before France. There was no natural frontier; and the artificial line, separating the three empires, itself ran through the body of Poland. When William II had decided to 'lunch in Paris and dine in St. Petersburg' and the German forces swept westward, the Austrians were to invade alone, from the south. It was expected in Russia that they would attack from as far east as possible.

For those interested in the question of war origins, it is significant that the Russian plan was much more of a defensive

[1] Golovin, 38-40.

character. Behind where Russian Poland joins on to the main empire, there is a geographical feature of extreme strategical importance. It is the vast Pinsk Marshes, a great tract of marsh and forest, which had forced itself on the calculations both of Charles XII and of Napoleon. Following the dictates of Nicholas I, the able War Minister of Alexander II Dmitry Milyutin, and his brilliant successor as Chief of Staff, Obruchev, desired to concentrate east of the Pinsk Marshes; and therefore a system of fortresses had been constructed to convert this region into what was called a van theatre, making of Russian Poland a great salient, which would enable the Russians to strike whether to north or south. This idea was challenged in 1910 by the light-minded War Minister, Sukhomlinov; and though the commanding chiefs of the time, including the Grand Duke Nicholas, protested vigorously, the original plan was so much altered as to lose its whole value. There was a corresponding hesitation in the attention that was paid to the fortresses. Russia seemed not to know whether she wanted them or not, and some of them were falling into disrepair.

The plan on which Russia acted at the outset of war was therefore a mixture and a muddle. It naturally adopted two variants for the different events of a simultaneous attack from Germany and Austria or an Austrian attack while Germany dealt with France.[1] As the latter alternative was chosen by the enemy, the second variant was adopted on the sixth day of mobilization. By it, of the eight original Russian armies, two were to face the Germans and four the Austrians, while the two others were to remain in observation of Finland in the north and of Rumania in the south. As the dangers which they were to counter did not materialize, they were later thrown into the main struggle. The Caucasus was at first left almost denuded of troops.

It was Obruchev who in 1892 had signed the military convention with France. The regular staff conversations which had followed had in the main consisted of French requests and Russian concessions. The French insistence was not supported by knowledge, and, as a result, the Russians were committed hard and fast, in the event of a war with Germany, to put into the field against Germany alone, 700,000 men to balance the 1,200,000 men of

[1] Golovin, 'The Russian War Plan of 1914', *Slavonic Review*, No. 42, 575.

France. Austria was described, even by the French military authorities, as 'negligible' — no doubt for France, whom Austria could not attack, but by no means so for Russia. What was much worse, was that Russia had engaged to invade on the twentieth day of mobilization, which took no real account of the enormous distances that the Russian troops had to traverse and the exceedingly inferior transport.[1] But only a third of their effectives could get to the Front in fifteen days. Golovin has calculated that it was only on the twenty-second day of mobilization that the Russians could equal the minimum of enemy troops which by this time would be opposed to them, and the maximum only on the thirtieth day; and this did not allow for any delays.[2]

The rapidity with which the German army marched on Paris will be well remembered, and the French Ambassador in St. Petersburg as early as August 5th asked both Sazonov and the Grand Duke for a rapid offensive against Germany. On the 21st, he received instructions to become more insistent, and insistent he remained to the end of the war. In his remarkable diary he records the numerous occasions when he is to be found battering either at the Foreign Office or at the War Office or at Headquarters with demands for haste.[3] It is pleasant to remember that the attitude of the British Ambassador was far more understanding. 'I wish', he said to me, 'we did not ask them to do too much.' The readiness with which France at once came to the help of Russia is beyond praise; but we can already see the seeds of that dissatisfaction with the Allies which was to come later.

While the main German forces streamed westward into Belgium and France, only a much weaker force was left to defend East Prussia. Not waiting to defend its own frontier, the First Russian Army under Rennenkampf, after an insufficient concentration, on August 17th, at Stallupönen drove off the First German Corps of v. Francois, which had advanced without orders.[4] Pushing the Germans back, Rennenkampf engaged them again on the 19th at Gumbinnen and in a two days' battle drove them farther in. Rennenkampf was of the bulldog type of general, without much brains, and peculiarly careless about detail; for instance Danilov complains that his reports to headquarters were of the most vague

[1] Golovin, *Slavonic Review*, No. 42, 573.
[2] ibid., 576.
[3] Paléologue, 55-6.
[4] Hoffmann, II, 26.

and casual kind.[1] He appears to have sent cavalry to capture guns, and there were already many casualties of young scions of the oldest families in Russia. But the advent of the Russians into East Prussia aroused panic everywhere, which recalled the traditional fear of the Russian 'hordes' in the raid on Berlin in the time of Frederick the Great. The name of Cossack carried terror; these hardy men, ready for any odd job, who were a product of the mass revolt of Russian individualism against serfdom, raided, looted and took easy prisoners; I can remember one such who reported to his colonel that he had 'arrested' eleven Germans — presumably for being German soldiers; another Russian soldier slung over his shoulder a heavy sewing machine to take back to his sweetheart and marched for miles with it. East Prussia was the elect home of the Junkers, and many of them hurried off to Berlin, to demand reinforcements. On the 22nd Rennenkampf reached Insterburg. The German Commander, Prittwitz, simultaneously heard that his rear was threatened by the Second Russian Army of Samsonov, advancing from Warsaw. He hastily ordered a retreat to the Vistula and the abandonment of East Prussia. His senior Staff Officer, Hoffmann, persuaded him to reverse this decision and, while disengaging himself from Rennenkampf, to throw himself on the left wing of Samsonov.[2] The German Headquarters were only informed of the first decision and immediately deprived Prittwitz of his command. To replace him was sent General von Hindenburg. This splendid old soldier had fought in the Prussian Guard at Königgrätz (Sadowa), had mounted the murderous Poplar Allée with it at Gravelotte, had taken part in the actions of Beaumont and Sedan, and had witnessed the foundation of the German Empire at Versailles. He was now on the retired list.[3] For Chief of Staff he had Ludendorff, and the latter, who had entered Belgium with the Germans, and in fact been responsible for the capture of Liège, telegraphed from Coblenz to stop the German retreat.[4]

So far from confining themselves to Rennenkampf's invasion, the Russians had planned another attack much farther west, using undefended Poland as a base and launching the Second Army under Samsonov to take the Eighth German Army in the

[1] Danilov, 190. [2] Hoffmann, ii, 27.
[3] Hindenburg, 21-45. [4] Ludendorff, 46.

rear. Rennenkampf and Samsonov each separately outnumbered the defending German forces. Between them was the Tenth Russian Army, which, when ready, would connect them with each other. Samsonov had very much farther to go than Rennenkampf. There was a natural barrier between the two in the Mazurian Lakes. The country to the west through which Samsonov was advancing was very difficult, and largely covered with forest. It appears that the whole advance was based mainly on one great causeway. Rennenkampf had unpardonably lost touch with the Germans in front of him and halted. On August 23rd he resumed his advance and on the 25th turned aside northwards (i.e. farther away from Samsonov) under the lure of the fortress of Königsberg. While Rennenkampf turned farther away to the right in the direction of Königsberg, to which his attention had been directed by his Chief, Zhilinsky, commanding the Northern Front, Samsonov turned farther away to the left, presumably with the object of making his encirclement more complete. The Tenth Army, between them, was so far behind as to take no part in the action that followed; and indeed the Lakes acted as a shield to the Germans, dividing the field of operations into two halves, so that no joint action was possible. The inferiority of the Russian transport showed itself from the outset, and the 15th corps had to march four days without bread.[1]

In later operations the public became accustomed to German announcements 'according to plan', where preliminary organization had made the result a certainty; but no such depreciation can be cast upon the German plan of Tannenberg. Before Hindenburg and Ludendorff arrived, the German Eighth Army had disengaged itself from Rennenkampf. What was to be expected and what, as a matter of fact, the German commanders did expect was that Rennenkempf would again press forward to co-operate with Samsonov. 'He need only have closed with us', writes Ludendorff, 'and we should have been beaten.'[2] 'Any advance by Rennenkampf', writes Hoffmann, 'would have prevented the disaster'.[3] They had only such encouragement as may come from minor indications long before certainty can be established — the capture of a Russian officer's pocket book and a Russian wireless message recklessly given *en clair*. What they did, was to remove practically

[1] Knox, 80. [2] Ludendorff, 49. [3] Hoffmann, ii, 41.

the whole force facing Rennenkampf except two cavalry brigades and the garrison of Königsberg in line, and to throw them across to join those who were facing Samsonov. This could not have been done but for an excellent lateral railway in a direction admirably suited for the purpose.

Of the details of this movement the Russians had nothing which could be called knowledge. On the road the 17th German corps fell upon the right flank of Samsonov's 6th corps, and drove it somewhat backwards. On Samsonov's other flank the 1st corps under Artamonov, under mistaken orders, diverged farther from the main body. This left two big gaps between the wings and the central mass, consisting of the 13th, 15th and 23rd corps, and into these two gaps Hindenburg plunged to achieve what would have seemed impossible, an encirclement of the Russian centre. Some of his orders were delivered as he stood close to the monument commemorating the crushing defeat of the German knights by a vast Slavonic crusade on this spot in 1410.[1]

The two German wings advanced with stubborn courage and with success. The proper answer, it would have seemed, was for the great Russian central mass to advance and break the German centre. This is probably the reason why Samsonov, instead of staying outside the circle and directing his own two wings to close in, plunged into it. But the Russian centre could make no way; and the reason is clear — the great superiority of the German artillery, more than four times as strong as the Russian.[2]

The Russian guns were hampered in their firing by the great forest in which they stood. The pincers closed, and the Russian centre was doomed. The two central corps were shattered and surrendered, and vast numbers — for the most part wounded, but including the Corps Commanders — were taken prisoners. The 23rd, which stood slightly behind them, was thrown back, losing one division. Samsonov and the seven or eight officers of his personal staff tried to escape on foot out of the doomed circle. The British Colonel, Knox, whose book, *With the Russian Army*, is one of the best authorities on the eastern side of the war, had in the autumn of 1911 ridden a bicycle into East Prussia at this very point and was now with Samsonov. The Russian commander muttered that he could not face his sovereign after such a defeat;

[1] Hindenburg, 92. [2] Golovin to B. P.

he fell behind, a shot was heard and that was the last that was ever known of him till the medallion which he carried was discovered later.

Before the full news reached the now renamed capital, Petrograd, Paléologue again called on Sazonov to spur on the Russian advance. This deeply patriotic and religious man was already under the full influence of the catastrophe, and could only reply: 'Samsonov's army is destroyed. That is all that I know.'[1]

For all that, this reckless and chivalrous crusade in the allied cause is claimed by all military writers to have achieved its purpose;[2] for in spite of a message from Ludendorff that they were not necessary, two German corps were detached from the invading army in France — one from the critical wing of Von Kluck — on the eve of the battle of the Marne, and were hurried off to save East Prussia, arriving only after Tannenberg; and the battle of the Marne was the turning-point of the war. The Russian losses in this fighting are reckoned at 170,000.

Ludendorff has written of the Russian Commander-in-Chief: 'The Grand Duke was a really great soldier and strategist',[3] but what perhaps counted for even more than that, was that he was a man of splendid moral courage. He announced the defeat in a bulletin of the greatest frankness beginning, 'God has visited us with a heavy misfortune',[4] and then telegraphed orders to his southern armies, which were hard pressed by the Austrians, to hold good all along the line.

The position on that side was already critical. While the main German forces were engaged in the west, all the main bulk of the Austro-Hungarian active army — of about a million men — had been launched in a great invasion of Russian Poland. The Russians knew before the war that they had to expect this; but they were wrong in their conjecture as to where the enemy forces would be concentrated. The German territory to the north of the great protruding westward bulge of Russian Poland was not much more than a long, narrow tongue of land between the Russian frontier and the Baltic; but on the south side of the bulge, the mass of the territory of Austria-Hungary lies much farther back eastward, so that it was possible for the Austrians to debouch in the Russian

[1] Paléologue, I, 104.
[2] Hoffmann, II, 42.
[3] Ludendorff, 119.
[4] I quote from memory.

territory much farther to the east. As it would be their object to amputate Russian Poland at the neck, the Russians expected them to do this. But the Austrian director of operations, Konrad von Hötzendorff, of whom both Russian and German critics have nothing but good to say,[1] decided otherwise, and the Austrian concentration took place much farther back to the west than the Russians had expected. In this way less decisive results might be achieved, but the Austrian Army, in any case divided from the German forces by the great bulge of Poland, would at least remain in closer contact with them. The Austrians advanced north-eastward in a great convex line with the object of breaking the Russian centre. The Russians, on their side, had on this front four armies, the Fourth, Fifth, Third and Eighth — running from west to east along the Austrian front — but they had been posted in such a way as to counter an Austrian invasion from farther east. The changed Austrian direction made things easier for the Russian left wing on the east, who found no serious obstacles in front of them and advanced rapidly into East Galicia. On the other hand the Russian right wing, the Fourth Army, was vigorously attacked by superior forces on August 17th at Krasnik, and driven into a disorderly retreat. This greatly endangered its next neighbour, the Fifth Army, commanded by one of the ablest, firmest and most enterprising of the Russian generals, Plehve. This great soldier, already well on in years, kept quite cool and was equal to the strain thrown upon him. He manœuvred with such skill as to hold back the overwhelming Austrian forces, which were trying to break the Russian centre, but he could not prevent them from pushing on through the south of Russian Poland, well to the east of Warsaw, and approaching Lublin. At one time Plehve almost cut his own army in half to help his neighbours, with cavalry covering the wide gap in his centre, and in spite of that was almost surrounded by superior numbers.[2]

While Plehve held the enemy at arm's length, Headquarters sent hasty orders to his next neighbour eastward, the Third Army, of Ruzsky, to turn northward to his succour; but here again, as on the north-western front, a large town acted as a deceptive lure. Both Ruzsky and the Eighth Army under Brusilov, which formed the extreme Russian left wing, were advancing on Lemberg, the

[1] Hoffmann, ii, 73; Ludendorff, 75. [2] Note the figures 5 on Plan ii.

capital of East Galicia, a Polish city amidst an Ukrainian population. The Russians seemed to have imagined that it was well fortified, so that its capture would have been a spectacular success; but this was not the case and there was no serious obstacle on this side before the strong fortress of Przemysl, the strongest in Austria-Hungary, which lay farther westward. Brusilov with his Eighth Army was already approaching Lemberg. His method was, where possible, always to seize the initiative by attacking, which, with much reason, he regarded as the least costly form of defence.[1] By these methods he had already won two actions on the two branches of the River Lipa. Lemberg was his natural prey; but Ruzsky with the Third Army turned also in that direction. Possibly, like Samsonov in the north, he was aiming at a more complete encirclement of the Austrian centre; but by doing so, he exposed the Russian centre to just such a danger as had proved so fatal to Samsonov at Tannenberg, where the Germans had plunged into the gaps left between the Russian centre and the two wings and annihilated the former. In fact, Konrad von Hötzendorff seized the opportunity and sent the army of the Archduke Joseph Ferdinand to outflank Plehve's left wing. Also on September 1st Austrian and German forces were advancing together on the retreating Fourth Army and threatened to envelop it. The Grand Duke Nicholas paid a hurried visit to this army and replaced its incompetent commander by a very good soldier, Evert; and he had also by now been able to form on his right wing a new army, the Ninth, under one of the steadiest of the Russian generals, Lechitsky.

It was on August 30th that the Grand Duke ordered a general resistance along the Russian south-western front, and the next day he sent a message to 'hold out to the last man'. On September 2nd, Evert went forward with the strengthened right wing. The next day Lemberg fell without a blow; and Ruzsky, after repeated orders, at last turned in northwards towards the Russian centre. Plehve, meanwhile, was staving off the enemy's centre. His line was all but broken at Fazlawica; and the Russian Guard, which had been hurried up to save it, actually detrained under fire. On September 6th Ruzsky fell upon the flank of the Austrian centre and crushed it at Rawa Ruska. It was a tremendous struggle, in which much of the best Hungarian cavalry was

[1] Brusilov, 84.

destroyed. An advance of Austrian reinforcements from the south for a time threatened Brusilov's position in front of Lemberg; but by bold fighting he held off the attack. The gap between Ruzsky and Plehve was now closed and the whole Russian line swept forward. Heavy artillery, of which the Russians had so grave a lack, played little part in these actions; the Russian field artillery was admirably served, and, with the bayonet, the Russians were throughout the masters. The Austrian centre, which was now in serious danger, retreated with the utmost haste, losing, on its road, great numbers of prisoners and vast military material. It was keenly pursued on the Russian right by Lechitsky with his Ninth Army. It crossed the San, and only rallied at the Wisloka much farther westwards. The First Austrian Army of Dankl, in particular, had the greatest difficulty in getting away at all.

Thus it was in a battle beginning in the heart of Russian Poland that East Galicia was really conquered. Russian cavalry crossed the Carpathians, and Czernowitz, the capital of Bukovina, fell into Russian hands. The Russians had won on this side more territory than the Germans had won in the north. The main Austrian field army had been knocked out, and was for a time almost in dissolution. The news of the Marne arrived in the middle of this success. It was not only that Germany had been forced into an error of dispositions which lost that crucial battle, but the Austrian alliance was in itself in danger; for Austria was almost driven to think of a separate peace. For this great victory the Grand Duke and the Chief of Staff of the south-western front, Alexeyev, received the Order of St. George of the Second Class, which could only be granted for the conquest of a province. The First Class was reserved for a Commander-in-Chief who entered the enemy's capital at the head of his troops.

The Austrians' panic-stricken appeal for help had to be attended to by the Germans, though Hindenburg at this point complained bitterly of the intrusion of politics into military operations. But he had one job to deal with before he listened to Austria, and that was to drive Rennenkampf altogether out of East Prussia. On the day after Rawa Ruska, the turning point in the Austro-Russian battle, he drove back Rennenkampf's left and passed the Lakes on his south, thus turning the buttress which they offered; and on the next day he engaged the whole Russian line. On this day

(Sept. 8th) the German right broke past the Russian left wing and Rennenkampf was compelled to retreat. The Germans pressed through. Their right wing advanced farther to cut the Russian communications; and by September 10th Rennenkampf was in full retreat, with big gaps in his line, and the Germans reached Suwalki on Russian territory. As early as this, confident of victory, Hindenburg offered to send two corps to Silesia. By the 11th his right had gone farther forward to Goldap, was turning Rennenkampf's army through the forest, and crossed the Niemen, which was well to the east of the Russian frontier. Rennenkampf managed to escape, and the fighting on this side ended on the 15th.

On the 13th, while the First Russian Army was in retreat, Hindenburg doubled his offer to Austria for support in Silesia; he promised four corps and a cavalry division. Leaving part of his army to guarantee his new gains, he now passed south-westward, transversely through Russian Poland, making the usual disgusted comment on the Polish mud,[1] which Napoleon before him had described as a 'fifth element'. He took up his quarters at Thorn, and later at Posen; and now, as Commander-in-Chief of the German Eastern Front, with the Eighth and Ninth Armies, he set about remedying the *débacle* of the Austrians, and bringing their army back to some kind of stability. From this time begins the infiltration of German support into the Austrian Army which was to reach extravagant proportions before the end of the war. The Russians, then, by their conquest of Galicia, had at least made it necessary for the Germans, in their own interest, to hold up their direct impact on Russia.

The Marne had been won; but the French Government was still in Bordeaux; and Paléologue, with no thought of anything but the dangers of France, renewed his mischievous importunity. He got nothing out of the sly and sullen Sukhomlinov,[2] and on September 15th made extravagant demands to Sazonov, for whom he drew up the formula: 'As soon as the Austro-Hungarian armies of Eastern Galicia are put out of action, a direct offensive of the Russian armies against Germany will be developed with vigour.'[3]

[1] HINDENBURG, 116; LUDENDORFF, 82.
[2] PALÉOLOGUE, I, 128.
[3] ibid., 130.

The chivalrous Tsar gave orders in this sense, and the Grand Duke prepared to carry them out.

The main Russian and German forces were now face to face in the middle of Poland. Each was simultaneously preparing an offensive. The Russians were first with their plan, but the Germans, as was to be expected, were first with the execution of theirs. Hoffmann describes the Russian plan as 'a bold decision'; and adds, 'the idea was a good one'.[1] The Grand Duke almost denuded his front in Galicia and brought up two of his four armies there to face the Germans in Russian Poland; the other two were withdrawn to the San and ordered to stand firm. With the mass which he would thus have at his disposal he would cut the Austrians from the Germans and outflank the latter from their left, going forwards towards Berlin through Silesia. But as usual, the immense inferiority of the Russian transport, too often with vile roads in the place of railways, meant days of delay. Gurko declares that till a network of field bakeries had been established by the Red Cross, there were more sick than killed and wounded.[2]

Before the Russian plan could materialize Hindenburg was facing the Grand Duke, and launched Mackensen with the Ninth German Army on Warsaw. In the original hesitation and muddle as to strategy which has been described earlier, Warsaw had so far been left unguarded; but the Russian Poles, as we have mentioned, had put their national hopes in the triumph of the Entente, and eagerly begged that the city should be defended. It is an illustration of Russian muddle that there was no responsible officer in possession of a cipher to send this message to Headquarters, and Colonel Skachkov had to invent a cipher of his own, which, however, proved intelligible.[3] The Guard under Bezobrazov, which was not far off, marched in and was received with torches and flowers.

But the Grand Duke, whose own plans were in movement, was already making provision against the danger. He had brought northward from Galicia the Fourth Army of the capable Evert and the Fifth of the trusty Plehve. The Fifth Army, without any adequate transport, had to plough its way through the autumn mud, sometimes with twelve horses attached to one gun[4] — a figure which was at one point repeated identically on the

[1] Hoffmann, ii, 52.
[2] Gurko, 74.
[3] Related to me, by Colonel Skachkov
[4] Danilov, 275.

German side; but, unlike the Germans, the Russians had to go without bread for five days. While Plehve was hurrying northward, more immediate help was at hand in the 3rd Siberian corps, which had had one of the longest journeys of all to make on mobilization. The Siberians got to Warsaw just in time to hold Mackensen up at the western suburbs. Meanwhile both German and Austrian forces had advanced as far as the fortress of Ivangorod on the Vistula, which is here already a broad and spacious river. For all that, the splendid 3rd Caucasian corps of Irmanov forced the passage at Kozenice, under fire, and advanced through marsh and forest on the western side. Of the famous Shirvan regiment, which has been the subject of a well-remembered couplet of Pushkin, some five commanding officers in succession were struck down in the two days. Ludendorff writes of this field of battle: 'I shall never forget it . . . I look back with horror'.[1] But the Russians still swept forward, in their strange picnicking way, but with conquering vigour. Hindenburg, seeing that the Austrians had failed him, withdrew Mackensen on the night of October 18th. The German retreat was admirably carried out, all bridges and roads being smashed up efficiently; but the great Russian wave passed triumphantly over all obstacles to the new German line on the Rawa and Pilica, where Mackensen was again hotly engaged. They finally even got a footing in Silesia; but as Hoffmann had calculated, the mass came to a stop 100 kilometres in advance of the railways still intact. Southward the Russians almost reached the protruding western frontier of Russian Poland, and after an engagement at Leszczica, in which Austrian Poles were opposed by Russian Poles in fratricidal strife, the 3rd Caucasians swept forward again into Kielce, where they sang their great Mohammedan song 'Allah Verdi' (God has given us the victory).†

Again the tradition of German fear of the Russian hordes came back like a nightmare, and Hindenburg testifies to the tremendous anxiety surrounding him at Posen on the German side of the frontier. On October 29th Hoffmann writes in his diary: 'Of course we shall not be able to avoid giving up a bit of German territory.'[2] The neighbouring Austrians had retreated nearly as far as Cracow.

[1] LUDENDORFF, I, 87. [2] HOFFMANN, I, 43.

With German leaders and with German organization, it was certain that the clash would be renewed, and the Grand Duke also on his side was preparing for a further advance. Again there were two simultaneous offensives, and again the Germans moved first. Rennenkampf, with his reduced First Army, replaced in the north by the Tenth under Sievers, was now standing next to the new Second Army of Scheidemann and the Fifth of Plehve, in advance of Warsaw; and Rennenkampf's slackness left a gap through which Hindenburg was able to throw his 25th Reserve Corps, and Litzmann's Division of the Guard, with the object of cutting Scheidemann and Plehve from Warsaw. It succeeded in getting almost clean through, and Scheidemann telephoned to the watchful Plehve to be on the alert. He buttressed Scheidemann and set about closing in behind the advancing German corps. In such a situation it is daring and energy that count. Each side might hope to cut off the other. Scheidemann, it is said, telephoned to Ruzsky, who since September 19th, had replaced the incompetent Zhilinsky in command of the North-Western Front: 'I am surrounded'; and Ruszky is said to have replied: 'You have surrounded them; demand their surrender.' For some days it was touch and go. Plehve held good and completely saved the situation; but the already intercepted Germans fought their way back, and through Rennenkampf's failure to close the gap from the north, they broke through the enveloping Russian line from its rear at Brezina in the night of October 21st, destroyed the 6th Siberian Division, and managed to escape.[1] Thus the Battle of Lodz was drawn — with a heavy balance of losses in men on the Russian side. The Russian offensive, like the German, came to a stop. 'The colossal block', writes Hindenburg, 'lay still'.[2] The two sides were left facing each other to the west of Warsaw.

When two of the four Russian armies of the south had been moved up to the centre, the conquered territory in Galicia was guarded by the Third, now under Radko-Dmitriev, and the Eighth under Brusilov, with Brusilov in command of the whole force. The situation of the Russians on this side was very dangerous. It will be seen from a glance at a map that, while facing westward against the co-operating Austrian and German forces, it was exposed on its left, on the south, along the whole

[1] Danilov, 315. See Lodz on Plan III. [2] Hindenburg, 128.

line of the Carpathian Mountains, from which fresh Austrian forces could at any time penetrate into its extreme rear. Brusilov's custom of meeting offensive by attack now proved its full value. He was constantly threatened on this side, and in each case seized the danger with both hands. He had pressed for an early attack on the great Austrian fortress of Przemysl, now enveloped by Russian forces and beleaguered rather than threatened by a new army (the Eleventh), composed chiefly of militia. Brusilov was allowed to make his attack; but he was interrupted by a large Austrian force which had passed the Carpathians south of him. He broke off and drove away the Austrians, following them into the passes of the Carpathians, and each of their renewed attempts to relieve Przemysl he met with attack.

Brusilov and Radko not only held good on the San. They crossed it, and moved forward again to the Dunajec. The Russian Front on this side remained stabilized throughout the winter westward along this river and southward along the Carpathians. It was a huge salient, inviting an Austrian attack at any moment. The bulk of Galicia still remained in Russian hands. North of the Dunajec, the front passed between Warsaw and the protruding western frontier. On January 2nd there followed, at this part of the line, a frontal battle at Bolymow with murderous German fire and great Russian losses; it was here that gas cylinders were first used by the Germans, but without great effect.[1] This battle did not materially change the position, and here too the fighting died down. Farther to the north, however, where the protruding Russian line bent back again towards East Prussia, there was sharp fighting at Wloclawek on the middle Vistula and at Prasnycz, where the Russian Guard was engaged and both sides prevailed in turn.

Everyone in Russia, like many people elsewhere, had assumed that a heavy struggle under such terrific conditions would be settled one way or the other by Christmas. Such an excuse can be found for the remissness of the Russians and especially of the War Minister, who was officially responsible for all supplies, in disregarding the question of reserves of munitions. Once they were able to advance, the Russian armies in Galicia had gone forward without any regard for the future. They hardly

[1] Ludendorff, 121.

entrenched except to throw up a mere head-covering, because they knew the Austrians were not likely to come up to them with the bayonet. There was no provision for feeding points; the road transport provided by the War Office was so inefficient that it was almost set aside and was replaced by the intelligent efforts of the Civil Red Cross. Similarly, it was only through the Civil Red Cross that anything like adequacy was approached in the ambulance work. The Russian army, wonderfully picturesque with its variety of uniforms and its mixture of nationalities, was a glorious fighting force. Knox's excellent book is keen and critical wherever criticism is required; but while showing up the unpardonable weaknesses in command and supply, he is whole-hearted in his admiration for the Russian regular army of 1914. He paints a picture of mingled muddles and heroism; no patrols, 'dreadfully futile cross movements, wading through sand or mud', late orders, no telephone, no cipher, no notes of their units taken from the prisoners, enemy officers not questioned, no roads assigned for transport, petrol short; and on the other hand, triumphant good temper as a substitute for order.

After the defeat of Hindenburg's second offensive a council of headquarters was held at Sedlitz; and here it was realized that supplies of munitions were literally running out. 'The effectives of the army were melting', writes the Quartermaster-General, General Danilov, 'the lack of officers was taking alarming proportions.'[1] Regular officers were now counted in units; in some cases no N.C.O.s were left. In the Third Army of Radko-Dmitriev the effectives of the regiments were reduced to half. With the Ninth, of Lechitsky, some had only 400 left out of 4000. Danilov calculates that the wastage in men amounted to 300,000 a month.[2] Brusilov, speaking for the victorious Eighth Army, writes that he had now fought his last battle with trained troops; most of his army was gone. The drafts were 'disgustingly untrained'; and again he writes, 'our army is more like an ill-trained militia . . . such men could not be called soldiers.'[3] Knox, writing at the time without the final figures, but on the information gathered in his own personal visits, records that the 3rd Caucasians, normally 40,000, lost 8000 in four days at Kozenice.[4] One regiment of the

[1] DANILOV, 317.
[2] ibid., 321.
[3] BRUSILOV, 102-4.
[4] KNOX, 150.

Guards, he writes, had lost 50 out of 78 officers,[1] south of Lublin, and the famous Preobrazhensky regiment 48 out of 70.[2] In the 18th division 40 officers were left out of 370.[3] We must note that whereas the German and Austrian officers very sensibly took reasonable precautions for their safety, Russian officers went into action standing, while commanding their men to crawl forward. Ensigns had now charge of battalions. Knox calculates that there was now one officer per verst of the line. 'These people play at war', he writes sadly.[4] The position with regard to munitions was desperate; Brusilov records that they had practically run out by November. It was now officially announced to commanders that they could not hope for any real remedy of the situation till March 1915. Knox records[5] that under threat of court martial batteries were ordered to reduce their fire to three rounds a day, irrespective of what the enemy might do. So far the daily expenditure at the front was 45,000 rounds.[6] Men in training had to use one rifle for three. The drafts could not be sent to the front properly armed. In November all batteries were reduced from eight guns to six. The prospect as to cartridges was not so alarming, but where were the rifles? There was no organized collection of those left on the field.[7] Meanwhile the War Minister told Knox a direct falsehood as to his expectation of rifles from America;[8] and on September 25th, to a question from Marshal Joffre as to whether munitions were adequate, Sukhomlinov had replied that they were.

It was fortunate indeed that the great fighting was dying down, and this apparently on equal terms; indeed Russia still held more conquered territory than her opponents. But there was one more big battle. The German attacks at Bolymov and Mlawa were really no more than demonstrations. At this time, without full realization of the disastrous state of supplies, the conquering commanders of the south-western front, Ivanov and Alexeyev, were clamouring for a pursuit of the beaten Austrians towards Vienna; and indeed one adventurous divisional general, Kornilov, had descended into the Hungarian plain. They were even prepared if it were desired to substitute for this the march on Berlin so urgently advocated by the French. On the other hand, Danilov

[1] Knox, 177. [2] ibid., 185. [3] ibid., 194. [4] ibid., 249.
[5] ibid., 254. [6] ibid., 217. [7] ibid., 217. [8] ibid., 222.

at Headquarters was all for a further attack on East Prussia, where an advance would greatly shorten the front and eliminate dangers from the rear. Both these contentions were intelligible; for the Russian front, as now stabilized, still protruded far into Europe, leaving great enemy salients on both flanks. But no definite plan was adopted. By the Russian regulations the Commander-in-Chief had, in some respects, little more than a consultative or co-ordinating authority. Both wings were in motion, and their movement produced in the mind of Ludendorff the impression of what he calls 'a giant plan of the Entente'[1] for the encirclement of its enemies from both north and south, that is, from the Carpathians and from the Niemen. To strengthen the Austrians, von Linsingen was sent to the Eastern Carpathians with six German divisions; and at the northern end Hindenburg fought what is always called 'the Winter Battle' of February.

It started on February 7th in violent snow-storms with drifts man-high and on frozen ice, on which runners would not work.[2] In the middle of the action came a thaw, with bottomless mud. Even the Germans found communications almost impossible to maintain. Their object was to encircle the Tenth Army of Sievers; for they felt that they must as soon as possible knock out one of their many enemies, and were working hard to obtain decisive results. During the autumn Sievers had even recovered a small part of East Prussia. From this he was now expelled in spite of the splendid resistance of the 3rd Siberian corps.[3] Again the Germans used poison gas. Johannisburg was reached on February 7th, and on the other wing February 10th saw the Germans in Insterburg. The Russian Army was very lacking in pliability, and both flanks were turned.[4] The Germans were able to anticipate the Russians at the approaches to Grodno.

Meanwhile the Russian 20th corps, of which no news reached Headquarters, was fighting its way back through the forest. Little support reached it by way of weak counter attacks from Grodno. The 20th corps was at Suwalki on February 12th, but it was already outflanked to the north, and the German cavalry were capturing its convoys wholesale. Finally the corps was brought to a halt on February 14th. With superb gallantry its vanguard was still fighting its way through the Germans in the snow and mud.

[1] LUDENDORFF, 119. [2] ibid., 123. [3] ibid., 124. [4] DANILOV, 366-73.

Some units were reduced to ten per cent, but it had not as yet lost a single battery.[1] Even cartridges were running short; but in a night march through marshy country the vanguard got through. The main body, after the most stubborn fighting, was practically annihilated by February 21st. Sievers's army was half-crushed, and the loss in men and material was enormous. Later it transpired that Guchkov's old antagonist, Colonel Myasoyedov, now a high Russian intelligence officer, was indeed a spy in German pay, and had by aeroplane organized regular communications with the enemy. Yet the German commanders remained disappointed of their hopes. They had counted on encircling the whole of Sievers's army and not merely the main part of a single corps, and the decision on the eastern front for which they had worked so hard seemed as far off as ever. On the contrary, furious fighting with changing fortunes took place in March farther west, close to their frontier, at Prasnycz.

The Russians had now been driven entirely out of East Prussia, but very little farther; and, as so often before in Russian history, the sorely hammered army still stood its ground and faced the enemy. Meanwhile the greater part of Galicia remained in Russian hands.

[1] Danilov, 372.

CHAPTER VIII

THE GREAT RETREAT

O God of battles! Steel my soldiers' hearts!
Possess them not with fear; take from them now
The sense of reckoning.

King Henry V, 4, 1

With a lull in the fighting, the Allies were better able to review their situation and prospects. On September 5th, 1914, the three principal powers on this side — France, England and Russia — had severally engaged themselves not to make peace separately. The French Government, which had left Paris on September 2nd, had returned on December 9th. After the Marne there had been a kind of race northwards, to stabilize the Anglo-French line and to prevent the Germans from getting to the Channel.

So far the main demands for assistance had come from France; they had been addressed principally to Russia, and had always met with a chivalrous response both from the Emperor and from the Grand Duke Nicholas. Now arose a new consideration. The doctrine of the Russian steam roller, which was expected to crush all opposition, had died hard among the Western Allies. It was of course a direct encouragement to the fallacy, which has been mentioned by Golovin — that overwhelming numbers excuse one from taking any thought of material; and indeed the Russians had fully recognized, both in word and in practice, that deficiencies in technique on their side had to be made up by corresponding sacrifices of men. It was a cruel arithmetic, and even this sacrifice did not lead to real results. There was now springing up a more general appreciation of mutual needs. For instance, on March 21st, 1915, Paléologue varied his insistent demands for further Russian sacrifices by a belated suggestion that France should send a number of technicians to Russia.[1]

The question of mutual inter-Allied help gave emphasis to that of communications. The closure of the Straits and the war with Turkey cut Russia off from communications on that side. To

[1] Paléologue, I, 326.

restore them by a knock-out blow to Turkey in the Dardanelles was the object of the ill-planned Gallipoli expedition. On February 19th an Anglo-French fleet shelled the Dardanelles, and an Allied force landed at Gallipoli at dawn on April 25th. This raised the whole problem of the future of Constantinople, which for so long a time had been a cause of European contention. The Russian Slavophils had always wanted to 'restore the Orthodox cross on St. Sophia'. The Tsar was strongly fascinated by this dream. Intelligent Russians, even if very patriotic, sometimes asked how, with such disorder in her own Empire, Russia could deal with such a tangle of new problems as would face her in Constantinople. One thing was clear — if Russia sought to establish herself in absolute control of the Straits, Bulgaria, thus permanently locked up in the Black Sea and without access to the Aegean, must be forced into the ranks of her enemies. Sazonov, though more than doubtful about the wisdom of asking for Constantinople, continued to press his demand for the Straits. On November 14th France and England had promised consideration of this question 'in a sense favourable to the views of Russia'. On March 1st, 1915, Sazonov definitely asked for Constantinople, a request which his sovereign repeated on March 13th. On March 27th England notified her agreement, if the war were carried through by the Allies in union till the end.

The lack of southern communications attracted especial attention to those in the north. Englishmen travelling to Russia at the outset of the war passed through Norway and Sweden and crossed the Gulf of Bosnia to Finland; but this road was soon cut, for in the Baltic the Germans were in overwhelming force. Essen and Kolchak did all they could, and distinguished themselves by daring submarine and mining activities at Danzig and Kiel, but they were chiefly concerned with eluding direct German attacks. Report said that on one occasion the Tsar very thoughtlessly sent Essen a wireless message *en clair* asking: 'Where are you?' and the Russian Admiral ingeniously replied: 'I don't know.'

Sea communication for material could only pass by the original difficult road by which Sir Richard Chancellor in the reign of John the Terrible made the rediscovery of Russia, that is, by the North Cape. The one important Russian port Archangel was ice-bound during the winter. A dying wave of the Gulf Stream does reach Murmansk, farther west and almost on the frontier of Norway. Here, as Nicholas had intelligently desired in the early years of his reign,[1] was developed a subsidiary port, and on January 15th a cable connecting Murmansk with Scotland got to work; but railway communication from Petrograd to Murmansk was still lacking, and owing to the progressive breakdown of the Russian railways, this vital line was only completed not long before the Revolution.

The *Göben* and *Breslau*, now nested in Constantinople, were able to enter the Black Sea and bombard Odessa; but otherwise the Turkish war did not too seriously preoccupy Russia. Witte is even believed to have regarded it as at last giving Russia some object in the war. On January 5th the Turks were well beaten at Sarakamysh, and General Yudenich was more than a match for them in brains and efficiency. At this time neither the Tsar nor his army had any doubt of the ultimate victory of the Allies, and Nicholas played at the then fashionable game of redividing up the world. Paléologue records, perhaps rather loosely, an extraordinary conversation with him on November 21st, 1914.[2] Nicholas is for dictating fixed terms to the beaten enemy, as was later to be done without him. As to conditions, he says: 'I approve in advance, all that France and England would think they ought to formulate in their particular interests.' Russia must receive Posen, part of Silesia, Galicia and North Bukovina which will permit her to reach her natural limit, the Carpathians. In Asia Minor the Tsar felt that he really could not replace the Armenians under the Turkish yoke, though he would only annex them at their request. The Turks were to be driven from Europe; the Northern Straits might be Bulgarian, but the environs of Constantinople — Sazonov had not yet asked for the city itself — must be in the hands of Russia. Nicholas demands the deposition of the house of Hohenzollern.

Each of the opposing groups of States was anxiously soliciting even possible minor allies, and for that reason had to try or to pretend to try to be on its good behaviour; never was there such a market for small States to bargain for even preposterous gains. The cautious old king of Rumania, Carol I, who was himself a Hohenzollern, had died on October 11th, 1914, and his son and

[1] WITTE, I, 6. [2] PALÉOLOGUE, I, 197 & ff.

successor, Ferdinand, had a wife of English and Russian origin with strong Entente sympathies; but for Rumania, for whom even bargaining was dangerous, everything depended on who was likely to win. Italy also had long been gravitating away from the Central Powers, and was offered by the Entente territory which could only properly belong to one of its existing members, Serbia.

In the all important issue whether Russia was moving towards liberty or reaction, the country could not have any close contact with either England or France which did not at once reflect itself in the atmosphere of her own public life from the Emperor downwards. This had been noticeable before the war with the arrival of any new French or British deputation; and now this influence was becoming more and more emphatic. 'I understand', wrote Paléologue later, 'that any visit of a French statesman to Russia is of itself an act of democratic propaganda.'[1] The Tsar could not win the war without Russia; but beyond that, owing to Russia's lamentable lack of technique and munitions, he could not win it without the closest co-operation of the Allies. As soon as Buchanan or Paléologue had to discuss with Russia a request for equipment, which at that time we sorely needed ourselves in the west, they found themselves in a new intimacy, which necessarily brought to the fore the greatest problems of Russian internal politics. Buchanan, especially, through his close personal friendship with Sazonov, became more and more a central figure in Russian life, and, supported heart and soul by the important British colony in Russia, he made an admirable use of his opportunities, thinking, acting or refraining from action with the greatest restraint and delicacy, but always giving his views frankly and plainly. Allied influence was at this time penetrating the public life of Russia.

Paléologue can hardly be said to have made such a tactful use of this situation. One question, which both Ambassadors had to raise, was of peculiar delicacy; and both he and Buchanan were seriously embarrassed when they were called upon by their Governments to plead the cause of Vladimir Burtsev. This is one of the most remarkable characters in the whole of our story. He was closely in touch with the revolutionary parties, and he was specially interested in terrorism, as a weapon to be used only when the Government refused all concessions to public opinion. He was

[1] PALÉOLOGUE, II, 273.

at one time not inappropriately tried, sentenced and imprisoned in England for his frank publication of this view. But his interest was not that of an agent but of a scholar, and it is typical that he was arrested on coming out of the British Museum. He was the best expert on the history of the revolutionary movement and was in fact, so to speak, a revolutionary detective, with a 'flair' superior to that of any of the police. He was constantly exposing the Russian police agents abroad, with such success that at one time they all had to be changed: so we are told by Beletsky himself, who was then Director of the Police Department.[1] It was Burtsev, who, with unflagging cleverness and assiduity, had ultimately succeeded in proving to the leaders of the Social Revolutionaries that the president of their terrorist section, Azef, was serving simultaneously as a police spy. Burtsev, under certain circumstances, could defend or even advocate terrorism, but, as he has put it, 'he objected to murders by a police agent'. So unwilling were they to listen to him that at one time he was in danger at their hands; but ultimately his proofs were so thorough and convincing that Azef was tried by his colleagues, condemned and shovelled away into retirement, where later his accuser paid him a friendly and scholarly visit to verify some doubtful point. Burtsev used to talk freely to the heads of the Police Department. His method was to start by showing them a good part of what he already knew and thereby extract more. No one ever had such an intimate knowledge of the scum of Russian politics on both sides of that vague line which separated the police from the revolutionaries.

At the beginning of the war, Burtsev, who was living in Paris, came out with a strong lead to all revolutionaries to support Russia against the Central Powers, taking the opposite line to the outstanding champion of defeatism, Lenin, an example which was of the greatest service to Russia with French and British opinion. More than that, he boldly returned to Russia, where he was not unnaturally arrested and sent to the extreme north of Siberia. There is some piquancy in the picture of the courtly Paléologue, pressing the Tsar, on behalf of French opinion, to amnesty Burtsev. He was successful in his plea; but Nicholas very reasonably asked: 'Tell me in what cases my Paris Ambassador has intervened for condemned politicals.'[2]

[1] Beletsky, *Padenie*, III, 298.

[2] Paléologue, I, 248.

On August 6th, 1914, a decree had bestowed exceptional powers on the Russian Cabinet for the duration of the war; but friction between the Cabinet and Headquarters was already developing, and it was little more than a nominal remedy for the Cabinet to send Prince I. L. Obolensky as its representative to reside at Headquarters (Sept. 27th). On August 12th, the zemstva or county councils of thirty-five different provinces had united to form the Zemstvo Red Cross Union, and on the 21st to 22nd, at a meeting in Moscow the mayors of the principal towns followed suit by forming a Town Council Red Cross. The two unions later joined into one and were usually called Zemgor (*zemstvo* and *gorod*); this was the Civil Red Cross to which reference has already been more than once made. They were sanctioned on August 29th by the Tsar for the duration of the war, and received generous state support; their work was invaluable, and as we have already seen, the needs of the army could not have received adequate attention without them.

The renaming of the capital on August 31st to Petrograd, instead of St. Petersburg, was a symbol of the revolt against the almost traditional hold which Germany had obtained inside Russia. The new name had not the time or the conditions to become popular; but the revulsion against everything German which it signified was very widely felt. It was also expressed on October 22nd by violent anti-German riots in Moscow, which called urgently for repression. The cry of the day — and it was so general as almost to amount to an epidemic — was for the suppression of everything German, especially of 'German exploitation'.

The first year of the war, however, was in general a cleansing of the Russian conscience, especially in the sacred atmosphere of the front. On September 4th all manufacture or sale of alcohol was abolished by an imperial decree which was certainly the sincere expression of a deep desire of the Tsar, inherited from his father. Reforms by way of autocracy can be very efficient; and Russia did indeed, in the main, become teetotal for about a year. The temperance decree helped to fill the savings banks; and in all probability it saved the lives of many enemy prisoners in the first few dangerous moments of their capture, because their captors were sober. Agriculture did not at first seem to suffer; the sturdy women of Russia were well able to carry out the work; indeed it profited greatly by the increased prices; and large contracts were given by the Government to co-operative societies. Also the great amounts of food stuffs which Russia had exported had now to remain in the country. The needs of the national army were a kind of holy obligation which filled all minds to the exclusion of everything else,[1] and it was constantly being discovered that the government provision for them was utterly inadequate. The Empress, whose best instincts were called out by the war, set a striking example of personal service; she and her two elder daughters at once went through a thorough course of ambulance training; and from August 23rd she found her greatest happiness in performing even the most repulsive duties in dressing the wounds at the hospitals which she had set up. An order calling up students to the front on October 23rd was received by them with a patriotic demonstration.[2]

But as the deficiencies and disorders of the front came very slowly to penetrate the great curtain which divided front and rear, signs of criticism appeared. The Duma was summoned for a session of two days only on February 9th, and on the 7th some of the leading members asked their questions and laid their complaints at a private meeting with some Ministers; in particular they requested an early publication of the promise for autonomy to Poland. They were not able to get any real satisfaction from the aged and wily Goremykin or any clear answers from Sukhomlinov, and their discontent was reflected in the short public session of the Duma two days later. Another private meeting of Duma men with some of the Ministers gave no better result.

So far, in educated opinion, there was no lack of whole-hearted devotion and service in the defence of the country; defeatism was suspected only around the throne, and there was no ground whatever for this suspicion. From time to time came rumours of peace moves from the Central Powers, always inaccurate and distorted. At the end of March Prince von Hohenlohe-Schillingfürst sent a suggestion of peace with Austria; the Tsar was greatly irritated; clearly he felt that his loyalty to his Allies was challenged, but on the advice of Sazonov he left the message without any

[1] A very exact picture of this mood will be found in *The Dark Forest* by Sir Hugh Walpole, who himself won the medal of St. George in Red Cross work at the front.

[2] CARRICK, 7.

reply.[1] On April 30th the Empress received an overture in the same sense from her brother the Grand Duke Ernest of Hesse-Darmstadt, to whom she replied with a patriotic reproach.[2] There were other more substantial causes for public agitation. The Okhta munitions factory, situated in the capital itself, was blown up on April 12th, and in all probability that was an enemy act. A similar explosion took place in Petrograd later.

Much more agitating was the story of Colonel Myasoyedov. He was a worthless man known and despised by the more serious Ministers;[3] but he was intimate with the War Minister, Sukhomlinov, or rather with his young, restless and intriguing wife, and he had been pushed into several responsible posts. Before the war, when he was in charge at the frontier station of Wirballen, he appears to have formed connections with the German secret intelligence. His treachery had now been discovered. There was no defence, and it was even stated that he had admitted his guilt, saying that only the triumph of Germany could save the autocracy in Russia. For all his high connections, Myasoyedov was hanged as a traitor on March 10th.

As time went on the Tsar, who was himself all for winning the war, began to be conscious of the pressure of public opinion. The one persistent advocate of his autocracy was his Minister of the Interior, Nicholas Maklakov, who not a year ago had advised him to reassert it in full. An interesting private correspondence now passed between the two. On March 30th Maklakov, feeling himself powerless, wrote suggesting his resignation; four days later he received from the Tsar an intimate letter with the unusual beginning, 'My friend Nikolas Alexeyevich', in which, while emphasizing his personal affection, he showed that he felt how few now shared the views of this Minister; but Maklakov still remained in office. The public thought more of two other and more formidable personalities both of them frankly opposed to the war. The first was the ex-Premier, Count Witte. He had never swerved from his conviction, firstly, that Russia must avoid war at all costs, and, secondly, that she must work for economic friendship with France and Germany to counteract the preponderance of England. He came back to Russia soon after the outbreak of

[1] Paléologue, I, 333-4. [2] A. F. to N., Ap. 17th/30th.
[3] Kokovtsev, II, 61.

war; he asked that an end should be put as soon as possible to this 'stupid adventure',[1] and everywhere preached his views with such energy that Buchanan sought an audience of the Emperor to protest against them, and issued a public reply.[2] Nicholas detested him, and now more than ever; but on March 13th Witte died suddenly.

The other formidable opponent still remained. Rasputin was opposed to the war for reasons as good as Witte's. He was for peace between all nations and between all religions. He claimed to have averted war both in 1909 and in 1912, and his claim was believed by others. We recall his telegram to Anna Vyrubova for Nicholas just before the World War and Nicholas's irritation at it; according to his daughter, who claims to have seen them, he sent several other such telegrams at that time for the Emperor's reading. After an extraordinarily quick recovery from the wound which Guseva had given him, by September 11th, 1914, he was back in Petrograd speaking, like Witte, against the war.

Strange as it may seem, it is clear that there was a friendship between the two men. Rasputin spoke of it to Illiodor,[3] and often to Simanovich.[4] But perhaps more authoritative is the evidence of Mosolov, head of the Emperor's civil chancery and brother-in-law both to Dmitry Trepov and to A. F. Trepov who became Prime Minister later. Much against his will he had to meet Rasputin several times, and he records a drunken scene at the Hotel d'Europe where Rasputin talked to him of his political friendship with 'Vitia' (his pet name for Witte).[5] Rasputin often spoke of his wish to bring Witte back to power, of which Kokovtsev knew as early as the spring of 1911, and we have also the testimony of Izvolsky and Beletsky.[6] This is proof of his political courage, as was later his advocacy of the Jews; for he must have known how hard a task he was setting himself; but there is nothing surprising in all this. Rasputin's views were very long-sighted and they coincided with Witte's. He had a special antipathy to 'English diplomacy'. On Witte's side, with his rather obvious cunning and his predilection for intrigue, it was almost certain that he would be one of the first to gauge Rasputin's political importance and to make use of it.

[1] PALÉOLOGUE, I, 121.
[2] BUCHANAN, I, 220.
[3] ILLIODOR, 101.
[4] SIMANOVICH, 113, 114, 115.
[5] MOSOLOV, 156.
[6] KOKOVTSEV, II, 22; IZVOLSKY, 139; BELETSKY, IV, 147.

On October 2nd, 1914, before setting out for the army, the Tsar first saw Rasputin privately; and on the 5th Rasputin spent three hours with Anna Vyrubova. Since the debate in the Duma on his promiscuous scandals, his meetings with the imperial family generally took place at her 'little house' instead of at the palace, and she regularly transmitted messages from him to the Empress. On October 7th the Empress came to the little house to meet Rasputin. On November 1st Rasputin, through Vyrubova and another lady friend, tried to sound the political views of the French Ambassador.[1] Rasputin went away, and returned on December 28th. On the following day he telephoned to the Empress. The evidence for all these meetings is contained in the correspondence (with dates in the Eastern calender) between the Empress herself and her husband. They were for the most part quite unknown to the public, and only vague and distorted rumours of them transpired; but these gave rise to all sorts of suspicions. On February 24th he met Paléologue, who had to submit to a lousy embrace, and questioned him sharply on the war.[2]

Anna Vyrubova went regularly into town from Tsarskoe Selo, usually visiting Rasputin and acting as a kind of newsagent of the Empress. While on her way on January 15th, 1913, she came in for a severe railway accident. A heavy iron girder fell on her head and pinned her in, so that it was with the greatest difficulty that she was extricated. Her skull and spine sustained serious injuries, her right leg was crushed and her left broken in two places. She was carried on the torn-off door of the compartment to a neighbouring sentry's lodge, and the Empress herself took her to the hospital of Princess Gedroitz, who declared her to be dying. The Emperor was sent for, and came to her bedside. Rasputin, according to the detailed account which he later gave to Beletsky,[3] did not hear of the accident till the next day. He was at that time in disgrace with the Emperor because of a report of Dzhunkovsky on his conduct. Mosolov recounts how he started up from supper to go to her.[4] He was at this time cut off from the palace and could not command a car, but Countess Witte lent him hers. The patient was lying in delirium, murmuring from time to time 'Father Gregory, pray for me'. The Holy Communion had been

[1] Paléologue, i, 183.
[2] ibid., 308-11.
[3] Beletsky, *Padenie*, iv, 501-2.
[4] Mosolov, 162.

administered to her. The imperial couple were watching by her. Rasputin, without asking leave, entered the room and without a word to the bystanders took her hand and said: 'Annushka, wake up! Look at me!' She opened her eyes and murmured: 'Gregory! That's you! Thank God!' Rasputin turned to the august bystanders and said no more than 'She will recover, but she will remain a cripple!' He tottered from the room and fell outside in a faint from which he awoke in a strong perspiration, feeling that all his strength had gone from him.[1] The Empress, writes Mosolov, on returning to the palace declared that he had performed a miracle;[2] Rasputin, when speaking of this incident, would say 'When I resurrected Anna'. She outlived all the other principal characters in this story.

On January 19th a troika, driven furiously along the Kamenno-Ostrovsky Prospect, only just missed running Rasputin down. Those who were in it admitted that they had come from Tsaritsyn, the special fortress of Illiodor, and it was generally supposed that they were his agents.[3] On February 11th Rasputin again had an interview with the Empress, and on the 24th again met Paléologue. On March 12th the Tsar, on the eve of setting out for the front, was blessed by him. Nicholas noted in a later letter to his wife that he was trying to account to himself for the special peace of mind which he felt; and he curiously attributed this to Rasputin's blessing, to Witte's death, which had just happened, and to a pleasant and satisfactory talk with Sir George Buchanan, no doubt about the Straits and Constantinople.[4]

On April 8th Rasputin created a public scandal worse than any before. He had been visiting Moscow, as he explained to the Empress and others, in order to pray at the tombs of the patriarchs. Apparently the praying had been too much for him, or he felt that he now had some credit in hand. Anyhow he visited one of the most notorious places of entertainment, Yar, and there, according to the police report, which is extant, sat in the public eye with his clothes in such disarray as can only be described in print as the grossest indecency; and when those who saw it expressed their disgust, again according to police reports, he suggested that he could behave in this way in the presence of the

[1] Vyrubova, 56-7.
[2] Mosolov, 162.
[3] Paléologue, I, 275.
[4] N. to A. F., Ap. 30th/Mar. 13th.

imperial family. Bruce Lockhart, who witnessed part of the scene, describes how he was taken off by the police, 'snarling and vowing vengeance'.[1] It was now generally assumed that this would finish him. The Moscow Prefect of Police, Adrianov, sent the particulars to the Police Department and in this way they reached Dzhunskovsky. This honourable man had had Rasputin watched, particularly in connection with his interventions in politics, which he felt to be the greatest danger not only to Russia but to the Emperor and the dynasty. He had seen Rasputin's increasing influence in political appointments. At an audience with the Emperor on recent disorders in Moscow he boldly reported on the outrage at Yar. The Emperor listened to him attentively without a word, only asking at the end for the written report, which he put in his desk. Dzhunkovsky now asked leave to continue his investigations. The Emperor not only gave leave, but begged him to do so and detained him till 12.30 p.m. in friendly conversation.[2] According to Beletsky, Nicholas spoke angrily to Rasputin on the matter and Rasputin gave his usual excuse — which would carry more weight with a Russian than an Englishman — that he was 'a sinful man'.[3] It is not clear that this meant anything more than that he admitted having been drunk, as he did on some other occasions, with the explanation that the simple peasant had been tempted purposely by others. This was in June 1915. It seems that Nicholas was extremely annoyed, but it does not appear that his wife was informed.

Though Nicholas had been dissuaded from taking the Command, he had a constant urge to be with his army and, as far as possible, to share its dangers and privations. In this he was always encouraged by the Empress, in spite of the personal sacrifice which it meant to her. It was not only that she felt this to be his duty but that she was intensely jealous of the popularity of the Grand Duke and wished the Emperor to assert himself by frequent contact with the troops. He made extensive visits to it in this period (Oct. 2nd/9th, Nov. 3rd/15th, Dec. 1st/Jan. 1st, Feb. 4th/15th, Mar. 12th/24th, Ap. 17th/May 5th). In the course of these visits he traversed almost every part of the army and a great part of his empire. He writes to the Empress with a simple enthusiasm on the

[1] Bruce Lockhart, 128. [2] Dzhunkovsky, *Padenie*, v, 104.
[3] Beletsky, *Padenie*, iv, 151-2; Vasilyev, 108.

various picturesque regiments and their fighting spirit and vigour. He says no more than would be confirmed by anyone who lived with the Russian Army in those days — for instance General Knox or myself.

The last of these visits was certainly very unfortunate. He had been strongly dissuaded from making it, both by Rasputin and the Grand Duke Nicholas, especially the former, on the ground that it was too soon.[1] It was to the conquered Galicia, where already a Russian Governor-General was installed. Here he visited Lemberg and some sections of his army, being particularly delighted with the spirit of the splendid 3rd Caucasians of Irmanov, who had just been brought up to strength and were quartered at the foot of the Carpathians. At Lemberg he slept in the bed of Francis Joseph. Rodzyanko, whose principal defect was that he overdid his importance and his activity, also visited the city at this time, and the welcome given to him by the population as President of the Duma was a matter of great vexation to Nicholas Maklakov. Without much tact, Rodzyanko predicted impressively to Nicholas that the Russians would soon be driven out again.[2]

The Russian occupation of Galicia had brought out many of the best features of the Russian Army and people. The Staff of the military district of Kiev before the war had included many of the most brilliant soldiers in the army, of whom one after another was later to find higher employment elsewhere. Old Ivanov, commanding the south-western front, was ordinary enough, cautious and rather hesitating; but Alexeyev, who had risen from comparatively humble origins by sheer merit, was quick in perception and a really able strategist. The Kiev Staff had always been kept alive by the neighbourhood of danger; and its Chief, Alexeyev, had been warned as early as the crisis of 1909 to be ready to take measures to repel an invasion any time within forty-eight hours.[3] On this front were Ruzsky, who had now been sent to command the north-western front, Brusilov, who was later to be Commander-in-Chief, and Kornilov and Dukhonin, both of whom were later to succeed to the same post. Nearly all these distinguished officers were in the general sense Liberals, and there was a breath of liberation in the Russian advance into Galicia. It was not

[1] A. F. to N., Ap. 6th/19th. [2] RODZYANKO, 125-6.
[3] Alexeyev to B. P.

difficult in Russia for persons of consequence to fix where they would go; and this atmosphere brought to Galicia in the service of the Red Cross precisely the most liberal-minded members of the Duma, such as Nicholas Homyakov, its former president, that typical English Liberal Michael Stakhovich (now a member of the Upper House), Alexander Zvegintsev, recognized as the Duma's intermediary between Russia and England, Milyukov's friend Igor Demidov, and several others; Demidov was in charge of the Duma's field hospital, which was also here.† The troops sent to Galicia were wisely drawn in the main from Russian Ukraine, and were, therefore, closely akin in language and spirit to the inhabitants of East Galicia. The Ukrainian troops of Austria sometimes welcomed them by simply firing in the air. Many made their way of themselves over to the Russian side. The Russian Red Cross wisely made medical provision for the service of the population as of the Russian troops, and enlisted the help of the native surgeons, who worked admirably under the Russian authorities. The invading soldiers and the population could and did speak to each other with a facility which had often been denied to the Austrian officers. Farther westward, in those parts of Polish Galicia which the Russians occupied, there were the same happy relations; and those who witnessed the simple friendliness of the Russian soldiers when quartered in the neat Polish huts would have said that for the peace of the two peoples nothing was required but to leave them to themselves. This, however, was not the policy of the Russian Government; and in particular the Church authorities regarded the occupation as an opportunity for extending the reign of formal Orthodoxy as far as possible. The troops resented this intrusion of ecclesiastical politics almost as much as the inhabitants themselves.

The Austrians, who had now occupied Belgrade (Dec. 2nd) again attacked in the Carpathians, with the hope of still saving their beleaguered fortress of Przemysl; but there the Austrian garrison largely consisted of Slavonic troops, and though the surrounding Eleventh Russian Army, mostly composed of militia, was hardly more effective, the fortress surrendered on March 19th with 120,000 prisoners and 900 guns. Though strengthened on the extreme east by German support, the Austrians were held up without great difficulty. A memorandum of March 2nd from

Ivanov to Headquarters obtained for him permission to advance in the direction of Budapest and Vienna.[1]

As has been already mentioned, Ludendorff had mistaken a hesitation between two different schools of military thought on the Russian side for a single great plan to outflank their enemies in the extreme north and the extreme south; that is why, in the Winter Battle, he had pushed the long northern Prussian salient farther into Russia, and that is why the extreme Austrian right wing had been strengthened by German troops. The Russian Headquarters wished Ivanov to move from the extreme east of his line inward, gradually driving the enemy back westward; but Ivanov went straight ahead southward from the middle of Galicia. This, as Ludendorff soon noticed, put Ivanov's right wing, the Third Army of Radko Dmitriev in a position of danger, as the line of the Dunajec, which it held, was far too much forward to the west. This part of the Russian line made a great protrusion facing south-westward towards Vienna, and it was very vulnerable from the Carpathians, which turned the whole line into a huge salient.

However, the Russians went on ploughing their way through the mountains. The Carpathians are a very thick belt of mountains, with one height after another, often with a slope of one in six and covered with timber. Owing to the pitiful lack of artillery ammunition, each of these hills had to be stormed separately with the bayonet, and this task was carried out at a ruinous cost with the greatest chivalry and courage. The Russian knew that, with the exception of the Hungarians and the Tyrolese, if he could get to his enemy he had a beaten man before him, and innumerable prisoners were taken in the advance. The mountain range was actually passed. By April 10th, with what Danilov[2] rightly describes as 'super-human efforts' and Ludendorff as 'a supreme contempt for death',[3] the Third Army secured the summit of the central range of the Beskides, and to its left Brusilov with the Eighth Army was already descending the other side. By now, all the passes through the Carpathians except that of Uzhok were in Russian hands. The population of the mountains themselves was mostly Ukrainian or Slovak, that is Slavonic; and the advance still had the character and atmosphere of liberation.

[1] DANILOV, 385. [2] ibid., 389.
[3] LUDENDORFF, 141 (he is here quoting from von Seeckt).

Local actions of a more or less desultory character had been proceeding on the opposite flank in the extreme north. A limited offensive of three Russian armies on March 2nd had given no great result. There was a great deal of fierce fighting around Prasnycz, where the courage of both sides won the admiration of Ludendorff; but nothing of real moment occurred until the end of April, when on the 30th the Germans launched a systematic offensive along the Baltic coast in the direction of Riga. Ludendorff was anxious to prevent any outflanking Russian movements on this side; and he was already preparing for the great events of the summer by stretching out a claw almost past the extreme Russian right. On May 3rd the Germans entered Mitau; on the 7th they occupied the Russian port of Libau; and they continued to advance in the direction of Shavli and Riga.

Plenty of warning had reached the Russians of a great Austro-German concentration on the other wing in the south, near Cracow, where the command had been entrusted to one of the best German generals, Mackensen. He had with him his Eleventh German Army and the Fourth Austrian;[1] and in his neighbourhood, especially on his eastern side, several German units had been filtered into the wavering Austrian army, under Linsingen at Munkacz, Marschall in Bukovina and Marwitz in the Beskides. The German Staff had itself at this time moved to Pless in order to co-operate the better with the Austrians, and all reserves were now being sent to the eastern front. Without this co-operation it is likely that Austria would have made a separate peace; the more so as Italy had just joined the Entente Powers on April 26th, declaring war only on Austria and not yet on Germany.[2] Already in April an Austrian force, largely Tyrolese, had been launched without effect on the Russian positions at the extreme point of the salient southwestward, near Tuchow.

It was near here that the blow fell on May 2nd. Of the long Russian line which extended over 800 miles, it attacked the southern side assigned to the Third Army of Radko Dmitriev and the Eighth of Brusilov. Radko alone had a front of something like 115 miles, with a force probably numbering something over 300,000 men. Though he had sent several warnings to his superiors without effect, he can hardly have anticipated the

[1] Danilov, 410. [2] ibid., 404-9; Ludendorff, p. 141.

suddenness of the attack; for on the previous day he advised me to visit exactly this part of his line. The blow fell in a gap between the 10th and 9th corps. The 10th corps was in complete confusion. From a neighbouring height one could see an uninterrupted line of enemy fire from the heaviest guns for five miles to each side. The Russian artillery was practically silent. The elementary Russian trenches were completely wiped out and so, to all intents and purposes, was human life in that area.† The Russian division stationed at this point was reduced in this and the immediately succeeding operations from a normal 16,000 to 500. Several other divisions were reduced to 1000.[1] The enemy did not risk any advance until he had practically eliminated his opponents by metal. His technique was to concentrate an overwhelming mass of heavy guns at a given point, to begin usually by shelling the immediate Russian rear so as to cut off communications with the front, and then to bore a hole clean through, after which the same operation would be repeated farther along the line till a great gap had been opened. Very belatedly Radko had received some reinforcements, in particular the splendid 3rd Caucasian corps; but he had never prepared any second line, because the whole experience of the Russians in Galicia was that the Austrians did not come up to the attack; and as he thus could not retire to an entrenched position farther back, he threw in his reinforcements and reserves as they came, and they were swallowed up in the general ruin. Irmanov's Caucasians, without any artillery support, did actually reach the neighbourhood of the enemy guns, and later covered the retreat, but they were quickly reduced from a normal 40,000 to 8000.[2]† In this way the whole salient was driven in. Tarnow on one side, and Gorlice on the other, had to be abandoned. Ivanov gave orders to make a stand on the line of the Wisloka, but this was quite impossible; and the Third Army, fighting back bravely, whenever it had a chance — especially at night, when the bayonet still gave it a complete superiority — was rolled back on to the San.† The 24th corps had lingered in the south of the Carpathians till it was nearly enveloped. One of its divisions, the 48th, was commanded by Kornilov, so well known later after the Revolution. He had shown himself a lover

[1] PARES, *Day by Day with the Russian Armys*, 201-7.
[2] ibid., 207-12.

of daring risks, both when he had commanded the rear guard at Mukden and when in 1914 he had dashed forward almost of himself into Hungary. He was now met by a cross fire from Germans on the north and Austrians on the south; his division was destroyed or taken captive, and he himself, after hiding in the forests, was discovered and became a prisoner; but he managed to escape on foot together with a Cossack private in the uniforms of Austrian officers, and returned to Russia to play an outstanding part later.

After some kind of a stand on the San, Jaroslav fell to the enemy on May 15th.[1] The 3rd Caucasians, now reduced to 6000, had in a bayonet attack at night at Sienawa taken 7000 prisoners. The Third Army, to quote the expression of its commander, 'had literally lost all its blood'. He had not maintained the proper communications with his neighbours, Evert of the Fourth and Brusilov of the Eighth Armies, and they were now also ordered to retire. This meant the surrender of the Carpathians, won with such heavy sacrifices; but Brusilov made an extremely able retreat, first dispatching baggage by duly assigned roads and standing from time to time to repulse the enemy. For a moment he was in charge of the now useless fortress of Przemysl, which as he truly remarked was no longer a fortress in the lack of any shell to fire.[2]

Headquarters replied to the blow by sending reinforcements for a shock counter-attack in the neighbourhood of Lyubachev. Here the new units were thrown into the line in driblets, and the retreat continued. Any attack from the enemy's side on the temporary lines at this point found the troops condemned simply to sit under fire without any defence from their own guns, and Irmanov when outflanked on both sides was even short of cartridges.[3] In this way the Russians were bundled out of Galicia; but the retreat was still gradual and deliberate; Irmanov seldom went back farther than three miles a day, and at Krasnustaw in Russian Poland, on the site of the first great Austro-Russian clash of 1914, one of his divisions in a night attack dealt such a blow to the two Austrian divisions opposed to it that they did not move again for a fortnight.

This was the moment of the worst disorganization as to drafts. Recruits, young or elderly, drawn from anywhere without any

[1] LUDENDORFF, 145. [2] BRUSILOV, 126. [3] PARES, *Day by Day*, 254-7.

local cohesion, were hurried up into the line, often without a rifle, with instructions to wait for one till a neighbour was wounded; and having had no proper training in taking cover, these men were often back at the first aid station in a day or two. Brusilov, who himself set about giving the recruits a training in the actual neighbourhood of the line, had now five to six of his original officers per regiment, and four to six of the old regular privates in a company of 250. 'In a year of war', he writes, 'the regular army had vanished. It was replaced by an army of ignoramuses.'[1] His average division numbered between three and four thousand instead of sixteen.[2] With the battered Third Army of Radko, it was very much worse; at points which I visited the average company numbered 40. Irmanov, when he was pressed over the frontier, had no cartridges. The soldiers' letters were full of the word 'exasperation'.[3] I recall some of their comments: 'You know, sir, we have no weapon except the soldier's breast.' 'This is not war, sir, it is slaughter.'

In this condition, the Third Army, now attached to the North-Western Front, went slowly back under a new commander to Brest Litovsk. This meant that the Fourth and Second had necessarily to retreat from the neighbourhood of Warsaw, which there was now no hope of saving. At the end of January a council was held at Headquarters. The army was declared to be short of half a million men. The War Office had only received 40,000 rifles of poor quality. The Grand Duke wrote to the Tsar describing the training as 'beneath all criticism'.[4]

The enemy plan, designed to meet an imaginary co-ordinated outflanking Russian movement from north and south, had been to counter it by a similar outflanking. It was as if two great pincers were thrust out from Galicia and the Baltic coast; and we shall recall that, before launching the great offensive of Mackensen in Galicia, the Germans had already pressed forward along the coast in the direction of Riga. Thus, whatever the Russian movements of retreat, their centre still protruded and was exposed on both sides, north and south. What Hindenburg now wanted to do, as he tells us in his book,[5] was to take Kovno, follow on to Vilna and then, being in a position to turn the Russian right, to

[1] BRUSILOV, 138. [2] ibid., 141. [3] Told me by a military censor.
[4] DANILOV, 435. [5] HINDENBURG, 142.

press in both Russian wings on to the impracticable Pinsk Marshes and cut their communications with their rear. He had always been for enveloping the enemy, in order to get a final result as soon as possible; in the war conditions of the Central Powers, this was an imperative need, as it was absolutely necessary to achieve a definite victory on one front, east or west. Envelopment had succeeded with him on the smaller tactical scale to a surprising degree. He had enveloped the Russian centre at Tannenberg, and he had enveloped part of the Tenth Army in the Winter Battle in the forest of Augustovo. Hoffmann tells us that the orders had actually been given and Hindenburg and Ludendorff had only to telephone from Headquarters, whither they had been summoned, for them to be put into effect.[1] But, as to the direction of the next German drive in the north, he and Ludendorff were overruled. Without extending so far north, they were to strike almost direct on to the Narew. This in itself would be sufficient at least to envelop Russian Poland, but not the Russian Army. Gallwitz, with the Twelfth German Army, started forward on July 13th. The Narew was reached twenty-six days later, and Ostrolenka on August 4th. 'The Russians', writes Ludendorff, 'offered a stubborn resistance everywhere, and suffered very heavy losses.'[2] Meanwhile Woyrsch, who had several times played a distinguished part in the centre, moved forward on Warsaw. But the 'fierce' Russian resistance gave time for their centre to withdraw. The Twelfth German Army which turned southwards, at least to cut off some Russian units, failed to do so.[3]

In the south, the Austrians, though strengthened by German units, had failed to turn the Russian left.[4] The Eleventh Russian Army had stopped them at the Dniester, and Brusilov with the Eighth, who had somewhat farther to go back, had, as we know, made a competent and courageous retreat, to which Ludendorff himself pays a tribute;[5] and here the Russians settled down for the winter with a very diminished south-western front. Far the greater part of the Russian Army was now engaged in contesting the German advance in the centre and north, with a greatly increased North-Western Front under Alexeyev. His one object was to prevent encirclement, and the measures which he took

[1] HOFFMANN, II, 109. [2] LUDENDORFF, I, 150. [3] HOFFMANN, II, 113
[4] LUDENDORFF, I, 146. [5] ibid., I, 146.

have in general received nothing but praise from both sides. With terribly shrunken units — Gurko describes corps as 'miniature regiments'[1] — and with no prospect of any relief in munitions, he could only delay the retreat with vigorous counter-attacks, especially at night when the Russians maintained their superiority, though actually at this stage in the war, owing to the overwhelming Russian losses, the advantage in numbers had for the time passed to the other side.

It was now perfectly clear that Warsaw must fall. The Russian Poles under the leadership of Dmowski had from the outset declared themselves on the side of the Entente, and the sincerity with which they had rendered any services they could to the Russian Army had been acknowledged in a public proclamation to the population by Evert, the commander of the Fourth Russian Army. They now set themselves to consider how even under German occupation they could remain faithful to the Allied cause.[2] Perhaps no people suffered in the war so much as the Poles. Even in Belgium the tide of invasion had rushed over the country once for all; but in Poland, which had been the main area of the fighting, it had flowed to and fro, carrying new ruin with it each time. This was greatly aggravated by the measures of the Russian Headquarters. On an entirely illusory analogy with the campaign against Napoleon in 1812 it adopted what were called 'Moscow' tactics,[3] and ordered not only the complete destruction of all materials in this the best developed part of the empire, but the actual retreat of the population. The inhabitants were driven out of their homes and herded eastward through country which was less and less provided with railway transport, and even that was entirely taken up with the needs of the army. Infinite suffering went with them on their road; they had no fixed destination, and even the great generosity of the Russian public could make no adequate provision for them in a time of such complete confusion. Numbers were to die of typhus and other epidemics on their wanderings; and those who survived were not to see their homes again till the war was ended or even at all. Many remained permanently stranded in Siberia.

[1] Gurko, 121.
[2] At the end of June, I had discussed with Dmowski in Warsaw the steps which Poland could take under German occupation with this object.
[3] Danilov, 465.

On the night of August 2nd, the Second Russian Army crossed to the east side of the Vistula at Warsaw, retaining only the forts on the other side.[1] On the 4th, the Fourth Army of Evert left the Vistula line at the fortress of Ivangorod, and the same night, the Second Army left it at Warsaw.[2] By August 11th the Russian centre was east of Sedlitz. The provisional line which Alexeyev had fixed for the North-West Front was reached and passed by the enemy by August 12th; and Alexeyev could prescribe nothing more effective than vigorous delaying actions. By the middle of the month the German pressure was increased.

The enemy were now passing the immature and uncoordinated system of Russian fortresses in this area. Ludendorff has expressed the opinion that fortresses in future have no further importance, except as strengthened sectors in the line of an active army, and at this stage of the retreat this opinion prevailed at the Russian headquarters. Novo-Georgievsk, now behind the enemy line, had been invested and shelled, and fell on August 19th. Kovno was still in the line and was now subjected to a tremendous bombardment. Its commander, Grigoryev, showed no energy whatever in its defence, and himself vanished into the rear before the fortress fell on August 17th. The magnificent little garrison of Osovets, which had already fought off three attacks in the course of the war, made another splendid resistance, but was ultimately taken from the south. Knox mentions that at this time one corps had no shell at all, and that all the rifle ammunition was used up in one defensive action.[3] The Germans again threatened envelopment by landing forces so far to the north-east along the coast as Pernau near Reval, and German mine-sweepers entered the Gulf of Riga.[4] The Russian Guard was sent to hold up this outflanking movement, and measures for the evacuation of St. Petersburg were under consideration; but again the tide was stayed. The Russians, as Ludendorff wrote, always succeeded in escaping: 'They frequently made fierce counter-attacks with strong forces, and again and again took advantage of the many marshy areas in the neighbourhood of rivers and streams to rally and offer prolonged resistance.'[5] The Germans had the greatest difficulty in advancing, and were always exposed to such counter-

[1] DANILOV, 444. [2] ibid., 445. [3] KNOX, 318.
[4] DANILOV, 454. [5] LUDENDORFF, I, 152.

attacks, though assisted by excellent railway work in the rear, to which there was no equivalent on the Russian side. Grodno was only taken after violent street fighting,[1] and Gallwitz could only force the Russians back 'fighting all the way'.[2] 'As always', writes Hoffmann, 'they defended themselves energetically.' The northern defence was entrusted to the cool and steady Plehve, who extended his strengthened forces in a fan-like formation to stem further advance. Ludendorff marks a crisis in his drive on Vilna, when the Russians attacked heavily on the north bank of the river, and he comments: 'We passed once more through a period of great anxiety.'[3] On September 9th there was a further German advance with 'fighting long and severe'. It was only possible to 'force the Russians back across the river by degrees'.[4] They 'were not able to hold Vilna against this pressure and retired slowly, fighting along the whole front'.[5] The Germans were ever farther from their base, and their offensive had now only the impetus to carry it to the region west of Smorgoni and the neighbourhood of Baranovichi and Pinsk. Konrad tried to support with an Austrian offensive farther south, but was repulsed. 'The idea was right', says Hoffmann, 'but the instrument failed him.'

This was the farthest eastward that the offensive was to reach. The Russians had already lost a ruinous proportion of their best railways, but they still had an important main line, close behind the new front. For this railway the Germans made a dash with their cavalry in September. They succeeded in reaching it at Molodechno; but the tired infantry was late in following up, and by prompt measures on the Russian side Molodechno was recovered and the gap was filled. Strong Russian counter-attacks fixed the line at this point; and Brusilov in the south ended the campaign with another challenge in December. In the course of the winter the new Russian line was stabilized, and it remained fixed to the end of the war, except where in its southern half it was to be gloriously re-extended in the next year by the wide sweep of the offensive of Brusilov. In the northern part, this line which takes no account either of geography or of population, has remained to the present time the frontier of Russia.

How much had been lost? Russian strategy which, with a

[1] HOFFMANN, II, 116. [2] LUDENDORFF, I, 162. [3] ibid., 167.
[4] ibid., 168. [5] ibid., 169.

threadbare army, had just written one of the finest pages of its history, had been justified in the use that it had made of the vast and comparatively empty spaces of Russia. Even now, the Russians had not yet been driven back to the farthest western scenes of the battles of Napoleon's campaign in 1812. Above all, Alexeyev, like Kutuzov before him, had succeeded in keeping the Russian Army in being, and it was again to show its mettle in the following year. Ludendorff thus sums up his results: 'The great campaign against Russia was at an end. The Russians had been defeated and forced back . . . the enemy had been able to thwart the enveloping movement with which they were threatened on the Vilya'.[1] He describes the failure at Molodechno as 'immensely tragic' and the position of two of his armies as 'precarious and dangerous'. 'The great anxiety of those September days had once again resulted only in a tactical success.'

But at what price? The figure for the full Russian losses (killed, wounded and prisoners) up to July and exclusive of the last fighting, which I was asked to bring back from the Russian War Office to the British Government, was 3,800,000. That for ten months of war! It corresponds pretty nearly with Danilov's estimate of 300,000 a month, made before the shortage or absence of munitions had taken its full effect; and I have every reason to think that it was an understatement.

[1] LUDENDORFF, 170.

CHAPTER IX

THE CONSTITUTIONAL CRISIS

The means that heaven yields must be embrac'd
And not neglected. Else, if heaven would
And we will not, heaven's offer we refuse,
The proffer'd means of succour and redress.

Richard II, III, 2

You pluck a thousand dangers on your head:
You lose a thousand well-disposed hearts.

Richard II, II, 1

THE NATIONAL MOVEMENT

It is probably no overstatement to say that we now reach the major crisis in the whole of Russian history. This could not be generally perceived at the time, because in all countries the question of victory in the World War overrode all others. By many it is not perceived now; there has grown up on the wide basis of theories, economic and otherwise, a tendency to regard everything that has happened as inevitable, and those who have not lived through this period or have not made a really detailed study of it sometimes rest content with such an assumption. The opposite is the view of those who saw the issues at the time and realized how easily things might have moved and nearly did move in quite a different direction, and that at the point which we have reached in this story we were really at the parting of the ways. Sergius Shidlovsky, a Liberal in Russia who might have been an intelligent Conservative in this country, and later Chairman of the Progressive Bloc, had said just before the war: 'Give us ten more years and we are safe.'[1] Ivan Petrunkevich, the veteran Liberal leader, had pointed out in 1905 the path which led to a 'new order of things, without convulsions, without bloodshed, without thousands of unnecessary victims'. Shidlovsky meant

[1] To Professor S. N. Harper.

that those essential changes which were required in Russia could come without convulsions, and they very nearly did.

From the sketch of Russia's past in the first chapter it may be seen that there were certainly some elements favourable to a constitutional regime, though they were infinitely less developed and articulate than with us. Probably the firmest of all of them lay in the instincts of the peasant farmers, who accepted state burdens, including the defence of the country, as long as they were fairly distributed, and asked before all things for public order, with freedom of transport and trade and local development. The great traditions of the fundamental reforms of Alexander II, which were acts of the Government itself, were in this sense liberal. The zemstva were grounded on the very idea of liberty. The cry for reform since 1905 was even predominant within the body of the Church itself, when the Synod itself had asked for the summons of a Church Council and the re-establishment of the Patriarchate.[1] As to the army, whether one is thinking of the peasant rank and file or of the majority of the officers and commanders, there was no doubt at all of the prevalence of the same spirit. The war itself was popular because Russia was allied with the democratic powers; the very object of it, as presented by Tsar and Government, was the liberation of 'the younger brothers', the lesser Slavonic nations. If any lesson had been required to drive home the evils of the obsolete but still existing system of government, it had been taught wholesale to officers and men alike in the succeeding heavy phases of war.

The Emperor's constitutional manifesto of October 30th, 1905, had itself been the promise of everything that was still being asked for: a legislative national assembly, and no law to be passed without it. Publicity of finance had already become a practice, and typical first class officials such as Kokovtsev had taken real pleasure in their co-operation with the Duma. The Fourth Duma, however unrepresentatively elected, had come more and more to voice the needs of the people, and most of its active members had learned in eight years of parliamentary life to work together, to respect each other's opinions, to understand the main problems of the Empire, to recognize the difficulties of administration and to discriminate between those who were working for the good of

[1] WITTE, I, 325.

the country and those who were not. At the great moment of national solidarity in face of the German challenge, an instinct of patriotism had sent the best of them up to the front, in the sure conviction that the apparatus of government had made no adequate preparation for the needs of the army; and there they were, working heart and soul as leaders of Zemgor, which represented the people's devotion to its national army. Inside that curtain which still separated front from rear, they came to know all the terrible realities of the unequal struggle against almost perfect organization and the highest technical efficiency, and this was a tremendous human lesson which, more than ever before, practically made patriotism and liberalism identical.

The Tsar himself, as has been recorded in his letters to his mother, had realized at the time that in his charter of 1905 he was creating a constitution. At the first dissolution, when public opposition was dying down, he had taken the premiership from an out-and-out reactionary and had committed it to 'a constitutionalist though not a parliamentarist', Stolypin, and it was Stolypin who restored order in the country. Loud voices had demanded the abolition of the Duma, but he had since accepted it as something that had come to stay, and regarded it even as a creation of his own of which he might be proud. His own conscientious joint labours with his Ministers had much of the character of constitutional work. The months preceding the war, under the influence of the quarrel with the Duma and the Romanov Tercentenary, had made him think more of his autocracy; but at the deeply stirring time of the German challenge, no one had felt more strongly than he the sacred moment of unity. Nicholas's strong and fatalistic conception of his anointed mission took the direction that he was before all things the victim, the sufferer for his people. He loved his army passionately and there was no one in the empire who took more deeply to heart every heavy blow that fell upon it. He particularly admired all those of its qualities which most called for admiration: its broad jollity, its variety, its conquering friendliness, its humour, its calm and easy patience, and its wonderful spirit.

This devotion to the army was fully shared by the whole nation. With the public the first effect of these heavy reserves was wholly good. Whatever may have been read into this story in the light of later events, the opposition to the Government, which was practically common to the whole country, was at this time entirely loyal, and much more patriotic than the Government itself. The worst economic effects of the war were only now beginning to make themselves felt; the chief of them was a great rise in prices, making life perhaps forty per cent dearer for town workers. The peasants, on the other hand, were better off than before, except that it was now much more difficult for them to get what they needed from the towns. As to food, in reality there was plenty of it and it was only a question of its circulation. Of course, there was discontent, but it was inarticulate, and had not so far taken political form. The chief lesson which Russia had been taught at the front was the same as that which she had had to learn on a far smaller scale in the Crimean War; all the difficulties were those of organization; all the glory was that of the simple fighting man.

The Duma and, beneath it, the zemstva, were the only legal mouthpieces which the nation possessed. The Duma was only very seldom in session and at other times could only speak through its President, Rodzyanko who, as such, might claim a right of access to the Tsar. For this immense responsibility Rodzyanko did possess the essential and primary qualities: absolute loyalty to the throne, a broad intelligence of what the nation wanted to say, and unflinching courage in saying it. It was inevitable that if one man had to speak for the nation, the nation's cause must suffer from any of his personal defects. Rodzyanko was quick and excitable; he was a superficial investigator of the matters brought before him; he was fussy, and much too ready to interfere in everything. It was too often that he claimed to see the sovereign on matters not concerned with the Duma. That he magnified the importance of the Duma was in its way good; but this led him to magnify his own personal importance, which was not the best way of approach to a man like Nicholas II. At an almost casual request of the Commander-in-Chief, he had taken it on himself to organize the boots supply for the army through the zemstva, and this had brought him into sharp personal conflict with the reactionary Minister of Interior, Nicholas Maklakov, who had but little sympathy with the zemstva or any of their works and regarded them as endeavouring to form an alternative government of the country.[1] Consequently the two men were always reporting to the Emperor against each other, and Maklakov was very much the more congenial to the sovereign.

But this time Rodzyanko had a cause which there was no denying, and the measures which he urged had the support of the whole nation. The public, especially through the Civil Red Cross, was longing to supply the crying gap in munitions. The War Minister knew so little about his work that he had even disregarded a considerable supply at his disposal until it was brought to his notice by Guchkov,[2] and he had been refusing wholesale the offers of big industrialists to adapt their factories to this need. Rodzyanko wanted a special 'Defence Council' which might serve as an equivalent to the Ministry of Munitions in England. He could not ask that this should be a mere department of the activity or inactivity of Sukhomlinov, and that is why he asked for a new special organ, which was not a Ministry, though, as he recognized, the War Minister would inevitably have to preside over it. He wanted it to carry the work of the whole country in army supply and to include not only representatives of the War Office, but of both Houses of the legislature, and the finance and commerce of the country. He laid this idea before the Grand Duke, who approved of it.

On May 17th, after the first crushing blows in Galicia, the Emperor arrived at Headquarters and heard the report on the conditions at the front, which the Grand Duke gave him with bitter tears. The Tsar too was deeply distressed. The Grand Duke later telegraphed to Rodzyanko: 'Your scheme must wait,' but the following day came a second telegram summoning him to Headquarters and asking him to bring those whose support he considered useful. Rodzyanko took with him Litvinov-Falinsky, Head of the Department of Industry, and Putilov, Director of the greatest heavy industry factory in Petrograd. He thus describes his reception by the sovereign.

> The Emperor looked extremely pale and worried; his hands trembled. He seemed particularly impressed when, myself deeply affected and scarcely able to restrain my tears, I spoke to him of the troops' unswerving devotion and love for their Tsar and motherland, their readiness to sacrifice themselves,

[1] RODZYANKO, 118-22. [2] Guchkov to B. P.

> and their simple unaffected response to the call of duty. The Emperor was pleased with the idea of a Special Council, and its outlines were drafted on the spot.[1]

Among those summoned to take part in it was even the inacceptable, but inevitable Guchkov.

At a later audience on June 12th Rodzyanko warmly pressed for the dismissal of those Ministers who were most unsympathetic to the war.[2] These were, in particular, the reactionary Nicholas Maklakov, the War Minister Sukhomlinov, the reactionary and pro-German Minister of Justice Shcheglovitov, and the Procurator of the Holy Synod, Sabler, who was so complacent to Rasputin. The aged Prime Minister, Goremykin, was not yet an object of attack; but no one could have been more unsuited to his post and to his work, and he himself spoke cynically of the candles which were only waiting for his coffin.[3] He said he was only too ready to be relieved of his duties at any time, in fact he had asked leave to resign, and only stayed on in obedience to the orders of his sovereign.

At this time the foremost personality in the Cabinet was the Minister of Agriculture, Krivoshein. He could himself have been Premier on the dismissal of Kokovtsev — in fact he had twice been offered this post — but, possibly with some foresight of future developments, he had preferred to remain in reserve and to guide the policy of Goremykin, who so far had been ready enough to take his lead. Krivoshein was an opportunist, — as Milyukov has described him, with several different cards in his hands and watching which to play; but he was much too clever to be in any doubt as to the issues now involved, and by May he had definitely aligned himself with those who were working for co-operation with the public.

Of the other Ministers, several were able and honest administrators fully capable of rising to the needs of the situation. Sazonov was a statesman not of the first class but of the second, fully acquainted with all the details of his work, loyal, and deeply patriotic. Count Paul Ignatyev, the Minister of Education, was bound to the Tsar by personal memories of their common military training, which did honour to both of them;[4] he

[1] RODZYANKO, 132.
[2] ibid., 137.
[3] PALÉOLOGUE, II, 4.
[4] IGNATYEV, *Padenie*, VI, 5.

stood as close as possible to Sazonov in all matters of policy, home or foreign, and both were entirely well disposed to the Duma. Haritonov, the State Auditor, was a man of shrewd wisdom and experience with a common-sense instinct for honesty, efficiency and co-operation with the nation. Sazonov enlisted other recruits, such as Peter Bark, the able Minister of Finance; his department was more than ever vital, especially to the connections with the Allies, whose assistance became every day more and more necessary. It would not, therefore, take very much to make the Ministry one which the public could trust and support.

The Emperor listened to Rodzyanko for over an hour with the closest attention, his elbows on the table and his face buried in his hands. At the end he took Rodzyanko's hand in both of his own and said to him, 'Thank you for your straightforward, frank and courageous report'. 'The Emperor', Rodzyanko writes, 'was visibly affected, and after uttering his last words, pressed my hands once more and passed quickly out through another door, unable to conceal his emotion.'[1] Clearly at this time he felt again at one with the public.

Rodzyanko's proposal of a Special Defence Council was sent on by the Tsar to his Cabinet. Here we have one of the best instances of the importance of capturing the word of the sovereign which, short of revolt, was the only way to secure changes in the government policy. In this way even the support of Goremykin was won. His principle was that an imperial order should simply be obeyed; and, in presenting the project, he declared that as the sovereign's wishes were clear, he imagined that there was no need of long discussion. But Nickolas Malakov was a man of principle, and he persisted in voting against the measure. Shcheglovitov and Sablin also expressed their disagreement, but in view of Goremykin's statement, they did not dare to record their votes against it. Nicholas could not feel any satisfaction with Maklakov's conduct; he was especially a champion of the autocracy, and now he was opposing his sovereign's own wishes. His dismissal followed immediately on June 16th, and those of the other dissentients were soon to follow.

Maklakov was succeeded at the Interior a fortnight later by Prince Shcherbatov. The appointment was made at Headquarters

[1] Rodzyanko, 138-9.

under the influence of the Grand Duke Nicholas, who as Inspector of Cavalry had been well acquainted with Shcherbatov's able work in charge of the army studs. At his first interview Shcherbatov told the Tsar that he could not regard the all-important Ministry of the Interior as simply a Ministry of Police, to which Nicholas cordially agreed.[1] Shcherbatov was all for co-operating with the public, and persistently resisted any promptings to dragoon the Press or to stifle public opinion. He gave his own quiet advice to the leaders of the public organizations, warning them not to put forward excessive claims;[2] but he consistently defended them at Cabinet meetings. On the other hand, he was always asking for the sorely needed delimitation of powers between the civil and the military authorities; and he raised another vital matter when he asked for a definition to distinguish between the duties of the Prime Minister and those of the Minister of the Interior—a question which was to give all sorts of trouble later.[3]

Meanwhile, on June 18th, the efficient head of the Zemgor, Prince George Lvov, a thorough-going Liberal, had called in Moscow a conference on munitions. He declared that only a united effort of all the forces of the country could save it.[4] The principal speaker was Guchkov. He had lived on the Warsaw front throughout the war as a head of Red Cross, and had seen units sent under fire without rifles. He knew of the orders limiting the fire of a battery to five or six shells a day. He had even travelled adventurously far into the no man's land in front of the line to ascertain from the Germans the fate of Samsonov. He had been to Sukhomlinov, but could get no satisfaction from him, and other Ministers were timid about interfering in a province not their own.[5] He now openly denounced Sukhomlinov.† The fall of the War Minister soon followed. Nicholas had been at home at Tsarskoe Selo since May 26th. Sukhomlinov had gone so far as to reply to the French Government's inquiry, as to how he stood for munitions, that nothing was required. This letter was shown by the French Ambassador Paléologue to Sazonov, who had repeatedly been urging the Emperor to dismiss Sukhomlinov. Sazonov showed the letter to the Emperor, and this proved the

[1] SHCHERBATOV, *Padenie*, VII, 209. [2] ibid., 227.
[3] ibid., 211. [4] PALÉOLOGUE, II, 9.
[5] Guchkov to B. P., who was present.

last straw.[1] Nicholas greatly regretted parting company with this agreeable visitor and made this clear to him in a warm, personal letter. 'After long thought and consultation with the Grand Duke,' he had finally decided that this was necessary.[2]

On June 23rd Nicholas again set out for Headquarters, and on the 27th all the remaining Ministers were gathered there under his chairmanship, with the exception of Shcheglovitov and Sabler, who received their dismissal soon afterwards. It was the Grand Duke again who really fixed Nicholas's choice of Sukhomlinov's successor and, with him, Krivoshein and Prince Vladimir Orlov, the Head of the Emperor's military chancery, both of whom were now at Headquarters. Their candidate was General Polivanov. Badly wounded in his first action in the Russo-Turkish War of 1877, he had since held one important post of military administration after another. Before the war, when Sukhomlinov maintained such indifference to the Duma, Polivanov had visited it as his deputy on behalf of the War Office and rendered it every assistance, resulting as has been said, in the increase of the Duma's votes for army equipment.[3] Sukhomlinov had quarrelled with him and dismissed him from the post of Assistant Minister. The Grand Duke sent an urgent summons to him and steered through his appointment — only, it is true, as Acting War Minister, as was done in cases where the Emperor's decision was not final. In this case he had reservations, and Polivanov, acting on the Grand Duke's advice, elicited them in his first audience. In sum they were simply due to Polivanov's association with Guchkov, with whom he had worked in the closest collaboration when the Third Duma was insisting on army reform. The Emperor advised him against too much intimacy on that side. He asked both Shcherbatov and Polivanov to visit the Empress, whom he no doubt hoped thereby to reconcile to their appointment.'[4] Sukhomlinov had relied for his maintenance in power on easy and superficial explanations and entertaining conversation. Polivanov, on the other hand, was vigorous and even brusque; he knew his work through and through, and went straight to the point in his reports to the Emperor. Shcherglovitov was replaced at the Ministry of Justice by a nominee of Goremykin, A. A. Hvostov,

[1] Sazonov, 287.
[2] Polivanov, 141.
[3] ibid., *Padenie*, vii, 56.
[4] Polivanov, 131-7.

who had served as head of Goremykin's chancery. This was a strong Conservative, an excellent jurist, with an instinctive insistence on order and regularity, a sound judgment and fearlessness in expressing it.

The Cabinet meeting at Headquarters on June 27th was of critical importance. It was the most decisive step taken so far towards co-operation between the Government and the public. A rescript was issued on the subject of munitions instituting the Defence Council. The Emperor appealed to the country for its united help to save the army and win the war. This appeal, drafted by Krivoshein, with valuable suggestions by the Grand Duke, summoned the Duma for, not later than August, (Aug. 14th) 'in order to hear the voice of the land of Russia'.[1]

Now that Russian Poland was being lost to Russia, the question of its recovery automatically became one that called for a joint effort of Russia and her Allies. Already in January in the representations of the Duma men to the Government, Milyukov had pressed for a realization of the autonomy promised to Poland at the outset of the war by the Grand Duke with the approval of the Emperor. The Poles, too, particularly those who had access to the sovereign, such as Count Sigismund Wielepolski, were pressing for something more definite as a counterpoise to anything which the Central Powers might promise on their side. General Evert, when commanding the Fourth Russian Army in Poland, had published a special tribute to the cordial help of the Polish population in the war, and even the reactionary Purishkevich was now entirely converted to their cause. It was decided to set up a commission of twelve to give shape to the promised autonomy.

It remained to fill the post of Sabler as Minister of Religion. Again on the advice of the Grand Duke, Nicholas summoned to Headquarters the elected Marshal of the Moscow nobility, Samarin, a strong Conservative and deeply loyal. He came of a family with great Slavophil traditions, which held in Russia a position very similar to that of the Cecils in England. They did not seek office and in fact were even reluctant to take it when it was offered to them — Samarin had refused appointment to this post in 1906 — and if they did so, their very independence was a guarantee of faithful service in the interests of the Church. Samarin

[1] Polivanov, 137.

was unwilling to give his agreement to the Emperor's invitation without clearing up the question of the influence of Rasputin in church affairs, and he asked for an interval of a fortnight before giving his definite acceptance. Rasputin, about this time, went off to Siberia, and the public accredited this to Samarin's insistence. Anyhow Samarin accepted the post.

It was at this point that the Empress intervened. She, too, by her pervading love for her husband was all-Russian at heart. There are passages of real beauty in her letters to him, expressing her deep sense of the sublimeness of this time of world cleansing by suffering, with the banishment of everything petty, the return of God and the simple virtues to their old place in the minds of men.[1] So she would write as she came away from the bedside of some patient and noble sufferer whether colonel or peasant, for whom alike she had been doing all the offices of a trained nurse; 'really saints and heroes all of them', she writes.[2] She has no doubt whatever of the issue of the war, because she believes in God and He could not allow the insolence of the challenge to prevail. William she regards as 'dragging his country into ruin' and having committed the greatest of sins;[3] even before the war, Mosolov tells us, 'she could hardly maintain ordinary civility at their personal meetings';[4] of the brutalities of German warfare she writes exactly as a middleclass Englishwoman might have written at the same date: 'the Schadenfreude of the Germans makes my blood boil',[5] and again, 'We must show that we stand higher than they with all their culture';[6] and it is in these letters that we can see the triumphant and even scornful refutation of the personal slanders that have been circulated against her.

But it is precisely in these letters, written in imperfect English, and there alone, that we can find the central key to all that was to happen later. Before the War Nicholas and Alexandra were very seldom parted; during the War she wrote to him every day of his absence from her and sometimes twice in the day. She wrote an easy, running hand, very legible, and at one point she stops to wonder at how much paper she has covered in half an hour. Sometimes the reader will wonder on his side how the Emperor

[1] A. F. to N., Ap. 5th/18th, 1915, Ap. 8th/21st, 1915.
[2] Jan. 28th/Feb. 10th, 1915.
[3] Sept. 27th/Oct. 8th, 1914.
[4] MOSOLOV, 203.
[5] June 12th/25th, 1915.
[6] Sept. 5th/18th, 1915.

found time to read it all. Each of her letters she carefully numbered. At the Revolution she destroyed many of her papers; apparently all the correspondence between herself and Vyrubova, who was then lying ill in the palace. But her correspondence with her husband was ultimately found in a black leather suitcase at Ekaterinburg after their death.

Once they were published, these letters became the most important historical source for the subjects with which they deal, and the main subject of them is the governance of the Russian Empire.

On this subject the mind and thought of the Empress are compellingly clear and whole-hearted and she knew her own mind better than anyone else in the whole story. It coloured every instinct, every fear, every suspicion. She had married into the Russian autocracy. This was something different from every other monarchy. Repeatedly she marks this distinction: 'But *we* are anointed by God.' She is all for peasant Russia, 'who are our strength and the devoted souls of Russia',[1] but peasant Russia is all for the Tsar. While she worships him for his superiority over her by the charm of his character, she recognizes, like a mother, all his gentleness and weakness; as he is gentle and weak, it is her wifely duty with her wholeness and firmness and courage to save his autocracy for him and her little heir, in whom she believes she sees a firmness which will tolerate no indecision and no opposition. She has a well-founded contempt for all the loose living in high Petrograd society; she has a well-founded scorn for the gossip, the scandals, the impure suggestions against herself, the monstrous supposition that she is the friend of Russia's national enemy, Wilhelm. 'They will be telling you next', she says once, 'that I am a German spy,' which indeed came to be the current report throughout the capital.

For the first year of the war Alexandra, constantly troubled by her bad heart, often only able to move about in a wheeled chair, literally shared in the humblest work of her hospitals. With her sense of the sanctity of the imperial authority, she seldom even in her intimate letters intervenes with suggestions on politics and still less in military questions. She is content to surround her loved one with flowers, scent, little presents of all sorts to make him feel that

[1] A. F. to N., June 24th/July 7th, 1916.

he is never parted from her presence. 'All my soul will follow and surround you everywhere.'[1]

The letters are, of course, full of the simple doings of the children, but already there is a marked and personal animosity against the Commander-in-Chief. He is one who has abandoned 'a man of God' because he has turned against Rasputin, who keeps her boy alive with a power that can only be from God. The Grand Duke was deeply religious, and foreign guests at Headquarters were struck with the multitude of icons there. It appears that Rasputin suggested a visit in order to hang up a new one, and the Grand Duke telegraphed: 'Come and I'll hang', which effectually kept Rasputin away.[2] But the Empress's main complaint was the one which she had made to Kokovtsev against Stolypin, that he was overshadowing her little husband, as he could hardly help doing, whether physically or otherwise. Scandal repeated, with direct untruth, a tale that the Grand Duke had even spoken of himself as Nicholas III; in reality, he was touchingly loyal throughout. Alexandra is, therefore, constantly suggesting that her husband should show himself more often to the troops, 'that they may see whom they are fighting for', and evidently relies on his strongest quality, his personal charm, to counter what she believes to be the Grand Duke's ambition. Just as Anna Vyrubova used almost daily to visit Petrograd to gather up the prevailing scandals, so the same troublesome lady corresponded with irresponsible young aides-de-camp at Headquarters, collecting any sufficiently tasty and spiteful rumours against the Grand Duke. And now Rasputin had declared that the war would lead to wholesale bloodshed and losses, and so it had proved. No wonder! The Commander-in-Chief had abandoned the guidance of 'a man of God', in whom he had once believed.

On June 10th/23rd, in a letter written to follow her husband on his departure for Headquarters, practically for the first time she goes far beyond the anxieties of a wife over the colossal task imposed on her husband. On May 4th/17th when encouraging him to 'continue bravely bearing your heavy crown', she had added, 'I

[1] A. F. to N., Feb. 27th/Mar. 12th, 1915.

[2] The ordinary version current was somewhat cruder and was repeated by Rodzyanko to the Grand Duke, who smiled and admitted there was something of the kind. It is more likely to have been as described above.

yearn to lessen your burden; you were born on the day of the long-suffering Job, too, my poor Sweetheart . . . Be firm, remember you are the Emperor', though she half apologizes, 'I meddle in things not concerning me'. But now she is faced with the first Ministerial changes. Like the Tsar, she was sincerely attached to Nicholas Maklakov. 'Let me help you, my treasure,' she writes '. . . the Ministers are all squabbling amongst each other', (she regards it as a noisy dispute in the servants' hall). 'It makes me rage. In other words it is treachery . . . and then the Left profit by it. If you could only be severe, my love . . . they must learn to tremble before you . . . harken [*sic*] unto our Friend'; but again she writes next day, 'I hope my letter did not displease you . . . Share all with me', and on June 13th/26th, 'if you have any questions for our Fr., write at once'. On the 14th/27th, 'Perhaps I can be of some use . . . Be more autocratic my very own Sweetheart'. On the 28th, 'The town is full of gossip on the Ministerial changes', and she gives a message from Rasputin, 'Pay less attention to people; use your own instinct'. 'He regrets you did not tell him more . . . Oh! how I long to help you and give you faith in yourself.' Nicholas writes on the same day from Headquarters, 'These changes must be brought about'; but next day she has heard of the invitation to Samarin, and writes, 'I am simply in despair . . . All will go badly . . . as he is against us — once he is against Gr: (Gregory); . . . my heart feels like lead . . . Oh! why are we not together to speak over all together . . . our Friend's enemies are ours . . . come back . . . nothing is trivial now — all is grave'; and on the 29th, 'Ah! my Boy, my Boy, how I wish we were together . . . think more of Gr:, Sweetheart . . . Oh! let me guide you more.' Nicholas telegraphed the same day, 'Please do not worry, and see Goremykin, who will calm you', but she writes, 'Never forget that you are and must remain an autocratic Emperor . . . Nobody knows who is the Emperor now', and on July 5th,[1] 'Oh! my Boy, make one tremble before you . . . I fear I aggravate you by all I write'. On July 8th she writes about 'that horrid Rodzyanko asking to call the Duma . . . Oh! please don't, it is not their business . . . they must be kept away . . . Russia, thank God, is not a constitutional country and these creatures try to play a part . . . it is fright if one gives in, and their heads will go up . . . I loathe your

[1] June 22nd, O.S.

being at Headquarters'. On the 9th she begs forgiveness for vexing him and excuses it by her 'misery at not being able to help', and at last he returns to his home.

Of what happened there, we know less; for the direct source of the letters ceases and this bombardment is now superfluous. But we should be wrong if we assumed that Nicholas was now cut off from his people. At the launching of a warship he says to Paléologue, 'Nothing does me more good than to feel myself in contact with my people; I needed that to-day'.[1] On her side, she complains at one point later that she could see so little of him, though he was back with her. What we know is, that she continued to fight her battle; and the very extremeness of the expressions in her letters is a proof that she realized how extraordinarily difficult it was. In order to magnify his authority, she had almost to override it; and this is not a nagging wife, but one who is heart and soul devoted to him. While she will use to the utmost his personal charm, she is at the same time trying to cut off the exercise of it on his beloved people. And what has she got against her? In a word, history. She is an Englishwoman fighting Germany wholeheartedly for her adored husband's Russia. At the same time she is pushing away the equally wholehearted efforts of the Russian people in the same cause. She adores the Russian Army, and she is standing in the way of the satisfaction of its most urgent needs. While she expresses typically English instincts and takes pleasure in any meetings with English men or women, she is repulsing vigorously the influence of England in Russian internal affairs.

There is, as Paléologue admitted, a certain grandeur in the struggle. And has she been proved wrong in questioning whether Russia was ripe for constitutional rule? In this question Rasputin was not for her merely a man who had kept her boy alive, but the channel between her and the simple and wise instincts of the Russian peasantry, illustrated by countless little anecdotes at each of his visits to her.

Valery Carrick, the distinguished caricaturist who had been one of the later Narodniks and was always most at home 'in the bosom of the people', at the outset of the war writes in his shrewd diary (Aug. 5th, 1914)[2] 'And somewhere at once a curtain was let down which separates us from the lower classes'. His old housekeeper

[1] Paléologue, ii, 11. [2] July 23rd, O.S.

asks him, 'Why don't all the gentlemen go (to the front)?'[1] One sees at once the broad and sound base on which Lenin was to set his propaganda. A dying soldier mutters to me: 'It had to be! The Emperor had to be rich!' Or put it as it was put later, 'The rich man gains a market; the poor man loses a leg'. What pathetic life stories did Rasputin bring to the palace from his lone rambles in a country now covered with cripples? 'Getting empty in the villages,' says a peasant to me with a kind of cheery objectiveness; and he tells how all his three brothers have died at the front, and now he is looking after all their families. The first two had some little time to distinguish themselves; but of the third he says, 'Him they put up like a sheep!' Rasputin, says Simanovich, told them of 'the tears of the life of the people', and to Paléologue he said, 'Too much bloodshed!' 'Which do you think most of', he asked the Tsar, 'the 150 thousand (the thin layer of gentry) or the 150 millions?'[2] For him and for the Empress only this was the people, and the chatterers in the Duma and in the capital were not Russian. One recalls the comment of Maurice Baring, who has seen deeper into the Russian nature than any other foreigner; he said he would rather trust the political judgment of a peasant cab-driver than that of any Member of the Duma; and I myself have to remember that the best summaries on the course of Russian politics were made to me by peasants.

But meanwhile the public concern was rising higher and higher. We must bear in mind that since May 2nd, as we know from the last chapter, the most distressing and agitating news was coming in from the front in quick succession. On June 15th the fortress of Przemysl was lost; on the 22nd was also lost Lemberg, almost the last footing that the Russians had in Galicia. On June 17th the Germans were launching a new advance from the Narew on the eastern frontier of Russian Poland, which quite outflanked Warsaw. On July 4th the line at which Alexeyev had hoped to stop the German advance was broken, and the Commander-in-Chief had to make a hurried journey to the front; the enemy was about to threaten the Gulf of Riga. Yanushkevich was writing panic-stricken letters to the new War Minister. On July 8th/21st, 'Why, no science has taught this method of waging war, without cartridges, without rifles, without guns!' And on July 18th/31st, 'I

[1] CARRICK, 6-7. [2] SIMANOVICH, 154.

beg pardon for my importunity, but like a drowning man clutching at a straw I seek salvation for the distressing situation in a number of measures'.[1] Almost as menacing was the news from Moscow where great riots began on June 10th. German shops were sacked and there was a fierce outbreak of hooliganism, with street fighting which had to be repressed with the use of the troops. The elder Prince Yusopov, who was the civil authority in charge, evidently relying on his intimacy with the Emperor, put forward the most extravagant demands, which in substance would isolate Moscow both from the rest of the army and from the rest of the country. There were also riots and shootings in the great industrial town of Ivanovo-Voznesensk.

The two most vital Ministries at this time were those of the Interior and War; and both were now administered by 'new brooms', Shcherbatov and Polivanov; the latter's concise published notes are invaluable for the study of this most critical period. Both of them were appalled by the chaos and confusion in which their easy-going predecessors had left their Departments — 'such a muddle', says Shcherbatov, 'as I could not reconcile myself to.'[2] For Polivanov it was even worse. By the Statute of Field Administration, hastily adopted at the beginning of the War on July 29th, 1914 — Sukhomlinov had only then submitted it for the Emperor's approval — the army authorities had absolute and unrestricted control, not only over all areas within the field of operations, but also over all military institutions in the rear, for which they did not have to give any account to the Cabinet or other civil authorities. Only the Ministers were allowed to correspond with them, and even they had the greatest difficulty in obtaining replies, and could not challenge any of the decisions which had been reached; in most cases where they heard of them, it was only after the event. The Commander-in-Chief had the right to dismiss any local official, whether of the central or the local government — for instance, governors, mayors or heads of county councils. Nothing whatever was said of the relations of the army to the civil government. The Prime Minister and the Cabinet were not even mentioned in the Statute. It is to be realized that this military control extended to Finland, Poland, the Caucasus, the Baltic Provinces, Archangel, Vladivostok, and

[1] Polivanov, 185-6. [2] Shcherbatov, *Padenie*, vii, 211.

even to the capital, Petrograd, which was under the military rule of the Commander of the Sixth Russian Army with a purely military censorship. To secure an explanation of any kind, the Ministers had necessarily to travel to Headquarters.[1]

All this authority was summarily exercised by the young Chief of Staff, General Yanushkevich, who was not the choice of the Grand Duke, but had with chivalrous weakness been taken over by him on his appointment. Like his rival the War Minister, Sukhomlinov, Yanushkevich did not show any particular ability, and the main work of Headquarters was done by the able and industrious Quartermaster-General Danilov; but in every way Yanushkevich magnified his authority in open defiance of the civil government, which included the War Minister, responsible for army supply. The Grand Duke, himself, had always welcomed co-operation with the Government, but this was defeated by Yanushkevich, who, for instance, would not tolerate the presence of an authoritative ex-Minister at Headquarters, and claimed that any representative of the Central Government there should report to him and correspond with Petrograd only through him.[2] The worst of all the disorders which arose through this state of things was due to his wholesale removal, not only of Germans and Jews, but of the population itself from the abandoned territory, which flooded the interior with a huge stream of fugitives marking their way by numberless corpses, especially of children, and a wide spread of typhus — a problem with which it was quite impossible for the local governors to cope.[3]

These were the conditions in which the Cabinet met on July 29th. Already at a meeting held in the palace on the 21st under the chairmanship of the Emperor, it had unanimously begged for the summons of a military and civil council, to include commanders of the various Fronts and the Ministers. The sitting of the 29th was opened in a dramatic way by a speech of Polivanov, who began with the words, 'I hold it to be my civic and service duty to declare to the Council of Ministers, that the country is in danger'.[4] We have for all the Cabinet meetings of this period the notes of its Assistant Secretary, Yakhontov, sometimes taken on chance slips of paper in the midst of cross currents of passionate debate. Polivanov's words, he tells us, even discounting the rhetoric of his statement,

[1] YAKHONTOV, 10 ff. [2] ibid., 12. [3] ibid., 12. [4] ibid., 15.

fell like a bomb on the meeting. He had to explain that as he could get no information from Headquarters, he had to depend in part on the evidence obtained in the capital from the enemy intelligence! He described the panic of some of the units, the numerous surrenders, the recruits under fire waiting for rifles, and curtly stated that there were no corresponding losses on the German side, which indeed was well known to those living at the front. In reply to criticisms Yanushkevich had said that he did not propose to take any account of the Cabinet's reproaches; he described his measures against the Jews as 'extremely weak' and proposed to reinforce them; he had not even consulted the commanders of the different fronts. On Polivanov's suggestion, it was agreed that Goremykin and he should again beg the Emperor for a military council at the palace and that other individual Ministers should report in this sense. In the course of the debate Krivoshein compared the chaos to that of an asylum. Shcherbatov reported the plaints of the local governors. The Duma was to meet in three days; it had no right to interpellate the Commander-in-Chief, and could only entrust its grievances to the Ministers, who had no means of obtaining redress. Krivoshein denounced the dualism of military and civil authority, and declared, 'Over Russia there is hovering some irreparable tragedy'. Shakhovskoy, the Minister of Industry, cited the arbitrary oppression of factory workers by the military authorities in the capital. Rukhlov, Minister of Railways, declared that the work of transport was becoming intolerable; the military were disturbing all dispositions of the Ministry by entirely arbitrary counter-orders.

It was peculiarly unfortunate that the indignation of the Cabinet should, at this time, have been justifiably directed against one who exercised the authority of the Grand Duke Nicholas; and Goremykin, in very plain words, gave a wise warning that the Empress, whom he mentioned by name, was already the Grand Duke's enemy.[1] It remained to the meeting to decide on the terms of the Government's statement at the opening of the Duma. Goremykin accepted the wording of his proposed speech as drafted by Krivoshein, and this was generally approved. Especial importance was attached to the question of Poland, which was already in the course of being lost to Russia. It was decided to

[1] Yakhontov, 21.

repeat in the name of the Government, and even of the sovereign, the promise of autonomy made at the beginning of the war by the Grand Duke. Sazonov asked for greater emphasis on the keen interest which Russia's Allies took in this question. He wanted an immediate grant of autonomy, announced in a manifesto of the Emperor, which could be published in Warsaw before the Russian troops left. To this the other Ministers were opposed, and Polivanov grimly closed the discussion by saying 'The days of Warsaw are already counted'. The Russian Second Army was to evacuate the city four days later.

Behind the Government there was to come the Duma; and neither the Government nor the Duma could be taken to measure the resentment of the whole country. It has been mentioned that as far back as February 7th some Ministers had privately met a number of prominent members of the Duma, in anticipation of the short two days' session which began on February 9th; and there the Ministers had been interrogated on various questions, particularly the liberty of the Press and the treatment of non-Russian nationalities. By the end of May, under the impression of the great reverses at the front, public opinion was demanding a new session with a full discussion of the burning questions. Throughout, the Duma leaders had kept their colleagues in touch with their negotiations with Ministers.

Gradually there had now come to completion a movement which had been in progress for several years back. Long parliamentary co-operation, together with an increasing intimacy with the details of the administration of the empire, had brought the parties together. The Socialists, it is true, continued to go their own way, but the Mensheviks were not at all unpatriotic. Close to them the Labour Group, led by Kerensky, was all for the defence of the country, sometimes even more unreservedly than the Cadets of Milyukov.[1] But the Cadets themselves were now drawing much closer to the more conservative parties of reform. Of the latter the most distinguished members were at the front with the Red Cross; as the Cabinet fully realized, they had witnessed all the disorders at the front, and it was really their growing understanding of the essence of the constitutional issue that was bringing them nearer to the Cadets. The nationalist Shulgin relates[2] how, on his return

[1] Milyukov to B. P. [2] RODZYANKO, 134; SHULGIN, 61.

from the front, where his Red Cross service had been adventurous and efficient, he rang up the Cadet leader, Milyukov, and visited him in uniform. So far they had had no personal relations, but Shulgin opened the discussion by saying at once, 'Paul Nikolayevich, I have come to ask you straight out — Are we friends?' 'He did not answer at once', says Shulgin, 'but all the same he answered, "Yes, I think so, I think we are friends".' With this beginning they came without difficulty to an agreement. The Duma would stand whole-heartedly for the war; and for that very reason it would call attention to the crying abuses of administration. This, both agreed, was the only way of averting a violent convulsion. The same idea of a Duma united for patriotism and reform had occurred to Rodzyanko, and for Basil Maklakov it had always been a long-desired dream.[1]

It was in this atmosphere of united effort that the Duma met on August 1st. Goremykin's speech met with a cold reception; but Polivanov, who had insisted on speaking also, made it clear that in every way he meant to work with the Duma, and was applauded with enthusiasm. The Nationalist Count Vladimir Bobrinsky, by an understanding with his colleagues to the left, put forward a demand for a 'Ministry of Confidence', which became the watchword of the reformers up to the Revolution. This meant that the Tsar should choose as Prime Minister a man who commanded not only his confidence but that of the country, and that there should be no one in the Cabinet who was not in line with him in his intention to co-operate with the public. This was the least that the Cadets could ask, and they accepted this formula in order to present a mass of united opinion. Milyukov, who supported Bobrinsky, went on to outline a series of necessary reforms, touching several questions with which the Cabinet was itself preparing to deal. There was in his own party a restless left wing under Nekrasov which wanted more. They demanded that the Ministry should be directly responsible to the Duma; and so did Labour, the Socialists and Zemgor; but this was premature. In the first place, it would at once have split the ranks of the reformers when it was all-important that they should remain united. But besides that, there were so many different groups in the Duma that it was only now, under the pressure of the national danger, that

[1] V. Maklakov to B. P.

there was forming any solid majority which could have served as a basis to a Cabinet.

On August 3rd the very able Cadet, Shingarev, was elected chairman of the Duma's Commission of Imperial Defence, and without delay he submitted a whole series of detailed questions on this subject to the willing Polivanov.[1] On the 5th, a Bill legalizing the Defence Council, brought in by Polivanov, was up for discussion. Shingarev denounced the 'disgusting state' of the railways and the arbitrary abuses under the Statute of Field Administration, which he declared to be an infringement of the rights of the legislative chambers.[2] The debate was continued on the 14th. In confirming the Defence Council, the Duma put forward the suggestion that there should be an additional Assistant to the War Minister to deal with it under his direction and that this Assistant might be a civilian. It was freely assumed that a post was being created for Guchkov, and Polivanov, realizing at once that this move would be credited to him at the palace, hastened to get the approval of the Emperor for the appointment of General Lukomsky.[3]

The Defence Council was nominated by the sovereign. Its constitution was as follows: The President of the Duma; four members each from the Council of State, the Duma, and representatives of the trade and industry of the country; officials of the War Office, Admiralty, and the Ministries of Finance, Transport, Commerce, and the State Audit. Krivoshein had secured that it should regulate not only military equipment, but also fuel and food supply, and eventually there were four separate councils: for munitions, food, fuel and transport, with a fifth added later to deal with the overwhelming inflow of refugees. Polivanov has reasonably explained that it would have been quite impossible for the War Office alone to deal with all these closely interconnected problems.[4]

But in the course of the debate there was an incident which later reached the Emperor and must have greatly disturbed the Empress. The writer ventures to recall that on his first report to Mr. Lloyd George, then Minister of Munitions, on July 26th, he drew him aside and urgently warned him that if the conditions were not changed in Russia, the war must bring a disorderly revolution, on which subject he was asked to write a memorandum

[1] POLIVANOV, 191. [2] ibid., 193. [3] ibid., 194. [4] ibid., 200.

to the British War Cabinet. Speaking at Bangor on August 5th Mr. Lloyd George remarked:

> The Eastern sky is dark and lowering. The stars have been clouded over. I regard that stormy horizon with anxiety, but with no dread. Today I can see the colour of a new hope beginning to empurple the sky. The enemy in their victorious march know not what they are doing. Let them beware, for they are unshackling Russia. With their monster artillery they are shattering the rusty bars that fettered the strength of the people of Russia.[1]

His speeches were eagerly read in Russia, and this one was quoted in the Duma with rapture by a keen little radical lawyer Adzhemov, and was later read by the Emperor.[2] If the Empress wanted confirmation that allied influence was always a danger to the interests of the autocracy, she might certainly find it in this incident.

Very early the Duma decided by 345 votes to 30 to impeach the fallen War Minister, Sukhomlinov.[3] He found no defenders in the Cabinet; it was Goremykin himself who proposed a commission of representatives of the two legislative chambers to examine all charges against those responsible for the tragic lack of shell in the army, and such a commission was appointed.[4] Another claim of the reformers was easy to satisfy, for it had become almost academic. This was the abolition of the so-called Jewish Pale of Settlement, from which Jews were allowed admittance to the rest of the empire only under very harsh conditions. The army itself, on the orders of Yanushkevich, had been driving all Jews into the interior; and the better part of the Jewish Pale had already been conquered by the enemy. Here too Goremykin himself showed alacrity in recognizing the accomplished fact and Jewish refugees were admitted to the interior, though not to the capital.[5]

Meanwhile the Duma was organizing a more or less solid majority to serve as the natural support of a 'Ministry of Confidence'. On Aug. 18th/19th the leaders of all the central groups met at a special sitting of the Senioren-Konvent. On the 22nd they met again at the President's flat. Two days later they joined hands with the more liberal groups in the Upper House.

[1] PARES, *My Russian Memoirs*, 389, footnote. [2] PALÉOLOGUE, II, 43. [3] ibid., 35. [4] YAKHONTOV, 27. [5] ibid., 30.

A joint committee met on August 27th and 28th, and its detailed proposals were accepted after long consideration by all the members of the groups concerned on September 4th. Thus was formed a 'Progressive Bloc'. Whether wisely or not, in order to be able to appeal for a common effort of the whole nation in the war, the Bloc decided to ask for certain definite reforms of a moderate character, most of which were long overdue.[1]

All this took time, and, of course, both the Government and the public had a general idea of what was going on. It was the main body of the Duma and the best brains in it that were represented in the Progressive Bloc. The Socialists, to the left, were in sympathy with it; and to the right, the Bloc itself contained most of those who could have been elected under an open franchise, and several of the rest were drawing closer to it. It might have contented itself with the very reasonable preamble to its programme. 'The Duma asked little,'[2] wrote Sazonov later; and certainly its central demand was for something which practically the whole mass of educated opinion in the country wanted, namely a united Cabinet which could command its confidence.

On the other hand, was the Bloc wise in putting forward at this moment a mass of prospective legislative reform? We can understand that its members had wished to know to what extent they were agreed on questions of detail, but a far-reaching demand for a radical change in the whole order of Government was a challenge which would need to be supported by action or even by revolt; and that was exactly what the right wing of the Bloc most wanted to avoid, especially in time of war. It is therefore very questionable whether they should have agreed. The draft of the programme was evidently in the main the work of the leader of the left wing, Milyukov. He was infinitely the most fitted for the task by his wide knowledge of Western constitutional history; but he was not a good tactician. It is true that Shulgin, of the right wing, could see little ground for objection to any of the points raised.[3]

The Tsar, from the first, while not expressing opposition to reform, was clear that it must be deferred till after the war, and this continued to be his attitude throughout. But even to the Cabinet the programme was a fresh challenge. Krivoshein regarded it in the same light as the military dualism, that is, as

[1] YAKHONTOV, 109. [2] SAZONOV, 281. [3] SHULGIN, 65.

a claim of another alternative Government, and, therefore, a challenge to the existing one; and he maintained that the Cabinet should either assert its authority or resign. To Rodzyanko, who paid a visit during a Cabinet sitting, he said, 'I suppose you have come to preside over us?'[1] Far more insistent was the opposition of the Empress, who recognized quite clearly that this meant the end of the Russian autocracy, already questioned and half displaced by the concession of October 1905, and she set herself to resist the challenge in every way.

The Cabinet meanwhile continued to meet frequently, and its more conservative members expressed great annoyance at the delay of the Duma in passing the necessary laws for calling up what were called the second-class reservists, namely persons exempted in all other cases than those of a grave national emergency. The Duma was all for the army; but it distrusted the Prime Minister and was still calling for a united Cabinet. On August 16th Kovno, one of the strongest Russian fortresses, fell without any adequate resistance; the timely individual exit of its commander, Grigoryev, made the worst impression; it was some time before he could be traced and brought before the court martial which was immediately set up by the Grand Duke.

On August 17th Yakhontov records an unusual occurrence.[2] Guchkov is present at a Cabinet meeting on the invitation of Polivanov. He has come to ask for sanction of a network of unofficial war industry committees which he is setting up all over the country. The origin of this movement was a Congress of the Trades and Industries of the country (this was an established and recognized institution with a permanent office).[3] The Congress elected a committee for this special purpose, and chose Guchkov as chairman.[4] The new organization contained sections for every branch of army supply; and it included delegates from the workers themselves, who held separate meetings and had their own office. At first, partly owing to defeatist instructions sent from abroad by Lenin, there was some unwillingness among the workers to elect delegates, but later this became one of the most vigorous sides of the organization. Guchkov's network spread all over the country, mobilizing the smaller factories to war uses. It was in

[1] RODZYANKO, 149. [2] YAKHONTOV, 36. [3] See p. 116.
[4] Guchkov to B. P.; Konovalov to B. P.; FLORINSKY, 133.

close alliance with Zemgor which was co-ordinating the artisans and the cottage industries for similar work. Both Guchkov and the Ministers felt anything but comfortable at meeting each other, and later he wrote a letter to Goremykin, which was taken as confirming the impression that he claimed to have set up a separate and independent authority; but the committees were accepted and continued their work till the revolution. The Empress loathed that 'rotten war industry committee'.[1] As to Guchkov, her letters were full of the bitterest hatred for him. 'Oh, could not one hang Guchkov'?[2] 'Could not a strong railway accident be arranged in which he alone would suffer?'[3] 'Guchkov is very ill — wish he would go — it's not a sinful wish.'[4] Meanwhile Kerensky and the socialists were discussing the sequels to peace; among these they were demanding the restoration of universal suffrage and the principle of self-determination for the nationalities of the empire.

On August 19th after a series of preparatory discussions came the following message from the town council of Moscow, soon to be followed by Petrograd and other towns:

> (1) Moscow knows that a whole number of our towns and even fortresses are in the hands of the enemy. But Moscow unflinchingly and firmly believes in the Russian Army and its leader, the Grand Duke, and is ready to strain every nerve to create the conditions which will guarantee victory. The War must be carried to the end. Peace must be concluded only after complete victory over the enemy and in unanimous agreement of all the Allies.
> (2) The War has entered a new phase. The situation which has been created sets new and more responsible tasks. At this moment all the forces of the country, all sections of the population must unite in a common arduous endeavour to undertake all that leads to work.
> (3) The foundation for the winning of victory is the union of the national Government with the Country. Moscow is convinced that the Imperial Duma will know at this hour how to carry out the wishes dictated by the country.
> (4) The present standing responsible task demands the calling of a Government strong in the confidence of the public and unanimous, at whose head must stand someone in whom the country believes.

[1] A. F. to N., Mar. 15th/28th, 1916.
[2] Sept. 2nd/15th, 1915.
[3] ibid., Sept. 11th/24th, 1915.
[4] ibid., Jan 4th/17th, 1916.

Long before the Progressive Bloc was formed, there were signs of another direction at the palace. Very early in the session of the Duma (Aug. 3rd) Nicholas had said to Polivanov, 'In general I don't pay attention to what they say — or to what they understand either'.[1] On the 11th after a Cabinet meeting under his chairmanship, which discussed a proposal of Krivoshein to divert land of German colonists to soldiers who had distinguished themselves in the war, Nicholas drew Shcherbatov aside and asked him if he could not replace his Assistant Dzhunkovsky by Beletsky.[2] What had happened? Since Dzhunkovsky's report in June on Rasputin's outrageous conduct at Yar, he had accompanied his sovereign on some of his journeys and had been treated with special consideration. On July 5th the Empress had written a furious invective against him: she had at last been acquainted with the report. It was in her eyes 'that vile filthy paper',[3] and so it was, but the filth was Rasputin's. She asked her favourite aide-de-camp, N. P. Sablin, who was going to Moscow, to inquire into the matter. Sablin admitted that Rasputin was drunk, and so did Rasputin.[4] But the rest she treated as a simple invention of the malice of the police, for which none of the family had any love, nor did their reputation stand high with anyone else. She had a special grudge against Dzhunkovsky and the police of Moscow, because when he was Governor there, they had failed to intercept the book of Illiodor before its passage abroad.

On August 19th came a new and sharp turn of events. Sazonov had been urging the interest of the Allies in the Jewish and other questions, and it was on this day that it was finally decided to abolish the Jewish Pale. The Minister of Finance, Bark, had declared that foreign credit was at present closed, and in view of the great influence of Jewish international figures, the Cabinet was prepared to bargain for their help by concessions to the Jews in Russia. Polivanov had so far said nothing at the meeting, but sat heavily brooding throughout. Goremykin now called on him for a report on the army, and the picture which he gave was more agitating than anything which they had so far heard. At the end

[1] POLIVANOV, 189. [2] ibid., 199. [3] June 2nd/3rd, O.S. [4] Sablin to B. P.

he added, that he had something even more serious to report, and that he was breaking faith in doing so. The Emperor had told him in confidence that he intended to displace the Grand Duke, and to take up the high command himself. Polivanov had said everything he could to dissuade his sovereign from this 'humanly impossible' dual task, but quite in vain. Goremykin, who spoke more quietly than anyone else, revealed that he had known of this decision for some days, and he was vigorously attacked by Sazonov and most of the Cabinet Ministers for leaving the Cabinet in ignorance and not dissuading the Emperor from his intention. Goremykin had himself tried to do so. The effect of this news was as great as that of Polivanov's original declaration on July 19th. One after another, most of the Ministers gave urgent reasons why this step must be regarded as fatal. Shcherbatov pointed out that there would be no authority in the rear and spoke boldly of the influence of Rasputin; Samarin did the same. All that Goremykin could think of, was to try to change the subject. Bark again pleaded the importance of foreign credit, and Sazonov the faith which the Allies placed in the Grand Duke. Most of the Ministers must have been sorry that they had not taken more account of Goremykin's warning, when they had directed their first indignation against the army administration. But of course, the Empress's communications with her husband, so hostile to the Grand Duke, were entirely unknown to them. With Goremykin driven farther and farther into a minority, it was agreed that Polivanov and Shcherbatov should again try to dissuade the sovereign. They were to explain to him that any reverse at the front would be charged to his responsibility, that the rear urgently required his attention, and that the dynasty would be in danger. At this time the Germans were close to Riga; but that danger was dispelled. Still, it was the worst possible moment for the sovereign to take command of the beaten army; and with the disorder caused by the great stream of refugees, it was felt that even his personal safety could not be guaranteed at the front.[1]

On August 27th Polivanov reported that all his representations had remained without effect, and Shcherbatov was asked to try his luck. He, too, failed. The most agitated of the Ministers was Samarin, probably the most conservative and loyal of all. He

[1] YAKHONTOV, 53-57.

compared the decision of the Emperor to a spark among barrels of gunpowder. In this and a subsequent debate the same question was discussed. Some were for at least trying to persuade the Emperor to postpone his decision. Samarin was against any acceptance of it, and wanted himself to beg his sovereign on his knees. He again introduced the subject of Rasputin, whom he quite rightly regarded as the prompter of Nicholas's decision, and declared excitedly, 'I am ready to the last drop of my blood to serve my lawful sovereign, but not — '.[1] Krivoshein pursued his earlier theme, that the Government was no longer the Government, and that as it was not allowed to have any control over events, its only alternative was to resign. The Cabinet had already had to face the challenge to its authority from the military administration and the challenge from the Duma; now there was also the challenge of the Emperor's private advisers — the Empress and Rasputin. Goremykin alone adhered firmly to the principle that when the sovereign had declared his will it was only left for the Ministers to accept it. However, he agreed to the suggestion that the Cabinet should ask for a special meeting under the chairmanship of the sovereign.

Samarin's outburst was fully justified. No other question had ever yet so starkly revealed the impossibility of governing a country under such conditions, where the reputed autocrat might as often as not be expressing a suggestion of others than his appointed advisers. In such an atmosphere no responsible Minister could tell where he stood; nor was it in any way possible for the Cabinet to trace and counter the promptings of which they were ignorant. On such a background, misunderstandings of the first importance were almost inevitable. With public gossip denouncing the Empress as pro-German and doubting the constancy of Nicholas in the War, his decision was completely misinterpreted, though not by members of the Cabinet. His desire to take command of the army was prompted by the same burning patriotism which was at this time common to the whole country. This was his personal sacrifice. By taking the command he committed himself finally to the war, with all its responsibilities and all its reverses. For this very reason he had wished to go to the front in the Japanese War, and it was only with difficulty that he had been dissuaded from

[1] Yakhontov, 70.

the same course in 1914. It was precisely when the army was being beaten that he yearned to be with it. With the Empress it was somewhat different. This was her definite and effective reply to the challenge that had been given to his autocracy. The dualism of the military and civil authorities would now disappear, for the Emperor would be at the head of both. But for her too, this victory was bought at a heavy price. It took from her the dearest source of her happiness and it exposed her husband to all sorts of other influences at the front, of which she was from this time forward deeply suspicious. To the one counsellor whose advice counted for anything with her, the choice was self-evident. With anything like a constitutional regime, the ties between Rasputin and the palace must inevitably be broken. Shcherbatov tells us that the prophet had left St. Petersburg on the day after his own appointment as Minister of the Interior. He was back there on August 19th. On the 29th a violent attack on him appeared in the *Bourse Gazette*, which caused the Empress and Emperor to call for further restrictions of the liberty of the Press.

There was a curious new turn at this point. Polivanov had been entrusted by the Tsar with a letter to the Grand Duke announcing his decision to take the command; he had also been sent to Alexeyev to inform him that he was to be Chief of Staff to the sovereign. He had executed this commission with discretion; and the Tsar, who was heart and soul in his new undertaking, felt sincerely grateful to him. He even embraced Polivanov solemnly three times and said that he should never forget this service. One of the Tsar's chief reasons for assuming the command was to abolish the dualism between front and rear which had caused such confusion. Krivoshein, who was full of strategy, decided to avail himself of the Tsar's new confidence in Polivanov. He surprised Polivanov by asking him to be his candidate for the Premiership, which he was himself again unwilling to take. He even spoke to Nicholas on the subject, and the idea found favour. The Tsar declared that he had come to feel real confidence in Polivanov. The idea was that Polivanov, as in charge of the War Office, without being formally appointed Prime Minister should act as such and take the chair in the Cabinet. The Tsar actually helped Krivoshein to draft the new title, incidently substituting for 'Acting Minister of War' the words 'Minister of War' and saying that he now wished to confirm Polivanov in that post. With this were associated the words, 'and presiding in the Council of Ministers'. Krivoshein, seeing the Tsar's new mood, even went so far as to recommend Guchkov for service. 'I know you do not like Guchkov', he said, 'but if you call him, you will thus create an admirable impression in the country and you will win a devoted servant' (Aug. 30th). In such a light the new situation would become much more reasonable. The sovereign united front and rear and as his deputies had, in the army, his best strategist and, as Head of the Cabinet, his best military administrator. Next day Polivanov had to report at the palace, but there was no sequel to this conversation. The suggestion was to come up again in another form; for in the next year we find Alexeyev calling for a 'Minister of National Defence', who is to preside in the Cabinet.[1]

On September 1st came a sign that the crisis was moving in another direction. It was announced that General Dzhunkovsky was discharged from the post of Assistant Minister of the Interior. Shcherbatov had received a communication couched in the unusual terms, 'I insist on the immediate dismissal of General Dzhunkovsky'. In view of all the circumstances it is perfectly clear that it was the Empress who was insisting.[2] Prince V. Orlov, another old and faithful servant of the sovereign, who was with the Grand Duke and for the reformers, was dismissed about the same time. He was reputed to have said that the Empress should be sent to a convent or to Livadia for the rest of the war.[3] Both men were too loyal to let their friends defend them. Orlov wrote to Polivanov to prevent this. They were both allowed to join the deposed Commander-in-Chief in his new post. The Empress never ceases to speak of them with malice in her letters, especially of 'my enemy Dzhunkovsky'.[4]

Sazonov, also, in his representations to the Tsar had not omitted to refer to Rasputin.

> I did not dot the 'i's' or mention any names [he writes] and indeed there was no need to do so. The Tsar easily grasped the unsaid meaning and I saw how distasteful my words were to him. It was painful to me to refer to the dangerous part that the Empress had begun to play since Rasputin gained

[1] POLIVANOV, 223-5. [2] DZHUNKOVSKY, *Padenie*, V, 103.
[3] DUBENSKY, VI, 386. [4] A. F. to N., June 22nd/July 5th.

> possession of her will and intellect. The Tsar did not contradict me, but as I spoke he seemed to recede farther away from me till at last I felt that a deep gulf lay between us.[1]

The Cabinet wanted to make a collective warning to the Emperor in person, but this Goremykin refused to transmit to him. He had offered to resign and said to his colleagues, 'Ask the Emperor to dismiss me, it would be doing me a service'. However, on September 2nd, as the majority had so long desired, the Cabinet met at the palace at Tsarskoe Selo under the chairmanship of the Emperor. Yakhontov can give no record of this meeting, as at such sittings the secretaries were not present. We have, however, mentions of it both from Sazonov, who gives the wrong date, from Polivanov, and from Ignatyev, and also from the Empress and Vyrubova, who describes how the two went out on the balcony and looked in at the window, while the 'long-nosed' Sazonov was presenting his case. Vyrubova tells us that Nicholas held firmly in his hands throughout a small icon, which she and the Empress had given him beforehand and that he returned in a high state of perspiration.[2] It would appear that even Goremykin again urged the grave dangers of the Emperor's decision, and so did the other Ministers, especially Krivoshein, Sazonov and Samarin, who implored him to realize its possible sequels. At the end he got up: 'I have heard what you have to say,' he said, 'but I adhere to my decision.'

Yakhontov describes the scene of utter helplessness when the Cabinet met by itself next day.[3] The majority decided to make one more effort. Cabinet resignations had hardly any precedent in Russian history, though when Alexander III on his accession decided to take the path of reaction his principal minister Loris Melikov and the majority of his colleagues resigned simultaneously; but the present Ministers saw no way of carrying out their duties, if their advice remained without effect on a question of such capital importance; nor could they accept a situation in which the Prime Minister, not of their choice or of their opinion, was able to override the rest. In October 1905 Nicholas had committed the direction of and responsibility for the Cabinet to Count Witte, and this was at the time a definite step in the introduction of the

[1] SAZONOV, 292. [2] VYRUBOVA, 60; A. F. to N., Sept. 16th/29th.
[3] YAKHONTOV, 60.

Cabinet system of government; but he had never ceased to regret this experiment, and his wife's view was even more clear than his own, that the Premier, appointed exclusively by the Tsar, had the task of keeping the other Ministers in order.

Ultimately the great majority of the Cabinet informed Goremykin that they would make their joint statement to the Tsar without him. The majority met at Sazonov's quarters in the Foreign Office, and there, by common request, Samarin drew up a joint letter to the Tsar. It was signed by eight members of the Cabinet out of thirteen. Goremykin, of course, did not sign it. Two of the rest, Polivanov and Grigorovich, as Ministers for War and the Navy, were under special obligations of military service to the sovereign, but they signified their full support of the statement. The other two who did not sign were Rukhlov (Transport), who was ill, and the elder Hvostov (Justice). The letter ran as follows:[1]

> Most gracious Sovereign, Do not find fault with us for appealing to you boldly and frankly. Our action is dictated by loyalty and love for you and our country and by our anxious recognition of the menacing character of what is happening around us. Yesterday at the meeting of the Council, at which you presided, we unanimously begged you not to remove the Grand Duke Nicholas from the High Command of the Army. We fear that Your Majesty was not willing to grant our prayer, which is, we think, the prayer of all loyal Russians. We venture once more to tell you that to the best of our judgment your decision threatens with serious consequences Russia, your dynasty and your person. At the same meeting you could see for yourself the irreconcilable difference between our Chairman and us in our estimate of the situation in the country and of the policy to be pursued by the Government. Such a state of things is inadmissible at all times, and at the present moment it is fatal. Under such conditions we do not believe we can be of real service to Your Majesty and to our country.
>
> *P. Haritonov, A. Krivoshein, S. Sazonov, P. Bark, Prince N. Shcherbatov, A. Samarin, Count P. Ignatyev, Prince V. Shakhovskoy.*

It was a thousand pities that the breach had come from Nicholas's

[1] SAZONOV, 291-4.

own personal contribution to the imminent danger of his army and people.

At 11.0 a.m. on September 3rd, the Emperor himself started the first session of the new Defence Council in the White Hall of the Winter Palace. He wished to give the greatest significance to this event, and had surrounded it with impressive ceremony. He desired to take the chair on later occasions when not at the front. Accompanied by the Empress, he opened the Council with an excellent and spirited speech drafted for him by Krivoshein and Polivanov. He received the chairman of the Duma Commission of Imperial Defence, Shingarev, and accepted from him a memorandum of the Commission on the state of munitions. It was not till the meeting was over that Sazonov handed the Ministers' letter to Polivanov, and he gave it to an officer to deliver to the Emperor. That evening after his audience at Tsarskoe, where he said good-bye to the Emperor on his departure to the front, he learned from Sablin that the letter had been read by Nicholas in the train on his way back from the capital, and, no doubt, shown to the Empress. To make it clear to Sablin that he shared the view of the other Ministers, Polivanov said that such a Premier as Goremykin would lead the country to revolution.[1]

On the very day of this opening ceremony was published the full programme of the Progressive Bloc in the form in which it is given here.[2]

> On Sept. 7th (Aug. 25th o.s.), 1915, representatives of fractions of groups of the Imperial Duma and of the Council of State (the Upper House) signed the programme and agreement of the newly formed Progressive Bloc, consisting of Members of the Imperial Duma: the Progressive Nationalists [Shulgin's group], the group of the Centre, the Zemstvo-Octobrists, the Left Octobrists, the Progressists, the Constitutional Democrats [the Cadets of Milyukov]; and members of the Council of State: the Academic Group, the Centre, and, conditionally, the group of Non-party Union. [The final text of the programme runs as follows]:
>
> The undersigned representatives of parties and groups of the Council of State and of the Imperial Duma, out of the conviction that only a strong, firm, and active Government can lead the country to victory, and that such can only be a

[1] POLIVANOV, 237-8. [2] YAKHONTOV, 109.

Government based on the confidence of the public, and capable of organizing an active co-operation of all citizens, have come to the unanimous conclusion that the most essential and important task of creating such an authority cannot be realized without the fulfilment of the following conditions:
The formation of a united Government, consisting of persons who have the confidence of the country and are in agreement with the legislative institutions as to carrying out, at the earliest time, a definite programme.
A decisive alteration of the methods of government hitherto employed, founded on distrust of public initiative;
in particular:
(*a*) A strict observance of the principle of legality in administration.
(*b*) A removal of the dualism of military and civil power in questions which have no immediate relation to the conduct of military operations.
(*c*) A renovation of the personnel of local administration.
(*d*) An intelligent and consistent policy directed to the maintenance of internal peace and the removal of racial and class antagonisms.
For the realization of such a policy, the following measures must be taken both in administration and in legislation:
(1) By way of amnesty of the sovereign, the withdrawal of cases initiated on the charge of purely political and religious offences which are not complicated by offences of a criminal character; the remission of punishment and restoration of rights, including that of taking part in elections to the Imperial Duma, zemstva, and town councils, for all persons condemned for such offences, and some mitigation for others who have been condemned for political and religious offences, with the exception of spies and traitors.
(2) The return of those exiled administratively (that is, without trial) for offences of a political character.
(3) Full and decisive cessation of persecutions for religion under any kind of pretext, and a repeal of circulars in this sense limiting and distorting the meaning of the decree of April 17 (30), 1905.
(4) A settlement of the Russo-Polish question, that is: a repeal of limitations of the rights of Poles over the whole surface of Russia, the earliest preparation and introduction into the legislative institutions of a law on the autonomy of

Russian Poland (Tsarstvo-Polskoe) and a simultaneous revision of the legislation on Polish landownership.

(5) A beginning of abolition of the antagonism against Jews — in particular, further steps for the abolition of the Jewish Pale, facilitation of access to educational institutions and a repeal of limitations in the choice of a profession; the restoration of the Jewish Press.

(6) A policy of appeasement in the Finnish question — in particular, a change in the personnel of administration of the Senate (the Cabinet of Finland), and the cessation of prosecutions of officials.

(7) Restoration of the Little Russian (Ukrainian) Press; the earliest revision of cases of inhabitants of Galicia kept under arrest or exiled (for instance to Siberia), and the liberation of those of them who have been arrested without guilt.

(8) The restoration of the work of professional unions (trade unions), and a cessation of persecution of the workers' representatives in hospital savings banks, on suspicion of belonging to any unlegalized party; restoration of the Labour Press.

(9) Agreement of the Government with the legislative institutions as to the speediest introduction:

(*a*) of all laws which have the closest relation to the national defence, the equipment of the army, the care of the wounded, the regulation of the lot of refugees, and other questions immediately connected with the War.

(*b*) The following programme of legislative work, directed to the organization of the country for helping victory and toward the maintenance of internal peace; equalization of peasants with other classes, the introduction of cantonal zemstva, the revision of the zemstvo law of 1890, the revision of the municipal law of 1892, the introduction of zemstvo institutions in the frontier provinces, for instance, in Siberia, Archangel, the Don region, the Caucasus, and so on; laws on co-operative societies, rest days for shop assistants and improving the lot of postal and telegraphic employees, on the permanent confirmation of temperance, on zemstvo and town congresses and unions, on the statute of revision, on the introduction of Justices of the Peace in those provinces where their introduction has been arrested for financial considerations; and the carrying out of such administrative measures as may be found to be necessary for the execution of the above-described programme of action in the sphere of administration.

This programme was signed by the leading representatives of each of the groups named.

Nicholas was followed to the front by a letter from the Empress, which was a very paean of triumph.[1] She writes:

> I cannot find words to express all I want to — my heart is far too full . . . I only want to whisper words of intense love, courage, strength, and endless blessings . . . You have fought this great fight for your country and throne . . . Our souls are fighting for the right against the evil . . . It is all much deeper than appears to the eye . . . You are proving yourself the Autocrat without which Russia cannot exist . . . God anointed you at your coronation. He placed you where you stand, and you have done your duty . . . Being firm is the only saving — I *know* what it costs you, and I suffer hideously for you; forgive me I beseech you, my Angel, for having left you no peace and worried you so much — but I knew too well your marvelously [*sic*] gentle character — and you had to shake it off this time, had to win your fight alone against all. It is to be a glorious page in your reign and in Russian history, the story of these weeks and days — and God, who is always near you will save your country and throne through your firmness . . . Our Friend's prayers arise night and day for you to Heaven, and God will hear them . . . Your sun is rising. [She ends] Sleep well my sunshine, Russia's Saviour.

In the same letter she is already proposing a substitute for Shcherbatov at the Interior.

The Grand Duke had learned from Polivanov's visit what was impending. He was a man of obstinate loyalty to the throne. He at once accepted the change, and it is reported that he only wrote to ask that it should be deferred till he had himself made the inevitable surrender of the fortress of Brest-Litovsk, which had followed on August 26th. Nicholas writes on his arrival:

> Nicholas came in with a kind brave smile and asked simply when I would order him to go. I answered in the same manner that he could remain for two days; then we discussed the questions connected with military operations, some of the generals, and so forth, and *that was all*.[2]

On taking up the command, the Emperor issued a spirited message

[1] A. F. to N., Aug. 22nd/Sept. 4th. [2] N. to A. F., Aug. 25th/Sept. 7th.

to the Army and nation, making it perfectly clear that he had committed himself to war to the end. He did not in any way interfere in the military operations, though he studied them carefully every day, and practically left all decisions to his new Chief of Staff, General Alexeyev, the best appointment he could possibly have made (Sept. 5th). The North-Western front, which Alexeyev had commanded, was now divided into two; a Northern front confided to Ruzsky, and a new Western front to Evert.

The Cabinet meanwhile was busy with the discussion of the programme of the Progressive Bloc.[1] Goremykin had tried to bring divisions into the ranks of the Bloc by offering to meet members of its right wing alone; but they had told him that they could not confer with him without their colleagues.

On August 31st was held in Moscow an Industrial and Commercial Conference. It was intended to make a vehement pronouncement; but Rodzyanko, who attended the Conference, managed to confine it to a support of the demands of the Duma for a 'Ministry of Confidence', and its example was followed by other bodies such as town councils and zemstva in the provinces. On September 1st the resolutions of the Moscow Town Council were discussed in the Cabinet; Krivoshein declared that the situation of the Cabinet had become impossible and that it was now definitely at the parting of the ways. The Cabinet discussed the programme of the Bloc on the 6th, and resuming this discussion on the 8th, it decided to authorize some of its members to meet the leaders of the Bloc. Goremykin had not responded to the invitation from his colleagues to take part in this meeting, and on the 9th members representing various views in the Cabinet, conferred with the leaders of all the groups in the Bloc at the house of Haritonov.[2] Even old Hvostov, who took part in this meeting, found little in the programme of the Bloc that presented any insurmountable obstacle to agreement; and indeed its requests had been so long before the public, that the one grave question was whether they should have been put forward at a critical moment in time of war. On the following day the Cabinet received and considered the report of its delegates; before the meeting, Goremykin had been received in audience

[1] Yakhontov, 111.
[2] ibid., 119; Milyukov to B. P.

by the Empress, who described the Ministers to her husband as 'fiends worse than the Duma',[1] and 'needing smacking'. The Cabinet regarded the report not unfavourably; and it was suggested that it might go into negotiations with the Bloc, to bargain with it as to the acceptance of some parts of its programme. Meanwhile there might be a decent and friendly prorogation of the debates of the Duma. Goremykin tried, as best he could, to arrest these discussions; but he could find no better alternative to propose than open measures of repression; he expressed himself more and more cynically on the public demands; but one Minister after another spoke in a sense of conciliation. It was openly declared that the sovereign had come to the point where he must choose his road, and that there was no real alternative to a responsible Ministry — by which was meant one that was united and had the confidence both of the sovereign and the country. It was agreed to ask for a friendly prorogation of the Duma debates, and to request the formation of a new Cabinet. Goremykin, on the other hand, stood for a blunt prorogation of the Duma, without any prospect of further negotiations. There was all the difference in the world between these two proposals.[2]

Next day Goremykin went off to Headquarters. He was received there by the Emperor on September 12th, and returned with authority to prorogue the Duma forthwith. When he announced this decision to the Cabinet (Sept. 14th) it almost broke up in indignation and confusion.[3] Sazonov said in the lobby 'il est fou, ce vieillard'; he described the proceedings as a pantomime.

> Krivoshein [writes Yakhontov] looked hopelessly sad and agitated. Ignatyev, as always at difficult moments, scratched his thin hair in agitation; and the discussion proceeded with an unusual feverishness, leaping from one question to another and inevitably returning to the prorogation and its consequences.

He had the greatest difficulty in following their debate. At the resumed meeting next day Krivoshein declared that there was no longer a Government; 'It must be he (that is Goremykin) or we,'

[1] A. F. to N., Aug. 28th/Sept. 10th. [2] YAKHONTOV, 119-24.
[3] ibid., 128.

he said. Goremykin announced that he had the imperial order definitely to close the Duma the following day (Sept. 16th) till November. All the Ministers were commanded to stay at their posts. Sazonov declared that the State was in danger; Goremykin returned to his favourite argument of repression and closed the sitting.

On the following day Rodzyanko, suppressing his fury, declared the Emperor's will to the Duma, and by great personal exertions persuaded its members to disperse quietly.[1] There followed at once a two days' strike of all factories in Petrograd. It is really from this day that is to be dated a wide growth of defeatism in the country. On the 19th the Civil Red Cross met in Moscow, and demanded the recall of the Duma, and the appointment of a 'Ministry of Confidence'; but the deputies whom it appointed to present its resolutions to the Emperor were not received at Headquarters, and Rodzyanko's request for an audience was also refused.[2] Already the Empress was sending her husband suggestions, drawn-up by herself with the help of Goremykin and of other very much less reputable advisers, of candidates to replace the recalcitrant Ministers, and was asking for rapid decisions; she even begged him to come to the capital for the purpose. It is probably to this moment that may be referred a draft letter from Rasputin to the Emperor proposing that Goremykin should receive the exceptional title of 'Chancellor', and should also be entrusted with the Foreign Office in the place of Sazonov.

On the 27th Goremykin was again at Headquarters and brought back a summons to the whole Cabinet to assemble there. The Empress had actually begged her husband to comb his hair several times with Rasputin's comb before he received them.[3] Several Ministers put their view plainly, but Nicholas looked bored throughout. In reply to the letter of the majority of the Cabinet and to the representations which these Ministers still made to him, the Tsar spoke to them as a master rebuking them for their disobedience, and ordering them to go on with their ordinary duties until he might choose to replace them. He telegraphs to his wife, 'The conference passed off well. I told them my opinion sternly to their faces.'[4]

[1] Rodzyanko, 154.
[2] ibid., 156.
[3] A. F. to N., Aug. 23rd/Sept. 5th.
[4] N. to A. F., Sept. 16th/29th.

In October, the parasite reactionary 'Union of the Russian People' which in the summer, according to Shcherbatov, had only existed on paper, revived its activities; and the reactionary ex-Minister Shcheglovitov spoke spitefully of 'the lost charter'.[1] It is Kerensky, not a member of the Progressive Bloc, who pithily sums up what had happened. 'Nevertheless', he writes, 'the Empress Alexandra Fedorovna challenged the whole nation on this question — and won.'[2]

[1] Milyukov, 27. [2] Kerensky, C.L., 202.

CHAPTER X

THE EMPRESS TAKES OVER: 'FRIEND' AND 'TAIL'

Their defeat
Doth by their own insinuation grow.
Hamlet, v, 2

THE DOUBLE PLAN

AND so the Russian Emperor was compelled by his wife to flout all thinking Russia, his Ministers, the Duma, the organs of local government and the general public, and go off to the front to win the war without them, leaving her to manage the rear for him. Rodzyanko mentions that at this time there were strong rumours of an unofficial and secretly appointed Regency of the Empress.[1] It was simpler than that, it was the most intimate co-operation of husband and wife; but he was not far from the truth. On September 7th Nicholas had written, in words, whose very simplicity shows the domestic character of the arrangement, 'Think, my wifey, will you not come to the assistance of your hubby now that he is absent?'[2] In this casual way the management of the estate is handed over, and several times later he expresses his encouragement and thanks. She continues at times to half apologize for her interference, but her slight scruples gradually vanish altogether. 'I must be your notebook,' she writes on October 1st, and later she definitely describes herself as 'his wall in the rear'.

As time goes on, her direction and even control becomes more and more absolute; and indeed absolute control can only be exercised by one whose mind is absolute. All the trouble lay in that proprietary idea which had been traditionally inherited from the old Grand Princes of Moscow, when a chance order, whether relating to the household or the State, resulted in the setting up of an office to satisfy it. Nothing will better illustrate how

[1] RODZYANKO, 152. [2] August 25th, O.S.

persistent was this idea in the Russian imperial family than a conversation which I had, after the Revolution, with the Tsar's cousin and brother-in-law, the Grand Duke Alexander Mikhailovich, who was later to give his warning like others. When asked, 'Wasn't it rather a pity that she should have governed the country?' he replied, 'When the Emperor went to the war, of course his wife governed instead of him'.

Everyone outside this narrowest of home circles realized the character of Rasputin; his sexual outrages, by the most glaring proofs, were known to anyone in Russia who could read and write. The soldiers in the army all took it for granted that there was some kind of sexual connection between Rasputin and the Empress.[1] Society in Petrograd openly discussed this question. Anyhow it was becoming evident to those who were closest to the throne that power could only be sought by his mediation; and as his disgusting record was so well known, especially after the blatant scandal at the Yar restaurant, any decent person, except the unusually ignorant, was precluded from seeking office by this road. Rodzyanko in his memoirs complains several times of the indifference of those who might be called 'the neutrals', and he is quite right. As to the Empress, we shall miss the whole tragedy of this story, if we do not realize that it was a Victorian English prudery in her which simply refused to face the facts, as too disgusting for belief, in the light of the 'prophet's' conduct in the palace, his talk of religion and what he was doing for her son in answer to her agonized prayers.

It is thus that we must understand what the Empress Alexandra gave to Russia in lieu of a constitution; and even the worst anticipations of the protesting Ministers proved to be far short of the real consequences. We must not forget that we are writing the history of the government of Russia in the twentieth century during a world war in which she was allied with France and England, and when even the most honest, able and patriotic administrators could hardly have balanced her chances in the field against the wonderful German military machine. But the materials for this narrative are too convincing. We have chapter and verse at first hand for every detail. Letters, diaries, records of conversations, are all there; and no instance is known to us in which those concerned have protested that they have been per-

[1] I was living in the army at this time.

verted or falsified. Immediately after the Revolution of March 1917 Kerensky, as the new Minister of Justice, set up his investigating commission manned by some of the best lawyers in Russia which interrogated in detail all the chief actors in this period. The questions put to them, according to the most clement procedure of western justice, were exactly those on which we should most desire information, and we have verbatim their answers.

It is from this last-named abundant material that we draw our principal information on the period which is now being described. Two of the chief villains of the piece — for this period S. P. Beletsky, and for a later period A. D. Protopopov — proving amenable in examination to give in detail all that they knew, were invited by the Chairman of the Commission to write it out in full; and one of the seven volumes of this report is devoted entirely to these two men, and mainly to the record of Beletsky. He took a certain curious literary pride in writing it, though it is in a florid and involved style, almost German in kind, suggestive of an official police report; in fact he calls it 'an act of accusation against myself';[1] but it is full of detailed and balanced statements, which can often be verified from other sides. Burtsev, who knew Beletsky well, considers that it can be trusted entirely.[2] It is quite frank and tells the story exactly as any intelligent person would see it, almost without self-consciousness and quite without any mercy for his own part in it. He begins with the words: 'I will write my evidence or rather my confession'; and he stops at some of the most extravagant facts which he has to relate, to say how even he was compelled to blush for his part in them,[3] or to exclaim: 'I was bathing in dirt.'[4]

Stephen Beletsky, who was personally known to me, was a typical professional police official, a thorough man of the world, very careful and resourceful in detail, who by years of able service in various posts had before the War risen to that of Director of the Department of Police. He was not an honest man, and could never have been regarded as such, whether by himself or by others; but he had exactly the abilities required by his office. At that time the reactionary Nicholas Maklakov was Minister, and the Assistant Minister concerned was the upright and

[1] BELETSKY, *Padenie*, III, 347.
[2] Burtsev to B. P.
[3] BELETSKY, *Padenie*, 331, 432.
[4] ibid., 396, 432.

honourable Dzhunkovsky, who hated all little tricks such as those of Beletsky. Dzhunkovsky purified the police and that was why he felt that he must dismiss Beletsky.

In that period little was yet known of Rasputin's political influence, and Beletsky had at first regarded him simply as a scandalous personage, and learning that he was taking lessons in hypnotism, expelled his teacher from the capital.[1] At the point which we have now reached in our story, it was clear to Beletsky that power was only to be sought by the mediation of Rasputin.

But Beletsky was nothing more than a glorified hack official; and he would have to make his bid with the help of someone who was a member of the ruling class. Mention has been made of one, Alexis Nikoleyevich Hvostov, who must on no account be confused with his uncle, the honourable Minister of Justice, Alexander Hvostov. Alexis Hvostov belonged to a not uncommon type of Russian provincial governor, in which capacity he had served at Vologda and at Nizhny Novgorod, a restless careerist who, within the limits of his rather crude wiles, sought to pose as the intelligence and benefactor of his province. He was also a member of the Duma, sitting on the extreme right and always trying to catch the accents of an old fashioned loyalty to the throne, though naturally in a complete minority. It was now the fashion to inveigh against German exploitation and German espionage. During the summer, while others were demanding reforms, Hvostov in a vigorous speech made himself the spokesman of this fashion, and his speech found favour at Court. Shortly before the murder of Stolypin, Nicholas had thought of him for a moment as a possible Minister of the Interior, and Rasputin had been sent 'to look at his soul'.[2] At that time (in 1911) Rasputin's political importance was by no means realized, and Hvostov, not recognizing the character of his errand, had been very curt with him and sent him off to the station. Rasputin used to complain that though he had only three roubles in his pocket, Hvostov did not even give him a meal. This man now went into joint partnership with Beletsky. His evidence, which is offhand and evasive, is also available in the records of the post-revolution commission.

But Hvostov and Beletsky needed an introduction to the palace, and here they sought the assistance of an even stranger coadjutor,

[1] BELETSKY, *Padenie*, IV, 501.
[2] HVOSTOV, A. N., *Padenie*, I, 3.

a certain Prince Andronikov, one of the most sinister personages in the public life of Russia. He had very small means which were soon exhausted, and he lived in the main on speculations and on credit, but his title and his education in the aristocratic Corps of Pages enabled him to move about in higher society. He had no definite position, though he was formally attached without duties, successively to the Ministries of the Interior and of Religion. 'Allow me to put you direct the question — In what does your work consist? Who are you?' asks the President of the Investigating Commission later, and all the answer that he gets is, 'a person, a citizen, who wishes to make himself as useful as possible'.[1] In less formal circumstances he described himself as 'A.D.C. to the Almighty'.[2] Acclimatized to a regime where everything went by favour, Andronikov made a speciality of picking up gossip in the evening hours in various Ministries and learning of the variations in the political atmosphere, and especially of possibilities in the nature of new appointments. These he would anticipate by congratulations to the prospective candidate, usually accompanied by the gift of an icon. He was also a member of what seems to have been called by friends and enemies alike the 'reptile press', and was constantly begging subsidies from the secret funds of the police. By cultivating the palace officials, and even the Prime Minister, Goryemkin — he brought the old gentleman sweets[3] — all of whom affected to treat him with indifference, he was sometimes even able to bring his effusions to the notice of the Emperor; both the Minister of the Court and the commandant of the palace had later to admit having received them. Andronikov became to be regarded as a kind of semi-official mystery.[4] He carried about a portentous portfolio, which was credited with exciting contents, but as a matter of fact seems to have only contained old newspapers. He had been associated with Prince Meshchersky, who had direct access to the Emperor through his periodical *The Citizen* and was always intriguing for political appointments of a reactionary kind. Andronikov was a type of busybody very common in Russian life. He set himself to know everyone who counted or might count.[5] But he had the most unsavoury moral reputation,

[1] ANDRONIKOV, *Padenie*, II, 11. [2] MOSOLOV, 164; POLIVANOV, 141.
[3] GOREMYKIN, *Padenie*, III, 319. [4] FREDERICKSZ, *Padenie*, V, 46.
[5] He was so good as to approach the writer.

and Beletsky himself has confirmed the general belief that he was a homosexual.

Andronikov had earlier been a supporter of Beletsky, and in the summer his political flair had told him to draw nearer to Rasputin. By means of his various ties, he was able to scrape acquaintance with the empty-headed Anna Vyrubova, who definitely acted throughout all this period as the principal agent and informant of the Empress. This lady had no idea of his moral character, but her parents were greatly alarmed at this connection. At this time Rasputin was away from the capital. A sharp dispute was in progress between him and the honourable Minister of Religion, A. D. Samarin, for whose dismissal the Empress was constantly calling in her letters to her husband. One of Rasputin's protégés, Bishop Varnava of Tobolsk, had irregularly sought the canonization of a previous Bishop John of that See, and this was vigorously opposed by Samarin and the Synod. The Empress was equally furious with the Minister of the Interior, Prince Shcherbatov; she hated him for his courage in refusing the measures suggested by her for silencing public opinion, more particularly on Rasputin, and because he would not trample on the protests of the local governing bodies at the prorogation of the Duma. The Empress had no knowledge whatever of the personnel of public life in Russia. She met only those who happened to come to her, whether as Ministers or as officials connected with charitable organizations of which she was president, and she was entirely lacking in judgment of men. It is only in this way that one can explain her references to Andronikov, whom she describes in one of her letters as 'my Andronikov'.[1]

Beletsky records that for a fortnight on end he and Hvostov worked out together a full political programme, on the basis of which they would seek official appointment.[2] It was complicated in the extreme, and they almost tripped over themselves in their ingenuity. Rasputin's influence was to bring them to power, but in view of his public ill-fame they were to pretend to have nothing to do with him. This was specially necessary for Hvostov, as he still hoped to use his influence as a member of the Duma; and to the President, Rodzyanko, he explained that he was trying to

[1] A. F. to N., Dec. 1st/14th.
[2] BELETSKY, *Padenie*, IV, 119.

ruin Rasputin, whom he hoped to compromise by making him drunk in public places.[1] The Premier, Goremykin, was no more than the servant of the autocracy, who proposed that no account at all should be taken of the Duma. In reality throughout this period Rasputin was thoroughly scared by the Duma, and consequently also his patronesses, the Empress and Vyrubova. Hvostov and Beletsky proposed themselves to avert the possibilities of scandal by holding Rasputin in check and threatening him if necessary with exposure. For such a purpose they had plenty of ammunition in the police reports of Rasputin's various outbreaks. These they were going to keep from the Empress as far as possible; to her they recommended themselves in the first place as securing the personal safety of Rasputin, who under previous Ministers, for instance Kurlov and Dzhunkovsky, had been watched with careful hostility. They too would also watch him and indeed collect as much material as possible for eventual use; but to the Empress they were the guarantors of his safety and would limit the possibilities of scandal.

In the Empress's letters we come suddenly on vehement recommendations of Hvostov for the Ministry of the Interior.[2] She is busying herself at this time in a hunt for Ministers to replace all those who had signed the famous letter, and she continues it exactly in the spirit of a housewife who has always to complain that it is so hard to get respectable servants and trusts to their chief (in this case Goremykin) to keep them in order; but Hvostov really fascinated her with his programme, or rather with that part of it which he told her. She writes on September 7th/30th, 'I yearned to see a man at last, and here I see and hear him'. Hvostov was equally impressed. He describes her later as 'clever and brilliant'. On this day she writes two colossal letters, and also telegraphs twice to urge his appointment. For her, in this and subsequent appointments, the chief test is the candidate's attitude to Rasputin. For instance, in recommending a successor to Samarin, a General Shvedov, she writes: 'He calls our Friend Father Gregory.' She is also seeking to replace Sazonov. The Prime Minister, Goremykin, never insisted on his recommendations, and the only Ministers whom he later claims to have put into office were the elder

[1] Rodzyanko, 158.
[2] A. F. to N., Aug. 22nd/Sept. 4th.

Hvostov and Ignatyev.[1] In the present case he recommended for the Interior a very experienced bureaucratic official, Kryzhanovsky, like himself thoroughly trained in the tactics of his milieu, who was responsible for drafting the Second Electoral Law, which had made the Duma cryingly unrepresentative of the country; but Kryzhanovsky was at least a possible choice, and Goremykin represented to the Emperor that Alexis Hvostov could not be regarded as such. Hvostov's own uncle, the one Minister who had stood by Goremykin in the summer crisis, when consulted by the Emperor gave his nephew the following helpful testimonial.

> This is a person absolutely inexpert in this work, one who by character is entirely unsuitable . . . I expect nothing good from it and in some ways I expect even harm. This is a man very far from stupid, but who cannot be critical of his own instincts and judgments. He is inclined to intrigue, and I think he won't content himself with this, for him, so desirable promotion, and in all probability will try to become Premier; in any case all his activities in the office of Minister will not be devoted to the work, but to considerations which have nothing to do with it.[2]

I have given the uncle's opinion in full because it was to be so fully verified. The Empress, however, was ecstatic on the subject. She had already invented a pet name for her candidate derived from the meaning of his surname in Russian (hvost — tail) and writes of him as 'my Tail' and later 'my honest Tail', and the appointment duly follows. Hvostov for his Assistant Minister for the police work takes Beletsky, combining with that post the Direction of the Police Department.

As Goremykin was simply passive, these two men are in fact such government as Russia possessed for the next five months of the World War. It must not be supposed that they were without ability. On the contrary, Kafafov, Beletsky's mild deputy at the Police Department, describes them as 'two volcanoes'.[3] In their own way, they did govern Russia. If the Empress was in no way in touch with public opinion, they certainly were; and it is from this time that Beletsky, like all the other best sources, dates the beginning of defeatism and even of a tendency against the dynasty.

[1] Goremykin, *Padenie*, iii, 317. [2] Hvostov, A. A., *Padenie*, v, 467.
[3] Kafafov, *Padenie*, ii, 137.

Still he thinks that the further organization of what he calls 'the workers' movement' had no such direction as it was to take later and was prompted less by political conditions or social theories than by the growing rise in prices and shortage of goods. To this question he devotes a great part of his furious energy and organizes everywhere food shops subsidized by the Government, in which work he welcomes the co-operation of many with whom he has nothing in common in his political views. Another vast question which he has to attack is the enormous wave of refugees which has flooded the interior through the ruthless and stupid policy of Yanushkevich. The generosity of the Russian public was everywhere active in this cause; and Beletsky, by frequent journeys to the provinces and his use of the ex-governors of those which had been abandoned, did what he could to meet this evil.[1] He also took measures to counteract the incipient movement against the dynasty. Some of these were superficial and even stupid — for instance, the tracking of all such references in private correspondence (such details were regularly supplied through Vyrubova to the Empress) and all sorts of publications to glorify the Emperor's prowess at the front and the Empress's solicitude for the rear. He carefully measured the support which he gave from the secret funds to the parties of the Right; Shcherbatov had told the Emperor that practically all these subsidized associations had no real existence,[2] and Beletsky does not seem to have thought much better of them.

Hvostov meanwhile undertook all questions of high policy and especially relations with the Duma. Hvostov, this 'friend of the Duma', had a wonderful plan for rigging the next elections to it. There was to be no blunt buying of Press organs by the Government, but a wide and vague shareholding company, apparently public, but directed from the first by a whole number of secret agents specially enlisted for the purpose and paid in advance. The company was to make itself master of newspapers, including the provincial press, printing presses, book stalls, advertisements, cinemas, cinema factories, and even telephone communications. A certain number of Press organs of the capitals were to be directly subsidized, with a preference for those of the left, with the sole exception of the Bolsheviks. By this means public opinion was to

[1] Beletsky, *Padenie*, iv, 120 ff. [2] Shcherbatov, *Padenie*, vii, 221.

be 'steered', and even the Opposition was to be directed by the Government. Very large sums of money were paid out on credit, but the organization never got to work.[1]

The two fellow conspirators had to deal with the replacement of several of the Ministers, which gave them occasion for the display of their cunning. Shcherbatov had been replaced by Hvostov's own appointment, and the next to go was the Minister of Religion, Samarin, dismissed by a message from Nicholas to the Prime Minister immediately after a reception at which the Emperor had given no warning of it. Samarin was proposed for re-election to his old position as elected head of the nobility of Moscow, but loyally discountenanced any demonstration in his favour. Hvostov's candidate for the vacancy was one Volzhin, a decent enough person to face the Duma, who made the condition that he should not have to meet Rasputin; this was difficult enough to carry out while the control of church affairs was practically abandoned to Rasputin's discretion, and we soon read in the Empress's letters of her and Rasputin's dissatisfaction with the new Minister.[2] Krivoshein, Minister of Agriculture, recognized that he had made his bid when he sided with his colleagues against Goremykin in the summer crisis, and ultimately he asked himself to be relieved of his office. Hvostov, who posed as an authority on this subject, only helped to give him the last push. This Ministry played an essential part in the food supply. It was practically impossible, in view of the next meeting of the Duma, to give it to a man who was either dishonest or incompetent; besides, Hvostov wanted to keep up his double game there. He fixed on an honourable zemstvo worker, Naumov; but Naumov expressed the same aversion to office and to Rasputin as so many of his predecessors. He refused the post; but on Hvostov's suggestion the Emperor, as his sovereign in time of war, overrode the refusal and published the appointment. Even then, Naumov made it clear to the Tsar that his sympathies were with the public.[3]

Sazonov was also in great danger, and the Empress was full of complaints against him in her letters. Rasputin had committed the indiscretion of inditing a letter in which he suggested that the

[1] Hvostov, A. N. *Padenie*, vi, 94 ff.
[2] Beletsky, *Padenie*, iv, 164-8.
[3] ibid., 202-4; Naumov, *Padenie*, i, 329-32; Hvostov, A. N., vi, 85.

Foreign Ministry should be confided to the ancient and incompetent Goremykin, who would remain Prime Minister and receive the title of Chancellor. This letter was purloined from Rasputin's flat; it would have been no surprise to the sovereign, but it would have made a great scandal with the public, and it was only with the greatest difficulty and by a large expenditure that Beletsky prevented it from falling into the hands of the Liberal newspaper *Rech.*[1] Whether or not she was frightened by this incident, the Empress later recommends that Sazonov should be retained. Another Minister who had signed the famous letter was Peter Bark. If there was any Ministry that could not be made the play of caprice in the middle of the war, it was that of Finance, and Bark was not only an able and capable financier, but also a very clever politician. The candidate of Hvostov, Rasputin, and the Empress was Count Tatishchev. Hvostov, who here again had no special knowledge, tells us that he selected him because he would be 'completely subordinate' and 'would have no personal influence'. The Cabinet strongly protested against his interference with other offices than his own. Bark had supporters on many sides; and though he had to receive more than one professional 'instruction' from Rasputin — such as a criticism of his stamp money — he made his peace with him and even got a good report from him to the Empress. Waiting his time — 'like a first rate chess player', as Beletsky remarks — at the moment when the attack on him was about to materialize, Bark casually declared to Beletsky his intention of inquiring into Tatishchev's stability in money affairs, with the result that the candidate threw up the game and retired to Moscow.[2]

Another no less vital Ministry, that of Transport, fell vacant through the retirement of the Conservative Rukhlov. The railways were in dreadful disorder, and Hvostov got the Empress to recommend that they should be inspected by his candidate, Neidhardt. He even himself made a demonstrative visit to Moscow to disentangle the railway connections with Petrograd, but it does not appear to have had any real results. This time Hvostov was again unsuccessful. The new minister, A. F. Trepov, though a strong Conservative and with little special knowledge of transport, was an independent man with courage enough to resist the

[1] Beletsky, *Padenie*, iv, 318. [2] ibid., 244, 256-7.

insinuations of Rasputin, who, through the Empress, sadly lamented the appointment to the Emperor.[1]

Many of the lesser appointments of this time were simply fabulous; for instance, one Zhevakhov, who happened to have been recommended to the Empress, though she gets his name wrong, was proposed by her for the creation of a new supplementary post of Assistant in the Ministry of Religion. This was only staved off by Hvostov by dangling before the Empress the danger of the coming debates in the Duma, and the appointment was brought about later.[2] A certain Reshetnikov, a friend of Rasputin and of Anna Vyrubova, with no qualifications whatever for any official post and no bureaucratic standing, was with difficulty prevented from getting appointed as Assistant Minister of Commerce, on no other ground than that he had contributed large sums to the Vyrubova's hospital.[3] Rasputin's point of view in these matters was very simple. He merely demanded to have 'his own man' in one Ministry after another.

In all these appointments the two chief conspirators had increasing difficulties with Andronikov. He expected to be consulted about everything. He had a number of personal enemies for whose dismissal he was clamouring, and he also had his own candidates for several posts, though not as a rule the principal ones. One sharp conflict with him led in the end to a surrender by Hvostov, for there were plenty of points in his programme which he could not afford to have shown up to his patronesses. Gradually, however, he and Beletsky were reinforced by a growing dissatisfaction of Rasputin with Andronikov. Andronikov's idea was to be the broker of Rasputin's favours and to act permanently as the intermediary between him and the Ministers. At the outset the three met regularly with Rasputin in Andronikov's quarters; their host had even insisted on a special meeting, in a room which was a curious combination of bedroom and chapel, for a religious service to celebrate their appointment; and Andronikov claimed that the agreed sums (at first £1800 a year and later £3600) should pass to Rasputin through his hands; he had offered Anna Vyrubova to act as Rasputin's business manager.[4] Rasputin on his side claimed to have detected inaccuracies in Andronikov's

[1] A. F. to N., Nov. 1st/14th. [2] Beletsky, *Padenie*, IV, 220-4.
[3] ibid., 247. [4] Beletsky, *Padenie*, IV, 158; Andronikov, I, 379.

deliveries, and in any case had no intention of making him his intermediary in these or any other relations. After a while the meetings were removed from Andronikov's quarters and different 'conspirative apartments' — such were always at the disposal of the police — were found for them. Ultimately and after many small conflicts, the quarrel became definite; and at this point Beletsky undermined the confidence of Anna Vyrubova by carefully shaded information on Andronikov's moral delinquencies.[1]

Hvostov and Beletsky intended to keep Rasputin out of Petrograd until the approaching session of the Duma was over; and for this purpose they planned a great demonstrative journey for him, in which he was to show his sanctity by visits to well-known monasteries. The details of this story are peculiarly disgusting. Rasputin was to be supplied with all his requirements, including a large stock of Madeira wine (this, no doubt, was the basis of Hvostov's misleading report to Rodzyanko), and the priests who were to accompany him so clamoured for promotion and other advantages that Beletsky himself says that he was compelled to blush for them.[2] The difficulty was to get Rasputin to go; and on any pretext, without actually refusing, he postponed the journey. The two conspirators determined to intimidate him. Before Hvostov's time, official information had been received in the Ministry of the Interior from the honest Governor of Tobolsk, Stankevich, of an outbreak of Rasputin on a river boat in his province. We will print Beletsky's account of this incident in full; it is perhaps the least offensive illustration that we could choose of what Rasputin was and what harm he did to his sovereign.

> But already in the war, in the last days of Maklakov's Ministry [early in 1915], Rasputin on a steamer, when he was not sober, started entertaining some recruits, singing and dancing with them; and when at the request of the passengers, who complained of his annoying them, the captain moved him from the first class to the second, he wanted to treat the recruits to dinner in the second class; and when the steward refused to lay the table, and it seems, to serve wine for him, he inflicted a physical insult on the steward. On the demand of the public the captain, who had witnessed this scene, in spite of Rasputin's protests, put him ashore at the nearest

[1] Beletsky, *Padenie*, iv, 242. [2] ibid., 173.

pier, where the captain and steward insisted that the police should draw up a report. The police, taking into account that it was Rasputin, and knowing the demand circulated at that time to smother up facts of this kind in Rasputin's conduct, before sending the case to court, to avoid wide publicity, addressed their report to the Governor; and Stankevich, as he later himself explained to me, having no instructions from Prince Shcherbatov as to Rasputin, with a letter of his own 'to be delivered in person', sent a copy of the correspondence to Prince Shcherbatov. The last-named sent it to the Minister of Justice, A. A. Hvostov, asking for his instructions; Hvostov sent it back to the Prince stating that reports of this kind were in no need of being sanctioned by the Minister of Justice, as the law declared them to be proper cases for trial. Prince Shcherbatov also informed the President of the Council of Ministers, I. L. Goremykin. Reports of the matter also reached circles in the Duma. Such were the conditions in which this correspondence was inherited by A. N. [Alexis] Hvostov. The case was brought before the cantonal [peasant] court on the plea of the plaintiff with whom, as the Governor replied to my question in cipher by telegram, no reconciliation had taken place.

This state of the case very much alarmed A. A. Vyrubova and greatly disturbed Rasputin, who explained the matter to A. N. Hvostov and myself in a somewhat different light. Rasputin maintained to us that he was not drunk, that he did not annoy women and passengers, but they provoked him to a scandal, that the captain of the ship took their side for reasons of principle in consequence of his liberalism, knowing that it was Rasputin, that it was entirely under the influence of the captain that the steward made his official complaint against him, which the police did not want to report, but that the captain insisted on this; and that in general there was no drunken hooliganism, as in entertaining a party of recruits on their way to the war he, Rasputin, acted on purely patriotic motives and besides that, in his talks with them he had emphasized the attitude of the Emperor and Empress to the war in the highest tones of patriotism, and that he was offended with the steward because he had not let recruits, who were setting out to shed their blood, into the saloon of the second class, whither he had himself gone as the public there were simpler folk. This was

> the light in which Rasputin put this story 'above' and in the eyes of A. A. Vyrubova; but taking it all round, it was clear that the matter did not stand as he said, for he was afraid of this case being made public. This was what was also asserted to me by Abbot Martemian [one of Rasputin's clerical companions], whom I asked about it when he came later to see me in my flat.
>
> According to Martemian it was clear that Rasputin was very drunk and annoyed the public, and that when no one wanted to drink with him he went to the recruits, and while entertaining them, himself drank with them. For Martemian it was very humiliating to leave the boat with Rasputin, under a storm of derision from those present, whether on the boat or on shore, and that his, Martemian's request to the captain not to land them and not to draw up a report, had no effect on the captain of the boat.[1]

But this was not the end of the matter. Rasputin was also about to be prosecuted for a second drunken incident, also on a river steamboat, and this time, as at the Yar, he had used scandalous expressions about the Empress and Emperor. This case had also come before the Governor, and had separately reached Beletsky by another channel. He called Stankevich to Petrograd and the Governor brought all the papers with him. Rasputin and Vyrubova did not yet know of this second prosecution, but were already clamouring for Stankevich's dismissal. When Beletsky told him quietly of the second prosecution, Rasputin consented that Stankevich should be promoted to a more central province, but named his own candidate for his native Tobolsk where, he said, 'he must have his own man'. He was however seriously frightened by the second report, and Hvostov and Beletsky hoped to use it to send him off on his journey to monasteries, for which all the details, including the supply of Madeira, had now been planned. But as soon as they handed over the police reports to Anna Vyrubova, he refused to move.[2]

As Andronikov's offices as intermediary came to be dispensed with, some new arrangement was required, and some more precise technique for the relations with Rasputin. For this Beletsky found the man he wanted, a certain General of Gendarmes, Komissarov.[3] This was a broken official who might be

[1] Beletsky, *Padenie*, IV, 177-8. [2] ibid., 179-84. [3] ibid., 338 & ff.

set to such a job. He had been exposed in the most notable speech ever made in the First Duma (1906) by the Liberal, Prince Urusov, who till lately had been Assistant Minister of the Interior and had resigned his office under Witte because of open incitements to pogroms circulated by Komissarov directly from the Department of Police. Komissarov himself has represented in his evidence to the post-revolution commission that he was really a scapegoat,[1] and whether or not that was true, Beletsky had a tender spot for him, which we can understand the more readily because Komissarov was always faithful to him. He had a curious blunt frankness, and indeed he does not come out as the worst character in this story; but he was used to doing other people's dirty work. He gave to the Commission a most interesting description of how at one time he was employed by the Ministry of the Interior to steal and decipher the correspondence of various foreign embassies; he even boasted that his Ministry was able in this way to secure earlier information on foreign policy than the Ministry of Foreign Affairs itself.[2] Beletsky, in his anxiety to rehabilitate Komissarov, had employed him as a personal agent for the safety of Stolypin and Krivoshein during an official visit which they made to Siberia, and Komissarov had done this job discreetly and well. Hvostov and Beletsky now decided to put him in charge of Rasputin. He was to be assisted by a squad of police with very definite instructions. To minimize the likelihood of public scandals, they were to prevent Rasputin as far as possible from surprise visits in unexpected directions, and this they would do on the plea that they were securing him against assassination, of which he was always in danger. They were to obtain his confidence; but at the same time they were to spy on him and collect further materials which could be used against him if necessary. A whole procedure was worked out. It was the custom for Rasputin to be in telephone communication with the palace early in the morning, and Komissarov was to keep before him any point which Hvostov and Beletsky specially wanted to emphasize. Next, all personal petitions of Rasputin in favour of his very varied and very shady clients were to be granted where they did not touch any major issue; these were to be forwarded for the purpose by Komissarov to Beletsky, on whom all through Hvostov was trying

[1] Komissarov, *Padenie*, III, 158-60. [2] ibid., 141.

as far as possible to put all responsibility for his relations with Rasputin. Beletsky, who was, as we know, a furious worker at his ordinary duties, describes how crowded his day became with such additions, and generally he had not finished till half-way through the night.[1] To the Empress, of course, it was represented that Rasputin was at last effectively protected against assassination.

Very curious relations grew up between Komissarov and his charge. They were by no means without a certain cordiality; and whenever Rasputin was capable of seeing reason, he must of himself have felt that Komissarov in his reproaches was often acting in his own interests. Rasputin, when talking to strangers, had the habit of prefacing his conversations with a mystical muddle of religious talk; but Komissarov would cut in with genial brusqueness: 'Now, Gregory, drop the theology.' On one occasion when Rasputin was summoned by telephone to Tsarskoe Selo, he was dead drunk. His meetings there now always took place at the 'little house' of Vyrubova, where Beletsky and Hvostov sometimes dined. Rasputin ordinarily had a genius for recovering his sobriety almost instantaneously, but on this occasion — the Empress was not present — he was still tipsy at Vyrubova's table, and she showed her annoyance. On the way out Rasputin had demanded to dash out of the carriage, saying outrageous things about the intimacy of his relations with the Empress. Komissarov shook him and told him he would strangle him if he disgraced himself in this way.[2] This probably gave the occasion for the entry in a letter of the Empress relating to a subsequent interview, in which she says: 'He was not tipsy.' Komissarov's squad was inside the house, and there were times when Rasputin himself invited them into his quarters. Outside were the agents of Globachev, Head of the Gendarmes, and the palace police of Spiridovich also took a hand in the protection of Rasputin.

The most sinister part of Beletsky's record is his account of the sort of petitioners that came to him in this way. Rasputin used to hold a kind of levée, attended among others by leading bankers and speculators of more than dubious reputation. They constantly pressed large gifts upon him, which he often handed on immediately to poor petitioners; on occasion he would directly bleed the rich

[1] Beletsky, *Padenie*, IV, 359.
[2] ibid., 251-2; Komissarov, III, 172.

for the poor. Beletsky was aware that Rasputin was taking part in some very fishy speculations.[1] He does not say so much on this subject as Rasputin's man of business, Simanovich, who tells all the sordid details in the frankest way and quite possibly with some exaggeration. Rasputin's relations with shady financiers had begun long before this; but the worst details which Simanovich gives seem to relate to the latest period of his power, when he was absolutely shameless. But already Beletsky and Hvostov had noticed that when he returned from Siberia, shortly after their appointment, he showed a far greater confidence than before. He knew that he had really won his duel with Samarin, and that his power was now practically unlimited.[2]

It was Rasputin's smaller petitions that went to Beletsky, but he was also in regular communication with Vyrubova, who, as we learn from the Empress's letters, at his request, had been allowed by the Emperor to write straight to him at Headquarters.[3] As a matter of fact Anna Vyrubova adored the Emperor, and Alexandra showed signs of jealousy at this direct approach, but herself accepted it because it was the arrangement of Rasputin.[4] The Empress's own letters are not the source for Rasputin's shady financial petitions; but at times Rasputin addressed his requests direct to the Emperor. When Nicholas saw clearly how unwarranted they were, Rasputin would simply say that he did not himself know the value of his suggestions, but had been asked to hand them over. The receipt of gifts to himself he invariably explained by saying that he only accepted them to hand them over to others. However, many of these ugly profiteering deals related directly to such matters of major importance as the munitioning of the army. In fact, under a regime of favour, this subject was a playground for all sorts of tomfoolery, especially by Grand Dukes. The Emperor's brother, Michael, supported a scheme of an adventurer named Bratolyubov to project liquid fire; it did not go beyond the stage of experiment, but caused several deaths, and, according to Rodzyanko, brought a subsidy of three million pounds from the Treasury to the inventor.[5]

The greater number of Rasputin's personal petitions went to

[1] BELETSKY, *Padenie*, IV, 324.
[2] ibid., IV, 161.
[3] A. F. to N., Nov. 3rd/16th.
[4] A. F. to N., Nov. 3rd/16th.
[5] RODZYANKO, 164-5.

Beletsky. His general instruction from Hvostov was to satisfy all of them if possible; but as he came to get a clear idea of the character of Rasputin and the nature of the petitions, he found that he could not do this. Many of them were concerned with exemptions from military service; and there were cases in which even the names of the persons to be assisted were not given to Beletsky. Of course the satisfaction of such demands was a gross dereliction of public duty. Other petitions asked for subsidies or for promotions.

Beletsky was especially exercised by the moral character of the petitioners. Nearly all of them were women, some of them of loose character, and others from whom he learnt that Rasputin, as the price of his favour, was demanding the satisfaction of his lust. This is one of the foulest parts of the whole story, and we can have no wish to linger over it; but there is no understanding of all the issues at stake, if it is left out. Beletsky gives three particular examples. In one case, that of a quite respectable petitioner from Moscow, whom he names, it is only Beletsky's warning as to the real character of Rasputin that just saves her in time, but not before Rasputin had violently tried to force his way into her bedroom; and afterwards he said resentfully to Beletsky: 'She cheated me.' In another case Rasputin gets one of his loose lady friends a place in a Red Cross office and by his midnight visits creates a serious scandal, which he explains away with the plea of 'visiting the sick'. In a third case, this time again with a respectable petitioner, he promises to refer her case direct to the Empress, but only on the condition of her surrender to him; and when his insistence has reduced her almost to hysterics, he actually rapes her, though he does not later make the appeal for her to the Empress.[1] The cynical and unscrupulous police officer is again compelled to blush for his associate; and indeed Komissarov has to report that his squad of guards and spies are for the same reason disgusted with their job. Earlier a high police authority had given much the same account of the attitude of his men to Rodzyanko, when commenting on Rasputin's visits to the mixed public baths in the company of women.[2]

Beletsky's record, on this side of his story, culminates in his description of the celebration of Rasputin's name day — as it

[1] BELETSKY, *Padenie*, IV, 328-34. [2] RODZYANKO, 62.

happens, for the last time — on January 23rd, 1916.[1] The Empress, in her daily letter, greets the morning with the words, 'Why, there is the sun for our Friend; that is lovely, indeed it had to be for Him.'[2] Rasputin begins the day with the traditional and religious visit of Russian peasants to the church and to the bath. On his return he meets a great display of the most handsome presents from the secret funds of Beletsky, and from the rich bankers and other financiers who are in with him. The plain apartments glitter with gold and silver, pictures, carpets and furniture which is later removed to Rasputin's Siberian home. Anna Vyrubova, timid and correct, is present at lunch; and while she is there nothing outrageous takes place; she brings the thankful congratulations of the imperial family. The apartments are now crowded with equivocal, prosperous business men of all kinds who also shower their grateful presents on the author of favour. Rasputin and his many lady friends next engage in furious bouts of dancing and drinking, until he is removed unconscious to his bedroom. However, before long he recovers; and by now, his favourite musicians, the gipsies, whose entertainment, as a rule, went much beyond the farthest limits of an English music hall, are also come with their congratulations, and the orgy of excitement goes on until the gipsies themselves leave in disgust. Rasputin and a number of the ladies sink unconscious on the floor, and the next morning two husbands with drawn swords, who have come to look for their wives, are with difficulty fended off by Komissarov's squad, and the ladies escape by the backstairs.

None of these particulars would have been given except to mark the actual background in the life of the man who had become the arbiter of Russia's destinies in the middle of the World War. It is in this sense that the reader should understand Rasputin's petitions to Beletsky and his constant and direct access to Vyrubova, with her direct approach to the Emperor. We have also to bear in mind that for the considerable periods which Nicholas still continued to spend with his family we have hardly any record of the satisfaction of Rasputin's demands through that channel. But if we take the single source of the Empress's own letters to her husband during his absences, where we have the advantage of month and date and can know easily enough from later events which of the major

[1] BELETSKY, *Padenie*, IV, 354-6. [2] A. F. to N., Jan. 10th/23rd, 1916.

demands were satisfied, we find them permeated with Rasputin's insistence, of which the following are examples for this period.

On Sept. 7th/20th, 1915, she sends a list of possible successors to Samarin. Guryev (one of them) 'likes our Friend'.

On Sept. 8th/21st she asks him to put Bishop Pitirim on the Synod, and adds: 'He venerates Our Friend.'

On Oct. 3rd/16th Rasputin begs the Tsar to telegraph to the King of Serbia. She adds: 'So I enclose a paper . . . Put the sense in your words.' In the same letter Rasputin condemns the new stamp money, and she says she will report this to the Finance Minister, Bark.

On Oct. 10th/23rd Rasputin already foresees what is to be the actual cause of the Revolution, namely the disorder in the food supply. 'He says you must give the order that waggons with flour, butter and sugar should be allowed to pass: there are to be no other trains for three days. He saw the whole thing in the night in a vision.' Rodzyanko tells us later how the whole passenger traffic was hung up not for three days, but for six, and entirely without result, for no proper arrangement had been made to bring the goods to the point of embarkage.[1]

On Nov. 1st/14th Rasputin is 'very grieved' at Trepov, nominated as Minister of Transport in place of Rukhlov, as 'he knows he is very against him'. It is in this letter that she writes: 'Our Friend was always against the War, saying that the Balkans were not worth troubling to fight about.'

On Nov. 8th/21st: 'He dictated to me the other day I saw Him, walking about, praying and crossing himself, about Rumania and Greece and our troops passing through.' He also gives his plans for the Russian entry into Constantinople; the Empress's favourite regiment is to lead.

On Nov. 10th/23rd Rasputin has recommended the dismissal of the Premier, Goremykin. Now he asks the Tsar to wait until he has seen the elder Hvostov, to form his impressions of him as a possible successor. The results of Rasputin's call on this rugged and honest Conservative are not favourable, for the Empress describes him as having received Rasputin 'as if he were a petitioner'.

On Nov. 12th/25th Rasputin pushes Pitirim 'as the only suitable

[1] Rodzyanko, 159.

man' for the office of Metropolitan of Petrograd, the most important post in the Orthodox Church. He also proposes Zhivakhov as Assistant Minister of Religion.

On Nov. 13th/26th, he spends an hour and a half with the Empress and tells the Tsar to delay his decision as to the Premiership 'according to God'. He suggests a surprise visit of the Tsar to the Duma to avert scandals, which, as we shall see, took place later.

On Nov. 15th/28th, 'prompted by what he saw in the night', he orders an advance near Riga. He 'says it is necessary, begs you seriously, says we can and we must'. He repeats the suggestion of a surprise visit to the Duma, though, she adds, 'he loathes their existence, as I do, for Russia'.

In her letter of Dec. 12th/25th, among his instructions is one that 'He cannot exactly remember', but, she adds, he says 'we must always do what he says'.

These instructions run through the whole of the period, and this selection will for the present perhaps be sufficient.

At the turn of the year Rasputin repeated, almost simultaneously his famous 'double' of 1915, namely the 'resurrecting' of Vyrubova and his scandal at a public restaurant. On December 16th the Emperor, now accompanied by his little son, was starting from Headquarters for a trip to the southern front. The train was moving over the points, and the boy was standing with his nose pressed to the window, when a jolt suddenly started serious bleeding. Nicholas at once turned back for Tsarskoe Selo. Gilliard, who was with the boy, describes his condition as serious.[1] They reach home on the morning of the 11th, and a telephone message is sent to Rasputin. However, according to Beletsky, he does not come for a whole day, and later explains this to him by saying that he did not want to cut short the Emperor's anxiety; but on his appearance the bleeding stops directly, and the confidence in Rasputin is correspondingly increased.[2] In January, however, at a night orgy in which he was taking part at a notorious haunt of the gipsies in St. Petersburg named the Villa Rodé, where special arrangements were always made for his entertainment, he was set on by a number of officers, but according to his account and that of some others, he stood up to them so boldly that their arms were paralysed, and anyhow he escaped.[3]

[1] GILLIARD, 114. [2] BELETSKY, *Padenie*, IV, 307. [3] SIMANOVICH, 239.

With such a Government it can be imagined in what kind of spirit the Russian rear met the mortifications of the winter of 1915-16. The front was not driven farther back; on the contrary the army showed signs of its recovery in some fine local actions, though the general position was not altered. But Bulgaria, liberated by Russian arms in 1877, had now come out on the side of the Central Powers, and pouncing on the Serbian rear, had driven army and people alike in the depths of winter over the mountains to the Adriatic, where the remnants of the Serbian troops were with difficulty salvaged and sent for recuperation to Corfu. Serbia was overrun wholesale; Poland had been lost, never to be recovered, and streams of refugees were crowding the interior. Very definitely, even for the Russian private soldier, the war had been accompanied by the hope of a more free and happy life in Russia itself; and now that that hope had failed, defeatism, depression and demoralization were growing apace. The higher society in Petrograd, not likely to be restrained by the example of Rasputin, was showing a scandalous indifference to the war, which was almost forgotten in the personal pursuit of pleasure. Here is its true picture in some anonymous satirical verses of the beginning of 1916:

OUR MOODS

We do not take defeat amiss,
  And victory gives us no delight;
The source of all our cares is this:
  Can we get vodka for to-night.[1]

The victories we can do without.
  No! Peace and quiet is our line,
Intrigues and scandal, evenings out
  Trimmed up with women and with wine.

We only want to know, next day
  What Ministers will be on view,
Or who takes who to see the play,
  Or who at Cuba's sat next who:

[1] An allusion to the prohibition edict of the Tsar.

Has Vyrubova had to go?
  Or can Kuvaka[1] give you joy.
Or how the Germans knead their dough,
  Or why on earth there's Shakhovskoy.[2]

And does Rasputin still prevail,
  Or do we need another saint,
And is Kshesinskaya quite well,
  And how that feast at Shubin's went:

If the Grand Duke took Dina home,
  What kind of luck MacDiddie's had—
Oh, if a Zeppelin would come,
  And smash the whole of Petrograd.

Here is another satire on the personnel of the Cabinet; one must own that the writer mingles good and bad in his ridicule:

THE WOEBEGONE CABINET[3]

In lack of system there's a system,
  And I'm prepared to show you how:
Though even with verses to assist 'em,
  In such ideas there's danger now.

The very thought of progress[4] banish;
  Those forward steps you'll never see.
So if our woes are not to vanish,
  Then Woebegone should Premier be.

Drag by the tail, as serves occasion,
  Your citizens, your judges too.
And that your Tails in combination
  (The uncle and the nephew) do.[5]

The sweep of spiritual endeavour
  No longer must the flesh besmirch;
Then surely the idea was clever
  To run our Volga[6] through the church.

[1] Natural waters which their owner, Voeykov, the commandant of the palace, tried to make the most of, profiting by the prohibition edict.
[2] The Minister of Trade, supported by Rasputin.
[3] The name of the Prime Minister, Goremykin, means Woebegone.
[4] An allusion to the Duma (which means 'thought') and to the Progressive Bloc.
[5] The two Hvostovs. Hvost=Tail.
[6] Volzhin=man of the Volga.

To disengage a railway junction,
  You only need to give a shake;
And so for such a simple function,
  Why, Shaker[1] is the man to take.

Suppose your stock of money's failing,
  Then postage stamps will help you out;
And on a Bark[2] you'll still go sailing,
  Suppose there's not a ship about.

Then Agriculture: well, what of it?
  We know that corn won't grow on Clay:[3]
Of course with Clay we should not profit,
  But say, will Nahum humbug? Nay.

And so a choice symbolic ranges
  Each time a Minister is made,
And now the point of all these changes
  I'll whisper, if you aren't afraid.

We see no end to dissolution;
  The future's grey with clouds, you'll own;
So by our curious constitution
  The Dissolute must rule alone.[4]

Goremykin, trained and wily old bureaucrat as he was, had at least some record of public service; but he was entirely lacking in initiative and by his theory of implicit obedience he had condemned himself to a passive role. In the light of the ages and characters of the two men, it was inevitable that Alexis Hvostov should aim at undermining him. At this point, appeared on the scene a new public figure in the person of Pitirim. He had been Exarch of the Church in the Caucasus, and was a personal friend of Rasputin. The death at this time of the Metropolitan Flavian of Kiev created a vacancy near the top. Kiev, in fact, was the senior post, and on Rasputin's insistence — after all he had lately brought about the canonization of a new saint, St. John of Tobolsk — the

[1] Trepov (Minister of Transport). Trepat = to shake up.
[2] An allusion to Bark's stamp money.
[3] The choice for Minister of Agriculture had lain between Glinka, which means clay, and Naumov. Nahum is a Russian Christian name derived from the Hebrew Prophet.
[4] A word for dissolution is *rasputie*, and the name Rasputin means 'the Dissolute'.

Metropolitan Vladimir was moved from Petrograd to Kiev, and Pitirim was appointed to his place in Petrograd. The new hierarch was a born intriguer. He was already in the good graces of the palace. He brought with him as his secretary one Osipenko, whom Beletsky recognized at once as worth bribing. Goremykin had never, since the Duma existed, talked of it with anything but contempt, and he had successfully defied it in the summer. However, even then, the date had had to be given for its next meeting, which was rapidly approaching. Hvostov on the other hand was himself a member of the Duma and kept up his equivocal ties with Rodzyanko. Rasputin and the palace were sincerely afraid of the Duma; the Empress herself recognized that account had to be taken of it, and her reliance on Hvostov was grounded on a belief that he would be able to control it. Rodzyanko, as its President, was insisting that it should be called. Goremykin was for postponement; at the most its Budget Commission, which sat behind closed doors, should meet and do its work first, and any general meeting should be confined to the ratification of its decisions. The question was referred to Rasputin, who declared that Goremykin was 'quite wrong'. Rasputin's view was much the more intelligent. Had not the Duma dispersed quietly in the summer? He had described it to Illiodor as 'dogs collected to keep other dogs silent',[1] a definition of which the clever Shulgin himself need not have been ashamed. He even tried to get in touch with some of the members: not at all from the Rights, whom he regarded with contempt as men of straw.[2] His view naturally suited Hvostov, as it was excellently adapted to his tactics.

This verdict the Empress on Nov. 15th/28th sent on to her husband. This was why the elder Hvostov was sounded; he was approved, as one who had not signed the letter of the Ministry, but he could never have been made the tool of Rasputin, and was rejected as unsatisfactory. His restless nephew was constantly pressing Rasputin to urge his own claims; to which Rasputin only replied 'All in good time'; and the Empress, who knows Rasputin's mind, tells her husband that: 'he is too young'. Rodzyanko had no knowledge of these intrigues; and indeed throughout this period one can only measure the depth to which

[1] LODYZHENSKY, *Padenie*, VI, 153; MILYUKOV, VI, 312; ILLIODOR, 98.
[2] BELETSKY, *Padenie*, IV, 281.

the underground government of Russia had sunk by the almost complete ignorance of public men as to what was taking place. Rodzyanko, with his memories of the summer, regarded Goremykin as the principal obstacle to a national policy, and addressed to him at the New Year a stinging letter;[1] he not only showed it to others, but actually on the 9th handed a copy to the Emperor; it ran as follows:

> Dear Ivan Logginovich,
>
> I am writing under the impression of what I have just heard at to-day's meeting of the Special [Defence] Council concerning the catastrophic state of the railway transport. This question had already been raised by the members of the first Special Council and a commission formed to deal with the matter, but its work was confined to talk, references and estimates, and the catastrophe which was then merely foreshadowed has now become a reality.
>
> The President of the Special Council has doubtless informed you of conditions in the munition factories, where a stoppage is imminent, and also of the prospect of a famine with which the population of Petrograd is menaced, and which may lead to unrest and consequent disorders.
>
> Both I myself and the members of the Special Council are fully persuaded that our country is heading for ruin owing to the Government's apathy and complete lack of initiative in taking the steps necessary to avert the terrible calamities which are approaching. I consider it the bounden duty of the Council of Ministers, of which you are President, immediately to give proof of that solicitude for the destinies of Russia, which, as a body of statesmen, it is its duty to show. A year ago the members of the Special Council had already foreseen what is happening now, and you, Ivan Logginovich, cannot deny that I myself have warned you more than once. The only answer, however, that I ever got from you was that this was no concern of yours and that you could not interfere in matters concerning the war.
>
> Such answers are now inadmissible. The turning-point in the war is approaching,[2] but a general disintegration in all branches of our national life, coupled with a lack of essential commodities, is growing in the rear of our national armies.

[1] RODZYANKO, 166-8.

[2] The words, as translated in the English edition of Rodzyanko's memoirs, are 'the fatal end' but the Russian words mean 'the final decision'.

> The victorious spirit of the people and their faith in their own powers are being crushed by the inactivity of the Government.
>
> Your paramount duty is, without losing a moment, to manifest at last the greatest zeal to remove all obstacles from the path to victory.
>
> I beg definitely to state that we, the members of the Imperial Duma, possess a merely consultative voice,[1] and cannot, therefore, be held responsible for the inevitable and imminent collapse.
>
> If the Council of Ministers fails to take such steps as may yet save our country from disgrace and humiliation, the entire responsibility will rest upon you. If you, Ivan Logginovich, feel that you lack strength to bear this heavy burden, and to use all available means to help the country to emerge on to the high road to victory — have the courage to own this and make way for younger and more energetic men.
>
> The decisive hour has struck; events, stern and inexorable, are drawing near, pregnant with consequences which may prove fatal to Russia's honour and dignity. Do not delay, I earnestly beg of you — the Fatherland is in Danger.

This was another nail in Goremykin's official coffin. At this point Pitirim took a hand in the game. This intriguer, whose moves seemed in the main to have been inspired by Osipenko, paid a demonstrative visit to Rodzyanko and offered his friendship to the Duma. He did not get an over-sympathetic reception. The burly President saw no room for their co-operation, as the estimates for the Synod, the only church matter in the province of the Duma, were in the hands of the Minister of Religion.[2]

There now comes into the picture another figure from the underworld, one Manasevich Manuilov, as unscrupulous as Andronikov and much more formidable, whose acquaintance we shall have to make more closely later. Manuilov was one of those parasites who moved about with confident dexterity on the fringes of the Press and the secret police. As a correspondent of the principal Petrograd newspaper, the *Novoe Vremya*, he had at one time had an interview with Rasputin, in which the latter boastfully gloried in

[1] Rodzyanko wishes to intimate that, contrary to the existing law, the Duma has practically been reduced to a consultative status.

[2] Rodzyanko, 171.

his visits with women to the public baths, and Manuilov had written a scorching article on the subject. Like others, he had since realized that Rasputin was the one sure source of favour, and ingratiated himself with him. Pitirim, whom he had met in Georgia, called on him on his arrival in Petrograd, and Manuilov, seeing the kind of part which the new prelate wished to play in the capital, had put himself at his disposal. Pitirim was also in favour of conciliating the Duma; and Manuilov now advised him to recommend for the Premiership the reactionary Stürmer, known to him when Governor of Yaroslavl, whom hardly anyone could have thought of except Manuilov. Stürmer was a shallow and dishonest creature, without even the merit of courage. He was a born dissimulator with almost a preference for the equivocal. Stürmer was prepared to pose as a semi-liberal and to try in this way to keep the Duma quiet. After a meeting between the two, Pitirim even made a journey to Headquarters to recommend Stürmer to the Emperor. Rasputin backed Stürmer, and also the Empress, and he was suddenly appointed Prime Minister on February 2nd to the surprise of every one, and most of all to that of Goremykin, who, as was usual with the Emperor, had never been given the idea that he was even in danger.[1]

There is an amusing specimen of the tricks which all these intriguers were constantly playing on each other. They all depended on Rasputin, but they all pretended not to know him, because otherwise they would have lost all respect with the public. Pitirim had indulged himself in this pretence, speaking of 'that awful man'; and Hvostov, having watched for a time when they were together in Pitirim's quarters at the Alexander Nevsky Monastery, made a sudden raid on them in a car and surprised them in intimate converse.[2]

The Duma was now to be summoned and the new Premier presented to it; but there could hardly be any doubt as to how he would be received. He had drawn up a kind of inaugural lecture, expatiating on his liberalism with such emphasis as was sure to make it incredible, and even comparing himself to the greatest Liberal statesman of Russian history, Ordyn-Nashchokin, Minister of the Tsar Alexis, in the seventeenth century. Little as it was known at the time, it was Rasputin who had first suggested that

[1] BELETSKY, 286-7. [2] KOMISSAROV, *Padenie*, III, 168; HVOSTOV, I, 25.

the Tsar himself, who had never visited the Duma, should now pay it a surprise visit, which would practically make it impossible to hiss the new Prime Minister. The references in the letters of the Empress will be found under the dates Nov. 13th/15th in the summary which we have just given of his political interventions.[1] The same advice was given by Hvostov and Beletsky. Part of the policy of conciliation, also due to Rasputin, was that Rodzyanko should at this time be given a decoration, and with the reluctant consent of the Empress he was granted the Order of St. Anne, not indeed as President of the Duma, but as warden of a school. Rodzyanko quite correctly understood that this was definitely an attempt to compromise him with public opinion; but otherwise he was completely in the dark.[2] He was himself trying at this very time to bring about what Rasputin wanted, namely a visit of the Tsar to the Duma.

It was no wonder then that the visit took place (Feb. 22nd, 1916) and Rasputin was clever enough to mystify not only the Russian public, but France and England, whose parliaments sent congratulations to the Duma on this first visit of its sovereign. However, the weakest link in the chain was always the last, namely the so-called autocrat, Nicholas himself. The kindly little man who, not unnaturally, at first looked pale and nervous, was completely overwhelmed by the ardent and enthusiastic loyalty of these good country gentlemen. The short, but devout religious service completed the temporary cure, and Nicholas, who was a very good speaker, made an admirable address to the Duma in which, for the first time, he saluted them as 'representatives' of his people.† Rodzyanko pressed him to seize this happy moment to announce that he was about to appoint a 'Ministry of Confidence'; but Nicholas got no farther than a promise to 'think it over'. All this was not at all according to the programme of Rasputin, and the Empress herself later writes her dissatisfaction. The Emperor's speech was mutilated by the censorship. The next day he again departed for the front.[3]

Alexis Hvostov recognized that he had been outwitted. He had been disappointed of the Premiership, but still the post which he occupied, that of Minister of the Interior, was the most powerful in Russia. For a time he and Stürmer played together at concilia-

[1] See p. 300. [2] Rodzyanko, 163. [3] ibid., 175-6.

tion, and at the latter's request Hvostov even left to him some of his own important functions. But what was more serious for Hvostov was the growing inconvenience of his relations with Rasputin. For a time, after Andronikov had more or less dropped out, things had seemed much easier; but the increasing pride of Rasputin and his domineering methods were becoming less and less tolerable. Both Hvostov and Beletsky had wives of whom they were not worthy, and neither had dared to tell his consort to what extent they were tied up with Rasputin. Hvostov had deliberately from the first put the relations with Rasputin in Beletsky's hands, and Beletsky was constantly finding that he could not grant given demands of Rasputin without forfeiting all official respectability. When Beletsky refused, Rasputin would refer to Hvostov. He would ring up the one or the other in their homes, so that it was impossible for them to keep the scandal from their wives.[1] In one case, when Madame Hvostov was entertaining her friends, one of the minor officials burst in with an abrupt message from Rasputin. Madame Beletsky, who knew more, had always been pleading her utmost with her husband to break off the connection.

This brought Hvostov to a strange decision. He decided to murder Rasputin, and of this he informed Beletsky and Komissarov. They left his house together; of course, they both saw that Hvostov intended to leave all the blame to them, and they agreed that they would not fall into any such trap. Hvostov continued to be insistent, and demanded a definite plan. Komissarov, to humour him, proposed an assault on Rasputin by some of his own squad disguised as hooligans. Rasputin was to be strangled in a back street, as the quietest way of extinction, and his body taken out to a point at the river mouth not far from where it was actually to be found at the end of the same year with another set of murderers. For this purpose Rasputin was to be enticed to dinner and Hvostov himself was to come down in a private car to see the business put through. But the whole plot was make-believe, and as was not unnatural, from whatever quarter he had been informed, the principal actor, Rasputin himself, failed to put in an appearance.[2]

Hvostov demanded a new plan, and this time poison was suggested. When it came to details, there was the danger in

[1] BELETSKY, *Padenie*, IV, 335-7. [2] ibid., 364-7.

approaching an ordinary chemist. Komissarov declared that he knew the man required, but that he lived far away in Saratov, where Komissarov had once been Prefect of Police, and he asked leave to go and consult him. Once in Saratov, he had evidently no intention of coming back, and lingered on until he was sharply summoned by Hvostov. Beletsky describes how, visiting the two, he found them side by side on a sofa — Komissarov, with the authority of a professor, showing a number of poisons to Hvostov and explaining their nature and effects. Beletsky noticed that some of the bottles looked alike. Komissarov told the Minister that he had already tried them on a stray tom cat with complete success and recounted how it had died in agony, to the great relish of Hvostov. Beletsky, being in Komissarov's confidence, did not believe he would really poison Rasputin, and indeed the next time that he saw him pour out a glass of Madeira for the starets, he asked for one too. On being pressed, Komissarov said that the drugs which he had shown to Hvostov were really household remedies from his wife's medicine-chest and that he himself had written the labels on them from a cheap handbook of dangerous drugs which he had bought. Anyhow, the plan was approved by Hvostov, and Komissarov did put poison not into Rasputin's Madeira but into the milk prepared for his cats, which rolled over and expired. A further tangle in this absurd story was that Rasputin attributed the deed to Andronikov, and both he and Vyrubova finally broke off all relations with him.[1] Very likely, that was what Komissarov wanted.

Hvostov, who has admitted that he gave these various orders, must have seen that he was being hoaxed. At one time, so he tells us, he tried to get an unscrupulous Cossack to do the job instead.[2] In the end, in desperation he turned to an adventurer of even a lower type, one Rzhetsky, whom he had employed for the most questionable services when Governor of Nizhny-Novgorod; Rzhetsky was a man who was incapable of keeping faith with anyone. Hvostov was aware of the bitter hostility between Rasputin and the monk Illiodor, who was already credited with one attempt to assassinate Rasputin. Illiodor was now living in Denmark. He had written his famous book, *The Holy Devil*, and

[1] Beletsky, *Padenie*, iv, 370-1; Andronikov, i, 384, 389-90.
[2] Hvostov, i, 43.

he was now supposed to be offering it to an American publisher. So far the story, as told by Beletsky, does not seem to call for comment. Hvostov dispatched Rzhetsky on a mission to Illiodor. Rzhetsky, in a confession which he made later, declared that the object was to try to organize the murder of Rasputin, though he withdrew this in an amended version. When, later, all telegrams from Illiodor were intercepted by the police, one was found to be a demand for money to arrange for some of Illiodor's adherents in Tsaritsyn to come to Petrograd; and it was from Tsaritsyn that had been drawn the participants in the unsuccessful attempt on the Kamenno-Ostrovsky Prospekt. Rzhetsky was the stupidest of conspirators, for when questioned by the passport authorities at the Finnish frontier at Beloretsk, he boasted that he was a special emissary of Hvostov, and followed this up with threats and insults to the local officials. This was all reported to Beletsky as Chief of the Police, and on Rzhetsky's return from his mission he was again challenged at Beloretsk and showed even more indiscretion than before. Rzhetsky was in any case wanted for another offence, and Beletsky had him arrested. In his account Beletsky declares that he was prepared to limit the matter to the elimination of Rzhetsky, if he could once be sure that Hvostov was playing straight with him. In three conversations which he had with him, he came to the opposite conclusion. Meanwhile Rzhetsky, through a friend, had himself warned Rasputin, and Beletsky, who, according to his account, had always opposed the idea of assassination, also advised Rasputin to stay at home till the danger was over.[1]

Beletsky's further account may be given, and it is very circumstantial. He strongly urged Hvostov to give up his plan of assassination, and, on the contrary, to mobilize at once all the information against Rasputin to be derived from Komissarov's squad and from the spies of the Chief of Gendarmes, Globachev, who had also been keeping watch on Rasputin. Globachev and Komissarov were summoned and set to work on a report to be handed to the Emperor by Hvostov on the next day, which was his day of reception by the sovereign. The two worked all night, and by Beletsky's orders produced in three copies a report of which Hvostov approved. Two copies were to be taken by Hvostov to

[1] BELETSKY, *Padenie*, IV, 400 & ff.

Tsarskoe Selo — one to leave with the Emperor, and one to bring back. The third remained with Beletsky. Next day, Beletsky himself accompanied Hvostov to the station, and saw him off. He met him again on his return and went with him to his house. When he asked the result of the audience, Hvostov gave a detailed account of how the Emperor — as was usual in such cases — drummed with his fingers on the window and showed other signs of great nervousness, but ultimately accepted the report. Beletsky was not satisfied, and invited one of his colleagues to look in Hvostov's dispatch case. He records the fact that Hvostov had brought both his copies back. As a matter of fact, Hvostov had asked the Emperor for the dismissal of Beletsky himself, who was to be appointed Governor-General of Siberia. This decision was announced to the public on March 1st.[1]

Let us compare this with the version of Hvostov. At his first examination by the commission after the revolution he was not yet on trial and treated it in an offhand casual way, frequently changing the subject when faced with an awkward question; but his story, full of falsehoods and evasions, contradicted itself at point after point. He posed as one who had been for the Duma and against Rasputin throughout, and made a free use of Beletsky as a lightning conductor for each charge. Rasputin was an agent of Germany, and he himself was a patriot trying to save the country from him. He admitted all the murder plots, except that of Rzhevsky which he declared to be a trap of Beletsky, and even later added another of which Beletsky apparently did not know; after the revolution it was self-recommendation to claim to have tried to kill Rasputin.[2] When he was examined again, and this time on trial, the commission had had time to study Beletsky's evidence; and in answer to straight and searching questions, his defence broke down altogether, and substantially he confirmed Beletsky in the essentials. The report which Beletsky gave him to take to the Tsar he claimed to have composed independently, and to have himself collected all the proofs against Rasputin which were attached to it; but these he said he had destroyed. He makes out that they were proofs of espionage by Rasputin for Germany, which in all probability, did not exist. All that he meant to do through Rzhevsky was to get hold of Illiodor's book. Hvostov

[1] BELETSKY, *Padenie*, IV, 406-7. [2] HVOSTOV, *Padenie*, I, 7-51.

himself tells us that he did everything he could to complicate the task of his successor, though he describes a grim scene where he and Stürmer, alone in the Ministry of the Interior, burnt all the papers there relating to Rasputin. He also tells us that he later offered his services to the Opposition.[1] He certainly tried to approach Milyukov.[2]

Beletsky felt sure that all blame in the matter was now to be put on himself, with the result that in the shortest time he would be dismissed from his new post. He and Hvostov were now bitter rivals. Both sides brought Anna Vyrubova into their quarrel, and the Empress was horrified. Rasputin himself was almost in terror. 'It is a damnable story', wrote the Emperor,[3] but of course it was impossible to bring it before a law court. Hvostov now played a last game of bluff. He set about arresting some of the intimates of Rasputin, including Simanovich, who was to be sent to Narym in Siberia, but did not actually get farther than Tver. Perhaps Hvostov, who was now playing the Duma side of his connections, wanted to terrify Rasputin and Anna Vyrubova back into submission and, presumably, co-operation. Anyhow, a meeting between the three at the lady's house was arranged; but Beletsky managed to persuade her to put it off. Hvostov now lost all restraint, and to his Duma friends and others gave his own version incriminating Beletsky; he himself, he said, had all along been trying to oust Rasputin and had evidence enough to charge him with espionage for Germany.

The Jewish editor of a prominent Petrograd newspaper, the *Bourse Gazette*, one Hackebusch, who was greatly indebted to Beletsky, warned him of these reports, and asked for an account of the whole matter. Beletsky gave his account, though for the information of Hackebusch rather than for publication. A circular had just gone out prohibiting any reference to the subject. This, however, had not been received at the *Bourse Gazette* and the interview was published in the form in which it was given. There was no subject on which the Emperor was more sensitive than public scandals of this kind affecting his private affairs. Beletsky was so indiscreet as to write a letter to the Press, which only confirmed

[1] Hvostov, *Padenie*, vi, 74-113.
[2] Milyukov to B. P.
[3] N. to A. F., Mar. 5th/18th, 1916.

the authenticity of the interview; and his appointment to Siberia was cancelled.[1]

Almost simultaneously the question of Rzhetsky's mission was referred for investigation to Manuilov, and thus came into the province of Stürmer. There were plenty of other causes of dissatisfaction with Hvostov—one of them was the question of the use which he had made of the large sums of secret money granted him to rig the elections to a new Duma — and his final dismissal followed shortly after. Rasputin remained supreme, and the whole story was hushed up as far as possible.

Thus ended the Empress's first attempt at governing Russia; it might have been thought that it would be the last; but it was not. The experiment was continued — only, instead of Hvostov, with Stürmer, who now in addition to the Premiership received the Ministry of the Interior.

There is a curious epilogue to this story which can be given here. Both Hvostov and Beletsky were shot by the Bolsheviks, but while they were waiting for their death, they were confined in the same common cell and fought over their old battles without any bitterness; and of all people in the world, their companion in prison and the recorder of their conversations was, by a strange historical appropriateness, the most distinguished student of the history of the Russian underworld, the revolutionary Burtsev, who escaped to tell the story.[2]

[1] Beletsky, *Padenie*, IV, 418 ff. [2] Burtsev to B. P.

CHAPTER XI

THE STATE IN DISSOLUTION

A cutpurse of the Empire and the rule.
Hamlet, III, 4

This Land of such dear souls, this dear dear Land,
Dear for her reputation through the world,
Is now leas'd out . . .
Like to a tenement or pelting farm.
Richard II, II, 1

STÜRMER'S MYSTERY CABINET

RASPUTIN is reported to have said of Stürmer's appointment as Prime Minister: 'I begat Pitirim and Pitirim begat Stürmer. But it was Manuilov who recommended Stürmer to Pitirim and brought them together.' I. F. Manasevich-Manuilov was one of the most unlovely of those shady figures that lurked in the background of Russian public life. At this very time there was lying in the Department of Police a detailed report on this scoundrel. There were many such that clustered around the source of favour, combining the various functions of police agent, newspaper correspondent, pimp and blackmailer; but Manuilov is perhaps the most eminent member of this noble army.

Let us take his police record. Born a Lutheran Jew in 1870 he became one of the 'young men' of the mischievous and spider-like Meshchersky, and was early acclimatized both to luxury and to dirty work. He now joined the dominant Orthodox Church. At 25 he was taken up by Rachkovsky, the head of the Russian police in France, to which, according to Witte, President Loubet said that he would rather entrust his safety than to his own police. Here he was employed in spying on revolutionaries; soon Rachkovsky accused him of spying on himself. Betraying others and himself betrayed, he was transferred to Rome, presumably to direct police relations with the Catholic priesthood, whom he bribed. He was now also a political spy; but his subordinate agents accused him of cheating them. He secured the favour of V. K. Plehve, the reactionary Minister of the Interior (1902-04), and was sent again to Paris for relations with the French Press, controlling large subsidies to it. In 1903 he betrayed Plehve's agents to Witte, who thanked him for his kindness. His next notable work consisted in tapping ciphers, his best performance being in Holland, where he photographed the Japanese cipher in the Hague Legation of Japan. He claimed to have overheard the talk of Colonel Akashai and to have stolen his diary. He also obtained documents from the French secret police. Out of all these exploits he made money, but always spent it rapidly; he even received the order of Vladimir (fourth class). With false keys he managed to steal documents of Count Witte for Plehve, and for this he was dismissed. Plehve made the dry comment: 'This blockhead steals what is not wanted.' On August 10th, 1905, he was dismissed from the Police Department, but was sent by Witte to bring back the Priest Gapon to his former police allegiance. Kokovtsev refused him any employment in the Ministry of Finance, and Stolypin in 1909 remarked: 'It is time to stop this blackguard.' Manuilov got into touch with the famous revolutionary Burtsev to whom he gave police information; this enabled Burtsev at one time to make the position of most of the Russian agents in Western Europe untenable; Burtsev still declares that though Manuilov would say to him, 'I am a vicious man; I love money; I love life', he never gave him any information which did not prove to be true.

Meanwhile he was living on his wits and chiefly on sheer brag. He conducted innumerable swindles, which bore the character of blackmail. He had a rather imposing reception room from which he would pretend to his petitioner to be telephoning direct to the Ministers or other high authorities; but he was careful to insist that the sums which he received from his victims should be described as 'loans'. All this time he was making urgent requests for re-instatement. He described himself as 'thrown on the street' by the Police Department 'to which I have given the best years of my life, never sparing myself and always exposing my life to the blows of revolution', and he claimed that he had always remained the faithful executant of any task entrusted to him. 'If it pleased Your Excellency', he writes to Kurlov, Assistant Minister of the Interior, on Jan. 6th, 1911, 'I could give you data which would to a certain extent paralyse the disgusting trick of Burtsev[1] and the agents bribed by him', and he signs himself 'your devoted servant'.

On April 15th, 1911, the Vice-Director of the Police Department, Vissarionov, reports to Kurlov on the more recent activities of Manuilov, and describes in detail several of his latest frauds. 'However', he sums up, 'if we turn to the decision of the question of the expediency of sending this case for trial, it seems right to come to a negative conclusion.' He explains that the record of this former agent of the police department is too bad for publication, and the trial would compromise too many others. It is decided to stop the case on the ground of inexpediency. This is the man who now intervenes to settle the government of Russia. Manuilov calls on the French Ambassador, who is fully acquainted with the record of his underground activities in France, and with smiling face announces himself as secretary to the new Premier. He did really act as such, though his principal charge was the security of Rasputin. 'What a title to our respect!' writes Paléologue.[2]

No anticipation of Stürmer's appointment was possible to the public, and least of all as a friend of the Duma. 'A crushing blow', says the honest Minister of Agriculture, Naumov. Among the sensible appointments of the summer had been that of Prince V. M. Volkonsky as one of the two Assistants of the Minister of the Interior. Volkonsky had previously for several years been Vice-President of the Duma; he was a typical Conservative of intelligence and honour, and he has described himself as 'horrified'. 'Stürmer was about as suitable as the last person I could think of', he says.[3] Rodzyanko's verdict is 'an utter nonentity';[4] Shulgin's: 'absolutely unprincipled and a complete nullity'.[5] Honest Uncle Hvostov calls him 'a false man and double faced',[6] and, not unexpectedly, that is the estimate of Manuilov himself, who adds with contempt '*ramoli*, finished at fifty, constantly dosing'.[7] Yet Nicholas, back with his army, writes on February 10th that he has

[1] Burtsev, after all, had a sneaking liking for Manuilov, and has told me that he owed to him his escape from prison and from Russia after the Revolution.

[2] PALÉOLOGUE II, 172.

[3] VOLKONSKY, *Padenie*, VI, 138.

[4] RODZYANKO, 178.

[5] SHULGIN, 79.

[6] HVOSTOV, A. A., *Padenie*, V, 458.

[7] MANUILOV, *Padenie*, II, 34, 79.

'unlimited confidence in Stürmer', and he is so glad that the Empress has him to lean on.[1]

Who was Stürmer? He was best known as Master of Ceremonies (Ober Hofmeister) at the Court. He had served as head of Department in the Ministry of the Interior under the out-and-out reactionary, Plehve; he had been a reactionary provincial Governor in Yaroslavl and had left there highly unpleasant suggestions as to his financial integrity. Sazonov describes him as 'a man who had left a bad memory wherever he had occupied an administrative post'.[2] 'Do you remember Tver?' replied Ignatyev, the Minister of Education, to Stürmer's protestations of liberalism.[3] Stürmer was the man who had cleared out wholesale an elected Liberal zemstvo in Tver, on illegal grounds, for its proposal to appoint agricultural experts to advise the peasants as to the sowing of their crops. On Plehve's assassination in his first indignation Nicholas had thought of him for a moment as a possible Minister of the Interior, before he went to the other extreme by appointing the liberal-minded Svyatopolk-Mirsky. In his reactionary mood of the winter of 1913-14 he had thought of removing the elected Mayor of Moscow and putting Stürmer in his place. He was now a member of a group of reactionaries. Yet his opening statement of policy to the Duma contained exaggerated professions of Liberalism. His appointment was received with consternation, as an open affront to the whole nation. Being a man of small wiles, he thought to hoodwink the Duma by inviting the more prominent of its members to a great evening party, but only the extreme Rights and the Nationalists accepted his invitation. Honest Uncle Hvostov looks back with regret to the time of Goremykin. 'From then', he says, 'everything went down';[4] and the War Minister, Polivanov, dates this as the beginning of the end.[5]

At one of Stürmer's earliest meetings of the Cabinet the Ministers were already dispersing when a fresh paper was handed round, which had not been mentioned on the agenda. It was a decision to assign five million roubles from the military fund to the Premier for purposes which were not to be disclosed, and each

[1] N. to A. F., Jan. 28th/Feb. 10th.
[2] SAZONOV, 306.
[3] IGNATYEV, *Padenie*, VI, 15.
[4] HVOSTOV, A. A., *Padenie*, V, 459.
[5] POLIVANOV, *Padenie*, VII, 77.

member of the Cabinet was asked to sign it. Ministers used to sign automatically the various resolutions which had been duly adopted at the meeting, and this paper was slipped in among the rest without explanations. Count Ignatyev stopped to look at it and called the attention of the War Minister, Polivanov, who could get no explanation from Stürmer except a vague reference to counter-espionage. Vigorous protests came also from Naumov and the Finance Minister, Bark. This was the first Cabinet meeting attended by the newly appointed State Auditor, Pokrovsky, and he also insisted on a further explanation. The only reply vouchsafed was that this was a special decision of the sovereign, who called upon the Ministers to affix their signatures. It was noticed that in the course of the discussion, Stürmer more than once whispered to Alexis Hvostov, who was then still Minister of the Interior (one of Hvostov's many falsehoods later was a denial that he was present at this meeting). Hvostov's gigantic plan for rigging the next elections has already been described. Both he and Stürmer also contemplated the purchase of the leading Russian newspaper, *Novoe Vremya*, and this last idea was mentioned at the Cabinet. Stürmer endeavoured to put the whole responsibility for the matter on Hvostov. Pokrovsky and Naumov later worked out a proposal to put the disbursement of this sum under the usual control of the State Auditor. Ignatyev reported strongly to the Emperor on the subject, protesting that 'such scandals were not to be tolerated in Russia', and Nicholas at once gave the order for this matter to take the usual course. Stürmer tried in vain to compromise Pokrovsky by getting him to mention it in the Duma. In his later evidence he had the impudence to claim that it was he who had demanded the ordinary procedure. Ultimately the whole sum was returned unused to the Treasury.[1]

It will be seen that there were still many honest men in the Cabinet. Pokrovsky, who had succeeded the dying Haritonov and had been recommended by him, had a long record of honourable official service. He had himself far back in 1899 been head of the Cabinet Chancery, and had had a long training in the Finance Ministry, where he had been Assistant to Kokovtsev. He is described by one of his colleagues as 'clear as crystal' and even the

[1] IGNATYEV, *Padenie*, VI, 18; POLIVANOV, VII, 78; NAUMOV, I, 342, 344-5; POKROVSKY, V, 342; STURMER, I, 272-3.

Empress speaks of him as 'a known Left — their nicest, luckily' (March 17th/30th); for her, Lefts included all independent Conservatives. Ignatyev, nominated Minister of Education in January 1915 on the death of the reactionary Kasso, had from the first made it clear to his sovereign that he stood 'not for juggling and politics', but for 'close union and blending with the forces of the public',[1] and he had received steady support from Nicholas in his claim for independence in his own province of education. He enjoyed the full confidence of the Duma, whose liberal ideas on this subject he shared. 'Get rid of the Fourth Duma', he said, 'and you will not get such another.'[2] Naumov, both to the Emperor and to Stürmer, repeatedly spoke out sturdily for the Duma, and never left any doubt of his desire to co-operate heartily with the public. Indeed, without the help of the elected local governing bodies how could he cope with the colossal task of food supply, which kept him busy for eighteen hours out of the twenty-four. Trepov, the new Minister of Transport, if not specially competent, was a patriotic and independent Conservative. But according to the idea which the Empress was always enforcing upon her husband and which he was not altogether unwilling to hear, these men were there as specialists — Naumov was the gardener, Trepov the coachman. Each was to do his job, but in other matters to take his directions from the butler, and how could they tolerate Stürmer in this position? Ignatyev records that the spring and summer were a period of 'constant conflict', in which he had frequently to appeal to the sovereign, not without effect, to guarantee him the independence of his department.[3] Sazonov at one point comments: 'Stürmer disagreed from me on this subject (Rumania) as indeed on every other';[4] Pokrovsky can only credit him with 'small cunning', 'chancery cunning'; he had no broad lines of policy and was constantly changing his views (this is confirmed by the Secretary of the Cabinet, Lodyzhensky); he could not even talk plainly or grasp the subject of discussion; in the more serious questions he 'sat there like an image and nothing else'.[5] Under these circumstances few questions were submitted to the Cabinet which were not almost uncontroversial or at least quite

[1] IGNATYEV, *Padenie*, VI, 2. [2] ibid., 19.
[3] ibid., 17. [4] SAZONOV, 266.
[5] POKROVSKY, *Padenie*, V, 338-40; LODYZHENSKY, VI, 157.

simple. For the most part, matters of importance were dealt with otherwise. Stürmer had the habit of asking a few of the Ministers to settle them with him outside.

Clearly, then, it was not in the official Cabinet that we shall find the Government of Russia in this period. Nor in Stürmer's small Inner Cabinet either; for Stürmer was himself a puppet. Stürmer was in frequent conference with the Empress. Such were the express orders of Rasputin, who, according to Manuilov, even shouted at Stürmer that he would put the 'lid on' (*kryshka* — an exact equivalent of the English expression) if he did not do what he was told by 'Mother' (Rasputin's name for the Empress).[1] She also received the Ministers in turn, and forwarded accounts of her conversations regularly to Nicholas.

This has Nicholas's full approval and encouragement. On May 10th,[2] he asks her to discuss with Stürmer and Bark a proposal of Rasputin for a colossal loan for railways. On June 11th/24th he begs her to speak with Stürmer on all current questions mentioned by her, adding 'he is an excellent honest man, but irresolute'. He writes, 'The Ministers persist in coming here and take up all my time'. And on July 17th/30th, 'It is a good thing you receive Stürmer — he likes your suggestions'. On Sept. 4th/17th, in reply to her apologies for importunity and thanks for agreement, he writes, 'It is I who ought to thank you'. With a singular want of imagination, she later at one point notes to him with pride that she is the first Empress to receive the Ministers regularly since the great Catherine, who disposed of her husband in a much less loving and more summary way.

We have to remember that she was throughout in wretched health. Her heart had never been right since the birth of her boy, and was constantly dilated. She had all sorts of other troubles; for instance, she writes that her face is being electrified, and that she has had three visits in one day from the dentist. She spent much of the morning in bed, writing at a tremendous rate those long letters on politics in a beautifully clear hand; she is dealing with a whole number of subjects of which she has no idea: food supply, transport, fuel, the medical service at the front (in which she tried to push a man named Rein, whom Nicholas would not accept), even naval appointments, which were particularly in the

[1] MANUILOV, *Padenie*, II, 48-9. [2] Ap. 27th, O.S.

province of the husband at the front. To one of them he replies (March 10th/23rd), 'Shir Shikh (Shirinsky Shikhmatev) is an excellent man, but he has not been on a ship for many years'. There are in fact as many interventions that come direct from herself as the instructions of Rasputin which she conveys with them.

Nicholas delighted in the open air life of the army. To the writer, who saw him at Headquarters in March, he spoke of it with a boyish and simple pleasure. He did not interfere in the conduct of operations, though he took his daily lesson in it from Alexeyev, whom he sincerely liked and appreciated. On his side, Alexeyev had told Polivanov at the outset that he would not know how to play the courtier; he dined with his staff, and had stipulated for independence of all ceremony. But at Headquarters Nicholas was gradually becoming more and more enveloped in an intense loneliness. Sazonov's graphic impression that the Tsar was receding from him had been realized by so many others of his most intimate and faithful servants; Dzhunkovsky, Orlov, and Drenteln — the only one who could keep up with him on his long walks — all had gone, because they had dared to express their honest opinions, and the rest learned their lesson. With his old faithful Count Fredericksz relations were only maintained by a tacit abstention from all serious conversation. Sablin was the only one whom the Empress could describe as 'one of ours', and even he had wavered, Nicholas had succumbed to the stronger will of his wife; and wife and family were almost all that were now left to him.

There was no period in which his letters showed a more tender or even passionate affection. 'I have seldom longed for you as much as I do now,' he writes on June 6th/19th. On the other hand she received at times a few gentle, but definite snubs. He asks her to take no notice of the 'stupid tale-bearing' of Vyrubova (Sept. 8th/21st). He refuses to be rude to her rival in Petrograd, the elder Grand Duchess Maria Pavlovna, or to interfere in the private affairs of one of the regiments. She, on her side, exclaims at one moment: 'There I am meddling again'; and it is in this period that she thanks him humbly for twenty-one years of perfect happiness. In a word, these are love letters, and it was as easy for her to secure agreement from him as for any fiancée during the period of her engagement. Nicholas was of course useless or perhaps worse than useless at the front, but it was his playing at command that filled up his time. Shcherbatov had pointed out to him before he went to the front that the Minister of the Interior alone was expected to report to him every five days, and now he expresses vexation because the various Ministers, each of whom has to make the tiresome journey to Headquarters, expect to be received separately. On March 12th/25th we come across a mention of a special direct telephone communication established between the palace at Tsarskoe Selo and Headquarters. As time went on, he arranged for visits of his wife and the whole family to Headquarters when, of course, national affairs in the capital were left without any direction.

Alexandra, in her letters, fights her way through all the troubles that surround her. At the news of a German gas attack she writes on Feb. 3rd/18th), 'The soul, where is it in all this?' And on the general break up of morality, 'Sodom and Gomorrah verily' (March 8th/21st). She takes refuge in the hope that the world may be better after the terrible lessons of the war (March 5th/18th). For her Rasputin is their one real stay and support. At Easter she takes the communion with him and writes that she is coming even to identify him with Christ in her thoughts. 'He bears all slanders for our sakes' (April 5th/18th); 'Everything had a double meaning' (April 8th/21st). 'At that time' she writes (during the crisis of 1915) 'I fought for you even against yourself' (April 7th/20th). 'I am so glad our Friend came to bless you before leaving' (April 24/May 7th). 'It is thanks to Him that you . . . took over the commandment' (Aug. 3rd/16th). 'God sent Him to be your help and guide' (Sept. 7th/20th).

On Jan. 30th/Feb. 12th Rasputin wants General Ivanov to be appointed War Minister in the place of Polivanov. On March 6th/19th he declares that a responsible Ministry would be 'the utter ruin of everything'. On March 15th/28th she writes: 'I wish you would shut up that rotten war industry committee', on the ground that it is 'anti-dynastic'. On March 17th/30th, 'For Baby's sake we must be firm . . . it is your war and your peace'. On May 8th[1] Rasputin protests against the imprisonment of Sukhomlinov. On June 4th/17th Rasputin forbids an offensive which is planned on the northern front (Hoffmann has described

[1] April 27th, O.S.

this sector as the most vulnerable part of the German line). The Empress is constantly asking for the exact dates of intended operations that Rasputin may pray for success, and the Emperor repeatedly begs her to keep any such information entirely to herself. On June 9th/22nd Rasputin sends five urgent questions on the Duma, the administration of the capital, fuel, the Zemgor (who are on no account to be publicly thanked), and one that his medium, Vyrubova, 'can't remember', and answers by telegraph are requested. On June 18th/July 1st she writes 'they (Rasputin and the Minister of Industry, Shakhovskoy) have been thinking over things together'. On June 25th/July 8th, as Rasputin is dissatisfied with the Minister of Religion, Volzhin, the Emperor receives her candidate, Rayev, who 'made an excellent impression'.

We can see from the examples quoted how absolutely the Empress had surrendered her judgment to Rasputin and how far-reaching was his dictation. The question was, therefore, who, if anyone, prompted the suggestions of Rasputin, and this brings us back to Manuilov. It is true that he had a rival with Stürmer, one Gurland, but his significance is that he was a direct intermediary between Rasputin and Stürmer. Stürmer in his later evidence, which was typically evasive and mendacious, is perhaps truthful when he declares that he never visited Rasputin at his flat. Klimovich, Stürmer's Director of the Police Department, appointed in the last 'Duma' phase of Alexis Hvostov, states that he several times had information of visits of Rasputin to Stürmer. To Klimovich, who is very careful in his evidence and was much too honest for him, Stürmer pretended not even to know Manuilov, though he was frequently to be found with him smoking casual cigarettes. After the first such meeting that he witnessed, Klimovich faced Stürmer with the police record of Manuilov, which has been quoted above, and Stürmer shaking his head said, 'Yes, yes, what a scoundrel! A fine gentlemen!' and flatly denied that Manuilov was attached to his service. That did not save Klimovich from having to pay out to Manuilov on Ministerial order a salary of £1800 a year, which he did later succeed in reducing by half.[1] Manuilov, on his side, was always trying to extend his influence and wanted to create a sort of super-depart-

[1] Klimovich, *Padenie*, I, 56-60.

ment of secret service, of which he would be the head.[1] But there is also direct evidence that Stürmer met Rasputin at night, of all places, in the fortress prison of St. Peter and St. Paul, with which he was later to make a more intimate acquaintance.[2] This, we are told, was arranged by one of the palace clique, a friend of Vyrubova and Rasputin, Nikitina, the daughter of the governor of the fortress, whose appointment had in an earlier period been brought about by Stürmer. Alexis Hvostov and Beletsky had at least stood up to Rasputin's effrontery; but Stürmer was an easy prey. On his side, Stürmer was from the beginning in a fright of him and would do anything to pretend that he hardly knew him. It was to Manuilov that their relations were entrusted, and it was principally in this sense that he could describe himself as the secretary of the Prime Minister; but this position put him at the centre of things, both in the Government and at the source of favour.

The personal security of Rasputin had become a cardinal question for the Empress. Since the Hvostov episode, anonymous and threatening letters had also reached Vyruvoba. Rasputin himself, in spite of his courage, was constantly in a state of nervous excitement. Manuilov now took up on a larger scale the role of Komissarov, who had been sent flying to a provincial post from which he was later dismissed. Manuilov probably was more successful in managing Rasputin than anyone else. Rasputin was very clever, but so was Manuilov, and for a time he enjoyed his more or less complete confidence, though Rasputin never gave it entirely to anyone. He had an amusing and clever way with him, and made his presence acceptable. He appears to have introduced Rasputin to the typewriter. He accompanied him everywhere in a very swift motor suspiciously secured from the War Ministry, and thus shared his dangers and guarded his safety. He was far less of a subordinate than Komissarov, and had no more respect for Stürmer than anyone else had. He must often have met Vyrubova, as she came to see Rasputin almost daily when he was in the capital, and it seems that he did secure the entrée to the little confabulations at her house in Tsarskoe Selo, as had been the case with Hvostov, Beletsky, Simanovich and even Komissarov.

[1] Beletsky, *Padenie*, iv, 514; also see Paléologue, ii, 291.
[2] Manuilov, *Padenie*, ii, 47; Stürmer, v, 163.

In his last period of hostility to Stürmer and Rasputin, Alexis Hvostov called the attention of Polivanov to the scandal caused by the visits of Rasputin and Manuilov to low places of entertainment in a War Office car which was too fast to be followed by the police. The brusque Polivanov was just the man to bite at this bait. He sharply questioned Stürmer, who again denied any connection with Manuilov and said that he was in the service of Hvostov. Hvostov in turn denied, in this case truthfully, and Polivanov gave Stürmer the lie direct.[1] Since the episode of the five million roubles he had realized that his days in office were counted. He had always explained the army estimates to the Duma and asked for its support. He was as enthusiastic for the work of the war industry committees as Guchkov himself. The Empress had disliked him from the outset. Since the Emperor had assumed the command, he had felt isolated during his visits to Headquarters. It was primarily on the War Minister that the front depended for men, equipment, and supply; and, on indirect testimony of Hindenburg himself, Polivanov had restored the Russian Army.[2] Knox regarded him as 'undoubtedly the ablest military organizer in Russia'.[3] He had carried into effect the response to the appeal which Nicholas himself had made at the opening of the Defence Conference for the whole-hearted support of the country in the war. He had organized the tremendous effort which all Russia was making in this cause, and the results were astonishing.

At the same time he had been able to secure the most generous help from the Allies. While the Grand Duke Nicholas was still in command, Lord Kitchener had dispatched to him Colonel Ellershaw, one of the most radiant figures in the war, asking him how he could serve him for the needs of Russia, and the Grand Duke in his soldierly reply had practically authorized Kitchener to act as a munition agent for Russia. It was to complete this work that Kitchener himself later went to his own death on the *Hampshire*; but already Ellershaw, who was to perish with him, had been buying right and left on the credit of Russia.

Polivanov's success had been no less on the side of training. The worst moment in the war in this respect had been the autumn of 1915, when men of any age and with no local cohesion were sent up from anywhere to fill the gaps. Now the Tsar himself comments

[1] POLIVANOV, *Padenie*, VII, 78-9. [2] HINDENBURG, 243. [3] KNOX, 412.

on the splendid appearance of the new recruits. He writes that they are 'just as fine as their predecessors' (Feb. 14th/27th).

On Jan. 9th/22nd the Empress had written to her husband 'Get rid of Polivanov'! On Feb. 9th/22nd Rasputin has recommended a successor to him. On March 4th/17th the Empress writes 'Remember about Polivanov'. On the 19th she returns to the charge, and on the 25th, she makes another violent attack on him. 'Lovy, don't dawdle', she writes. Before the letter is finished comes the news that she has been obeyed, and she concludes 'O! the relief! Now I shall sleep well'. And what of the Russian Army, which Polivanov has re-created? Polivanov was refused the ordinary letter of thanks which accompanied dismissals. The Emperor wrote to him, 'The work of the war industry committees does not inspire me with confidence, and your supervision of them I find insufficiently authoritative'[1] (March 13th/26th).

The Empress had for some time been vigorously urging the candidature of General Beliayev as the next War Minister. Beliayev was a harmless person and an efficient subordinate, but lacking in initiative and independence and ready enough 'to go with the stream'. It was precisely for that reason that he was recommended by Alexandra; for he had not shown any vigour in repulsing appeals for exemptions from military service for the protégés of herself and Vyrubova; but Nicholas shared the ordinary opinion and later described Beliayev as 'an extremely weak man who always gives way in everything and works slowly' (Aug. 16th/27th). The appointment was made at Headquarters, and his choice fell on General Shuvayev, an entirely honest and courageous soldier, who had done very good work in the post of Intendant; but Shuvayev himself was surprised and scared by the appointment to an office to which he felt himself in no way equal. When receiving General Knox for the first time, he was in tears and frankly expressed his insufficiency.[2] However, in the war, service was a duty, especially for a soldier, and in this spirit he undertook the heavy task; and no one reported with more frankness and courage to the Emperor.[3]

[1] POLIVANOV, *Padenie*, VII, 82. [2] KNOX, 416.
[3] SHUVAYEV, *Padenie*, VII, 285-6.

CHAOS AND DEFEATISM

The result of all this atrocious mismanagement was complete confusion and chaos. It is true that since the removal of the Grand Duke Nicholas to the Caucasus Front there was no longer the former friction between Headquarters and the Government; but there was no longer any effective criticism or control. Since the fall of Alexis Hvostov, the two strongest posts in the country, those of Prime Minister and Minister of the Interior, were both occupied by Stürmer, but there is no sign of his ever having dealt or attempted to deal with the real work of either. Klimovich tells us that he never received from Stürmer a single general direction of policy and that in his six months as Director of the Police Department, he never got more than five hours of conversation in all with him, of which one half was taken up with the affairs of Rasputin, 'Chaos' is the word which he uses to describe the Government;[1] the same is the word used by the Grand Duke Nicholas in the Caucasus: 'It is now a reign of chaos.'[2] Klimovich's colleague at this Ministry, Prince Volkonsky, found himself so much in the dark as to the intentions of the Minister that he thought of putting up over his very important Department: 'Piccadilly: new programme on Saturday.'[3] As Klimovich was convinced that the existing regime was gravely threatened, he circulated, with Stürmer's permission, a report to all the Ministers to this effect, and was then brought to book for doing so.[4] He was constantly begging leave to resign. So far as can be seen, Stürmer was exclusively interested in keeping his place. It is true that he did devise a misty scheme of a total reform of local administration; but all that could be gathered from it was that he wished to give the Duma a bone to gnaw at.[5] Even the reform of the underpaid and short-handed police, which was a most pressing need and should have appealed to him in his two capacities, was left to his successor at the Ministry of the Interior.

The most pressing of all needs had come to be the regulation of

[1] Klimovich, *Padenie*, I, 67-73.
[2] N. N. to N., June 24th/July 7th, *Lettres des Grands Ducs*, 25.
[3] Volkonsky, *Padenie*, VI, 138.
[4] Klimovich, *Padenie*, I, 61.
[5] Hvostov A. A., *Padenie*, V, 465.

the food supply. The army so far got all that it wanted; this was a vast proportion of the whole supply of population, at a time when the productive forces had been heavily encroached on by conscription. Krivoshein had been an able Minister of Agriculture; and his successor, Naumov, was both honest and capable. His whole heart was in his work; and as a lifelong zemstvo worker, he felt that he could do nothing without enlisting the help of the local governing bodies in the task of distributing supplies. Stürmer in his first official visit to him, flooded him with effusive praise of zemstva and Duma for an hour and a half; but it was his constant practice to prevent or postpone any real co-operation. In the end he even stopped him from explaining the position in reply to urgent questions of the Chambers, on the ground that there was 'such a sympathy' between Government and Duma that all questions — and this was that of the nation's food supply — should be put off till the autumn.[1] In July Naumov at last got his resignation accepted, but the successive subterfuges and falsehoods of Stürmer brought him to ask direct: 'What is one to say to the President of the Council of Ministers, when he tells you an untruth?'[2]

Rasputin more than once predicted the certainty of great riots if the matter were not attended to. Never was the abnormal position of Petrograd more fatal than in relation to this question. The capital, with a population of over two millions and with the seat of authority, was placed in a far corner of the north of the empire, in an area which could not grow crops to feed itself. Yet the position was not really irreparable. We may emphasize the verdict of one of the greatest Russian economists, Professor Peter Struve:

> The student of economic factors will not ascribe the political catastrophe that overwhelmed Russia in 1917 to the economic condition of the country in general and the food question in particular. For an understanding of the Revolution, first and foremost, political forces should be considered. Herein lies the profound difference between Russia's war time economy and that of the Central Powers, whose defeat was almost automatically prepared by the inexorable march of economic forces and, especially, by those of the food supply.[3]

[1] NAUMOV, *Padenie*, I, 342-3. [2] ibid., I, 344-5.
[3] Introduction to *Food Supply in Russia during the War*, 20: FLORENSKY, 48.

Russia was used to roughing it; she had proved self-sufficient enough to muddle her way through conditions nearly as bad with some kind of satisfaction of her crudest needs. But no society could survive such gross mismanagement. She never better deserved a national government: and we have had to study those forces which gave her a government directly anti-national.

Let us take a survey of the condition of the country at this time, with the valuable help of the summary of M. T. Florinsky.[1]

On the outbreak of war Russia automatically became much richer in food supply for its vast area. Primarily agricultural, with a population of which 85 per cent was rural, she could not now export to other countries. Another important factor in the improvement was the Emperor's Temperance Edict at the beginning of the War (Aug. 22nd, 1914)[2] which of itself tended to fill the savings banks. All serious critics agree in dating the beginning of the ruin from the miserable end of the constitutional crisis in September 1915, and the pace was vastly accelerated on the advent of Stürmer. The national factories were now absorbed in the munition needs of the army, and were no longer turning out goods which made it worth while for the peasant to send his grain to market, and through this and the succeeding period he hoarded it more and more. It was not at all a question of a sufficiency of food supply in Russia; the whole point was that it was not utilized;[3] the framework of the national economy was of itself still sound.[4]

The question was, therefore, one of transport, and if of transport, also of fuel, and this too became an increasing preoccupation of the Government. Not only of the Government; Alexeyev, the very capable Chief-of-Staff to the Emperor, was bound also to be exercised by it, as it lay at the root of all the requirements of the army and even of its power of movement. The Minister of Transport, A. Trepov, was honest and did what he could, but the rate at which the evil progressed was past his power to deal with it. Here too the confusion of authority between the military and civil proved specially noxious. In a word, the only one of the five conferences set up which had been able to produce remarkable results was the first — that of national defence, and that chiefly owing to the conspicuous ability and cordial co-operation of Polivanov. The honest Shuvayev, not a great organizer but by no

[1] *The End of the Empire.* [2] Florinsky, 37. [3] ibid., 49. [4] ibid., 44.

means an incapable administrator, continued to give the support of the War Office to the Defence Council; and for that reason it continued to play an important part, both militarily and politically, up to his dismissal—that is, nearly up to the eve of the Revolution.

Let us follow the effects of these failures into the story of the living conditions of the country, again with the use of Florinsky's helpful summary. Prices were rising all the time. Here is the food index for thirteen articles. In the last half of 1914 it had risen to 110.1 per cent of pre-War; in the first half of 1915 to 141.9; in the second half of 1915 to 155.5; in the first half of 1916 to 195.6; by August 1916 to 221.6. In July 1916 the rise in the price of meat represented 332 per cent, in that of flour 265, in that of salt 585! In Moscow in June 1916 the figure for butter was 220 per cent, for fat 273, for sugar 153, for milk 171, for potatoes 144, for fuel 224, for petrol 210, for textiles 262, for boots 334.[1] The distress in fuel was extreme. Now that Cardiff coal was cut off from the north, the capital was dependent on the Donets region far away to the south, and for the transport it had available less than one half of the cars required. By 1916, writes Florinsky, town life was 'a virtual ordeal'.[2] Several of the flour mills were stopping work.

If we pass to the corresponding question of wages, we have the following figures for the average monthly earnings of employees in all industries in 1913-17 taken by Florinsky from appendices 3 and 4 of Strumilin's *Wages in Russian Industry:* (*Zarabotnaya Plata Russkoy Promyshlennosti za 1913-1922*).[3]

Year	*Nominal* (in paper roubles)	*Real* (in gold roubles)
1913	85.5	85.5
1914	85.5	84.6
1915	103.0	79.2
1916	142.0	69.8
1917	255.6	38.0

The caricature contained in the difference between the final figures, will leap to the eye. Another useful table which Florinsky takes from Strumilin[4] gives the average monthly wages in the textile and metal industries in 1913-16.

[1] Florinsky, 124. [2] ibid., 122-3. [3] Florinsky, 126.
[4] Strumilin, 90: Florinsky, 159.

Year	Textile Industry Nominal	Textile Industry Real	Metal Industry Nominal	Metal Industry Real
	(in roubles)			
1913	17.9	17.9	33.5	33.5
1914	17.6	17.4	38.0	37.6
1915	19.5	15.0	46.4	35.7
1916	(28.3)[1]	(13.9)	(78.6)	(38.7)

Meanwhile rents rose in Petrograd to 200 per cent and even 300 per cent of pre-war. The lesser towns, where hectic rescue enterprises of the Government were less likely, were in many ways in a worse condition than the capitals. From the summer of 1916 rationing was introduced, and supplies became worse and worse as time went on.

Equally, it is from the autumn of 1915 that we must date the serious growth of national discontent, and even then by no means in terms of any revolutionary organization. Rodzyanko in a striking pronouncement as late as the summer of 1916 is right when he bluntly tells the Ministers that revolution is their obsession and that it is they and they alone who are making it. Revolution was indeed the everyday preoccupation of the police even in peaceful pre-War times; and that is no surprise, if we remember the persistent delay of the most urgent reforms. The police throve on the threat of revolution. They even played on this instrument; near the beginning of the War their agents were deliberately instructed by circular to promote a division of revolutionary forces by direct provocation.[2] Similar was the tendency of the infamous circular of January 1916 to Governors, directing their animosity against all Jews as revolutionaries, which formed the subject of a debate in the Duma.[3]

So far the effects even of this provocation were nugatory. Lenin, the Bolshevik leader, was at this time abroad. He was at one moment arrested in Austria, but was set free, apparently on the insistence of the German General Staff, and in September 1915 he, with a small number of extremists from various countries, took part in a conference at Zimmerwald in Switzerland, at which he demanded with his accustomed vigour that the imperialist war must be turned into a class war; and at a

[1] Figures given in parenthesis indicate incomplete data.
[2] Beletsky, *Padenie*, III, 286. [3] Kafafov, *Padenie*, II, 125.

further conference at Kienthal in April 1916 he again urged the same course. His defeatist literature was circulated without difficulty among the Russians in the prisoners' camps in Germany and Austria. His theses reached Russia early in 1915, but did not produce any marked effect, except that the five Bolshevist members of the Duma, men of no particular eminence, were arrested for circulating them and sent to Siberia, in spite of strong protests from the leader of the rival Labour Group in the Duma, Kerensky, who pleaded their cause in a personal visit to the Minister of Foreign Affairs. He urged that so far the country hardly knew of Lenin's defeatist policy and that this trial was the best way of advertising it.[1] For the Police Department, as we know from Beletsky, the bogey of revolution was still Kerensky;[2] And Kerensky was not only travelling all over Russia clothed with the inviolability of a member of the Duma, but was taking a vigorous and eloquent part in its discussions and invariably pleading for the admission of the nation to active co-operation in winning the war. As is testified by the President of the Duma, Rodzyanko, Kerensky sometimes surprised him by being even more whole-hearted in his support than the leader of the Liberals, Paul Milyukov. But if there was no organization of revolution there was inevitably an ever-rising expression of economic dissatisfaction with the Government, sometimes passing into organized political support of the Duma.

The prorogation of the Duma in September 1915 had at once led to an organized political strike of two days by all the factories of the capital; and from that time onwards strikes were recurrent all over Russia. The significance of this will be better realized if we give the total number of strikes for the periods concerned: 1914, January to July (that is before the War) 4,098; August to December of the same year, 68; 1915, 1,034; 1916, 1,410. But we believe the reader will like to have the table taken by Florinsky from *Rabochee Dvizhenie v 1917 godu (the Labour Movement in 1917)*.[3]

[1] Kerensky to B. P.
[2] BELETSKY, *Padenie*, IV, 145.
[3] Edited by M. G. Fleer, Moscow, 1925, pp. 4, 6 and 7. Quoted by FLORINSKY, 165.

	Economic		Political		Total	
	No. of strikes	*No. of strikers*	*No. of strikes*	*No. of strikers*	*No. of strikes*	*No. of strikers*
1912	732	175,678	1,300	549,813	2,032	725,491
1913	1,370	384,654	1,034	502,442	2,404	887,096
1914:						
Jan.-July	1,560	413,972	2,538	1,035,312	4,098	1,449,284
Aug.-Dec.	61	31,907	7	2,845	68	34,752
1915	819	397,259	215	155,835	1,034	553,094
1916	1,167	776,064	243	310,300	1,410	1,086,364

Fleer, writing in Moscow after the Revolution, recognizes that the work of the Bolshevik Party up to the late summer of 1915 was quite disorganized. He remarks that its activities at that time consisted only of the publication of propaganda leaflets and attempts to re-establish contacts in the prisons. He agrees that the arrest of the five Bolshevik members did not stir the masses. He does not date any active part in the influencing of public opinion by the Bolshevik Party earlier than the end of 1915.[1]

But from the same date that we have given, the autumn of 1915, begins also the gradual growth of ordinary defeatism, that is, of popular despair as to the issue of the war. This did not yet seriously affect the army. The writer, living at the front and accompanied always by peasant soldier guides in his night excursions, did not hear even ordinary grumbles till this date; but, from his visits of the same date he recalls a wonderful night spent alone with privates in an advance dug-out, in which all the talk, which was of the freest kind, was full of a glorious spirit of courage, the different men capping each other with the exploits of their various regiments. There was all the difference between front and rear; and in the rear life was, with very many, one long grumble.

The centre of Russian articulated opinion still stood solidly for the war and victory. It was on two opposite sides that defeatism throve. The first notable expression of it came near the top of Russian society, and it was at first little more than the usual impulsive disappointment of Russians at the delay in the realization of their hopes. But throughout there was a certain section which stood against the war. Rasputin, as we know, strongly held this view; and to Simanovich, who kept warning him of the

[1] Florinsky, 171.

danger of his position and of the threats of assassination, he replied: 'I will make peace first, and then I will go to Jerusalem'. He would tell the Tsar, 'You gave life to no one; why should you take it from them?'[1] Rasputin was no ordinary German spy. His position was far too strong for him to run the risk of being bribed and found out; as it was, he could get anything that he liked. He knew Germans through his wanderings, which had brought him into contact with the admirable industry of the German colonies planted by Catherine on the Volga. According to Simanovich he even suggested to the Tsar that German girls should be given as wives to Russian peasants, just as Admiral Bruce, the advisor of Peter the Great, recommended him to import little Jewish boys into the province of Yaroslavl, bringing them up as Christians and marrying them to the peasant girls. Rasputin greatly suspected all diplomats, and, in particular, Sir George Buchanan and the English. As we can gather from her letters, he had warned the Empress that England was going to catch Russia out in the terms of peace when the war had been won.

This reaction was inevitable. The Russians were in dire need of our help and that of France in munitions; and as both these Allies wanted them very badly for themselves at the same time, we were bound to inquire what use was being made of them in Russia in the common cause. The answer would have been a very sorry one. Our only two roads into Russia, till the Murmansk Railway was completed, were through Archangel and Vladivostok, and at both places enormous masses of material were piled up without hope of any early transport, so that they were even sinking into the ground. England, with her navy, guaranteed the navigation of all her Allies and therefore claimed a measure of control of the Russian merchant fleet; and this suggestion aroused the patriotic indignation of even such a firm friend of England as Rodzyanko.[2] It was to complete the Allied work in the supply of munitions that Lord Kitchener started for Russia. 'How awful about Kitchener! A real nightmare!' writes the Empress on learning of the tragedy of the *Hampshire* (May 25th/June 7th), but she later quotes Rasputin as having said to Vyrubova, 'It is good for us that Kitchener died, as later on he might have done Russia harm' (June 5th/18th).

[1] SIMANOVICH, 153. [2] RODZYANKO, 161.

Certainly there was now, as always, a really considerable section of the higher world which was inclined to friendship with Germany. It was an obviously reasonable view; and apart from good-neighbourhood, convinced supporters of absolutism were not wrong in foreseeing that the fall of the German autocracy, the strongest in Europe, might naturally be followed by that of the Russian. There were ex-officials of high standing who took this view, for instance the dismissed Minister of Justice Shcheglovitov and the dismissed Minister of the Interior, Nicholas Maklakov. He begged to see the Empress during this period, and she records her pleasure at the meeting with the words 'True devoted soul' (Mar. 16th/29th).

At this time defeatism of the right was much more articulate and threatening than defeatism of the left. It was a popular phrase at the time that England would fight to the last drop of Russian blood. French and British military writers, as well as Russians, have said that the great sacrifice of Tannenberg led up to the turning point in the war. It is in this light that we must understand an insult which the irresponsible Grand Duke Boris at this time offered to an able British officer, Captain Thornhill. The incident and its sequel are recorded by Knox.[1]

> *Saturday, June 24th, 1917.* Petrograd.
> Thornhill (Chief of the Intelligence Section) told me that he and two other British officers dined last night at Tsarskoe Selo at the mess of the Depot Battalion of the 1st Rifle Regiment of the Guard. About 1 a.m. the Grand Duke Boris, who was also a guest, made some astonishing statements. He said he was sure that the very next war would be between England and Russia, owing to the greed of our Government, that our attempt at the Dardanelles had all been bluff, that he knew for a fact that Russia had offered to take Baghdad, but that the British Foreign Office had declined, 'because England wanted to take it herself'.

With the strong support of Buchanan, Knox and Thornhill went without delay to Boris and demanded and obtained a withdrawal. Later the Emperor spoke severely to the Grand Duke on the subject. He was extremely indignant with Boris and the Empress shared his indignation in full. 'The insolent fellow,' she writes; and she expresses her satisfaction that her husband 'has washed Boris's

[1] Knox, I, 429-31.

head'. The exigences of the French Ambassador, Paléologue, had aroused even sharper comment, especially in the army, and the friendship with France and England was quite seriously criticized.

STÜRMER TAKES HIS LAST TRICK

Rodzyanko during this period did a good deal of harm to his cause. His only foundation for reports to the Emperor was his position as President of the Duma, and this could be, and was, questioned at a time when the Duma was not sitting. As a prominent member of the Defence Council, he interfered in all sorts of military matters in which he could not have been an expert, for instance the supply of aeroplanes, and received a resentful snub in a letter from Alexeyev himself. He had given another plain warning to Nicholas on March 8th in an audience lasting an hour and a half, begging him to send away Rasputin and warning him of the direct danger to the dynasty; but Nicholas no longer listened to him with the same seriousness. At a dinner given on May 25th to all the Ministers and some members of the two legislative Chambers, he was indeed a true spokesman of the nation. He writes:[1]

> I accepted the invitation in order to take advantage of the intimate surroundings to give free vent to my feelings of anxiety and indignation. After dinner, when coffee was served in the drawing-room, I addressed the company somewhat as follows:
> 'Just think of what is taking place . . . In these momentous days, when the spirit of the nation and the gallantry of our army stand revealed in all their beauty, when torrents of blood are being freely shed — the Government reveal themselves as incapable of leadership and, in pursuit of their own interests, never get farther than a petty control over public organizations. You, the representatives of the Government, see nothing, realize nothing, and clinging to your powers and privileges, remain the passive spectators of the great patriotic upheaval which sweeps the country irrespective of parties and nationalities . . . When the people long for work in order to ensure final victory, and ask for a firm and wise Government, you spend your time in trying to discover an imaginary

[1] Rodzyanko, 188-90.

> revolution . . . You organize Monarchist congresses, persecute public organizations, provoke endless inter-departmental disputes and intrigues, which paralyse the work of administration, and deliver the country into the hands of self-seekers . . . Bribery, extortion, plunder are growing on all sides, and nothing is being done to prevent it. Persons who deserve the gallows continue to remain in high favour, and instead of patriotism, personal patronage and vested interests are the moving springs of the Government's actions . . .
> 'The whole nation', I said, 'has rallied to the motto: "Everything for the war", but the Government pursues its course of petty officialdom, completely out of touch with the great events of the moment . . .' I pointed out the Government's utter incompetence to foresee or deal with the stupendous problems of reconstruction with which the nation would be faced after the end of the war, and which were already engaging the attention of the more advanced Allied statesmen. 'You should realize', I said, 'that you are neither beloved nor trusted by the nation . . . In your senseless search for a bogey revolution, you are murdering the living soul of the people and creating unrest and discontent which sooner or later may breed an actual revolution . . . The time will come when you will be called upon to render an account of your deeds . . .'

No answer could have been given; and according to Volkonsky this denunciation, delivered in Rodzyanko's great voice, had the effect of a thunderbolt on his audience. On his side, General Alexeyev was becoming more and more anxious about the supply of the army and handed in to the Emperor at Headquarters a memorandum proposing the appointment of a Minister of National Defence under whom would be co-ordinated the whole Government, uniting front and rear. The two key posts in the Government, those of Prime Minister and Minister of the Interior, were already united in the person of Stürmer, who knew little of the duties of either. It was at one time suggested to associate with him a sort of committee of five or six Ministers, no doubt limited to those whom Stürmer consulted apart from the formal meetings of the Cabinet. Alexeyev, who could not abide Stürmer, could hardly have had anything of this kind in view; he was no doubt in favour of appointing an eminent 'public man' outside the Cabinet, presumably Rodzyanko, as the public had been asking all along, and it is perhaps in this connection that we may understand certain proposals which were made to Rodzyanko later. The Emperor, when saying good-bye to Naumov, whom he followed out of the room and embraced, even showed Alexeyev's memorandum to him and asked whether a 'public man' should be appointed to such a post.[1] Alexeyev, though no doubt thinking in military terms, apparently had not used the word 'dictator'; but in this atmosphere of confusion and rumours, that is how his proposal was interpreted, arousing the indignation, among others, of Rodzyanko. Different candidates for such a post were talked of, including the Grand Duke Sergius, the Inspector General of Artillery; and this called forth resentful comments from the Empress who, after the events of the preceding summer, was deeply distrustful of all that was done without her at Headquarters. Even Naumov, as a departing Minister, thought that if there was a Prime Minister, such an authority could only be properly wielded by him. Indeed, it appears that a decree was actually drawn up assigning the task to Stürmer.

But Stürmer was getting entirely out of his depth and could not face such a fresh increase of responsibility. Even the Ministry of the Interior was altogether too much for him, and was practically administered by deputies. Besides, this was the Ministry to which were addressed much the major part of the scandalous importunities of Rasputin. Stürmer was pretending throughout that he had nothing to do with Rasputin; and almost from the start Rasputin, who had a very contemptuous nickname for Stürmer, was less and less content with him. Each of them was getting more and more sick of the other, and, in these circumstances, Stürmer worked out the most ingenious 'double-shuffle' of his shady career.

Sazonov was the most important of the older Ministers still remaining in the Cabinet. He had been in recurrent danger since the famous letter of the Ministers to the Tsar. There was no one on whom the alliance more directly depended. Since Russian Poland had been conquered by Germany, the question of its recovery had really become an international question, at least for the Allies. It was known that Germany and Austria were devising a plan of apparent concession to Poland which

[1] NAUMOV, *Padenie*, I, 339.

would warrant the use of the word independence. They were now in a position to unite the whole of Poland, if only they could agree between themselves; and for the Poles unity came even almost before independence. The one card remaining in the hands of the Allies was that the Central Powers would probably never do so. Buchanan, in deference to Sazonov's opinion, continued to regard the question as at present one for Russia alone;[1] but the over-active Paléologue, who was in touch with the Poles, did not show the same restraint. The Poles had been asking for something definite ever since the Grand Duke's appeal, which had promised them autonomy. Even Goremykin, when challenged in the Duma, had at least confirmed the promise which had already been made. Sazonov had, therefore, asked and received from the Emperor permission to draw up a definite scheme.

This scheme was just and liberal. It did not go beyond the limits of autonomy. We will give it as Sazonov communicated it in confidence to the French and British Ambassadors when next he saw them.[2]

> (1) The Government of the Kingdom of Poland will consist of a Lieutenant of the Emperor or Viceroy, a Council of Ministers (Cabinet) and two Chambers.
> (2) The whole administration of the Kingdom will depend on the Government, except the army, diplomacy, customs, finance of common interest, and railways with a strategic interest, which will remain affairs of the Empire.
> (3) Administrative disputes between the Kingdom and the Empire will be laid before the Senate of Petrograd; a special section will be set up to that effect, with equal participation of Russian and Polish Senators.
> (4) The ulterior annexation of Austrian and Prussian Poland will be provided for by a formula of this kind: If God blesses the success of our arms, all Poles who become subjects of the Emperor-King will benefit by the dispositions which have just been decreed.

With this scheme he went to Headquarters.

The Tsar [writes Sazonov] listened attentively and sympa-

[1] Buchanan to B. P.

[2] PALÉOLOGUE, II, 314-5.

> thetically to what I had to say about Poland . . . Gentle and good-natured, he was pleased to meet any desires that seemed to him just . . . In this case too, as almost always, his intentions were good, but his will was not his own.[1]

Nicholas approved of the scheme and instructed that it should be communicated to the Cabinet. Paléologue has described how while he and Buchanan happened to be in the Foreign Office, Sazonov returned radiant on July 13th. Without taking off his great coat, he said to these two friends: 'I have won all along the line'; he was on his way to Finland for a short holiday.[2] The Empress without delay expressed her vehement opposition. Sazonov reported to Stürmer, who, well knowing the Empress's view, dashed off to Headquarters and was received by Nicholas on the 16th. On the 18th the Empress received him at Tsarskoe Selo, and even directly ordered him to send a telegram to Nicholas telling him to wait before any decision about Poland,[3] and on the 20th she was herself at Headquarters, accompanied by the family and Vyrubova. Her argument was that 'Baby's' future rights were challenged, and she quoted Rasputin in this sense. Sazonov while in Finland suddenly heard of his abrupt dismissal. The scheme was indeed laid before the Cabinet, where only three Ministers voted for it, but the Emperor could, of course, have persisted. On hearing the disastrous news of Sazonov's dismissal, Buchanan and Paléologue instructed the British and French representatives at Headquarters to approach the Emperor and beg for an alteration of his decision. Delicately as their request was put, Count Frederickz, the friendly Minister of the Court, had to tell them that it was impossible.[4]

But this was only a part of Stürmer's double shuffle. Uncle Hvostov was still Minister of Justice. Before Goremykin's removal and Stürmer's appointment, Rasputin had been sent to sound him as a possible Premier, but Hvostov had refused to receive him on any other than his day of general reception among the usual crowd of petitioners and had sharply cut him short as soon as he began to talk politics. Hvostov was not courting popularity; he has explained that he only wished to save the credit of the Government by showing that there were limits to Rasputin's political

[1] Sazonov, 305.
[2] Paléologue, ii, 314.
[3] Stürmer, *Padenie*, v, 181.
[4] Buchanan, ii, 16.

influence. Early in 1916, Hvostov, who had duly set up the commission of both Chambers to inquire into the case against Sukhomlinov, had learned the results of its preliminary examination, in which there were implications connecting Sukhomlinov with the proved traitor Myasoyedov; he ordered that Sukhomlinov should be imprisoned in the fortress where, by the way, he would have better treatment than under an ordinary prison regime. Sukhomlinov had never shown favour for Rasputin and had relied for his influence with the Emperor exclusively on his own talent as a *charmeur*; but his young and restless wife, who played an adventurous part in society and public affairs, now sought Rasputin's help. Rasputin, as he told others, was specially attracted by her. Several signs now appear in the Empress's letters of the pressure which Rasputin is exercising upon her in favour of Sukhomlinov. The honest Minister of Justice is inexorable, and Stürmer urges him to go and see her. He does so, taking the evidence with him, and the Empress is greatly alarmed. Hvostov was not strong in health, and the Emperor had agreed that he should himself report if he did not feel up to his work. Stürmer knew of this, and suggested to the Emperor that Hvostov should be given a rest — but only as Minister of Justice, and that he should then take up the far more onerous duties of Minister of the Interior, from which Stürmer himself wished to escape; it would be a neat stroke to put on his enemy the answering of the petitions of Rasputin. On July 13th, the day of Sazonov's return to Petrograd, Hvostov was himself at Headquarters and showed the Emperor the evidence against Sukhomlinov; and to his great surprise Nicholas suggested to him that he should take a rest. When Stürmer informed him of the further appointment, this rugged man, who had never minced his words with Stürmer, asked: 'How did you dare to do me such a dirty trick (*pakost*), without saying a word to me?' (July 17th).[1] But the new appointment was an order in time of war. Hvostov pleaded in vain that his health was not up to this new and heavy task; but he accepted it purely out of obedience to his sovereign. We may weary of Stürmer's deceits, as his colleagues did — Naumov had always been asking himself when he could 'escape from this hell'; but we are tracing the breakdown of a great State.

[1] Hvostov, A. A., *Padenie*, v, 449.

The Empress, too, had made her own double stroke, for she had hung up the Polish settlement and the trial of Sukhomlinov; but it certainly seems that neither she nor Rasputin knew of Stürmer's intrigues and their object, and they do not appear even to have been warned of his flying visit to Headquarters. And now comes the point of his little plan: he is suddenly presented to the public as the new Minister of Foreign Affairs. This subject had always been regarded as especially in the province of the sovereign, and the Foreign Minister, according to this view, was so to speak the technician to carry out his intentions. Stürmer, therefore, now held two decorative and honourable posts, those of Premier and Foreign Minister, and no doubt he congratulated himself on having slipped out of the clutches of Rasputin, who could hardly come to the Foreign Office for the satisfaction of his requests. But this manœuvre, probably his neatest, was in danger of being his last. Rasputin was furious and ordered him to go and see the Empress at least once a week; and the Empress, in consequence, from now onwards gave him only faint support.[1]

Their alienation will be the better understood because in the course of all these cunning manipulations Stürmer had made one very big mistake. When shifting Hvostov against his will to the Interior, he had not been as ready with a successor to him at the Ministry of Justice. Presumably on a hasty suggestion of his, Makarov was appointed. It was Makarov who, when at the Interior, had committed the grave *faux pas* of handing back the Empress's letter to Rasputin not to her but to the Emperor. This was an offence which it was impossible for her to forgive, and we find her at once expressing her vexation and alarm: 'I must have our Friend guaranteed against them' (July 16th/29th).

In all this, none of the intriguers took the slightest account of the welfare of Russia. Stürmer was a man of the shallowest personal ambition, and again fully justified the invective which Rodzyanko in his voice of thunder had shouted at him at his evening party. It is only because we absolutely know the real mind of the Empress with regard to Russia, Germany and the War that we cannot fall into the mistake — which was made by practically the whole Russian public — of regarding her almost as a traitor. I myself ordinarily heard no other view except from one person,

[1] MANUILOV, *Padenie*, II, 51.

Sir George Buchanan, who assured me earnestly that he could stand guarantee for her loyalty.

The Duma could no longer expect the frank explanations to which Sazonov had accustomed it; and it was now for the two Ambassadors to continue with Stürmer the connections formed with Sazonov. The picturesque Paléologue thus describes their first meeting:

> His look [he writes in his diary], sharp and honeyed, furtive and blinking, is the very expression of hypocrisy. I do not know if he will die 'in the odour of sanctity', as the mystics say; but I do know that he emits an intolerable 'odour of falseness'. In his 'bonhomie' and his affected politeness one feels that he is low, intriguing and treacherous.[1]

Here is another little scene which he gives out of their meetings. Paléologue notices, in the cabinet of the new Foreign Minister, three pictures which were not there before. They represent the great European Congresses of Vienna (1814-15), Paris (1856) and Berlin (1878); and Stürmer points to a fourth place, which has been left empty. 'That,' he says, 'is the place which I am keeping for the picture of the next congress, which, if God listens to me, will be called the Congress of Moscow.' He makes the sign of the cross and shuts his eyes for a moment, as if for a short prayer, and he repeats: 'How fine it will be at Moscow! How fine it will be! God grant it! God grant it!'[2]

Paléologue evidently shared the general idea that Stürmer might at any time conclude a separate peace with the Central Powers. Buchanan's view is different: 'It was Stürmer's appointment', he says, 'that first caused me to take a really serious view of the *internal* situation';[3] but though he formed just the same estimate of Stürmer's character as his French colleague, he again showed his greater foresight by saying that there would be no change in foreign policy. Writing to the Foreign Office on August 18th he says:

> I can never hope to have confidential relations with a man on whose word no reliance can be placed, and whose only idea is to further his own ambitious ends; but [he adds] self-interest compels him to continue the foreign policy of his predecessor.[4]

[1] PALÉOLOGUE, II, 270. [2] ibid., III, 34. [3] BUCHANAN, II, 18. [4] ibid., 18.

Buchanan, as soon as he knew of the dismissal of Sazonov, inquired of the Emperor, who was still at Headquarters, whether, in view of the invaluable services of Sazonov to the Alliance, he would allow him to ask King George V to grant him the honour of a G.C.B., as already the K.C.B. was being given to the commanders of the Russian armies. Nicholas expressed his pleasure, the distinction was conferred, and Buchanan communicated a short note to the Press to explain this honour. This communication was rejected by the censorship. Not long afterwards appeared an article by one Bulatsel, who was regarded as simply a pen man of Stürmer, vehemently attacking England, impugning her influence as revolutionary and even implying that King George, as a Freemason, was also probably a revolutionary (the two things went together in the minds of the Russian die-hards). Buchanan at once called on Stürmer and demanded an explanation. Stürmer referred the publishing of the article to the slackness of the censorship. 'The censorship was not slack', said Sir George, 'when it dealt with my communication about M. Sazonov.' He demanded and obtained that Bulatsel should be sent to the British Embassy to apologize. At the meeting Buchanan refused the proffered hand of the reptile writer, and simply read to him a stern *communiqué* on the incident, which he had forced Stürmer to admit to the Press.[1]

For the public the simple inference was that Stürmer would as soon as possible make a separate peace, thus betraying Russia's allies. At his appointment his German name had been a source of much merriment. The use of foreign languages was forbidden in the Duma, but the witty Purishkevich, who was the strongest of Conservatives, begged leave of the President to say three German words, which he at once proceeded to utter: 'Ober-Hofmeister Stürmer'. It had even been suggested that Stürmer should change his name to one of distinction in Russian history, that of the Panins, which was anything but agreeable to the Panins themselves. The following clever anonymous verses deal with all this incident:

Fresh comes Stürmer from the Palace
  In his diplomatic role.
Deutschland, Deutschland über Alles!
  Russland, Russland, lebe wohl!

[1] Buchanan to B. P.; BUCHANAN, II, 20-1.

STÜRMER TAKES HIS LAST TRICK

Friend of Russia's bold freemasons,
Cursing Petrograd and all,
See how Lord Sazonov hastens
To his Finnish waterfall.

'Stürmer, Stürmer, very shocking!'
Mutters Grey in far Hyde Park.
'He may say he is Nashchokin;
I suspect he'll be Bismarck.

'Not for nought he looks a villain,
Fur as red as fox — the pup!
And exactly like friend William,
His moustachios twisted up.'

As he dines with dames of fashion:
'Ah, the future's full of fog',
Ruminates in deep depression
Our poor Monsieur Paléologue.[1]

'Seems as if our work is undone:
New appointments — very strange.'
So Buchanan writes to London
On the Ministerial change.

'Shall we run upon the shallows?
Does it sound our friendship's knell?
Deutschland, Deutschland über Alles!
England, England, fare thee well!'

. . . . .

And when ends our warfare Punic,[2]
Nesselrode, Kotzebue,
Biren, Ostermann and Munich,[3]
Just as if they lived anew,

In their graves will shake with malice,
And above the bells will toll:
Deutschland, Deutschland über Alles!
Russland, Russland, lebe wohl!

[1] There are frequent references in Paléologue's diary to his social contacts with higher Russian society.

[2] In the Russian: 'and when he (Stürmer) signs a (separate) peace'.

[3] Names of German Ministers or favourites who ruled Russia under unpopular or reactionary Russian sovereigns.

It should be said at once that this estimate has no foundation in evidence. Ludendorff writes that there was no contact with Stürmer, 'nor the remotest suggestion of any move on his part'. So his Government informed him.[1] Stürmer of course knew, if others did not, the loyalty of the Empress to the War. As Paléologue has described it, his shallow thoughts went no farther than the glory of his own chairmanship of a victorious peace conference; and Buchanan, who was again more generous than the Russian public, was no doubt right when he assumed that the same policy would be continued.

The new Minister of the Interior, the elder Hvostov, was the first honest administrator which that office had seen since Shcherbatov and much more capable. His colleague, Volkonsky, has described his period of office as 'two bright months'.[2] He instituted a regular order of work, and he was just to everyone. Klimovich found himself under a chief whom he could respect. While refusing, when Minister of Justice, to pardon the five Bolshevik deputies, he had offered to forward Kerensky's request for a free pardon to the sovereign;[3] and as Minister of the Interior he even righted a wrong which he considered had been done to that twice-broken man, Komissarov, by his dismissal after long service without a pension.[4] But, as he had always realized, it was not for long that he was to be left at the Interior. Stürmer was always trying to make him dismiss Klimovich, whom Hvostov esteemed as an honest man and refused to give up. After constant nagging on this question, Hvostov in a plain talk made it clear that Stürmer could only get rid of Klimovich by getting rid of himself.[5] Stürmer's chief grievance against Klimovich was that he had exposed Manuilov to him, with whom he still claimed to have no connection. Manuilov had meanwhile returned to his favourite game of blackmailing; and Klimovich, with the approval of Hvostov, set a trap for him: marked money was used and the bait was taken. There were three charges, all of them well substantiated: one was for £1000 obtained for exemptions from military service. Hvostov announced the arrest to Stürmer as, 'an interesting piece of news which at first will probably frighten you, but later will please you'.

[1] Ludendorff, 401.
[2] Volkonsky, *Padenie*, vi, 139.
[3] Hvostov, A. A., *Padenie*, v, 454.
[4] ibid., v, 470.
[5] ibid., v, 456.

Stürmer threw himself round his neck, denouncing Manuilov as 'a blackguard and a blackmailer', but this was only pretence. The Empress identified Manuilov with the security of Rasputin, who a week later returned with Vyrubova from a visit to his Siberian home; a trial of Manuilov would involve Rasputin — in fact, Manuilov himself made that quite clear. The immediate result was first the dismissal of Klimovich, without reference to Hvostov, and then the release of Hvostov himself from his duties at the Ministry of the Interior. In bidding good-bye to Stürmer he said, 'It is the first time that I leave you with a feeling of sincere pleasure'.[1]

There was now a new vacancy at the Interior through the dismissal of the elder Hvostov. The man who, after some delay, was selected for this office was the last choice of the Empress and Rasputin, and was to lead Russia direct to revolution. His appointment opens a new and different chapter.

The dismissals of Polivanov and Sazonov were definitely the work of the Empress. The dismissals of the elder Hvostov, first from the Ministry of Justice and then from that of the Interior, were also due to her wishes. At one point poor Nicholas himself had entered a mild protest. 'I cannot change my mind every two months — this is simply unthinkable' (June 4th/17th). She must take the responsibility before history of having broken down the government of Russia. The whole apparatus of administration was crumbling away of itself.

[1] Hvostov, A. A., *Padenie*, v, 457.

CHAPTER XII

LAST GLORIES OF THE ARMY

O, farewell honest soldiers, who hath reliev'd you?
Hamlet, I, I

ALL through this miserable and disreputable period in the government of Russia the front remained extraordinarily sound. This fact was borne in on all who lived there, and with certain reservations, mostly local, it holds good up to and in some parts even after the March Revolution.[1] One will find it in whatever records one reads. Knox, the best and most objective of all observers, repeatedly bears testimony to it. In February 1916 he comments on the improved morale, the fine spirit at the front. In spite of what he describes as 'foul conditions', the 'men seemed excellent as usual'.[2] And later he bears testimony to 'the rare gallantry: no one is depressed'[3] even after colossal losses. 'The Seventh Army', he writes on November 3rd, 'has lost 200,000 men in the summer fighting. Every shell it has lacked has been paid for in blood.'[4] And a few pages later this fine soldier breaks out: 'I wonder when people will realize that the real hero of the War is the plain infantry private or second lieutenant.'[5]

There was a wonderful unity in mind, thought and speech between those who lived in the constant reach of death, in the actual front line, whether in Russia or in France.[6] There was a zone which, in a very true sense, remained clean and even holy throughout. It was the range of a rifle bullet or machine-gun, about 1000 yards, and the Russian divisional staffs repeatedly stood close up within this zone. Here it seemed as if there could be no mean and petty thoughts, and certainly there could be no care for the morrow; no reading matter could be acceptable save the best (for instance, the Bible, Shakespeare or Thomas Hardy),

[1] I lived at the front throughout the greater part of the period mentioned, at various points in the centre, north and south.
[2] KNOX, 387-91. [3] ibid., 452. [4] ibid., 492.
[5] ibid., 496. [6] In this year I visited both fronts, Russian and British.

the place which is usually filled by light reading was more than taken up by the subconscious atmosphere of hourly peril fully faced. As to news, the main facts got known everywhere, and the rest, including rumour, was only mentioned to be dismissed. It almost seemed as if every one knew the same jokes, and all of them robust and healthy. Friendships made here had the firmest foundation.[1] Passing out of this zone one felt at once the relaxation of spirit, accompanied by a semi-humorous reflection that one had come out of it, and now looked back on it almost with a kind of affectionate amusement. The staffs of the army corps had still a touch of this atmosphere:

> The youth who daily further from the East
> Must travel, still is Nature's priest,
> And by the vision splendid
> Is on his way attended;
> At length the Man perceives it die away
> And fade into the light of common day.

At the staffs of what were called Fronts — with us, Groups of Armies — it had disappeared altogether, and General Headquarters was a nest of intrigues and jealousies. The rear, especially Petrograd, was a different world, going fouler and more rotten every day. It bore no comparison whatever to our own vigorous rear. But as one again entered the closed circle of the army at Charing Cross, one began to pass back into something which seemed strangely familiar and became more and more so with every step to the British Front, till in the actual front line one was living on the very same thoughts as in the line which one had left. On my return to the Russian Front I was asked by a Russian officer what we were thinking over here, and I could only reply, 'The same thoughts as you have just expressed, and we put them into the same words'.

We left the Russian Army at the close of the great retreat in September 1915. It was terribly shaken; as Ludendorff has said, the enemy reckoned that it was henceforth incapable of active operations; but the same writer at the same time sums up the result of the campaign of 1915 as a constant disillusionment.

[1] An old Russian lady who followed her sons in the Guard with a Red Cross unit remarked that it seemed as if the only real friends whom she had ever made had been made here.

The two great pincers, starting in the south near Galicia and in the north from the Baltic, in spite of the marvellous industry and endurance of the magnificent German Army, had never succeeded in closing on the enemy. Every time, with desperate courage and furious rearguard actions, the Russians had got away. It was, indeed, on the two extreme wings that the firmest front had been shown. Brusilov in the far south, next to the almost annihilated Third Army of Radko-Dmitriev, from which he was separated by a big gap, had at once appreciated the lessons of the disaster. He got his men out far better. He had three lines of entrenchments, and fought hard on the way, retreating by stages and holding firm on the river Bug where he inflicted a severe check on the advancing enemy. Here he dug himself in and set himself at once to repair his damaged army by regular training at the front itself.[1] Brusilov had earlier declared that the army had become a mere militia. Regiments possessed no more than five or six of their old officers. 'In a year', he writes,[2] 'the regular army had vanished.' But it was very soon that a new atmosphere began to take shape — it is true, from the rear. The chief point of the difference was that there was no longer the same curtain between front and rear, and that the army was becoming, more truly than ever before, the nation.[3] This was largely due to the zemstvo Red Cross (Zemgor), for which Brusilov can find nothing but praise.[4] Its close proximity to the front, made absolutely necessary by the crying defaults of the official military organization, had a strongly humanizing influence on the front itself; and the 'off days' of the winter presented here and everywhere opportunities for many interludes of happy holiday in the immediate rear.

Brusilov gives a charming description of a masquerade got up entirely by the soldiers for the entertainment of their officers close up to the front line. 'It is astonishing', he says, 'what our soldier can do: what he can simply arrange by himself with the greatest art. On a broad field in front of the forest, in which were scattered the dug-outs of this division, they set us down as spectators of an extraordinary sight. Soldiers, dressed up as men of all nations or as animals, paraded and danced and engaged in the sports of a

[1] Brusilov, 127-37. [2] ibid., 138.
[3] The same change took place more gradually on the German side.
[4] Brusilov, 158.

country fair, and gave us a whole programme of amusing items, dances, competitions, tricks, choral singing, or rude country games. The laughter and merriment were endless; all this music, noise and hubbub were interrupted by the discharges of the enemy's artillery, which were here considerably more audible than at the staff; and among men and officers there reigned such carefree merriment, as was a sheer joy to watch [*lyubo-dorogo smotret*].'[1]

The firmness of Brusilov in the south was matched by Plehve in the extreme north. This remarkable little man, elderly and worn, always steady and at need full of daring initiative, holds a place of his own in the Russian military records. It was he who had borne the main brunt of the resistance to the first initial Austrian invasion of Russian Poland, when he had had, so to speak, to hold himself with arms extended, to prevent the penetration of the Russian centre while the Russian wings were closing in. It was he who had closed the gap when the Germans made their daring break through near Lodz in the autumn of 1914; and but for the usual slackness of Rennenkampf, he would have turned their bold venture into a brilliant Russian victory. In the last stages of the retreat it was he who held good near Riga, and saved that city, with an extended salient along the coast to give promise of an advance later on. The last German exploit on this side was the audacious dash of German cavalry to cut the most important lateral railway that remained between the enemy and the capital. The railway saved, the Russians, in their turn, ended the campaign with a vigorous counter-attack.

We have noted that the Germans had not yet reached any of the battlefields of Napoleon's invasion of 1812. The lessons of 1915 had been taken to heart, and the whole line was put into a proper state of defence. The line was still inordinately long, because Europe broadens widely as it passes into Russia; but it was much more like a straight line. In the middle of it, as its most distinguishing feature, lay the enormous forest marshes of Pinsk, where both sides had abandoned operations of importance and had little more than a series of outposts. This district and that to the north of it were covered by the new Western Front under Evert. The Northern Front, running to the Baltic, which Alexeyev had handled during the retreat, before he was called to

[1] BRUSILOV, 153-4.

Headquarters, as Chief-of-Staff of the whole army under the Emperor, went for a time to Ruzsky, and, when he fell ill, was held by Plehve. But in the course of the winter Plehve's health proved to be completely worn out, and as Ruzsky was not yet recovered, after many hesitations, this Front was in February given to Kuropatkin, the Commander-in-Chief of the Japanese War, already a back number and always deficient in initiative.

Apart from this constant work of entrenching and training, the Russians were not long in showing fight again. In the late autumn Bulgaria joined in on the enemy's side, to the extreme mortification of the Tsar and the Russian public, and a joint encircling movement of Austrians and Bulgarians drove not only the whole Serbian Army, but as much of the population as could follow it over the great *massif* of mountain which separated it from the Adriatic coast, the Serbians fighting splendidly all the way. In December the broken Russian Army made a belated attempt at help in an offensive in the south in the neighbourhood of Trembovlya, and though it had no permanent success, it was marked by furious fighting with alternating successes. Meanwhile in the Caucasus, where the Grand Duke Nicholas was now Viceroy, seconded by a very able General, Yudenich, the Russians were at issue with their old enemy the Turk; and in conditions which were reminiscent of earlier types of warfare, they drove back the invading forces, and in February crowned their counter-advance with the conquest of Erzerum. In these operations the greatest assistance was given by the Russian Black Sea fleet, now commanded by Admiral Kolchak. The first naval officer to join his ship by aeroplane, he immediately took the initiative, drove the *Breslau* back to the Bosphorus, and mined the Straits, converting the Black Sea into a Russian lake, over which transports could pass with security to the advancing Russian Army on the farther side. The Turks were no longer able to use the sea for transport to Constantinople, and it even became necessary for the Germans to send them coal from Upper Silesia.

All this time really great progress was being made in the supply of the Russian Army under the vigorous direction of Polivanov. Polivanov has complained that under the casual regime of Sukhomlinov training had aimed at the parade and not at preparation for action in the field. All this was now completely changed. His new and systematic methods soon yielded remarkable results. Instead of the haphazard collection of men of all ages of the late summer, there was now a fine pick of well-built, soldierly men, who excited enthusiastic comment on all sides: from the Emperor, who speaks of them as 'real Guardsmen', from Rodzyanko who admired them as splendid material, and from Knox. Their training was largely completed in the front zone itself, and partly even in front of that. They showed remarkable keenness and I recall how after the regular regimental and company scouts had gone out to the most 'interesting', that is most dangerous, spot, a considerable party, without an officer, came and asked leave to go out there too.[1] One thing was painfully lacking: the officers, who had for a long time insisted on going into action standing, while they told their men to crawl on the ground, had been knocked out at twice the rate of the men, and as a result the number of promoted N.C.O.s had greatly increased. These were excellent fellows, but for the most part uneducated, and could bear no relation for efficiency to the promoted N.C.O.s in the German Army.

Equally important was Polivanov's work for munitions. Here he was enthusiastically supported by the network of War Industry Committees created all over the country by Guchkov. Polivanov, it will be remembered, was definitely told at his dismissal in March 1916 that his mild control of the public organizations was his chief crime, but his successor, Shuvayev, plainly told the Emperor that to carry out the work of the army without the help of the country was 'like trying to swim against the current',[2] and he continued the helpful attitude of the War Office to these Committees. They were much criticized in other quarters and not without reason; the big ordnance factories resented both their interference and their popularity — it will be remembered that Guchkov had set up workers' sections with representatives of labour — and certainly the conversion of small factories of any kind to munition work could only be an accessory to that of the established factories, such as Putilov's; but they did represent a great common effort of the whole country and a most substantial increase of munitions, and

[1] I was so much impressed by what I saw of this improvement that I was preparing to entitle my next issue of notes on the front 'The Recovery'.

[2] SHUVAYEV, *Padenie*, VII, 286-90.

the atmosphere which they created was as important as their actual work.

Of like importance, though equally subject to criticism, was the extensive work of the town and county councils Red Cross (Zemgor). At the start they had confined themselves to provision for the wounded, who without them would have been in a parlous state. Then they discovered one deficiency after another in food stations, transport and other needs of the army, and made good the worst gaps. Over and over again, their work made all the difference between lack and supply. Unfortunately they became cover for many who did not wish to be called up to the fighting line and thereby lost some of the goodwill which the army had reason to feel towards them. They were receiving large subsidies from the Government, and they were extremely casual in their accountancy. It appears that they had never sent in any financial accounts, even from the period of the Japanese War, and the Empress was not unreasonable in challenging them on this point. She regarded them, not without cause, as a budding nucleus for a new government of Russia, and indeed it was by his work as Chairman of Zemgor that Prince George Lvov qualified for appointment as the first Premier after the Revolution.

All these efforts, added to the extensive sacrifices of the Allies to Russia, led to a very marked improvement in the equipment of the army. The most difficult question was that of rifles, which have peculiarly complex requirements for their manufacture, and these had largely to be bought ready-made from abroad, but Knox is able to write on February 20th that 'the rifle situation had improved enormously'.[1] What the Russians had done for themselves is summed up by him a little later (Ap. 27th).[2] He puts the output of Russian rifles as averaging 100,000 a month, and giving an account of the position in the middle of May, he writes:

> All units at the front possessed their full complement. The number of machine-guns had increased to an average of 10 to 12 per 4-battalion regiment. Most of the infantry divisions had now 36 field guns, and there was a reserve of some 8 million of 3 in. shell. Most of the corps had a division of eight 4.8 in. howitzers. A considerable number of trench mortars and hand grenades had been provided.

[1] Knox, 395. [2] ibid., 421-3.

Danilov commenting on the same improvement, mentions that, by February 1916, cartridges and shell were enough for one major operation, heavy artillery in a better position, and ammunition nearly sufficient.[1]

In the winter the Inter-Allied Military Conference meeting at Chantilly laid down its proposals for the campaign of 1916. Owing to the Russian losses in the preceding year, it was established that the main effort should be made by the French and British on the Somme; and in order to distract the attention of the enemy, the Russians were to move a little earlier with a secondary operation. But the Allied plans were, for the time, completely forestalled and upset by the enemy. In February the Germans started their tremendous mass assault upon Verdun, which was to last for four months, with ruinous sacrifices of men and yawning gaps in both armies. Urgent appeals for early help were again made to Russia and received the usual chivalrous reply. Though the Emperor inevitably left the conduct of all operations to Alexeyev, a decision of this kind could only be taken by him; and it was taken without account of anything but chivalry and without regard for the difficulties which it involved. General Evert, commanding the western front, was ordered to move forward in the direction of Vilna, which was a critical part of the German line of advance, and a group of corps of the Second Russian Army was entrusted for this purpose to a shrewd old general, Baluyev. The Germans were completely surprised by the intensity of the Russian artillery preparation: Hoffmann describes it as 'such an expenditure of ammunition as we had not yet seen in the East'. 'The infantry attacks', he writes, 'were conducted, as usual, with the utmost bravery and determination and with complete disregard of loss of life.'[2]

The Russians advanced with the greatest ardour, wading through the mud, and carried the first two enemy lines. Baluyev made successful attacks on March 25th, 27th, 31st, April 3rd and 14th.[3] The Russian batteries, however, anchored on their several islands in the midst of the general morass, remained idle spectators of the slaughter of their advancing infantry.[4]

On the night of the 22nd there were five degrees of frost (Réaumur), and in the morning 300 men of a division of the

[1] DANILOV, 496. [2] HOFFMANN, II, 131-2. [3] KNOX, 407. [4] Quoted by KNOX, 409.

> 5th Corps had to be hacked out of the ice where they lay. The marsh in the centre of Baluyev's front soon became impassable . . . Continual fog prevented artillery observation.[1]

A peculiarly sinister hill, commanding the Russian position, proved untakable. The soldiers named the hollow which it commanded the Valley of the Shadow of Death, which their officers revised to 'The Valley of Good and Evil'.[2] For all that, the German General Staff were very seriously perturbed, and Ludendorff, who describes the Russian gunfire as of 'unprecedented intensity', declares that the situation from March 18th to 21st was critical for the Tenth German Army.[3] The climax of the attack was on March 26th when the Russians wading, in the words of Ludendorff, 'through swamp and blood', suffered extraordinarily heavy losses.[4] At this point, the Russian Headquarters recklessly deprived Baluyev both of his heavy artillery and nearly all his aeroplanes, and on April 28th the Tenth German Army, strongly reinforced, especially with artillery, regained in a single day all that had been lost.

Ludendorff mentions that this was the first occasion on which the methods of the western German front were fully used on the eastern side.[5] Hoffmann writes: 'This attack of the Tenth Army, which was preceded by an admirably carried out artillery preparation, can serve as an example of all our subsequent attacks in the East.'[6] The gunnery work in this action was the debut of a brilliant officer, Colonel Bruchmüller, who was later put in regular charge of this work to the great satisfaction of the German troops. The Russians lay in marshy ground with the most inadequate trenches, which hardly gave any cover at all. The Germans had brought up their heavy guns to the near neighbourhood of this line, and starting at 5 a.m. in clear weather their field guns, practically brought up to the German trenches, pounded the Russian lines at a range of some 400 yards, supported also by poison gas, which had so far seldom been used on the eastern front. The Russians were entirely unprovided either with gas masks or even steel helmets. After each hour of the bombardment the enemy paused to ascertain the effects, and on the resumption of rifle firing from the Russian trenches gave them a fresh turn.

[1] KNOX, 409. [2] I was present at this point. [3] LUDENDORFF, 210-11.
[4] ibid., 211-12. [5] ibid., 213. [6] HOFFMANN, II, 132-3.

After five hours of this attack every battalion in the Russian front line was reduced to a figure between 90 and 100 men. When the German infantry at last advanced it was not for a frontal attack, but to outflank with machine-gun fire. The one bayonet charge in the action was on the Russian side. Russian infantry reserves were rushed up, but with little or no artillery to support them. Yet the Russian line was not driven farther back than a mile and a half, and the men, bivouacking as best they might in the marsh, continued nightly to sing as before the Easter hymn with the words 'Christ is arisen from the dead, conquering death by death'. One wondered whether that was not the only weapon they had to fight with. Their losses were tremendous; the Smolensk regiment, for instance, which had been specially decorated for its courage, was left with only seven out of its thirty-five officers.

After this battle, which was concealed from the Russian public, Headquarters sent down a commission to investigate the causes of the defeat; it might as well have investigated its own decision to denude Baluyev of his equipment at the critical moment. When the commission had departed, the poor old general was entertained by his staff in the little garden of the cottage which he occupied with a cinema show in which the picture arrived upside down. The corporal who was operating it called out nervously: 'Your Excellency, I beg leave to discontinue this picture,' and a grumpy voice came back through the darkness: 'I command you to continue upside down.'† [1]

The action on Lake Naroch was only local, and the Russian pledge to a more general offensive remained unchanged, the more so because at this time the French were hard pressed at Verdun. On April 14th the Emperor presided at a conference of the military chiefs at Headquarters. Alexeyev's proposal was that Evert should undertake the principal offensive, supported by subsidiary movements by the northern and south-western fronts. Evert was to have the main artillery and reserves. It was Evert who had been responsible for the Naroch operation; naturally cautious, he was now even more so, and he reported that with the Germans in front of him he saw no prospect of breaking the enemy front. Kuropatkin was asked what he could do, and this old general,

[1] PARES, *My Russian Memoirs*, 376-8.

who had exaggerated caution in the Japanese War and also had the Germans in front of him, gave the same answer.

There remained the South-Western Front. It had recently received a new chief, Brusilov, who had taken the place of the elderly and somewhat irresolute Ivanov. This was a man of original ideas. At one time head of the cavalry riding school, he had had close touch with the Grand Duke Nicholas, then Inspector of Cavalry, whom he greatly admired and regarded as the best possible Commander-in-Chief of the Russian Army. Alexeyev was too cautious for him. His tactics during his brilliant work in the Galician campaign had always been those of attack, and he maintained that it was only by seizing the initiative that great results could be achieved. In other matters, including politics, he had a big touch of the spirit of adventure. He resented the monopoly of the military academy and of staff officers, and was content to make his own way with something like a demonstration of democratic tendencies; his memoirs are unnecessarily full of disclaimers of personal ambition, but that was not the impression that he left on those who met him.[1] He now spoke out vigorously, offering to take the lead himself. We must remember that it was the Austrians that he had opposite to him, and that the Russian generals on that side had a sense of superiority over them, which their troops fully shared. Brusilov only claimed that he should have support from the two other Fronts.[2]

Brusilov's proposal was accepted; he was to start, and Evert was to come in later. But the artillery and reserves were still in the main to be kept for Evert. The French military authorities, whose views carried especial importance while they were desperately defending Verdun, as usual asked for a direct blow at the Germans, and the direction in which they would be most sensitive was still that of Vilna.

Brusilov, as we know, had been hard at work entrenching throughout the winter, and now he carried forward this work in the most systematic way. The Austrian trenches were particularly strong, and every care had been taken to survey them with the help of engineers and aeroplanes so thoroughly that, when in

[1] Including the writer, to whom he said at their only meeting: 'Why don't Evert and Kuropatkin do anything? Why do they leave it all to me?'

[2] Brusilov, 163-6.

the subsequent operations an Austrian staff officer was captured, it was found that his chart of the Austrian lines was no more correct than Brusilov's. Following a precedent of the greatest of Russian generals, Suvorov,[1] Brusilov even went so far as to construct models of the Austrian entrenchments some way behind his own lines and to practise his men in storming them so that, to use the words of one of his most brilliant officers, Golovin, when the men at last found themselves in the actual trenches, they felt quite 'at home'. Regular training courses were instituted, especially for those junior officers who had joined up during the last six months; there were periodical visits of the staff for daily instruction, and the charts of the lines in front of them were communicated even to company commanders.

Brusilov's tactical idea was original and, as it turned out, decisive. He was entirely opposed to a servile following of German methods. With the marvellous regularity of the German fighting-machine, it was possible to arrange a concentration of men and guns at a single given point with such surety and rapidity that the ensuing result was practically a certainty, and it was sometimes even declared in advance. But the Germans had behind them a splendid network of railways and even in the conquered territory their supply of lateral railroads was such as altogether to eclipse that of their opponents. On the other hand, the best of all the Russian railways were in the west of the empire, that is in the territory which had already been conquered. It was perfectly clear to Brusilov, and indeed to anyone, that any similarly laborious effort on the part of the Russians to concentrate on a given part of the line must be known to the enemy long in advance, and would give him plenty of time to collect even stronger forces at the threatened point. Brusilov's idea was to 'tap along the wall'. Trench work might just as well be conducted simultaneously at several points in the line; and it would then be impossible for the enemy to know which point was most threatened.[2]

This was what Brusilov did. In some parts the digging was carried out only to half the ordinary depth; and by an ingenious device of spraying the ground, there was created what was called a horizontal camouflage, which, as it proved, often succeeded in

[1] Before the assault on the Turkish fortress of Ismail in 1791.
[2] Brusilov, 168.

misleading the enemy. On the other hand, Brusilov himself never had one single part of the line in view. There were to be four simultaneous offensives conducted by the four different corps under his command. The north of his line was close to the southern end of the Pinsk Marshes, where serious operations were practically impossible. Proceeding southwards from this point he had the Eighth Army, formerly his own, and now under Kaledin, the Eleventh under Sakharov, the Seventh under Shcherbachev and the Ninth under Lechitsky. All the four generals were competent, especially the two last-named. Lechitsky had done splendid work throughout the war; Shcherbachev had been head of the military academy and his chief of staff, Golovin, was one of its professors.

Secrecy was carefully safeguarded. Everything possible was done in preliminary care and training of the troops. *Places d'armes*, or military shelters for the attacking units were constructed in advance, and these units were as far as possible kept in the rear till the time should come for attack. Advance lines were brought up as close as possible to the enemy in order to diminish the distance necessary for the actual assault. The one deficiency was the comparative absence of reserves, and that was not Brusilov's fault.[1]

It was left to the responsible General to settle how to carry out an operation entrusted to him, and in this matter Brusilov was able to get his own way. The essential factor of his plan was the element of surprise. He was asked by the Emperor to pay a visit to the Empress, but he was very careful to deny her any indication of the date chosen, which was all the more necessary because, as we know, the Empress more than once claimed in her letters to be told the proposed dates in advance in order to engage the prayers of Rasputin for that particular moment. Rasputin's chief associates were, like himself, friendly to the enemy; and he himself might in any of his drunken revels communicate the information to others.[2]

But now intervened another urgent call from the side of the Allies. The Austrians had engaged in a great offensive against Italy, and were at first sweeping all before them. Cadorna, the Italian Commander-in-Chief, urgently begged for an immediate move on the Russian side. According to Hoffmann, the complete victory of the Austrians in Italy was then a matter 'of days or even of hours'.[3] Another disturbing factor was the question when the

[1] BRUSILOV, 174-6. [2] ibid., 172-3. [3] HOFFMANN, II, 136.

cautious Evert would be prepared to follow up Brusilov's attack, as according to the German commanders, he ought certainly to have done. There were negotiations by telephone between Brusilov and the General Staff, in which he had almost to clamour for his rights. At one time he was told that a decision could not be obtained because the Commander-in-Chief, that is the Emperor, was asleep, to which he claims to have replied: 'The sleep of the Commander-in-Chief doesn't concern me.' The dates had to be changed more than once; but ultimately Alexeyev summed up: 'Well, do as you think.'[1]

The strongest section of the Austrian line was in the middle, covering the approach to Lemberg, which was only about a hundred miles off. Clearly an attack on this section might be anticipated and would not have the element of surprise. Brusilov struck at four different points. His principal blow, backed by four army corps, was delivered by Kaledin's Eighth Army on his north wing as close as possible to Evert, who was still expected to follow with the main attack. At the south end of the line, Lechitsky's Ninth Army was to break through near the Dnieper with two army corps. Sakharov's Eleventh Army and Shcherbachev's Seventh in the centre were closer to the strongest section of the enemy line, and were to attack respectively with one and a half army corps and with one. On June 4th at dawn the guns opened fire along Brusilov's front: the artillery preparation varied from forty-five hours with the Seventh Army to six hours with the Eleventh. The result was extraordinary and exceeded all expectations. When the infantry went to the attack, they carried the Austrian lines at nearly all points straight off and swept the enemy back in a condition approaching to panic. By June 9th the Eighth Army had reached the River Styr and captured Lutsk, making a breach in the enemy's line of over twenty-five miles in depth and widening it from fifteen to fifty miles. Its next neighbour southward, the Eleventh Army, was not able to break through; but the Seventh, with only seven infantry divisions, carried a width of twenty-five miles by the same date. Lechitsky and his Ninth Army, dealing with the Austrian right flank, first attacked southward so as to be able to outflank it, and then swept their line northwards in the direction of Shcherbachev, penetrating to a depth of twenty miles.

[1] Brusilov, 177-8.

In four days Brusilov had taken no fewer than 125,000 prisoners. This astounding number has not only a military explanation. Little as it was realized on the Allied side, something like three-fifths of the subjects of Francis Joseph had no affection for his rule. There were Serbs, who naturally longed for an Allied victory; there were Poles, most of whom, as has been mentioned, had decided before the war that the best hope of the resurrection of their country lay with the Allies; there were Ruthenians, who in nationality were identical with the Russian Ukrainians; above all there were Czechoslovaks, and in their country a moral movement of the first value had long since been led by scholars such as Palacky and Masaryk, supported by a whole network of the gymnastic associations of the Sokols. As early as 1914 Czechoslovaks resident in Russia had formed special legions, which were later reinforced by whole numbers of their fellow countrymen in the Austrian army. There was a constant flow of Czechoslovaks to the Russian line, sometimes in driblets, sometimes in whole units as large as regiments of four battalions, one of which came over in that year *en masse*, under fire with colours flying and band playing. It became routine at the Russian front to put to the Czechoslovaks, not the question, 'Where did you surrender?' but 'Where did you come over?' And these men, instead of accepting the release from the war involved by captivity, in nearly all cases sought service on the Russian side. Thus when Brusilov attacked, as soon as the Austrian line was broken, the flow of transfer began of itself. But this does not diminish the credit of the attack. The enemy in his victorious advance in 1915 had employed metal to bore holes through the Russian line at one point after another. By the terrible arithmetic of the conflict, the Russians could only achieve the same results by the sacrifice of men. General Dukhonin, who, as Brusilov's Quartermaster General, had the responsibility of issuing each order of attack, said[1] that each such order gave him a 'wrench of the heart', because he well knew what price he had to pay. Still, at this cruel sacrifice Brusilov did with men what the Germans in the preceding year had done with metal.

After the initial successes arose a critical question. The Austrian line was broken, and it was now necessary to decide in what

[1] Dukhonin to B. P.

direction this great success should be followed up. All the circumstances which had led to it were tactical, and now, for the carrying home of the blow, strategic considerations became predominant. Kaledin was aware that he had almost broken the Fourth Austrian Army, and wanted to complete his victory by pursuing it directly westwards towards Vladimir-Volynsk. Brusilov, if left entirely independent, might have preferred this direction; but he knew that all his efforts were meant to be subsidiary to the main attack, which was later to be made by Evert. Correspondence with Headquarters only produced the news that Evert was not yet ready. If Brusilov took a north-westerly direction — as it was proper to do if his operation was only regarded as a part of a larger whole — he would be best helping Evert in his more difficult task against the Germans by reaching the extremely important railway junction of Kovel, and would also in this way hinder the transfer of German troops to the panic-stricken Austrian Army. The directions of Headquarters were not clear. Brusilov was not told that he was free to act independently; yet Alexeyev suggested to him an advance south-westward, that is even more to the south than the direction proposed by Kaledin. Six infantry divisions which had been sent in June to the South-Western Front were all given to Kaledin; but owing to the confusion of plan he advanced simultaneously in two directions on Kovel and on Vladimir-Volynsk; this of course slowed up his progress.

It must be borne in mind that there were always two schools of thought in the Russian Army. Those who had been so successful in the south-west were always longing to complete their triumph by finishing with Austria and compelling her to a separate peace; and indeed it was largely through the defection of her Allies that Germany was finally defeated. The other view — that no substantial success could be won without a direct defeat of the Germans — was of course strongly reinforced by the French Staff and the French Ambassador in Petrograd. Had Brusilov simply followed up the beaten Austrian Army, it is almost certain that he could have finally knocked it out; as it was, he dealt it its final blow, and it was for Evert to see that the Germans were kept busy to the north of him.

However, Brusilov continued to go forward, and his next most notable success fell to Sakharov's Eleventh Army, which was able to advance as far as Brody. The two armies to the south of him, the Seventh and the Ninth, also greatly extended their gains, and the Ninth even won the capital of Austrian Bukovina, Czernovitz. By the beginning of July, the gains had been very much further extended. On the north of Brusilov's front the Eighth and Eleventh Armies had widened the breach to close on a hundred miles, with a maximum depth of forty. In the south, the breach was about eighty-five miles with a depth of twenty-five. By now, only forty miles of the original Austrian line were still in enemy hands.

The German Staff was exceedingly alarmed by what Ludendorff describes[1] as Russia's 'amazing victories over the Austro-Hungarian troops', and everything was done to concentrate a German front between Lutsk and Kovel. The first German reinforcements to arrive were simply carried away with the retreating Austrians. German troops covered the Austrian retreat at Korokov, and there were some local German successes round the beginning of July; but the reinforcements had to be launched in driblets; Hoffmann writes, 'We scraped together all the reserves we could find, thinned the quieter fronts and obtained in this way a few regiments'.[2] In the main all that could be done was to attempt to stem the rout, and the very thin German line had great difficulty in resisting the fierce Russian attacks, which were continued with the greatest violence. Evert did at last move on the side of Lake Naroch and Baranovichi, and here too the fighting was fierce; but it was not prolonged.[3] On July 8th the Russian advance on Kovel was stopped, but Ludendorff describes these moments as 'terribly anxious days' and 'one of the greatest crises of the war';[4] and even till the end of July he regarded the German prospects 'with a sinking heart'. It was decided between the Staffs of the Central Powers that Hindenburg's command was to extend as far south as Brody.[5] In the beginning of July a powerful German counter-offensive against the Eighth Russian Army was repulsed.

The number of prisoners taken so far reached 225,000, quite apart from the Austrian and German losses in killed and wounded; the Russian sacrifice in casualties had already reached the colossal figure of 300,000; but Italy had been saved, and the Austrians, breaking off their offensive on that side, were now hurrying up

[1] Ludendorff, 220. [2] Hoffmann, ii, 141.
[3] Ludendorff, 222-5. [4] ibid., 226. [5] ibid., 226-9.

forces to face Brusilov's front. The German pressure on Verdun had also slackened and that huge operation had begun to peter out. The Germans were now directing all reserves to their eastern front, sending from the west as many as twenty-five divisions, and were also dispatching heavy reinforcements from in front of Evert to stop Brusilov. Evert did advance once more, but with a half-hearted effort, directing four army corps against a point to the north of Baranovichi. The twenty-fifth Russian corps, now under the command of Danilov, succeeded in piercing the junction of the Austrians and Germans at this point; but he received no support from his neighbours and was recalled.[1] On July 1st at last began the belated Franco-British advance on the Somme, which was to last for five months; but it only gained some twenty-five miles and was stopped by the famous Hindenburg line. In all, the Germans were able to send as many as thirty-five divisions to their eastern front.

On July 9th Alexeyev instructed that the leading part was now to be assigned to Brusilov, and the Russian reinforcements were in the main directed to the south-west. These consisted in the main of a new army composed of the Guards, which, being the Thirteenth, to spare the superstitions of the men, was named the Special Army. There were long delays in bringing it to the front. One might have thought that, as Brusilov was now to lead, his forces should have turned more directly on the routed Austrian army; for he no longer had the responsibility of acting as second to Evert. In this case the natural direction would have been Lemberg; but Brusilov himself continued to aim at Kovel, perhaps in order, to make it more difficult for the Germans to send help south. Thus he pursued simultaneously the two directions of Kovel and Lemberg. At this time he had also been given, temporary control over Evert's southern army, the Third, encamped in the Pinsk Marshes; and on Kovel he now directed this army, together with the Special Army of the Guards and the Eighth of Kaledin. The lie of the country was in the highest degree unfavourable, especially in the marshy and wooded district on the River Stokhod, and prolonged foul weather further diminished his chances. Bezobrazov, the commander of the Guards' army, had previously incurred criticism for his obstinacy.

[1] Danilov, 504.

One of his corps was entrusted to the Grand Duke Paul, a sick man without any kind of military competence. On July 28th began a fierce struggle on the Stokhod, in which the Russian losses were tremendous. Bezobrazov took little account of his neighbour on the right, the Third Army of Lesh; and the Guards were led to a frontal attack through a hopeless swamp where many of them sank while the German aeroplanes circled over them. They actually succeeded in reaching their objective, which they were then ordered to abandon. Rodzyanko, who was at this time on a visit to his son in the Guards, gives a terrible picture of the losses of the splendid recruits known as the Polivanov men.[1] Bezobrazov was superseded by the capable Gurko, who refused to send his men to such another attempt.[2]

Meanwhile, the three southern Russian armies continued their victorious advance, and this time the three were acting in conjunction on a strategic plan, and all of them advancing in the direction of Lemberg. The forty miles of front which the Austrians still held in the centre of their original position, were completely turned by the advance of Sakharov from Brody, Shcherbachev on the Koropets and Lechitsky farther south; and by the beginning of August the whole of the original Austrian line, some 260 miles in length, had been captured. Originally Brusilov had in front of him an enemy force of 400,000. He had now taken 375,000 prisoners, but to balance this, together with the enemy losses in killed and wounded, he had himself paid the price of 550,000 men. Hindenburg later pays a magnificent tribute to the Russian courage:

> In the Great War ledger the page on which the Russian losses were written has been torn out. No one knows the figures. Five or eight millions? We too have no idea. All we know is that sometimes in our battles with the Russians we had to remove the mounds of enemy corpses from before our trenches in order to get a clear field of fire against fresh assaulting waves. Imagination may try to reconstruct the figure of their losses, but an accurate calculation will remain for ever a vain thing.[3]

No wonder that the bleeding wounds of Russia drove almost every other thought from the public mind; and the Empress, who

[1] Rodzyanko, 201-5; Knox, 458-72. [2] Gurko, 157. [3] Hindenburg, 273.

had almost the same passionate love for the Russian Army as her husband, kept writing to him to urge Brusilov to stop. She constantly quotes the insistent plea of 'Our Friend'. According to Simanovich, Rasputin had urged Nicholas to pay any price to end the war. 'The soldiers', he prophetically told him, 'will return like wild beasts.'[1] 'Our Friend', writes the Empress on Aug. 8th/21st, 'hopes we won't climb over the Carpathians,' and on Oct. 8th,[2] 'Oh give your order again to Brusilov to stop this useless slaughter.'

All attempts in the direction of Kovel were now abandoned and Brusilov continued to advance on Lemberg. We may quote the summary of results so far from the admirable article by Golovin on Brusilov's offensive, on which the preceding account is chiefly based:

> When the Galician battle began, 39 Russian infantry divisions were opposed to 37 Austrian units and 1 German division. Towards the beginning of the third period (that is, up to August 12th) we had — taking into account all our six armies (of the South-Western Front) — 61 infantry divisions against 72 of the enemy; and now not 1 but 24 divisions were German.[3]

Brusilov's advance was no longer so effective; and on August 17th came a political event which robbed it of its significance. On that day the Rumanian Government at last signed a military alliance with the Entente Powers. It had been bargaining for terms throughout the war. Rumania had originally been connected with the Triple Alliance; but there were two parties in the country and the astute Bratianu had been balancing the chances on either side.[4] Sazonov had thought — correctly, as the event proved — that Rumania was more useful to the Entente as a neutral than as an ally; but when Stürmer replaced him, the Rumanians were given a time limit which, in spite of some procrastination, brought them to the point. There can hardly be any doubt now that this was a capital mistake of Allied diplomacy, and it had always been sturdily opposed by Alexeyev. Till

[1] SIMANOVICH, 153. [2] Sept. 25th, O.S.

[3] 'Brusilov's Offensive' in the *Slavonic Review*, vol. XIII, No. 39, 590.

[4] A Rumanian prisoner of the Austrian Army when asked by me 'When are you coming into the war?' replied: 'When we do, you will know which side is going to win'.

Rumania came in, the southern Russian flank was covered by her neutrality, which also prevented the Germans from any regular access on that side to her Bulgarian and Turkish Allies. However, though there was no merit in bringing Rumania into the war on the Allied side, it was self-evidently a result of the success of Brusilov's offensive.

His position was now completely altered. The Rumanians had been urged to attack the Bulgarians southward and join hands if possible with the Allied forces in Salonica, but by the unjust Treaty of Bucarest in 1913 they had already obtained Bulgarian territory in the Dobrudja, and their national aspirations led them to insist on an invasion of Transylvania. Rumania, like Poland, had a considerable population on both sides of the lines in the Great War — Transylvania, which was in Austria, and the larger part of Bessarabia, which was in Russia — so that only an invasion of the former could satisfy the national spirit. This altered all the military objectives and brought Brusilov's offensive to a close, and this change in the situation was to put Russia in greater difficulties than ever.

On August 27th the Rumanians, without declaration of war, began their Transylvanian offensive against their former allies. Hindenburg has declared that at this moment the forces of Germany and Austria were exhausted.[1] It would seem that the German diplomacy in Bucarest may have relied too long on the continual haggling on terms between the Rumanian Government and the Allied Powers. The Rumanians found little difficulty in penetrating even to the capital of Transylvania, Hermannstadt, which they reached on September 6th. At this time a new offensive began in the west on the Somme: the Allied force under Sarrail at Salonica also attacked on August 29th, but was repulsed. The Germans now made a magnificent effort of organization. While Falkenhain attacked the Rumanians in Transylvania, Mackensen, passing through Bulgaria, invaded the Dobrudja, which the Rumanians were abandoning by September 15th. Originally the Rumanians had been very chary of admitting Russian help, so that only one single Russian corps was sent, but they now began to ask for more. It was by Russian troops that Mackensen was temporarily stopped on September 16th, and

[1] HINDENBURG, 197.

meanwhile Sarrail, with splendid work of the reorganized Serb troops, regained lost ground near Salonica. Hindenburg has confessed to the surprise which he felt in seeing the Serbian Army, re-trained in Corfu, again take the field with vigorous effect. On September 19th the Ninth German Army in Transylvania passed over the Carpathians near Petrosany, and the two German wings were now converging on the heart of Rumania. Again Russian efforts in the Pinsk Marshes and at Dorna Vatra were ineffective, though the Russians were able to get somewhat nearer to Lemberg. On October 3rd Mackensen drove the Rumanians over the Danube, and in Transylvania they were beaten badly at Kronstadt and driven to a general retreat. Attacks by Gurko in the direction of Vladimir-Volynsk, though successful in occupying two lines of the enemy, were eventually repulsed. Mackensen had by now broken through into Rumania proper: the port of Constanza was lost on October 23rd. The German successes followed one after the other, though the Serbs coming from the south were able to re-enter their country. It was in this atmosphere of temporary success that the aged Austrian Emperor Francis Joseph at last died on November 21st. Mackensen crossed the Danube on the 23rd and the German and Bulgarian forces were soon surrounding Bucarest, which was abandoned on December 3rd. The Rumanian Army retreated to the Sereth (Dec. 24th) closely followed by the now united Austro-German forces. By January 6th the Russians were pressed hard on their own frontier on the Danube. A Russian offensive at the other end of the line at Riga stopped on January 10th.

By now Lechitsky's Ninth Army and Kaledin's Eighth were both defending Rumania, and before long a quarter of the whole Russian Army was engaged in this task. This involved difficult questions of command which were settled, unsatisfactorily enough, by making the Rumanians responsible for the centre of their defences and Brusilov for the two wings. The tremendously long line of the Russian Front had thus been greatly extended, and Rumania instead of being a help had turned out to be a trap. The Rumanians had started the war as if they had taken no account of its military lessons, especially in supply. They were hopelessly short of all the main accessories, and they depended for their munitioning on what might be likely to reach them through the whole length of Russia, where the railways were by now in a deplorable state.

Till now, whatever had been the privations of the rear, the army had somehow or other continued to be well supplied; now things were running short all round. In the north, which was normally short in food-production, the men were put on short rations, especially with regard to meat, which they could only obtain once or twice a week. At the other end of the line in Bukovina a Russian General of Division, who was a humane man, could find no other means of supplying his men with food than raiding any resources in the neighbourhood. The difficulty in supplying the heavy ordnance requirements of Rumania can be imagined. What the Allies sent from the west had but a poor chance of reaching these distant fronts. However, with their sympathy for another 'Latin' nationality, the French sent General Berthelot, who with great ability and success set about a reorganization of the broken Rumanian Army; it now occupied only a fragment of its territory in the north in the neighbourhood of Jassy.

In view of what was to follow, any first-hand example of the Russian conditions of fighting at this time may be of interest. I was present at an engagement at Kirli-baba, at which the opposing German troops were definitely surprised and the line broken, but only for a Russian regiment to fail in its direction in a thick mountain fog and to lose three-quarters of its men in an hour or two. Other regiments were reduced in the same proportion. All the front line ambulance section was destroyed, and a detachment of the Civil Red Cross had to be brought up to take its place. The wounded were lying for the most part in the winter snow and mud; there were no litters and only one tent; and as the distance to the first-aid point was considerable and the transport entirely ineffective, most of them must have reached it already with the beginnings of gangrene. It was calculated about this time that the Russians restored to fitness and to the fighting line 40 per cent less than their opponents, and one must not forget that the Russian Army by now had practically been renewed three times over. Inquiries in each unit, as to how many men were left of the original company of 250, were usually answered with a figure between five and six; and the question as to how many times the unit had been brought up to strength, which ordinarily represented the renewal of half its personnel, received a reply varying between eight and ten times. Here is a description of the conditions in which these troops lived on the eve of the Revolution:

> Several times I took some of my English companions with me on my visits to the front. One day, Dr. Flavell, head of the Anglo-Russian hospital, came up with me. We went to a grisly place, a slope which it was impossible to descend except by daylight, and which was then always commanded from the rear by German machine-guns. On the top the men had tried to scrape trenches out of the rock; the wind constantly swept the snow about, even when none was falling, and it was a heavy day's work simply to keep these shallow lines from being silted up. When we got back, I asked Dr. Flavell his impressions. He possessed a standard of comparison, for he had done a lot of winter war-work in the Vosges. He told me that his conclusions were three: first, that the officers absolutely shared the privations of the men, in which I can entirely bear him out; second, that human life in these conditions was impossible for more than a fortnight; a fortnight was exactly the time that each regiment stood in line, and then it only went into the reserve for a week; thirdly, he said that anyone wounded here in the head or the stomach was a lost man, for in these conditions it was practically impossible to get the heavily wounded to the rear. Our line was terribly thin — generally about one man to five yards, and sometimes with no second line behind it. The troops in this long thin line were spread out over great distances, and in many cases they were commanded by young officers barely trained, who had only lately come up to the army.[1]

It was not only on the Rumanian front that the conditions behind the lines were deplorable. Danilov, now Chief of Staff of the northern front, gives the same picture.[2] 'Life', he says, 'was almost completely paralysed in the army zone.' The troops had often only one or two days' reserve of food. Transport, under the ridiculous administration of the rear, had almost completely gone to pieces. And the food question, especially in the north, as foreseen by everyone, including Rasputin, was now becoming far the most serious of all.

[1] *My Russian Memoirs*, 408-9. [2] DANILOV, 526.

The depots in the capital and in the rear were crowded with innumerable young recruits who, through the insufficiency of the necessary armament, could only be very inadequately trained, and, therefore, having little to do, were an easy prize to defeatist or even revolutionary agitation. 'Idle mobs', writes Danilov, 'without guns or instructors, presented a vast field for agitation and secret propaganda.'[1] And he rightly insists that this propaganda was born in the rear. Owing to the neighbourhood of the northern front to Petrograd, its effects were much earlier felt there than farther south.

In the south there was still a splendid spirit; though one might have to own it was markedly stronger among the officers than among the men, the general testimony is conclusive. The army was very different from the regulated machine of the beginning of the war, but it had become in a sense one great family. The fact of living together in conditions of danger, with every encouragement of individual initiative and courage, of itself tended to this result, and it seemed as if this spirit of free co-operation between officers and men might be a real asset in the future. The very close co-operation of the Zemstvo Red Cross, now even reaching to the front line, was also an influence in the same direction. The evident deep depression of spirits among the enemy, as shown conclusively in the bearing of the prisoners taken, was a lively encouragement to the Russians; it has since been confirmed by the German military writers.[2] By now there were humorous exchanges between the two lines. The Germans put up a notice: 'Our William has gone to get some bread.' In a single day enemy detachments twice strayed across the interval to beg for food and were driven back. Even after the Revolution when the enemy set up a notice: 'The English have chased your Tsar from Petrograd,' there was posted up a reply: 'So much the worse for you.' Even in this remote part of the line it was now calculated that munitions on the Russian side were now on a level with that of the Austrians and not far behind that of the Germans.† Hindenburg, summing up his conjectures for the New Year, declares that whereas the Austrian Army was breaking, there was no real news of disintegration on the Russian side. 'We had to anticipate', he writes, 'that in the winter of 1916-17, as in previous years, Russia would succeed in making

[1] Danilov, 527. [2] Hoffmann, ii, 156-9.

good her losses and renewing the offensive powers of her armies.'[1] He declares[2] that he had 'ceased to believe' in the coming of revolution in Russia. Ludendorff observes[3] that 'Russia in particular had produced very strong new formations', and that 'its reorganization meant a great increase in strength' especially by the re-arrangement which gave 12 battalions to the division and 6 guns to each battery. He declares that 'there was no hope of a collapse of any of the Entente Powers'.[4] On December 12th the German command had been assured by the Chancellor that 'there was no hope of a separate peace with Russia'. Ludendorff notes the effects of the food shortage on the German morale.[5]

In July 1916, in reply to propaganda on the other side, a military branch for this purpose had been set up at the German Headquarters; but Ludendorff himself complains that the direct propaganda on the Russian front had produced but little effect.[6] I can add the same testimony: I was frequently invited to hear the examination of German prisoners; one of them would stand forward with an obviously prepared speech, for instance explaining that Germany was bound to win because she was much richer than her enemies, as she was not spending enormous sums in the purchase of munitions abroad; and the effects of this propaganda fell dead flat both among officers and men. At the Inter-Allied meeting of Staffs at Chantilly in November 1916, a decision had been taken for a simultaneous offensive on both Eastern and Western Fronts, and it was arranged that a Russian offensive should be planned for the early spring. This was well known on the Russian front, and never were there such confident anticipations of final victory in the war. The Emperor sent his cousin the Grand Duke George to distribute rewards in the south. This was perhaps the most level-headed of the not untalented Grand Dukes of the branch of Michael, and while writing to Nicholas a peculiarly outspoken letter on the demoralization of the rear and even emphasizing the bitter discontent of the army with the administration of Stürmer and the consequent general chaos, he insists, after visiting eighty-two different divisions, on the 'excellent impression' of the troops which he received, describes their condition as 'splendid', and adds 'it would be difficult to say which is the best

[1] HINDENBURG, 243. [2] ibid., 270. [3] LUDENDORFF, 305.
[4] ibid., 307. [5] ibid., 349. [6] ibid., 379-83.

corps'. He echoes the general feeling when he adds, 'I believe that the hour of victory may be much nearer' (Jan. 14th/27th, 1917).[1] Even on the actual eve of the Revolution, the experienced French General Castelnau, returning from a visit to the front, reported, 'the morale seems excellent'.[2]

This may be qualified by one pathetic prophecy. General Snezar, addressing his soldier Knights of St. George on the feast day of that Order (Dec. 9th) in the Carpathians, said to them: 'Somehow I have a feeling that, after it is all over, we are not going to be thanked for all the hardships and privations which we are going through, but rather that all this is going to be held against us.'†[3]

[1] *Lettres des Grands-Ducs*, Jan. 24th, 223-4.
[2] PALÉOLOGUE, III, 195.
[3] *My Russian Memoirs*, 406-7.

CHAPTER XIII

THE LAST CRISIS

And is't not to be damn'd
To let this canker of our nature come
In further evil?

Hamlet, v, 2

PROTOPOPOV

WE are witnessing two significant processes: the gradual conversion of all the members of the Duma to a corporate interest in its work; and the gradual isolation of the Tsar and his wife from their last friends. The most striking examples came from the Right. These were men who but for a crippled franchise would hardly have had a chance of being elected, and they were a considerable section of the House. Some of them had been regularly receiving subsidies from the police department. Others had moved over to Stolypin's new party of Nationalists or country Tories, who were patriotic and vigorously independent. Such was Shulgin, admirably equipped by a quick mind and a lively humour for getting the best out of a parliamentary education. More to the right of him, the two principal reactionary leaders, Markov and Purishkevich, had both been subsidized, and Markov still was; but Purishkevich, who had a sparkling intelligence and a fearless spirit, had been gradually emancipating himself and was now quite clear of all government or even party ties. As a Russian patriot, throwing himself with ardour into the war, he had created a very efficient organization for the soldiers' needs. 'Wonderful energy and a remarkable organizer' wrote the Emperor after a talk with him at the front (June 1st/14th). The measure of the national alienation from the Government is to be measured by his brilliant attacks on it in this period.

It was Purishkevich who, to describe the rapid succession of Cabinet appointments, coined the phrase 'the ministerial leapfrog'.

'THE MINISTERIAL LEAPFROG'

The surprise nomination of Protopopov as Minister of the Interior[1] drew from him the following clever verses:

THE STORMERS[2]

On the appointment of the respected
A. D. Protopopov

The 'Stormer' period still goes on;
  The pace it goes is simply mad;
Whatever else we lack, there's none
  Could count the Ministers we've had.

The order of our State is sage;
  It's founded on a solid plan:
Portfolios[3] are now the rage,
  And those who want to get them can.

They've just to make their bow, you see;
  No programme needed — that's all right:
Some talkative, like Bobrinsky,[4]
  And some that keep the mouth shut tight.

They come, they sniff the dainty spread,
  But never reach the feast, alack!
Then, cursing all in terms illbred,[5]
  They turn and leave the beaten track.

There's scarce a day but 'one in grey'[6]
  Drives up to the Fontanka's[7] side;
Again you hear the couriers say:
  'Here, take these things away to hide.'

With flashing folds of uniforms,
  With stars and crosses in a shower,
Demure officials come in swarms
  To hail the idols of the hour.

[1] At first as Acting Minister; confirmed later.
[2] A pun on Stürmer. [3] i.e. Ministerial posts.
[4] The very incapable Minister of Agriculture.
[5] Original: 'in Russian', which here has the same meaning.
[6] A vague and unknown figure in Leonid Andreyev's play *The Life of a Man.*
[7] A canal in St. Petersburg close to the Ministry of the Interior and the Department of Police.

But, well received, they grow more bold,
  And scratch their heads and whisper low;
'I don't suppose that *he* will hold;
  About a month — and out he'll go.'

A bird of passage! Look around —
  The gossip of the town is new;
You'll see your Minister uncrowned
  Within a month — or rarely two.

By minutes now we count their term;
  They go, and leave a sulphurous smell;
Only Rasputin still holds firm —
  And long-maned Pitirim as well.

Who was Protopopov? One might well ask this question as in the case of Stürmer, but with more curiosity and interest, for Stürmer was a nullity and Protopopov was not. He might be generally described as one of those busybodies who try to get a finger into every pie, or, as Milyukov has put it, 'the typical noble in debt who is always prepared to do anything that is wanted'.[1] Coming of the gentry of Simbirsk, the home both of Kerensky and of Lenin, where he had a very poor reputation, he did his military service, studied in the law school and became director of a large cloth factory inherited from his father, always taking a part in public affairs, especially those of commerce. He was a man whom it was very difficult to run down to a definite address at any time of the day. He had the over-done politeness of a tradesman. Suffering from ill health, which was later to develop into progressive paralysis, he sought the attentions of Rasputin, who put him through a prolonged 'cure'; he was also in touch with the strange professor of Tibetan medicine, Badmayev, who appears from time to time as one of those associates of Rasputin who had access to the Emperor. Protopopov served on different commercial committees, and sometimes made a very good chairman, smoothing away all difficulties. He was elected to the Duma, and was actually chosen as Vice-President; there he posed as a moderate Liberal (Left Octobrist) asking for an extension of parliamentary rights. Rodzyanko, who was a poor judge of men, took account of him; so also did Guchkov, who regarded him as a man who could get things done. In the Duma, as elsewhere,

[1] Milyukov to B. P.

Protopopov played for popularity, and was thus to be considered as a member of the Progressive Bloc, especially on that side of its work which related to the munitioning of the army. In June 1915, when I was collecting from my friends in the Duma information relating to the Russian shortages, it was Guchkov, the founder of the War Industry Committees, who entrusted me to the care of Protopopov. In the summer of 1916 the Duma was invited to send a deputation to England and France to strengthen the ties of the alliance, and Rodzyanko, who could not himself go, sent Protopopov to lead it. Milyukov, a member of the deputation, who knew England intimately, was his principal adviser throughout, and the conciliatory Protopopov was a quite adequate spokesman at those exaggerated demonstrations of friendship between the Allies, which were in fashion at that time. While the Deputation was in Paris, he surprised the Cadet Shingarev by coming into his bedroom at 1.0 a.m. to ask for his collaboration in a new great newspaper, non-Party but Liberal; he expected to have the help of Korolenko, Gorky, Amfiteatrov, the author of a famous skit on the imperial family, and Menshikov, the reactionary leader-writer of the *Novoe Vremya*. He was quite sanguine of enlisting Milyukov![1] On the way back I twice met Protopopov, who overwhelmed me with profuse expressions of affection for England and ardour for the Allies. The second of these occasions was at Christiania; and at Stockholm, his next stop on the way back, Protopopov sought an interview with one Warburg, a financier, who was in touch with the German Minister there, Lucius. He was strongly suspected of having discussed a separate peace, but when brought severely to task by Rodzyanko and the Duma, he declared that he took the opportunity to assure the Germans of the firmness of the Allies. Shortly afterwards he asked me to introduce him to Sir George Buchanan; he wished to found a newspaper, *The Will of Russia*, to champion the Allied cause.

Rodzyanko's suggestions of detail were sometimes extremely ill-judged and indiscreet. In his summer audience with the Emperor, when calling for the dismissal of Stürmer, he suggested as Premier, the able and honest Naval Minister, Grigorovich; but he followed this up by suggesting for the Ministry of Commerce Protopopov, no doubt regarding him as his own man. Protopopov

[1] SHINGAREV, *Padenie*, VII, 35.

obtained an audience to report on the visit to England. He followed the favourite line of Sukhomlinov; that is, he set himself to ingratiate, please and amuse, and Nicholas reported to his wife the favourable impression which Protopopov had left on him.[1] Meanwhile Protopopov was in reality not Rodzyanko's man, but Rasputin's; in fact Beletsky, who always knew so much about everyone else's affairs, states that Rasputin was far more intimate with him than either with the young Hvostov or with Stürmer. Hvostov was an unscrupulous man, who tried to make use of Rasputin; Stürmer was Rasputin's timorous puppet, always anxious to pretend his independence; Protopopov was a friend,[2] and it is significant that afterwards he made no such vigorous attempts as his predecessors to disclaim the connection. He had an unhealthy mind and was definitely fascinated by the then fashionable mysticism of which Rasputin was the outstanding exploiter. Protopopov was brought into touch with Stürmer, for whom he suddenly, and quite publicly, expressed an admiration. He was also made acquainted with the Empress, and Rasputin through her insisted vehemently on his appointment to the key post of Minister of the Interior. The idea of 'the ladies' half' (*zhenskaya polovina*)[3] of the palace was simply to have their own man, and to manage the empire as if it were their farm, without any regard for established formalities; the Empress even offered the post of Assistant Minister to Mosolov, head of the Emperor's civil chancery.[4]

Time after time, the Empress bombards her husband with appeals to appoint Protopopov. The little man jibs at first. He declares that these constant changes of Ministers are extremely upsetting to the public service, and he even expresses doubt as to the wisdom of Rasputin. The Empress writes again and again. On September 7th/20th: 'Gregory begs you earnestly to name Protopopov . . . he will know how to be with them . . .' — again we have the idea of using a Duma man to curb the Duma. 'He likes our Friend since at least four years.' On Sept. 9th/22nd

[1] Protopopov, replying to questions after the Revolution, naively compared his personal disposition to that of the Emperor, saying that they were both men who avoided plain utterance.

[2] MANUILOV, *Padenie*, 91. Also N. P. Sablin to B. P.

[3] An expression used by Rasputin, Illiodor and Manuilov. They also used the words 'the tsars' for the two sovereigns.

[4] In December, 1916; MOSOLOV, 119.

she writes: 'Please take Protopopov as Minister of the Interior. As he is one of the Duma, it will make a great effect and shut their mouths.' It is here that Nicholas kicks a little. 'Our Friend's opinions of people', he replies, 'are sometimes very strange, as you know yourself — therefore one must be careful (Sept. 9th/22nd). The Empress meanwhile returns to the charge; and the very next day (Sept. 10th/23rd) Nicholas telegraphs: 'It shall be done.' Vyrubova describes this appointment as one of the most momentary of all the Emperor's decisions.

Rodzyanko and the Duma were furious; and at the best, the appointment could only be regarded as a very bad joke. Rodzyanko records an interview in which he takes his former junior to task in the roughest way. Protopopov is servile, and declares that he has taken office in the hope of making valuable changes. He even hints at the appointment of Rodzyanko himself as Premier and Foreign Minister, though of course by now he is perfectly well aware that the Empress would die sooner than consent to anything of the kind. With the words: 'Here are my terms,' which he asks Protopopov to transmit, Rodzyanko declares that he must have the choice of all his colleagues, with a guaranteed term of tenure of three years, that the Empress should be sent to Livadia for the rest of the war, that no Grand Dukes should hold posts, that the inacceptable Polivanov should reside permanently at Headquarters, and that the Duma should be publicly told of all these arrangements. Protopopov, still conciliatory, suggests in reply that Rodzyanko should go to see the Empress![1]

Protopopov was a small man, and now his head was turned by the glory of his new post. His old friend and fellow member in the Duma, Vladimir Lvov, told him that his appointment was a scandal and he ought to resign; and Protopopov naively replied: 'How can you ask me to resign? All my life it was my dream to be a Vice-Governor, and here I am a Minister!'[2] Not a few of those who approached him thought him increasingly queer in the head.[3] He still courted the favours of the Duma, and had kept his large portrait of Guchkov, the pet bugbear of his sovereigns. He also had an icon to which he referred for advice on all decisions — so he told the unsympathetic Kerensky. 'That's He', he said, 'I do nothing

[1] Rodzyanko, 213-5. [2] Guchkov to B. P.
[3] Milyukov to B. P.; Maklakov to B. P.

without Him. He advises me on everything.'[1] He drew up marvellous schemes, not merely of a new order of government, but of a whole social system for Russia, expressed in a series of graphs or tables, such as take the fancy of Russian idealists when scheming the welfare of the world in general.[2] At one time during his short period of office he was seriously ill. To Rodzyanko and other critics of Protopopov's sanity the Emperor not unreasonably replied that 'they', that is the public, had made Protopopov Chairman of this or that commission and Vice-President of the Duma and head of the delegation to England, and had even recommended him as Assistant Minister;[3] but now that he was Minister, they declared that he was mad. The Empress was more permanently deceived. She went into raptures about Protopopov's honesty and goodness; but even she and Rasputin soon found that Protopopov, like Stürmer, was exceedingly timid in carrying out their orders. As Minister of the Interior, Protopopov was titular head of the gendarmes, and it was probably at their command that he donned the unusual uniform of this post, and in it took up his seat at the Duma; but the result was nothing but ridicule, of which Protopopov was helplessly conscious. On the testimony of the Director of his Police Department Vasilyev, he never got to know anything about his Ministry, and so difficult was it to see him that his subordinates were limited to written reports.[4] In spite of his planning on paper, he seems never to have had any effective proposal for the solution of any of the grave and critical problems which he was there to settle.

Protopopov tried to cover his ignorance by inviting to help him an old fellow student at the law college, who had served as Assistant Minister of the Interior. This was Kurlov, who according to official investigation at the time, ought to have been tried for criminal negligence in connection with the assassination of Stolypin. For this reason Protopopov did not dare to announce any formal appointment, but Kurlov all the same signed official documents as responsible. The Senate returned such documents as illegal, and in face of public scandal, Kurlov after a time was released from this work.[5]

Scandal was all the more important because the Duma, which

[1] Kerensky to B. P. [2] Pokrovsky, *Padenie*, v, 358. [3] Rodzyanko, 197. [4] Vasilyev, 155. [5] Kurlov, *Padenie*, iii, 205.

had been put off and put off, had definitely to meet on November 14th. The dominant question was the food problem, and this, too, as well as those of transport and fuel, the Empress had taken into her hands without any kind of understanding of them; she describes how her head goes round in long conversations while the details are explained to her. Bobrinsky, who had succeeded Naumov, talked a lot and did nothing but hinder the zemstva from taking the part they longed to take for the army and for the country. Rasputin, not without reason, considered that this responsibility should be transferred to the Minister of the Interior, who had the police to enforce his orders, and even the State Auditor, Pokrosvky, supported this idea when it came before the Cabinet.[1] The transfer was about to be made when Protopopov turned coward. He was wondering, no doubt, how he could face this burden in the coming explanations which were bound to be demanded in the Duma. However, his real master, Rasputin, was not to be denied; and the Empress, at his dictation, dispatched urgent messages to the Emperor to listen not to Protopopov but to Rasputin. She practically gave the order herself.[2] Nicholas himself had recognized that the food supply was 'the most damnable problem'.[3]

Any close examination of the materials will make it clear that it was only at this period, the autumn of 1916, that revolution began to be regarded as almost inevitable; but from now onward the question was whether it would come from above by way of a palace *coup d'état*, or from below.[4] The leaders of the Duma were still doing all they could to postpone it till after the war.

The Progressive Bloc, to use an expression of Shulgin's, was 'creaking'. Since the crisis of the summer of 1915, the small so-called Progressist party had demanded not merely a Ministry possessing the national confidence, but a Ministry directly responsible to the two chambers. Some of its members had joined hands with a rebellious left wing of the Cadets led by an ambitious man, Nekrasov. The same demand came from Labour, the Co-operatives, the war industry worker representatives and Zemgor. These were now calling for action of some kind — if not constitutional, by way of terrorism. The Bloc itself was quite opposed to

[1] POKROVSKY, *Padenie*, V, 355.
[2] A. F. to N., Oct. 30th/Nov. 12th.
[3] N. to A. F., Sept. 20th/Oct. 3rd.
[4] Kokovtsev to Paléologue, III, 134.

this; Milyukov never believed in conspiracy; but he was anxious to be more explicit in his denunciations of the Government than some of the members to the right of him, Octobrists or Nationalists. At a meeting of the Bloc the question was debated whether Milyukov, who would lead the attack in the Duma, was justified or not in using the word 'treason'.[1] It was really the worst word to choose; for the public suspicions as to the loyalty of the Emperor and Empress to Russia, though they were now expressed in the most extravagant form everywhere, were entirely without foundation.

Meanwhile the tide, elemental as it might be, was surging up from below, and at least some kind of direction had to be given to it. According to A. I. Konovalov, Moscow merchant and Progressist Member of the Duma, it was in October that living conditions became really alarming, and it was from this time that the revolutionary mood must be dated; Kerensky gives the same date.[2] Defeatist propaganda on a large scale began to pervade the factories and barracks of the rear, and backed by the colossal casualties of Brusilov's campaign, it was taking more and more effect. General Manikovsky, who was the principal director of the munitions campaign of the Defence Council, had an interview at Headquarters with the Emperor on this subject. The police reports of the time were fully alive to the danger. In a report for the Russian October (Oct. 14th to Nov 14th) we read:

> In the opinion of the spokesmen of the labour group of the Central War Industries Committee, the industrial proletariat of the capital is on the verge of despair and it believes that the smallest outbreak, due to any pretext, will lead to uncontrollable riots, with thousands and tens of thousands of victims. Indeed, the stage for such outbreaks is more than set: the economic position of the masses, in spite of the immense increase in wages, is distressing . . . Even if we assume that wages have increased 100 per cent, the cost of living in the meantime has risen by an average of 300 per cent. The impossibility of obtaining, even for cash, many foodstuffs and articles of prime necessity, the waste of time involved in spending hours waiting in line in front of stores, the increasing morbidity due to inadequate diet and anti-sanitary lodgings (cold and dampness as a result of lack of coal and firewood),

[1] SHULGIN, 81. [2] Konovalov to B. P.; Kerensky to B. P.

etc., all these conditions have created such a situation that the mass of industrial workers are quite ready to let themselves go to the wildest excesses of a hunger riot.

. . . The prohibition of all labour meetings, even those for the organization of co-operative stores and dining-rooms, the closing of trade unions, the prosecution of men taking an active part in the sick benefit funds, the suspension of labour newspapers, and so on, make the labouring masses, led by the more advanced and already revolutionary-minded elements, assume an openly hostile attitude towards the Government and protest with all the means at their disposal against the continuation of the war.

In the opinion of some of the more thoughtful Social Democrats, groups of responsible workers find it difficult to prevent the masses from bursting into demonstrations growing out of the lack of necessities and the rise in the cost of living. . . .

. . . The question of a lasting general strike has been frequently and repeatedly discussed in many factories and workshops; and if it has not met with unanimous support, it is only because the workers are in favour of putting forward their economic grievances, while the Social-Democrats advocate a purely political platform. Nevertheless the Social-Democrats are firmly convinced that a general strike is bound to come in the very near future. Many of them believe that it will concide with the prorogation of the Duma, which is expected to take place before long.

Revolutionary circles, then, have no doubts that a revolution will begin soon, that its unmistakable precursors are already here, and that the Government will prove incapable of fighting against the revolutionary masses, which are the more dangerous because they consist largely of soldiers or former soldiers.[1]

At the end of October an incident in Petrograd made the danger vividly evident. On October 29th, all the factories in the capital were on strike. Four hundred trains a day were required for army food and fodder,[2] and a conference of all the Quartermasters of the Front met to discuss this pressing need. Protopopov spent two hours with the Emperor. Two days later the police were called in to suppress the strike; and two regiments of the Petrograd

[1] Quoted by Florinsky, 175-7. [2] N. to A. F., Oct. 16th/29th.

garrison, which were summoned to their help, fired not on the strikers but on the police. Four regiments of Cossacks were called up, and drove the mutineers back to barracks; and on November 9th, 150 of them were shot; this was followed by another strike in the factories.[1]

At this point, more emphatically than at any other, the government of Russia was in the hands of Rasputin. 'A colossal figure,' says Beletsky; and again, 'Rasputin was at that time the axle on which revolved the destinies of Russia'.[2] To put them in the order in which they counted — he, the Empress and Protopopov were in constant conference, though not necessarily together, and their wishes were then communicated to the Emperor for confirmation. At times the Empress actually wrote out a list of all the decisions that were to be taken and asked for a simple telegram to confirm them.[3] They ranged in every direction. The City Prefect of Petrograd, Prince Obolensky, had watched the movements of Rasputin, and his wife was even more hostile to the favourite. The Empress sends her husband repeated complaints against Obolensky, calling for his dismissal. At one time Obolensky succumbs, and receiving Rasputin, actually shows him the many petitions which he had sent in to him, all tidily tied up in ribbon, to convince him of the deference which the City Prefect is showing him.[4] Rasputin even expresses himself as 'very content' with Obolensky, and this, too, is reported to the Emperor, whose consent suggests that he is surprised at Obolensky's self-humiliation.[5] The Prince is not only pardoned by Rasputin, but is even recommended by him as an Assistant Minister of the Interior; but apparently Obolensky again becomes unsatisfactory and is finally dismissed in favour of 'Rasputin's own man' Balk. It was Balk who was to be responsible for the failure of the city authorities to suppress the revolution when it came.

The chief invectives of the Empress at this time were directed against the honest Minister of Justice, Makarov. He had taken over from his honest predecessor, the elder Hvostov, the burden of receiving the entirely illegal demands of the Empress for the withdrawal of cases which might lead to any exposure of Rasputin.

[1] Paléologue, III, 67.
[2] Beletsky, *Padenie*, IV, 521.
[3] For instance, A. F. to N., Sept. 27th/Oct. 10th.
[4] A. F. to N., Sept. 28th/Oct. 11th.
[5] N. to A. F., Sept. 30th/Oct. 12th.

The principal scandal was that of Manuilov, whom the elder Hvostov had arrested for blackmail on two charges, both supported by the necessary evidence. In the course of the investigations Manuilov had a serious collapse, which apparently was not feigned, and the trial was, therefore, suspended. Manuilov was the most impudent scoundrel, and had given every reason to expect that he would defend himself without regard for any of his patrons, and for this reason the Empress demanded that the case should be withdrawn. Makarov gave a brave refusal. He was overridden by an imperial command, but eventually Manuilov was sent to prison.[1]

Another important arrest was that of the very wealthy banker, Rubinstein, regarded as one of the principal pro-Germans in the capital, and certainly the favourite financial supporter of Rasputin, whom he often visited at his receptions. Apparently all that Rubinstein had done was to transfer certain important financial interests to Sweden. No proof has been given of any treasonable activity; but his trial was sure to implicate Rasputin, and if there was no treason, according to Simanovich there had been any amount of profiteering. Rubinstein had also acted in a business capacity for the Empress, who very naturally had at one time or another tried to send some help to poor connections in Germany. Anyhow she was insistent that the Rubinstein case should also be stopped. In default of compliance by Makarov, Rubinstein was released by imperial order.

Lastly there was still the case of Sukhomlinov, for which the elder Hvostov had been driven from office. It was clear that there was a case for trial, and Makarov was as firm as Hvostov.[1] The Empress was not the kind of woman who could naturally have tolerated Madame Sukhomlinov, but the lady sought an interview on behalf of her husband, and the Empress, prompted by Rasputin, constantly insists that this case also shall be withdrawn.

Rasputin made his own proposals on the food question, such as that rations should be weighed in advance to prevent the long waiting in queues, which gave the best of opportunities to the propagandists of discontent — Rasputin's suggestions of this kind were communicated to the relevant Ministers. He also foresaw the

[1] MAKAROV, *Padenie*, II, 128.

difficulties which would follow from demobilization, and wanted the establishment of a big loan for this and other purposes. He even repeated the programme of the Cadets in the First Duma, asking for the appropriation of state and monastery lands for the demobilized,[1] and he anticipated the Communist Revolution by suggesting that the manors of the squires should be turned into schools.[2] He wanted a Tsar who would stand primarily for the peasantry, and would have liked him to receive frequent visits from representatives of this class. Most interesting of all is the definite action which he took on behalf of the Jews, a bold thing to do at a Court where Jew-baiting had always been popular. To the credit of Simanovich, he was always urging Rasputin to do something for his people, and there are several signs that this was attempted. Rasputin had always believed in tolerance for all religions and insisted to the Emperor that all his subjects, of whatever race, claimed the same care; 'the blood of the minorities is precious', he said.[3] We find the Empress interesting herself in kindly treatment of Jews, and Protopopov definitely made suggestions in this sense to the Cabinet. To the Jews Rasputin used to suggest that, as they had the power of the purse, they should simply buy up anyone on whom the decision depended.[4] On this subject he seems to have even welcomed the sympathies of the Lefts. He had already removed the unsatisfactory Volzhin, Procurator of the Holy Synod, who had insisted that he should not have to meet him, and replaced him by one Rayev, described by Simanovich, who helped to recommend him, as 'insignificant' and 'comic'.[5] He greatly desired to remove Makarov, and to Simanovich he insisted that they must have their 'own' Minister of Justice. His candidate, Dobrovolsky, was a man of doubtful financial integrity who owed a large sum to Simanovich.

Rasputin treated each of his political or personal operations on the mind of the sovereigns as a difficult physical effort. At such a moment he went through a regular procedure. He would go to the steam bath, and on his return consume bottle after bottle of Madeira. He would write on a piece of paper a note of the object which he aimed at, and would put this under his pillow (earlier,

[1] SIMANOVICH, 187. [2] ibid., 153. [3] ibid., 107. [4] ibid., 95. [5] ibid., 146.

before he learned to read and write from Madame Lokhtin, he used a notched stick for the purpose). The next morning he would rise entirely calm in mind, and would say: 'My will has prevailed.' Simanovich comments: 'His word had to come last.' His riotous 'evenings out' and his sexual excesses apparently lasted right up to the end. They were in the main now localized to the Villa Rodé, where such privacy as he wanted was assured to him, with his favourite company of the gipsies.

From time to time, warnings from all sides came in to the Emperor. Outsiders, not knowing that Protopopov was now the special confidant, concentrated their attention on Stürmer. At Headquarters he was repeatedly warned by Alexeyev, who was now lying ill there; when Nicholas visited him, he is said to have simply called out in his fever: 'Clear out Stürmer!'[1] He was warned by his field-chaplain Shavelsky; and Kaufmann of Turkestan, a former Minister of Education, who had a permanent post there, warned him and was dismissed for doing so.[2] The Flag-captain in attendance on him, Admiral Nilov, whom Nicholas had once saved from committing suicide, certainly did so, though it is not clear at what time. On November 5th Sir George Buchanan visited him there and spoke to him very clearly; he referred to Protopopov,[3] and the disorders in the capital, and warned him also against the dangers of repression. Nicholas listened to him with friendly attention for an hour and a half and particularly emphasized his determination to go through with the war.

On the 10th the Tsar went to Kiev and visited his mother, who had lived there for some time. She was always able to re-establish the atmosphere of intimacy, and warned him gravely against Stürmer. Gilliard, who was with him, records that the Tsar was much impressed.[4] On the 14th, after his return to Headquarters, he received a visit from his cousin Nicholas Mikhailovich, who had written out what he wanted to say, in case he could not get a chance of saying it in person. He had a long talk with the Emperor and handed him his letter. This Grand Duke had a reputation for Liberalism, and used sometimes to be smilingly described as 'Philippe Égalité'. He was a considerable

[1] Bazily to B. P. [2] ibid.
[3] BUCHANAN, II, 25-7. [4] GILLIARD, 133.

historical scholar, and President of the Imperial Historical Society, but he discounted the value of his influence by his reputation for inquisitiveness and gossip. The letter was a good one, and dealt boldly with the interventions of the Empress.

> You trust her [he wrote], that is quite natural. Still what she tells you is not the truth; she is only repeating what has been cleverly suggested to her. If you are not able to remove this influence from her, at least protect yourself from constant systematic manœuvres that people are attempting by the intermediary of the wife that you love . . . When the hour comes — and it is already near — from the height of the throne you could yourself give the Ministers responsibility to yourself and to the legislative institutions, and that simply, naturally, without pressure from outside, and in another way from the memorable act of Oct. 17th/30th, 1905. You are on the eve of an era of new troubles, on the eve of an era of *attentats*. Believe me, if I insist so much on your freeing yourself from the chains that have been formed, I do so . . . only in the hope of saving you and saving the throne of our dear country from the irreparable.

Nicholas did not read the letter but mentioning the conversation in his next letter to his wife, he sent it on to her. She was positively furious, and demanded in vain severe punishment.[1]

The brother of Nicholas Mikhailovich, George, after a visit to Brusilov during his tour in the south also wrote as follows from Berdichev on November 24th:

> The hatred for Stürmer is extreme . . . I can tell you, everyone asks for the dismissal of Stürmer and a responsible Ministry to protect you from the deceits of the Ministers. If I had heard that from the lefts and Liberals, I should have paid no attention to it, but it is those who are devoted to you and who with all their heart desire your happiness and that of Russia who have spoken like that to me. That is why I have decided to write to you. I own I did not expect to hear in the army what I have heard everywhere in the rear . . . I am sure the Lord will help you to meet the universal wish and avert the imminent storm which is coming from the interior of Russia.[2]

[1] *Lettres des Grands-Ducs*, appendix; A. F. to N., Nov. 4th/17th; N. to A. F., Nov. 4th /17th; A. F. to N., Nov. 10th/23rd.
[2] *Lettres des Grands-Ducs*, 218.

In his admirable record of this last period, *Days*, which is at once the fullest in colour and the truest in interpretation, Shulgin pauses in his lively narrative to picture an imaginary conversation between a chance husband and wife in higher Petrograd society on the Empress. In the mist of confusion and misunderstandings which surrounds them, they seem to see the situation exactly as it really is:

> She is very clever . . . she is far above all her surroundings . . . she has a contempt for — well, *just us* — in a word, Petersburg . . . she is sure the simple folk adore her . . . She and Rasputin? — no, that is impossible . . . anything you like, but not that. Her domination over her husband is itself an open revolt against the autocracy, and is terribly misleading for everyone else. What kind of autocracy is that? Even for the most devoted loyal hearts, for whom respect for the throne is a sixth sense, it is poison. It poisons the very instinct of monarchy. . . Just because of the weakness of one husband to one wife, the sovereign offends his people, and the people offend their sovereign. The scandal is too foul to discuss; he cannot clear it up, and you cannot ask him to. [They conclude] How awful to have an autocracy without an autocrat![1]

EMPRESS OR DUMA?

The inevitable session of the Duma, which could no longer be postponed, began on November 14th. The foreign ambassadors were present, and Stürmer had expressed the wish that they should leave when he did, presumably in order to avert an immediate demonstration against himself.[2] No sooner had he gone out in silence than the storm broke. It was Milyukov who led off for the Progressive Bloc. The War Minister, honest old Shuvayev, was reported to have replied to public criticism: 'I may be a fool, but I am not a traitor,' and Milyukov denounced one abuse of the Government after another, ending each time with the refrain: 'Is this folly, or treason?' As we know from members of the Bloc, it had wished to avoid the utterance of this last word, and Milyukov had found this way of introducing it. It was a

[1] SHULGIN, 90-101. [2] PALÉOLOGUE, III, 86-8.

tactical mistake, and more than that. There was no real evidence of 'treason' on the part of the Government, unless inefficiency was treason. It laid the emphasis exactly on that charge of public gossip against the Government which was farthest from the truth; but the word once uttered passed in manuscript all over the country — for the speech was deleted from the reports. Milyukov went farther and, taking advantage of the fact that the Vice-President, Varun-Sekret, was in the Chair and did not know German,[1] he quoted a passage from the *Neue Freie Presse* of Vienna which spoke plainly of the influence of *die junge Zarin* and the group surrounding her. Stürmer demanded the report of the speech, and Rodzyanko sent him the official one, from which the obnoxious words had been omitted. Stürmer then asked for the original stenographer's wording, and Rodzyanko would not supply it.[2] Stürmer proposed to the Cabinet that Milyukov should be arrested and put on trial. He obtained no support there, except from Protopopov.

On the 16th Basil Maklakov, who was a Right Wing Liberal, made one of his most eloquent speeches. He marked the progress of defeatism, poured ridicule on the 'small manœuvres by which Stürmer thought he could cover things up', and asked where was 'the Government of Great Russia in the Great War?'

> All this is no chance [he said] when we know that the confidence of the country overthrows a Minister and its hatred confirms him in office. No! That is no chance — it is the regime, that cursed old regime, which is obsolete but still lives on. The old regime and the interests of Russia have now parted company; and every Minister is faced with the dilemma: he has to choose whether he will serve Russia or serve the regime. [He quoted from Pushkin] 'Woe to that country where only the slave and the liar are close to the throne.'

The applause that followed in this respectable assembly came from every quarter of the House.[3]

Stürmer asked in vain for the dissolution of the Duma. He did not dare to go to it again, and on the 20th the monarchist Shulgin pointed in scorn at the empty Ministerial benches to illustrate the

[1] Milyukov to B. P. [2] RODZYANKO, 225-7.
[3] *Tribuna:* Vypusk, XI, Stenographic report, 126-35.

complete isolation of the Cabinet from the country.[1] Stürmer's colleagues did not relish this taunt. Most of them sincerely wished to work with the Duma and, in sign of this, they asked the War and Naval Ministers to go and show that they desired its co-operation and that of the country in the national defence. Plain old Shuvayev was no politician, and he went so far as to shake hands warmly with Milyukov, who had held him up to criticism a few days before.

The Empress very much resented this incident. She felt that every support except Protopopov was failing her. She blamed Stürmer for his lack of courage, and she wrote to her husband, quoting Rasputin and recommending that Stürmer had too much work and should be given a rest.[2] The Emperor was still at Headquarters, and was still under the influence of the grave warnings which he had received, especially from his mother. Stürmer went to try his luck there, but for once it seemed that even the Empress concurred in the general opinion. Nicholas acted boldly and gave him his dismissal (Nov. 22nd). Paléologue describes how he watched him later shuffling slowly across a snow-covered road in the capital, a broken old man.

The Emperor was still at Headquarters. The senior of the remaining Ministers was A. F. Trepov, Minister of Transport, at least conservative, patriotic and honest, and entirely opposed to the influence of Rasputin. To him was temporarily offered the post of Premier, and he accepted it, but he explained clearly that he could not be responsible for carrying the burden at this time without drastic changes in the personnel of the Cabinet. In consequence the incompetent and garrulous Bobrinsky, Minister of Agriculture, was replaced by the best permanent official whom they could have chosen, Rittich, who, under Krivoshein, had directed with conspicuous success the land settlement of Stolypin. As Stürmer had by his dismissal also been displaced from the Foreign Office, here too an excellent choice was made, though not at once, in Pokrovsky, trained in long service, under Kokovtsev and, like him, conspicuously upright and honest. Pokrovsky had already served nearly a year as State Controller, and in this post he was replaced by Feodosyev. It remained to deal with the Ministry of the Interior. The public and the Duma may still

[1] Shulgin, 86. [2] A. F. to N., Nov. 7th/20th.

have thought that Stürmer had been the leading man in the Cabinet, but Trepov as a member of it knew that the real trouble now lay with Protopopov, and he insisted on a change in that Ministry. The Emperor agreed, and on November 10th/23rd wrote as follows to his wife:

> When you receive this you will probably know already from St[ürmer] about the changes which it is imperative to bring about at once. I am sorry for Prot. — he is a good, honest man, but he jumps from one idea to another, and cannot make up his mind on anything. I noticed that from the beginning. They say that a few years ago he was not quite normal after a certain illness [when he had sought the advice of Rasputin]. It is risky to leave the Ministry of the Interior in such hands in these times.
> Old Bobrinsky will have to be replaced too . . . While these changes are in progress the Duma will be prorogued for about eight days, otherwise they would say that it was done under pressure from them. In any case Trepov will try to do what he can. In all probability he will return on Sunday bringing with him the list of persons whom we had discussed with him and St. Only, I beg, do not drag Our Friend into this. The responsibility is with me, and therefore I wish to be free in my choice.

All this time the Empress had been pressing the opposite view. In face of the speeches in the Duma she saw her whole position and that of Rasputin vitally threatened and, in the words of Simanovich, she became 'like a furious lioness defending her lair'.[1] On the 12th[2] she had written of Protopopov and Stürmer: 'They both believe in Our Friend's wonderful, God sent wisdom . . . Protopopov will have all in his hands and finish up all the Unions [Zemgor, etc.] and by that will save Russia.' Of the Duma, whom she describes as 'impertinent brutes', she writes: 'It is war with them and we must be firm,' and adds, 'Tell me you are not angry with me. They (Protopopov and Stürmer) bow before His wisdom.' 'All my trust', she writes on the 13th,[3] 'is in Our Friend, who only thinks of you, Baby and Russia, and guided by him we shall get through this heavy time. It will be a hard fight, but a Man of God is near to guard you safely through the reefs, and little Sunny is standing as a rock behind you, firm and unwavering,

[1] Simanovich, 167. [2] Oct. 30th, O.S. [3] Oct. 31st, O.S.

with decision, faith and love to fight for her darlings and our country.' 'Had we not got him', she wrote on Nov. 4th/17th, 'all would long have been finished', and on the 18th she demands that Rodzyanko's court rank should be taken from him. 'They must feel your power. It's time for the saving of your country and your child's throne . . . you are an anointed one.' On the 21st: 'Oh lovey mine, how I live with you all the time — soul burns — head tired — weary — but spirits up, to fight for you and Baby.' On the 23rd: 'If he (Trepov) does not trust me or Our Friend, things will be difficult.'

On hearing that Protopopov is to go she is in despair. On the 24th she writes, 'Don't go and change Protopopov now . . . Change Makarov, he is not for us . . . Don't change anyone until we meet, I entreat you . . . Quieten me, promise, forgive. It is for you and Baby I fight.' This she follows up next day: 'My head goes round in a ring . . . They feel I am your wall . . . It is more serious than you think . . . I am but a woman fighting for her Master and her Child . . . Only don't pull the sticks away on which I have found it possible to rest . . . Darling, remember that it does not lie in the men, Protopopov or XYZ, but it is a question of monarchy and your prestige now . . . They will drive off all friends and then ourselves . . . You were alone with us two (herself and Rasputin) against everybody . . . The Tsar rules and not the Duma . . . But I am fighting for your reign and Baby's future.' She is already expected at Headquarters, and as soon as she joins him, she wins again and Protopopov is saved.

On the 27th Trepov was at Headquarters and found the Empress there. He asked in vain to resign on the 28th and reported for an hour and three-quarters, but with no result. Trepov, now entirely helpless, was told to come to some kind of compromise with Rasputin. He could not have chosen a more tactless way. He commissioned his brother-in-law, Mosolov, who has given a full account of the incident,[1] to offer Rasputin a house and living expenses in Petrograd, a bodyguard, and £20,000 down as soon as Protopopov was dismissed. On his side he was to refrain from all further interference in government, but he would be left free to do what he liked with the clergy! He had given himself into Rasputin's hands. The favourite of course refused the offer and

[1] Mosolov, 170-3.

revealed it to his sovereigns; their enemies, he said, had tried to deprive them of his counsels, but had of course failed to shake his honesty and independence.

The Duma resumed its sittings on December 2nd. Trepov had to appear as the new Premier with a statement of his policy, and his trump card was the long deferred agreement of England and France to Russia's possession of Constantinople after the War. This fell entirely flat. There were even many conservative Russians who questioned how the great Turkish capital could be administered under Russian rule and regarded such a prospect as nothing but an immense complication; 'merely an unwelcome hindrance', writes Sazonov.[1] Besides it was impossible in this way to divert attention from the rot that had set in within. The Duma had no conception of what was happening behind the scenes. Trepov was even hissed, and made three unsuccessful attempts to secure a hearing. In the Cabinet his relations with the triumphant Protopopov were of course impossible. His colleagues took his side strongly, and vigorously opposed a proposal of Protopopov to make his own pronouncement in the Duma. He was told he could only do so as a private member. On December 8th they demanded that he should go to the Emperor and resign, which this obsequious man promised to do; but he readily accepted the sovereign's request to remain at his post.[2]

And now, with all the Ministers present, came the most stinging denunciation of all from Purishkevich, the most ardent monarchist in the Duma. He had dined with the Emperor at Headquarters on November 16th and compared the Government of Russia to that of 'caliphs of an hour' in Turkey. On December 1st he had separated himself from the group of the extreme Rights, the only fraction in the House which did not share in the general indignation. 'As before', he said, 'there burns in me an endless love for my country and an unbounded and deeply loyal love for my sovereign.' But he declared that this was a time when the tocsin must be rung from the belfry of Ivan the Great (the central tower of the Kremlin). Purishkevich went straight to the root of the whole matter — Rasputin, whom he regarded as the destroyer of the dynasty and compared to that adventurer of the seventeenth century, Grishka Otrepyev (another Gregory) who had climbed

[1] SAZONOV, 245. [2] PROTOPOPOV, *Padenie*, IV, 17.

on to the throne of the House of Rurik (1605-06). He held up to scorn the 'Ministerial leapfrog' and the 'dark forces' behind all these appointments. He pilloried Protopopov, Andronikov 'and others who make the infamy of Russian life'. Turning to the Ministers, he said, 'If you are truly loyal, if the glory of Russia, her mighty future, which is closely and inseparably bound up with the brightness of the name of the Tsar, is dear to you, be off to Headquarters, throw yourself at the feet of the Tsar and beg his leave to open his eyes to the awful reality'.[1] In the crowded audience sat an intent listener, the young Prince Felix Yusupov, who had already formed the design of assassinating Rasputin.

Nicholas was at Tsarskoe from December 8th to 17th, and wrote at parting: 'I am now completely calm, only thanks to you. I admire you more than I can say. Forgive me if I was moody or unrestrained . . . Henceforth I intend to become sharp and bitter', which he must have known was outside his character, and even his ability. The Empress writes on the same day of her deepest 'faith' in their Friend, and 'the great and beautiful times coming for your reign and Russia . . . Let them (the critics) pass by as something unclean. Now comes your reign of will and power'. On Dec. 5th/18th: 'I shall stand against them (Trepov and Rodzyanko) with God's holy man . . . He has kept you where you are . . . My spirit is firm and lives for you, you and you — my heart and soul . . . Always with you, sharing all — the good is coming, the turn has begun.' On Dec. 13th/26th, having evidently learned of Trepov's offer to Rasputin, she writes a furious letter against him: 'Horrible . . . not decent . . . only believe more in Our Friend . . . and we must give a strong country to Baby, and dare not be weak for his sake . . . draw the reins in tightly which you let loose . . . I am your wall behind you . . . take no big steps without warning me . . . Only not a responsible Cabinet which all are mad about . . . Russia loves to feel the whip . . . How I wish I could pour my will into your veins . . . I have had no sleep, but listen to me, which means Our Friend. I suffer over you as over a tender, soft-hearted child. Pardon, believe and understand.' On Dec. 14th/27th, she writes the last of her tremendous letters: 'Be the Emperor, be Peter the Great, John the Terrible, the

[1] PURISHKEVICH, *Diary*, 6.

Emperor Paul — crush them all under you — Now don't you laugh, naughty one . . . Send Lvov to Siberia . . . Milyukov, Guchkov, and Polivanov also to Siberia. It is *war*, and at such a time *interior* war is *high treason* . . .' She calls herself by the name which Rasputin has given her. 'Russia's mother, blessed by Our Friend'. 'We have been placed by God on the throne, and we must keep it firm and give it over to our son untouched. I kiss you, caress you, love you, long for you, can't sleep without you, bless you.'

Nicholas writes on Dec. 16th/27th, 'Tender thanks for the severe written scolding . . . Your poor little weak-willed hubby', and she replies: 'Forgive me for my impertinent letters.'

MURDER OF RASPUTIN

After the denunciations in the Duma Rasputin was thoroughly alarmed for his personal safety, and indeed even avoided going out as much as possible. On one occasion, it is said, he returned saying he had been walking by the Neva and the river was full of the blood of Grand Dukes; if true, this is an extraordinary anticipation which no one would have shared at the time. It will be remembered that a number of attempts had been made to kill him. The first known was that of the Prefect of Yalta, Dumbadze, to attack him when on a steamboat in the Black Sea.[1] Then there was that of Guseva at the outset of the War, which, possibly without justice, had been ascribed to the machinations of Illiodor. There was the accident to his carriage when returning from the Islands which was certainly the work of men who had come from Tsaritsyn, Illiodor's fortress. There were the machinations of the younger Hvostov of which a full account has been given. He now expected another attempt, but least of all from the side from which it was to come. There is an extraordinary letter which Simanovich has attributed to him, written at this time.[2] It is headed 'The Spirit of Gregory Efimovich Rasputin-Novykh of the village of Pokrovskoe'.

[1] Beletsky, *Padenie*, IV, 150.

[2] I acquainted myself with Simanovich and have seen a facsimile of the letter. I cannot vouch for anything further.

> I write and leave behind me this letter at St. Petersburg. I feel that I shall leave life before January 1 [of course, Old Style]. I wish to make known to the Russian people, to Papa, to the Russian Mother and to the Children, to the land of Russia, what they must understand. If I am killed by common assassins, and especially by my brothers the Russian peasants, you, Tsar of Russia, have nothing to fear, remain on your throne and govern, and you, Russian Tsar, will have nothing to fear for your children [obviously an allusion to the health of the boy], they will reign for hundreds of years in Russia. But if I am murdered by boyars, nobles and if they shed my blood, their hands will remain soiled with my blood, for twenty-five years they will not wash their hands from my blood. They will leave Russia. Brothers will kill brothers, and they will kill each other and hate each other, and for twenty-five years there will be no nobles in the country. Tsar of the land of Russia, if you hear the sound of the bell which will tell you that Gregory has been killed, you must know this: if it was your relations who have wrought my death then no one of your family, that is to say none of your children or relations, will remain alive for more than two years. They will be killed by the Russian people. I go and I feel in me the divine command to tell the Russian Tsar how he must live if I have disappeared. You must reflect and act prudently. Think of your safety and tell your relations that I have paid for them with my blood. I shall be killed. I am no longer among the living. Pray, pray, be strong, think of your blessed family. Gregory.[1]

Simanovich declares that this letter was later conveyed by him to the Empress with an entreaty not to show it to the Tsar. He also claims that the letter and many other notes of Rasputin's were later returned to him by the Empress, and I have seen in his possession her prayer book with her favourite sign of the swastika, which she appears to have had with her at the time of her own death.[2]

Often in the society news, recurred the name of Prince Felix Yusupov. His family on the mother's side was originally of Tartar origin. It is said to spring from a Nogay prince of the time of Tamberlane and from Yusup-Murza, who died in 1556; their descendants became Christian in the last years of Tsar Alexis.

[1] SIMANOVICH, 256. [2] This Simanovich showed to me in Paris in 1934.

One of them was a court official under Peter I.[1] By a series of marriages in successive generations, the male ancestors had risen to the present title; and young Felix, just before the War, having returned from Oxford, had married the niece of Nicholas II, Irina. This was one of the richest families in Russia; and Yusupov's mother had at one time been intimate with the Empress, but like others had expressed her antipathy for Rasputin. Felix Yusupov was now in the Corps of Pages, a training college for higher official posts in the army and elsewhere. He tells us that he had contemplated the murder of Rasputin from 1915.[2]

Yusupov was on friendly terms with the Golovin family, related to Princess Paley and connected with Vyrubova, who were devoted adepts of Rasputin, especially with the daughter Munya, a young girl of great piety. By her he was brought into close touch with the 'starets'. He meant first to try to induce Rasputin to give up his sinister influence, and, if not, to assassinate him; but Munya Golovina was of course kept entirely in the dark. Besides the more obvious motives for the murder, Yusupov mentions two others. He believed that the Tsar was systematically drugged by Rasputin, and for this there is no evidence. He also believed, like so many others at the time, that Rasputin was in touch with German agents, and he even gives a mysterious picture of strange persons with Teutonic faces, seen by him through an open door at Rasputin's flat, and records mysterious talks of the starets about the 'Greens' and the 'Greenishes', of whom the former were described by Rasputin as living in Sweden.[3] There is of course, no doubt whatever that Rasputin wanted to end the war. It is possible that he was actually in touch with German agents. What is in no way likely, is that he was himself a paid agent of Germany.

Yusupov's plan, as he has described it in his book, was to seek closer acquaintance with Rasputin, win his confidence and investigate his activities and methods;[4] and he went so far as to ask Rasputin to cure him of a slight malady from which he suffered. He gives a graphic picture of the 'cure', especially in his description of the workings of Rasputin's very unusual eyes, which sank to pinpoints or mingled in a circle.[5] He also gives

[1] PURISHKEVICH, 14. [2] YUSUPOV, 59. [3] ibid., 112.
[4] ibid., 80, etc. [5] ibid., 114.

specimens of Rasputin's utterances: 'The Empress is a very wise ruler . . . but as for him, well, he is a child of God.' 'She is a second Catherine.' 'He is no Tsar Emperor, he is just a child of God.' 'He won't budge, and even she is obstinate' (evidently on the question of peace). He suggests that the Tsar should be replaced by his son, with the Empress as regent; Nicholas should be sent down to his favourite Livadia and engage in his favourite pastime, gardening. Then there would be a general clear out — 'of the chatterboxes first of all — with the people it is different'. He also speaks of emancipating the Jews.[1]

Yusupov finds that Rasputin is not to be persuaded to give up his privileged position, and being now resolved on the murder, decides to seek help. First he approaches the Liberal Basil Maklakov. Both Yusupov and Maklakov have described these interviews, the latter in order to correct mis-statements;[2] his version is more likely to be accurate. Yusupov declares that the centre of the mischief is Rasputin, and here he is certainly right. Maklakov, who has no contact with the palace, wrongly regards him only as a symptom; he has never mentioned his name in any of his speeches. Yusupov gives instances of Rasputin's absolute power over Nicholas, and suggests that he must either be bought or killed. Maklakov replies: 'We go other ways', and points out that Rasputin, even if bribed, would in any case be a very untrustworthy ally; besides, he might easily be replaced by another Rasputin. Yusupov thinks with good reason that if Rasputin is killed, there cannot appear another man like him. In a fortnight he thinks the Empress will be in a mental home, as her balance entirely depends on him, and Nicholas will become a good constitutional sovereign. Maklakov, who here shows better insight, warns the Prince against the vengeance of the Empress. Yusupov says he is not thinking of killing Rasputin himself, as he almost belongs to the imperial family, and that would be almost revolution. He suggests that the revolutionaries should do it. Maklakov replies, 'He is their best ally'. Yusupov suggests hiring someone, and Maklakov interjects, 'Why, do you think I keep an office for assassins?' Yusupov is about to go. Maklakov warns him to avoid

[1] Yusupov, 118-25.

[2] 'Certain supplements to the accounts of Prince Yusupov and Purishkevich on the murder of Rasputin.' *Sovremennye Zapiski*, 1928, *No.* 34

anyone who is ready to kill on hire. 'It will pay him better to give you away; but if you think of doing it yourself, come to me and I might warn you against unnecessary mistakes.' Maklakov regarded the whole conversation as mere talk, such as was common enough in the capital at that time.

Directly after Purishkevich's speech of December 2nd in the Duma, Yusupov sought a meeting with him, and here he met with a very different reception. Purishkevich at once explained that the murder of Rasputin had long been his own dream.[1] The two proceeded without delay to plan the murder. There is another ally, the Emperor's favourite cousin the Grand Duke Dmitry Pavlovich, now twenty-six years old and a cornet in the horse bodyguard. On his father's second morganatic marriage he had been entrusted to the care of the Grand Duke Sergius and regarded the imperial palace as a second home, addressing the Tsar in his letters as 'uncle'. Knowing that none of their daughters wanted to marry out of Russia, the imperial couple had even apparently at one time regarded him as a possible husband for the eldest of them, Olga, and the Empress's letters contain frequent allusions to her interest in him and her cares for the training of his character, at times regarding him as one who is rather drifting away from them. Dmitry Pavlovich receives Yusupov's suggestion with alacrity, and his alliance is welcomed as indicating that the murder will not be a demonstration against the dynasty.

Two others are brought into the plot, a young officer, Sukhotin, who figured in Petrograd society, and a doctor, Lazavert, recommended by Purishkevich on the ground that his services would be useful. Purishkevich, who is described later by Rasputin's daughter as 'the soul of the plot',[2] had an ambulance train which made frequent journeys between the capital and the front. Of this it was decided to make use. On December 4th the conspirators met at 10 p.m. and on the 7th they discussed the details further in Purishkevich's train. On the 10th Purishkevich was shown over the cellar of the magnificent house of the Yusupovs. Yusupov is to go alone to bring Rasputin, driven by Lazavert. The rest will be collected upstairs; and when Rasputin has been

[1] RODZYANKO, 21. Rodzyanko has confirmed this; he writes that Purishkevich had told him so even before the War.

[2] MARIE RASPUTIN, 125.

killed, Sukhotin will don his fur coat and making a bundle of his other clothes drive to Purishkevich's train and burn them there.[1] The closed car of Dmitry is to be brought to Yusupov's house and Rasputin is to be taken thence to a spot on the river, finally fixed as a place in the island suburbs on that branch known as the Little Nevka. There, attached to weights which are to be provided by Purishkevich, it is to be dropped into the river.[2]

It had been agreed between the conspirators that all were later to deny any knowledge of the affair and never to make any statements about it,[3] but the two principal leaders both showed their disregard for this. Maklakov describes how — apparently on December 11th — Purishkevich approached him in the great lobby of the Duma, which was thronged, and to his astonishment began telling him that the murder had been planned. Maklakov drew him aside under the bust of Alexander II, and Purishkevich gave him all details and the date. 'Why do you tell me all this?' asked Maklakov. Purishkevich dismissed the idea of secrecy as superfluous, and asked if Maklakov would again receive Yusupov. Maklakov did so, though he still doubted of success. He suggested that if the corpse were concealed, it might be thought that Rasputin was still alive; but Yusupov assured him — as it proved correctly — that no very energetic investigation would be made. To mislead investigators, Maklakov suggested that the conspirators might telephone a message to Rasputin's favourite place of entertainment, the Villa Rodé, asking if he had not arrived there. He was also willing to give any legal help after the event, and for this reason was to be notified by telegram in Moscow when the murder had taken place. Yusupov, when leaving him, asked for a steel press with a bent handle which he saw on Maklakov's desk.

To his intense surprise, shortly afterwards, Maklakov was approached by one of the Duma journalists, a lady named Becker, who gave him correctly the full details of the plot, as derived direct from Purishkevich in the journalists' room there. This excitable little man, with the words, 'I am in the plot myself' had named the various conspirators and given the date. Maklakov now felt free to mention the matter to Kerensky, like himself a barrister, who was very indignant and observed, 'Don't you understand that this

[1] PURISHKEVICH, 22. [2] ibid., 23. [3] YUSUPOV, 136.

murder will strengthen the monarchy?' — which was indeed to be its immediate effect.

On December 20th an extra session was held of the United Nobility, the most conservative body in Russia, who protested against 'the dark forces behind the throne' and discussed a proposed address to the Emperor. In the Duma the Empress was spoken of as 'disposing of Russia as if it was her boudoir'. In the army the soldiers were talking freely of an imaginary illicit connection between her and Rasputin.

For the last month, as Vyrubova has recorded, Rasputin was constantly thinking of death. At his last meeting with the Emperor, instead of giving the usual blessing, he said, 'To-day you bless me!' He was certain that his death would be followed by great misfortunes.[1] Meanwhile, Simanovich was on the watch. He had set up a large gambling club which had become very fashionable, and through its attendants he was able to get some information. He was told that Purishkevich, while being treated by a doctor, had blabbed in the same way that he had done in the Duma.[2]

Yusupov had issued an invitation to Rasputin to come and visit him at his house. His wife had never met the prophet; Rasputin was anxious to meet her, and Yusupov used this prospect as the lure which was to bring him to his death.[3] She was at this time in Crimea, which was well known to the Empress. Rasputin accepted the invitation. He regarded Yusupov, for whom his nickname was 'the Little One', with no great concern.[4] Simanovich tried to dissuade him from the visit. Two days before, Rasputin was in a state of great apprehension and indulged himself as usual by a night out. But the following day he was entirely calm and to Simanovich's warnings he made it clear that he relied entirely on his will power. On the evening of the 29th he received a visit from Vyrubova, who, at the Empress's desire, came to bring him an icon brought back by her from her recent visit to Novgorod and begged him not to go to Yusupov. He said to her somewhat mysteriously, 'All that you still needed from me, you have received already'.[5] Protopopov also paid an evening visit, and found that the usual triple guard at Rasputin's flat had been

[1] Vyrubova, 91. [2] Simanovich, 238.
[3] Yusupov, 142, 158; Purishkevich, 31-2.
[4] Simanovich, 241-4. [5] Vyrubova, 72.

dismissed by Rasputin himself. Protopopov exacted a promise from him that he would not go to Yusupov's; but later to Simanovich Rasputin declared: 'I am master of my own word,' a view which he claimed to have expressed more than once to the Tsar.

The cellar of the Yusupovs' house had been carefully furnished for the occasion. It contained among other things a bearskin and a beautiful labyrinth cupboard full of mirrors and little columns of crystal and silver surmounted by a seventeenth-century crucifix.[1] The conspirators were established in a room above with a gramophone which was playing 'Yankee-Doodle'.[2] In the cellar were prepared some remains of a tea party, with chocolate and almond cakes, of which some had been carefully poisoned with cyanide of potassium by Dr. Lazavert. There was wine, too, some glasses of which were also poisoned.[3]

At midnight Yusupov went alone to Rasputin's flat. The 'starets' was waiting for him, smelling of cheap soap and dressed in a white silk blouse and black velvet trousers. At every point in his narrative Yusupov indicates that he was himself almost trembling with nerves. He brings his guest to the cellar and there sits alone with him.[4] Rasputin took an especial interest in the labyrinth cupboard, which charmed his peasant mind. At first he was not willing to take any tea or wine, but later asked for tea, and Yusupov gave him some biscuits, which were unpoisoned. The cakes Rasputin at first refused, but eventually he took two. Later he asked for Madeira, and Yusupov, letting fall an unpoisoned glass, which was in his hand, substituted one of the poisoned glasses. Rasputin now drank freely of the poisoned wine. It took no effect, but Rasputin regarded him for a moment with a look of hatred. 'My head reeled,' writes Yusupov.[5] Rasputin now drank some tea, and knowing that Felix was an adept with the guitar, he asked him for a song. He sat listening with drooping head and called for one after another, but though the murderer sang on, the murdered man did not collapse.

Meanwhile the rest of the party sat on upstairs, anxiously waiting for something to happen and listening to the interminable 'Yankee-Doodle'. According to Purishkevich, Yusupov came up

[1] YUSUPOV, 146. [2] PURISHKEVICH, 69.
[3] YUSUPOV, 149; PURISHKEVICH, 65.
[4] YUSUPOV, 159. [5] ibid., 163.

three times in all, first to say that Rasputin would not eat or drink, next to report that he had both eaten and drunk without visible result, and last in despair to discuss what else should be done. Yusupov records only one visit at 2.30 a.m. Dr. Lazovert's nerves had altogether failed him; and going out into the fresh air, he had for a moment fallen in a faint in the snow. Dmitry Pavlovich suggested calling it all off. It was Purishkevich who strongly opposed this, and after the three chief conspirators had each volunteered to finish off the business, Yusupov, who alone could go down without enlightening Rasputin, returned to him, carrying behind his back Dmitry Pavlovich's revolver.[1] Rasputin was sitting at the table, with drooping head and breathing heavily. He drank some more Madeira and, reviving, even suggested a visit to the gipsies. 'With God in thought', he said, 'but with mankind in the flesh.' Yusupov rose and went over to the crystal crucifix. Rasputin followed him, and gazed with fascination at the labyrinth cupboard. Yusupov asked him to look at the crucifix and say a prayer before it. The reason which he later gave to Maklakov, was that Rasputin would then have to cross himself, and this would for the time subdue the devil in him; for Yusupov was throughout in terrible fear of his victim's supernatural power. Maklakov makes the amusing comment: 'A "common front" of cyanide of potassium with the miraculous power of crossing — of murder with a call for the blessing of God.' As Rasputin stood still looking at the crucifix, Yusupov shot near the heart, and with a roar Rasputin fell backwards on the bearskin rug.[2]

Yusupov's friends now dashed down into the cellar, which one of them reduced for a moment to darkness by rubbing against the switch. The body was examined and declared to be dead. 'We all felt elated,' writes Yusupov.[3] Sukhotin, dressed in Rasputin's fur coat, was now dispatched in the car with Dmitry to Purishkevich's train, and from thence a cab was taken to the Sergius Palace, where Dmitry lived. Meanwhile Yusupov and Purishkevich remained talking in the upper room. Deciding to have another look at the corpse, Yusupov went down to the cellar. He even shook the body, which fell back limply. But he noticed that there was still a twitching of the eye and face, and then, as he looked at it, to his speechless horror, Rasputin rose from the

[1] PURISHKEVICH, 69, 74. [2] YUSUPOV, 167-8. [3] ibid., 171.

ground, seized him, tore an epaulette from his shoulder and fell again. Yusupov no longer had the Grand Duke's revolver. In sheer fright he rushed upstairs. 'In an instant', he writes, 'I found myself in my study.'[1] But even here he is not safe. A noise is heard on the stairs. It is Rasputin. He comes clambering up the stairs on all fours, pushes heavily against an outside door which, though locked, bursts open and runs quickly across the snow-clad courtyard roaring with fury. Purishkevich dashes out into the courtyard and fires twice. He misses and bites his hand in vexation. Two more shots, and Rasputin falls in the snow. Purishkevich stands over him and kicks him on the head.'[2]

The conspirators had wished at all costs to avoid the noise of shooting; that is why, like Alexis Hvostov, they had preferred poison; but Purishkevich was not the man to think of that. Four shots in the open air were very audible. He dashed through the house to the front door where two soldiers were on guard and said to them, 'I have killed Grishka Rasputin, the enemy of Russia and the Tsar'. They promised silence; the excited Purishkevich embraced both of them and they helped him to drag the body to the house. Yusupov was violently sick, but when with Purishkevich's support he approached the body, he threw himself on it and battered it with the steel press of Maklakov. Rasputin still showed some signs of life, and one eye was still open. Yusupov went on hammering his head till at a word from Purishkevich the soldiers dragged him away.[3]

A policeman was on duty outside and had called to ask the soldiers about the shooting. Purishkevich sent them to summon him, told them they had killed Rasputin, and dismissed him. The other conspirators now returned with Dmitry Pavlovich's car. Yusupov, half unconscious, was handed over to the care of one of his servants. The two soldiers had wrapped up the body in a blue blind or curtain fastened with a rope, and with it they drove to the islands; Purishkevich has declared that it was still warm. Rasputin's fur coat and snowboots had not been destroyed as intended, and were in the car. The agreed telephone message to the Ville Rodé, to ask if Rasputin was there, had been duly sent.

At the appointed spot, on the other side of the bridge, there was

[1] YUSUPOV, 175. [2] PURISHKEVICH, 80-1.
[3] PURISHKEVICH, 81-5; YUSUPOV, 179-81.

a sentry box, which apparently they had not noticed on their first investigation. Fortunately for them, the sentry was asleep; but this they did not know. The car was stopped, the lights put out and the engine turned off; and in a great hurry, Rasputin's body was bundled over from the bridge into the river. They had entirely forgotten to attach the weights, which they threw after it, also the fur coat with chains attached, and one of Rasputin's snowboots — the other by mistake they left in the car. Thoroughly unnerved, they returned to the Sergius Palace, and discovering the second snowboot, they burnt it together with the curtain in which Rasputin's body had been wrapped. There were still stains of blood on the floor of the car.[1]

The steps which the conspirators took afterwards were equally inconsequent. As blood had been shed, Yusupov called in the house servants to clean up the mess. On the other hand, though Purishkevich had officiously announced himself to the police as a member of the Duma, and declared that they had killed Rasputin, their answer on further investigation was that they had shot a dog; in fact they even shot a dog for that purpose.[2] They had agreed that nothing was to be said on the subject; but after a talk with Munya Golovin, who of course was told nothing about it, Yusupov rang up the Empress to ask to see her; and when she would not do so and requested him to write, his letter was an assertion that he had had nothing to do with the matter.[3]

The Empress knew that Princess Irina was in Crimea, and when she learned of the invitation from Vyrubova, had been very suspicious. To the Emperor she wrote at once of a big scandal at Yusupov's house in which Purishkevich ran out screaming to the police that 'Our Friend' was killed. She asked Protopopov to stop Yusupov from his proposed journey to Crimea. 'Felix', she writes, 'pretends that he never came to the house and never asked him . . . I still trust in God's mercy that one has only driven him off somewhere . . . Shall keep her (Vyrubova) to live here, as now they will get at her next. I cannot believe that he has been killed. Such utter anguish (am calm and can't believe it) . . . Come quickly.'[4]

In the meantime she asked Maximovich, a high police officer,

[1] PURISHKEVICH, 90-1. [2] YUSUPOV, 183-8. [3] ibid., 190-3.
[4] A. F. to N., Dec. 17th/30th.

to confine Yusupov and Dmitry to house arrest. Such an order, as concerning members of the imperial family, could only be given by the Emperor himself and it infuriated the rest of the Grand Dukes. They had already held a kind of family council a little earlier to persuade the Emperor to grant some kind of a constitution in time,[1] and they were now acting in concert. Several of them, in particular Nicholas Mikhailovich, paid visits to the arrested. The Minister of Justice was still the threatened Makarov, and directly after the murder, the conspirators had telephoned and asked to call on him. As two of them were connected with the imperial family, he had given no direct order: Purishkevich, who demonstratively put himself in the forefront in order to challenge arrest, could hardly be treated separately, and he was left free to depart for the front. Under urgent exhortations from the Empress, the police were making every effort to find the body of Rasputin; but Yusupov had rightly forecast the difficulties of the situation, and they made no real effort to press home the guilt of the murderers. On January 1st the body was traced by the son of Simanovich, who noticed a snowboot lying on the ice, and was recovered from the river by divers.[2] One hand of Rasputin had freed itself from its bonds and was bent in the sign of the cross. There were at least two wounds — one in the back and one in the neck — which must have proved mortal. It was taken to the Chesmé Chapel between Petrograd and Tsarskoe Selo, where the Empress and Vyrubova knelt in prayer beside it. A post-mortem was arranged but was stopped by the Empress, who removed the body. It has been stated, however, that the lungs were full of water, which would indicate that Rasputin was still alive when he was thrown into the river.[3]

Nicholas, when he received the Empress's message, was at that very time presiding over a most important military council at Headquarters. He well knew what must be his wife's state of mind and left it to go back to Petrograd; the council, summoned from all the Fronts, could take no steps without him; and Gurko, who had temporarily replaced Alexeyev, was himself only a deputy Chief of Staff. No one should have failed to foresee what would be the Tsar's attitude to the murder. The Grand Dukes asked in a joint letter for the pardon of Dmitry Pavlovich; and he

[1] PALEY, 13. [2] SIMANOVICH, 249. [3] Protopopov to Beletsky, *Padenie*, IV, 503.

replied: 'It is given to nobody to occupy himself with murder.'[1] Yusupov was sent to his country estate and Dmitry Pavlovich exiled to the Russian forces operating in Persia; the sentence was to save his life, as he did not come in for the sequel of the Revolution. The Empress's sister, the Grand Duchess Elizabeth, sent him a sympathetic message that she was praying for him. The breach between the imperial couple and the rest of their family 'could not have been more complete'.[2]

Rasputin was buried in a fog in the palace park on January 3rd, with the imperial family as mourners. There was an intention to set up a church on the spot. After the Revolution the coffin was dug up and the body taken out of it and consumed on a bonfire, so that, as was said, it suffered all the extremities of water, earth, fire and air. An icon signed by Nicholas, Alexandra and their children had been buried with him. It went through various vicissitudes and reached the hands of Kerensky.[3] Everyone in society who had had anything to do with Rasputin was now anxious to deny or minimize it. He left a peasant wife, a son who was not quite right in his mind, and two daughters. The Empress went out of her way to be kind to the two girls, inviting them to the palace twice a week;[4] and Simanovich, at considerable personal expense, saw to their quarters and their needs, and continued after the Revolution to care and provide for the family.

Yusupov had naively imagined that the deed would be the signal for a vigorous public movement to save the monarchy, but the result in no way corresponded to his expectations. As to the peasants, a common view was that expressed to Maklakov just afterwards by a soldier: 'Yes, only one muzhik has got through to the Tsar, and him the masters killed.' The view of society may be summed up in a remark of Sazonov to Paléologue: 'According to all our precedents the era of *attentats* is opened'; the act was indeed to be followed later by terrorism on the vastest scale. The criminals' names were known everywhere, but it was evident that the Government did not dare to prosecute them; the silence imposed on the Press only emphasized this conclusion.

Simanovich claims that the Emperor sent for him and asked to learn the last political wishes of Rasputin. This might be true;

[1] MISS BUCHANAN: *The Dissolution of an Empire*, 150.
[2] MOSOLOV, 73. [3] Kerensky to B. P. [4] MARIE RASPUTIN, 157.

for it is clear that in the period that followed the policy — rather of the Empress than of the Emperor — was to follow out in detail every idea that Rasputin had indicated. In any case Trepov, whose resignation was again declined on January 3rd, was on the 9th allowed to retire; the Emperor had made it clear in his letters to the Empress that he was only using Trepov as long as was convenient; after that, he would be 'kicked out'.[1] Ignatyev also had asked to retire from the Ministry of Education; he told the Tsar that he could be of no use in such a Cabinet.[2] Such was the exit of possibly the best Minister of Education that Russia had had. He was replaced by Kulchitsky. The War Office was again completely upset by the removal of Shuvayev, whom the Empress had sharply criticized for his visit to the Duma. She now at last secured the appointment of Beliayev, for which she had been clamouring for months past; this amiable little official was entirely unequal to his task. Makarov was at last dismissed – to the very end he had refused to obey the Empress in the withdrawal of pending suits from the law courts – and Dobrovolsky, the client of Rasputin and Simanovich, who was heavily indebted to the latter, was appointed in his place (Jan. 15th). The Premiership was a more difficult matter. There was an honest old gentleman in weak health, Prince N. N. Golitsyn, who was known to the Empress as her deputy-chairman of a charitable committee. Nicholas summoned him and after beating about the bush said: 'I am not being straight with you' (*ya s vami hitryu*) and offered him the Premiership. Poor Golitsyn was horrorstruck and begged 'that this cup might pass from him'. He appealed to his age, his ill-health and his inexperience, but he did not feel able to reject a command from his sovereign in time of war.[3] Thus when the Revolution came, a good part of the Cabinet, including the Prime Minister, consisted of persons almost unknown and almost without administrative experience. But these appointments meant little. The one thing that counted was that the all powerful Ministry of the Interior was still in the hands of Protopopov.

[1] N. to A. F., Dec. 14th/27th. [2] IGNATYEV, *Padenie*, VI, 22.
[3] GOLITSYN, *Padenie*, II, 251.

CHAPTER XIV

WARNINGS, PLOTS AND COUNTERPLOTS

My soul is full of discord and dismay.
Hamlet, IV, I

The people muddied,
Thick and unwholesome in their thoughts.
Hamlet, IV, 5

For the imperial couple the murder of Rasputin removed a lynch pin. Or it was as if the base of a triangle were taken away and the two other limbs, leaning against each other, stood up as best they could. Vyrubova writes: 'Their Majesties went into themselves'. She has recorded how the still beautiful Empress sat with tear-stained face, staring in front of her with her big grey-blue eyes;[1] but she still held high the flag of the autocracy; and she was not one to go down otherwise than with her colours still flying. From this time begins the real test of her character, which she was to pass through with growing courage to the end.

Can we follow them into this period, which is at once the most mysterious and really the darkest in their lives? The letters cease, for they are together. We have his diary, but apart from receptions of Ministers or advisers, of course reactionary, it tells us no more than that on January 4th he took a walk in the dark. Her case is clear enough. Her earthly support had failed her, and she could only hope for heaven. Rasputin had always told them that when they had lost him, on earth they were doomed. Did she need him to make her way to heaven? In no sense. The loss of her guide only brought out all her native strength; and once she knew what she had to face, never did her faith in God shine more purely or more brightly.

She is, in the long run, far the easier to understand of the two, and much the less interesting to study. However much her chosen remoteness had made her unintelligible to the outside world,

[1] Vyrubova, 74-5.

once we know her as we do now, there is no mystery left. But with him it is different. The half-tones of his nature, the reticence in which his delicate soul took refuge, his ability to see two sides, and even to see them in a just perspective, make a study of him largely a matter of guess-work. Some thought they definitely saw in him even a lightening of spirit when he learned in the atmosphere of Headquarters of the death of Rasputin. On the other hand, a photograph of this period is unique in presenting his face as actually a harsh one; and Protopopov, who saw most of him in this period, tells us that he was truly a 'Right', and that even at home in his palace he was jealous of his authority up to the end.[1] That is what she has told him that he must be. With so good a mind as he has, he must have had many conflicting thoughts. He realized that he had put his wife and her counsels first, and that even she had now no hope to offer him. Above all, he realized that he was cut off from his people; and it is here I think that we get the key to his character. The weight that crushed him was his sense of duty, of responsibility to his father and to his son, constantly kept before his eyes by his wife. Take that responsibility away, in whatever way short of his own treason to it, and his return to the instincts which nature had given him would be free and spontaneous.

Apart from the murder, which he must have in one way regarded as an affront, he knew well that the wife whom he so tenderly loved was generally detested in his capital. There is even a report of an attempt to shoot her while she was still discharging the most irksome of duties at her hospital, and Vyrubova received threatening anonymous letters one after another. The naively ingenious Protopopov countered these by arranging a number of letters and telegrams from simple folk in the provinces to the Empress assuring her that she was the saviour of Russia, and she still held to this pathetic illusion.

Though Nicholas had so strong a distaste for any intrusion into his personal affairs, he had ordinarily listened with singular patience and restraint to the many detailed warnings which had been given him against Rasputin. As we know from his letters, he did not share the whole-hearted obsession of his wife on this subject, and was capable of questioning the prophet's wisdom.

[1] PROTOPOPOV, *Padenie*, IV, 6, 8.

With him, as with her, Rasputin had been a link with the Russian people, and had known how to calm him and reassure him in anxious moments, and that support was now gone. In the words of Simanovich, 'he accepted his own ruin', [1] the more so as he had always been a profound fatalist. She had deprived him of one of the principal joys of his life, the feeling that he had succeeded with his simple charm in making those around him happy. She had set him an impossible task. How could he possibly be John the Terrible or Peter the Great? 'One cannot snap at everyone', he says in one of his last letters before the crash, and his determination to be 'sharp and bitter' rings hopelessly insincere. He had succeeded in alienating practically everyone at Headquarters; even in his suite there was no one but Sablin who could still be reckoned one of 'ours'. Drenteln had been dismissed. Nilov had warned him. Voyeikov was never more than a palace servant. The good and kindly Fredericksz had made clear his sad if silent reproof; his chaplain Shavelsky the same. Alexeyev, once so entirely trusted, was now alienated. The Emperor was possessed of an overwhelming loneliness, and he did not again return to Headquarters till the eve of the Revolution, making his position as Commander-in-Chief more than ever a caricature. In the palace he was little more than a loving father of a family, and it was the Empress, deprived of her chief support in Rasputin, who now practically governed with the weak help of Protopopov. Outsiders found him sunk in the most hopeless and helpless apathy. The main telephone in the palace was in the Empress's drawing room, where she sat at her writing-desk, staring at a portrait of Marie Antoinette which stood facing her. From this room had been constructed a plain wooden staircase which, passing through the walls, debouched on to a high platform at the back of her husband's audience room, concealed by a curtain, behind which she could lie on a couch and listen to the reports of his visitors. [2] Both Buchanan and Kokovtsev, in their last visits to the Emperor in this period, could not help the feeling that they were being overheard. The picture given by the faithful Kokovtsev

[1] SIMANOVICH, 26.

[2] These arrangements had been preserved when I visited these apartments in 1936 and 1937. That they were there at the time I have verified from Kerensky, who, as Minister of Justice of the Revolution, was almost the first to penetrate into the palace. He himself mounted this staircase.

is peculiarly pathetic. He knew the Emperor far too well to make the mistake common at the time of thinking his apathy habitual. He had wondered at his remarkable quickness of thought and his exceptionally good memory. On February 1st he was received in connection with the feast of the Alexander Lyceum (the nearest thing in Russia to Eton), of which he was curator or provost. The Tsar stood uncertain of himself with the door open. 'Is it Friday?' he asked abstractedly. His face was lined with wrinkles which had never been there before, his eyes yellow with a grey dullness in the pupils. He smiled, looking about him, spoke as if only half conscious, promised to write, and opened the door for his guest to leave.[1] Not long before, the Empress had written to him at Headquarters including this obstinately loyal man in her general indignation.

The Council of State, where the party of the Rights was led by the dismissed Trepov, so long separated in its political attitude from the Duma, had now joined hands with it, and was likewise insisting on a Ministry that could carry the confidence of the country. 'Sweep away the dust and dirt', was Alexandra's comment in one of her last letters to Headquarters.[2] The Council was composed in equal proportions of members nominated by the Emperor and of those elected by the higher official institutions of the country; and it had become the custom at each New Year for the sovereign to nominate afresh those of his choice for the given year. As the Russian New Year (Jan. 14th) approached, the lists had been made up and presented by Trepov. Stürmer, now entirely discarded, no longer appeared in them. The purge suggested by the Empress included the choice of a new Chairman; and the old and honourable Kulomzin was replaced by a pronounced reactionary, Shcheglovitov, who had been summoned to Headquarters on December 28th just before the death of Rasputin. Shcheglovitov had been an opponent of Rasputin before the favourite's omnipotence, but he had now made his peace with him; indeed Rasputin, before his death, had actually telephoned offering him the premiership;[3] but though he might succeed in suffocating the discussions of the Council of State, he was too constant an evader of difficulties to be of any real support in the present critical times.

[1] KOKOVTSEV II., 401-3. [2] Dec. 16th/29th. [3] SHCHEGLOVITOV, II, 434.

The government of Russia was now managed as a kind of personal concern between the Empress and Protopopov with the auxiliary assistance of Vyrubova. Rasputin had telephoned to the palace at ten every morning, and this habit was continued by Protopopov, who also frequently visited either the palace or the hospitals of the two ladies at Tsarskoe Selo. With the equivocal Dobrovolsky Protopopov, who was deeply tinged with a vague and unintelligent mysticism, appears to have held spiritual séances, at which he endeavoured to recall the spirit of Rasputin and to back with this assurance his recommendations to the Empress. The Cabinet was a thing apart and of no consequence. Protopopov did not even always attend its meetings. When he did, he ordinarily found his colleagues in indignant opposition to him, and more than one of them (Golitsyn on Jan. 15th and also Pokrovsky) urgently asked the Emperor for his dismissal; Golitsyn even recommended Kryzhanovsky as his successor.[1] To this had sunk the administration of the empire. Anonymous verses which were widely circulated in manuscript and read with the greatest delight, give the true public view of Protopopov; they were written shortly before the death of Rasputin.

PRETTY POLLY SEES TO IT

(*Pro to Popka vedayet*)

Premier Trepov keeps a bird,
  Pretty politician,
Listening to every word
  Of the Opposition.
Who says he agrees to it,
  Who says he'll oppose it —
Pretty Polly sees to it,
  Pretty Polly knows it.

Times are so inferior,
  Everyone grows thinner.
That concerns Interior —
  What we'll get for dinner.[2]
Who has beef with peas to it,
  Who goes short, and shows it —
Pretty Polly sees to it,
  Pretty Polly knows it.

[1] Vasilyev, 161.

[2] An allusion to the transfer of the food supply to the Ministry of the Interior.

Too much for our puny forms,
  Posing as dictator;
Profiteering uniforms
  Pays a good deal better.[1]
Make your man say 'Please' to it;
  Make him pay: he owes it.
Pretty Polly sees to it,
  Pretty Polly knows it.

You have full facilities
  In our strange conditions,
Trader with abilities
  Less than your ambitions.
Show the pie, he'll freeze to it;
  That's how you'll dispose it.
Pretty Polly sees to it,
  Pretty Polly knows it.

What's our state authority
  Though there's plenty of it?
Much superiority –
  Precious little profit.
Grisha bends his knees to it,
  Annie asks: 'How goes it?'[2]
Pretty Polly sees to it,
  Pretty Polly knows it.

Sow as you know how; and then,
  Crops will come, and pay too.
Keep your secret: now and then,
  Bow the other way too.[3]
Then, some sharp decrees to it!
  That will soon disclose it.
Pretty Polly sees to it,
  Pretty Polly knows it.

Protopopov did not know his work, and his ideas of government, which for the most part remained on paper, merit little attention. He was merely a political agent; but his intentions as to policy, considering the post which he held, are of historical

[1] An allusion to Protopopov's cloth factory.
[2] Grisha, Rasputin. Annie, Vyrubova.
[3] i.e. to the Opposition, of which Protopopov had formerly been a member.

interest. In addition to his complete and wholly apologetic evidence to the post-revolution commission, written in prison, we have a most interesting document in what is called his 'memorandum before death'[1] after the second Revolution in November 1917, before he was shot by the Soviet Government. It is vague, like most things that come from him, but indicates certain general lines. He wished like his predecessors to establish more control over army administration, where, he says, 'complicated economic problems were cut through with the aplomb of ignorance, by the blade of the sword'.[2] And he, like Nicholas, wished to re-establish political inspection in the army, a task which it was thought at the time, might be entrusted to Beletsky. There is no doubt that he intended, after the dissolution of the Duma, a drastic revision of the constitution, as is suggested in the last stanza of the verses just quoted. In his graphs there are to be found only general lines, but the Ministers were apparently to be independent of each other — that is, directly under the sovereign through his principal adviser. He intended to suppress the public organizations, especially Zemgor and the War Industry Committees, to win back the support of the industrial world, which he knew better than anything else, to rule through local committees, to alleviate the lot of the Jews, to institute an elective clergy with regular salaries, in place of their existing dependence on fees from their parishioners, and to distribute land to the peasants. The soldiers would act as rural police. The workers were to be under the War Minister, with palliatives such as conciliation courts. Strict control over the Press was also one of his objects.[3] Ministers would answer for their actions before a special body replacing the Duma. As to foreign policy, he has made his ideas perfectly clear. He would demand of the Allies the conclusion of peace, giving notice that if this were not done in six months, Russia would come out of the War.[4]

It must have been quite evident even to Nicholas that Protopopov was not the man to carry through such a policy, and both he and the Empress for a moment turned from him to the most reactionary of all their ex-Ministers, Nicholas Maklakov.

[1] In *Golos Minuvshago*, 2/xv, 1926, *Predsmertnaya Zapiska.*
[2] Protopopov, *Predsmertnaya*, 175. [3] ibid., 177 & ff.
[4] Protopopov, *Predsmertnaya*, 169.

Maklakov had been received by the Empress before the death of Rasputin. Directly after it he had written to the Tsar, advising the strongest measures for the restoration of his authority. He was the one real and resolute diehard in the official hierarchy. Even in 1913, as will be remembered, he had clamoured for the reduction of the Duma to a merely consultative capacity and he was behind Nicholas's suggestion in that sense to his Ministers on the eve of the War. He now handed to the Emperor a memorandum by another reactionary, Govorukho-Otrok, but he does not seem to have made any study of it, and even let parts of it fall on the platform when glancing through it on his way to Tsarskoe Selo.[1] He was very clear as to the entire inefficiency of the subsidized reactionary associations. Nicholas asked him to draw up a dissolution manifesto as the preface to a *coup d'état*, and this was actually done,[2] but the Tsar wavered irresolutely, and let Maklakov drop out of contact with him, continuing to leave things blindly to Protopopov, whose attitude to Maklakov was simply one of the narrowest official jealousy.

In this period a number of warnings in the opposite sense streamed in on the Emperor from nearly every honest person who had a claim to approach him. Before Rasputin's death a meeting of the imperial family in the palace of the Grand Duke Andrew had requested the Grand Duke Paul, the one remaining uncle of the Emperor, to convey to him a request that he would take advantage of his name-day, the feast of St. Nicholas on December 19th, to announce the grant of a constitution, and on the 16th Paul sought and obtained an audience. He was entertained at tea by the Emperor and Empress. She shook her head at his request, and Nicholas replied that he had sworn at his coronation to leave his power intact to his son. Paul then asked for a Ministry possessing the national confidence, and spoke quite plainly of the influence of Rasputin. Nicholas went on smoking, and it was the Empress who answered with a long and earnest defence of her prophet, who, she declared, was calumniated by everyone, and she dismissed as impossible any change in the Ministry.[3] Just before Rasputin's murder, the Grand Duchess Elizabeth, strongly urged by a loyal friend in Moscow, went specially to Petrograd to

[1] N. Maklakov, *Padenie*, v, 289. [2] On Feb. 24th or 25th, ibid., 287.
[3] Paley, 15.

make one more attempt to warn her younger sister. To quote the report of this friend: 'Her journey proved a complete failure. Though she was able to speak to the Empress, well-informed persons said that as soon as she mentioned Rasputin, the Empress at once cut the conversation short and said that the Grand Duchess could return to Moscow by a train which was shortly due to start; she even gave orders for a carriage to be fetched to convey her sister to the station.'[1] They were never to meet again, and both were to be assassinated in Siberia within a day of each other.

Directly after Rasputin's death the Emperor's cousin and brother-in-law, who was father-in-law to Prince Yusupov, the Grand Duke Alexander Mikhailovich, hurriedly arrived from Kiev. He visited the palace (Jan. 4th), and by Nicholas's consent was allowed to speak to his sister-in-law, the Empress, who was lying up in her bedroom. Heated voices were heard from outside, and Nicholas, entering with some of his children, gently interrupted the interview. Then Alexander asked leave to write down in the study what he had wanted to say.[2] At a later date (Feb. 7th) he completed a long letter written at various intervals, expressing his fears and warnings.

> There must be [he wrote] an organism responsible and carrying all the burden of responsibility before the people. The present system where you are alone in carrying this responsibility is inadmissible . . . The President of the Council of Ministers must be a man in whom you can have full confidence; he will choose the other Ministers and be responsible for them.

The Grand Duke opposes the principle of a Ministry responsible to the Duma; but he continues:

> The nominations which have taken place in these last times [Jan. 14th] show that you have definitely decided to follow a home policy quite opposed to the wishes of your faithful subjects . . . This situation cannot last long; I again repeat, one cannot govern a country without listening to the voice of the people . . . In conclusion I will say that, strange as it may appear, it is the Government which is preparing the revolution: the people do not want it; but the Government is

[1] Communicated by V. F. Malinin.
[2] G. D. ALEXANDER, *Once a Grand Duke*, 313-6; VYRUBOVA, 74.

employing all possible means to increase the number of the malcontents, and it is perfectly successful. We are watching an unwonted spectacle, revolution coming from above and not from below.[1]

Of the generals, Alexeyev, as we know, had repeatedly warned the Tsar against Stürmer, but he had now fallen ill and had had to be given some six weeks' leave. He had a competent successor as Chief of Staff of the Army in Gurko, whose energy and ability had brought him rapidly to the top. In view of the recent bid for Polish support made by the Central Powers the question of Poland was still vividly before the public. As Ludendorff has testified, the so-called 'independent Polish State', conceded by Germany and Austria, had quite failed to rally any real support from the Russian Poles,[2] and the friction between the two victorious Powers became more and more evident. An Inter-Allied Conference was timed to meet shortly in Petrograd, and some recognition of Russian promises had again become imperative. Gurko, while the Emperor was still at Headquarters, had again raised this question. In spite of the opposition of the Empress and Rasputin, he was able to secure a renewal of the promise in a pronouncement which the Emperor consented to sign after the New Year;[3] and indeed some kind of a shadowy commission on Poland, though with no Polish representatives, was set up by the Cabinet (Feb. 31st). Gurko had always been in touch with Guchkov; and on January 25th, after two hours' talk on the preceding day with Rodzyanko, to whom most of the critics went for advice, he again urged the Emperor to make peace with the Duma and to dismiss Protopopov.[4] No sooner did Nicholas return to Headquarters on March 8th than Alexeyev, now recovered and back in office, again begged for concessions to the nation.

It was more than ever a delicate matter for a foreign ambassador to interfere in the internal affairs of Russia, and could hardly be attempted otherwise than on the ground of allied policy in the War. On January 7th Paléologue, at an urgent request of Pokrovsky, who himself begged in vain with both hands for wiser measures, tried to give something of a warning. He began by suggesting that he had come for 'consolation', but the courtly Frenchman lost

[1] *Lettres des Grands-Ducs*, Appendix.
[2] Ludendorff, 396.
[3] Gurko, 204-6.
[4] ibid., 233.

courage and allowed himself to be sidetracked by the steady though gentle evasiveness of Nicholas.[1] Buchanan, before his audience of November 5th, at which he had spoken so plainly, had asked leave of the Foreign Office to give his counsels not as an ambassador, but in his own name.[2] Now that the position had become so much worse, he decided to give one more warning, and this time asked leave to speak in the name of his Sovereign and Government. To this the Foreign Office did not consent; but he was allowed to speak again in his own name. On January 12th he was received at the palace not as before, in the study, but in the audience chamber. Buchanan began by expressing a pessimistic view of the prospects of the Inter-Allied Conference, adding that there was no guarantee 'that the present Russian Government would remain in office or that the decisions of the Conference would be respected by their successors',[3] and after asking permission to speak frankly, he came bravely to the main point:

> The Duma I had reason to know [he had asked Rodzyanko just the day before] would be satisfied if His Majesty would appoint as President of the Council of Ministers a man in whom the nation had confidence and would allow him to choose his own colleagues. . . .

He even said:

> The Ambassadors never knew whether the Ministers of to-day with whom they were treating would still be Ministers on the morrow. Your Majesty [he went on], if I may be permitted to say so, has but one safe course open to you — namely to break down the barrier that separates you from your people and to regain their confidence.

The Emperor, drawing himself up, asked whether he was to regain the confidence of his people or whether they were to regain his confidence.

> Both, Your Majesty, for without such mutual confidence Russia will never win this War. [He mentioned by name Protopopov] who, if Your Majesty will forgive me saying so, is bringing Russia to the verge of ruin.

The Emperor answered resentfully, but Buchanan concluded with these remarkable words:

[1] PALÉOLOGUE, III, 147-50. [2] BUCHANAN, II, 42. [3] BUCHANAN, II, 44.

> Your Majesty must remember that the people and the army are but one, and that in the event of revolution only a small portion of the army can be counted on to defend the dynasty. An Ambassador, I am well aware, has no right to hold the language which I have held to Your Majesty, and I had to take my courage in both hands before speaking as I have done. I can but plead as my excuse the fact that I have throughout been inspired by my feelings of devotion for Your Majesty and the Empress. If I were to see a friend walking through a wood on a dark night along a path which I knew ended in a precipice, would it not be my duty, Sir, to warn him of his danger? And is it not equally my duty to warn Your Majesty of the abyss that lies ahead of you? You have, Sir, come to the parting of the ways, and you have now to choose between two paths. The one will lead you to victory and a glorious peace — the other to revolution and disaster. Let me implore Your Majesty to choose the former. By following it you will, Sir, secure for your country the realization of its secular ambitions and for yourself the position of the most powerful Sovereign in Europe. But above all else, Your Majesty will assure the safety of those who are so dear to you and be free from all anxiety on their account.[1]

The position of foreign ambassadors was becoming almost impossible. The Emperor was at war with his people, and they were accredited to the Emperor. In different ways Paléologue and Buchanan had sought such contact with the public as they could get in these circumstances. Paléologue moved more in the higher society of Petrograd, which was the most incensed with the Tsar. He had also much earlier invited public men to his Embassy, including Milyukov and the Cadets. But Buchanan had been in much closer contact with Duma circles, though perhaps in a less direct way, and was much more trusted by them. At this time, as was almost inevitable, his contact with them was becoming more direct. His plain warning to the Emperor was deeply resented. Vyrubova records that the Empress even discussed with her husband the question of Buchanan's recall, but the gentle Nicholas replied: 'That would be too harsh'.[2] Protopopov asked that the British Embassy should be watched. It is practically from this episode alone that has been derived the calumny which represented Sir George (who did not know Russian) as visiting

[1] BUCHANAN, 48-9. [2] VYRUBOVA, 96

revolutionary meetings in false whiskers, the kind of absurdity which passed currency even in the little circle of the palace.

The last of the great warnings was appropriately delivered by Rodzyanko on January 20th. At the New Year reception at the palace on January 14th Protopopov had sidled up to him and held out his hand, and Rodzyanko had replied: 'Nowhere and never.'[1] He began by apologizing to the Tsar for his rudeness in his palace, but remarked that Protopopov could not have greatly felt the insult as he had sent no challenge, which the Tsar received with a laugh (according to Protopopov he had forbidden him to do so). Rodzyanko then proceeded to his report, as follows:

> Your Majesty was able to gather from my second report that I consider the state of the country to have become more critical and menacing than ever. The spirit of the people is such that the gravest upheavals may be expected. Parties exist no longer, and all Russia is unanimous in claiming a change of Government and the appointment of a responsible Premier invested with the confidence of the nation. It is necessary to organize, on the basis of mutual confidence between the Government, the legislative chambers and public bodies, the work for the attainment of victory over the enemy and order at home. To our shame, chaos reigns everywhere. There is no Government and no system, neither is there, up to the present, any co-ordination between the front and the rear. At every turn one is confronted with abuses and confusion. The nation realizes that you have banished from the Government all those in whom the Duma and the people trusted, and replaced them by unworthy and incompetent men. The constant changes of Ministers at first have created confusion among the officials, which finally has given place to complete indifference. Think, Your Majesty, of Polivanov, Sazonov, Count Ignatyev, Shcherbatov, Naumov — all of them honest and loyal servants of yourself and of Russia, who were dismissed for no cause or any fault whatever . . . Think of such venerable statesmen as Golubev and Kulomsin. They were removed for the sole reason that they refused to silence honest men in the Council of State. As if purposely, everything is being done to the detriment of Russia and the advantage of her enemies. No wonder monstrous rumours are afloat of treason and espionage in the rear of the army. Sire,

[1] RODZYANKO, 251.

there is not a single honest or reliable man left in your entourage; all the best have either been eliminated or resigned, and only those who have bad reputations have remained. It is an open secret that the Empress issues orders without your knowledge, that Ministers report to her on matters of State, and that by her wish those whom she views with disfavour lose their posts and are replaced by incompetent and inexperienced persons. Indignation against and hatred of the Empress are growing throughout the country. She is looked upon as Germany's champion. Even the common people are speaking of it . . .

'Give me facts,' said the Emperor, 'there are no facts to confirm your statements.'

There are no facts, but the whole trend of policy directed by Her Majesty gives ground for such ideas. To save your family, your Majesty ought to find some way of preventing the Empress from exercising any influence on politics. The heart of the Russian people is tortured by the foreboding of awful calamities, the people are turning away from their Tsar because they see that, after all their suffering and bloodshed, fresh trials are in store for them. . . .
Your Majesty [I continued] do not compel the people to choose between you and the good of the country. So far the ideas of Tsar and Motherland were indissoluble, but lately they have begun to be separated.

The Emperor pressed his head between his hands, then said:

Is it possible that for twenty-two years I have tried to act for the best, and that for twenty-two years it was all a mistake?

It was a hard moment. With a great effort at self-control I replied:

Yes, your Majesty, for twenty-two years you have followed a wrong course.

He adds:

In spite of these frank words, which it could not be pleasant to hear, the Emperor bade me a kind farewell and manifested neither anger nor even displeasure.[1]

[1] RODZYANKO, 252-4.

The centre of opposition to the palace among the Grand Dukes was the Grand Duchess Maria Pavlovna (to be distinguished from the much younger lady of the same name, the sister of the Grand Duke Dmitry Pavlovich). She was herself a German from Mecklenburg-Schwerin, but hated the Kaiser as perhaps only some of the minor princely families of Germany knew how to hate him, and she was the widow of the Tsar's eldest uncle the Grand Duke Vladimir. Had Alexander III had no children, she would have been Empress of Russia. As it stood, she was the third lady in the empire, coming immediately after the two Empresses. The Grand Duke Vladimir had been an out-and-out conservative, and it was he who was most responsible for the shooting on Bloody Sunday, but her relations with the palace had always been strained. The Empress disliked her and in particular her son Boris, for whom she had asked the hand of the Emperor's eldest daughter Olga. Boris did not enjoy a good reputation, and the Empress's reaction in her letters to her husband might have been expressed in the same words by her grandmother, Queen Victoria. Maria Pavlovna was still very embittered by the refusal. Paléologue was a frequent visitor in her house. Maria Pavlovna had often spoken to him of politics and talked of the Empress with very little restraint.

The palace of the Vladimir branch had now become the centre of meetings to discuss joint action of the imperial family, and more than one council was held here. To his great surprise Rodzyanko, at about one in the morning, received a telephone call from the Grand Duchess asking him to come and see her at once on an 'urgent matter'. The sturdy man replies: 'To tell you the truth, I was just going to bed', and comments: 'The President of the Duma calling on a Grand Duchess at one o'clock in the morning — it would savour too much of a conspiracy.' So he put off the meeting till luncheon the next day. We will let him describe in his vigorous language what happened:

> On my arrival next day I found the Grand Duchess and her sons, as if assembled for a family council. They were all most cordial to me, and not a word was said about the 'urgent matter'. At last we passed into the Grand Duchess's boudoir, the conversation still revolving round trivial topics. Cyril Vladimirovich, turning to his mother, said: 'Why don't you speak?'

The Grand Duchess then began to talk of the general state of affairs, of the Government's incompetence, of Protopopov and of the Empress. On mentioning the latter's name she became more and more excited, dwelt on her pernicious influence and interference in everything, and said she was driving the country to destruction; that she was the cause of the danger which threatened the Emperor and the rest of the imperial family; that such conditions could no longer be tolerated; that things must be changed, something must be done, removed, destroyed. . . .

Wishing to understand more precisely what she was driving at, I asked:

'What do you mean by "removed"?'

'Well, I don't know . . . Some attempt must be made . . . The Duma must do something . . . She must be annihilated . . .'

'Who?'

'The Empress.'

'Your Highness', said I, 'allow me to treat this conversation as if it had never taken place, because if you address me as the President of the Duma, my oath of allegiance compels me to wait at once on His Imperial Majesty and report to him that the Grand Duchess Maria Pavlovna has declared to me that the Empress must be annihilated.'[1]

This passage gives us the tone of the Grand Ducal opposition, and the measure of its inefficiency. There were resounding banquets ('trimmed up with women and with wine'), at which champagne glasses were emptied to openly disloyal toasts. At a dinner at the house of the Grand Duke Gabriel of the Constantine branch, which had always kept more or less apart from the palace, there was open talk of the assassination of the Emperor Paul in 1801;[2] and, as Basil Maklakov has noted, books on that subject were sought out with interest. The general suggestion was a removal of the Tsar, to be replaced by his son with either Nicholas's brother Michael or the Grand Duke Nicholas as regent.

Similar, though conceived in a different spirit, was the plan of the Progressive Bloc. At the last meeting of the Duma before the short break for Trepov to prepare his programme, on December 27th, there was a vigorous speech from Milyukov about the 'coming

[1] Rodzyanko, 246-7. [2] Paléologue, III, 137.

storm', to be followed up next day by a meeting of Zemgor in Moscow under the chairmanship of Prince George Lvov. This meeting was immediately closed on the orders of Protopopov, but not before a resolution condemning 'the dark forces' and the fatal inefficiency of the Government was read out and carried by acclamation, to be circulated everywhere. The Bloc were more or less prepared with their programme. Nicholas was to be replaced by his son Alexis, and the Grand Duke Michael was to be the regent. The Cadets, who early in 1905 had come out for a republic, were now for a constitutional monarchy, especially Milyukov, and such was the view of the bulk of the Bloc, including the Octobrists and Nationalists. The Bloc prepared a future Cabinet, which, as a matter of fact, with a few alterations, was to come into office as the Provisional Government after the Revolution. Milyukov had successfully set himself to eliminate Rodzyanko from the Premiership, and to substitute Prince George Lvov, the President of Zemgor. Rodzyanko had his defects but he was a real asset, and this was very probably a grave mistake. Guchkov was to be War Minister, and Milyukov Foreign Minister. It was the Nationalist, Shulgin, who later proposed the invitation of the Labour leader Kerensky.

At this meeting no methods were proposed to bring about the transfer of power. Guchkov said bluntly that after the revolution the power would fall to those who had made the revolution. He later received visits from Nekrasov and Tereshchenko, who wanted to know what he proposed to do; and between them they outlined a plot by which the Emperor was to be held up on the railway in the province of Novgorod on one of his journeys between the capital and Headquarters, and compelled to abdicate in favour of his son. For this purpose it was necessary to concentrate at the given point units of troops which would carry out the plan, and this presented great difficulty and delayed its execution. However, the plot was timed to materialize in March, and was only anticipated by the Revolution itself.[1]

Another separate plot was that of Prince George Lvov, and was to be carried out in concert with Alexeyev. The General was a simple straightforward soldier with liberal convictions but no politician. He was amazed at having to deal with Ministers who

[1] Guchkov to B. P.; also GUCHKOV, *Padenie*, VI, 279.

came up to the worst charges that had been laid against the Government. The Emperor was very fond of him, and the Empress at first liked him. On one of her visits to Headquarters she took him by the arm and led him into the garden to suggest that Rasputin should come to Headquarters to bless the troops. Alexeyev replied simply that if Rasputin came he would not be there, and the Empress jerked her arm away.[1] But what most seriously alarmed him was his discovery that she possessed the Emperor's copy of a secret map of the operations of which there was only one duplicate in his own possession. And he rightly guessed that it was not likely to be kept secret from Rasputin. This was for him a military question of the greatest gravity. He received at least one letter from Guchkov, saying that he alone was in a position to find a remedy for the evil; and, as we know from her letters, this through the police became known to the Empress. Alexeyev agreed with Prince Lvov that at one of her frequent visits to Headquarters he would arrest her and demand of the Emperor that she should be sent to Livadia for the rest of the war; if he refused he would be asked to abdicate in favour of his son. Prince Lvov was to organize public support for this demand. It appears that the Grand Duke Nicholas in the Caucasas was informed of this plot, but would not have anything to do with it. It is said that an emissary of Lvov visited Headquarters to ask Alexeyev at what time he proposed to act, and that the General, without replying, began detaching leaves from a calendar and his hand stopped at a certain date. This plot was frustrated by the serious illness of Alexeyev, who, as we remember, had to go on leave for several weeks.[2] In justice to the Empress we have to recognize that when, in her last tremendous letter before the death of Rasputin, she demanded of her husband that he should send Guchkov and Lvov to Siberia she was not speaking without a reason, and in fact she at this time regularly received from the censorship copies of private letters which were often revealing and were full of animosity against her.

There was no connection between these plots and a visit to Petrograd in mid-January of General Krymov, though Krymov, like Polivanov and Gurko, was one of the leading soldiers in close

[1] Alexeyev to I. P. Demidov and N. Bazily.
[2] G. Lvov to A. F. Meyendorff.

touch with Guchkov.[1] We may give Rodzyanko's account of this incident:

> At the beginning of January [1917] General Krymov arrived from the front and asked to be given an opportunity of unofficially acquainting the members of the Duma with the disastrous conditions at the front and the spirit of the army. A large number of members of the Duma, the Council of State and the Defence Council assembled at my flat. The gallant General's tale was listened to with profound emotion. His was a painful and grim confession. There could be no hope of victory, said Krymov, until the Government had changed its course, or given way to another which the army could trust. The progress of the war was heavily handicapped and all temporary successes brought to nought by conditions in the rear. Krymov wound up his statement more or less as follows:
>
> 'The spirit of the army is such that the news of a *coup d'état* would be welcomed with joy. A revolution is imminent, and we at the front feel it to be so. If you decide on such an extreme step, we will support you. Clearly there is no other way. You, as well as numbers of others, have tried everything, but the Emperor attaches more weight to his wife's pernicious influence than to all honest words of warning. There is no time to lose.'
>
> Krymov ceased speaking, and for a few seconds an ominous and painful silence filled the room. It was first broken by Shingarev.
>
> 'The General is right. A *coup d'état* is urgent. But who will have the courage to undertake it?'
>
> Shidlovsky said fiercely:
>
> 'No need to pity or spare *him*, when he is driving Russia to ruin.'
>
> Many members of the Duma agreed with Shingarev and Shidlovsky; heated arguments arose on every side. Someone quoted Brusilov's words: 'If I had to choose between the Emperor and Russia, I follow Russia'.
>
> The most implacable of all proved to be Tereshchenko. His words greatly agitated me, and I rebuked him.
>
> 'You do not take into account', I said, 'what will follow on the Emperor's abdication . . . I shall never countenance a

[1] Guchkov to B. P.

revolution . . . I have taken the oath of allegiance . . . I desire you not to speak this way in my house . . . If the army can insist on an abdication, let it do so through the medium of its leaders; as for me, I will continue to act, not by violence, but by persuasion, to the very last.'

The conference lasted far into the night. One felt the gathering of the storm, and the future loomed dark and menacing: some fatal destiny seemed to be drawing the country into a fathomless abyss.[1]

The Progressive Bloc was still following out the motto 'For the War, and criticize the Government'. The French statesman Doumergue revisited Russia for the Inter-Allied Conference, and on February 8th he lunched with a party of Liberals at the French Embassy — Milyukov, Polivanov, Basil Maklakov and Shingarev — and again, as earlier, he insisted on patience, in order that there should be no great disturbance in Russia till after the War. Milyukov and Maklakov replied that 'there has been enough patience; we have exhausted it all . . . Besides if we do not act soon, the mass will not listen to us any longer'. Doumergue tried to soften down his demand, yet he ended: 'Before all, think of the War.'[2] But this was just why the Left Cadets and Progressists were breaking away, so as not to be behind the mood of the country. Words without deeds were becoming inadequate, both with the country and for the support of the mild new Premier, who had declared that he wished to work with the Duma and the public.

On the other hand, if one seeks for signs of any organization or definite plan among the workers, one can find no more than before. Valery Carrick, the excellent caricaturist, always on familiar terms with the man in the street, in his valuable diary, in which he noted all the turns of opinion, especially in the masses, had written earlier: 'The inhabitant sees no place at all from which can come men capable of organizing and directing the revolution.'[3] The same was the verdict of the military governor of Petrograd, General Habalov,[4] and a leading revolutionary, V. B. Stankevich, said later: 'The mass moved of itself.'[5] The best summary of all

[1] RODZYANKO, 244-5.
[2] PALÉOLOGUE, III, 188.
[3] CARRICK, 31.
[4] HABALOV, *Padenie*, I, 209.
[5] MILYUKOV, 41.

is that of Shulgin: 'They (the revolutionaries) were not ready, but all the rest was ready.'[1]

The fact is that in the Russia of that time, with its millions of illiterates, the people as a whole were still politically too immature to give practical shape to their thoughts; and the socialist leaders themselves, many of them men of the highest education and deep thinkers, were really no more part of the masses than the politicians to the right of them. Even at the beginning of 1917 the actual revolutionary Parties, S.R.s and S.D.s are estimated by Kerensky as numbering no more than 35,000 registered members of which no more than 15,000 can be assigned to the one defeatist section, the Bolsheviks.[2] The Social Democrats or Marxists at this time anyhow numbered no more than forty thousand on their list of active members — a figure given to the writer by one of them shortly afterwards — and of those the majority were still Mensheviks or moderates, though many of them were, no doubt, now going through the process of Bolshevization. Plekhanov, the veteran Menshevik leader, who was still abroad, had called for patriotism and the winning of the War, and the Chairman of the Social Democrat group in the Duma, the clever and bitter little Georgian Chkheidze, who had come to be quite a favourite figure with his opponents, was a Menshevik. The Bolshevik leader Lenin and all his principal lieutenants were at this time in Switzerland, where they had been able to obtain facilities for circulating defeatist literature among the Russians in the prisoner camps in Germany; Trotsky was still a Menshevik and was in America; and it was only by the most devious ways that in war conditions they could exercise any influence in Russia. It is significant that in the records of the post-revolution commission set up immediately after the first revolution and working up to the second, in which the most comprehensive evidence is taken from all responsible for the fall of the monarchy, the name of Lenin is hardly mentioned.[3] The bugbear of the police was Kerensky; and he tells us that 'no party of the left and no revolutionary organization had made any plan for a revolution.'[4] On February 27th, in a flaming speech in the Duma, he boldly declared:

To prevent a catastrophe the Tsar himself must be removed —

[1] SHULGIN, 139.
[2] Kerensky to B. P.
[3] Only four times, and then incidentally.
[4] KERENSKY, C. L., 206.

> by terrorist methods if there is no other way . . . If you will not listen to the voice of warning now, you will find yourselves face to face with facts — not warnings. Look up at the distant flashes that are lighting the skies of Russia!

But Kerensky had been throughout a strong supporter of the War for the best of reasons — that if the victory of Germany put Russia at her feet, there could be little hope for a Russian revolution, and he was drawing into closer personal contact with the rest of the Opposition, for instance even with the nationalist Shulgin. After the speech that has been quoted, Dobrovolsky wanted the Duma to surrender him, but Rodzyanko said to him: 'Be assured we will never give you up to *them*.'[1]

But if we are speaking not of political plans and programmes, but of the alienation of the masses from the existing system, the bitter discontent was rising higher and higher and ready to flood the country at any moment. We have no such excellent evidence as the police report of October, already quoted, but all the features described in it were by now tremendously aggravated, and calling for the earliest expression. While the Progressive Bloc preached patriotism and the War, the two great longings of the masses were peace and bread, the words which Lenin was later to inscribe on the banners of all the first Bolshevik processions. Even after the Revolution, General Selivachev regarded these two yearnings as superseding all others. There were extravagant rumours among the troops of the treachery of the Generals, which spread even more widely among their kinsfolk in the rear. As to bread, the disproportion between the rise of prices and the increase in wages had become more fantastic than ever. The peasants, unable to secure anything like a just equivalent in the market, were hoarding on a large scale, and the new Minister of Agriculture, Rittich, experienced and capable as he was, could not find a way of dealing with the situation, and was violently criticized in a Duma debate which nearly split the Progressive Bloc.[2] The Cabinet was constantly discussing the food problem, but the man who held the power, Protopopov, was often absent, and the hostility of his colleagues to him was increasing every day.

[1] KERENSKY, C. L., 231-2.
[2] SHULGIN, 136.

On January 29th began the mockery of the Inter-Allied Conference in Petrograd, and the delegates remained in Russia till February 1st. There could not be any result. The War Minister, Beliayev, who had after all had sufficient experience in his long tenure as Chief of the General Staff, did not even know his own details — the tonnage which he asked for his munition orders was one-fifth of what was required,[1] and the Allied delegates could not have failed to see the monstrous disarray of their stranded gifts as they passed through Murmansk. Lord Milner sat impatiently moving his chair and saying: 'We are wasting time.'[2] Buchanan, at the Emperor's reception, did find a chance of again suggesting that the zemstva, whose congress had been closed by Protopopov, should be admitted to participation in the work of food supply.

While the Inter-Allied delegates were still in Russia, Protopopov, on February 12th, arrested the workers' section of the Central War Industry Committee. This was the one legal organization through which the workers could express themselves; it was working enthusiastically for the War, and served as the focus of patriotic labour opinion. There was at this time an increasing avalanche of strikes, ever growing in volume. On January 22nd, 12,000 workers had taken part in a strike of demonstration; soon 70,000 metal workers were out in Petrograd, and there were similar movements in the provinces. The interminable queues gave opportunity for interminable speeches of strike agitators. Protopopov's ideas on the conclusion of peace have already been noted; he was a loose thinker and a vague speaker, and some of his remarks more than indicated an intention to call up a small disturbance and suppress it, so that later he might be able to turn to the Allies and explain the difficulties which Russia had in continuing the War. The arrest of the War Industry workers' delegates was based on a speech advocating an armed rising, by one Abrosimov,[3] who turned out to be a police agent, and was not himself kept under arrest. So little had the police learnt their own lessons that they were resorting again to their nasty tricks of the times of Azef and Malinovsky. It was expected that on February 27th, at the reopening of the Duma, it would be visited by a great procession of workers; and Protopopov, who was deeply

[1] RODZYANKO, 257. [2] PALÉOLOGUE, III, 181.
[3] GUCHKOV, *Padenie*, VI, 286.

superstitious, on the advice of a foreign spiritualist, had noted this among the dates which he expected to cause him anxiety.[1] Milyukov issued a strong warning to the workers not to be caught in a trap, but it was refused publication. There is sufficient evidence that another person, no doubt a police agent, resembling him and calling himself Milyukov, was seen among the workmen, trying to stimulate an ill-considered outbreak. Anyhow, the march to the Duma did not take place.

Meanwhile one notable person after another, for instance, Samarin and Prince George Lvov, visited Rodzyanko to ask what could be done to make the Emperor see the imminent danger. On February 23rd he had the last of his audiences. He was coldly received, and Rodzyanko therefore limited himself to reading his written report. The Emperor's attitude was not merely indifferent, but 'positively harsh'. He constantly asked the reader to hurry.

> When I mentioned Protopopov, he said irritably:
> 'Protopopov was your deputy-president in the Duma. Why do you dislike him now?'
> I explained that since he became Minister, Protopopov had positively gone mad. In the course of our talk about Protopopov and home policy in general, I alluded to Maklakov [Nicholas, the reactionary brother].
> 'I very much regret Maklakov', said the Emperor, 'he at least has certainly not gone out of his mind.'
> 'He had none to go out of, your Majesty,' I could not refrain from saying. . . .
> I was obliged to conclude my report:
> 'I consider it my duty, Sire, to express to you my profound foreboding and my conviction that this will be my last report to you.'
> 'Why?' the Emperor asked.
> 'Because the Duma will be dissolved, and the course the Government is taking bodes no good. There is still time; it is still possible to change everything and grant a responsible Ministry. That, apparently, is not to be. You, Your Majesty, disagree with me, and everything will remain as it is. The consequence of this, in my opinion, will be revolution and a state of anarchy which no one will be able to control.'
> The Emperor said nothing and curtly bade me farewell.[2]

[1] Cf. Protopopov, *Padenie*, II, 8. [2] Rodzyanko, 260-1.

One of the last visitors to Rodzyanko was the Emperor's brother, the Grand Duke Michael Alexandrovich. He had made a morganatic marriage with a twice-divorced lady, which, for a time, had caused a breach between them. He had been allowed to return to Russia in the War, and had held a command at the front. The Grand Duke Michael lived more or less among the general public, and could not fail to know what it was thinking. He at this time visited Nicholas to urge him to return to Headquarters, no doubt in order to get him away from his wife. Nicholas was still nominally Commander-in-Chief, and himself felt that he ought to go. According to Rodzyanko, on the eve of his departure, he told the Prime Minister, Prince Golitsyn, in answer to another earnest warning, that he was prepared to go to the Duma the next day and announce that he would give a responsible Ministry. Rodzyanko writes:

> That same evening he was again summoned to the palace, where the Emperor announced to him his intention to leave for Headquarters.
> 'How is that, Your Majesty?' asked Golitsyn, amazed. 'What about a responsible Ministry? You intended to go to the Duma to-morrow.'
> 'I have changed my mind . . . I am leaving for Headquarters to-night . . .'[1]

Before leaving, Nicholas had his last interview with Protopopov (Mar. 7th). The Minister well knew that anything might happen at any time, and plans had been made for the suppression of a rising. Petrograd contained an inflated garrison of something like 170,000 men; of these the mass were raw recruits — what would have been called in this country 'the last combings out'. We are already aware that the Russian regular army, which had at first contained quite a large number of volunteers, had practically been exterminated some three times over. These late recruits were most unwilling to go to the front, especially in the existing conditions. Owing to the shortage of arms in the rear they had had little regular training, and, therefore, more time to listen at meetings to propaganda. Now that there was also a shortage of food at the front, their conditions were far preferable where they were. It was therefore recognized that no dependence could

[1] Rodzyanko, 263.

be placed on any but the actual training staffs which numbered some 5000 men — or little more than a tenth of the number of regulars who had garrisoned the capital in the troubled years 1904-07. Many officers had gone to the front sooner than be ordered to shoot on a crowd of their fellow-countrymen; and in Petrograd there had been meetings of protest in which both officers and men had foregathered. The City Prefect, Balk, who had been appointed simply because, in the words of Rasputin, 'he was our own man', was responsible for public order; but he was subordinated to the general commanding. As late as January, the capital had been detached from the Northern Front, where Ruzsky was again in command, and became a separate unit under a rear general of no ability, Habalov. It had been arranged that in the event of disturbances the police should shoot first, then the Cossacks and finally the regulars, and one battalion was responsible for each ward of the city. Batteries of heavy artillery were lying at Tsarskoe Selo, and had several weeks earlier been tampered with. According to Beletsky, Protopopov had sent for a supply of machine-guns, and had told him that they had arrived.[1] Afterwards he most vigorously denied all responsibility for this and threw it on the military commanders; but certainly the machine-guns were there and were used.

The Emperor had recently commanded Gurko to send to Petrograd four regiments of the Guard Cavalry, but Gurko, who had already given his warnings, knew very well that the Guard were disgusted at the prospect of being called in to suppress a popular rising.[2] He had sent instead three crews of sailors. Protopopov, reporting to the Emperor on March 6th, had asked to return next day. On the 7th he was received by the Empress; the Emperor, she told him, insisted on spending a month at the front, and she had done her utmost to dissuade him. The Emperor entered the room while they were talking; he took Protopopov off to his study, and there he told him what Gurko had done. Protopopov exclaimed that the sailors, who were recruited from the town workers, were the most revolutionary element in the fighting forces. The Emperor in deference to the Empress, had consented to reduce his stay at Headquarters to three weeks. 'The time is such, Sir', said Protopopov, 'that you are wanted both here and there . . . I

[1] BELETSKY, *Padenie*, v, 264. [2] KNOX, 515.

very much fear the consequences.' The Emperor had seldom seemed so agitated, but he kindly took Protopopov by the arm, and promising to be back if possible within a week, he said good-bye to him, begging him to take care of the Empress.[1] He left the next day (Mar. 8th). From the station of Bologoe he sent his wife a telegram: 'Feel again firm, but very lonely', and in a letter to her, he says: 'I am terribly sad.' He has a bad cough. In reply to her next letter, he writes: 'It is a great comfort to me in my loneliness.'

On the day that Nicholas left his home, measles broke out in the family. The first to take it were Olga and the boy, and the next day Tatyana, who was the most useful to her mother, followed suit, and also Vyrubova, whom since the murder of Rasputin the Empress had removed from her 'little house' to the palace. The Empress always nursed her own children in spite of her very bad heart trouble.[2] She had direct communication with Headquarters by telephone, which public scandal had altered to communication with Berlin.

On reaching Headquarters the Emperor found Alexeyev returned from his leave, and adds: 'On his face there is a calm expression such as I have not seen for a long time.' Probably Alexeyev's mind was made up, if not long since, for he again begged for concessions for the nation. 'Here in the house', writes Nicholas, 'it is so still. No noise, no excited shouts' (his boy is not with him). And the absurdity of his situation is illustrated by his writing at such a critical moment: 'I shall take up dominoes again in my spare time.' 'The stillness here', he writes, 'depresses me when I am not working . . . You write about my being firm, a master; that is quite right. Be assured that I do not forget, but it is not necessary to snap at people right and left every minute.' On the 9th he suggests that the two remaining children, Maria and Anastasia, should be allowed to get the measles too, so as to get it over, and recommends that they might perhaps be sent to Crimea for their recovery. 'My brain is resting here', he writes, 'no Ministers, no troublesome questions demanding thought. I consider that this is good for me, but only for my brain.' The suite to which in other days his cheerful kindliness had given animation, were now nearly all alienated from him. The heavy snowfalls had

[1] PROTOPOPOV, *Predsmertnaya Zapiska*, 191-3. [2] VYRUBOVA, 96.

so blocked the transport that the army was within three or four days of a shortage of food supplies; 57,000 trucks were said to be held up.[1] 'It is terrible,' writes the Tsar. At the same time, he is complaining of an 'excruciating pain' in his chest, which however passes away while he is at his prayers.

No wonder that Mosolov has written of the staff, 'We were living on another planet.'[2]

[1] Paléologue, 213-4. [2] Mosolov, 125.

CHAPTER XV

REVOLUTION

The ocean (overpeering of his list)
Eats not the flats with more impiteous haste.
Hamlet, IV, 5

On the very day of the Tsar's departure (Mar. 8th), while the Duma violently attacked the food policy of the Government, disorders broke out in the city, where already thousands of workers were on strike. Crowds wandered about the streets, calling for bread and peace and singing the Russian version of the 'Marseillaise'. There was some looting in the poorer parts to the north of the Neva, and on the Nevsky Prospekt itself there were conflicts with the Cossacks.

On the 9th (Friday) the disorders increased, and in the northern wards the crowd began to sack the bakeries. It has since been declared that there were really supplies of bread in the city for several days, and that the trouble was due to the extremely tardy distribution;[1] the bakers, in their turn, complained that they could not get the necessary fuel for doing their work. The Cossacks were brought into play to assist the police; but Carrick noted that there was still a certain amount of good humour, and in reply to the crowd the Cossacks shouted back: 'We won't shoot.'[2]

Rodzyanko got into touch with the Prime Minister. An urgent meeting of the Cabinet was held, though so far the only question seemed to be that of the food supply. Protopopov was again absent; but by invitation Rodzyanko and the Mayor of Petrograd were present. They insisted that the food distribution should be committed to the town council, to which the Cabinet readily agreed, though there would necessarily be some little delay in organizing the change. The Cabinet also decided to seek the co-operation of the Duma; and two of its members, who could command respect there, Pokrovsky and Rittich, paid a visit to it and talked with Basil Maklakov and others. The Duma men

[1] HABALOV, I, 186. [2] CARRICK, 64.

made it quite clear that they could not support any Cabinet where the members were not responsible to the Prime Minister for the unity of their policy, and this was reported to the Cabinet.

On the Saturday (Mar. 10th) the crowds were even larger. They bore red flags and shouted 'Down with the German woman' (the Empress). The police fired, and there were a hundred wounded. Police patrols paraded the streets. The Cabinet met again, and sat till five in the morning. This time Protopopov was present. The Duma's answer was reported. Nearly all the Ministers were only too ready to be replaced by men whom the country would follow. They communicated this wish by the long telephone to the Emperor at Headquarters, but they were commanded to stay at their posts. They begged him to return. They also decided to prorogue the Duma not at all out of hostility to it, but on the ground that it could hardly work in the existing conditions, and as they had offered their resignations, time would be required for the appointment of a new and popular Cabinet.[1]

It was really something like a repetition of the situation in the summer crisis of 1915, when the majority of the Cabinet, who were in favour of a popular Ministry and offered their own resignations, had considered a similar friendly prorogation, which Goremykin managed to convert into a hostile one; but it was hardly to be expected that all this would be understood by the public.

Even before the War, it had been the practice for the Emperor to leave with the Prime Minister during his absence blank orders of prorogation or of dissolution, where in case of urgency the date was to be filled in by the Premier, and originally these dates had been settled in consultation with the President of the Duma, a practice which had latterly been abandoned. Golitsyn had in his possession such 'blanks', both for prorogation and dissolution. Protopopov, though he afterwards protested that this was not so, according to the evidence of his colleagues had throughout stood not for prorogation but for dissolution.[2]

Protopopov told the truth when he compared himself and the Emperor as persons who both evaded plain speaking where possible, and in his report over the long telephone to Headquarters we know from that side that he quite failed to bring home

[1] Golitsyn, *Padenie*, II, 264; Beliayev, *Padenie*, II, 237.
[2] Golitsyn, *Padenie*, II, 259.

the seriousness of the situation.[1] Even in Petrograd itself the question was still in the first place one of food; and the Emperor, away in the wilderness of a small provincial town, had no means of judging the situation. In reply to the nerve-wracked Habalov, the Emperor at 9 p.m. sent a telephone message:[2] 'I command that the disorders in the capital shall be stopped to-morrow, as they are inadmissible at the heavy time of war with Germany and Austria. Nicholas.'[3] By this message he signed his own dethronement. It is significant of the complete disorder that the War Minister in Petrograd was never informed of this telegram till after the Revolution. Habalov showed the telegram to Protopopov.[4] He himself was in dismay, and from this moment completely lost what balance he had, but he saw no way of disobeying the order.

On Sunday, March 11th, the people of the capital read the posters in which Habalov announced that crowds were forbidden and that if they gathered, he would open fire. The crowds were huger than ever; the troops fired four or five times and many persons were killed. The Pavlovsky regiment mutinied and killed its colonel, but it was disarmed for the time being by the crack regiment of the Guard, Peter the Great's Preobrazhensky. By the evening order was restored, and Protopopov even made a tour of inspection through the quiet streets.

In the course of this day there were urgent Cabinet consultations. Its meeting of March 10th had ended only at four o'clock in the morning; but the War Minister, Beliayev, who as such was specially responsible, consulted the Premier in the morning and asked for another meeting in the evening. The Cabinet met at nine o'clock and sat till 2 a.m. Protopopov, who was present, spoke at great length, but very vaguely, though it was clear that he strongly desired the dissolution of the Duma.

But the worst was now to come. The Volynsky regiment of the guard had at first participated in the firing on the people, but in disgust had retired to its barracks. Here there were heated discussions, and in the end the regiment mutinied and killed one of its officers. At this time most of the regiments in the capital were

[1] Voeykov, *Padenie*, iii, 71.
[2] They were usually called telephonograms.
[3] Habalov, *Padenie*, i, 190; Voeykov, *Padenie*, iii, 71.
[4] Protopopov, *Padenie*, iv, 46.

short of officers, and these were nearly all either wounded men or those who had successfully escaped being sent to the front. Habalov's own deputy was away ill, possibly by design, and of the colonels next under him, the two senior were not to be found.

On receiving the order of prorogation, the Duma had refused to disperse. For all that happened there in these hectic days the best record — at once the most objective and the most picturesque — is that of Shulgin. On the 11th, he, the Conservative, urged the others to get ready as soon as possible their own list of new Ministers; as we know, it had already been drafted; he was also the first to recommend the inclusion of Kerensky; but no action was taken. 'We had not the courage', he writes, 'or rather the saving cowardice, to think of the gap yawning.' On the other hand Kerensky, young Labour leader, in the early thirties, was in his element. 'We must do something,' he said. 'Are you going to do something?' He only insisted that the power should not be given to bureaucrats, that is, those already associated with the official world. Another Labour man, Skobolev, declared: 'You have the confidence of the people.'[1]

On this day Rodzyanko sent an urgent telegram to the Emperor, reporting the disturbances, and ending: 'May the blame not fall on the wearer of the crown.' Nicholas, on receiving it, put it aside with the comment: 'Some more rubbish from that fat Rodzyanko.'[2] At the same time Rodzyanko got into connection with all the generals in the highest commands, asking for their support, which he very soon received from Ruzsky and Brusilov, and later from all the rest.

On the Monday (the 12th) the Volynsky regiment, whose barracks lay not far behind the Duma, was out, and that was the turning point in the whole story. Three hours before they came out, the leaders of all the groups of the extreme Left were conferring in Kerensky's quarters. The representative of the Bolsheviks, Yurenin, declared: 'The reaction is gaining strength, the unrest in the barracks is subsiding. Indeed, it is clear that the working class and the soldiery must go different ways. We must not rely on day dreams and preparations for revolution, but on systematic propaganda at the works and the factories in store for better days.' This confirms Kerensky's picturesque statement:

[1] SHULGIN, 144-7. [2] FREDERICKSZ, *Padenie*, v, 38.

'The Revolution came of its own accord, born in the chaos of the collapse of Tsardom.'[1]

The regiment came out with only one officer accompanying it, the young Astakhov. Their invitation to other units went round like a snowball. Kerensky, the moment he heard they were out, telephoned to a friend to go straight to them and direct them to the Duma, and that is where they went, and not only they, but regiment after regiment as it joined them.

Habalov had news of the Volynsky about 6.30 a.m. The regimental commander was at this time a sick man, and Habalov sent a substitute and went himself to the regiment. It had by then drawn itself up outside its barracks fully armed, and had already been joined by a company of the Preobrazhensky from their neighbouring barracks and a number of factory workers. Great crowds were coming over the Alexander Bridge from the Viborg suburb in the north-east, which contained the Finland Station and a number of ammunition factories. The insurgents marched towards the Duma and wrecked the barracks of the gendarmes and the School of Ensigns. Habalov formed a column of reserves, which he had very great difficulty in obtaining — 6 companies with 15 machine-guns. It was to push down towards the Duma and confine the revolt to the loop of the Neva which almost surrounded it. The column was commanded by a badly wounded officer from the front, Col. Kutepov, the same who in 1930 was mysteriously kidnapped in Paris. No news came back from this column. The Assize Court near the bridge had now been sacked and was on fire, and the firemen who arrived on the scene were driven off by the crowd. Two detachments of the Moscow Regiment endeavoured to isolate the Arsenal but were overwhelmed and the Arsenal taken. A huge crowd filled the Sampson Prospekt and the troops quartered there stood doubtfully in front of their barracks. By noon 25,000 were arrayed on the side of the revolution. The military forces were now divided, and fighting went on the whole day. Government troops were firing with machine-guns on the Nevsky, but the military headquarters were captured and as many as twenty of the police stations; all these were set on fire. By the evening Habalov only had under his control the central part of the city, where he drew up his small remaining

[1] Kerensky, C.L., 235-6.

forces in front of the Winter Palace: three companies of the Ismailovsky (from the other end of the city) and three of the Chasseurs of the Guard. One commander after another had replied to his requests that if he sent him his few dependable units, the rest would break away at once. An appeal to the garrison at Kronstadt brought the same answer. He was joined for a time by some of the Preobrazhensky and strangely enough by the Pavlovsky which arrived with its band playing. He had hardly any shell or cartridges, and access to the northern factories was of course out of the question. Some of his officers were already urging him to make his peace with Rodzyanko. The fortress of St. Peter and St. Paul, on the north side of the river, was besieged. There were barricades on the broad Liteiny Prospekt near the Duma. Most of the troops, including the Guards, had now gone over. The prisons were opened and the prisoners set free. Again, there was no sign of general direction other than what has been mentioned.[1] The revolted regiments made for the obvious marks, just as in July 1789 the whole of Paris, without organization, made for the Bastille; and the great wave went over them like a flood. Amidst the blaze of the burning buildings fighting continued on all sides in the evening.

Of this day's happenings, March 12th, we have a vivid picture from the Director of Police, Vasilyev. The night before, Protopopov had been supping with him and his family before going to the Cabinet meeting, and Vasilyev was sent for at midnight to report on the police measures taken for the tranquillity of the city.

> It was three in the morning [he writes] when I came back home. The Ministers had let me see their anxieties and their discouragement. The feeling of their heavy responsibilities oppressed me, and their nervousness had passed on to me. Crushed with fatigue, I was a long time unable to get to sleep.
>
> At six in the morning the telephone bell woke me sharply; the City Prefect informed me that an N.C.O. of the Volynsky Regiment of the guard named Kirpichnikov had just killed his superior officer, Training-Captain Lashkevich; the assassin had disappeared, and the attitude of the regiment was threatening. The news crushed me; I now saw how far anarchy had infected the barracks. The murder had taken

[1] Habalov, *Padenie*, I, 198-200.

place on military ground; so I could do nothing direct, and called General Habalov to the telephone. No use; the Governor could not be found, and from the vague answers which were given me, I could not know where he had gone. The N.C.O. Kirpichnikov, who escaped abroad, has later naively confessed that he fled without knowing whether an hour later he would be a national hero or hanged. This remark is a picture of the situation; no one in Petrograd had then the least idea of the turn which events would take.

Through my window I could see an unusual excitement in the street. Soon there passed hurrying military cars; in the distance shots resounded. The telephone rang again, and again the City Prefect gave me bad news; Brigadier-General Dobrovolsky, commanding a battalion of sappers of the Guard, had been killed by his men. Then events moved fast; the Volynsky Regiment, which had risen after the murder of Captain Lashkevich, had chased its officers out of the barracks. The mutineers joined the Preobrazhensky and Lithuanian regiments of the Guard, whose barracks were near their own. They had succeeded in taking the Arsenal on the Liteiny.[1] Soldiers were dashing about the streets armed with guns and machine-guns. A roaring crowd invaded the quarters of the prison of preliminary confinement (before trial) and opened the cells; soon it was the same in all the prisons of the city. The police stations of the various wards were carried by the mob. Policemen, who were not able to change into mufti were torn to pieces. The fire finished off the rest. Most of this took place in the Liteiny[1] quarter. I was told on the telephone that the criminals freed by the mutineers had set fire to the offices of the Regional Assize Court of Petrograd; this meant an irreparable loss and the destruction of archives which could not be replaced.

There could no longer be any doubt; the situation was extremely serious. Petrograd had for several days been in the hands of the military authorities, who proved powerless to prevent the murder of officers by the revolutionary troops and to overcome the insurrection. The sequel proved this only too clearly. The mutinous troops disarmed their officers; any resistance meant death. One detachment of engineers, which had remained faithful and was doing all it could to resist the mutineers, was crushed. The insurgents succeeded in seizing

[1] Vasilyev writes 'Lithuanian'. The right word is 'Liteiny', the Foundry Prospekt.

the Officers School on the Kirochnaya and disarming its occupants. Their number increased under one's eyes. The mob was rushing to the centre of the town, not to miss so fine an opportunity for plunder.

The bridge connecting the Liteiny quarter with the Viborg quarter to the north of the Neva was held for some time by police officers armed with machine-guns, but soon they were overwhelmed by numbers. The crowd rushed on the barracks of the Moscow Regiment of the Guard. Some detachments resisted, arms in hand. They were soon overflowed and the Moscow Regiment joined in the revolt.

I was preparing to go to my office and try to see Protopopov, who lived in the main building. As I was getting ready to start, a courier came up and told me that a sharp fusillade made the Liteiny Prospect impracticable. The police were making a last effort to prevent the insurgents from crossing the bridge. The courier begged me not to risk my life uselessly and wait till things were quiet again.

The only thing left to me was to get into telephonic communication with the (Police) Department. My secretary told me they were going on working as usual in the office, though not without great nervousness. As I had several reasons to fear an assault by the insurgents, I gave orders to send all the staff away. My orders came just in time. A little later my secretary rang me up and told me that a furious crowd had made its way into the building. I at once gave orders to burn the books with the personal addresses of the employees and secret agents. As I learned later, the 'free people' had ransacked all the offices. Some of the leaders had tried, no doubt out of personal interest, to find the section of identification of criminals. All the records, photographs, finger-print albums relating to ordinary criminals, thieves, swindlers and murderers were thrown out into the court and solemnly burnt. The insurgents also forced my tills and appropriated the sum of 25,000 roubles of public money. From the Police-Department the crowd made its way to the quarters of Protopopov and sacked them. Afterwards, according to eye witnesses, cloaked women of respectable appearance came out of the Minister's flat carrying objects of value. I pass over the innumerable telephone calls which I received in the hours that followed. The Moscow authorities wanted at all costs to know what was happening in Petrograd. I replied to Colonel

Martynov, chief of the Okhrana, that a serious mutiny had broken out and I would do my best to keep him informed. The disorder was so great on all sides that neither the insurgents nor the military authorities thought of occupying the telephone exchange. It continued to work normally, maintaining a perfect neutrality and thus allowing both the representatives of order and the revolutionary leaders to coordinate their action. Still it was not long before the employees abandoned their work to get off home as soon as possible, and it became more and more difficult to get a connection. In the end the direct line through to the Winter Palace was interrupted. After that I could not ring up the Okhrana.

I was also surprised to get a telephone call from Protopopov, who had taken refuge at the Marie Palace. I gave him in a few words a rough sketch of the situation, adding that the military authorities appeared absolutely powerless, as the troops were making common cause with the insurgents.

I soon left my quarters, accompanied by my wife and my friend, Gvozdev. To tell the truth, I did not know where to go, though I had on me a passport for abroad under a borrowed name. I thought for a moment of joining my brother who lived in the Astoria Hotel; on reflection I did not do so, and the event proved I was right. The hotel was about to be occupied by the insurgents. I then went to a friend, an engineer named A——, who lived near the hotel. We were well received. All the same it was impossible to think of sleeping. Rifle and machine-gun fire was raging. Heavy lorries, crammed with armed men, were dashing through the streets. We passed a very restless night.'[1]

Let us follow the events of this day in the Duma. Shulgin and the Cadet Shingarev, who now lived with him on the north side of the river, made their way thither, with difficulty. On their road they passed the funeral procession of one of the authors of the pre-war prosperity, Alexeyenko, formerly Chairman of the Budget Committee of the Duma. As they crossed the river, Shingarev ironically remarked: 'Both banks recognize us at present.'[2] But as they came nearer through the crowded and agitated streets, Shulgin observed: 'I think our role is over.'

At 11.0 a.m. Kerensky, Nekrasov and Chkheidze asked Milyukov to support an immediate summons of all Four Dumas, including

[1] VASILYEV, 166-70. [2] SHULGIN, 153.

the two first which were elected by general franchise. This might have given the necessary basis for popular support, but Milyukov refused. The news went round that open elections by show of hands were proceeding at various points in the city. These elections were for a new Soviet or 'Council of Workmen Delegates', such as had intervened in 1905 after the general strike had begun and endeavoured to give it direction. Word came that a crowd of 80,000 was on its way to the Duma. The leaders of groups met in the President's cabinet. It was understood that, as in 1905, Labour would be sure to ask for a constituent assembly, and to this Milyukov was opposed. An officer dashed in, asking for help. Kerensky confirmed that urgent action was necessary if any control were to be maintained, and he was himself preparing to start for the barracks to establish it. 'I must know,' he asked, 'what I can tell them. Can I say that the Imperial Duma is with them, that it takes the responsibility on itself, that it stands at the head of the movement?' No answer was given: but his figure, writes Shulgin, seemed to grow to significance that minute. 'He spoke decisively, authoritatively, as one who had not lost his head. His words and his gestures were sharp and clear-cut, and his eyes shone.'[1] His eloquence, direct and whole-hearted, was essentially that which could take command of a crowd. It was decided to set up a 'provisional committee' of all the leading parties except the Rights. Shulgin was on it, Rodzyanko, Milyukov, Nekrasov, Kerensky and the Social Democrat Chkheidze – in a word it was the committee of the Progressive Bloc with the addition of the two last names. Kerensky, by his authority alone, had managed to create some kind of a guard for the Duma.

And now the crowd arrived, and flooded the halls, so that there was no room to move. It was a great unwashen crowd, and the pressure, though friendly, was overwhelming. As Shulgin amusingly writes: 'Ils viennent jusque dans vos bras.' Most of the Duma members were still mazed, and no wonder, at this sudden happening. It was not fear of death, Shulgin writes, death did not seem to matter; they were simply lost in amazement. But Kerensky, as he puts it, was 'one of those who can dance on a marsh', and this marsh was one that had 'little hillocks on which he could find a footing', like those on the marshy front from which

[1] Shulgin, 160.

Shulgin had come; or again, changing his metaphors, that there were 'little hooks' at which he alone could catch.

> He seemed to grow every minute. The soldiers who had streamed in consulted him and took his orders without question.
> And look! One of the first prisoners of the Revolution, Shcheglovitov, [the evasive reactionary ex-Minister of Justice] is brought in. He is in near danger of lynching, but Kerensky strides up to meet him, and says in his vibrant voice: 'Ivan Gregorevich, you are arrested. Your life is not in danger. The Imperial Duma does not shed blood'.

And this was like a watchword, everywhere received with reverence. After all there was someone in the Duma who could command, and Shulgin describes the crowd as standing in the great lobby 'as if in church'. As to the rest:

> We did not have an idea of what was happening, and certainly no plan or idea of how to deal with it.[1]

All were feeling as if they were in some strange new country. One of Milyukov's opponents dashes up to him: 'Let me introduce myself,' he says, 'your bitterest enemy'.

> In one of the smaller rooms of passage was a group of men particularly excited about something. In the middle of this group was a man in a winter overcoat and scarf rather rumpled, grey-haired but still young. He was calling out something, and they were pressing on him. Suddenly he seemed to see an anchor of salvation; evidently he recognized someone. This 'some one' was Milyukov, who was pushing his way somewhere through the crowd, as white as a ringtail, but clean-shaven and 'quite respectable'. The slightly rumpled man threw himself at the well-preserved Milyukov: 'Paul Nikolayevich, what do they want of me? I have been six months in prison; they have dragged me here, and they say I have got to take the lead of the movement. What movement? What is happening? You see I don't know anything. What is it all? What do they want me for?' I did not hear what Milyukov said to him; but as he got away and drifted past me, I asked him 'Who is that man?' 'Why, don't you know? That's Hrustalev-Nosar'.

[1] SHULGIN, 171.

It was the famous president of the first Soviet of 1905; the Vice-President Trotsky was still far away in America. Meanwhile, poor old Tory Rodzyanko is saying: 'I don't want to revolt.' But Shulgin, who is even more conservative than Rodzyanko, urges him: 'Take the power, the position is plain; if you don't, others will.'

At night the city was arming. The executive of the new Soviet, hastily and very irregularly elected, had by now established itself in the hall of the budget committee of the Duma; one of the Vice-Presidents was Kerensky. Shulgin was by now convinced that the monarch must be sacrificed if there was to be any chance of preserving the dynasty, and, among other reasons, for this — it was the only way of saving his life.

While all this was going on, the Cabinet was also busy. In the morning some of the Ministers met at the Premier's quarters. None of them had expected such quick developments. Habalov arrived before the rest, and it was evident that he was completely distracted and quite incapable of taking any responsibility; Golitsyn observes that his report was a hopeless jumble. The colonels in charge were inexperienced men; and Beliayev suggested that the Cabinet should give Habalov an assistant in the person of General Zankevich, who had held a command at the front. He himself visited the City Prefecture, and could find no plan, organization or presence of mind. Beliayev insisted that the first step must anyhow be to dismiss Protopopov. Golitsyn saw difficulty in doing this without the sovereign's authority, but was prepared to take the responsibility if necessary.

The Cabinet met between six and seven p.m. Golitsyn at once addressed Protopopov and requested him to retire from his post, giving the plea of 'illness', if he desired; and Beliayev adds the comment that, as a matter of fact they very well knew that Protopopov was 'ill' all along. The man, who was to have saved the monarchy and taken all care of the Empress, makes no objection; this tragi-comical figure passes out. 'Now there is nothing left me, but to shoot myself,' he says, but that was to be left to others. No one says good-bye to him as he walks out. Beliayev makes a haphazard suggestion that he should be replaced at the Ministry of the Interior by one, General Makarenko; but someone remarks at once that Makarenko is at the head of the military discipline, and that at such a moment this would be a most unsuitable choice; in fact Makarenko points this out himself. The Grand Duke Michael has come to the meeting; he and Beliayev go off to the War Minister's residence, and there the Grand Duke speaks direct to Headquarters. He urges that there should at once be appointed a Minister who can command the confidence of the country, and suggests the name of Prince George Lvov; he asks leave to announce the appointment immediately. General Alexeyev, who comes to the telephone, asks him to wait half an hour for an answer. In forty minutes he speaks again, this time on behalf of the Emperor. The Tsar tells his brother to announce that he is coming at once himself, and will take his decision on his arrival. The Grand Duke lingers on with Beliayev till two o'clock in the morning, and then sets off home for Gatchina. Meanwhile, the Cabinet has dispersed of itself in various directions and most of its members by this time are already in hiding. Protopopov has taken shelter in a tailor's shop.[1]

On the early morning of Tuesday, the 13th, as soon as the Grand Duke had left, Beliayev went off to the Winter Palace, where the staff was still protected by a few loyal troops, drawn up on the Palace Square. The Preobrazhenksy, the Pavlovsky, the sailors of the Guard had all gone. General Zankevich had been introduced to his small command. Attack was out of the question. As it was now known that the Emperor was sending General Ivanov from Headquarters, the only hope was to hold on to one last fastness till he arrived. Zankevich wanted this to be the Winter Palace, at whose gates he thought that the last defenders of the sovereign should die fighting. Habalov, now half superseded, preferred the neighbouring Admiralty, so placed by Peter the Great that it commanded a free range down the three great diverging arteries of the capital; but what was the use of a free range with only eighty shells to fire and hardly any cartridges? The little band moved from one to the other, first the Admiralty, then the Winter Palace. The Emperor's brother, Michael, who at this point arrived from the last Cabinet meeting, asked that the Palace should be evacuated, so the Admiralty was occupied again. As there was no water supply or fodder, the few Cossacks were allowed

[1] Beliayev, *Padenie*, II, 240-2; Golitsyn, ibid., II, 266-7; Protopopov, IV, 101.

to go. But there was also no food, except a short supply of bread obtained with difficulty and distributed to the men, of whom in all there were about 1500. From time to time single gun shots are fired at the garrison to which there is no reply. At noon the Naval Minister Grigorovich intervenes. The fortress of St. Peter and St. Paul has been taken and will turn its guns on the Admiralty unless it is evacuated in twenty minutes. The troops lay down their weapons and go out unarmed; there was no authority with which a surrender could have been negotiated. By now captured machine-guns were dashing along the streets with red flags, and fires blazed up at one new point after another in the city. Police and officers were being hunted down, and urgent appeals for help were made to the Provisional Committee of the Duma. In particular, a group of officers were still defending themselves at the Astoria Hotel. As the early evening closed in, fighting continued in the dark; but the battle was really over.[1]

The centre of direction was now at the Duma, where both the Provisional Committee and the Soviet had their headquarters, and throughout that Tuesday it was flooded out, as before, by invading crowds singing the 'Marseillaise'. Its members were constantly called out, to address one deputation after another. Rodzyanko in particular, with his bull-like voice, had to make speech after speech. His bulk and gravity, as well as his office, made him the most suitable spokesman. He was doing all that he could to shout into his hearers some enthusiasm for the defence of the country against the foreign enemy.

By now no government controlled, no officers commanded. The committee was hard at work and appointed commissaries to deal with the most urgent tasks. Appeals streamed into the Duma, and prisoners were dragged thither, mostly from the police, who were still firing from some points of vantage with machine-guns down the broad straight streets of the city. These men owed their lives to the motto that had been set by Kerensky. 'For that', writes Shulgin, his political rival, 'let us say thank you to him; let it at some time or other be reckoned to him.'[2] 'They were pitiful . . . these policemen,' he says. 'One could not even look at them: in

[1] BELIAYEV, *Padenie*, II, 242-3; HABALOV, ibid., 201-6.
[2] SHULGIN, 188.

mufti, disguised, frightened humbled like the small shopkeepers whom they used to bully, there they stood in a great coiling queue, which led to the doors of the inner chamber of the Duma. They were waiting their turn to be arrested.' By now the President's cabinet was full of prisoners, and the more important of them were housed appropriately enough in the pavilion set apart for the Ministers.

> Suddenly [writes Shulgin] out of Volkonsky's room [the Vice-President's] there was coming something specially exciting; and at once the reason was whispered to me: 'Protopopov is arrested'; and at that moment I saw in the mirror the door burst open violently, and Kerensky broke in. He was pale, his eyes shone, his arm was raised: with this stretched-out arm he seemed to cut through the crowd; everyone recognized him and stood back on either side, simply afraid at the sight of him. And then in the mirror I saw that behind Kerensky there were soldiers with rifles and, between the bayonets, a miserable little figure with a hopelessly harassed and terribly sunken face — it was with difficulty that I recognized Protopopov. 'Don't dare touch that man!' shouted Kerensky — pushing his way on, pallid, with impossible eyes, one arm raised, cutting through the crowd, the other tragically dropped, pointing at 'that man'. This was the arch criminal against the revolution, the ex-Minister of the Interior.
>
> 'Don't dare touch that man!' It looked as if he were leading him to execution, to something dreadful. And the crowd fell apart. Kerensky dashed past like the flaming torch of revolutionary justice, and behind him they dragged that miserable little figure in the rumpled great-coat, surrounded by bayonets. A grim sight!
>
> Cutting through 'Rodzyanko's cabinet' Kerensky, with these words, burst into the Catherine Hall [the great lobby] which was crammed full of soldiers, future Bolsheviks and every kind of rabble. It was here that the real danger for Protopopov began. Here they might throw themselves on that miserable little figure, drag him from the guards, kill him, tear him to pieces. The feeling against Protopopov was as incensed as possible. But that did not happen. Struck dumb by this strange sight, the pallid Kerensky dragging his victim, the crowd fell away before them. 'Don't dare touch that

man!' It seemed 'that man' was no longer a man, and they let him through.[1]

The Duma was now sending speakers in all directions to restore some measure of control, and men of the most various parties took part in this work. The day passed like a nightmare, writes Shulgin. He felt as if they had all been let down into some deep, sticky hole. Night came, and the hubbub grew less. Everyone camped out as best he could. In fact, as Kerensky has written, 'all Russia was now camping out'. The members slept where they could find room — on chairs or on the floor.

On this day (Tuesday, Mar. 13th) lorries, crowded with revolutionary soldiers, made their way to Tsarskoe Selo, which was only fourteen miles off. No special steps had been taken for the protection of the palace, though at one moment the City Prefect, Balk, had offered to Protopopov to try to cut his way through. Gilliard has described how after the death of Rasputin the Empress had seemed to be 'painfully waiting for some unavoidable misfortune'.[2] Her confidence had been smashed; but she was not one to break down, and she had found a spur to new exertion in the claims of her sick children. The troublesome Vyrubova, who had been moved into the palace and had also caught the measles, writes, 'I kept seeing her beside my bed dozing, now preparing a drink, now smoothing the cushions, now talking to the doctor'.[3] She had had full reports by telephone of the disorders in the capital. About 10.0 on the Monday evening Beliayev had urged that she should leave at once, which was of course impossible with the children in bed with measles. She communicated with Voyeikov at Headquarters, and the answer was that the Emperor was coming. In the night Habalov, evidently quite overwrought, telephoned that he was still holding the Winter Palace and begged for food supplies; but soon afterwards he finally moved to the Admiralty, and this line was closed. By midday on the Tuesday, Count Apraxin had come with full news. The railway lines were already being interrupted. It was now that the lorries came; and when they arrived the Empress was perfectly calm and courageous. In the evening rifle shots were audible in the palace. The whole garrison of the little town had marched off fully armed without its officers; but the palace guard had assembled in the courtyard;

[1] SHULGIN, 189-91. [2] GILLIARD, 138. [3] VYRUBOVA, 96.

it consisted of two battalions of the Picked Composite Regiment, one of the Guard, two squadrons of the Cossack Escort, one company of the First Railway Regiment, and one heavy field battery. Songs, music and shots were heard from the town. The reserve battalions of the three rifle regiments of the Guard had joined the insurgents and thrown open the prisons. The night was full of alarms. There was a skirmish with a palace patrol, and it was felt that some of the defending troops were doubtful. Accompanied by her plucky daughter of seventeen, Maria, who was already sickening for measles, the Empress went out into the snow and visited her defenders. It was bitterly cold — 40 degrees below zero — and she had them brought in by groups into the palace to get warm, and served them with tea. She herself brought pillows and blankets for those of the staff of the Court to whom she had given refuge. She slept fully dressed, but rose several times to see that all was well and to give the news that came in. By 2.0 a.m., the noise outside was dying down.[1]

The next morning (Wednesday, Mar. 14th) the little town was quiet. General Ivanov arrived that day with his small force and had a short audience of the Empress. No more news came in except that the Emperor's train had not been able to get through. The family, as we know, had been completely alienated from all the Grand Dukes and no Christmas presents had been sent to them this year; but the Empress summoned the one remaining uncle of the Emperor, the Grand Duke Paul, who lived in Tsarskoe. He came, says Count Benckendorff, at 5.0 p.m. in a very excited state, and a heated talk took place. He wanted her to sign on behalf of the Emperor a muddled kind of 'constitution' which he had drawn up with the Grand Duke Michael. He sent it to her typed out next day, but she gave it no attention. Paul therefore signed it himself with some other Grand Dukes and sent it to Milyukov, who received it with the professorial comment: 'It is an interesting document.'[2] The night of the 14th passed with frequent alarms. In the course of it, the railway company killed its two officers and started for Petrograd. The battalion of the Guard also left, alleging orders from the capital and leaving its colours and officers behind. An armistice was arranged by which the troops facing each other before the palace donned white

[1] BENCKENDORFF, 2-7. [2] PALEY, 46; BENCKENDORFF, 15.

armlets and engaged themselves not to attack each other. In the town the wine shops were looted.[1]

Meanwhile the Emperor was starting for the capital. He had committed the task of dealing with the disorders to General N. I. Ivanov, the former commander of the South-Western Front, who, when replaced by Brusilov, had been brought to Headquarters as a military adviser. Nicholas knew that he was acceptable to the Empress, who in several letters had urged his appointment as Minister for War. Ivanov was an old, loyal, and tried Conservative, the typical Russian general of the old style, honest and human and always at home with his troops. He has given his plain and impressive record of his journey. At 8 p.m. on the 12th he received his orders to go to Petrograd; two regiments from the Northern Front and two from the Western were to be sent to support him. He, like others, had already urged reform; and for this he had felt that the Emperor was displeased with him. Alexeyev, who was entirely opposed to any forcible attempt at suppression of the revolt, recommended that he should only take with him a single battalion, composed in the main of soldier knights of St. George. In that splendid order of chivalry, established by Catherine the Great, there were distinctions alike for officers and men, and the soldier knights were always the pillar of a regiment in an advance. Nicholas had spoken of the troubles as only food riots, but Ivanov told him that the true cause lay much deeper, and that the garrison of Petrograd was not to be trusted. He proceeded to get into contact by telephone with Habalov, with whom he was even able to converse as late as the morning of the 13th, when the Government's troops were on the verge of quitting the Winter Palace. He set out in the early hours of Tuesday, the 13th, and heard at the last moment that the Tsar was coming too, though by a different route. They conversed at the station at 3.0 a.m. Ivanov was given full powers to act in the capital, and Nicholas said to him: 'We shall probably meet to-morrow at Tsarskoe Selo.' Ivanov did not fail to get in a last word: 'Remember the reforms.' With only one battalion, he had of course no intention of attacking, and he told Nicholas that if he found the capital still in revolt he would not take his men in, to which the Tsar replied: 'Of course.'[2]

Ivanov and his men travelled by way of Vitebsk on the direct

[1] BENCKENDORFF, 14-15. [2] IVANOV, *Padenie*, V, 315-19.

line from Kiev to Petrograd, which passes through Mogilev, where the Headquarters still stood. They reached the junction of Dno very late at 6.30 a.m. on the 14th, and at once they were in the thick of things. A number of soldiers who had come from Petrograd were disarming the officers at the station; the local commander of gendarmes begged his help, telling him that Nicholas was also expected at Dno. Other trains arrived from the capital, simply crammed with disorderly soldiers. The windows were all smashed. Agitators were busy making vehement speeches. A soldier dashed straight at him with an officer's sword in each hand. Ivanov recalled an occasion where he had had to deal with mutinous troops at Kronstadt; he laid his hand on the man's shoulder and called out, 'On your knees!' Old habits held good, and the mutineer was removed.[1]

He proceeded farther north, and reach Vyritsa at six in the evening. Here he heard that the Ministers had been arrested and there was mutiny at Tsarskoe Selo; but he still pushed forward, after attaching a second engine to the back of his train in case he was compelled to retreat. He did succeed in reaching Tsarskoe Selo, where he had anyhow intended to stop, and here he had a short audience with the Empress, to whom he spoke clearly of the cause of the troubles and especially about Protopopov. The palace was still guarded, and he was told that Members of the Duma were now charged with its protection; but his own position was ominous. The town was quiet; but armoured cars, manned by revolutionary soldiers from Petrograd, probably dispatched to oppose him, began to appear. It would have been quite impossible for him to rely on his own men, and his presence could now only be a source of trouble. He received a telegram from Alexeyev saying that order had been restored in the capital, and that there was even hope of saving the monarchy. It ended: 'So it would be best not to attempt anything.' So Ivanov and his troops left the little town, and the whole enterprise petered out ignominously at a point on a branch line farther west.[2]

Nicholas had also started, going by Orsha, Vyazma and a branch railway which at Likhoslavl joins the main line from Moscow to Petrograd. Had he travelled behind Ivanov by the same direct route, he would have come straight to Tsarskoe Selo.

[1] IVANOV, *Padenie*, V, 320-1. [2] ibid., 321-3.

He chose the other to avoid dislocating the movements of the troop trains. His train left Mohilev between four and five on the morning of the 13th. At Likhoslavl, and also at Bologoe, he received telegrams from the capital. At Likhoslavl he learned that a Provisional Government was being set up under Rodzyanko, and that the Winter Palace had fallen; the City Prefect, Balk, and his assistant Wendorff were reported to be killed; the railways were now in charge of a member of the Duma, Bublikov; the travellers were warned that they would probably not be able to reach the station of Tosno. Revolutionary troops were said to be in Lyuban; a railway officer who had just come through declared that they had machine-guns.[1]

The Emperor had two trains, one preceding the other, and when this news reached the first train, it was decided to stop in Malaya Vishera and inform the sovereign, who was in the second. At 2 a.m. on the 14th the second train arrived. Everyone in it was asleep, and Voyeikov, the palace commandant, had to be waked. He went straight to the Tsar, and it was suggested that they should turn aside due westward and proceed by Bologoe to Pskov, the headquarters of General Ruzsky, who commanded the Northern Front and would have the military firmness and experience required to deal with such a situation. Nicholas accepted this suggestion with complete calm. Several writers, some hostile like Guchkov, have commented on his extraordinary self-command and restraint in critical circumstances, which, they insisted, were not at all to be identified with apathy; and the picture given of him at this time is very different from that of Kokovtsev's last interview. 'Well then, to Pskov,' he said; and General Dubensky, who gives much the most intelligent account of this journey, comments on his simple courage, and declares that he slept and talked just as at ordinary times.[2] The two trains, therefore, turned aside and passing through the junction of Dno, reached Pskov on the evening of the 14th. It had been rumoured that Rodzyanko was coming to Pskov, and the telephone was busily at work between him and Ruzsky throughout the night of the 14th.

This brings us back to the Duma. On the 14th there was still fighting in the city, and fires were still blazing. Officers and police were being hunted down by the soldiers and the mob.

[1] DUBENSKY, *Padenie*, VI, 402. [2] ibid., 405.

Troops were rallying at the Duma. They included the pet regiments from Tsarskoe Selo — the imperial convoy, the Cossack bodyguard, the Tsar's railway regiment and even the palace police. The Grand Duke Cyril of the Vladimir Branch, demonstratively hostile to his cousin, arrived leading the sailors of the Guard, who were under his command; we must credit him with the belief that this was the only way in which he could continue to keep them in control. The Soviet had already established itself at the Duma. It was a large body of about a thousand delegates. Its significance had been entirely altered by the fact that it was now not merely a Soviet of workmen members, but a Soviet of workmen and soldiers' delegates. The principle that a thousand workmen elected one delegate was supplemented by a representative from each company. The change was vital; for to all intents and purposes it made the Soviet master of the capital. It sat first in the huge lobby of Catherine; but later it moved into the actual hall of debates, crowding the Provisional Committee and its new commissaries, whose authority it did not challenge, farther and farther into corners of the Duma's own house. The Soviet did a good deal of valuable work in the restoration of order; but its attitude to the Duma and its Provisional Committee was more than doubtful. It did not take the responsibility, but it held the whip hand.

Let us continue Shulgin's lively narrative.[1] As he passed through the streets on his way to the Duma, they looked to him like 'known streets seeming unknown'. Great lorries rushed past crowded with revolutionary soldiers with fixed and pointed bayonets, bellowing as they went by. Shulgin paid a daring visit to the fortress. He managed to keep the peace there and arranged for the transfer of the fortress and the liberation of prisoners. He gets a ride back. He describes those whom he passes as 'men who seemed to come from some other kingdom'. All the time Kerensky maintains his commanding position. 'You can go,' he says in the old way to a man who has just delivered a packet to him; the soldiers retire and Kerensky, throwing it on the table, says: 'These are our secret treaties with the Powers; hide them!' and off he goes in the same dramatic way. As the Duma is crowded out and there is no chest available, the secret papers are hidden

[1] Shulgin, 208 ff.

under a table. Under another table are hidden two million roubles which could not be stowed elsewhere. When Cyril arrives with the sailors of the Guard, Rodzyanko makes them a speech on country and discipline and, 'touched for the moment', they greet him with a hurrah. Work is almost impossible; people come in from all sides to beg advice of the members. Kerensky is calling for Rodzyanko; officers are being killed, and something must be done at once. Some of the invaders almost attack Rodzyanko, who exclaims: 'What a rabble!' They are accusing him of being a capitalist. He thumps on a table and shouts: 'Take my shirt, if you want, but save Russia.' Rodzyanko is in communication with Headquarters, which the Tsar has now left. Alexeyev is for abdication. Rodzyanko wants to go to the Emperor, but no train can be found for him; and the Soviet, scenting danger, demands that he should not go unaccompanied. Meanwhile we find the monarchist Shulgin sending the Labour member Skobolev to arrange things at the fortress.

Now is posted up the famous Army Order Number One, which is one of the first products of the debates of the Soviet. It has already been put up all over the town. As will be seen from its title, it was originally intended for the local garrison, which had made the revolution, but its disruptive message was to break down the front.

> *March 1st* (14th), 1917. In the garrison of the military district of Petrograd to all soldiers of the Guard, army, artillery and fleet for immediate and exact execution and to the workmen of Petrograd for information.
>
> The Soviet of Workers and Soldiers Deputies has decided:
>
> (1) In all companies, battalions, regiments, parks, batteries, squadrons and separate services of every kind of military administration and on ships of the fighting fleet there must at once be elected representatives of the lower ranks of the above named fighting units.
>
> (2) In all fighting units which have not yet elected their representatives to the Soviet of Workers Deputies there must be chosen one representative per company who must present himself, with written certificate, in the building of the Imperial Duma by 10.0 a.m. on this 2nd (15th) March.
>
> (3) In all its political actions the military unit is under the Soviet of Workers and Soldiers Deputies and its committees.

(4) Orders of the military commission of the Imperial Duma should be carried out only in those cases where they do not contradict the orders of the Soviet of Workers and Soldiers Deputies.

(5) All kinds of armament such as rifles, machine-guns, armoured cars, etc., must be in the hands and under the control of company and battalion committees and in no case are they to be given to officers, even on their demand.

(6) In line and when carrying out service duties, soldiers must observe the strictest military discipline, but outside service and the line, in their political, ordinary and private life, soldiers can in no way be reduced in those rights which all citizens possess. In particular, standing to attention and saluting outside service are abolished.

(7) In like manner are abolished the titles used to officers: 'your excellency', 'your nobility', etc., and they are to be replaced by addressing them as Mr. General, Mr. Colonel and so on. Rude behaviour to soldiers of any fighting units and in particular the addressing of them as 'thou' is forbidden and any violation of this or any misunderstandings between officers and soldiers must be reported by the latter to the company committees.[1]

This was the first sign of a positive political purpose. The revolution had been made by the soldiers of Petrograd, mostly recruits. The real army was in the field, facing the enemy. The Soviet could not know what it would do, though those who were living at the front could probably have told it. Officers themselves were in a helpless position: there was no recognized civil authority to which they could turn for orders. It might all still prove to be a simple *émeute* which was ultimately suppressed. It would seem that Chkheidze, who was President of the Soviet, had this fear, for as he lay down to snatch some sleep in the Duma that night close to Shulgin, he murmured: 'It has all failed — I tell you, it has all failed. To save it, we shall need a miracle!'[2]

Shulgin urges Milyukov at once to write down the names of new Ministers, and this chivalrous Conservative pictures the conditions in which his courageous Liberal colleague sets about this task:

[1] DENIKIN, *Ocherki Russkoy Smuty*, I, 64-5.
[2] SHULGIN, 232.

> Amidst endless talks with thousands of people, plucking him by the arm, receiving deputations, speeches at interminable meetings in the lobby of Catherine, wild journeys to the regiments, discussions of long-phone telegrams from Headquarters, wrangles with the growing insolence of the Soviet Executive, Milyukov, squatting for a minute somewhere on a corner of a table, wrote down the list of Ministers. 'Minister of Finance? Yes, look here, that's difficult. The others all seem to work out somehow, but Minister of Finance' — 'Why Shingarev' — 'No, Shingarev must have Agriculture' — 'Alexeyenko's dead — happy Alexeyenko'. [The Prime Minister is to be Lvov, not Rodzyanko.]

So writes Milyukov

> holding his head in both hands . . . [He stood] a head and shoulders above others in mind and character.[1]

Guchkov of course is to have the War Office, and young Tereshchenko, the beet-sugar millionaire, who has thrown himself heart and soul into the Revolution, is eventually to be the Minister of Finance.

Of the two impromptu additions from the left, Chkheidse was offered the Ministry of Labour but refused it. Kerensky was offered that of Justice. As a Vice-President of the Soviet he was aware that it was opposed to any of its members joining the Ministry; but after brief but earnest consideration he consented, and carried its approval.[2] By this he established an all-important link between the two rival authorities.

In the evening arrives a deputation from the Soviet next door consisting of Sokolov (its secretary), Steklov, and Sukhanov; and Shulgin exclaims: 'Either arrest us or leave us to work.' Milyukov is engaged in long debates with these visitors: 'With a stubbornness which belonged only to him, he demanded that the Soviet should issue an appeal against violence to officers.' And Milyukov 'persuaded, entreated and cursed them. This went on a long time, it was endless. It was not a (regular) session. It was like this: A few men, quite worn out, lay in arm-chairs, and the three visitors sat at a little table with the grey-haired Milyukov. Really it was a debate between these four. The rest of us only occasionally replied out of the depths of our prostration. Kerensky dashed in,

[1] SHULGIN, 223. [2] KERENSKY, C. L., 259.

dashed out, lightning-like and dramatic. He threw in some tragic phrase and vanished, but in the end he too was completely worn out and sank into one of the arm-chairs. And there still sat Milyukov, stubborn and fresh, with pencil in hand. He jumps up, saying: "I want to speak to you alone." He goes out and gets agreement again.'[1]

Milyukov's persistent patience and equanimity was, as often before, a marvel: the more so as for four days on end he slept as best he could in the Duma.[2] He did indeed succeed in obtaining an agreed statement from the Soviet. There was to be a constituent assembly based on universal suffrage. The constituent assembly was to settle the form of government. All nationalities of the empire were to be equal (here the Liberal would have no difficulty in agreeing). Soldiers, apart from the requirements of discipline, were to enjoy all civil rights. But more immediately practical, and in the end fatal, was the agreement that the garrison of Petrograd should stay, as it was, in the capital; for the garrison meant the soldiers, and the soldiers were the reality in the Soviet.[3]

Late at night Rodzyanko is called out to make another speech in the snow. However, '"Mother Russia" works again, and they shout hurrah.' Rodzyanko reads out endless telegrams from Headquarters. He thinks the Emperor must absolutely resign. Guchkov comes back from the regiments, very gloomy; his friend, Prince Vyazemsky, a senior usher of the Duma, has been shot dead sitting by him in his car. Rodzyanko, Milyukov and Shulgin are all for saving the monarchy. 'Russia can't live without it,' says Shulgin. Then if the monarchy is to be saved, and Nicholas's life too, someone must go and bring back his abdication, and this task is entrusted to Guchkov and Shulgin. At five o'clock in the morning Guchkov writes out the text for the Emperor — not nearly as well as Nicholas was to write it himself. The two of them in the early dawn make their way to the station, which they find empty. A train is supplied in twenty minutes, and they start.[4]

According to N. Sokolov, the Emperor had a prolonged talk on the long telephone with the Empress before leaving Headquarters.[5]

[1] SHULGIN, 236. [2] MILYUKOV, *Padenie*, VI, 353.
[3] MILYUKOV, 47-8. [4] SHULGIN, 238-41.
[5] N. Sokolov, the investigator of the end of the imperial family, may well have got this from Gilliard, with whom he was intimate.

The agitating reports which he received in quick succession on the train must have shown him that the position was desperate. On his arrival at Pskov he did at last offer serious concessions, which Ruzsky communicated to Rodzyanko by telephone. He was now ready to satisfy the request of his Prime Minister and others to appoint a Premier who had the confidence of the country, presumably Rodzyanko, and to give him full authority for control over his colleagues and direction of policy, leaving to the sovereign as imperial prerogatives only foreign policy and the fighting services. Rodzyanko was himself already losing out in Petrograd, and he replied that these concessions came too late, as was only too evident there. Ruzsky reported the result of his talk at one o'clock at night.[1] The four divisions to be sent respectively from the northern and western fronts had failed to materialize; the two northern divisions revolted between Luga and Gatchina on their way to the capital, and the two from the western front never got anywhere.[2]

Alexeyev, on hearing from Rodzyanko, had on March 14th consulted by telephonogram all the Generals in command of Fronts, putting to them the question of abdication. From all five he received the same answer: they all regarded it as indispensable.[3] These answers were all communicated to Ruzsky on the morning of Thursday, March 15th, and he reported them to the Emperor. He also asked both his two next subordinate officers, Danilov and Savich, to give their opinion, and it was the same. Nicholas was greatly disturbed. They put it to him that, in face of the foreign enemy, this was the only course which could unite the nation. What guided him throughout, was the fear of a civil war on his account, and he readily answered that there was no sacrifice which he was not ready to make for Russia. A form of abdication had been sent by Alexeyev, and the Emperor, using his own words gave over the throne to his son, Alexis, for whom the Grand Duke Michael was to act as regent. This was the programme of the Progressive Bloc and the Duma committee, and had no doubt been communicated to Alexeyev. The document was dated 3 p.m. March 15th.

[1] DUBENSKY, VI, 404, 409. [2] DANILOV, 532.

[3] The Grand Duke Nicholas, Caucasus; Sakharov, Chief of Staff, Rumania; Brusilov, south-west; Evert, west; Ruzsky, north.

The abdication was to have been sent on by telephone to Rodzyanko by the commandant of the palace, Voyeikov, who was still with the Emperor. But it was now known at Pskov that Guchkov and Shulgin were on their way thither. Ruzsky therefore decided to hold it up till Guchkov and Shulgin had arrived; and it was well that he did so. In the interval Nicholas consulted his own doctor, who travelled with him, Fedorov, asking him if his son's ailment was incurable. Fedorov, a devoted and loyal servant, had to say that it was.[1] Nicholas decided, therefore, to abdicate in favour not of his son, but of his brother Michael. This was, as a matter of fact, directly illegal; the order of succession to the throne had been definitely settled by the Emperor Paul on his accession in 1801, and no departure could be made from it except by a formal renunciation, which in the boy's tender years would not have been in order; nor was he there to make it, as he was with his mother at Tsarskoe. On the other hand, the whole plan of the Duma Committee to save the monarchy depended on the accession of Alexis, as a regency was the obvious way of establishing a constitutional regime. To the country Michael would simply be another Romanov Tsar.

Guchkov and Shulgin, after a bleak journey through the mournful winter landscape of north Russia, reached Pskov at ten in the evening. They were the right men for the occasion. Guchkov would be sure to bring back the abdication, and Shulgin would see that the demand was presented in the most delicate way; his presence alone would make it clear that this demand was universal. Both men have given their accounts of what happened.[2] Guchkov was full of pity at approaching his arch-enemy at the moment of his deepest humiliation. Shulgin was affectionate and deeply distressed, and, above all, awed by this fateful crisis in the history of the Russian monarchy.

In the sympathetic accounts of this scene which both men have given, one feels at once that it was Nicholas who was master of the situation. Here was a part to play which was entirely in keeping with the best and highest in his character. There was no real difficulty about the abdication itself — had he not been abdicating

[1] There was no Rasputin. He had always said that after the age of thirteen the boy would be much stronger.
[2] SHULGIN, 266-77; Guchkov to B.P.

through the whole time of his reign? — and he was returning to the role for which nature had all along fitted him, that of the good loser, the willing accepter of defeat. The whole scene was one of a triumphant simplicity. He greeted them kindly, and in the sitting-room of his train they sat down to a simple talk. Guchkov spoke much too long; and the only gesture of impatience which Shulgin remarked was a look which seemed to ask: 'Is all this necessary?' But Guchkov spoke extremely well. He laid a quiet emphasis on the abandonment of the palace by the picked troops of the Guard, as the proof that there was no other way open. He and Nicholas had one thing in common, a burning Russian patriotism, and it was on this ground that he asked for abdication. The Emperor, speaking in a quiet voice, made no difficulty at all; but he communicated the all-important change which he had made in the order of succession, adding simply 'You will understand a father's feelings'. The two messengers were taken aback; they saw at once the difficulties of the change, and they asked if they might not discuss it between themselves, but they did not insist. The Emperor went for the corrected document, and handed it to them with the dignity of simplicity. The text, which is well known, in its final form runs as follows:

> In this great struggle with a foreign enemy, who for nearly three years has tried to enslave our country, the Lord God has been pleased to send down on Russia a new, heavy trial. The internal popular disturbances which have begun, threaten to have a disastrous effect on the future conduct of this persistent war. The destiny of Russia, the honour of our heroic army, the good of the people, the whole future of our dear country demand that whatever it cost, the war should be brought to a victorious end. The cruel enemy is gathering his last forces, and already the hour is near when our gallant army, together with our glorious allies, will be able finally to crush the enemy. In these decisive days in the life of Russia, we have thought it a duty of conscience to facilitate for our people a close union and consolidation of all national forces for the speedy attainment of victory; and, in agreement with the Imperial Duma, we have thought it good to abdicate from the throne of the Russian State, and to lay down the supreme power. Not wishing to part with our dear son, we hand over our inheritance to our brother, the Grand Duke Michael

> Alexandrovich, and give him our blessing to mount the throne of the Russian State. We bequeath it to our brother to direct the forces of the State in full and inviolable union with the representatives of the people in the legislative institutions, on those principles which will by them be established. In the name of our dearly loved country, we call on all faithful sons of the Fatherland to fulfil their sacred duty to him by obedience to the Tsar at a heavy moment of national trials, to help him, together with the representatives of the people, to bring the Russian State on to the road of victory, prosperity and glory. May the Lord God help Russia! — NICHOLAS.

Shulgin suggested two insertions. The first was that the new document should be dated at the same hour as the earlier one. The Emperor understood that this was to absolve the messengers from having used pressure, and he agreed at once. Shulgin further suggested that the reference to the Grand Duke Michael should include a public pledge to the new regime, and this too Nicholas accepted, improving on the wording suggested to him.

There was also the need of appointing a new Premier, and the Emperor no doubt assumed that this would be Rodzyanko. He simply turned to them: 'Who do you think?' They replied, 'Prince Lvov', and the Emperor, in a curiously suggestive tone said: 'Oh, Lvov? Very well, Lvov.' He recognized that Rodzyanko was passed over, and that the man chosen was the head of the Zemstvo Red Cross, which he had learned to regard as the prospective organization of revolution. The appointment was made in the form of a message to the Senate, the highest legal authority in the country.

The Emperor stood up, and he and Shulgin had a few words of conversation in a corner of the compartment.

> The Emperor looked at me, and perhaps he read in my eyes the feelings which were distressing me, because in his own there was something like an invitation to speak, and my words came of themselves: 'Oh, Your Majesty, if you had done all this earlier, even as late as the last summoning of the Duma, perhaps all that — ' and I could not finish. The Tsar looked at me in a curiously simple way: 'Do you think it might have been avoided?' [1]

[1] SHULGIN, 277.

Even his enemy Guchkov could feel only the deepest pity, as he noticed how those around him, who were the Emperor's own men, showed a complete indifference to his fate.[1] We cannot be surprised that Nicholas wrote in his diary that night – the very economy of words made it the more impressive.—'All around treachery, cowardice and deceit'.[2] The isolation was complete.

While the messengers were away, very much had happened in Petrograd. Order had been comparatively restored; but now that the masses had their own voice in the Soviet, things were moving at a breakneck pace to the left. The deed of abdication and the appointment of Lvov as Prime Minister had been dispatched in advance of them by telephone, and the names of the new Ministers were now published; Guchkov was to find that without his being consulted, the Naval Ministry had also been entrusted to him.[3] To one of the deputations which in constant succession were visiting the Duma, Milyukov committed the new Government to the principle of constitutional monarchy. He was at once shouted down. The crowd would have no more Romanovs. Guchkov, immediately on his arrival, was invited to address the railway men in a hall at the station, and was faced with a demand to hand over the deed of abdication. Shulgin, addressing another audience in the station, had announced the accession of Michael in words of fervent patriotism, and had even obtained a fairly vigorous hurrah; but he was directly afterwards called to the telephone and, speaking in a voice so hoarse as to be unrecognizable, Milyukov begged him to say nothing about the document and to send it as best he could to the Provisional Government. Bublikov, now responsible for the railways, had sent an emissary to fetch it. Meanwhile Guchkov had had to face a number of angry questions from the railway men, and in fact the doors had been closed to prevent his departure. Shulgin managed to get him out, and another emissary of the new Government brought them with difficulty through the crowd to a motor which was waiting for them. It took them straight to No. 10 on the Millionnaya, where the new Ministers were assembled with the Grand Duke Michael, discussing whether or not he should ascend the throne.[4]

[1] Guchkov to B. P.
[2] N., diary, Mar. 2nd/15th. KRASNY ARKHIV. XX, 137
[3] Guchkov to B. P.
[4] SHULGIN, 284.

The Grand Duke, a tall youngish man with a pale face, looking, as Shulgin thought, the very picture of fragility, sat in an arm-chair in a private drawing-room, surrounded by the new Ministers whose authority was so fragile. The question was keenly debated. Both Rodzyanko and Lvov spoke against his acceptance of the throne. On the other side, as Shulgin writes, Milyukov, looking for the time quite worn out, in a voice hoarse from innumerable speeches, almost croaked out the last plea for the monarchy. How strange his words would have sounded to the Liberal leader ten years before. The monarchy was the axle of Russia; there was no Russia without it; the oath to the sovereign was the one thing that bound the country together; it was the people's sanction, its approval, its agreement; the State could not exist without it. It was a passionate plea. Guchkov simply expressed his entire agreement. On the other side was Kerensky. He, like Rodzyanko, expected that if the Grand Duke accepted, his life could not be guaranteed. The Grand Duke asked for half an hour to think it over, and retired. He invited to consult with him Lvov and Rodzyanko. Then he came in and announced that he would only accept if invited by the coming Constituent Assembly; and a second deed of abdication within twenty-four hours, apart from the dismissal of the claim of Alexis, was typed out at one of the desks in the children's school-room next door.

The Russian monarchy, which had stood for over a thousand years, had crumbled to pieces, and all the pieces, whether they were called Nicholas, Alexis or Michael, had fallen to the ground of themselves, one after another.

There was an old legend that when Michael II reigned in Russia, she would win Constantinople; the founder of the Romanov dynasty was Michael I, and this would have been Michael II. At this moment the hereditary opponents of the Russian claim to Constantinople, France and England, had both agreed that it should be hers when the War was won; and in the end the War was won, but not with Russia.

And she, the foreign princess, who was everywhere recognized as truly an Empress? In the late afternoon of the same day she learned from the kind-hearted Grand Duke Paul of her husband's abdication. It was already in the papers, together with Michael's renunciation and the names of the new Ministers. She persisted in maintaining that Nicholas had only abdicated in order not to break his coronation oath by recognizing a constitutional regime.[1] Count Benckendorff in the evening confirmed the news to her and she faced it with unconquered courage; but, he writes, 'as we went out, I saw that she sat down at the table and burst into tears'. And to one of her ladies she said, 'Abdicated! And he all alone down there!'

[1] BENCKENDORFF, 17.

EPILOGUE

Antiquity forgot, custom not known,
The ratifiers and props of every word.

Hamlet, IV, 5

The worst is worldly loss, thou canst unfold:
Say is my kingdom lost? Why 'twas my care:
And what loss is it to be rid of care?

Richard II, III, 2

THE reign of Nicholas II had gone bankrupt of itself. The Government did not need to have any anxiety whatsoever as to the prospects of a restoration. There was no force which could have brought it about, and not even any body of men which would have attempted it. Nicholas, 'the very negation of the idea of autocrat', was himself the first obstacle; and Kerensky is right when he says, 'Nicholas, as a monarch, was deleted from the nation's thoughts'.[1] So it is in no way surprising that after Guchkov and Shulgin had received his abdication, they should have agreed to his suggested return to Headquarters to say good-bye to the army. As General Dubensky has put it, he had 'abdicated from the throne of Russia as if he were handing over a squadron.'[2] He did, however, issue a most dignified farewell into which he had poured all his heart; but the Government did not allow it to be made public. It ran as follows:

> For the last time I address you, the troops which I so fervently love. Since my abdication, for myself and for my son, from the throne of Russia, the power has passed to the Provisional Government, which has arisen on the initiative of the Imperial Duma. May God help it to lead Russia along the road of glory and prosperity. May God help you too, gallant troops, to defend our Country from the cruel enemy. For two and a half years you have hourly carried the heavy service of war; much is the blood that has been shed; many are the efforts that have been made; and near is the hour when Russia, bound to her gallant allies by one common striving for victory,

[1] KERENSKY, M. R., 100. [2] DUBENSKY, VI, 393.

will break the last efforts of the adversary. This unprecedented war must be brought to full victory.

Whoever now thinks of peace, whoever wishes it, is a traitor to the Fatherland, its betrayer. I know that every honest soldier thinks so. Do your duty then, stand on defence of our gallant Country. Submit yourselves to the Provisional Government, obey your commanders. Remember that any weakening of the order of service is only a help to the enemy.

I firmly believe that unbounded love for our Great Country is not extinguished in your hearts. May the Lord God bless you and may the Holy Martyr and Conqueror St. George lead you to victory.

At Headquarters, *March* 8th (21st), 1917.[1]

In the five days which he spent there he was already completely disregarded, except for the maintenance of the skeleton of the old forms of ceremony. His mother came at once to meet him from Kiev, to comfort him in his fall. Then arrived commissaries of the new Government to put him under arrest, a form which was as necessary for his own safety as for any other reason, and the corresponding step was carried out with the Empress and her family at the palace by Guchkov and the new commander of the Petrograd military district, General Kornilov. When the late Tsar reached his home at 11.15 a.m. on March 21st, as soon as the train arrived at the platform, there was a hasty general dispersal of his suite, of whom but a few faithful ones even thought of coming to the palace to present their last respects. The Empress rushed out to meet him, says Vyrubova, 'like a girl of fifteen'.[2] There was a long talk in private between them, in which Nicholas seems to have completely broken down; but from that time both faced all that befell them to the very end.

It was Kerensky who, as Minister of Justice of the Revolution, had charge of their arrangements, and to anyone but personal dependents who regarded any limitation as an insult, they must appear very humane. The soldiers had lost all discipline, and Kerensky first arrived at the palace accompanied by a large group of them. They expected from him little but insult and humiliation for the captives, so the restrictions were before all things in the interest of the imperial family. They continued to live in their

[1] SOKOLOV, 7 [2] VYRUBOVA, 100.

own pretty palace, or rather in a part of it, with access to a part of their park, which gave scope for Nicholas's love of hard work and hard exercise, though never unaccompanied by an escort. The troops in charge of them were taken from a reserve regiment of the Guard, of which some of the battalions had completely gone to pieces. The men, without their belts, slouched about or sat smoking, a sore sight for Nicholas's acute sense of military smartness. His own conduct was ideal. He behaved from the first like a simple comrade and, when his extended hand was rejected, he simply exclaimed: 'My dear fellow, why?'[1] There were many little vexations: shots in the park were followed by the news that disorderly soldiers had been shooting down the palace deer; the accident of a flapping curtain, shifting the light of a lamp by which one of the girls was sewing, resulted in a scare of 'signalling'. Vyrubova has given a distressing picture of the boy's alarm and confusion as his sailor nurse, Derevenko, who had been loaded with favours by the family, ordered him about the room.[2] The child's toy gun was taken from him and only restored privately and in pieces by the kindness of the commander of the garrison, Kobylinsky. To the men who succeeded each other as commandants of the palace Nicholas showed uniformly the completest kindness and courtesy, even inviting them into some of the little family amusements, and that though one of them was an embittered man who found difficulty in accommodating himself to the strangeness of his new office.[3] The family worked hard every day: Nicholas cutting down trees for fuel or joining in shovelling away the snow, or with the girls preparing for their use a kitchen garden, which later gave them vegetables. In the evening he would read to the family. As his imprisonment went on he took more and more pleasure in the Russian classics, and towards the end set about reading the whole Bible through from the beginning. It was Nicholas who gave the lead in patience. Gilliard writes on April 30th: 'He is an example and an encouragement to all of us.' By this time the family has been organized into a school, Nicholas being the teacher of history and geography, and he salutes Gilliard with the words, 'Good morning, dear colleague.'[4] For her it was different. Her native shyness and

[1] SOKOLOV, 13.
[2] VYRUBOVA, 104.
[3] BENCKENDORFF, 68.
[4] GILLIARD, 174-5.

apartness were enhanced now that she was a fallen empress, which was something that she could never forget. Kerensky could not fail to see at once the difference between the two.

It was no intention of the Provisional Government to keep the family in such dangerous proximity to the disorderly capital. King George V had at the very outset transmitted through Buchanan an offer of asylum in England till after the war. The nervousness of the Provisional Government in the face of criticism had prevented the King's telegram from being communicated direct to the fallen Emperor, but the invitation was transmitted. Nicholas would have preferred to go to his palace of Livadia in Crimea, but readily accepted the invitation, and so did the ex-Empress, although to the very end she was most unwilling to leave Russia, and the family began to sort our their things for the journey. Kerensky was away at the time in Moscow, where, addressing the Moscow Soviet, he set his motto of humanity with the words: 'I will not be the Marat of the Russian Revolution.' He was eagerly questioned as to the Government's plans for the imperial family, and very ill-advisedly he declared that he would himself escort them to Murmansk. A cry of indignation broke out when the news reached the Petrograd Soviet, and orders were at once circulated to the men's committees on the railways to hold back the train. A group from the Soviet even made the short journey to Tsarskoe and insisted on seeing the ex-Emperor. Their intentions were uncertain. They pushed their way into the palace, but Nicholas himself advanced simply down the corridor to meet them. There was a striking pause and after he and the leader had stood for a few moments looking at each other, they retired of themselves.[1]

Kerensky, as Minister of Justice, had set up the commission to which we owe so much of our information on our subject. In the months that followed nearly all the Ministers and other actors in the story, such as Andronikov and Manuilov, were interrogated by trained jurists. It must be remembered that the models of the Provisional Government were England and France, and they carried out their work with all possible consideration and courtesy. It was obvious, especially in the state of public opinion, that the chief role in this examination would naturally fall to the

[1] KERENSKY, M. R., 109; BENCKENDORFF, 49-50.

ex-Emperor and the ex-Empress. It is true that neither Kerensky nor anyone else had anything like the measure of the intervention of the Empress in politics which serious investigation has since brought to light. Vyrubova, for instance, who was a special mark of public detestation, boldly declared at her examination Rasputin never talked politics to her,[1] and it was only much later that the whole story became known. The question of a detailed examination of the ex-sovereigns themselves was a critical one. Kerensky has described his first entry into the palace in a striking passage, where he admits the excitement in his mind which was so obvious to onlookers such as the palace Marshal, Count Paul Benckendorff; and he tells how it was only a matter of a few seconds, after the kindly and simple greeting which Nicholas gave him, for him to see in the fallen sovereign not the Emperor of republican legend, but a man in misfortune.[2] Count Benckendorff, noting this result, comments that it was only the same as with all who ever approached Nicholas. Later he writes: 'He tried to make their Majesties believe — and he succeeded — that he was their sole protector.'[3] And later still: 'The confidence which the Emperor felt in Kerensky increased still more . . . and the Empress shared this confidence.'[4] This from a man to whom the whole appearance of the tribune of the people in the palace was intensely distasteful. Kerensky took upon himself, as Minister of Justice, the examination of the principals in the story, and it was in a single conversation of two hours with the Empress that he won the confidence which Count Benckendorff has described. It is Benckendorff who tells us that no mention was made in the inquiry of relations with Germany or a separate peace.[5] For some weeks, while the examination was proceeding, Kerensky thought it necessary to separate Nicholas and his wife, to avoid the possibility of any concerted answers to his questions, except at meals when an officer was always present, but even this hardship did not alter the impression which he had made on them.

The rising had been unorganized and elemental. It was as if a corpse had lain on the top of a passive people till with a single push from below it had rolled away of itself — by no means the least effective way for the termination of a whole period of history.

[1] Vyrubova, *Padenie*, III, 241. [2] Kerensky, M. R., 122-5. [3] Benckendorff, 67. [4] ibid., 77. [5] ibid., 78.

The first character of the revolution was therefore destructive. The whole fabric of administration of the country fell away of itself. There were no organs of local government. The police had fired on the crowds, and the police were abolished. When Army Order No. 1 reached the front, the army too began to crumble of itself, and in two months' time there were two million deserters.[1] 'The soldiers did not want to fight any more,' writes Brusilov. 'The officer at once became an enemy in the soldiers' mind, for he demanded continuance of the war; and in the soldier's eyes represented the type of master in military uniform.'[2] Bread and Peace — these were the two elemental demands; and it was the genius of Lenin that later harnessed to these two crying needs the doctrine of the class war and the rule of the proletariat.

The new Government was faced with three overwhelming tasks. The first was to restore the administration of the country. The second was to give it such a new shape as would represent the colossal change which had taken place; and this was one which might well have brought down Cabinet after Cabinet in time of peace. The third task, which the Government assumed in loyalty to its Allies, made the first two impossible; it was to keep Russia in the war. History sometimes foreshortens events for us. The war had still more than a year and a half to run. A year after the Russian Revolution the Germans were at the gates of Amiens. And the great majority of Russian revolutionaries were right in thinking that if Germany won the war, the Russian Revolution was as good as finished.

There was one programme before the Government, that of Liberalism. The new Cabinet was Liberal, and in obedience to the whole tradition of the long struggle against autocracy it applied almost automatically a system of super-democracy, universal suffrage for men and women throughout the empire, including, for instance, the nomads of Central Asia, and a Constituent Assembly, which would decide all questions not only of politics, but of property. Meanwhile, the present Government was even officially 'Provisional' and the new Premier, Prince Lvov, even suggested that each province or area should reorganize itself!

[1] *My Russian Memoirs*, 420; General Bredov to B. P.
[2] BRUSILOV, 209-10.

All political prisoners in Siberia were released, and returned bubbling with energy. Revolutionary emigrants made their way back to Russia from all sides. On April 16th (1916), exactly a month after the fall of the monarchy, through the practically open frontier at the north of the Gulf of Bosnia, came the general staff of the Bolsheviks, Lenin and his principal followers, to be joined a little later by Trotsky, still a Mensevik, from America. Dismissing the fears of his colleagues, such as Kamenev and Zinovyev, Lenin every day in public speeches on the balcony of the expropriated house of the dancer Kshesinskaya preached fraternization at the front, immediate peace and the class war — which was at first received with alarm even by the Soviet.

On May 3rd the continual street meetings bubbled up into a crisis. Armed bands of Bolshevized soldiers and workmen demanded the dismissal of Milyukov and Guchkov and the transfer of all power to the Soviets. The new Foreign Minister, Milyukov, with a fatal lack of political perspective, had been actively preaching the conquest of the Straits. Guchkov, as War Minister, had been straining every nerve to restore order in the army. The rising met with little public sympathy and was repressed without great difficulty; but Guchkov, unable to get firmer support from his colleagues, resigned and joined the front line Cossacks — as he has told me, in hope of death — and Milyukov, in deference to the pressure of his colleagues, also resigned.[1] Thus, within two months, two of the three principal challengers of the autocracy followed their ex-sovereign into the dust-heap of Russian history.

In the next period the dominant figure was Kerensky. There was little wisdom either in the Allied pressure or in Kerensky's activity which brought about the Russian offensive of July 2nd. The enemy was at first surprised and driven back; and Nicholas, who followed the fate of the army with the tensest anxiety, ordered a private service of thanksgiving;[2] but the enemy's counterstroke led to a complete Russian débacle. Meanwhile, with Kerensky away at the front, the Bolsheviks made their second attempt on Petrograd and very nearly succeeded. For a few hours, but for the resistance of the Cossacks, the city was practically in their hands and the Ministers were dispersed in various refuges; but the Preobrazhensky Regiment came out for the Government, and in

[1] *My Russian Memoirs*, 435-8. [2] BENCKENDORFF, 94.

the evening the Soviet itself, only a minority of which was Bolshevik, rallied to the same side and order was eventually restored (July 17th).

It had now become urgent to get the imperial family to some place of safety. On July 30th a meeting of sailors at Kronstadt had threatened violence to the palace. As soon as the Government had obtained better control of the railways, it had raised again with England the question of asylum for the Tsar. Through the Swedish Minister, Skavenius, Germany had been persuaded to guarantee that the British cruiser conveying him and his family would not be attacked. On the other hand Mr. Lloyd George had been frightened by agitation in Labour quarters in England against any welcome to the Tsar, repeating a similar challenge to the visit of Nicholas to England in 1909. In consequence a Foreign Office communication announced that the offer was no longer 'insisted on', and Buchanan, as has been described by Kerensky, with tears in his eyes and shaking hands, had to deliver a verbal message to the new Russian Foreign Minister, Tereshchenko, which amounted to a withdrawal of the offer of asylum. It contained an unsavoury reference to the entirely unfounded suspicion that the Russian sovereigns had pro-German proclivities. With this avenue closed, Prince Lvov committed to Kerensky the task of finding some other refuge.[1]

After the July attempt of the Bolsheviks on the capital Kerensky succeeded Prince Lvov as Prime Minister, and on July 8th/21st Nicholas wrote in his diary, 'This man is certainly in his right place at the present moment. The more power he gets, the better it will be'. Nicholas had hoped that he might go to his favourite Livadia; but this would have involved a journey through the heart of Russia, passing through big towns and a peasantry which was now engaged in appropriating the land of the squires. Kerensky, with whom the choice lay, decided on Tobolsk; and this time keeping his secret as far as possible to himself, he carried out the final arrangements for the move in a night of uphill work at the palace on August 13th.[2] Nicholas was allowed to take with him, besides his Deputy Court Marshal, Dolgorukov, an older

[1] Kerensky, M. R., 116-18; Miss Buchanan, *The Dissolution of an Empire*, 196-7.

[2] Benckendorff, 106-12; Kerensky, M. R., 128.

officer of his choice; and as the first whom he named hesitated, General Tatishchev came at the shortest notice, carrying a small suit-case, and accompanied him to the end. Kerensky had arranged a short meeting between the two brothers, Nicholas and Michael; but they had little to say to each other in his presence. After long delays the promised train was ready, and the ex-Empress, who was ill, was hoisted into it. The service on the train was well arranged and met with Nicholas's approval. It travelled under a Japanese flag, and the curtains were drawn at the stations. At Zvanka, near the capital, there was a momentary danger that the railway men would stop the party, but this passed off. Each day the train stopped for half an hour in the open country for the ex-Tsar to have his usual walk. The party reached the farthest railway point at Tyumen in the Urals on the evening of the 17th, and in the presence of a silent and respectful crowd passed on to the steamer *Rus*, which then started down the river for Tobolsk. The next day they passed a village standing high on the bank, with one house that dominated all the rest. The village was Pokrovskoe, and the house was Rasputin's home. As the level-headed Gilliard reports in his diary, this occasioned no surprise, for Rasputin had always told them that they would some day visit this place.[1] On the 19th at four o'clock the citadel of Tobolsk with its old churches rose before them; but the governor's residence which they were to occupy was found by the two officials accompanying them to be in insufficient repair, and for the next four days they remained in the centre of the river, making little excursions up and down it, and getting their customary walks.

On August 26th the house was ready for them.[2] Tobolsk, which was off the railway, was old-fashioned and patriotic. The local authorities were Mensheviks or S.R.s, and the attitude of the population has been described on all sides as definitely sympathetic. Nuns from a convent frequently brought food, passers-by crossed themselves or gave other signs of sympathy as they went past. The house[3] was pleasant and comfortable, though the garden gave little space for exercise. A section of the Guard at Tsarskoe had been sent with the party, and Kerensky had addressed it before its departure demanding the fullest consideration

[1] Gilliard, 183. [2] Visited by the writer in 1919.
[3] Kerensky, M. R., 128.

for the captives, with the words: 'No hitting a man when he is down.'

The family lived here quietly through the months that followed. They were allowed at first to go to church in the city. The bishop, curiously enough, was now Hermogen, who did his utmost to show them respect. At Tsarskoe they had organized the education of the children. The English tutor, Gibbs, to his honour, had also followed them to Siberia. The house across the street, which bore the name of Kornilov, supplied room for those who could not be accommodated in the governor's residence. The family physician, Dr. Botkin, had complete freedom of movement, and even set up a small practice in the town. The servants could also move freely, and in this way the family had plenty of facilities for correspondence with their friends.

Very striking are some of the letters which the ex-Empress wrote at this time. As Gibbs has put it, she was never more worthy of herself. Living, as before, 'an intense inner life', she found in it a complete answer to every trial which faced them. 'God's love is higher than all,' she writes to Vyrubova on Nov. 24th/Dec. 7th. 'Yes, the past is finished. I thank God for all that there has been, that I had; and I shall live on memories, which no one shall take from me' (Dec. 8th/21st). 'The Lord is so near, one feels his support. I have peace at heart, though often I suffer greatly, greatly, for the country and you . . . little daughter. After a year I think the Lord will have pity on the country. He knows better than we' (Dec. 9th/22nd). 'Pray for our dear country' (Dec. 15th/28th). Let them come to themselves . . . He (Nicholas) is simply astonishing, such strength of spirit, though he suffers without end for the country . . . None ever complain . . . Oh, God save Russia!' 'I am so pleased at their thoughts (the children's). They are rich soil . . . I feel myself mother of the country and suffer as for my own baby, and love my country in spite of all the horrors and all the sins. You know it is impossible to tear the love out of my heart — and for Russia too, in spite of the black ingratitude to the Emperor which breaks my heart' (Dec. 10th/23rd).[1]

Kerensky had probably prolonged the life of the imperial family for nearly a year; but he failed to deal with the increasing difficulties of his position as Prime Minister. Following the rapid

[1] VYRUBOVA, 148-56.

shifts to the left in opinion, he each time sought some new coalition in his desperate task of fighting the class war by national solidarity in defence of the Revolution. The failure of the second attempt of the Bolsheviks to seize the capital was allowed to pass without any measures for strengthening the hold of the Government, and it was in the fortnight that followed that the population began to feel that there was little to be done to help a Government which did so little to help itself. For a time there was definitely a lull in the progress of the Revolution;[1] and even the Soviets had begun almost to look at themselves as a temporary expedient, when there came a new convulsion, this time from the Right. On August 1st Kornilov, who had alone shown energy in restoring discipline in the army, was appointed Commander-in-Chief. He was a simple Cossack, a man of fearless bravery and a sincere patriot; but he had the vaguest understanding of politics. He himself stood for the March Revolution, but he allowed himself in political matters to be directed by a financier, one Zavoyko, who was out to stage a reaction. Under such influences Kornilov rapidly drifted apart from Kerensky, and prompted by his advisers, was preparing to march on the capital and dissolve the Soviet. His claim, as it ultimately reached Kerensky, was for a dictatorship of Kornilov surrounded by a Minister of nobodies, among whom Zavoyko himself was to be Minister of Finance. It is no wonder that Kerensky would have nothing to do with such proposals. The army did move, but its men at once began fraternizing with those sent to oppose them. Kerensky ordered the replacement of Kornilov by Alexeyev, who in vain tried to act as mediator, and Kornilov was put under arrest.[2]

This move from the Right was the final cause of the fall of the Provisional Government. Its main supports were now hopelessly disintegrated, and the Bolsheviks with rapid and able organization advanced into the space thus left empty. In this work the ablest part was played by Trotsky, now an ardent Bolshevik and President of the Soviet. He captured one after another of the committees which had been set up in each military unit soon after the March Revolution. Kerensky's difficulty was that till the Constituent Assembly met, there was no public body that could speak

[1] Golovin, 276; Gurko, 293; Hindenburg, 273.

[2] Related to me in detail by V. N. Lvov, the would-be mediator between Kerensky and Kornilov.

with the authority of the Russian people. He parried with one expedient after another: a Democratic Convention (in deference to the Soviet) and a Directory composed of four members (Sept. 12th), the proclamation of a Republic (Sept. 15th), a fresh Cabinet (Oct. 3rd), and the opening of a provisional Council (Vorparlament) of 450 members (Oct. 21st). On November 5th this Council itself voted against the Government. At this last stage negotiations had been practically completed for Austria's withdrawal from the war, and envoys were being selected to go to London. Bulgaria and Turkey were negotiating with the same object.[1] This was the last effort of the Provisional Government to help its Allies. On November 6th the revolutionary military committee established by the Bolsheviks in Petrograd decided to act. The next day the whole town was in their hands and all the troops on their side. The *Aurora* from Kronstadt lay in the river, and armoured cars paraded the streets. The Winter Palace was attacked, and was defended only by a women's battalion. Kerensky dashed off to Pskov to get support from the troops outside and did indeed return with the Cossacks of General Krasnov and fought a small battle outside the city at Pulkovo. But the Central Committee of the Cossacks, alienated by his breach with the Cossack general, Kornilov, ordered Krasnov to leave him. At two in the morning the Bolsheviks were in the Winter Palace. The Ministers were arrested and dispatched to join their Tsarist predecessors in the fortress of St. Peter and St. Paul. A Bolshevik Government was formed, consisting of People's Commissaries, with Lenin as Prime Minister and Trotsky at the Foreign Office. On the 9th the nationalization of all land was decreed. The example of Petrograd was followed with no long delay in Moscow, where a number of military cadets alone defended the Kremlin. On the night of the 20th a message was sent by the new Government to the Commander-in-Chief at the front, Dukhonin, ordering him to open negotiations for a separate peace, and on his refusal he was lynched by the soldiers, led by his successor, Ensign Krylenko (Dec. 1st). Kerensky himself had fled and like Guchkov and Milyukov had passed into the rubbish-heap. On December 3rd negotiations were opened with the enemy by Joffe at Brest-Litovsk.

[1] Kerensky to B. P.

EPILOGUE

It is only in the barest outline that we will carry this story further. The new Government put the whole of its programme into action at once in order at least to give a demonstration of its principles to the world and to encourage, in the conditions of the war, similar movements among the proletariats of other countries. The land had been nationalized; house property followed, and also the banks; private trade was declared illegal and the shops were closed, although there had been no time to replace them by adequate government stores. The Bolsheviks were a militant force, owing their power to the war, and admirably adapted to war conditions. They had as leader the one man of genius, Lenin, who had a perfectly clear conception of his objects and even of the tactics which were required to face every turn of fortune. By 1917 every old-established idea in Russia had been wiped out in hopeless discredit; the State had dwindled to the Empress and her group; the official Church had been demoralized by Rasputin; and the new Moses, descending from the mountain with his tablets, carried with him the support of the workers of the large towns, of the peasants, who had been rapidly expropriating the estates of the squires, and especially of the young, who saw the outlet for bravery and initiative which was given them in this new world. The Constituent Assembly, for which the elections began on November 25th all over the empire, did not give them anything but a minority and was, therefore, dispersed with violence after a single continuous sitting on January 18th-19th; two of its best members, the Liberals Shingarev and Kokoshkin, were murdered in hospital directly afterwards. It was replaced in reality by the Communist Party, or rather by its leaders, but to appearance by a vast pyramid of Soviets elected not by the ballot, but by show of hands on a franchise limited in principle to manual workers. The peace negotiations, in spite of the extreme disadvantages of the Russian position, were carried on, and peace was finally concluded on March 3rd at Brest-Litovsk with the abandonment of most of the territory won by Russia since Peter the Great.

All these events took place in the atmosphere of the World War, which the Bolsheviks hoped to convert into a universal class war. It was inevitable that this should lead to a civil war in Russia, and in the course of time forces of opposition matured at all points of the compass: in Yaroslavl, where a rising of officers was suppressed by the energy and ability of Trotsky; on the Volga, where the dispersed Constituent Assembly set up its flag; in the south, where Kornilov and Alexeyev gathered round them a number of young Russian officers; in Siberia, where the instinct of autonomy was strong and an independent government was established at Omsk. The Allies saw breaking under their eyes the eastern barrier so necessary to their blockade of Germany, who now had her own ambassador in Moscow, in place of those of the Entente. The insurgent forces in Russia stood for the continuation of the war against Germany, and asked for help from the Entente; many Russian officers actually passed into its service, among them Admiral Kolchak, who now offered his sword to England and was asked to go to Siberia.

Perhaps the strangest episode of this time was the story of the Czech legions. Kerensky had given them freedom to organize after his summer offensive, in which they had played a prominent part. When the Bolsheviks made peace, for a moment they treated with Trotsky on the basis of a free dispatch by way of the Pacific to the western front, as for them no peace with the Central Powers was possible. When the bargain was not kept, they established themselves on the ground where they happened to stand at point after point along the Trans-Siberian, and as the railway was the vital nerve of Siberia, from whose supplies it was essential to exclude the exhausted forces of Germany, they were a valuable asset to the cause of the Entente. Much of this was to happen later, but it is in these conditions that we can carry the story of the imperial family to its close.

For this we have two main authoritative records. The one is given us by N. A. Sokolov, a trained legal investigator of rare integrity and unusual ability who, during the eight months that the Whites were in control of Siberia, carried out his commission with the utmost devotion and courage in the difficult conditions of civil war with all sorts of impediments and interruptions. The other is that of P. M. Bykov, who as President of the Soviet of Ekaterinburg is intimately concerned in the story. Sokolov died in Paris before he could know that in all essentials his very detailed report was fully confirmed from the other side. We have also the invaluable evidence contained in the diary of Pierre Gilliard, who shared the captivity at Tobolsk.

It will naturally be asked why there were such few and feeble attempts at a rescue of the family. This, so long as the Provisional Government lasted, need not have seemed very urgent; that Government had itself earlier tried to assist the passage of the family out of the country and still entertained the idea of conveying it through Siberia to Japan.[1] We have seen that correspondence of the Empress with her friends was still comparatively easy, and the commander of their guard, Colonel Kobylinsky, the first revolutionary commandant of Tsarskoe Selo, was an officer twice wounded at the front, and so devoted to the interests of his prisoners that the ex-Tsar describes him as 'my last friend'.[2]

The fatal futility of Anna Vyrubova again enters into the story. There was a young adventurer named Lieutenant Solovyev, who after studying mysticism in the school of Madame Blavatsky in India, had launched an equivocal career in the stormy waters of the Revolution. At one time we find him engaged in Bolshevist propaganda; at another he appears, of all places, in the chapel of the Duma as the bridegroom of Mara Rasputin, the daughter of the famous starets. He had secured the full confidence of Vyrubova, and it would appear that it was almost by hypnotic suggestion that Mara, who did not care for him, was induced to accept him as a husband.[3] In August 1917 Vyrubova and Solovyev had paid a visit to Siberia, where the lady had twice been the guest of Rasputin in his village; and later Solovyev returned to take up his position at Tyumen as the official rescuer of the imperial family, a task of which he claimed the monopoly.[4] There were small monarchical groups, both in Moscow and Petrograd, associated with former Ministers such as Trepov and Krivosheim, and others of Conservative views, such as Neidhardt, who had been one of the Empress's candidates for the Ministry of Transport. There was also N. E. Markov, a man with an extraordinary personal resemblance to Peter the Great, who was till the end the leader of the extreme Rights in the Duma. These collected sums of money which they sent to the imperial family, and they dispatched two officers to work for a rescue. On several occasions Solovyev headed off their emissaries, and even handed over at least two of them to the Bolshevik authorities. He

[1] KERENSKY, M. R., 118.
[2] *See* SOKOLOV, 36; GILLIARD, 183.
[3] SOKOLOV, 89-94.
[4] ibid., 95-8.

did not utilize the valuable services of the honest Botkin, but those of two lady's maids, Romanova and Utkina, the first of which names sometimes occurs as apparently a substitute for that of the ex-Empress in her correspondence; one of these later married a Bolshevik official. There is no doubt that he had contact through these with the ex-Empress, and she appears to have entrusted to him some of her jewels.[1] On the other hand there is strong evidence for saying that the major part of the money sent from Russia did not reach her and remained in the hands of Solovyev. There is evidence in Gilliard and elsewhere that the Empress actually spoke to her fellow prisoners of three hundred officers, 'good Russians', who had settled at Tyumen, which, as the last railway head before Tobolsk, was the obvious place for their concentration.[2] Solovyev appears to have even organized military parades, which he showed to visitors as evidence of his preparations for the rescue, but he systematically hindered in every way their further progress to Tobolsk.

Nothing definite was done and, with the advent of the Bolsheviks to power, the whole position was radically changed. The news that they were in power did not reach Tobolsk for a fortnight afterwards, and it was long after this that their authority made itself felt in this remote town; but as time advanced, various restrictions and humiliations were introduced into the house regime, which were invariably opposed as far as possible by Kobylinsky and to a certain extent by some sections of the Guard which had come with the imperial family from Tsarskoe. On November 3rd, presumably with the approval of Hermogen, the bells had pealed in Tobolsk in commemoration of Nicholas's accession; on December 5th the old prayers for the imperial family were read through, and on the 25th was sung the salute known as *Mnogoletie* ('Many Years!'). The result was that the family were no longer allowed to go to church in the city.[3] On January 12th was introduced a new scale of the family expenses, 600 roubles a month for each person; the rouble was by now immensely depreciated. On the 16th an order was given for the removal of epaulettes. Nicholas obeyed it though with extreme distaste, and when Kobylinsky expressed his own mortification the ex-Emperor

[1] Sokolov, 94. [2] Gilliard, 196, 198.
[3] Kerensky, M. R., 136; Bykov, 47-8; Gilliard, 190.

said to him: 'You see we are all patient; you must be patient too.'[1] The Commissary of the Provisional Government, Pankratov, a strange little religious revolutionary, who had behaved with kindness, was now dismissed; and on February 23rd the prisoners were put upon soldiers' rations. On March 1st a number of the soldiers of their guard were sent home.

The news of the negotiations for a separate peace was a bitter grief to the family. The ex-Emperor, remembering the accusations so often brought against his wife, asked indignantly, 'Who are the traitors?'[2] and she in a remarkable letter of December 22nd wrote, 'What an infamy! That the Lord God should give peace to Russia, yes, but not by way of treason with the Germans'. In all her letters there is the same indignation and, above all, at the thought of the offer of any German protection. Another strain that runs through all of them is the constant unwillingness to leave Russia, which she regarded as 'breaking the last link'. She even says that this is the one consolation which has still so far been left to them.[3] One does not find in Nicholas any strong desire to escape. On her side one feels that there was still a hope not only of rescue, but even of a possible recovery of power. Her view was that Russia could not do without the Tsar and some day must again turn to him.

In March the atmosphere in the town came to be more heavily charged. Ekaterinburg in the Urals was perhaps the most vehemently Bolshevik spot in Russia. This district had inherited traditions of hatred of Tsarism from the old serf factories of this area. Even before the Bolsheviks seized power in the capitals, the local Soviet had nationalized the mines, and it was mortally anxious to prevent any rescue of the family.[4] It sent a small band of Red soldiers to Tobolsk for this purpose, but there appeared from Omsk, which lay farther to the east, a stronger body of troops, whom the Empress took for the 'good Russians' of which she had been told; and she actually waved to them from her balcony. Their intentions are still obscure. They were led by two men, Demyanov and Degtarev, of whom the latter had been known at the university as an extreme Right, and Demyanov certainly tried to support the authority of Colonel Kobylinsky. Anyhow, they

[1] SOKOLOV, 37.
[2] ibid., 109.
[3] GILLIARD, 196-7.
[4] BYKOV, 62.

forced the detachment from Ekaterinburg to retreat. Later, Ekaterinburg sent a larger force; and its leader, Zaslavsky, tried to interfere with the guard of the house, but was hissed by them and retired in confusion.

Meanwhile on April 22nd, a direct emissary arrived from Moscow, one Yakovlev. When he visited the family, the boy was lying seriously ill, worse even than he had been at Spala, and Yakovlev was evidently upset at finding him in such a state. The reason became clearer when on the 25th he announced that he had instructions from Moscow to take the ex-Tsar thither, and no doubt he had also meant that the boy should accompany them. At first Nicholas refused to go; but Yakovlev, who treated him with the greatest courtesy, even addressing him as sovereign, urged him to submit, as he could not guarantee such treatment by others. Yakovlev conferred with Kobylinsky and assisted him in the routing of Zaslavsky. He was evidently in great haste to be off. The Empress was in extreme agitation. In intimate talks with Gilliard and her daughter Tatyana, she said that never till now in her life had she failed to see where her duty lay; now, she was divided between her husband and her child. She made it clear that what was troubling her was the fear that her husband, if again deprived of her counsel, might be forced into some action of which he really disapproved. Nicholas on his side was quite clear: 'What they (the Germans) want is that I should sign the Treaty of Brest-Litovsk, and I will sooner let them cut off my hand than do that!'[1] They were evidently convinced that the German Ambassador in Moscow, Count Mirbach, who, in Russia's military weakness could now speak as a master, had been instructed to demand that Nicholas be brought thither with this object; and indeed Mirbach had told the Russian loyalist Neidhardt that he would if necessary 'demand' the safety of the family.[2] For some time the ex-Empress paced up and down in the greatest distress, and then she made up her mind that her first duty lay with her husband, and asked Yakovlev that she should come too. He made no objection at all, saying: 'Whichever of you, you like.' The next morning, April 26th, Nicholas and Alexandra, with their daughter Maria and Dr. Botkin, started off in rough country carts at 3.30 a.m. It was noticed that Yakovlev saluted the ex-Emperor, and

[1] SOKOLOV, 45. [2] ibid., 106.

took especial thought about his wearing a warmer coat. By agreement with Kobylinsky, he took with him also eight soldiers, picked by the latter. The rest of the family were to stay in Tobolsk till the boy was well, and then to follow.[1]

The journey was a distressful one. The rivers were still frozen, so that it had to be accomplished in carts. The passage over the river Tobol had to be made on foot over the ice through standing water. At the halting places Yakovlev continued his care for the travellers and for Botkin, who was at this time seriously ill. There seems to be some strange instinct of drama in Russian history, even when it is just travelling forward of itself. The last place where they changed horses was actually under the windows of Rasputin's house in Pokrovskoe, with Rasputin's family looking out at them: Nicholas records this in his diary.[2] Yakovlev was followed closely by the detachment from Ekaterinburg, but managed to evade their attentions. On arrival at the railway head at Tyumen he learned that there was every intention to stop the party in Ekaterinburg, and therefore directed the train in the opposite direction towards Omsk! On the train he was often in conversation with Nicholas, who described him to others as 'not bad'. When it was suggested that Nicholas was going to Moscow to be tried, the ex-Tsar replied: 'Trial? Nonsense!' The idea which he seemed to have was that on reaching Moscow he would be conveyed out of the country to Sweden or more probably Denmark where he had royal kinsfolk.

Meanwhile Ekaterinburg, on getting word by telephone from its careful watchers, at once communicated with Omsk, and arranged that the train should be stopped there. Yakovlev, on reaching the station of Kulomzino, learned of this danger. He himself went into Omsk on a locomotive, and on his return had a long conversation on the telephone with Moscow. His orders were to return by way of Ekaterinburg. On arrival there, he was at once deprived of all authority by the local Soviet, and the soldiers of the escort were sent back to Tobolsk.[3] The captives were dispatched to the house of a merchant Ipatyev, a graceful little building in the old style, on the way into the town, on a slope that runs down from the road. Ipatyev (Hypatius) is not a common name in Russia.

[1] Sokolov, 39 ff.; Gilliard, 199, ff.; Bykov, 63-6.
[2] N., diary, April 14th/27th. Krasny Arkhiv, xxvii, 125. [3] Sokolov, 51-2.

Five years earlier, celebrating the tercentenary of their dynasty, the sovereigns had visited the Ipatyevsky Monastery close beside the town of Kostroma, where the first Romanov, the boy Michael, had received an urgent prayer from the most widely representative of all the old Assemblies of the Land (*Zemskie Sobory*), to accept the throne to which it had just elected him. This memory can hardly have failed to occur to the imperial captives. Ipatyev at the beginning, and Ipatyev at the end. Yakovlev protested, and went on to Moscow, but telephoned back that he had no longer any authority, and could not answer for the consequences. Later, so Bykov tells us, he fled to Kolchak.[1]

How is this strange story to be understood? It would certainly seem that Yakovlev, a former revolutionary but a man of good education and humane character, was anxious to save the prisoners from the Ekaterinburg Soviet. More than that, he possibly hoped to rescue them altogether. It is in any case certain that he carried a definite commission from Sverdlov, the Chairman of the Executive Committee of the Communist Party in Moscow. In interviews which Neidhardt and others had had with Count Mirbach, the Count spoke with confidence of the watch which he was keeping over the safety of the imperial family.[2] Was Sverdlov then, acceding to a demand when he dispatched Yakovlev to Tobolsk? There is no doubt that Ekaterinburg was in communication with him at the same time. Or was there any truth in the current report that the ex-sovereign was to receive a national trial in Moscow? That is much less likely.

Anyhow, if Nicholas was really to go to Moscow, it is hard to explain why, not long before this, the Soviet Government had arranged something like a general transfer of the Romanovs to the neighbourhood of Ekaterinburg. The Grand Duke Michael had on February 9th been sent from Gatchina to Perm, where he lived in comparative freedom in a hotel with his English secretary, Mr. Johnson. The Grand Duchess Elizabeth, sister of the ex-Empress, had been brought with her faithful attendant, the nun Yakovleva, from Moscow to Alapayevsk, not far, as Russian distances go, from Ekaterinburg, and with her had been collected there the Grand Duke Sergius Mikhailovich, three of the sons of the Grand Duke Constantine Constantinovich, and the young son

[1] BYKOV, 73; SOKOLOV, 53.   [2] ibid., 106.

of the Grand Duke Paul by his second, morganatic marriage, Prince Paley. There they lived in a rough and ready school building, also in comparative liberty, working in the garden or taking walks, and organized into a little community.

The regime in the house of Ipatyev, which was now called the House of Special Purpose, was very different from that of Tobolsk. It began with a rigorous search of all the belongings of the party, including even the most trifling possessions of the ex-Empress, which brought an indignant protest from Nicholas: 'So far I have had to deal with decent people.'[1] He was roughly told that he was a prisoner and that any such demonstration would be sternly punished. They were able to communicate in the briefest terms with the remainder of their family at Tobolsk, and a few last letters from the Empress did reach some of her friends. We know that she foresaw what was coming, and in one of the last we find the words: 'Behold the bridegroom cometh'. To Vyrubova she writes on April 8th/21st: 'Though the storm draws nearer, I am calm in spirit.'[2] Afterwards there was found on one of the walls her favourite emblem, the swastika, which she had put up at each of her halting places; the same emblem was used by the more or less fictitious 'brotherhood of St. John of Tobolsk', organized or not organized by Solovyev.[3] The family had now to take their meals out of a common pot, into which the chief of the guard, Avdeyev, a not entirely ungenial drunkard, would also dip his spoon, leaning over between Nicholas and his wife. The meals, which were not bad but very simple, were supplied from a kitchen outside, with long delays and with an inadequate apparatus to keep them warm.

On May 1st the sick boy, still at Tobolsk, was well enough to get up. Four days later came the Russian Easter, and on the 11th the family's 'last friend', Kobylinsky, was dismissed and replaced by a hooligan Rodionov from Ekaterinburg; he searched the priest and the nuns who visited the family, forbade them further access to it, and ordered that the doors of the girls' bedrooms were not to be locked. On the following day, May 20th, the whole party, including Gilliard and Gibbs, were shipped on to the steamer *Rus*, which could now travel up the river, and were brought by

[1] N., diary, April 17th/30th. Krasny Arkhiv, xxvii, 126.
[2] Vyrubova, 173.
[3] S. Markov in Sokolov, 103.

way of Tyumen to Ekaterinburg. They were followed by a young officer, Sergius Markov, foster-son of an old imperial official, General Dumbadze, and dispatched by Vyrubova with a commission from his better known namesake, N. E. Markov, the leader of the extreme Rights in the Duma.[1] Though they reached Ekaterinburg at nine in the morning of the 24th, the girls had to sleep the first night on the floor. The same day a faithful servant of the family, Chemodurov, was sent out of the house to the prison hospital, which proved the means of saving his life. Four days later two other servants were sent away, Nagorny, the faithful servant-nurse of the boy, who had taken the place of the unfaithful Derevenko, and the cook, Sednev.

Ekaterinburg has claimed to have had only a loose control over Perm and Alapayevsk. On June 12th two armed men made their way into the hotel where the Grand Duke Michael was living and ordered him to come away with them. The Grand Duke, who was under the jurisdiction of the Soviet of Perm, refused to leave without its instructions. A footman, who escaped, later told how the two intruders, after showing a document, which was apparently forged, had a few minutes' talk with Johnson: he smiled and said something to the Grand Duke, whereupon Michael agreed to accompany the two men. Did he suggest a rescue? Neither he nor Johnson was ever seen again, and later a desperado named Myasnikov told how he had shot both near the factory of Motovilikhi, and boasted that if only he were allowed, he could deal with Nicholas as he did with Michael. Later, as in other cases, the death of the Grand Duke was put down to an attempt to escape.[2]

Bykov naturally lays greater emphasis than Sokolov on rumours of plots to rescue the imperial family and join the Czechs, who were now in the neighbourhood, and also on correspondence with the family which passed through Doctor Derevenko, one of its physicians (not to be confused with the unfaithful sailor), who was able to live in the town and pay visits to them.[3] He mentions that the members of the old Academy of the General Staff were now living in Ekaterinburg, and that some of them were arrested. The Serbs were trying to save the Grand Duchess Helen, wife of the Grand Duke Ivan Constantinovich. Certainly there were a

[1] Sokolov, 95, 99. [2] ibid., 266. [3] Bykov, 77.

number of royalists in the town. Captain Paul Bulygin, a faithful officer who had served the Dowager Empress, has told us how he organized a band of officers at Kotelnichi, a small town in the province of Vyatka, to which, according to a Soviet newspaper, the imperial family were shortly to be transferred from Ekaterinburg because of the close neighbourhood of the Czechs. Bulygin and his friends had definitely made a plan to rescue the family and take them off by river steamer to the Artic Ocean. Finding that no transfer took place, Bulygin went off to Ekaterinburg to reconnoitre. There, while sitting at the station restaurant in company with a Soviet commissary, he was tactlessly saluted by an old soldier who had served under him, and was promptly sent to the town prison. In the crowded common cell there were at least two officers who had probably come to Ekaterinburg with a similar purpose. Both were shot while he was there, and he himself only escaped by an extraordinary piece of bluff, with the first story that came into his head. Later he made his way to Kolchak and assisted Sokolov in his difficult investigation.[1] Bykov goes on to tell of a definite communication with the imperial family. A note signed by a 'White' officer reaches Nicholas declaring that 'the time has come for action', and asking him to unfasten one of the windows as a signal. Arrangements, so it runs, have even been made for carrying away the sick boy. Nicholas replies indicating the second window and gives details, for instance as to the keys; he mentions the commandant, Avdeyev, 'who treats us well'. Later a plan is sent in a letter from 'our people'.[2] We read in the Emperor's diary for June 14th/27th: 'We spent an anxious night, and kept up our spirits, fully dressed. All this was because a few days ago we received two letters, one after the other, in which we were told to get ready to be rescued by some devoted people, but days passed and nothing happened, and the waiting and the uncertainty were very painful.' Workers' committees in the town were convinced that such an attempt would be made, and wanted to lynch the family themselves.

The atmosphere was all the more electric because of the close neighbourhood of the Czechs, who had reached this district in their wonderful Anabasis and indeed were to capture the town

[1] Bulygin, 'In Prison at Ekaterinburg', in the *Slavonic Review*, VII, 35.
[2] Bykov, 78-9.

on the morning of July 25th. According to Bykov, they had already outflanked it on two sides; and Bulygin records the anxious preparations for evacuation.

The military commandant of this area, Goloshchékin, a Jew of Vilna, as was later ascertained, went to Moscow and stayed in the quarters of Sverdlov, with whom he was well acquainted. On his communicating with Ekaterinburg, Avdeyev was dismissed, and even arrested, and his guard, consisting of Russians, was replaced. There was never better evidence of the charm of Nicholas's simplicity than in his relations with the various detachments sent to guard the family. At Tobolsk he sometimes crossed to the guard-house with his children and played draughts with the men, which reduced to amazement the meticulous, though kindly Pankratov, the commissary at that time, who happened to enter the guard-house while this was going on.[1] Nicholas, noting Avdeyev's dismissal in his diary, comments: 'I am sorry for Avdeyev.'[2] And one of Avdeyev's guard, Yakimov, later told how when he met the ex-Tsar at close quarters, the whole of the popular superstition that he was a terrible tyrant disappeared of itself: 'His eyes were good and kind . . . Generally, the impression that he made on me was of a man who was kind, simple, frank, ready to talk . . . We all thought that Nicholas Alexandrovich was a simple man, but she was not simple, that is, like an Empress . . . He looked younger than she did . . . Tatyana was like the Empress. The other daughters had no feeling of importance. You could see they were simple and kind . . . Nothing remained of my former ideas of the Tsar when I had come on guard. As soon as I had seen them several times with my own eyes, I began to feel quite differently towards them; I was sorry for them.'[3] Nicholas, indeed, was actually forbidden to speak to the guard. The girls, in the complete self-sufficiency of this closely-knit family 'talked merrily together to the end'. It was a complete conquest of their circumstances.

Avdeyev was replaced by a Siberian Jew, Yurovsky, a man with a most sinister face and record. Nicholas notes in the last published entry in his diary 'This specimen we like least of all'.[4] The rest of the new guard included no more than two Russians. They were

[1] Sokolov, 35.
[2] N., diary, June 21st/July 4th.
[3] Sokolov, 141.
[4] N., diary, June 28th/July 10th.

described by their predecessors as 'Letts' or 'Bolsheviks' (as distinguished from Russians).[1] The majority of them were prisoners of war. Inscriptions both in German and in Magyar were found scrawled up on the walls afterwards. One of them (from Heine) reads:

Belsatzar ward in selbiger Nacht
Von seinen Knechten umgebracht[2]

(Belshazzar was that same night done to death by his servants).

On July 4th Ekaterinburg telegraphed to Goloshchékin, that Avdeyev had been dismissed and Yurovsky was now in charge, and on the 12th Goloshchekin returned from Moscow. In the next few days he and Yurovsky made mysterious visits to a deserted mine-shaft close to four lonely trees known as the 'Four Brothers', near the village of Koptyaki, some fourteen miles from Ekaterinburg; this evidence was given later by peasants whom they scared out of their way, ordering them not to look behind them.[3] Voikov, a member of the Ural Soviet, purchased large quantities of benzine, and lorries carried this and supplies of vitriol to the mine-shaft near Koptyaki.[4]

On July 14th Father Storozhev, who had once before been allowed to read the service at the House of Special Purpose, paid his last visit. The hymns were sung by the family, who had organized themselves into a choir and were often heard singing them. Father Storozhev notes the great change which had taken place in them. At an earlier visit he had commented on the excellent health and bearing of Nicholas. Now all the family seemed to have no hope but in God. At the singing of the words, 'At rest with the Saints', the whole family fell on their knees. They were hearing their own requiem.[5] Religious verses of an English evangelical poet were later found in the hand-writing of the Empress, and also, in that of Olga, a beautiful Russian hymn of resignation and forgiveness, written specially for their circumstances, probably by their faithful lady-in-waiting, Countess Hendrikov, who had accompanied them to Ekaterinburg, but was not allowed to live

[1] SOKOLOV, 138. [2] ibid., 172. [3] ibid., 196.
[4] Voikov was later to be assassinated at the railway station at Warsaw, whither he had been sent as Soviet Ambassador.
[5] SOKOLOV, 146.

with them there.[1] The next day, the 15th, the young nephew of the cook Sednev was sent away.

Outside the house, from the beginning, had stood a very high double palisade, and inside the passage which it contained stood a large lorry. The outer guard was still composed of Russians. On the morning of July 16th Yurovsky told its chief, P. Medvedev, that they were going to kill the whole family that night, and ordered him to get together a number of revolvers. The family were told that they were to be moved elsewhere, and did not go to bed. In the late evening they were ordered to descend to the cellar, which was a half-basement, closed on the side of the road, but with small high windows on the garden side. The family came down, Nicholas walking first and carrying his sick boy in his arms. As there was some delay on reaching the cellar, they asked for some chairs, and three were brought, for the boy and his parents. Yurovsky and his band now entered, accompanied by Medvedev, who had been brought into the house. The Soviet of Ekaterinburg had passed a sentence of execution of the whole family, and this Yurovsky read out. Nicholas had only time to express his surprise before he was shot point blank by Yurovsky himself, and this was the signal for a volley directed against all the rest. Yurovsky carried two revolvers, and also shot the boy. Alexis was not killed by the first shot and groaned with pain, whereupon Yurovsky emptied the rest of his charge into him. The marks on the wall were all at a low level, and it is likely that the Empress and the girls, when they saw what was happening, fell on their knees. Anastasia also was not killed by the first discharge, and was dispatched with a bayonet. The faithful Doctor Botkin was killed with the family; also Nicholas's loyal manservant Trup and the lady's maid Demidova. She had brought cushions for the family, and as she was not hit by the first shots, she ran about trying to parry the bayonets with her cushions until she was finished off. The children's little spaniel, Jimmy, was also killed; his head was smashed with a blow, probably from a rifle. It is said that each of the bodies bore several wounds. While the shots were being fired, the lorry outside kept up a persistent hum with its engines, but on the garden side they were heard. 'You have understood?' said one of the outside guard to another. 'I

[1] Kerensky, M. R., 26.

have understood,' said the other: the Russian is shorter — 'Ponyal?' 'Ponyal.'[1] Medvedev declared afterwards that Yurovsky sent him out of the room just before the shooting began, but his wife asserted that he took part in it; anyhow, he came back to her in a miserable state, trembling all over. The bodies were then brought out on sledge-poles, used as litters, and laid in the lorry, which set off in the direction of Koptyaki. During the next two days there was busy work at the mine, with burning pyres and frequent discharges, and curious eyes were kept at a distance. The bodies were destroyed with vitriol, and the remains lowered into the mine. Voikov said: 'The world will never know what we did with them.'

A telegram was sent off to the Central Executive Committee in Moscow and reached it at a sitting where the Commissary of Health — Semashko, was reading a report. There was a moment of interruption, and Lenin announced the news; Semashko then resumed his report.[2] Communications passed between Ekaterinburg and Moscow as to the text of the public announcement to be made. At first it was only announced that Nicholas had been killed and that the rest of the family had been removed to a 'safe place'. Mirbach, on his next meeting with the monarchists, accepting this version, shifted his ground. He took Nicholas's death to be part of the lot of the conquered, using the words: 'Vae victis!' and claimed only to be advocating the safety of the Empress and the children, as connected by birth with Germany.[3] Later on, the death of the whole family was acknowledged and even for a time with satisfaction, but in September 1919, five Socialist Revolutionaries connected with the murder, out of twenty-eight who had been arrested, were executed by the Soviet Government itself for their part in it. Later still Bykov, as we know, has given us the whole story.

On the day following the murder, July 17th, the whole Grand Ducal party at Alapayevsk were done to death; there was again the plea of escape, but, as in the case of Michael, it seems to have been an artifice. The prisoners were conveyed in carts, two and two, singing hymns, again to a neighbouring deserted mine-shaft, and were thrown into it. The Grand Duke Sergius apparently showed fight and was shot dead first; but the rest were thrown in alive.

[1] Sokolov, 219. [2] Bykov, 82. [3] Sokolov, 108.

All the bodies were later recovered, and nearly all bore grave head injuries. Planks and even dynamite were thrown after them, but some may have lived on for some hours.[1] While Kolchak held Siberia, the remains of the sainted Grand Duchess Elizabeth and her faithful nun Yakovleva were conveyed out of the country and were later buried at Jerusalem (January 1921).

The remainder of the ex-sovereign's party at Tobolsk were, for the most part, dispatched afterwards. Countess Hendrikov, Madame Schneider, reader to the Empress, and the man-servant Volkov were taken out, carrying their baggage, to be shot on the edge of a wood near Perm. Volkov was missed at the first volley; he fell down and was taken for the moment to be dead. In the pause he jumped up, leapt over a ditch and ran for his life; shots were fired after him, but he escaped in the dusk. Sheltered by peasants, he was able in the end to make his way to Kolchak. General Tatishchev and Dolgorukov also answered with their lives for their loyalty. The faithful Nagorny was also shot.

Ekaterinburg was captured by the Czechs on the morning of July 25th. The first investigator of the murders did little more than dig up the garden at the house of Ipatyev. It was only by the most patient and thorough going investigation, with interrogation of members of the outer guard, such as Medvedev, and of the peasants of Koptyaki, and by long explorations at the mine itself, that Sokolov was enabled to establish the whole story, to be confirmed later by Bykov. It was the discovery of the body of Jimmy at the mine on June 25th, 1919, which put the seal of certainty on his efforts. The Empress and her children carried on them a number of precious stones, sometimes concealed in buttons, and many of these, not destroyed by the fire, were recovered and identified by Gilliard and Gibbs, together with such articles as the belt of the boy prince.

On July 22nd, Uritsky, the head of the Bolshevist secret police, the Cheka, visiting Count Kokovtsev in prison, where he had him under lock and key, in a long conversation of enthralling interest, tried to extract any evidence that he could get against Nicholas. The faithful Kokovtsev, had, as we know, not found the corresponding good faith on his sovereign's side, and the record of his answers to Uritsky's questions is a magnificent expression of

[1] SOKOLOV, 256-62; BYKOV, 86-7.

loyalty. In dignified language the ex-Premier refuted one after another the popular misconceptions as to Nicholas, and threw all the blame on the evil advice of others.[1]

In September Uritsky himself was assassinated, and a shot was even lodged in Lenin by a Socialist Revolutionary, Dora Kaplan. This was the signal for furious reprisals. By now the civil war was in full course and terrorism reigned on both sides, with this difference, that with the Whites it was sometimes concealed and sometimes punished, while with the Reds it was openly professed and even sometimes exaggerated to create fear in the enemy. Among the reprisals were the shooting of the Grand Dukes Paul, George Mikhailovich, Nicholas Mihkailovich and Dmitry Constantinovich in Petrograd in the following January. Paul is known to have died with dignity and courage.[2]

As was traditional in Russia, there appeared persons who claimed to be one or other of the dead. One such, who claimed to be the murdered boy prince, was examined by Gilliard before he left Siberia and was proved to be a naive impostor. Later came the impersonation of the Grand Duchess Anastasia, which for a time attracted some attention. Later still a young man, who claimed to be Alexis, appeared in Baghdad bearing some of the marks of the Tsarevich. He stated that he had been sheltered by peasants and had since made his way to Baghdad through Persia; but he too drifted back into obscurity.

Among the victims of the Bolshevist reprisals were a number of the ex-Ministers of the Tsar. Old Goremykin had already been strangled by a furious mob. The Government dispatched Stürmer, Nicholas Maklakov, Shcheglovitov, Protopopov, the younger Hvostov and Beletsky. Andronikov and Manuilov were both shot, the latter after helping Burtsev and others to make their escape. The honest and harmless old Prince Golitsyn, the Tsar's last Prime Minister, perished later, as an expiation of hostilities directed against the Bolsheviks by others. They had the habit, at one time copied on the other side by General Rozanov, of holding hostages whose deaths could be used as repayment in such cases, and it was as hostages that General Ruzsky and General Radko Dmitriev were shot at Pyatigorsk in the Caucasus, where they

[1] Kokovtsev, II, 460 ff.
[2] G. D. Alexander, *Once a Grand Duke*, 371.

were undergoing cures. Kaledin, who was Hetman of the Cossacks, killed himself when they deserted him. Sukhomlinov was set free and escaped to Finland. Polivanov and Brusilov took service with the Bolsheviks. Kornilov, who fought vigorously against the Reds, was killed by a shell behind the line, and Alexeyev died a little later.

All this was only part of the clean sweep which was made of all that had claimed authority in Russia before the Revolution. The other side of it is a wholesale emigration of more than a million Russians. The Dowager Empress Maria Fedorovna, who never lost her love for Russia, was rescued from Crimea by the invading Germans and lived for a time in England with her sister, Queen Alexandra, and later with her parents' family in Denmark, attended always by a faithful Cossack. The Grand Duke Nicholas entirely refused to be made a pawn in any calculation of the emigrants, declaring that the Russian people must settle its questions according to its own wishes. He died at Antibes in the south of France (Jan. 5th, 1929), and as the former Commander-in-Chief of an Allied army was accorded full military honours at his funeral by representatives of the other countries of the alliance. Kokovtsev, after being subjected to forced labour, was able to make the perilous passage over the Finnish frontier and came to live in Paris. Rodzyanko, escaping through Crimea with the part of Denikin's force, ended his life in Jugoslavia, harassed by the champions of unlimited autocracy, who had learnt so little from their own political bankruptcy. Purishkevich was also with the Whites in South Russia, and died of typhus there. The two ancient paladins of Liberalism, Petrunkevich and Rodichev, both ended their days abroad, the first in Czechoslovakia and the second in Switzerland. Guchkov, Milyukov and Kerensky, forgetting former differences, ultimately foregathered in Paris. Guchkov remained politically active up to his death from cancer in 1936; almost his last words were 'Read me what they are writing about Russia'. Milyukov, now well over seventy, continued with unabated vigour to play his part as scholar and politician.

This short list will give some measure of the colossal change which had passed over Russia. And now it was a new country throbbing with new activities and harassed by new conflicts. If twenty years after the March Revolution a stranger now visited the little palace at Tsarskoe Selo, he would find it kept exactly as it was on the night when the family gathered with Kerensky in the semi-circular hall, with luggage piled for the journey to Tobolsk, the French windows opened for them to go to the station, and the last leaf of the Emperor's calendar just torn off; and the guide might explain to him, without a trace of animosity, that the last Tsar was a healthy out-of-door man, delighting in his beautiful swimming bath, that the Empress's drawing-room was also almost a nursery, the centre of the family life, that the two sovereigns were excellent parents, and that their children were devoted to them. He would be left, as he came away, to shape his own memory of his visit; and what he would inevitably feel would be, that all this happened far back in the Middle Ages, when it was still thought possible to regard a sixth of the world as a personal estate and to govern a hundred and seventy millions of humanity from a lady's drawing-room. Then he would say to himself that all this was gone far, far away, never to come back again.

TEXT OF THE MANIFESTO OF OCTOBER 17/30, 1905

('THE LOST CHARTER')

ON THE PERFECTING OF THE ORDER OF STATE

THE troubles and disturbances in the capitals and in many places of our Empire, fill our heart full of great and heavy grief. The good of the Russian Sovereign is inseparable from the good of the people, and the affliction of the people is His affliction. From the disturbances which have now arisen there may follow profound disorder in the people, and a menace to the integrity and unity of the All-Russian Power. The great vow of the Tsar's service commands us, with every force of our understanding and authority to strive for the speediest cessation of a disturbance so dangerous to the State. After ordering the proper authorities to take measures to remove direct manifestations of disorder, excesses and violences, and for the safety of peaceful persons who aim at the quiet execution of the duty which lies on everyone, We, for the more successful execution of the general measures designed by us for the pacification of State life, have seen it to be necessary to unite the action of the Higher Government.

We impose on the duty of the Government the execution of our unchangeable will:

1. To grant the population unshakable foundations of civil freedom on the principles of real inviolability of person, freedom of conscience, speech, meetings and associations.

2. Without stopping the appointed elections to the State Duma, to bring to participate in the Duma, as far as possible in the shortness of the time left before its summons, those classes of the population which at present are altogether deprived of electoral rights, leaving afterwards the further development of the principle of universal suffrage to the newly established Legislative Order (that is, according to the law of August 6/19, 1905, Duma and Council of State).

3. To establish as an unchangeable principle that no law can obtain force without the consent of the State Duma, and that to the

elected of the people there should be guaranteed the possibility of actual participation in supervision of the legality of the actions of the authorities appointed by us.

We summon all faithful sons of Russia to remember their duty to the country, to help to stop the unprecedented disorder, and together with us to bend all efforts to the re-establishment of calm and peace in our native land.

NICHOLAS

TABLE OF THE PRINCIPAL REFERENCES

O.S.=dates given in Old Style.

Padenie Tsarskogo Rezhima (The Fall of the Tsarist Regime), 7 vols. Gosizdat, Moscow, 1924 27. (Verbatim report of the Extraordinary Investigating Commission of the Provisional Government.) Each reference gives the name of the witness and the word *Padenie* thus: STÜRMER, *Padenie*

Dnevnik Nikolaya Vtorogo (Diary of Nicholas II): Krasny Arkhiv, vols. 20-22 and 27 (O.S.) N. diary

Letters of the Tsaritsa to the Tsar: Duckworth, 1923 (O.S.) A. F. to N.

Letters of the Tsar to the Tsaritsa: Bodley Head, 1929 (O.S.) N. to A. F.

The Secret Letters of Tsar Nicholas (Correspondence with his Mother): T. & A. Constable, Edinburgh, 1938 (O.S.) N. to M. F.; M. F. to N.

A. Taneyeva (Anna Vyrubova): *Stranitsy iz Moey Zhizni* (Pages Out of My Life): Berlin, 1923. (English edition: Memories of the Russian Court: Macmillan, 1923) (O.S.) VYRUBOVA

Pierre Gilliard: *Imperator Nikolay i Ego Semya* (The Emperor Nicholas and his Family): Rus, Vienna (N.S.) GILLIARD

A. A. Mossolov: *At the Court of the Last Tsar.* Methuen, 1935 (O.S.) MOSOLOV

Count Paul Benckendorff: *Last Days at Tsarskoe Selo.* Heinemann, 1927 (O.S.) BENCKENDORFF

A. F. Kerensky: *The Murder of the Romanovs.* Hutchinson, 1935 (O.S.) KERENSKY, M. R.

Paul Bulygin: *The Murder of the Romanovs.* Hutchinson, 1935 (O.S.) BULYGIN

N. A. Sokolov: *Ubiistvo Tsarskoy Semyi* (Murder of the Tsar and His Family). Berlin, 1925 (N.S.) SOKOLOV

P. M. Bykov: *The Last Days of Tsardom.* Martin Lawrence, 1937 (N.S.) BYKOV

The Kaiser's Letters to the Tsar. Hodder & Stoughton, 1920 (N.S.) W. to N.

Lettres des Grands-Ducs à Nicholas II. Payot, 1926: the initials of the writer are given; for instance N. M. to N.

TABLE OF THE PRINCIPAL REFERENCES

Grand Duke Alexander of Russia: *Once a Grand Duke.* Cassell, 1932 (O.S.) G. D. ALEXANDER

Grand Duchess Marie of Russia: *Things I Remember.* Cassell, 1931 (N.S.) MARIA PAVLOVNA

Princess Paley: *Souvenirs de Russie.* Librairie Plon, 1923 (N.S.) PALEY

M. V. Rodzianko: *The Reign of Rasputin.* Philpot, 1927 (O.S.) RODZYANKO

A. Simanovich: *Raspoutine.* Librairie Gallimerd (O.S.) SIMANOVICH

Marie Rasputin: *The Real Rasputin.* John Long, 1929 (O.S.) MARIE RASPUTIN

Illiodor: *Svyatoy Chort* (The Holy Devil). Moscow, 1917 (O.S.) ILLIODOR

Prince F. Youssoupoff: *Rasputin.* Cape, 1927 (O.S.) YUSUPOV

V. M. Purishkevich: *Dnevnik* (Diary). Riga, 1924 (O.S.) PURISHKEVICH

V. A. Maklakov: *Nekotorya Dopolneniya* (Certain supplements to the reminiscences of Purishkevich and Prince Yusupov on the murder of Rasputin) (O.S.) V. MAKLAKOV

P. E. Shchegolev: *Russky Rokambol* (data of the record of I. F. Manasevich-Manuilov in *Okhranniki i Avantyuristy*). Moscow 1930 (O.S.) SHCHEGOLEV

Fülöp Müller: *Der Heilige Teufel.* Berlin, 1927 (O.S.) FÜLÖP-MILLER

Graf S. Y. Witte: *Vospominaniya* (Reminiscences), 2 vols. Berlin, 1922 (there is an English edition) (O.S.) WITTE

Graf V. N. Kokovtsev: *Iz Moego Proshlago*, 2 vols. Illyustirovannaya, Rossiya, Paris (there is an English edition *Out of My Past*) (O.S.) KOKOVTSEV

Iswolsky, *Memoirs.* Hutchinson, 1920 IZVOLSKY, M.

S. Sazonov: *Fateful Years.* Cape, 1928 SAZONOV

A. N. Yakhontov: *Tyazhelye Dni* (Grave Days). Arkhiv Russkoy Revolutsii XVIII. Berlin, 1926 (O.S.) YAKHONTOV

A. T. Wassilieff: *Police Russe et Révolution.* Bibliothèque D'Histoire Politique, Militaire et Navale, 1936 (O.S.) VASILYEV

A. D. Protopopov: *Predsmertnaya Zapiska* (Memorandum before death); *Golos Minuvshago Na Chuzhoy Storone*, 1926, No. 2, XV (O.S.) PROTOPOPOV, *Predsmertnaya*

P. N. Milyukov: *Istoriya Vtoroy Russkoy Revolutsii* (History of the Second Russian Revolution). Sofia, 1921 (O.S.) MILYUKOV

A. F. KERENSKY: *The Crucifixion of Liberty.* Barker, 1934 (O.S.) KERENSKY, C. L.

V. V. Shulgin: *Dni* (Days). Suvorin, Belgrade, 1925 (O.S.) SHULGIN

V. Carrick: *Dnevnik* (Diary in MS.) (O.S.) CARRICK

TABLE OF THE PRINCIPAL REFERENCES

M. Paléologue: *La Russie des Tsars Pendant la Grande Guerre*, 3 vols. Librairie Plon, 1922 (N.S.) PALÉOLOGUE

Sir G. Buchanan: *My Mission to Russia.* Cassell, 1923 (N.S.) BUCHANAN

R. H. Bruce Lockhart: *Memoirs of a British Agent.* Putnam, 1932 BRUCE LOCKHART

Meriel Buchanan: (Mrs. Knowling) *The Dissolution of an Empire.* Murray, 1932 (N.S.) MISS BUCHANAN

M. T. Florinsky: *The End of the Russian Empire.* Yale & Oxford University Presses, 1931 (O.S.) FLORINSKY

Gen. N. N. Golovin: *The Russian Army in the World War.* Yale & Oxford University Presses, 1931 (O.S.) GOLOVIN

Gen. Yu. Danilov: *La Russie dans la Guerre Mondiale.* Payot, 1927 (N.S.) DANILOV

Gen. Sir A. Knox: *With the Russian Army (1914-17)*, 2 vols. Hutchinson, 1921 (N.S.) KNOX

Gen. A. B. Brusilov: *Moi Vospominaniya* (My Reminiscences). Gosizdat, 1929. (There is an English edition: *A Soldier's Notebook*) (O.S.) BRUSILOV

Gen. V. I. Gurko: *Memories and Impressions of War and Revolution in Russia.* Murray, 1918 (N.S.) GURKO

Gen. A. A. Polivanov: *Memuary* (Memoirs). Vysshy Voenny Redaktsionny Sovet (O.S.) POLIVANOV

F.M. Hindenburg: *Out of My Life.* Cassell, 1920 (N.S.) HINDENBURG

F.M. Ludendorff: *My War Memories*, Hutchinson, 3rd ed. (N.S.) LUDENDORFF

Gen. M. Hoffmann: *War Diaries and other Papers*, 2 vols. Martin Secker (N.S.) HOFFMANN

When the author is the direct source of information the references are, for instance Guchkov to B. P.

TRANSLITERATION

As Russian has an alphabet of its own, Russians, when writing in other languages, spell their names in every imaginable way. Hence the vagaries in the titles of books. The transliteration used here is that of the *Slavonic and East European Review*, which, with slight variations, is that of the British Academy. It is consistent and gives a generally correct pronunciation.

PLAN IV. THE GREAT RETREAT

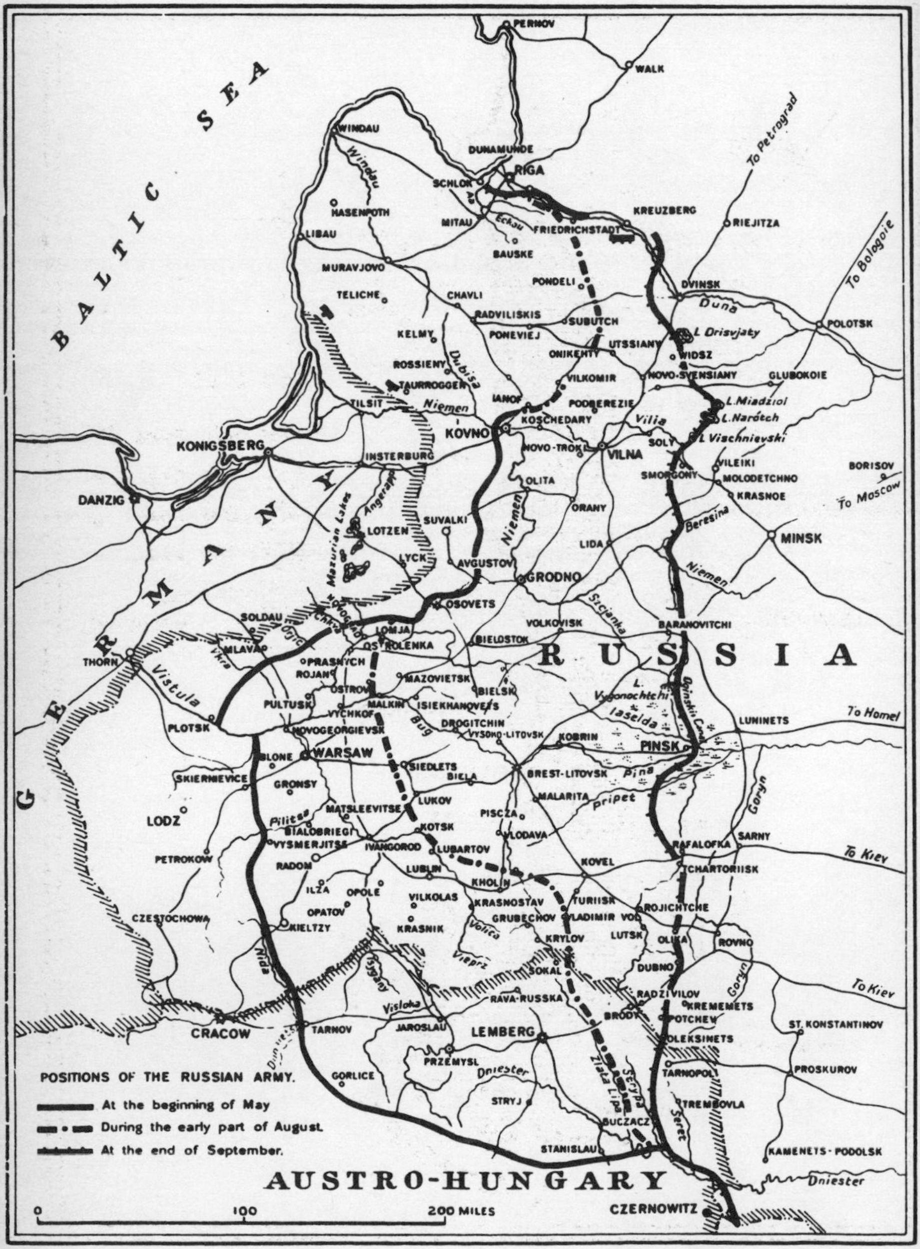

PLAN V. BRUSILOV'S OFFENSIVE

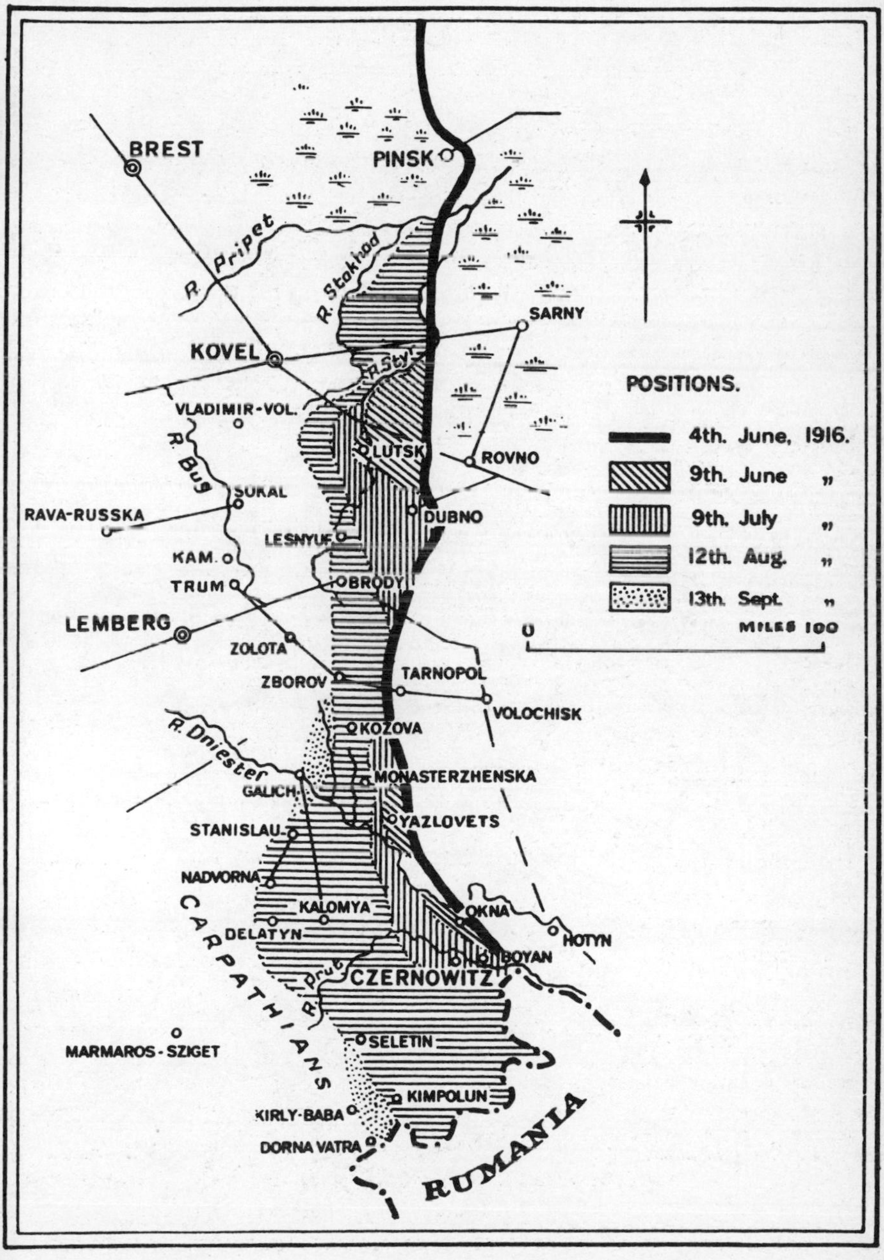

PLAN VI. PETROGRAD IN 1917

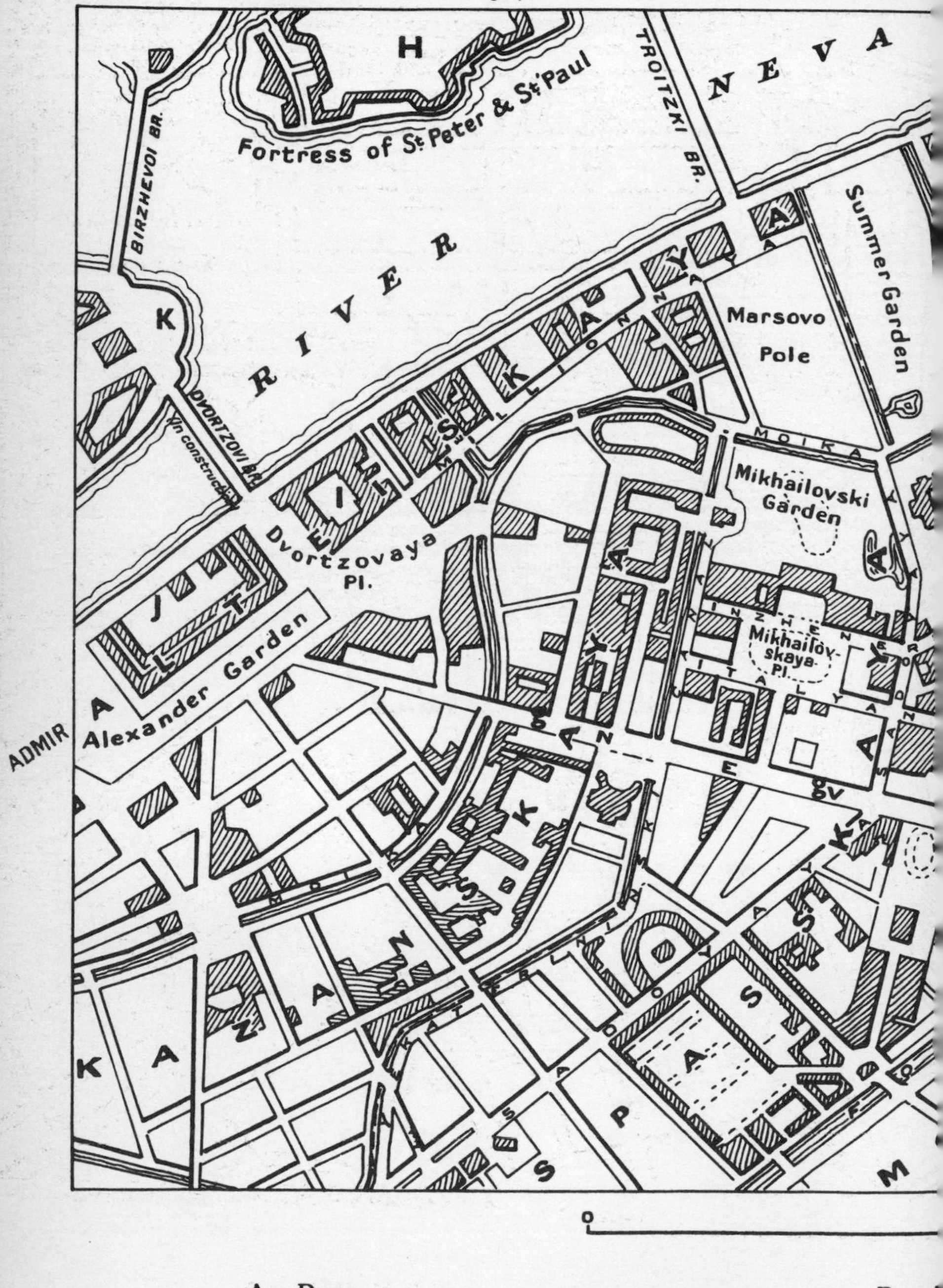

A	Duma	D	A
B	Barracks of Volynsky and Preobrazhensky Regiments	EE	I
C	Znamensky Square	FF	A
J	Admiralty		

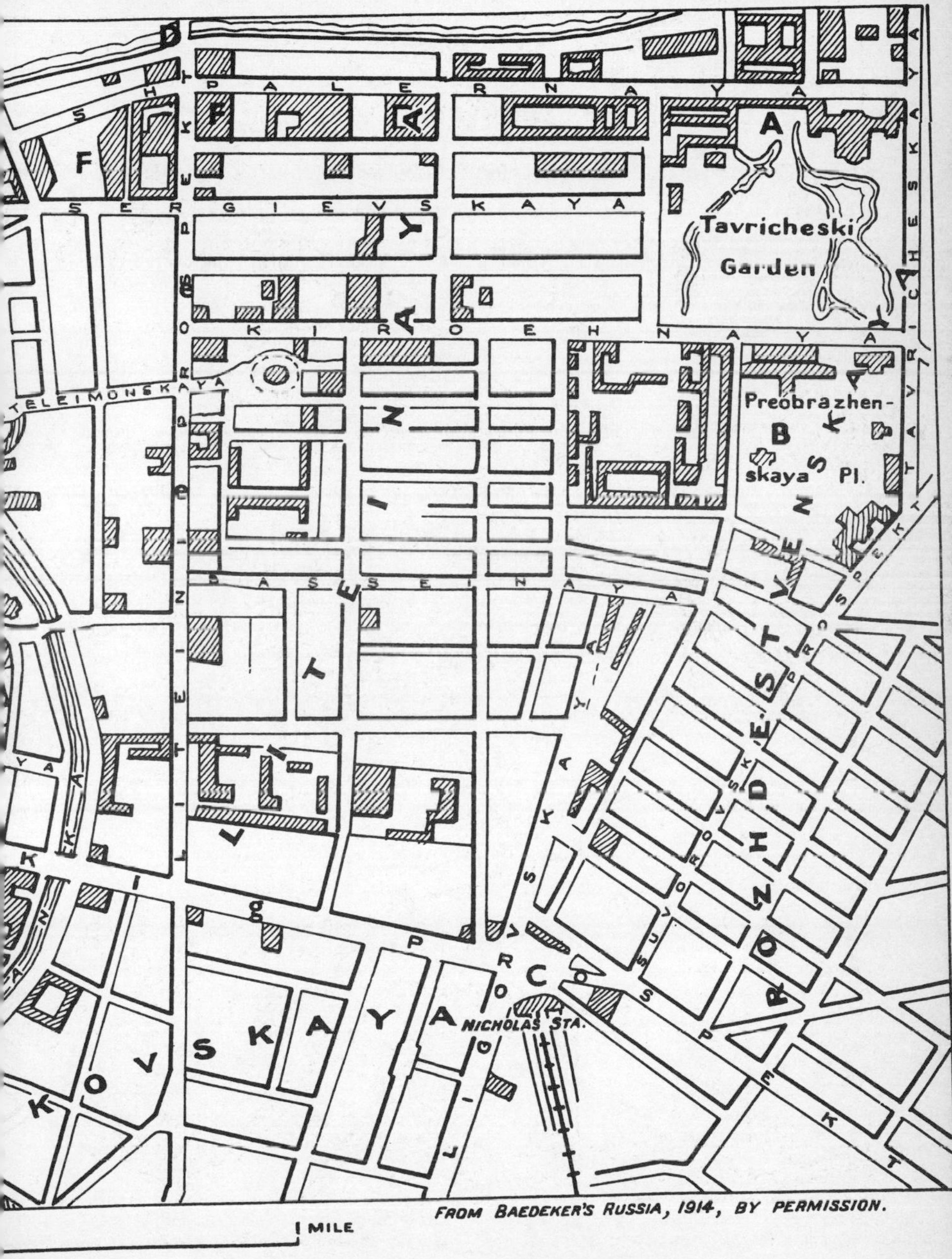

FROM BAEDEKER'S RUSSIA, 1914, BY PERMISSION.

er Bridge
Prospekt
Assize Court and Prison
K Basil Island (workmen's quarters)
GG Nevski Prospekt
H Fortress
I Winter Palace

INDEX

† Personally known to the writer

INDEX

INDEX

INDEX

INDEX

INDEX

On Sledge and Horseback to Outcast Siberian Lepers

KATE MARSDEN

Kate Marsden recounts her extraordinary journey, sponsored by Queen Victoria, from Constantinople to Yakutsk in north-east Siberia in the 1890s. A fervent Christian, Marsden was driven to research leprosy and its then widely differing treatments from the Middle East to Siberia. Illustrated with some of the author's own photographs and drawings.

Paperback
UK: £12.99 272pp + 24pp b/w 1 84212 397 1
USA: $19.95
CAN: $29.95

The History of Pugachev

ALEXANDER PUSHKIN

A history of Russia's greatest peasant rebellion by its greatest national poet. With a new introduction by Orlando Figes.

Paperback
UK: £9.99 160pp 1 84212 418 8
USA: $16.95
CAN: $24.95

Ivan the Terrible

HENRI TROYAT

Outstanding popular biography of one of the most violent and demented rulers in history, by the author of *Catherine the Great.*

UK: £14.99 304pp + 20pp b/w + Maps 1 84212 419 6
USA: $21.95
CAN: $31.95

Catherine the Great

HENRI TROYAT

The Prix Goncourt-winning French historian reveals the true nature of the ambitious and ruthless despot. 'Theoretically straightforward biography, it illuminates far more than the life of that amazing woman; a brilliant court, Russian itself, sparkle before our eyes' Antonia Fraser, *The Good Book Guide*

Paperback: £14.99   400pp + 16pp b/w   1 84212 029 8

Journey for our Time

THE JOURNALS OF THE MARQUIS DE CUSTINE

The 'de Tocqueville of Russia' provides a timeless insight into the divisions and distempers of one of the world's most enigmatic nations. With a new introduction by Simon Sebag Montefiore.

Paperback
UK: £9.99   240pp   1 84212 436 6
USA: $16.95
CAN: $24.95

Peasant Russia, Civil War

THE VOLGA COUNTRYSIDE IN REVOLUTION 1917–21

ORLANDO FIGES

Britain's most celebrated historian of Russia investigates why and how the October Revolution occurred.

Paperback
UK: £14.99   432pp + 8pp b/w + Maps   1 84212 419 6
USA: $21.95
CAN: $31.95

Cursed Days

IVAN BUNIN

This great anti-Bolshevik diary won Russia's first Nobel Prize for literature. Originally published in 1936 but banned by the Soviets, it relives the experience of civil war in 1918 Moscow and Odessa.

Paperback
UK: £12.99   304pp   1 84212 063 8
CAN: $24.95

A Lifelong Passion

NICHOLAS AND ALEXANDRA – THEIR OWN STORY

ANDREI MAYLUNAS AND SERGEI MIRONENKO

The love affair of Nicholas, the last Tsar of Russia, and his wife Alix, a granddaughter of Queen Victoria, was a lifelong passion with a tragic end. 'Reads like a thriller, filled as it is with stories of plots, betrayals and sexual intrigues.' *Sunday Telegraph*

Paperback £10.99 736pp + 16pp col 0 75380 044 6

Michael & Natasha

ROSEMARY AND DONALD CRAWFORD

The life and love of Michael, the brother of the executed Nicholas II. 'It is a long time since I have read so moving a story, and it is one that I defy any reader to put down once begun' Count Nikolai Tolstoy, *Sunday Times*

Paperback £9.99 464pp + 24pp b/w 0 75380 516 2

Peter the Great

HIS LIFE AND WORLD

ROBERT K. MASSIE

Peter the Great was a giant among men: he found Russia in Oriental semi-barbarity and left it a part of Europe. Massie's masterful biography has rightly become a classic. Peter the Great's life spanned a continent and marked an epoch of innovation and social revolution.

Paperback £14.99 928pp + Maps 1 84212 116 2